CW01272556

Applying Psychology to Criminal Justice

Applying Psychology to Criminal Justice

Edited by

**David Carson, Rebecca Milne, Francis Pakes,
Karen Shalev and Andrea Shawyer**

*Institute of Criminal Justice Studies at the
University of Portsmouth, UK*

John Wiley & Sons, Ltd

Copyright © 2007   John Wiley & Sons Ltd, The Atrium, Southern Gate, Chichester,
West Sussex PO19 8SQ, England

Telephone   (+44) 1243 779777

Email (for orders and customer service enquiries): cs-books@wiley.co.uk
Visit our Home Page on www.wiley.com

All Rights Reserved. No part of this publication may be reproduced, stored in a retrieval system or transmitted in any form or by any means, electronic, mechanical, photocopying, recording, scanning or otherwise, except under the terms of the Copyright, Designs and Patents Act 1988 or under the terms of a licence issued by the Copyright Licensing Agency Ltd, 90 Tottenham Court Road, London W1T 4LP, UK, without the permission in writing of the Publisher. Requests to the Publisher should be addressed to the Permissions Department, John Wiley & Sons Ltd, The Atrium, Southern Gate, Chichester, West Sussex PO19 8SQ, England, or emailed to permreq@wiley.co.uk, or faxed to (+44) 1243 770620.

Designations used by companies to distinguish their products are often claimed as trademarks. All brand names and product names used in this book are trade names, service marks, trademarks or registered trademarks of their respective owners. The Publisher is not associated with any product or vendor mentioned in this book.

This publication is designed to provide accurate and authoritative information in regard to the subject matter covered. It is sold on the understanding that the Publisher is not engaged in rendering professional services. If professional advice or other expert assistance is required, the services of a competent professional should be sought.

Other Wiley Editorial Offices

John Wiley & Sons Inc., 111 River Street, Hoboken, NJ 07030, USA

Jossey-Bass, 989 Market Street, San Francisco, CA 94103-1741, USA

Wiley-VCH Verlag GmbH, Boschstr. 12, D-69469 Weinheim, Germany

John Wiley & Sons Australia Ltd, 42 McDougall Street, Milton, Queensland 4064, Australia

John Wiley & Sons (Asia) Pte Ltd, 2 Clementi Loop #02-01, Jin Xing Distripark, Singapore 129809

John Wiley & Sons Canada Ltd, 6045 Freemont Blrd, Mississauga, ONT, L5R 4J3, Canada

Wiley also publishes its books in a variety of electronic formats. Some content that appears in print may not be available in electronic books.

Anniversary Logo Design: Richard J. Pacifico

Library of Congress Cataloguing-in-Publication Data

Applying psychology to criminal justice / edited by David Carson . . . [et al.].
    p. cm.
  Includes bibliographical references and index.
  ISBN 978-0-470-01515-5 (cloth : alk. paper)
 1. Criminal justice, Administration of—Psychological aspects. 2. Criminal investigation—Psychological aspects. 3. Judicial process—Psychological aspects. I. Carson, David, 1950–
  HV7419.A67 2007
  364.3—dc22   2007019140

British Library Cataloguing in Publication Data

A catalogue record for this book is available from the British Library

ISBN 978-0-470-01515-5

Typeset in 10/12pt Times by Aptara, New Delhi, India
Printed and bound in Great Britain by Antony Rowe Chippenham, Wiltshire
This book is printed on acid-free paper responsibly manufactured from sustainable forestry in which at least two trees are planted for each one used for paper production.

Contents

About the Editors		vii
Contributors		ix
Preface		xiii
Chapter 1	Psychology and Law: A Science to be Applied *David Carson, Becky Milne, Francis Pakes, Karen Shalev and Andrea Shawyer*	1
Chapter 2	Eyewitness Identification *Ronald P. Fisher and Margaret C. Reardon*	21
Chapter 3	Behavioural Science and the Law: Investigation *John G.D. Grieve*	39
Chapter 4	Investigative Interviewing: The Role of Research *Becky Milne, Gary Shaw and Ray Bull*	65
Chapter 5	Credibility Assessments in a Legal Context *Aldert Vrij*	81
Chapter 6	Fact Finding and Evidence *Jenny McEwan*	97
Chapter 7	A Psychology and Law of Fact finding? *David Carson*	115
Chapter 8	Criminal Responsibility *Susan Dennison*	131
Chapter 9	Criminal Thinking *Emma J. Palmer*	147
Chapter 10	The Mentally Disordered Offender: Disenablers for the Delivery of Justice *Jane Winstone and Francis Pakes*	167
Chapter 11	Decision Making in Criminal Justice *Edie Greene and Leslie Ellis*	183

Chapter 12	A Behavioural Science Perspective on Identifying and Managing Hindsight Bias and Unstructured Judgement: Implications for Legal Decision Making *Kirk Heilbrun and Jacey Erickson*	201
Chapter 13	To Decide or not to Decide: Decision Making and Decision Avoidance in Critical Incidents *Marie Eyre and Laurence Alison*	211
Chapter 14	Processes: Proving Guilt, Disproving Innocence *David Carson*	233
Chapter 15	The Changing Nature of Adversarial, Inquisitorial and Islamic Trials *Francis Pakes*	251
Chapter 16	Misapplication of Psychology in Court *Peter J. van Koppen*	265
Chapter 17	Identifying Liability for Organizational Errors *David Carson*	283
Chapter 18	Applying Key Civil Law Concepts *David Carson, Becky Milne, Francis Pakes, Karen Shalev and Andrea Shawyer*	299
Index		311

About the Editors

David Carson is Reader in Law and Behavioural Sciences at the University of Portsmouth. With Professor Ray Bull, he co-edited two versions of *Psychology in Legal Contexts* for Wiley (1995 and 2003), and co-founded the journal *Expert Evidence*. He organised the international conferences on psychology and law, under the aegis of the AP-LS, EAP&L and ANZAPPL in Dublin (1999) and Edinburgh (2003). His current research focus is on practical and inter-disciplinary approaches to fact-finding, evidence and proof.

Rebecca Milne (BSc (Hons). Ph.D. CPsychol AFBPsS) is a Principal Lecturer at the Institute of Criminal Justice Studies at the University of Portsmouth. She is the course leader of the FdA in Investigation and Evidence, a distance learning degree programme specifically for investigators. A chartered forensic psychologist and Associate Fellow of the British Psychological Society, she is and an Associate Editor of the International Journal of Police Science and Management and is the Academic lead member of the Association of Chief Police Officers Investigative Interviewing Strategic Steering Group. She has worked closely with the police and other criminal justice organisations through training of the Enhanced Cognitive Interview, Witness Interview Advising and also in the interviewing of vulnerable groups (i.e. Tier 3 and 5) and providing case advice.

Francis Pakes studied psychology at Groningen University in the Netherlands. His PhD, from Leiden University, was on decision making by Dutch public prosecutors. He has since published on comparative criminal justice, Dutch penal policy and on various issues in psychology and crime. He is, currently, a Principal Lecturer at the University of Portsmouth, UK.

Karen Shalev is a senior lecturer at the Institute of Criminal Justice Studies at the University of Portsmouth. She graduated with B.A in Criminology and English literature from Bar Ilan University, Israel in 1997. She then graduated with an MSc in Investigative Psychology at the University of Liverpool in 1999 and with a PhD in Investigative Psychology in 2004. Her research focuses on studying the relationship between the ways offenders perceive their environment and their offence location choice; identifying patterns of offenders' spatial behaviour; and on gaining knowledge about offenders' choices by interviewing them. She is also involved with research of missing persons and armed robbery.

Andrea Shawyer Andrea Shawyer is a tutor at the Institute of Criminal Justice Studies at the University Of Portsmouth. She studied Forensic Psychology at the University of Surrey, and her current research interests, and the topic of her PhD, is Investigative Interviewing with a specific focus on fraud investigation and detecting deception.

Contributors

Laurence Alison is the Academic Director of the Centre for Critical Incident Research and also Professor of Forensic Psychology at he University of Liverpool. His core area of interest is social cognition and the processes by which individuals make sense of ambiguous, complex or contradictory information within a forensic/policing context.

Ray Bull is Professor of Forensic Psychology at the University of Leicester. He was part of the small team commissioned by the Home Office to write the 2002 government document *Achieving Best Evidence in Criminal Proceedings: Guidance for Vulnerable or Intimidated Witnesses, Including Children* (ABE). In 2002/3 he led the small team commissioned by government to produce an extensive training pack relating to ABE

Susan Dennison is a senior lecturer in the School of Criminology and Criminal Justice at Griffith University, Queensland, Australia. She is also Director of the Prevention and Developmental Pathways Project within the Key Centre for Ethics, Law, Justice, and Governance Her publications include articles on child maltreatment, stalking and sex offending.

Leslie Ellis is a Senior Trial Consultant at TrialGraphix, a national litigation consulting firm. She received her M.A. in Psychology and Ph.D. in Social Psychology from the University of Illinois, Chicago, where she studied jury and judge decision making.

Jacey Erickson is a fourth-year graduate student in the Law-Psychology program at Villanova School of Law and Drexel University. She has published on the value of partnerships between corrections services and academic psychology and of gender-specific re-entry programmes for offenders.

Marie Eyre is a Research Associate at the Centre for Critical Incident Research (CCIR). CCIR is based in the School of Psychology at the University of Liverpool, Bedford Street South, Liverpool. She is interested in the relationships between broad cultural/organisational contexts and the ways in which they influence the cognitive processes of individuals in the dynamic environment of critical incidents.

Ronald Fisher is a Professor of Psychology at Florida International University (FIU). He is the Chair of the Psychology-Law Doctoral program at FIU. Dr. Fisher co-developed (with Ed Geiselman) the Cognitive Interview method of interviewing witnesses and victims of crime.

Edie Greene is Professor of Psychology at the University of Colorado in Colorado Springs. She is the author of many articles and book chapters on jury decision-making and co-author of *Psychology and the Legal System* (Wadsworth, 2007) and *Determining damages: The psychology of jury awards* (American Psychological Association, 2003).

John G D Grieve has a first degree in philosophy and a postgraduate degree, from research on Drugs Policy Analysis. Within the Metropolitan he served as a detective in every role from undercover officer to policy chair on drug squads, from the flying, robbery and murder to a Divisional Commander. As the first Director of Intelligence for the Metropolitan Police, he led the MPS Intelligence Project and the Anti-Terrorist Squad as National Coordinator during the 1996–1998 bombing campaigns. He was the first Director of the Racial and Violent Crime Task Force, from 1998 until 2002. He is now Senior Research Fellow at Portsmouth University and Emeritus at London Metropolitan University. He was awarded the QPM in 1997 and appointed CBE in the Millennium Honours list.

Kirk Heilbrun is Professor and Head of the Department of Psychology at Drexel University. His current research focuses on juvenile and adult offenders, legal decision-making, and forensic evaluation associated with such decision-making. His practice interests centre around forensic assessment, and he directs a practicum within the department in this area. He is a past president of both the American Psychology-Law Society.

Peter van Koppen (1953) is a psychologist senior chief researcher at the Netherlands Institute for the Study of Crime and Law Enforcement (NSCR) Leiden, Faculty of Law Maastricht University and Faculty of Law, Free University Amsterdam. He currently serves as President of the European Association for Psychology and Law.

Jenny McEwan is Professor of Criminal Law at the University of Exeter. Her particular, psychologically informed, interests in the consequences of adversarial trials and in vulnerable witnesses are reflected in such books as *Evidence and the Adversarial Process: the Modern Law* (Blackwell, 1992; Hart, 1998), and *The Verdict of the Court: Passing Judgment in Law and Psychology,* (Hart, 2003). She is a member of the Sexual Offences Research Initiative, funded by the British Psychological Society.

Emma Palmer is Senior Lecturer in Forensic Psychology in the Department of Health Sciences, University of Leicester. Her research interests are the roles of parenting and social cognition in the development of offending; design and evaluation of interventions with offenders; assessment of risk and need; and bullying in prisons.

Margaret Reardon has a Masters of Science in Psychology from Florida International University and is working on her Doctoral dissertation in the area of jury deliberation. Margaret has published research on juror evaluation of mental retardation and mental illness.

Gary Shaw is a Detective Chief Inspector who has 29 years police service with Northumbria Police, the majority within the field of criminal investigation. He is currently seconded to the National Centre for Policing Excellence (Operations) as the National Investigative Interviewing Co-ordinator. In his current role Gary acts as an operational consultant to forces investigating major crime and also supports them in formulating implementation plans around the ACPO National Interview Strategy.

Aldert Vrij is a Professor of Social Psychology in the University of Portsmouth. His research interests are deception, police officers' shooting behaviour, interviewing suspects, interviewing children, and ethnic prejudice. Most of his research deals with deception. He has published more than 250 articles and 6 books. His *Detecting lies and deceit: The* *psychology of lying and its implications for professional practice*, (Chichester: John Wiley & Sons, 2000) was the first book to incorporate research on both nonverbal and verbal cues to deception.

Jane Winstone is a principal lecturer in the Institute of Criminal Justice Studies at the University of Portsmouth. With Francis Pakes she is co-editor of *Community Justice: Issues for Probation and Criminal Justice* (Willan 2005) and co-author of *Psychology and Crime: Understanding and tackling offending behaviour* (Willan, 2007). She is researching the impact of organisations and culture on the management and delivery of community justice and professional training

Preface

Few things should go together better than psychology and law. Both are concerned with human behaviour: analyzing it, predicting it, understanding it and, sometimes, controlling it. Lawyers may, in the absence of empirical research, have made assumptions about human behaviour; for example that people who know they are dying will tell the truth (an exception to the rule against hearsay evidence). Judges had to make decisions to settle the dispute before them. But now there is research which can inform the law.

However few things are getting together less successfully than psychology and law. The specialist journals, books and conferences tend to be dominated, both in numbers and contribution, by academic psychologists. It can be complained that lawyers are insufficiently welcoming but that would fly in the face of the pragmatic imperatives of law. Both psychologists and lawyers, like all other professionals, need to keep up-to-date with developments in their discipline. Some, particularly the academic members, have a duty (and the licence of academic freedom), to push their ideas into new fields. But, when that is applied to lawyers, it is related to *current* law and practice. There is no economic incentive for practicing lawyers to be interested in psychological research on law unless it helps them to do their job more efficiently or effectively. Perhaps the law ought to be different, because of what the psychological research has revealed. But that is a normative proposition. Lawyers do not need to know about it until, if, the law is changed to make it relevant.

A consequence is that there are limited routes for the application of psychology to law. National differences can be identified reflecting different laws and opportunities. For example psychological reports to inform courts about the capacity of a defendant to stand trial are much more common in the United States of America (USA) and Australia than in the United Kingdom (UK). However government interest in the UK, first in the plight of child and then other vulnerable witnesses, led to a research focus on interviewing skills which has not been replicated, to the same degree, in other countries.

The basic thesis of this book is that more, and more imaginative, avenues for the application of psychology to law, particularly to criminal justice, ought to be found. The editors propose, and the contributors elaborate and exemplify, that there ought to be a proactive focus on the potential for applying psychology in practical contexts. It is no longer, if ever it was, sufficient to be reactive and wait for 'the law' to call for assistance such as through the means of expert scientific evidence in particular, relatively rare, one-off, cases.

We argue that there is a wealth of ways in which psychology can be, and needs to be, applied to law, from informing law reform agencies, through challenging legal concepts, to informing professional standards enforced via the civil law.

The Editors, four psychologists and a lawyer, are all members of the multi-disciplinary Institute of Criminal Justice Studies at the University of Portsmouth. The University also has, in its psychology department, one of the largest and most prominent groups of forensic and investigative psychologists in the world. In addition to making use of some of our own resources, we have been very fortunate to attract contributions from some of the most imaginative thinkers in psychology and law in the world. We hope that the individual chapters, and our theme of applying psychology in a more devolved manner, will inform and impress our readers. If not, please say so.

David Carson
Institute of Criminal Justice Studies
University of Portsmouth
St George's Building
141 High Street
Old Portsmouth
PO1 2HY
Mardi Gras Day, 20th February, 2007
Laissez les bons temps roulez.

CHAPTER 1

Psychology and Law: A Science to be Applied

David Carson, Becky Milne, Francis Pakes,
Karen Shalev and Andrea Shawyer

University of Portsmouth

'Psychology and Law' has seen a major growth over since the 1960s. Many books have been published. These include conclusions of major research studies into issues of relevance both to psychology and law, such as the prediction of violence from people with a mental disorder (e.g. Monahan *et al.*, 2001). They also include reviews of topics that have been widely researched for many years, such as identification evidence (e.g. Wells, 2002) and jury decision making (e.g. Greene *et al.*, 2002); topics that have become associated with relatively few researchers, such as confession evidence (e.g. Gudjonsson, 2003); and emerging topics, such as impulsivity (e.g. Webster and Jackson, 1997), offenders' reasoning (e.g. McMurran, 2002; Palmer, 2003), or failure to reason before acting (e.g. Libet, Freeman and Sutherland, 1999) where the implications, for law and practice are still emerging. There are reviews of the field (e.g. Kapardis, 2003), collected works covering a broad range of topics (e.g. Kagehiro and Laufer, 1992), and collections on specific topics, such as interviewing (e.g. Memon and Bull, 1999).

Several journals, dedicated to this ostensibly interdisciplinary domain, have also become established since the 1970s. In North America, *Law and Human Behavior* was founded in 1977, *Behavioral Sciences & the Law* in 1983 and *Psychology, Public Policy, and Law* in 1995. In Europe, *Expert Evidence* was founded in 1992 but, whilst (or possibly because) being the most interdisciplinary of the journals, it folded in 2000. Also in Europe, *Psychology Crime and Law* was founded in 1994 and *Legal and Criminological Psychology* in 1996. *Psychiatry, Psychology and Law*, the journal of the Australian and New Zealand Association of Psychiatry, Psychology and Law, was founded in 1994.

In addition, the interchange of ideas has been fostered through academic conferences. Each of the three main regional learned societies, the American Psychology-Law Society (AP-LS),[1] the European Association of Psychology & Law (EAP&L),[2] and the Australian

---

[1] http://www.ap-ls.org/.
[2] http://www.law.kuleuven.ac.be/eapl/.

Applying Psychology to Criminal Justice. Edited by David Carson, Rebecca Milne, Francis Pakes, Karen Shalev and Andrea Shawyer. © 2007 John Wiley & Sons, Ltd

and New Zealand Association of Psychiatry, Psychology and Law (ANZAPP&L)[3] hold annual meetings. Joint conferences have been organized: Dublin (1999), Edinburgh (2003) and Adelaide (2007)[4] although, unfortunately, in 2006 the AP-LS withdrew from the agreement to hold joint meetings every four years. (There had been an international conference, organized outside of these structures, in Swansea, Wales, in 1982 (Müller, Blackman and Chapman, 1984).)

Thus, the area where law and psychology intersect seems to be characterized by academic vibrancy. However, despite all this activity, there are a number of weaknesses in the underpinnings of the literature, which may harm the potential for substantial and appropriate development. This chapter will identify some of these problems and explain how the contributions within this book may begin to address some of them.

IS IT INTERDISCIPLINARY?

It is difficult to conceive of intellectual domains that should, once paired semantically, be more interdisciplinary than 'psychology and law'. Both psychology and law are, fundamentally, concerned with describing, analysing, understanding, explaining, predicting and, sometimes, shaping human behaviour. Most certainly there are major differences in methods (see below and Clifford, 1995, 2003). There are also differences in starting points that, to some, may seem like insurmountable obstacles. For example, it is said that lawyers assume that, and that many laws – particularly criminal – are predicated upon, offenders have free will, in the sense that they 'choose' to commit their crimes. However, psychologists would emphasize factors indicating that such 'decisions' are constrained or even determined. Lawyers might concede that there were pressures, in individual cases, which could mandate legal defences or mitigation of punishment, but they would insist that offenders, essentially, had an option to act differently. These are the sorts of issues, however, which should be the subject matter of critical debate, within psychology and law, rather than either ignored or sidelined as immutable differences, or excuses for lack of a more interdisciplinary approach.

Many of the alleged incompatibilities between law and psychology, indeed also between law and other behavioural and social sciences (Campbell, 1974), arise from law (like psychology) being an applied discipline (Haney, 1980, 1993; Schuller and Ogloff, 2001). In contrast with psychology, law dichotomizes, is orientated to past events, emphasizes responsibility rather than causation, and particularizes rather than generalizes. Dichotomous distinctions are needed, though, for example both to explain and to justify distinguishing the act of murder from manslaughter by the presence or absence of the defendant's intention. No criminal lawyer would claim that it has proved easy to construct a reliable dichotomy between the 'intentional' and 'unintentional' (e.g. Ormerod, 2005). Dichotomous categories exist because they are needed, in practice. Practicing lawyers need them just as practicing psychologists also need, and impose categories such as having, or not having, 'capacity'.

When we review an area of law, or psychology, we can recognize the impossibility of perfect models but identify, for the purposes of achieving practical improvements such as law reform, better categories. Practicing lawyers look backwards to analyse their clients'

---

[3] http://www.med.monash.edu.au/psychmed/anzappl/.
[4] http://www.sapmea.asn.au/conventions/psychlaw2007/index.html.

past behaviour. They must do so if they are to represent them appropriately when their clients are charged with a crime. So too must practicing psychologists look back at the behaviour of their clients, if they are to understand them and to devise suitable interventions. Lawyers can also look forward; contracts, a device also popular with psychologists when working with clients, are designed to shape behaviour in the future. So it has been argued that the implications of the alleged methodological differences, between law and psychology, have been exaggerated (Carson, 2003). They arise from the law when it is applied. However, it is as grievous an error to assume that law is limited to that which happens in practice (i.e. to the law in courts), as it would be to assume that psychology is an entirely academic discipline.

Psychology and law could and, at least in terms of the potential for improving the qualities of our laws, legal procedures and legal decision making, should be an interdisciplinary domain. However, at least as represented in the literature, in learned societies and their conferences, overwhelmingly, it is not. Psychology, when it is merely applied to legal issues, is a specialist domain of psychology and hardly 'truly' interdisciplinary.

Overwhelmingly, scholars in the area currently known as 'psychology and law', the authors, journal editors and editorial board members, are psychologists rather than lawyers. Where dually qualified, their orientation is primarily to psychology. Are lawyers not willing to write on psycho-legal topics? Why should anyone complain about the imbalance? Some lawyers do, directly, address such issues. For example, in the United Kingdom (UK), see Heaton-Armstrong, Shepherd and Wolchover (1999) on witness testimony and McEwan (1998, 2003; see also Chapter 6, this volume) on comparative disciplinary perspectives on trial procedures and fact finding. In the USA, many academic psychologists are also qualified in law. Many lawyers, who do not identify themselves with psycho-legal studies, write on issues relevant to psychology and law. Consider, for example, the three-year research project, funded by the UK's Arts and Humanities Research Board, to produce a normative theory of the criminal trial. Most of the authors, in the first volumes of proceedings, are lawyers, with some philosophers (Duff *et al.*, 2004, 2006). It is not a challenge, to the appropriateness or value of philosophy's contribution, to wonder why neither psychology nor any other behavioural science was involved. Academic lawyers have demonstrated a much longer, and more intense, participation with social sciences, such as criminology, sociology and economics, than with psychology. At least in the UK, criminology courses and teachers are often located within law schools and the Socio-Legal Studies Association[5] has a substantial and vibrant membership dominated by lawyers. The development of psychology and law, however, appears to have been significantly different in Australia and New Zealand; the relevant learned society (ANZAPP&L) incorporates psychiatry as well as psychology and law and a higher proportion of both practitioners and lawyers attend their conferences.

If psychology and law is ever to become a genuinely interdisciplinary venture then it is critical that more steps are taken to involve lawyers in both the design and the execution of research studies (King, 1986) and publications. This is not to advocate any legal hegemony, or suggest that the research should be limited to a legal agenda, and certainly not to inhibit appropriate criticism of legal assumptions, systems procedures or rules. Rather, it is to encourage an appreciation of why the law is as it is, after centuries of evolution, and an understanding of the pragmatic constraints it has to address daily. It is to encourage an

---

[5] http://www.kent.ac.uk/slsa/.

awareness of and research into key legal concepts, for example the processes by which certain behaviour is perceived, processed and maintained as being 'unreasonable'.

Unfortunately expectations and structures have already been established. The absence of many lawyers on a journal's editorial board speaks eloquently both to the readership sought and expected. Even though publishers have economic interests in achieving a broad readership, the implicit message is that it is not really an interdisciplinary topic. Currently, it is as if both lawyers and psychologists are too embarrassed and anxious to make significant overtures to each other outside of the instrumental needs of individual cases, such as for expert evidence. It is understandable that practicing lawyers would (not should) demonstrate limited interest in psychology. They earn their salaries from operating the law and legal system as it is currently. Investing in having their knowledge challenged and changed before it is strictly necessary (such as when legislation is amended) would be economically irrational. However, psychologists, academic and practicing, have no such excuse. Indeed, it is only too likely that many who would describe themselves as interested in 'psychology and law' really understand the phrase as psychology *of* law, as psychology *in* law (Haney, 1980) or 'legal psychology', a division of psychology and not an interdisciplinary topic. Even if research psychologists, employed in academic settings, can justify such non-interdisciplinary specialisms, they will be poorly placed to teach and advise the majority of their students who go on to become practitioner psychologists. They will regularly practice within legal contexts, relating, reacting and reasoning with law and lawyers. Many of those practicing psychologists will be interested in seeking laws and legal structures that are more appropriate for their clients. Unless it is genuinely interdisciplinary, the teaching of psychology and law will (1) handicap those students who wish to practice as psychologists and (2) further delay the day when lawyers must awake to the implications of the research.

Arguably therapeutic jurisprudence (TJ) and restorative justice (RJ) fall within 'psychology and law'. TJ studies demonstrate that laws can have anti-therapeutic effects, and can have consequences that either were unintended or were unnecessarily counter-productive (see generally Wexler and Winick, 1990, 1991, 1996; Winick and Wexler, 2003). Such studies, which regularly call on psychological research, enable their authors to identify and argue for law reform. RJ studies argue that our criminal justice system should focus more on restoring the balances disturbed by crime, particularly in the interests of victims, witnesses and the broader community, rather than on retribution on the offender (Miers, 2001). RJ also frequently involves psychological concepts and processes, for example mediation (Umbreit, 2001) and other processes designed to facilitate change for people involved in the criminal justice system. Despite this affinity, both with psychology and law and with the means they both provide for psychological research and insights to impact on the law and legal processes, both TJ and RJ are not, measured by the contents of the key psychology and law journals, edited collections and conferences, which are considered mainstream psychology and law. Is it coincidental, then, that lawyers are much better represented as authors of TJ research than in psychology and law? Note that many practicing judges, especially in the USA (Winick and Wexler, 2003), Canada (see the National Judicial Institute's report, Goldberg, 2005) and in Australia and New Zealand (e.g. Braithwaite, 1989; Schmid, 2001) have, through problem-solving courts or by developing restorative justice measures, actively demonstrated a vigorous interest and excitement in the possibility of achieving quantitatively and qualitatively greater justice.

Finally, in this critical introduction, consider the relative failure of both law and psychology to address some of the most important issues concerning human behaviour in legal contexts. It is likely that many psychologists, and other behavioural scientists, have – and indeed prefer – images of 'the law' that are associated with appeal courts determining difficult debates or interrogating scientific witnesses. But law, in terms of the daily practice of the courts and lawyers, is much more mundane. In particular, most court time is spent in determining the facts of past events, not in disputing the law. Few cases require expert witnesses. Indeed, the number of cases that ever proceed to an oral hearing, civil or criminal, are but a small fraction of all the cases in which lawyers are involved. Our legal systems are critically dependent on citizens not pressing their rights to an oral hearing; they rely on people (and include formal and informal measure to encourage them) to drop charges, to plead guilty, to accept an offer of settlement or to be too frightened about the costs of proceeding. Fundamental, within the daily life of our law and legal system, is the problem of proving (or sufficiently persuading judges about) what happened in the disputed past event. Justice, in practice, has little to do with the courts. Mediation, and other forms of alternative dispute resolution, are critical legal developments. Prevention and system analyses are budding perspectives. Yet this is hardly acknowledged, let alone represented in, the burgeoning psychology and law literature.

However fundamental psychology and law may be, it is a very underdeveloped field. Lawyers, for example, have demonstrated considerable interest in the law of evidence, but that relates to rules restricting who may say what in court, when and how (e.g. see Roberts and Zuckerman, 2004). Legal education provides instruction in the substantive rules governing (e.g. admissibility of a defendant's prior criminal record), not in the processes, logic or science (e.g. statistical tests of probability) of persuasion and proof. Much of the output of psychology and law is relevant or related to evidentiary issues (e.g. the reliability of offender profiles). The expectation is that that scientific evidence will be offered to a court as an expert's opinion, in a particular case. It is not focused on aiding fact finding and proof issues generally, such as required by the police and prosecutors on a daily basis (but see Saks and Thompson, 2003; Wagenaar, Van Koppen and Crombag, 1993). Very important work has been undertaken on how jurors may fill in evidential detail, and make decisions based on the quality of stories (theories about the evidence) presented to them, rather than just on 'the facts' presented to them, as legal theory assumes (e.g. Pennington and Hastie, 1986, 1988, 1991). That has not, however, made a major impact on the law, lawyers or legal practice. As Twining (2003) cajoles, fact finding, analysis, hypothesis generation, persuasion and proof are profoundly, multi- and interdisciplinary subjects, or rather should be! Whilst a number of researchers (mainly lawyers, but for a most important exception see Schum, 1994) have developed research into such processes (e.g. see Anderson, Schum and Twining, 2005; Murphy 2003), limited interest has been demonstrated by psychologists. Both psychologists and lawyers may be criticized, but it would be more productive to identify ways in which richer collaboration could be ensured. To that we turn.

APPLYING AN ANSWER

'Psychology and law' should become more applied. Greater attention should be paid to where and how it may have an effect. This might appear, initially, to be an appeal to think of the needs and wishes of practitioners, be they psychologists or lawyers. That is not our principal objective; it would be an unintentional – but valuable – by-product of our proposal. We would never, particularly given that we are concerned with such important, albeit often nebulous and contentious issues as 'justice' and 'quality', propose that psychology and law should only have a reactive role. Rather, psychology and law has an enormous potential to improve the quality of law and legal systems. It must always have a role in challenging assumptions about present practice and identifying alternative laws and procedures that might be demonstrated to be more effective and/or efficient in achieving agreed goals. Rather, we are thinking of the ways in which psychology might be applied in legal contexts.

Expert Evidence

Faigman and Monahan (2005), endorsing Borgida and Hunt (2003), recently stated: 'The field of psychology and law is inextricably bound to developments in the area of expert evidence' (p. 632). As a simple descriptive statement about a lot of such research, undertaken in North America, it has a ring of truth. However, it discounts a lot of work on emerging topics which is not yet, if ever it will be, admissible as expert evidence in that country. It certainly reflects the importance accorded, in the USA, to a number of Supreme Court decisions (*Daubert* v. *Merrell Dow Pharmaceutical Inc.* 579 US 563 (1993); *General Electric Co* v. *Joiner,* 522 US 136 (1997); *Kumho Tire, Ltd.* v. *Carmichael,* 526 US 137 (1999)), on when expert evidence is admissible (e.g. see Faigman *et al.*, 2002a, 2002b, 2002c). It is not accurate with regard to other countries, however. There are significant national differences in the development of psychology and law. There has, for example, been extensive research on juries, in the USA (Greene *et al.*, 2002), but not in the UK, where it is largely unlawful. Whilst the initial, major, stimulation for research in interviewing took place in the USA (Geiselman *et al.*, 1984), the major research and policy development on interviewing vulnerable witnesses has taken place in the UK, where there was government support (Department of Health and Home Office, 1992). If Faigman and Monahan's statement, above, is read as a normative statement, or as implying a necessary relationship – psychology and law is by definition bound up with expert evidence – then it is simply wrong. There is no restriction on the role or impact of psychology and law. Psychology and law can be, and should be, applied much more widely than as expert evidence.

Expert evidence is just one of the ways in which psychology can be applied to law. It may be considered to involve the ultimate challenge; it is about the status, of both the science and the scientist, and in court involves a pitting of wits and skills. But it is very inefficient. Unless a scheme, such as that advocated by Monahan and Walker (1986) is adopted, it will involve a case-by-case approach. That is expensive; many litigants will be unable to afford the additional cost of expert witnesses. It is slow; judges might have different opinions about the admissibility of the evidence, and juries might be influenced differently, so there is less cause for the parties to settle amongst themselves and not litigate. Judges may not understand the science, as has been demonstrated with regard at least to some topics (Gatowski *et al.*, 2001). That should not be too surprising as the evidence is only admissible, as expert evidence, because it is beyond the knowledge and experience of the judge and/or jury. Indeed, in what other context would it be considered appropriate (let alone sensible) to expect individuals, however knowledgeable and competent in other disciplines and areas of life, to understand – remembering that they are also expected to be critical of the scientific evidence, fresh information, and not just accept it on the authority of the witness – without a background and skills in the methodology and related topics on which it is based? (See Peter van Koppen, Chapter 16, this volume.) Chief Justice Rhenquist, in *Daubert* (1993), the leading case on the admissibility of scientific evidence in US Federal courts, albeit as dissentient, doubted the capacity of judges to understand such concepts as Popper's falsification theory. That theory has been challenged, as not describing how 'science' 'really' develops in practice, in a manual prepared and published to assist federal judges in making decisions about the admissibility of 'scientific evidence' (see Goodstein, 2000).

Monahan and Walker (1986; see also Walker and Monahan, 1987, 1988) proposed that scientific evidence could be recognized, by the courts, in a scheme analogous to legal precedent. Decisions, about the admissibility of different forms of expert evidence made by one court, would be treated as binding on all other courts which would be bound by an interpretation of the law made by that court. In this way, admissibility decisions could be overturned by courts higher in the court hierarchy but, otherwise, there would be much more certainty, predictability and consistency, which are critical if lawyers are to advise their clients to settle rather than to litigate their disputes. Such approaches have not been adopted, however. If they were, there is a risk that they might promote 'divisiveness.' Lawyers are skilled and practised in distinguishing legal precedents. They identify ways in which their case may be argued to be legally different from prior, precedent, interpretations of the law. The same skills might be applied to scientific evidence. For example, excellent research might inform experts' predictions of the dangerousness of a mentally disordered person (Monahan *et al.*, 2001), but what if a judge decides that the authority for that opinion is distinguishable because the individual before the court has never lived in any of the three areas (let alone the country) where the empirical work for that research was undertaken? It is not suggested that that would be a sound distinction. Rather, the 'pragmatic imperative', for lawyers, would be to find reasons for distinguishing, that is categorically rejecting, the science. Even if nobody can say, because it involves an inference from actuarial data, that the research applies equally to people outside the test sites, it still has relative value. Law has been criticized for dichotomizing, for example distinguishing concepts into mutually exclusive categories such as admissible or inadmissible, whilst science has been commended for recognizing degrees, that behaviour is relative, not simply reasonable or unreasonable (Campbell, 1974). The point is that scientific evidence may deserve to have a powerful effect upon judicial decision making, even if not overwhelming and determinative of the issue. Courts can cope with factual evidence which is of different degrees of relevance, reliability and credibility. The same is possible for opinion, expert, evidence.

Legislation

A much more efficient, and potentially effective, method for applying psychology to law is legislation. Psychological knowledge can be incorporated into legislation in a variety of ways. Instead of utilizing psychological expertise to decide whether Mr X, a unique individual, had capacity to perform legal act Y, when the expert witness could be pressed to concede that he or she cannot be sure about X, because his or her science is based on research conducted on other people, legislation could incorporate general insights and research from psychology. Instead of behavioural scientists seeking to have it both ways – to be entitled to give scientific evidence but not to be asked inappropriate questions which go beyond the general knowledge that they have developed – legislation provides a forum for lawyers and psychologists to meet and formulate the best laws possible.

Psychologists may object that law making is political. Legislators may, for example, wish to pass laws to punish certain mentally disordered offenders whom they consider blameworthy, when the science demonstrates that those individuals lacked understanding or control over their conduct. This must be acknowledged. It does not follow, however, that any science or discipline must accede to democratically elected ignorance. For example, judges, in the UK, have found themselves deciding that diabetes (*Hennessy* [1989] 2 All ER 9) and epilepsy (*Sullivan,* [1984] 1 AC 156) are 'diseases of the mind' (because they affect the operation of the brain) for the purposes of the common law defence of insanity under the *McNaghten Rules* ((1843) 10 Clark & Fin 200). It does not follow that those judges approved of the legal position they developed. Rather, they need informed legislation to replace the outdated common law. Hopefully, behavioural science may engage with law, on such topics, and over time develop better, more informed, humane and just laws. It is a dialectical process; it involves paradigm shifts (Kuhn, 1962). Just as new science can challenge old science, requiring a restatement of contemporary knowledge, so better psychologically informed laws can replace less informed former rules. Judgements should be made on efficiency and efficacy of the law reform process, not on 'snapshots' of the law at any one time. Pragmatic considerations must be taken into account. Law reform, especially if extensive research and consultation is involved, is time consuming. There is limited time for parliamentary debate. However, law reform proposals on relatively non-contentious topics, which have clearly been through a process involving informed and rigorous debate with relevant disciplines, will require less parliamentary time.

Psychology associations, and psychologists interested in law, should pay more attention to law reform agencies, submitting evidence-based proposals for law reform. However, those agencies should also be much more welcoming. For example, in the UK, although established by the *Law Commission Act 1965* to keep the law under review and undertake specific projects (such as the capacity of individuals to make legal decisions, leading to the *Mental Capacity Act 2005*), all of the Commissioners are lawyers. Other disciplines have much to offer, including alternative assumptions and perspectives, and skills in scientific research methods that do not form part of the educational background of lawyers. However, the psychology associations need to be proactive, not just reacting to invitations to respond to consultation papers. Without people from different disciplinary backgrounds such law reform bodies cannot know what they do not know, and so cannot know when to ask for special advice. In addition, there is the 'problem' that lawyers have been 'getting on with it' for centuries; they have taken things for granted, often not even articulating their assumptions as in a 'fireside musing' (Meehl, 1989), because it has been pragmatically necessary. For example, judges and jurors are regularly expected to retain and work on more data, at the same time, than the research on information overload suggests is either possible or desirable (Kahneman and Tversky, 1972, 1973, 1984). That a law or practice has been 'good enough' for several centuries may tell us quite a bit about how easily we have been satisfied in the past; it cannot justify continuing not to make use of current knowledge, provided attention is paid to the pragmatic issues involved in securing change.

Legal Criteria

A problem, with psychology and law taking the legislative route, is the pragmatic 'requirement' for legislation to be explicit, preferably adopting mutually exclusive categories. For example, the criminal law, of many jurisdictions, makes a critical distinction between those who 'intended' the harm that was caused and those that merely foresaw it (e.g. Ormerod,

2005). Without denying the possibility that the distinction may be dismissed as entirely tendentious, for example because action precedes thought (Libet, Freeman and Sutherland, 1999), in legal experience the distinction usually works. However, a form of intermediate category has been recognized, and treated as part of 'intention' at least for liability purposes, where there was extensive prior knowledge of the probability of the outcome and a willingness, if not a desire, for it to occur (*R. v. Nedrick,* [1986] 3 All ER 1, as amended by *R. v. Woolin,* [1998] 4 All ER 1). The law, particularly criminal law as it is concerned with liberty of the individual, needs exclusive categories to justify differential labels and responses (e.g. murder or manslaughter) and treatment (e.g. mandatory life or a discretionary sentence). The Law Commission for England and Wales (2005, 2006), for example, has suggested a reform in the law so that an intention to kill would constitute first-degree murder, with mandatory life imprisonment, whilst an intention to cause serious injury would be second-degree murder, where there would be sentencing discretion for the trial judge. Current behavioural science, however, may suggest that that is inappropriate on particular topics. Psychologists, and others, might feel it is inappropriate to support any particular formulation of a dichotomous test.

An alternative, to specifying dichotomous tests, is to identify relevant legal criteria that should be considered. These can inform and guide decision making by judges and juries. An example is provided by identification evidence. In *R. v. Turnbull* ([1977] QB 224) Lord Widgery, then Chief Justice, laid down a number of factors which trial judges should ensure that juries consider when assessing identification evidence. These include: the length of time over which the observation took place; how far away the incident observed took place was; and the lighting conditions at the time (see pp. 228–230). The Court, as Roberts and Zuckerman (2004, p. 494) stress:

> ... disavowed technical legal formulae and emphasised the substance of the warnings to the jury. The factors identified ... combine common sense assumptions, the accumulated wisdom of forensic experience, and pioneering behavioural science research ...

gleaned from an official Committee of Inquiry chaired by a senior lawyer (Devlin, 1976). This proved to be an exceptionally important development. The provenance of the criteria, in a Court of Appeal decision, necessarily commends them to all practicing lawyers. There are few more effective ways of ensuring that lawyers will learn about them! But there are dangers. First, note how they are considered to involve 'common sense' and 'accumulated wisdom.' These are labels that can be attached to almost anything that is perceived to be sensible and to have a history. They are not tests that can reliably be applied to identify criteria relevant to other legal tests, such as consent, capacity and freedom of choice. One person's common sense can be another's prejudice or ignorance; for example, that group decisions are always more moderate than those of individuals. Errors can accumulate as easily as wisdom. Evidence, not mere ascription of reassuring labels, is desirable. Second, no provision is made for automatic updating as fuller and better research findings become available.

Nevertheless the *Turnbull* case provides an excellent example of how psychological research might identify criteria relevant for determining legal tests. One approach would be to specify a procedure that identifies relevant considerations. This could be exceptionally important if the valuable research on predicting dangerousness, or risk, is to be utilized. Statute (Chapter 989, Virginia Acts of Assembly, § 37.1–70.4), in Virginia (USA), requires clinicians considering the continued detention of patients considered to be dangerous, who might be expected to prefer clinical tests and judgement) to have regard to an identified actuarial test (Monahan, 2004). This is important on many levels, not least because of the superior record of actuarial tests (Monahan et al., 2001). It also allows for the actuarial test to be substituted as new knowledge is developed, without the time and other resource expensive requirements of new legislation.

This approach could be used in legislation or through case law precedents. A 'sort of' statutory example exists in recent reforms to the law of rape in England and Wales. A core issue, in the offence, is the victim's absence of consent and the offender's belief, or otherwise, in the existence of that consent. The legislation is a response to a concern that offenders were committing the act but then maintaining that they believed that the victim was consenting. Given that belief is an 'inner' state of mind without explicit, 'externally' verifiable, referents, there has been concern that it is too easy to claim a belief in the 'victim's' consent, especially as that belief did not have to be reasonable. Now section 75 of the *Sexual Offences Act 2003* lists criteria that determine whether consent, or belief in it, existed: violence, threat of violence, detention, being asleep or unconscious, being unable to communicate because of a physical disability, and non-consensual taking of a stupefying drug. Surely the behavioural sciences could have offered a richer list of factors relating to the nature of consent, such as including the differentials in power and understanding?

An opportunity exists for using this approach in relation to the extensive research on interviewing, which has developed in recent years. Just as Lord Widgery, in *Turnbull* (above), identified the features of identification evidence that make it more or less reliable, so another judge could identify the features of an interview, particularly those leading to a confession of responsibility, which make the evidence more or less reliable. It may be objected that the factors, identified in *Turnbull*, were more concrete, tangible, such as lighting and distance, whereas the items likely to be listed, in relation to interviews, would be more qualitative, such as nature and order of the questions asked, degree of oppressiveness in the interview room. It is not the consonance with 'common sense', that is so important but that which has been tested, and its reliability.

Codes

Legal 'technology' is relatively limited. Statues are expensive to enact. Those who draft the legislation (who can have their handiwork spoilt by legislators) are required to predict difficulties in order to prevent as many as possible problems of interpretation. Every additional or alternative qualification adds to the number of potential interpretation problems. This makes it difficult to fit many statutes within a parliamentary timetable and does not put a premium on comprehensibility. It is not possible to simply declare an objective – the object of this Act is to proscribe dishonesty – or just to identify certain values. Our adherence to the 'rule of law' (although it involves improperly reifying 'law'), requires demonstrable clarity and applicability to individuals and facts if people are, in particular, to be punished. Legislation has to be about minimum standards; it has to specify the standards necessary for acts to be criminal or to create civil liability. Whilst it can, and does, contain sections that provide interpretations of key words and phrases, it cannot, realistically, include mission statements (fortunately), the articulation of best practices or statements of ideals.

Codes of practice, however, can. These have developed as an adjunct to legislation. They cover a wide range of topics, for example in England and Wales, from road safety (the

Highway Code), through industry (codes on employer and employee relations), to mental health. The *Mental Health Act Code* provides much greater practical detail on how patients should be treated than the *Mental Health Act 1983*, and the many sets of regulations made under it, ever could. The enforceability of a code depends on what is specified in the authorizing legislation. An Act may just authorize a government minister to have a code prepared and published. It could specify that any court or tribunal, hearing any dispute arising under the legislation, is to take the code into consideration. It could specify that any court or tribunal is to enforce the code. However, critically, codes are not subject to the same constraints as legislation. They can, for example state objectives and identify best practices in order to guide decisions. They can map out ways to better services or standards, and encourage movement towards them, without imposing liability. They can reflect and stimulate professional standards. They can be written and approved quickly without parliamentary debate. Alternatively, if participation and 'ownership' is important, a specified range of different people with immediate knowledge of the area, rather than members of the legislature, can be consulted about what the code should state. The Act which provides for the code can – but need not – specify who is to be consulted and it can require endorsement by a simple vote in parliament, but it is very much easier, cheaper and quicker to draft, or redraft, a code than to get a new statute enacted.

This is another way in which psychological research can be applied to law. It may not be as dramatic, or as closely associated with status, as providing expert evidence in a trial court, but it can be much more effective, in so many more cases. The compatibility problems (see discussion above), between law and psychology, can be reduced to a minimum where codes are the medium for applying psychology to law.

Practice Statements

A similar approach, to codes, is practice statements. The classic example, in the UK, is the *Memorandum of Good Practice for Video Recorded Interviews with Child Witnesses for Criminal Proceedings* (1992) drafted by a psychologist (Professor Ray Bull) and a lawyer (Professor Diane Birch) for two government departments, the Home Office (concerned with policing and related issues) and Department of Health (also concerned with social work issues). This both described and justified, with supporting research, a fresh approach to interviewing child victims of sexual and other violent offences. It led to very different, and it can hardly be disputed better, ways of interviewing these victims. Then, building on this foundation, the government established an *'Action for Justice'* programme to implement its *'Speaking up for Justice'* report (1998), which expanded on and replaced the *Memorandum of Good Practice* with *Achieving Best Evidence in Criminal Proceedings: Guidance for Vulnerable or Intimidated Witnesses, Including Children* (Home Office, Lord Chancellor's Department, Crown Prosecution Service and Department of Health, 2002). This, research based, work included legislative changes in Part 2 of the *Youth Justice and Criminal Evidence Act 1999*, which provide a range of special measures to support vulnerable witnesses through the courts. This is a paradigm of collaboration between psychology and law.

Practice statements can provide guidance on better ways of organizing services and undertaking a range of tasks. In the UK, the *Police Reform Act 2002* empowered the Secretary of State, for the Home Office, to publish codes of practice, as well as to prescribe practices and procedures, after consultation with relevant organizations. In this way, a hierarchy of 'practice statements' has been developed. Codes must be followed; but breach is not, per se, unlawful (e.g. *Code of Practice on the National Intelligence Model* (Appendix 1) (National Centre for Policing Excellence (NCPE), 2005a). Guidance (e.g. *Guidance on Investigating Domestic Violence* (NCPE, 2004) should be adopted by all police forces. Advice (e.g. *Core Investigative Doctrine* NCPE, (2005b)), however, is discretionary. These documents disseminate and advance best practices. Especially given the opportunities to see developments in research incorporated into professional policing practice, this approach offers behavioural scientists and lawyers so many opportunities to make a major difference – if they are open and willing to seize them.

Professional Practice Statements

This suggestion may appear very similar, and it certainly is related, to the discussion of practice statements, above. It is also, significantly, different. Note that breach of a code of practice does not, necessarily, constitute a breach of the law, civil or criminal. Any statement of good practice is liable to be seized on by a lawyer as an indication of a standard which, if breached, ought to lead to civil liability in the law of negligence. Even if the standard does not create liability, in litigation, its existence may cause concern. Considerable expense can be caused in dealing with claims of negligence, even if they never reach court. Some professionals can become so anxious about being sued that they avoid making decisions in the mistaken belief that that will prevent them from being liable. They are wrong because there can be liability for omissions as well as commissions (Rogers, 2006). (They are partly 'correct' in the sense that victims of failures to act professionally are less likely to realize they could sue than victims of commissions.)

To be liable in the law of negligence, at least in England and Wales, five conditions must be satisfied. The person responsible for causing the loss must have owed the person injured a duty of care. The standard of care, which applies to that duty of care, must have been broken. That breach must have actually caused the loss, which was reasonably foreseeable, and which was of a kind that the law compensates (Montgomery, 2003; Rogers, 2006). In practice, the most important of those requirements is the standard of care. Notably – and what makes this heading different from 'practice statements' discussed above – the standard of care does *not* have to involve best practice, even usual practice. If a responsible body of professional colleagues would support the standard concerned, in a particular case, then it is not breached (*Bolam v. Friern HMC* [1957] 2 All ER 118). That standard of care permits a great deal of variety. Whilst the House of Lords (which is also the UK's Supreme Court) has emphasized that professional organizations cannot be allowed artificially to lower standards in order to escape liability (*Bolitho v. City & Hackney HA* [1997] 4 All ER 771), their current standard practices will usually be adopted by the courts. The problem is that those standards are often inexplicit, particularly where several disciplines and professions are involved. The recommendation is that acceptable professional practice protocols are articulated to discourage inappropriate litigation. If an individual has made a decision, or otherwise acted in a manner consistent with such a professional protocol, then the standard of care will not have been broken. Fear of litigation, being blamed and losing motivation, leading to evasion of responsibilities can, in this manner, be discouraged.

It may be objected that such a device will deter progress because it only articulates basic standards. Many would protest that professionals should be encouraged to adopt best practices, not baseline standards, but that involves a misunderstanding. Articulating the standard of care is not incompatible with encouraging higher standards, especially when and where they are achievable with resources available. Any baseline statement of professional standards can only be provisional; it would need to be reviewed regularly. The courts expect to see standards rise as new knowledge, technology, practices, and so on become available, thereby stating that professional standards should be seen as part of an educational or learning circle where standards are improved over time. They can also be used to defend services against slippage in standards. If standards slip, or are not sustained, then there could be legal liability for any resulting loss. Managers and employers might be reminded of this if they should fail to support standards, such as by reducing resources inappropriately.

It might also be objected that not all professions involved with criminal justice services owe a duty of care to those they may injure. If they do not owe a duty of care then the question of a standard of care does not arise. In England and Wales, police investigators (*Brooks v. Commissioner of Police for the Metropolis and Others* ([2005] 2 All ER 489) and professionals involved in enforcing child protection legislation (*JD v. East Berkshire Community Health NHS Trust and Others* ([2005] 2 FLR 284), will rarely owe a duty of care, despite a decision of the European Court of Human Rights (EHCR) (*Osman v. UK* (2000) 29 EHRR 245). The ECHR only objected to a blanket prohibition on suing, not to making it a rarity (Hoyano, 1999). However, these obstacles to suing are most unusual. There is no such restriction on suing in, for example, Canada (i.e. *Jane Doe v. Metropolitan Police of Toronto* (1998) 160 DLD (4th) 697), France, Germany or South Africa (Hoyano, 1999). It is also unnecessary as investigators would rarely be liable. The standard of care, which would apply to such investigators, would be relatively low because of all the countervailing duties, for example to children possibly at risk, which the investigators would have to take into account. Social workers, for example, have to consider the harm that may befall a child if they do not remove it from potentially violent parents. They also have to consider harm that would be caused by removing the child. It may be lesser harm, but its likelihood is higher. Hence, there is an important role for articulating statements about baseline standards, particularly if this rule, at least in England and Wales, was replaced. Law has a particular contribution to make in terms of the clarity of the statement and ensuring it is consistent with case law, whilst psychology has a particular contribution in relation to system (see below) and learning factors.

'Training Manuals'

In essence, the documents on interviewing vulnerable witnesses, discussed above (Home Office *et al.*, 2002), provides guidance on how to perform an important psycho-legal skill, how to interview people in order to obtain the best (quantity and quality) evidence feasible. There is a potential for the application of psychology to law and the criminal justice system in the production of training manuals in a broader sense. For example, many disciplines and professions are concerned with undertaking risk assessment and risk management, and yet relatively limited attention has been paid to the psychological problems that risk decision makers can have with making risk decisions. Quality risk decisions require the availability of sufficient, relevant and accurate information, even though, by virtue of it being a risk decision, it will be incomplete. How should risk decision makers cope with the information overload, avoid inappropriate heuristics and manage information of very different natures (including value judgements)? It may be at a polar extreme from the drama of being cross-examined on scientific evidence given in court, but designing and writing quality training materials and programmes could have a much more profound value.

Indeed this could involve topics traditionally not included in academic psychology and law. For example, contracts are very important to practitioners, whether lawyers, psychologists (clinical, forensic, educational and others), probation officers, psychiatrists and so on. The professional can negotiate an agreement, contract, with another, for example with a client. They are a paradigm means of achieving change, with the additional benefits of reflecting the independence, competence and choice of both parties (Carson, 1999). Indeed, Bonnie and Monahan (2005), key members of the MacArthur Research Network on Mental Health and the Law, have advocated the potential of contract as a means of ensuring community treatment of people with mental illnesses. However, many contracts, between providers of professional services and their clients, are not binding in law. A key requirement, of a contract not under seal, is that both parties provide the other with a benefit, known as consideration. The relative or absolute value of this consideration is not legally relevant, provided it exists. Psychologists and others, employed by health, education, or other national or local government agencies, however, provide a service to their clients because they are employed, by others, to do so. Their clients do not provide them with consideration – outside of a private, contractual, relationship. That clients pay taxes, which in part go towards those professionals' salaries, does not constitute consideration. Hence, as they are not contracts, the courts cannot enforce them.

Perhaps this should be changed; perhaps the rights and obligations of clients would be enhanced if based more on individually negotiated contracts than on broad, impersonal, legislation (Carson, 1999). The reality is that 'contracts', as a tool for organizing behavioural change and managing 'legitimate' expectations, are very popular with practitioners. Their legal unenforceability does not appear to be much of a deterrent. In fact, the unenforceability of such contracts, with all the associated costs, complexity and confusion, may be an advantage. Nevertheless, training manuals designed to help people write contracts to realize their objectives, could only be valuable. Manuals on mediation and different forms of dispute resolution could be appropriate. It is submitted that these are key areas where psychology and law could productively interact.

Justice Systems

In recent decades a number of alternative models of justice have emerged, for example (as mentioned above) therapeutic jurisprudence (TJ), restorative justice (RJ) and preventive law perspectives. These have spawned a very substantial literature, which can only be hinted at here.[6] In essence, TJ demonstrates that laws can have therapeutic or anti-therapeutic effects and argues that, provided basic civil rights are not impugned, laws should have pro-therapeutic effects. Thus if, as has been argued, allowing clients to negotiate and to contract with their clinicians over their medication leads to them maintaining their treatment regime for longer, then the law should make this possible (Winick, 1997). TJ provides a very neat basis for utilizing psychological research to support law reform. It is both descriptive, in the sense that it depends on analysis of the effects of the law, and normative in providing policy guidance. It is relevant both to academic and to practitioner psychologists, and it can be used preventively, to avoid many legal problems during a life cycle (Patry et al., 1998).

---

[6] See: http://www.law.arizona.edu/depts/upr-intj/ and http://www.voma.org/bibliography.shtml.

Restorative Justice reflects an interest in restoring the balances upset by crime. It is concerned with the interests of victims, of witnesses, offenders' families and the communities affected rather just the focus on offender of retributive justice and formal legal systems. It is also concerned with effectiveness in the sense that it promotes interventions that will do more than just punish the offender, which will address the causes of offending and implications for victims. Once again psychology is very relevant to this alternative/additional model of justice. For example, it includes a focus on change by offenders (see Palmer, Chapter 9, this volume). Whether they are representative of TJ or of RJ does not really matter, but in many countries, particularly the USA, problem-solving courts have become very popular (Winick and Wexler, 2003). These focus on addressing the causes of frequent offenders' behaviour, such as domestic violence, misuse of drugs, or experience of mental ill health. They may cause concern to lawyers because they can appear 'process-light' in their emphasis on the quality of the courts' relationships with offenders rather than with formal rights. There may be a danger of valuable services becoming available, or quickly available, only if a court process is involved, so that individuals are tempted to plead guilty to get the service even when innocent. A key feature of these courts, however, is that they – and it is strange contrast with traditional academic legal perspectives – focus on the typical, the usual, and the norm, such as the fact that most people plead guilty and are dealt with in the minor courts. This is where most practitioner psychologists are likely to have clients. Again there is considerable potential for psychology and law working together, productively.

Services

A great deal of forensic psychology (contrasted with legal psychology) and psychiatry is concerned with the provision of 'services' or treatments to clients and patients, for example cognitive skills and anger management programmes or risk assessments. These can make a considerable difference for clients' well-being and community safety. Knowing what might be achieved, for a client, and understanding the real nature of the risks, should enable lawyers to assist their clients in more useful manners. (It is a great pity that the usage of 'advocate' has increasingly become limited to skills in asking questions, of witnesses, in court.) Lawyers should advocate for their clients in a much broader sense. Given that the vast majority of defendants, in criminal courts, plead guilty it might be expected that lawyers would be trained in the art of making effective pleas in mitigation. They are not. More effective interventions could be advocated if lawyers knew about the services and treatments available. This is another area where psychology and law could valuably collaborate.

Systems

The individualistic perspective, almost automatically adopted by legal analyses, is very apparent in inquiries into harmful events, from medical negligence, through child abuse inquiries to tribunals after disasters. The past is examined in order to identify the individuals who caused, and/or may be blamed for, the harm. We anticipate blaming human causes. We are not nearly so skilled in identifying, and appropriately blaming, other factors such as organizational structures, decision-making systems or working culture. Yet such factors may be highly relevant (Reason, 1990, 1997). The psychologists, undertaking these analyses and this research, are likely to consider themselves specialists in social or occupational psychology, rather than legal psychology, but that is a consequence of the artificial narrowness of legal psychology.

For example at the time of writing, the UK Parliament is considering government proposals, (the *Corporate Manslaughter and Corporate Homicide Bill*) to introduce a statutory crime of corporate manslaughter (Home Office, 2005). The current common law requires that a 'directing mind' has the *mens rea* for the offence. The result is that very small firms and organizations, where the directors are aware of what is happening in practice, can be held responsible. However, large firms, where the managers and directors are insulated (even if they ought not to be), from knowledge of dangerous working practices, are rarely liable even though many more people are killed by their accidents. The Bill proposes that an organization will be liable for corporate manslaughter if, because of the way in which its activities are organized by senior managers, it causes a death through a gross breach of a duty owed to the victim. It will be a 'gross' breach if it '...constitutes conduct falling far below what can reasonably be expected of the organization in the circumstances' (clause 3(1)). But what should investigators and lawyers look for when considering whether an organization's conduct fell far below what may be expected? Surely psychology could help by identifying poor working practices, structures, cultures, and so on. For example, in contrast with the proposals for England and Wales, which emphasize gross breach of duty, those for Scotland (Expert Group, 2005) emphasize degree of management failure. They suggest:

> an organisation should be liable where it fails to put policies, practices and systems in place to ensure the health and safety of its employees and those affected by its activities. This may include allowing, or failing to take all reasonable steps to prevent a corporate culture to exist which encourages, tolerates or leads to an offence taking place. (*Ibid*. para. 11.1.)

Their reference to corporate culture – which, it is submitted, organizational and social psychology ought to be able to help illuminate and operationalize into legal concepts or criteria – is based upon the *Australian Criminal Code 1995*.

APPLYING PSYCHOLOGY TO LAW AND CRIMINAL JUSTICE

Hopefully the foregoing has demonstrated the tremendous potential there is for psychology to be *applied* to law, and to criminal justice issues in particular. The examples may have highlighted the law and practice of England and Wales but similar issues and points apply in relation to most, if not all, other countries. The thesis of this opening chapter has been that, whilst there are problems in the relationship between law and psychology, much could be achieved by focusing on the range of ways in which psychology can contribute, particularly if law can become more aware and welcoming, through application to law and practice. We hope you agree that the following chapters substantiate this point.

REFERENCES

Anderson, T., Schum, D. and Twining, W. (2005) *Analysis of Evidence*, 2nd edn, Cambridge University Press, Cambridge.

Bonnie, R.J. and Monahan, J. (2005) From coercion to contract: Reframing the debate on mandated community treatment for people with mental disorders. *Law and Human Behavior*, **29** (4), 485–503.

Borgida, E. and Hunt, J.S. (2003) Psychology and law, in *Social Psychology* (eds S.E. Taylor, L.A. Peplau and D.O. Sears), Prentice Hall, New York.

Borodzicz, E.P. (2005) *Risk, Crisis and Security Management*, Wiley, Chichester.

Braithwaite, J. (1989) *Crime, Shame and Reintegration*, Cambridge University Press, Cambridge.

Campbell (1974) Legal thought and juristic values. *British Journal of Law and Society*, 1, 13–31.

Carson, D. (1988) Psychologists should be wary of involvement with lawyers, in *Lawyers on Psychology and Psychologists on Law* (eds P.J. Van Koppen, D.J. Hessing and G. Van Den Heuvel), Swets & Zeitlinger, Amsterdam.

Carson, D. (1999) From status to contract: A future for mental health law? *Behavioral Sciences & the Law*, 17 (5), 645–60.

Carson, D. (2003) Psychology and law: A subdiscipline, an interdisciplinary collaboration or a project? in *Handbook of Psychology in Legal Contexts* (eds D. Carson and R. Bull), Wiley, Chichester.

Clifford, B.R. (1995) Psychology's premises, methods and values, in *Handbook of Psychology in Legal Contexts* (eds R. Bull and D. Carson), Wiley, Chichester.

Clifford, B.R. (2003) Methodology: Law's adopting and adapting to psychology's methods and findings, in *Handbook of Psychology in Legal Contexts* (eds D. Carson and R. Bull), Wiley, Chichester.

Daubert v. Merrell Dow Pharmaceuticals, Inc. 509 U.S. 579 (1993).

Department of Health and Home Office (1992) *Memorandum of Good Practice on Video Recorded Interviews with Child Witnesses in Criminal Proceedings*, HMSO, London.

Devlin, L. (1976) *Report to the Secretary of State for the Home Department of the Departmental Committee on Evidence of Identification in Criminal Cases*, HMSO, London (HC 338).

Duff, A., Farmer, L., Marshall, S. and Tadros, V. (2004) *The Trial on Trial: Volume One*, Hart, Oxford.

Duff, A., Farmer, L., Marshall, S. and Tadros, V. (2006) *The Trial on Trial: Judgment and Calling to Account. Volume Two*, Hart, Oxford.

Expert Group (2005) *Corporate Homicide: Expert Group Report*, Scottish Executive, Edinburgh.

Faigman, D.L., Kaye, D.H., Saks, M.J. and Sanders, J. (2002a) *Science in the Law: Social and Behavioural Science Issues*, West, St Paul (MN).

Faigman, D.L., Kaye, D.H., Saks, M.J. and Sanders, J. (2002b) *Science in the Law: Forensic Science Issues*, West, St Paul (MN).

Faigman, D.L., Kaye, D.H., Saks, M.J. and Sanders, J. (2002c) *Science in the Law: Standards, Statistics and Research Issues*, West, St Paul (MN).

Faigman, D.J. and Monahan, J. (2005) Psychological evidence at the dawn of the Law's scientific age. *Annual Review of Psychology*, 56, 631–59.

Gatowski, S.I., Dobbin, S.A., Richardson, J.T. et al. (2001) Asking the gatekeepers: A national survey of judges on judging expert evidence in a post-Daubert world. *Journal of Law and Human Behavior*, 25 (5), 433–58

Geiselman, R.E., Fisher, R.P., Firstenberg, I. et al. (1984) Enhancement of eye-witness memory: an empirical evaluation of the cognitive interview. *Journal of Police Science and Administration*, 12, 74–80.

Goldberg, S. (2005) Judging for the 21st Century: A Problem-Solving Approach, National Judicial institute, Ottowa. Available at http://www.nji.ca/Public/documents/Judgingfor21scenturyDe.pdf (Accessed 16 March 2006).

Goodstein, D. (2000) How science works, in Federal Judicial Center. *Reference Manual on Scientific Evidence*, 2nd edn, Federal Judicial Center, Washington (DC), pp. 67–82.

Greene, E., Chopra, S., Kovera, M.B. et al. (2002) Jurors and juries: A review of the field, in *Taking Psychology and Law into the Twenty First Century* (ed. J.R.P. Ogloff), Kluwer, New York.

Gudjonsson, G.H. (2003) The Psychology of Interrogations and Confessions: A Handbook, Wiley, Chichester.

Haney, C. (1980) Psychology and legal change: On the limits of a factual jurisprudence. *Law and Human Behavior*, 4 (3), 147–99.

Haney, C. (1993) Psychology and legal change: The impact of a decade. *Law and Human Behavior*, 17 (4), 371–98.

Heaton-Armstrong, A., Shepherd, E. and Wolchover, D. (eds) (1999) *Analysing Witness Testimony: A Guide for Legal Practitioners and Other Professionals*, Blackstone Press, London.

Home Office (1998) *Speaking up for Justice: Report of the Interdepartmental Working Group on the treatment of Vulnerable or Intimidated Witnesses in the Criminal Justice System*, Home Office, London.

Home Office (2005) *Corporate Manslaughter: The Government's Draft Bill for Reform*, The Stationery Office, London.

Home Office and Department of Health (1992) *Memorandum of Good Practice for Video Recorded Interviews with Child Witnesses for Criminal Proceedings*, HMSO, London.

Home Office, Lord Chancellor's Department, Crown Prosecution Service and Department of Health (2002) *Achieving Best Evidence in Criminal Proceedings: Guidance for Vulnerable or Intimidated Witnesses, Including Children*, Home Office, London.

Hoyano, L.C.H. (1999) Policing flawed police investigations: Unravelling the blanket. *Modern Law Review*, **62**, 912–36.

Kagehiro, D.K. and Laufer, W.S. (eds) (1992) *Handbook of Psychology and Law*, Springer-Verlag, New York.

Kahneman, D. and Tversky, A. (1972) Subjective probability: A judgement of representativeness. *Cognitive Psychology*, **3**, 430–54.

Kahneman, D. and Tversky, A. (1973) On the psychology of prediction. *Psychological Review*, **80**, 237–51.

Kahneman, D. and Tversky, A. (1984) Choices, values and frames. *American Psychologist*, **39**, 341–50.

Kapardis, A. (2003) *Psychology and Law: A Critical Introduction*, 2nd edn, Cambridge University Press, Cambridge.

King, M. (1986) *Psychology in and out of Court: A Critical Examination of Legal Psychology*, Pergamon Press, Oxford.

Kuhn, T. (1962) *The Structure of Scientific Revolutions*, University of Chicago Press, Chicago (IL).

Law Commission (2005) *A New Homicide Act for England and Wales? A Consultation Paper*, Law Commission (Consultation Paper No 177), London.

Law Commission (2006) *Murder, Manslaughter, Infanticide*, The Stationery Office, London.

Libet, B., Freeman, A. and Sutherland, K. (eds) (1999) *The Volitional Brain: Towards a Neuroscience of Free Will*, Imprint Academic, Thorverton.

McEwan, J. (1998) *Evidence and the Adversarial Process: The Modern Law*, 2nd edn, Hart, Oxford.

McEwan, J. (2003) *The Verdict of the Court: Passing Judgment in Law and Psychology*, Hart, Oxford.

McMurran, M. (ed.) (2002) *Motivating Offenders to Change: A Guide to Enhancing Engagement in Therapy*, Wiley, Chichester.

Meehl, P.E. (1989) Law and the fireside inductions (with postscript): Some reflections of a clinical psychologist. *Behavioral Sciences and the Law*, **7** (4): 521–50.

Memon, A. and Bull, R. (eds) (1999) *Handbook of the Psychology of Interviewing*, Wiley, Chichester.

Miers, D. (2001) *An International Review of Restorative Justice*, Home Office, London.

Monahan, J. (2004) *Forecasting Harm: The Law and Science of Risk Assessment among Prisoners, Predators, and Patients*, Electronic Press, Berkeley, Paper 410. Available at http://law.bepress.com/cgi/viewcontent.cgi?article=1829&context=expresso (Accessed 21 March 2006.)

Monahan, J. and Walker, L. (1986) Social authority: obtaining, evaluating, and establishing social science in law. *University of Pennsylvania. Law Review*, **134**, 477–517.

Monahan, J., Steadman, H.J., Silver, E. *et al.* (2001) *Rethinking Risk Assessment: The MacArthur Study of Mental Disorder and Violence*, Oxford University Press, Oxford.

Montgomery, J. (2003) *Health Care Law*, 2nd edn, Oxford University Press, Oxford.

Murphy, P. (2003) *Evidence, Proof, and Facts: A Book of Sources*, Oxford University Press, Oxford.

Müller, D.J., Blackman, D.E. and Chapman, A.J. (eds) (1984) *Psychology and Law*, Wiley, Chichester.

National Centre for Policing Excellence (2004) *Guidance on Investigating Domestic Violence*, Centrex, Cambourne (Cambridgeshire).

National Centre for Policing Excellence (2005a) *The National Intelligence Model*, Centrex, Cambourne.

National Centre for Policing Excellence (2005b) *Core Investigative Doctrine*, Centrex, Cambourne.

Ormerod, D. (2005) *Smith and Hogan Criminal Law*, 11th edn, Oxford University Press, Oxford.

Palmer, E.J. (2003) *Offending behaviour: Moral Reasoning, Criminal Conduct and the Rehabilitation of Offenders*, Willan, Cullompton.

Patry, M.W., Wexler, D.B., Stolle, D.P. and Tomkins, A.J. (1998) Better legal counseling through empirical research: Identifying psycholegal soft spots and strategies. *California Western Law Review*, **34**, 439–55.

Pennington, N. and Hastie, R. (1986) Evidence evaluation in complex decision making. *Journal of Personality and Social Psychology*, **51**, 242–58.

Pennington, N. and Hastie, R. (1988) Explanation-based decision-making: Effects of memory and structure on judgment. *Journal of Experimental Psychology: Learning, Memory, and Cognition*, **14**, 521–33.

Pennington, N. and Hastie, R. (1991) A theory of explanation-based decision-making, in *Decision-making in Complex Worlds* (eds G. Klein and J. Prasanu), Ablex, Hillsdale (NJ).

Reason, J. (1990) *Human Error*, Cambridge University Press, New York.

Reason, J. (1997) *Managing the Risks of Organizational Accidents*, Ashgate, Aldershot.

Roberts, P. and Zuckerman, A. (2004) *Criminal Evidence*, Oxford University Press, Oxford.

Rogers, W.V.H. (2006) *Winfield & Jolowicz on Tort*, 17th edn, Sweet & Maxwell, London.

Saks, M.J. and Thompson, W.C. (2003) Assessing evidence: Proving facts, in *Handbook of Psychology in Legal Contexts* (eds D. Carson and R. Bull), Wiley, Chichester.

Schuller, R.A. and Ogloff, J.R.P. (2001) An introduction to psychology and law, in *Introduction to Psychology and Law: Canadian Perspectives* (eds R.A. Schuller and J.R.P. Ogloff), University of Toronto Press, Toronto.

Schum, D.A. (1994) *Evidential Foundations of Probabilistic Reasoning*, Wiley, New York.

Schmid, D.J. (2001) Restorative Justice in New Zealand: A Model for U.S. Criminal Justice. (Available at http://www.fulbright.org.nz/voices/axford/docs/schmidd.pdf (Accessed 16 March 2006).

Twining, W. (2003) Evidence as a multi-disciplinary subject. *Law Probablity and Risk*, **2**, 91–107.

Umbreit, M.S. (2001) *The Handbook of Victim Offender Mediation: An Essential Guide to Practice and Research*, Jossey-Bass, San Francisco (CA).

Wagenaar, W.A, Van Koppen, P.J. and Crombag, H.F.M. (1993) *Anchored Narratives: The Psychology of Criminal Evidence*, Harvester Wheatsheaf, New York.

Walker, L. and Monahan, J. (1987) Social frameworks: A new use of social science in law. *Virginia Law Review*, **73**, 559–98

Walker, L. and Monahan, J. (1988) Social facts: Scientific methodology as legal precedent. *California Law Review*, **76**, 877–96.

Webster, C.D. and Jackson, M.A. (eds) (1997) *Impulsivity: Theory Assessment, and Treatment*, Guilford Press, New York.

Wells, G.L. (2002) *Eyewitness Testimony. Encyclopedia of Psychology*, American Psychological Association, Washington (DC).

Wexler, D. and Winick, B. (1990) *Therapeutic Jurisprudence: The Law as a Therapeutic Agent*, Carolina Academic Press, Durham (NC).

Wexler, D. and Winick, B. (1991) *Essays in Therapeutic Jurisprudence*, Carolina Academic Press, Durham (NC).

Wexler, D. and Winick, B. (1996) *Law in a Therapeutic Key: Developments in Therapeutic Jurisprudence*, Carolina Academic Press, Durham (NC).

Winick, B. (1997) How to handle voluntary hospitalization, in *Therapeutic Jurisprudence Applied: Essays on Mental Health Law* (ed. B. Winick), Carolina Academic Press, Durham (NC).

Winick, B. and Wexler, D. (2003) *Judging in a Therapeutic Key: Therapeutic Jurisprudence and the Courts*, Carolina Academic Press, Durham (NC).

CHAPTER 2

Eyewitness Identification

Ronald P. Fisher and Margaret C. Reardon
Florida International University

Eyewitness identification is an influential component of the criminal justice system, affecting virtually every aspect of the process from the initial police investigation to the trial. An identification can guide the police investigation toward or away from a suspect, and is a particularly incriminating piece of evidence at trial (e.g. Cutler, Penrod and Dexter, 1990; Fox and Walters, 1986). In fact, some defendants have been convicted on the basis of eyewitness identification without the corroboration of any physical evidence. Unfortunately, not all identifications are correct and may lead to the imprisonment of innocent people. This fact has been illuminated by the number of recent exonerations made possible through DNA testing. Of the first 40 wrongful conviction cases in the USA, 36 (90%) involved faulty eyewitness identification evidence, in which one or more witnesses wrongly identified an innocent suspect as the perpetrator (Wells *et al.*, 1998).

These DNA exonerations brought the fallibility of eyewitness identification evidence to the forefront of public consciousness, spurring the United States Department of Justice to create a committee to look into eyewitness identification procedures. This committee, made up of prosecuting and defence attorneys, eyewitness researchers and police officers, drafted a set of guidelines for the collection of identification evidence, known as the National Institute of Justice (NIJ) guidelines (Technical Working Group for Eyewitness Evidence (TWGEYEE), 1999). Similar recommendations have been incorporated into law in the United Kingdom through the Police and Criminal Evidence (PACE) Act (1984, 1986). As a law enforcement guide, these recommendations concentrate on procedural factors that are known to affect eyewitness identification accuracy. This focus is very different from previous judicial standards, which have stressed the importance of event factors such as lighting and the distance between the eyewitness and the perpetrator (e.g. *Neil v. Biggers*, 1972 in the United States; *R v. Turnbull*, in England).

Laboratory Versus Field Research

Research in eyewitness identification takes place both in the field and inside the laboratory. Field research involves actual witnesses who try to identify the perpetrator after observing or being the victim of a crime. The obvious advantage of field research is that it is highly

---

Applying Psychology to Criminal Justice. Edited by David Carson, Rebecca Milne, Francis Pakes, Karen Shalev and Andrea Shawyer. © 2007 John Wiley & Sons, Ltd

realistic. This realism increases the likelihood that the results can be generalized to witnesses in other crime situations. A disadvantage of field research is that it lacks control. Witnesses are subject to a constellation of influences in a crime situation and this makes it impossible to determine which factors affected the identification. Another disadvantage of field studies is that it is often impossible to determine the accuracy of the witness's identification. Confession evidence or the conviction of the suspect as evidence confirming the witness's identification could be used, but these factors are often not independent of the identification itself. For instance, a positive identification of an innocent suspect by a witness may influence the suspect to confess if he believed that he would be found guilty anyway and wanted to cooperate with the police in an effort to reduce possible punishment. In contrast to field research, laboratory research takes place in a controlled setting and generally involves presenting a staged incident or crime to mock witnesses. The strength of laboratory research is experimental control, which allows causal relationships to be identified. Furthermore, in contrast to field research, laboratory research allows the investigators to know definitively whether a witness response is correct, because the witnessed event is set up by the researcher. The disadvantage of laboratory research is that, sometimes, it lacks ecological validity and does not (or cannot) capture some of the critical ingredients in a real crime (e.g. intense arousal). Whilst both laboratory and field research each have strengths and weaknesses, both are necessary in order to gain a clear picture of eyewitness identifications.

Research Paradigm

The typical eyewitness identification research paradigm includes two basic components: the witnessed event or stimulus, and the identification test. A witness observes a scene that contains the 'target' or the subject who is to be identified later. Often this scene is a mock crime, in which the target is the perpetrator of the crime. The scene can be conveyed to the witness via a live staged event (e.g. classroom interruption), video, or slides. At some point following the event, the witness is asked to identify the target from a line-up. This line-up may be constructed using live participants or photographs, although photographs are generally used for laboratory research. The line-up either contains a photo of the target/perpetrator from the original, witnessed event (target-present) or does not contain the target/perpetrator's photo (target-absent). Researchers use target-present line-ups to simulate those cases in which the police suspect is the perpetrator, and target-absent line-ups to simulate those cases in which the police suspect is innocent; that is, the real perpetrator does not appear in the line-up.

A witness can make one of several possible responses when faced with a line-up. In a target-present line-up, the witness may: choose the target (hit); select another person in the line-up (foil identification); or reject the line-up (miss). In a target-absent line-up, witness may: correctly reject the entire line-up (correct rejection); choose the innocent suspect (false identification); or select a foil (foil identification).

Estimator Versus System Variables

Many factors influence the likelihood of the witness correctly identifying the perpetrator, including the environment (e.g. lighting conditions), person characteristics (e.g. witness's age or perpetrator's ethnicity), type of interview (e.g. cognitive interview versus conventional interview), line-up procedures (e.g. live versus photo line-up), and post-lineup events (e.g. feedback to the witness). Research psychologists have divided these factors into two categories: system variables and estimator variables (Wells, 1978). System variables refer to those factors that may influence witness performance and which can be manipulated by the police (e.g. instructions to the witness), whereas estimator variables refer to those factors that may influence witness performance but which cannot be manipulated by the police (e.g. lighting conditions at the crime scene). We focus here exclusively on system variables. (For reviews of estimator variables, see Brewer, Weber and Semmler, 2005; Cutler and Penrod, 1995.) We concentrate on system variables because it is frequently difficult to implement knowledge about estimator variables in the analysis of a specific criminal case. For instance, if witnesses pay more attention to the perpetrator, they will make more accurate identifications. However, it is rarely known exactly how much attention a witness was paying to the perpetrator at the time of the crime. There are no concurrent measurements of witness attention that can be used to assess their attention at the time of the crime. At best, witnesses must be asked retroactively to assess their earlier level of attention. These judgements are (1) subjective, and (2) may be influenced by factors unrelated to the actual level of attention. Wells and Bradfield (1998), for instance, found that feedback to eyewitnesses following a line-up identification influenced witnesses' retroactive assessments of degree of attention paid to the perpetrator. In essence, we have only a vague idea of how much attention the witness was paying to the perpetrator at the time of the crime. Similar arguments can be made for a host of estimator variables, including the witness's (and especially victim's) level of stress, exposure duration, degree of intoxication, and so on. Furthermore, suppose the witness's level of attention could be measured at the time she observed the crime. All we could conclude is that the witness would have been less likely to identify the perpetrator had she paid less attention, and that she would have been more likely to identify the perpetrator had she paid more attention. But, the likelihood of a correct identification in the current situation cannot be assessed with any degree of certainty. Rather than calculating retroactively how to factor in such probabilistic information, it is preferable for police to conduct the investigation properly in the first place – increasing the likelihood of the witness making a correct identification – by implementing the existing knowledge of system variables. In this instance, an ounce of prevention (system variables) is truly better than a pound of care (estimator variables).

OVERVIEW

In this chapter we review the major system variables associated with eyewitness identifications. These variables are presented chronologically in the order in which they typically occur during the investigative process, beginning with interviewing the witness and ending with the presentation of eyewitness identification evidence at trial. A brief summary of the research literature on each topic is provided and, where possible, a recommendation regarding the 'best practice' procedure is given. Not surprisingly, many of these recommendations are included in the National Institute of Justice's Guide for Law Enforcement (TWGEYEE, 1999).

Interviewing the Witness

Some witnesses will have better memories of the crime scene than others, mainly due to factors not under police control (estimator variables). Regardless of the quality of the witness's memory of the crime, we may be able to promote better recollection by implementing more effective interview methods. An extensive body of research has found, for example, that the cognitive interview (Fisher and Geiselman, 1992) allows witnesses to recall considerably more information than does a typical police interview or a structured interview (for reviews and a meta-analysis, see Fisher and Schreiber, 2006; Kohnken et al., 1999). Do these interview methods also promote better witness performance on identification tests?

The literature on the effects of interview procedures on identification accuracy is mixed, with some studies showing positive effects of novel interview procedures and other studies showing non-effects. Fisher, McCauley and Geiselman (1994) describe a series of four experiments in which witnesses were exposed to an event (either a simulated, videotaped crime or a live, innocuous event). Shortly thereafter, between a few hours and two days, the witnesses attempted to identify the target person in either a photographic or live line-up. Just prior to the line-up test, some of the witnesses received a cognitive interview, whereas other witnesses were in the control condition (either a typical police interview or no interview). The results showed that the cognitive interview had no effect at all: It neither increased performance nor decreased performance on the identification test (see also, Gwyer and Clifford, 1997).

In comparison to the non-effects found with the cognitive interview, other researchers have found that modifying the interview procedure did enhance identification. Malpass and Devine (1980) conducted a study in which student witnesses observed a live event (disruption of an ongoing university lecture). Several weeks later, the witnesses participated in a test to identify the principal character. Just prior to the identification test, some of the witnesses received a 'guided memory' technique in which they were encouraged to visualize the details of the original event. The witnesses who went through this guided memory procedure correctly identified the target person much more often than did a control group of witnesses who were not instructed in the guided memory procedure. A conceptual replication of this study by Krafka and Penrod (1985) found similar results, namely, providing some clues about the original event to the witnesses just prior to the identification test facilitated witnesses' performance (see also Shapiro and Penrod's (1986), meta-analysis showing the effects of context reinstatement on identification).

It is not obvious why in some studies, reinstating the context of the original event facilitated witness's identification, whereas in other studies context reinstatement (a core component of the cognitive interview) had no effect. It may be that instructing witnesses to reinstate the context of the crime scene will be most valuable when much time has passed between the crime and the identification test (Malpass and Devine, 1980) or when witnesses have been exposed to many similar experiences in addition to the target experience (Krafka and Penrod, 1985), but it will be least valuable when witnesses have been exposed to a unique experience that has occurred recently (Fisher, McCauley and Geiselman, 1994). This reflects the expectation that reinstating context will be most valuable when the target event is difficult to discriminate from other events (long retention interval makes the target temporally nondistinctive). Context reinstatement will be least valuable when the target event is inherently distinctive, either in terms of content (no similar events) or temporally (recent event).

Verbal Overshadowing

A curious phenomenon has been observed whereby witnesses who provide extensive verbal descriptions of the perpetrator are sometimes less accurate in their identification performance than witnesses who do not provide any description of the perpetrator. This phenomenon has been referred to as verbal overshadowing (Schooler and Engstler-Schooler, 1990) and has been found with a variety of (nonverbal) materials including memory for faces, odours and wine tastes (Schooler, Fiore and Brandimonte, 1997). In the typical laboratory procedure, participants are exposed to several photographs of faces. Some participants are asked to describe verbally each face after they initially view the face, whereas others participants do not describe the face. All participants are asked later to attempt to recognize the face in a photo-identification test. The results of these experiments are somewhat mixed, as some investigators find the effect (poorer identification when earlier asked to verbally describe the face), whereas other investigators do not find the effect. There is no general agreement among researchers as to when the effect does and does not occur. Many have found that the effect occurs primarily when the identification test follows immediately after the description; however, some have found the effect even when the identification task follows long after the description task. It may be that the effect is most likely to occur when the participants are encouraged to adopt a lenient criterion and describe the face in extensive detail, providing facial descriptors that they may be uncertain about (Meissner and Brigham, 2001). If this is the case, then investigators should be wary when initially interviewing witnesses not to entice them to guess or to volunteer uncertain descriptors of the perpetrator.

Computerized Facial Composite Systems

A related question revolves around how best to elicit an initial description of the perpetrator, and especially of the perpetrator's face (see Davies and Valentine, in press for a review). Should the witness be asked to provide a verbal description of the perpetrator, or should an artist be used to render a sketch of the perpetrator's face, or should a computerized system be developed to generate a facial composite? Recently, researchers have expended considerable effort to take advantage of developments in computer science to elicit more accurate portrayals of perpetrators' faces. Unfortunately, most of these efforts have proved fruitless as computerized facial composites created by witnesses from memory bear little similarity to a face seen earlier (e.g. Koehn, Fisher and Cutler, 1999). Computerized facial composite systems have improved over time, so that one can now construct more life-like faces than in the past. If a computer operator is looking at a photograph of a person, he can use current computer programs to create a very similar looking face. The problem in a real police investigation, however, is that the perpetrator's face is not sitting in front of the witness at the time she is asked to create a likeness of the perpetrator. Rather, the witness must describe the perpetrator's face from memory. The limitation in all of these approaches seems not to be constructing the face itself but rather in extracting the information from the witness's memory (Taylor, 2001).

Line-up Administrator

A classic finding in social psychology is that the experimenter's knowledge of the research hypothesis may influence the experimental outcome (Rosenthal, 1969). Researchers therefore often use assistants who are blind to the experimental hypothesis to avoid influencing the data. A parallel situation exists in the police investigation, where the person who conducts the line-up test – usually one of the case detectives – knows which line-up member is the suspect. Does the line-up administrator's knowledge influence the witness's identification? Several studies have demonstrated that it may. The line-up administrator may influence the witness to select the person or photo known to be the suspect (Haw and Fisher, 2004; Phillips *et al.*, 1999) or to increase the witness's confidence that he selected the 'correct' person from the line-up (Garrioch and Brimacombe, 2001). We assume that line-up administrators will not blatantly tell the witness which person or photo to select, but that the influence will be more subtle, perhaps communicated through a change in intonation or in some nonverbal cue (Garrioch and Brimacombe, 2001). Although some researchers have found the effect of line-up administrator knowledge, others have not found any such effects (Russano *et al.*, 2006). It is uncertain why the effect is so ephemeral. Nevertheless, given the potential for perverting justice, the legal system should attempt to minimize any influence of the line-up administrator on the witness's behaviour. The ideal solution is to have a double-blind procedure, where the line-up administrator does not know the suspect's identity. Practically, this may pose problems for small police departments or in high-profile cases, as it may be difficult to find police officers who are unaware of the suspect's identity. Solutions that are easier to implement include presenting the entire identification test via computer, thereby completely eliminating the line-up administrator's influence, or simply having the line-up administrator sit behind and out of view of the witness (Haw and Fisher, 2004). Given the ease of overcoming the pernicious effect of the line-up administrator's knowledge, implementing some solution is strongly recommended. Some countries have already done so. The United Kingdom, for instance, now uses Video Identification Parade Electronic Recording (VIPER), a program that allows the presentation of moving line-up images on video. Similar solutions are also used in parts of Germany and Australia.

Show-Ups Versus Line-ups

Frequently, witnesses provide a thorough description of the perpetrator to the police immediately after the crime, and the police find someone in the vicinity of the crime who matches the witness's description. In our experience, this seems to occur often when the witness's description includes a distinctive vehicle, which the police spot near the crime scene. When this occurs, police may detain the person (now a suspect) to see if the witness can recognize him. In this test, called a show-up or field identification, the witness sees only the one suspect, whom the witness either positively identifies or indicates is not the perpetrator. Show-ups are desirable in that (1) the witness's memory is tested immediately, while it is still fresh, and (2) they allow the detained suspect to be freed immediately if he is not positively identified by the witness. The alternative procedure is to conduct a proper line-up, in which the witness is exposed to the police suspect plus several other people who are believed or known to be innocent (fillers or foils). The purported advantage of the line-up is that, if the witness (and especially a victim) is motivated to identify someone – either to assist the police or to seek revenge – but the witness has a poor memory of the perpetrator, the witness is likely to select one of the fillers. That is, if the witness is merely guessing, the likelihood is that she will not select the suspect, but rather will select someone from the line-up who is known to be innocent. This is a harmless error, as it will be obvious to the police that the witness has picked the 'wrong' person. By comparison, in a show-up, where only the suspect is shown, there are no fillers to 'absorb' witness identifications that are based on guessing. Witnesses who are motivated to guess, but who have poor memories, must select the suspect. For innocent suspects, this is anything but a harmless error.

A second way to conceptualize the difference between line-ups and show-ups is that, if a line-up is constructed properly, it should not be obvious which one of the line-up members is the police suspect (see later section on selecting fillers). In contrast, show-ups contain only one person, and so it is obvious that the detainee is the police suspect. The show-ups' inability to hide the suspect's identity has led research psychologists and legal systems to consider show-ups to be inherently suggestive.

Although show-ups are conducted frequently in some parts of the world, such as the USA and to a lesser extent Sweden, relatively little experimental research has been conducted about the show-up procedure. By comparison, research on line-ups is much more extensive. Nevertheless, there are some clear patterns emerging in the literature (see Steblay *et al.*, 2003, for a recent meta-analysis). Specifically, witnesses are considerably more likely to positively identify someone within a line-up than in a show-up. However, some of those line-up identifications are of fillers, known innocents, and hence they are not damning for the suspect. (Remember that, within the show-up, a witness cannot identify a filler, as there are no fillers.) The most important finding is that the overall likelihood of mistakenly identifying an innocent suspect is approximately the same for show-ups and line-ups. The hit rate is also approximately the same for show-ups and line-ups. Thus, although many have expressed concern about the inherent suggestibility of show-ups, the empirical data from controlled laboratory experiments suggest that false identifications of innocent suspects are no more likely for show-ups than for line-ups.

Some evidence even demonstrates that show-ups are superior to line-ups. Specifically, most of the laboratory research examining show-ups and line-ups follows the conventions of scientific research and controls for other important variables while manipulating whether witnesses are given either a show-up or a line-up. Thus, in laboratory research, show-ups are conducted after the same retention interval (time from crime to test) as line-ups. In real crime investigations, however, show-ups are typically conducted only a few minutes or hours after the crime, whereas line-ups are usually conducted after several days or weeks. Thus, laboratory research has not taken into account one benefit of real-world show-ups, namely that they are conducted immediately after the crime. A recent study by Dickinson, Fisher and Haw (2004; see also Dekle, 2006) compared show-ups and line-ups as they might occur in a real-world investigation, with show-ups occurring after only 0–3 h and line-ups occurring after one week (Davey and Behrman, 2001). When the different retention intervals that naturally occur between show-ups and line-ups were maintained, show-ups proved to be advantageous, with fewer false identifications and more hits. In overview, there is no very compelling evidence from laboratory research that, when real-world conditions are preserved, show-ups are inherently any more suggestive than line-ups.

One might argue that a critical ingredient of real-world crime scenes is not captured in laboratory research, specifically, a real victim's attempt to seek revenge on the perpetrator, and perhaps a greater likelihood of positively identifying anyone. If this were true, then the greater protection afforded by a line-up (the existence of fillers who are known innocents) may prove to be advantageous for an innocent suspect. Research psychologists should be encouraged to conduct more tests of the relative value of show-ups and line-ups, and specifically to incorporate the actual testing conditions that are likely to be found in real-world police investigations – at least to the extent that ethical constraints permit.

Selecting Fillers

The success of a line-up identification procedure will depend largely on how the fillers are selected. If the fillers look too similar to the suspect, even a witness with an excellent memory of the crime may not be able to identify which of the people or photos is the perpetrator. Alternatively, if the fillers are too dissimilar to the suspect such that the suspect stands out (e.g. she is the only blond-haired person in the group), then the line-up will be biased against the suspect, which may encourage the witness to identify an innocent suspect. Thus, the key question is: How are line-ups typically constructed and how effective are these methods?

When police conduct photo line-ups, they usually select fillers from photos of people who have gone through the criminal system, or from images of volunteers (e.g. VIPER). In doing so, police attempt to find fillers who match the suspect on some gross physical characteristics such as race, hairstyle and age. We refer to this filler-selection strategy as match-to-suspect. An alternative strategy is to select fillers who match the description that the witness provides. If the witness describes the perpetrator as a white female, mid-20s, with a round face, then all of the fillers would be white females in their mid-20s and with round faces. We refer to this strategy as match-to-description.

What difference does it make whether fillers match the suspect or match the witness's description? Logically, if all of the fillers matched the suspect perfectly, then a witness would never be able to identify the suspect except by guessing from among the line-up photographs. Clearly, we need some differences between the suspect's appearance and the fillers' appearance for the witness to recognize the perpetrator. The match-to-description strategy ensures that there are some differences among the line-up members, since witnesses never provide complete descriptions of the perpetrator. For instance, the witness may describe the perpetrator as in her 20s but not indicate whether it was early or late 20s. If fillers are selected to match only the characteristics that appear in the witness's description, and to match only at the level of precision indicated, there will be many differences between the fillers and the suspect. In the above case, for instance, the fillers would simply have to be white females in their 20s with round faces. They could differ from the suspect on other characteristics that were not mentioned by the witness (e.g. hair style, clothing) and they could differ along a dimension that was reported imprecisely (e.g. 20s but not specifying whether early or late 20s). With the match-to-description strategy there will be more differences among the line-up members, and as such, witness should find it easier to recognize the perpetrator.

Wells, Rydell and Seelau (1993) conducted a study to compare the effectiveness of the match-to-suspect and match-to-description strategies in target-present and target-absent line-ups. As expected, in target-present line-ups, witnesses were considerably more likely to identify the perpetrator when the fillers were selected to match the witness's description than to match the suspect. In target-absent line-ups, however, there were no differences in false identifications (of the innocent suspect) between the two filler-selection strategies. This combination of increasing hits without increasing false identifications of innocent suspects is the perfect, but often unattainable, goal of eyewitness research.

To what degree is a witness's response indicative (diagnostic) of the suspect's guilt or innocence, and how is that influenced by whether the foils are selected to match the suspect or to match the witness's description? Mathematical analyses of controlled experiments allow us to calculate the likelihood that the suspect is guilty or innocent (the diagnostic value of the test) depending on whether the witness selects the suspect or a foil. Recently, Clark, Howell, and Davey (in press) examined the data from four experimental studies in which witnesses attempted to identify perpetrators from line-ups constructed by match-to-suspect or match-to-description strategies. The results were mixed: For foil identifications, match-to-description line-ups were more diagnostic of the suspect's innocence than were match-to-suspect line-ups; for suspect identifications, however, there were no differences between match-to-description and match-to-suspect line-ups. Overall, then, the evidence is somewhat supportive of the match-to-description strategy, however, given the limited data base, we should wait for more empirical evidence before thoroughly endorsing one procedure or another.

Sometimes, a witness may describe the perpetrator, but the description does not match the suspect perfectly. For instance, the witness may describe the perpetrator as a thin, white male, with a scar on his forehead, but in fact, the suspect is a thin white male with a scar on his *neck*. If the fillers are selected to match the witness's description (scar on forehead), but the suspect appears differently (scar on neck), then the suspect will stand out from the fillers as being the only person who has a scar on his neck. Clearly, we do not want the suspect to stand out from the fillers, as this is highly suggestive. In cases such as this, when the witness's description does not perfectly match the suspect, it is recommended that the fillers match the suspect on the incorrect descriptor (here, all of the fillers should have scars on their necks), but that they match the witness's description for all of the other descriptors (here, thin white male; see NIJ Guidelines, TWGEYEE, 1999).

One way to determine whether a line-up is fair or suggestive is to provide mock witnesses (people who do not have any knowledge of the crime or the perpetrator) with the witness's description of the perpetrator and then ask the mock witnesses to identify the suspect from the line-up. If the line-up is fair, all of the line-up members should match the witness's description. The mock witnesses should then select the suspect's photograph only $1/N$ of the time, where N refers to the number of members in the line-up. If the line-up contains six members (one suspect plus five fillers), only 1/6 of all of the mock witnesses should select the suspect's photograph, with the other 5/6 of the mock witnesses choosing from among the five fillers. If the mock witnesses select the suspect's photograph considerably more often than chance ($1/N$), we should question the line-up's fairness, as, apparently, something made the suspect stand out from the fillers.

Format of Test Item

One approach to improving identification accuracy is to present high-quality test items (e.g. photographs) to the witness at the time of the test. In theory, the more similar the test item is to the original stimulus (the perpetrator as he appeared at the time of the crime) the better it should be recognized. Some of the different kinds of test item that have been used are photographs, sketch artists' renditions, computerized composite programs, live line-ups and videotapes. We might expect that live line-ups (sometimes referred to as corporeal line-ups) and perhaps videotapes of live line-ups will provide the highest quality image, followed by color photographs, and, last, black-and-white photographs. Despite the theoretical underpinning of this prediction, and its intuitive appeal, much of the research has found only relatively small or no differences across modalities (e.g. Cutler *et al.*, 1994).

Line-up Presentation Format

Police line-ups typically contain the suspect plus several fillers. How should police present the various line-up members to the witness? Traditionally, police showed all of line-up members at the same time (simultaneous line-up). For instance, police may display all of the line-up photographs on a table and allow witnesses to examine whichever photos they wish. When conducting live line-ups, police parade all of the line-up members in front of the witnesses, and again, witnesses can examine whichever line-up members they wish. Simultaneous line-ups allow witnesses to compare the various line-up members to one another and select the one who most closely resembles (their memory of) the perpetrator (referred to as a relative judgement). If a witness believes that the police have apprehended the perpetrator, this relative judgement strategy should increase his chances of selecting the perpetrator. A grave problem may occur, however, if the police suspect is not the perpetrator. If witnesses use a relative judgement strategy, they may well select an innocent suspect, simply because she looks *more* like the perpetrator than do the fillers (Lindsay and Wells, 1985). To reduce this relative judgement-induced error, Lindsay and Wells developed the sequential line-up procedure in which the police present only one line-up member at a time. Thus, the police present the first photograph (or the first live line-up member) and the witness decides whether that person is the perpetrator. If the witness says 'no', then that photograph (line-up member) is removed and a second photograph (person) is shown. The witness responds separately to each line-up member: Is this the person who committed the crime? (This is referred to as an absolute judgement.) In the optimal sequential line-up procedure, the witness does not know how many line-up members he will see, and the line-up terminates when the witness identifies someone or has rejected each of the line-up members. In the United Kingdom, however, where sequential line-ups on video are used routinely, witnesses are required to view all line-up members at least twice.

Several laboratory studies have been conducted to compare the effectiveness of sequential and simultaneous line-ups (see Steblay *et al.*'s (2001) meta-analysis). The overall pattern shows that when the police suspect is not the perpetrator (target-absent line-up), witnesses are considerably less likely to positively identify the innocent suspect in a sequential line-up than in a simultaneous line-up, confirming Lindsay and Wells's analysis. There is a cost, however. When the perpetrator is in the line-up (target-present), witnesses are somewhat less likely to identify the perpetrator in a sequential than a simultaneous line-up. Is the sequential line-up's reduction in false identifications worth the reduction in hits? Malpass's 2006 cost/benefit analysis demonstrates that the relative costs and benefits of simultaneous and sequential line-ups depend on a variety of factors (e.g. relative benefit of a hit or cost of a false identification), so that no one procedure is universally more valuable than the other.

Recently, several opinions within the research community have emerged about the mechanisms responsible for the difference between simultaneous and sequential line-ups. For example, Meissner *et al.* (2005) concluded that simultaneous line-ups simply entice witnesses to adopt a more lenient criterion before making a positive identification. Naturally, if witnesses make more positive identifications with simultaneous line-ups, they will make more hits (identify the perpetrator) but also more false identifications of innocent suspects. Other researchers have suggested more complex mechanisms to account for the differences between sequential and simultaneous line-ups (Gronlund, 2005). We expect that considerably more laboratory research will be conducted in the near future to explain the differences between simultaneous and sequential line-ups.

Instructions

The instructions that the line-up administrator gives to the witness at the onset of the identification test can influence the witness's identification behaviour. From social psychological research it is known that people often rely on others to help define an external social situation, especially if they are uncertain. Witnesses may be unsure of the perpetrator's identity, yet wish to help the police. Instructions from an authority figure to 'Pick out the person who committed the crime' may guide witnesses to make a positive identification, because they suggest that (1) the perpetrator is in the line-up, and (2) the correct response is to make a choice (Deutsch and Gerard, 1955). This may occur whether the administrator implies that the perpetrator is in the line-up ('pick him out') or even if the administrator fails to state explicitly that the perpetrator 'may not' be in the line-up. To avoid against this unwanted influence, researchers stress the importance of using unbiased line-up instructions, which warn the witness that the actual perpetrator may or may not be in the line-up (NIJ Guidelines, TWGEYEE, 1999; PACE Act, 1984, 1986).

Research examining the impact of line-up instructions shows that biased instructions, in which the administrator insinuates that the suspect is in the line-up and the witness's task is to pick him out, reduces identification accuracy (Malpass and Devine, 1981). Steblay (1997) conducted a meta-analysis of 18 studies and showed that the effect was different for target-absent and target-present line-ups. Specifically, when presented with a target-absent line-up witnesses were more likely to choose someone erroneously from the line-up when biased instructions were given rather than unbiased instructions. For target-present line-ups, however, instruction type (biased versus unbiased) had no influence on selecting the suspect. In overview, using unbiased instructions will provide protection for innocent suspects, but will not hinder law enforcement's ability to prosecute perpetrators.

Recording Confidence Judgements

After a witness makes an identification she is generally asked about her level of confidence in the decision. Recording the witness's confidence properly is critical, because many people in the legal system, and particularly jurors (e.g. Cutler, Penrod and Dexter, 1990; Wells, Ferguson and Lindsay, 1981), use confidence as an indicator of the accuracy of the identification: Confident witnesses are thought to be much more accurate than unconfident witnesses. Research shows that witness confidence at the time of the identification may be moderately predictive of identification accuracy, and especially when witnesses positively choose someone from the line-up (see Sporer *et al.*, 1995 for a meta-analysis). Unfortunately, many procedures may intervene between the time of the identification and the time of trial that can influence witnesses' confidence judgements. If these procedures influence witness confidence, but not accuracy, they will weaken the confidence-accuracy relationship and may distort jurors' judgements.

One such procedure that may alter confidence retroactively is to subject a witness to repeated post-event questioning. In practice, a witness may be asked to answer questions about the crime at multiple points in the investigative and legal process, such as in police interviews, depositions, and at trial. Shaw and McClure (1996) found that asking witnesses the same questions repeatedly over multiple interview sessions increased their confidence in the accuracy of their answers. Specifically, confidence ratings for questions that were asked multiple times were higher than ratings for questions asked only once. Preparing a witness for trial can also artificially inflate confidence judgements. Wells, Ferguson and Lindsay (1981) found that asking witnesses to rehearse answers to questions about their identifications increased their confidence in their identification. Unfortunately, such witness preparation does not increase the accuracy of the witness's identification. As a result, the witness's elevated confidence may mislead jurors to think that her identification was more accurate than it actually was.

Several procedures can artificially inflate a witness's confidence in her identification between the time of the actual identification and trial. Therefore, we strongly recommend recording the witness's confidence judgement immediately following the identification (see also the NIJ Guidelines, TWGEYEE, 1999). This practice ensures that the witness's confidence judgement will be based on her memory for the identification and not on other social processes. Furthermore, it is this confidence judgement that should be conveyed to the jurors at trial, and not the witness's confidence at the time of the trial, which may be distorted.

Police Feedback

Throughout the course of a police investigation, witnesses may receive feedback about how they performed on the identification task (e.g. 'good, you identified the suspect'). Such feedback can influence a witness's confidence about his identification decision (Luus and Wells, 1994; Semmler, Brewer and Wells, 2004; Wells and Bradfield, 1998). Wells and Bradfield (1998) presented a line-up to three groups of witnesses to a crime. After the identification, the three groups were equally confident about their identifications. The first group was then given confirming feedback indicating they had identified the suspect, the second group was told they failed to identify the suspect (disconfirming feedback), and the third group received no feedback. Later, when assessed for the amount of confidence they felt at the time of identification, witnesses given confirming feedback remembered feeling very certain whereas the group who received disconfirming feedback remembered being uncertain at the time of the identification. Additionally, Semmler, Brewer and Wells (2004) found that confirming feedback served to inflate witnesses' confidence in their identification regardless of the accuracy of the identification, so that even witnesses providing false identifications were significantly more confident in their decision after the confirming feedback. In fact, some research suggests that confidence inflation due to confirming feedback is greater for witnesses who make false identifications than for those who are correct (Bradfield, Wells and Olson, 2002).

Reinforcing feedback may influence, not only the witness's confidence judgement, but also the witness's perceptions of other aspects of the event and the identification task. Specifically, Wells and Bradfield (1998) found that witnesses who were given reinforcing feedback were more likely to indicate that they had a good view of the perpetrator during the incident, and that they easily identified the perpetrator from the line-up. Importantly, these aspects of the situation (quality of viewing conditions, behaviour during the identification task) are often used as objective indicators of identification accuracy.

Feedback can influence witnesses' judgements even when the feedback is about a co-witness, and not about their own behaviour. Luus and Wells (1994), for instance, found that information provided to a witness about a co-witness's identification behaviour influenced the witness's confidence judgements. Confidence was increased dramatically when the witness was told that the co-witness chose the same person, even when told that the co-witness later recanted the identification. Confidence was lowest when the witness was told that the co-witness identified a different person, or rejected the line-up.

Considerable research points to the distorting effects of feedback. The problem can be approached in either of two ways: minimize exposing the witness to feedback, or minimize the influence of feedback if and when it does occur. The police investigators can be instructed not to provide feedback to witnesses. Certainly, it is desirable to minimize direct feedback, and police may be able consciously to control providing feedback to witnesses. However, line-up administrators may inadvertently or nonconsciously influence witnesses through subtle body language or facial expressions. This type of inadvertent feedback is probably more difficult to control. One way to circumvent this nonconscious form of feedback is to have an officer unfamiliar with the case and the identity of the suspect conduct the line-up (see the section on the blind administration of line-ups). Realistically, though, even if we could completely eliminate all police feedback, witnesses can calculate that they must have identified the suspect simply because the prosecution has asked them to appear in court – presumably to strengthen their case against the suspect (now, the defendant). Furthermore, an administrator may feel compelled, for ethical reasons, to reveal the identity of the suspect to the witness if asked. It is difficult to imagine how to eliminate this form of feedback, given that it derives from the natural working of the legal system. For all of these reasons, it is probably more important to minimize the *influence* of feedback (to alter the witness's confidence) than to eliminate the source of feedback. The easiest and most efficient method of minimizing the influence of any post-identification feedback is to record the witness's confidence at the time of the identification, before the witness receives any type of feedback (Wells and Bradfield, 1998).

Search Through Mugshots and Multiple Identification Tests

When there are very few leads about the perpetrator's identity, police may ask witnesses to search through a large collection of photographs (mugshots) to see if they recognize anyone. Such collections of photographs (mug books) may contain hundreds of photographs of criminals from the past. If the current police investigation uncovers a viable suspect, witnesses who have searched through the mugshots may later be asked to participate in a line-up test that contains the suspect. If the suspect's face was seen earlier in the mugbook, it may 'stand out' in the line-up as the only familiar face. Witnesses may then mistakenly recognize the face because of its familiarity, even though the source of familiarity was the mugshot search (Johnson, Hashtroudi and Lindsay, 1993).

Researchers have attempted to simulate this process by exposing witnesses to an event (e.g. a staged crime) and then having some (but not other) witnesses search through mugshots before conducting a photo-identification test. Results of these tests have been mixed. Some studies find that exposure to the preliminary mugshot search impaired performance on the final photo-identification test (Brown, Deffenbacher and Sturgill, 1977), whereas other studies show no effects of the preliminary mugshot search (Shepherd, Ellis and Davies, 1982). Given the potential damage to innocent suspects, it is recommended that police do not encourage witnesses to search through mugshots prior to the final photo-identification test, unless police investigators have exhausted all other possible resources to identify the perpetrator.

A similar problem may arise in any police investigation that entails more than one identification test. For instance, a witness who initially identified a suspect in a preliminary show-up may be asked by police to participate in a later formal line-up test – in part, because prosecutors may believe that a line-up test is a stronger form of evidence than is a show-up test (see the earlier section on show-ups). The suspect may then be the only familiar person in the line-up, enticing the witness to identify him because of his (displaced) familiarity (Johnson, Hashtroudi and Lindsay, 1993). Another example of multiple testing occurs when witnesses are asked to identify the defendant in the courtroom, after having identified him in an earlier line-up test. In all of these multiple-test situations, suspects may appear familiar to the witness, and hence be recognized, even if the suspect is innocent.

A typical research study that examines this issue of multiple testing was conducted by Dickinson, Fisher and Haw (2004). Student witnesses observed an attention-grabbing event during a university lecture. Shortly thereafter, some of the student witnesses attempted to identify the target person in a show-up; other student witnesses did not participate in the show-up test. Half of the time, the suspect of the show-up was the target person (target present), and half the time the suspect was merely someone who looked like the target person, but who did not disrupt the lecture (target absent). A few days later, all of the witnesses then participated in a photo-identification test containing the 'perpetrator' (or his look-alike innocent suspect) plus photographs of five other people. The most startling result was that many more witnesses mistakenly identified the innocent suspect in the line-up test if they had seen him earlier in the preliminary show-up than if they did not participate in an initial show-up. That is, participating in a previous test (show-up) influenced performance on the later test (line-up), increasing the number of false identifications of innocent suspects.

Given the potential for a first identification test to influence the outcome of a second identification test – and especially to lead to positively identifying innocent suspects – it is recommended that police should not conduct multiple tests with the same suspect. Police should be especially mindful of conducting a sloppy first identification procedure, in the hope that they will be able to conduct a 'cleaner' procedure in the future. Using the same logic, it is recommended that in-court identifications should not be taken as strong evidence of a defendant's guilt.

In the Courtroom

Research suggests that jurors are unable to discriminate between accurate and inaccurate witnesses on the basis of courtroom testimony (Wells, Lindsay and Ferguson, 1979; Lindsay, Wells and O'Connor, 1989) and that they are insensitive to factors that are known to affect identification accuracy (Cutler, Penrod and Stuve, 1988; Cutler, Penrod and Dexter, 1990). In light of these findings, research has begun examining ways to improve jurors' assessment of eyewitness identification.

One suggestion to improve juror decision making is to instruct jurors whether law enforcement complied with the recommended guidelines for collecting eyewitness evidence. If jurors regard the guidelines as being authoritative (emanating from a government commission) then violations of the guideline's recommendations may influence jurors' perceptions of the case. To test this idea, Lampinen *et al.* (2005) presented mock jurors with one of three versions of a trial transcript. In one condition, the defence lawyer pointed out errors in the eyewitness identification procedures (biased line-up and biased instructions); in a second condition, the defence attorney pointed out the same errors and also noted that the procedures used were not in compliance with the guidelines recommended by the NIJ; in a third condition, there was no mention of how the line-up was administered. Jurors who were told how the procedures deviated from the NIJ guidelines found guilt less often than jurors in the other two conditions. Knowledge of the guidelines also influenced jurors' perceptions of the case: They rated the witness as less credible, rated the investigating officer as less professional, and were more likely to believe that the investigating officer had jeopardized the case for the prosecution.

Knowledge of the police's compliance with recommended guidelines can also help jurors make better decisions. In a mock jury study, jurors were told whether or not police officers followed the NIJ guidelines when conducting a line-up (Phillips and Fisher, 2001). This information sensitized jurors to the quality of the eyewitness identification evidence. Specifically, jurors rated the identification as more likely to be accurate when the police identification procedure complied with the guidelines, and less likely to be accurate when it did not comply with the NIJ guidelines. Information about law enforcement's adherence to the guidelines also improved jurors' decision making, leading to more guilty verdicts when the police followed the guide and fewer guilty verdicts when the police did not follow the guide.

When a witness is given an identification test, she may express some behavioural cues that can be used by others to infer the (in)accuracy of her decision. Such cues may include the amount of time the witness takes to choose someone from the line-up (decision latency), verbal qualifiers (e.g. 'maybe', 'kind of'), and facial expressions. These cues are likely to be lost or distorted, however, in the several months that intervene between the identification procedure and when the witness appears in court. As noted earlier, witness confidence is malleable and may be influenced by events that happen after the identification test is completed (e.g. police or co-witness feedback). As such, the witness's expressed confidence on the witness stand may not faithfully convey her confidence when she initially described or identified the perpetrator to the police. Jurors might profit from observing these earlier behavioural cues. To test this idea, Reardon and Fisher (2006) showed mock jurors either a sample of an in-court eyewitness testimony (including a direct and cross-examination) or the in-court eyewitness testimony supplemented by a videotape of the witness's original description of the perpetrator and the original identification test. Mock jurors who saw the additional videotape of the witness's original description and identification were better able to discriminate between accurate witnesses and inaccurate witnesses than were jurors who saw only the eyewitness testimony. Based on these findings, it is recommended that (1) police videotape witness interviews and identifications tests, and (2) these videotapes are made available to jurors. The videotaping of identification tests is already practiced in some countries, such as the United Kingdom, Australia and Sweden.

CONCLUDING REMARKS

One common pattern that has marked many of the system variables reported is that the effects were more noticeable – or sometimes noticeable exclusively – in the target-absent condition than in the target-present condition, for example instruction bias (Steblay, 1997), simultaneous-versus-sequential line-ups (Lindsay and Wells, 1985), and line-up administrator contact with the witness (Haw and Fisher, 2004). If this pattern holds, then it suggests that more can be done to reduce incorrect identifications of innocent suspects (target-absent) than to increase hits (target present). The one exception to this rule was the strong effect of selecting fillers to match the witness's description (rather than matching to the suspect's appearance). Perhaps there are other procedures that can increase hits. We certainly encourage other researchers to pursue both of these noble goals, increasing hits and decreasing false identifications, by developing novel system variables to enhance law enforcement's efforts to increase identification accuracy.

REFERENCES

Bradfield, A.L., Wells, G.L. and Olson, E.A. (2002) The damaging effect of confirming feedback on the relation between eyewitness certainty and identification accuracy. *Journal of Applied Psychology*, **87**, 112–20.

Brewer, N., Weber, N. and Semmler, C. (2005) Eyewitness identification, in *Psychology and Law: An Empirical Perspective* (eds N. Brewer and K.D. Williams), Guilford Press, New York, pp. 177–221.

Brown, E., Deffenbacher, K., and Sturgill, W. (1977) Memory for faces and the circumstances of encounter. *Journal of Applied Psychology*, **62**, 311–18.

Cutler, B.L., Berman, G.L., Penrod, S. and Fisher, R.P. (1994) Conceptual, practical and empirical issues associated with eyewitness identification test media, in *Adult Eyewitness Testimony: Current Trends and Developments* (eds D. Ross, J.D. Read and M. Toglia), Cambridge University Press, London, pp. 163–81).

Cutler, B.L. and Penrod, S.D. (1995) *Mistaken Identification: The Eyewitness, Psychology, and the Law*, Cambridge University Press, Cambridge.

Cutler, B.L., Penrod, S.D. and Dexter, H.D. (1990) Juror sensitivity to eyewitness identification evidence. *Law and Human Behaviour*, **14**, 185–91.

Cutler, B.L., Penrod, S.D. and Stuve, T.E. (1988) Juror decision making in eyewitness identification cases. *Law and Human Behaviour*, **12**, 41–55.

Davey, B. and Behrman, S. (2001) Eyewitness identification in actual criminal cases: An archival analysis. *Law and Human Behaviour*, **25**, 475–91.

Davies, G.M. and Valentine, T. (in press) Facial composites: Forensic utility and psychological research, in *Handbook of Eyewitness Psychology. Volume 2: Memory for People* (eds R.C.L. Lindsay, D.F. Ross, J.D. Read and M.P. Toglia), Lawrence Erlbaum Associates, Mahwah (NJ).

Dekle, D. (2006) Viewing composite sketches: Line-ups and showups compared. *Applied Cognitive Psychology*, **20**, 383–95.

Deutsch, M. and Gerard, H.B. (1955) A study of normative and informational social influences upon individual judgement. *Journal of Abnormal and Social Psychology*, **51**, 629–36.

Dickinson, J.J., Fisher, R.P. and Haw, R.M. (2004) *Showups: Probative or Perilous?* Paper presented at the American Psychology and Law Society 2004 Annual Conference, Scottsdale, AZ.

Fisher, R.P. and Geiselman, R.E. (1992) *Memory Enhancing Techniques for Investigative Interviewing: The Cognitive Interview*, Charles C. Thomas, Springfield (IL).

Fisher, R.P., McCauley, M.R. and Geiselman, R.E. (1994) Improving eyewitness memory with the cognitive interview, in *Eyewitness Memory: Current Trends and Developments* (eds D. Ross, J.D.. Read and M. Toglia), Cambridge University Press, London, pp. 245–69.

Fisher, R.P. and Schreiber, N. (2006) Interviewing protocols to improve eyewitness memory, in *The Handbook of Eyewitness Psychology: Volume One. Memory for Events* (eds M. Toglia, R. Lindsay, R.D. Ross and J. Reed), Erlbaum Associates, Mahwah (NJ).

Fox, S.G. and Walters, H.A. (1986) The impact of general versus specific expert testimony and eyewitness confidence upon mock juror judgement. *Law and Human Behaviour*, **10**, 215–28.

Garrioch, L. and Brimacombe, C.A.E. (2001) Line-up administrators' expectations: Their impact on eyewitness confidence. *Law and Human Behaviour*, **25**, 299–315.

Gronlund, S.D. (2005) Sequential line-up advantage: Contributions of distinctiveness and recollection. *Applied Cognitive Psychology*, **19**, 23–37.

Gwyer, P. and Clifford, B.R. (1997) The effects of the cognitive interview on recall, identification, confidence and the confidence/accuracy relationship. *Applied Cognitive Psychology*, **11**, 121–45.

Haw, R.M. and Fisher, R.P. (2004) Effects of administrator-witness contact on identification accuracy. *Journal of Applied Psychology*, **89**, 1106–12.

Johnson, M.K., Hashtroudi, S. and Lindsay, D.S. (1993) Source monitoring. *Psychological Bulletin*, **114**, 3–28.

Koehn, C., Fisher, R.P. and Cutler, B.L. (1999) Using cognitive interviewing to construct facial composites, in *Psychology and Criminal Detection* (eds D. Canter and L. Alison) Dartmouth, Brookfield, pp. 41–63.

Kohnken, G., Milne, R., Memon, A. and Bull, R. (1999) The cognitive interview: A meta-analysis. *Psychology, Crime and Law*, **5**, 3–27.

Krafka, C. and Penrod, S., (1985) Reinstatement of context in a field experiment on eyewitness identification. *Journal of Personality and Social Psychology*, **49**, 58–69.

Lampinen, J.M., Judges, D.P., Odegard, T.N. and Hamilton, S. (2005) The reactions of mock jurors to the Department of Justice Guidelines for the Collection and Preservation of Eyewitness Evidence. *Basic and Applied Social Psychology*, **27**, 155–62.

Lindsay, R.C.L. and Wells, G.L. (1985) Improving eyewitness identifications from line-ups: Simultaneous versus sequential line-up presentation. *Journal of Applied Psychology*, **70**, 556–64.

Lindsay, R.C.L., Wells, G.L. and O'Connor, F.J. (1989) Mock-juror belief of accurate and inaccurate witnesses. *Law and Human Behaviour*, **13**, 333–39.

Luus, E. and Wells, G.L. (1994) The malleability of eyewitness confidence: Co-witness and perseverance effects. *Journal of Applied Psychology*, **79**, 714–23.

Malpass, R.S. (2006) A policy evaluation of simultaneous and sequential line-ups. *Psychology, Public Policy and Law*, **12** (4), 394–418.

Malpass, R.S. and Devine, P.G. (1980) Realism and eyewitness identification research. *Law and Human Behaviour*, **4**, 347–58.

Malpass, R.S. and Devine, P.G. (1981) Eyewitness identification: Line-up instructions and the absence of the offender. *Journal of Applied Psychology*, **66**, 482–89.

Meissner, C.A. and Brigham, J.C. (2001) A meta-analysis of the verbal overshadowing effect in face identification. *Applied Cognitive Psychology*, **15**, 603–16.

Meissner, C.A., Tredoux, C.G., Parker, J.F. and MacLin, O.H. (2005) Eyewitness decisions in simultaneous and sequential line-ups: A dual-process signal detection theory analysis. *Memory & Cognition*, **33**, 783–92.

Neil v. Biggers, 409 U.S. 188 (1972).

Phillips, M.R., McAuliff, B.D., Kovera, M.B. and Cutler, B.L. (1999) Double-blind photoarray administration as a safeguard against investigator bias. *Journal of Applied Psychology*, **84**, 940–51.

Phillips, M.R. and Fisher, R.P. (2001, March) *The Reactions of Mock Jurors to the Department of Justice Guidelines for the Collection and Preservation of Eyewitness Evidence*. Paper presented at the American Psychology-Law Society.

Reardon, M. and Fisher, R.P. (2006, March) *The impact of viewing the identification process on juror perceptions of eyewitness accuracy*. Paper presented at the meeting of the American-Psychology Law Society, St. Petersberg, FL.

R v Turnbull, [1976] 3 All ER 549.

Rosenthal, R. (1969) Interpersonal expectations: Effects of the experimenter's hypothesis, in *Artifact in Behavioural Research* (eds R. Rosenthal and R.L. Rosnow), Academic Press, New York, pp. 181–277.

Russano, M.B., Dickinson, J.J., Greathouse, S.M. and Kovera, M.B. (2006) "Why don't you take another look at number three?" Investigator knowledge and its effects on eyewitness confidence and identification decisions. *Cardozo Public Law, Policy, and Ethics Journal*, **4**, 355–79.

Schooler, J.W. and Engstler-Schooler, T.Y. (1990) Verbal overshadowing of visual memories: Some things are better left unsaid. *Cognitive Psychology*, **22**, 36–71.

Schooler, J.W., Fiore, S.M. and Brandimonte, M.A. (1997) At a loss from words Verbal overshadowing of perceptual memories, in *The Psychology of Learning and Motivation: Advances in Research and Theory*, vol. **37** (ed. Medin, D.), Academic Press, San Diego (CA), pp. 291–340.

Semmler, C., Brewer, N. and Wells, G.L. (2004) Effects of postidentification feedback on eyewitness identification and nonidentification confidence. *Journal of Applied Psychology*, **89**, 334–46.

Shapiro, P.N. and Penrod, S. (1986) A meta-analysis of facial identification studies. *Psychological Bulletin*, **100**, 139–56.

Shaw, J.S. and McClure, K.A. (1996) Repeated postevent questioning can lead to elevated levels of eyewitness confidence. *Law and Human Behaviour*, **20**, 629–52.

Shepherd, J.W., Ellis, H.D. and Davies, G.M. (1982) *Identification Evidence*, Aberdeen University Press, Aberdeen.

Sporer, S.L., Penrod, S., Read, D. and Cutler, B. (1995) Choosing, confidence, and accuracy: A meta-analysis of the confidence-accuracy relation in eyewitness identification studies. *Psychological Bulletin*, **118**, 315–27.

Steblay, N.M. (1997) Social influences in eyewitness recall: A meta-analytic review of line-up instruction effects. *Law & Human Behaviour*, **21** (3), 283–97.

Steblay, N., Dysart, J., Fulero, S. and Lindsay, R.C.L. (2001) Eyewitness accuracy rates in sequential and simultaneous line-up presentations: A meta-analytic review. *Law and Human Behaviour*, **25**, 459–73.

Steblay, N., Dysart, J., Fulero, S. and Lindsay, R.C.L. (2003) Eyewitness accuracy rates in police showup and line-up presentations: A meta-analytic comparison. *Law and Human Behaviour*, **27**, 523–40.

Taylor, K.T. (2001) *Forensic Art and Illustration*, CRC Press, London.

Technical Working Group on Eyewitness Evidence (1999) *Eyewitness Evidence: A Guide for Law Enforcement*, U.S. Department of Justice, Washington, D.C. Available at http://www.ojp.usdoj.gov/nij/pubs-sum/178240.htm.

Wells, G.L. (1978) Applied eyewitness testimony research: System variables and estimator variables. *Journal of Personality and Social Psychology*, **36**, 1546–57.

Wells, G.L. and Bradfield, A.L. (1998) "Good, you identified the suspect": Feedback to eyewitnesses distorts their reports of the witnessing experience. *Journal of Applied Psychology*, **83**, 36–376.

Wells, G.L., Ferguson, T.J. and Lindsay, R.C.L. (1981) The tractability of eyewitness confidence and its implications for triers of fact. *Journal of Applied Psychology*, **66**, 688–96.

Wells, G.L., Lindsay, R.C.L. and Ferguson, T.J. (1979) Accuracy, confidence, and juror perceptions in eyewitness identification. *Journal of Applied Psychology*, **64**, 440–48.

Wells, G.L., Rydell, S.M. and Seelau, E.P. (1993) On the selection of distractors for eyewitness line-ups. *Journal of Applied Psychology*, **78**, 835–44.

Wells, G.L., Small, M., Penrod, S. et al. (1998) Eyewitness identification procedures: Recommendations for line-ups and photospreads. *Law and Human Behaviour*, **23** (6) 603–47.

CHAPTER 3

Behavioural Science and the Law: Investigation

John G.D. Grieve

SUMMARY

Psychology and behavioural sciences have made a contribution to police investigations for over 25 years. The chronology produced here is based on public inquiries into miscarriages of justice and has led to consideration of four areas of influence: (1) interrogation and investigative interviewing, (2) identification testimony, (3) profiling and behavioural advice and (4) bias and prejudice. These areas illustrate the importance of the breadth and depth in necessary skills and specialists required by police investigative teams.

INTRODUCTION

During the course of many hundreds of investigations, all important to someone, but of varying degrees of public significance or impact, I have worked with and had assistance from, a wide variety of academic practitioners.[1] Their knowledge and skills, their written material, advice and direct investigative and forensic interventions have contributed to a search for the truth, an investigation as opposed to the adversarial approach where, after the investigators have identified a suspect, they try to reinforce their suspicions whilst the defence try to prove innocence. The police investigator has been compared to the conductor in an orchestra, or perhaps more pertinently a craftsman with a toolbox. However, there is rarely a full orchestral score for the conductor-investigator. Biologists, chemists, physicists, pathologists, police surgeons, forensic medical examiners, and experts of: drugs, explosives, fingerprints, handwriting, fibres, soil metallurgists, tyres, feet and DNA, have compared, contrasted, mechanically fitted, analysed, considered continuity and integrity of exhibits

---

[1] The author served as a detective for 37 years, working as an investigator, senior investigating officer, officer in overall command and supervisor of many police enquiries both in the Metropolitan Police, London and as National Co-ordinator for counter terrorism. He was also responsible for policy change and implementation in respect of intelligence, psychological profiling as it was then known, analysis, leadership, diversity issues and at the end of his career a massive change programme after the public inquiry into the racist murder of Stephen Lawrence. This chapter therefore, draws on many policing experiences as well as the current research at University of Portsmouth.

Applying Psychology to Criminal Justice. Edited by David Carson, Rebecca Milne, Francis Pakes, Karen Shalev and Andrea Shawyer. © 2007 John Wiley & Sons, Ltd

whilst supporting or challenging the evidence produced by the teams I worked with (e.g. see Townley and Ede, 2004). They provided both the tools to help the craftsman-investigator to collect evidence as well as providing products of evidentiary or intelligence value, a distinction I owe to David Carson's thinking about Innes (2003, pp 144 et seq).

Since the late 1970s another group of individuals emerged from the behavioural sciences, largely driven to significance and importance by psychology and management studies, both academic and practical. These had sprung, ready armed, from the head of philosophy studies not least at the Police Staff College. It was therefore not just the push of late modernism to modernize policing as argued, for example by Bowling and Foster (2002), important though this was, but was also pulled into the service by psychologists such as Rob Adlam, working within policing at the England and Wales national Police Staff College, Bramshill (see, e.g. Watts, Pope and Weiner (1981) and Thackrah (1985)). Thus, this chapter looks at the utility and the rise in investigative importance of the behavioural sciences as a discipline and at psychology in particular. Like their predecessors, no one stands alone, as each provided from their toolboxes a saw to cut a part for a jigsaw puzzle of corroborative evidential pieces. The chronology produced here leads to four areas of influence that psychology has had on investigative processes: (1) interrogation and investigative interviewing; (2) identification testimony; (3) profiling and behavioural advice; and (4) bias and prejudice. There are many other areas of research and application of the behavioural sciences, but these four areas have long academic and practitioner histories and many interconnections with other aspects of the discipline.[2] In addition, the four areas identified here have all been used by me, as a detective.

Alan Wright (2002) argues from a postmodernist perspective that miscarriages of justice, challenges to the state and criminal justice system, are endemic in what he identifies as four modes of policing in the early twenty-first century: (1) criminal investigation; (2) community justice; (3) risk management; and (4) peacekeeping (Wright, 2002). Challenges to criminal justice come from many sources. The early external pressure to consider research being conducted in the behavioural sciences came from Fisher (1977), Irving and Hilgendorf (1980), Morris (1980) and Hayward (1981) together with Lloyd Bostock (1981) and Bull *et al.* (1983). Here were the foundations of many police investigators' knowledge of psychology. This led to interest in other social, behavioural and managerial sciences.

This chapter uses a chronology of challenges to policing in a context of police investigative use of behavioural science. There are other ways of looking at this progression, the influence of American studies, for example. The subjective chronology offered here starts much earlier than 1980. At the time, Hayward (1981) and Philips (1981) published, respectively, an account of forensic psychology and its practical application in a Royal Commission report, a new generation of police officers had become available. They had studied psychology, particularly the unpleasant realities of the police personality as taught by Rob Adlam (see Adlam, 1981, 1985), and were either reaching positions where they could use the materials and tools on offer, to impact on the service, or were leaving university ready to take advantage of the changes that were about to occur.[3]

---

[2] I have not considered psychology and psychiatry hostage negotiations (post Balcombe Street), firearms and other selection procedures nor training in, for example human awareness at Hendon Police College (post Lord Scarmans 1981 report). All these are important and fit the argument I am presenting of academic and practical pressures, internal and external to policing.

[3] For example, Albie McKew, Ian McKenzie, Tom Williamson, Geof Rees and John Grieve. Officers, such as Ian Johnston, had studied Social Policy at LSE. This may be contrasted with a large number of police officers who had previously studied law.

A wider context for Wright (2002) is the general fragmentation of society, the development of multiple perspectives on criminal justice and policing and experiences of communities and disciplines, which blur the edges of a definition of modern policing. He argues that the four overlapping modes of twenty-first century policing – mentioned above – cannot be undertaken by the police on the nineteenth-century model. That model, he claims, may have run its course. Policing, he believes, now requires multiple actors from many disciplines and skills as well as trained and sworn public police. Those actors include behavioural scientists, both as police officers and as academics. At the edges of different communities geographical and disciplinary, at the boundaries, physical and conceptual, things can go wrong. To some extent, the development of the investigative use of behavioural science was driven by the miscarriages of justice uncovered by public inquiries and other mechanisms not least the media. The argument is informed by an ongoing research project at University of Portsmouth's Institute of Criminal Justice Studies (Savage, Poyser and Grieve, 2006 in submission). This project is examining through structured interviews and the literature, the nature of campaigns for justice, the roles of families, professions and their skills, public inquiries and the lessons learnt.

A crucial milestone in this chronology is the 1980 Royal Commission on Criminal Procedure chaired by Sir Cyril Philips (1981), who commissioned the Tavistock Institute in general, and Barrie Irving in particular, to research current psychological practice of interrogation. More importantly, Barrie Irving and his associate used this as a vehicle to begin to outline the psychological aspects of the roles, behaviours, explanations for both suspects' and investigators' behaviours in interviewing and their practical implications for the search for the truth and justice (Irving and Hilgendorf, 1981). Also for Philips, Dr Pauline Morris reviewed the psychological literature pertinent to detention and interrogation (Morris, 1981). This important contribution to core investigative tasks, such as witness interviewing, interrogation, identification and custody guidance, cannot be underestimated. These research projects are often neglected in accounts of the importance of behavioural studies to policing, the lead up to the Police and Criminal Evidence Act 1984, associated Codes of Practice for investigators, and all that follows for policing and investigation.

The Royal Commission derived, in part, from the 1977 inquiry by the Hon Sir Henry Fisher into the trial of three young men, Colin Latimer, Ahmet Salih and Ronald Leigton. There were concerns about their role - or rather in some crucial aspects the lack of it - in a fire at 27, Doggett Road, London SE6, which lead to the death of Maxwell Confait (Fisher, 1977). Christopher Price, MP, and the press had been significant in drawing these to notice of investigators. Irving, however, had given crucial psychological theory evidence to that inquiry about the mental development of the suspects, the degree to which they were skilled verbally, and their ability to reason. With their skills deficits how could they cope with interrogation (Fisher, 1977, pp 52 and 53)? This had helped Fisher to reach conclusions (albeit amongst many others) that although the police suspicions were well grounded, some of their processes and methods, in respect of uncorroborated confessions and disclosure to the defence, had undermined confidence in their conclusions (Fisher, 1977, pp 29–32). Fisher, after hearing the psychological underpinning recommended, innovatively, the use of unannounced lay community visitors to suspects in police cells. This, over two decades later, led to structured lay independent advice from communities to police in times of crises, or critical incidents as they became known, of many kinds not just like the case considered by Fisher (TSO, 1999 and personal experiences). Later studies built on this background psychological underpinning, which Fisher had heard from Irving, of concerns of Black Minority Ethnic (BME) suspects and their communities, challenges to police interrogation and interviews more generally and the treatment in custody of juveniles and persons at risk in particular (see, e.g. Gudjonsson, 2003). All this should not be considered to be about behavioural science in isolation, rather it needs to be integrated in an analysis of the police investigation as a whole, including the role of physical and forensic sciences and expert evidence. Specifically, the Confait case can be seen to be about timelines, sequences and times of death, and how that all fits the psychological information available. The review of the case is an example of the jigsaw puzzle of trying to match the evidential pieces.

Hayward (1981) (Figure 1 p 19, Table 1 p 20, and thereafter) helpfully summarizes where things were at the end of the 1970s. He argues that clinical, community, correctional, criminological, developmental, educational, experimental, forensic, legal, occupational, prison and social psychology can each, or all, have a unique contribution to law and hence to police and other investigations. For example, I have experience that the policing role in the suppression of the illegal use and distribution of drugs involved all these categories (Grieve, 1998). Hayward produced 33 cases of considerable variety to illustrate these roles, including vulnerability, state of mind, mental illness and issues about corroborating police evidence (Hayward, 1981, summary p 64). From Hayward's description comes a prescient early indication of what has become known as knowledge-led policing – a development of intelligence-led policing. The behavioural sciences can be argued to be a branch of intelligence-led policing through the use of behavioural intelligence analysts amongst others (Grieve, 2004, p 30). In considering the role of behavioural sciences in investigations, I will now consider where the concept of knowledge-based policing sits with intelligence-led policing models. I am arguing for intelligent use of knowledge from those sciences.

EXPANDING THE IDEA OF INTELLIGENCE-LED POLICING TO KNOWLEDGE-LED POLICING USING BEHAVIOURAL SCIENCES

The evolution of the role of behavioural sciences can be described as springing, ready armed, from the head of philosophy. Therefore, it seems appropriate to introduce two modern philosophers whose thinking has helped us: Douglas Hofstadter (1980) on intelligence and Miranda Fricker (2002) on epistemic imbalance.

Hofstadter (1980) provides a useful framework for involving knowledge of behavioural sciences in policing and in the evolution of intelligence-led investigation specifically. His criteria for instantiation of the word 'intelligence' (not just as used in 'criminal intelligence analysis') includes eight elements:

1. the ability to respond very flexibly to situations,
2. taking advantage of fortuitous circumstances,
3. making sense of the ambiguous or contradictory,
4. recognizing the relative importance of different elements,
5. finding similarities between situations despite different elements in those situations,
6. drawing distinctions despite similarities,
7. synthesizing new concepts by taking old concepts
8. putting together new ways of approaching tasks.

Finally, he argues that coming up with ideas that are novel has considerable relevance for using the word 'intelligence'. The chronology about to be introduced includes examples of each of his elements using behavioural sciences and provides the basis for an investigator's open mind (as recommended by Lord Laming (2003) in his report into the care and killing of Victoria Climbie).

I do not pretend that this has been acceptable or easy for the Criminal Justice System or for policing. Miranda Fricker (2002), argues that, where particular pieces of testimony and hence particular lines of inquiry lead to the identification of significant witnesses, then that testimony can achieve greater or more significant influence than it might deserve. In other words, some parts of the evidence have a greater impact for some people, say investigators, than for others, say defence lawyers. This is a plausible account of what behavioural sciences have achieved, not just in respect of uncovering the unwitting bias, but also with decision making more generally about who might have relevant skills to an investigation team. This is not just noteworthy for applied psychology, and experiential learning, but also for experiment and theory.

To provide some bookends with Barrie Irving's work in 1977/1980 and Ray Bull's 1983 study, I have also examined some recent examples to derive some relevant behavioural current context. These examples are the Review of Operation Lancet (July, 2002) – a long term investigation into a complaint against police in Cleveland – and Sir Bill Morris' Inquiry into, amongst other issues, the police investigation of complaints made against black minority ethnic (BME) officers (2005). There are many valuable experiences in Lancet, but the following extract provided a functional preliminary framework for an ideal investigative methodology in which the behavioural sciences can sit. In some ways, what follows illustrates some deep ironies and paradoxes where key investigators and suspects are alike. I explore this powerful argument below.

> When dealing with alleged malpractice by police officers there is an understandable desire for a thoroughness and conclusiveness, which can border the search for perfection and result in an intoxicating cocktail comprising:
>
> - unachievable expectations;
> - investigatory activity disproportionate to the central issues;
> - apparently unconstrained expenditure;
> - inappropriate elongation of the enquiry;
> - unnecessary and debilitating pressures on the individuals concerns;
> - the setting of a 'threshold' of satisfaction by individual stakeholders that puts unrealistic (and often unintended) pressures on the other stakeholders; and
> - the 'suspension of reasonable and normal management measures.
>
> This cocktail, rather than resulting in effectiveness, which must be the outcome that best represents the public interest, can be a major contributory factor in creating widespread dissatisfaction.
>
> (Home Office, 2002, p 4).

I have quoted this section from the Lancet Review in its entirety. However, the three concepts that overarch all seven listed above are:

1. ... understandable desire for a thoroughness and conclusiveness ...
2. ... unachievable expectations ...
3. ... the suspension of reasonable and normal management measures ...

This possibly unrealistic ideal model, a conclusive comprehensive search for the truth, may be seen as a version of Bowling and Foster's (2002). Theirs is an omnibus model of policing as applied to investigative, detection modes for both proactive and reactive elements. Irving (1980) had already identified a 'complex of threats' to both suspects and investigators (1980, p 32), including uncertainty, failure, social stigma and economic as unpleasant consequences of being a suspect or a failure as an investigator. The management of investigators and the complexity of their decision making is another early issue raised by Irving (1980, p 28). Although he raised concerns initially about suspects' decision making, the conclusions he reached also apply equally to investigators, where problems with emotional arousal and impaired performance, limited capacity to take on board new information, memory deficit, inability to deal with diverse matters, inability to ignore other incoming but irrelevant information all can contribute to miscarriages of justice. All these matters concerned suspect behaviour; however, they are also relevant to everyone, not least police officers themselves. Small wonder that both Bull *et al.* (1983) and Ainsworth and Pease (1987) apply them to the problems of stress suffered by police officers not just when they are challenged or as suspects themselves in internal investigations but in their everyday work.

The report of Sir William Morris and his colleagues proposed an up-to-date route map for change in policing and how the behavioural sciences could help. The following categories are of immediate relevance to the behavioural sciences agenda:

1. People issues, including use of Advisory, Conciliation and Arbitration Service (ACAS) Code, mediation.
2. Managing difference.
3. Governance, accountability and scrutiny.
4. Professional standards including case management and ...
5. Capacity to deliver.
6. Building capacity. (Morris, 2005, pp 12–17).

A SUBJECTIVE[4] CHRONOLOGY OF PUBLIC INQUIRIES INVOLVING BEHAVIOURAL SCIENCES, CJS AND LAW,[5] 1949–2006

What follows is an extract from a literature review for on-going research, conducted at the University of Portsmouth,[6] where my principal interest is in the investigative lessons to be learnt from the chronology. In this chapter, I am specifically drawing attention to the links with behavioural sciences. The research constitutes an expanded version of a definition of public inquiries in miscarriages of justice cases since 1949, including trials, inquests as well as those inquiries set up under legislation and those independently undertaken.

---

[4] I am conscious that this is subjective covering the influences on my earliest interest in policing, philosophy, psychology and justice and my 37 years service.
[5] This is our expanded version of a definition of Public Inquiry in Miscarriages of Justice cases of three types. The inquiry has to be conducted in public domain with more than one dimension since the 1950s. Our typology is developed from an analysis or amalgam of ideas from cases and inquiries. Type I miscarriage of justice is convicting innocent, type II is a failure to act or to act effectively, thoroughly and competently, type III is a failure to explain and includes failure to provide a subsequent explanation.
[6] See footnote 1 above.

Ludovic Kennedy, the campaigning journalist who largely initiated interest in miscarriage of justice cases (Kennedy, 1961, 2002), is seen by many to be of great influence and thus the chronology starts in 1949 with the case of John Reginald Christie and the miscarriage of justice perpetrated on Timothy Evans. It concludes with current incomplete inquiries where there are relevant allegations and behavioural science potential.

The 55 year history, recorded in Table 3.1, highlights two important issues of relevance. First, the steady growth, breadth and increasing trajectory and incidence of external pressure on investigations from miscarriages of justice cases, public inquiries and causes celebres. Second, the table illustrates the increasing presence and use of behavioural science not just by those challenging the investigation from the outside but also by the investigators themselves and by subsequent investigators as reviewers. This is applicable both to police and other agencies. There are many other facets to be bought out from this work but I have chosen the four threads referred to above: (1) interrogation and investigative interviewing, (2) identification evidence, (3) offender profiling and behavioural investigative advice, impact assessment and analysis, and finally (4) mindset – bias and prejudice.

INTERROGATION AND INVESTIGATIVE INTERVIEWING

Although there are roots in American material, I have chosen to give credit to Barrie Irving (1980) for his hugely influential studies for the 1981 Royal Commission. These mapped out the effects of investing not just in the route for challenging some aspects of confession evidence, in improving investigative interviewing, vulnerable suspects and other witnesses. He also laid out the agenda, and some of the methodology, for the following 25 years. His review of the psychological approach and his case studies of current practice introduced investigators and their critics to typologies and models that clarified the dangers of manipulative strategies, the offering of alternatives and consequences of decision making by the suspect. He also highlighted the role of status, social pressures, isolation, approval and disapproval and their impacts on witnesses' self-esteem. His analysis of situational factors, environment, and fear of confinement, guilt and failure within the interview room led to arguments about risk, impaired performance and emotional factors in decision making. This research was ground breaking and contributed to the identification of false confessions and is still relevant today. It is worth reinforcing that his arguments and analysis applies equally to investigators as interviewers and senior investigator decision makers and suspects.

The issues that he had identified were picked up by serving investigators and academics alike; Tom Williamson, 1993, 2005), Ray Bull (Bull *et al.*, 1983) (Bull and Milne, 2004), Ian McKenzie (McKenzie and Dunk, 1999), Gisli Gudjonsson (1983, 1984, 2003 and many others), James McKeith (Gudjonsson and McKeith, 1982), Eric Shepherd (Shepherd, 1993; Shepherd and Milne, 1999), Becky Milne (Milne and Shaw, 1999; Bull and Milne, 1999), Graham Davies (Davies, 1999), Geoffrey Stephenson (Stephenson, Clarke and Kniveton, 1989), Steve Savage (Savage in submission), David Canter (Canter and Alison, 1999, 2000) and Peter Ainsworth (1995).

Out of this rich stew came improvements, not always welcomed by some police officers, in a wide variety of police interactions (Bull, 1983, p ix; Williamson, 2002; and many others personal communications and personal experience). It took nearly a decade to convince some less enlightened parts of the service. Unwelcome though it might have been, the conclusion that the police in general had no value-added ability to recall events

Table 3.1 A subjective chronology of Public Inquiries involving behavioural sciences, CJS and law, 1949–2006.

Chronology, year and title. The date cited is date of case and of the report published, where applicable.	(a) Nature of case/report/inquiry/allegations. (b) Types of behavioural sciences held to be of value. (c) Type I, II or III Miscarriages of Justice. Type I convicting innocent, Type II failure to act or to act in right way, Type III failure to explain.
1949. 10, Rillington Place. John Reginald Halliday Christie and Timothy John Evans (*) [8]	(a) Confession evidence. (b) Early example of psychology, psychiatry, suggestability and vulnerability. (c) Type I, II and III. The roles of Ludovic Kennedy (Kennedy, 1961). and his book 10, Rillington Place are cited by many campaigners and investigators as an inspiration to them.
1952. Murder of PC Miles. Bentley and Craig case.	(a) Incriminating evidence/confession at scene? Evidential weight, and clarity (or lack of clarity) of memory evidence. (b) Psychology. Mental age. (c) Defence trial issues. Alleged Type I.
1961. Hanratty (*).	(a) Eyewitness identification evidence. Subsequently DNA. (c) Alleged Type I. Paul Foot journalist as major campaigner.
1964. W.L. Mars–Jones Inquiry into cases of Halloran, Cox, Tisdall, Kingston and King–Burton.	(a) Early raising of 'police canteen culture' issues. (c) Type II with subsequent explanation. Internal and disciplinary investigations.
1965. A.E. James QC Inquiry into the circumstances ... Detective Sergeant Harold Challenor.	(a) Mental illness of a police officer and record keeping. CID culture and supervision. Raising of canteen culture issues. (b) Psychiatric evidence. (c) Type I, II and III allegations of perjury and conspiracy to pervert justice.
1969. 'The Times' Inquiry into New Scotland Yard (NSY).[9]	(a) Broadsheet disclosure of police malpractice and subsequent trials widely cited as highly influential. CID culture and behaviour widely discussed. Perjury, exhibit tampering and conspiracy to pervert the course of justice alleged. Informants – functional or dysfunctional relationships between criminals and detectives. (c) Types I and III. *Arrival of Sir Robert Mark at NSY, police reformer. Changes in complaints investigation*

Table 3.1 *(Continued)*

1971–1977. Inquiry by ACC Harold Prescott into NSY Drug Squad.[10]	(a) Derived from another agency's case – HM Customs and Excise – Investigation Branch. CID culture and behaviour further explored. Perjury, exhibit tampering and conspiracy to pervert course of justice in the form of recycling drugs and improper relations with informants alleged. Leading to discussion of ethics, drugs enforcement and moral ambiguity and contagion. (c) Type I, II and III.
1972. Pornography ('Dirty') Squad NSY.[11]	(a) CID culture and relationships with pornographers in London, moral ambiguity and contagion alleged questions about the role for detectives in this arena? (c) Types I, II and III.
1972. The original date of the murder of Maxwell Confait and the rise of community concerns (*).	(a) Lay visitors, subsequently independent advice, BME, interrogation generally and of juveniles and persons at risk issues alleged. Forensic and expert evidence challenged. (c) Types I, II and III.
1974. Birmingham 6 (*).	(a) Chris Mullin MP as change agent. Forensic science (Dr Frank Skuse) challenged. (b) Confession evidence subsequently challenged by psychology. (c) Types I, II and III.
1974. Guildford 4 (*).	(a) Forensic science (of Dr Frank Skuse) (b) Challenged by (amongst other disciplines) psychology of contested confession evidence. (c) Types I, II and III.
1974. Judith Ward(*).	(a) and (b) Gisli Gudjonsson (2003) and James MacKieth subsequently challenged with forensic psychology her terrorism confessions using concepts of susceptibility, suggestibility and compliance. (c) Types I, II and III.
1974 Terrorism cases.	*These three terrorism arrests of 1974, trials and the lessons for investigations from the challenges from the bar – culminating 15 years later in reversal and apologies – Michael Mansfield QC.*

(Continued)

Table 3.1 *(Continued)*

1974 Kenneth John Lennon.	(a) Murder victim allegations of collusion and agent provocateur/informant. Internal MPS Inquiry published in House of Commons (c) Type I, II and III.
1976 *R- v- Turnbull* (63 Cr App R 132)	(a) Culmination of 75 years of identification evidence alleged miscarriages and challenges results in (b) ADVOKATE model (see page below) guidance based on psychology to judge, jury, bar and investigator. (c) Not categorized.
1977. Publication of Hon. Sir Henry Fisher Inquiry ... trial of three person arising out of the death of Maxwell Confait. Colin Latimer, Ahmet Salih and Ronald Leigton and the fire at 27 Doggett Road London SE6. (*).	(a) Role of Christopher Price MP. Lay visitors, subsequently independent advice. (b) Background psychological underpinning by Barrie Irving of some aspects of Black Minority Ethnic, interrogation generally and of juveniles and persons at risk in particular. Forensic and expert evidence. (c) Types I, II and III. Forerunner of Philips Royal Commission.
1980 Royal Commission on Criminal Procedure Sir Cyril Philips. (Published January 1981).	(a) and (b) Barrie Irving research case study of current psychological practice in interrogation. Pauline Morris review of psychological literature on interviews and interrogation. Interview, interrogation, identification, and custody guidance proposed. Twelve research projects covering interrogation, confessions, trial issues, public role in solving crimes, tape recording, arrest, charging, prosecutions other than by police, and prosecuting authorities. Leads to PACE 1984 and Codes of Practice. Roles of social sciences, community policing, stop and search, training and complaints investigation all considered. (c) Considers Type I and II and raises questions for type III.
1981. Sir Laurence Byford. Yorkshire Ripper Inquiry.	(a) Leads to changes in major incident room procedures in serial murder case, training of CID, data rich environments. HOLMES computerized investigation system proposed as solution. (b) Psychology and management of decision making. (c) Type II.

Table 3.1 (Continued)

1980–1982. 'Operation Countryman'	(a) Detective culture especially specialist squads examined. Informants and police relationships thought through. (c) Type I and II.
1982. Roger Graef Thames Valley rape interview exposes low skill levels (*).	(a) Detective culture examined, stereotyping of victims challenged. Sexual Offences Investigation Trained officers as a specialist task (b) Application of developments in psychology of interviewing, victimology and sexual violence trauma. Unusual example as emerged from a TV documentary as a specific cause celebre without prior concern about that specific case. (c) Type II.
	Widening knowledge in UK of Behavioural Sciences, for example Hayward (1981), Lloyd-Bostock (1981) and Bull et al. (1983). Information about FBI use of Behavioural Science Unit becomes current in UK via exchange programs.
1983 Policy Studies Institute Report, Police and People in London.	(b) Four studies involving psychology, sociology and criminology in studies based on general attitude questionnaires, surveys and participant observations of police and young black Londoners and relationships.
1985 Bradford Fire. Lord Justice Oliver Popplewell Public Inquiry.	(b) Professor David Canter on crowd behaviour at scene of a disastrous fire at a football match. Conspicuous gallantry of police at scene. (b) Psychology techniques lead to early profiling then investigative psychology.
	Professor David Canter first becomes involved with New Scotland Yard and subsequently Surrey and Hampshire Constabulary over use of psychology, multivariate analysis for profiling and prioritising of suspects.
1985. Murder of PC Kieth Blakelock QGM.	(a) Murder of police officer during violent public disorder. Pace implementation period. PACE Code D on identification. (b) Development in interviewing techniques, refinement of role of psychology for vulnerable, young people issues during interrogation. Detective culture. (c) Alleged types I, II and III.

(Continued)

Table 3.1 *(Continued)*

1989. West Midlands Serious Crime Squad.	(a) Detective culture especially in specialist squads challenged. Leadership issues. (c) Alleged type I and II.
1992. (Final Report 1994). Sir John May (*). Interim Report of the inquiry into the circumstances surrounding the convictions arising out of the bomb attacks in Guildford and Woolwich in 1974 (See 1974 above).	(b) Consideration of behavioural science in challenging decision making about forensic and confession evidence. Development of PEACE model of interviewing and assisted recall techniques.
1993. Royal Commission on Criminal Procedure. Lord Runciman (*).	Overview of Criminal Justice System and police investigation role within it. Closed Circuit Television, forensic science and covert intelligence-led policing all considered, albeit the latter in enigmatic references.
1999. Stephen Lawrence Public Inquiry (*)	(a) Racist murder and failure of police and criminal justice system to bring peretrators to justice. Family Liaison as potential solution. Fusion and co-ordination of mainstream policing, investigative supervision, challenges and questioning of investigative tasking, hate crimes, race and community relations and community impact assessment and critical incident training derive from findings. Independent Police Complaints Commission proposed and implemented in 2003. (b) Psychology, sociology, criminology, political theory all applied to policing in wide ranging submissions. Behavioural sciences contribution to exploration of institutional racism – collective failure, unwitting, ignorant, thoughtless, stereotypical bias or prejudice. Bias in the lay sense, prejudice – literally prejudging an issue due to strong prior belief or motive. Found by inquiry to be broader and more subtle included a wide range of effects that influenced police thinking about minority groups and communities. ICAS (Intelligence cell analytic section) includes behavioural scientists and PhD students as part of Home Office and Metropolitan Police project on Understanding and Responding to Hate Crime Project. (c) Type I, II and III Miscarriage of Justice.

Table 3.1 *(Continued)*

1999. Patten Inquiry (*)	(a) Broader Inquiry into policing in Northern Ireland, not concerned with Miscarriages of justice directly but had an impact on 1600 outstanding murders over a 30 year period. Analysts, Community, Recruiting. Police Authority & Governance. Culture, structures, criminal investigation. Wide ranging study of policing Northern Ireland (NI), reform of Royal Ulster Constabulary and creation of Police Service of Northern Ireland (PSNI). (b) Criminology, Social Sciences, Politics, Journalism and media studies all contribute to analysis of policing style for twenty first century.
2000. MacGowan Inquests (*). West Mercia	(a) Allegations of racist lynching and institutional racism included many of the concerns raised in Stephen Lawrence Inquiry. Application of lessons learnt.
2002. Damilola Taylor Murder Inquiry (*)	(a) Murder of schoolboy. Progress on institutional racism recorded by Bishop John Sentamu. Persons at risk, juveniles, witness testimony community impact all considered and used psychology. Independent Advice to assist with community impact assessment and maintenance of open mind by investigators. Critical Incidents. Scene management. Cultural resources available amongst police staff. Proof of progress but took 5 years to complete trials. Justice delayed.
2003. Public Inquiry Victoria Climbie (*).	(a) Murder of young girl by guardians. (b) Psychology, sociology, criminology, education, media and social sciences all contribute. Lord Laming, assisted by Detective Superintendent John Fox, reach conclusions that investigators should: (para 14.108) Question and challenge (para 14.78) and that unquestioning acceptance of information undesirable in a social worker and unacceptable in a police officer... Police should bring to the arena • Healthy scepticism • An open mind • An investigative approach. (c) Justice delayed.

(Continued)

Table 3.1 *(Continued)*

2004. Lord Hutton Inquiry into the death of Dr David Kelly (leading government adviser before Iraq War).	Demonstrated practical use by Thames Valley Police of Critical Incident Management lessons learnt from Stephen Lawrence Inquiry..
2004. Lord Butler Inquiry into Espionage and Iraq war.	*Concerned Intelligence – Covert Human Intelligence Sources, Analysis, Assessment. Type III.* *Unusual example as not police but useful because wider context in governance of the intelligence led and knowledge based policing concepts considered.*
2004. Judge Peter de Cory NI/Irish 6 Inquiries. Announced completion of his reviews in 2004, proposed and accepted by two Governments, date of reporting of public inquiries unknown.	A wide range of challenges to six investigations in Ireland.
2004. Inquiry in to series of murders perpetrated by Dr Harold Shipman.	Changes proposed in 2006 to Coroners Inquests, and important category of public inquiry.
2004. Bichard Inquiry into Soham murders (*).	Data rich environment. Intelligence flow failures.
2004. Morris Inquiry (An Garda Siochana in Ireland).	Implications for some cases in Northern Ireland. Informants, includes summaries of Canadian and UK experiences plays a role in the creation of Ombudsman in Dublin.
2005. Sir W. Morris (Metropolitan Police Service)	(a) Examination of internal investigations and discipline inquiries, internal culture of police service (b) Psychology, social sciences, mediation, management, leadership.
2006. Lord Saville. Bloody Sunday Inquiry into military tactics and firearm use in Northern Ireland.	Long term review, largest ever public inquiry into alleged criminal activity and homicides during public demonstrations. Demonstrates changes in weighing of evidence, security and policing thinking and government policy over 30 year period,
2006. Deepcut Army Base investigations and inquests and demands for public inquiry into a number of cases of alleged suicide by young soldiers.	Use by external review of behavioural science challenges to mindset, stereotyping, sensitivity to victims families.
2006. Keith Inquiry. Murder of Zaid Mubarack in Prison	(a) Institutional racism in prisons. Early apologies offered by Director General of Prison Service, evidence of some learning from previous inquiries.

[8] (*) indicates case included in interview schedule at ICJS.
[9] Cox, Shirley and Short (1977).
[10] As footnote 11 above and Honeycombe (1974).
[11] As footnote 11 above.

or conversations than the wider public drove research into encoding, storage and retrieval of information. There is ample evidence that witness recall, their evidential statements and suspect's interviews are enhanced by the application of psychological research into memory and questioning. As a result, probably the most far-reaching practical outcomes for investigators have been the developments in interviews of all kinds. Work in Merseyside (Shepherd, 1993) and London (Williamson, 1993; Bull *et al.*, 1983) culminated in national programmes supported by the Association of Chief Police Offices (ACPO) and the Police Staff College and the birth in 1992 of the PEACE investigative interview model which had a far-ranging influence on police behaviour and continues to do so.

PEACE is a structured interview process; the acronym standing for planning and preparation of the interview, engaging with the interviewee and explaining the process, obtaining the account of what had occurred, closure and evaluation. In all, the reinstatement of the context of the original event is vital to recall. This process and the related GEMAC[7] model, from which PEACE evolved, are based on psychological experimental and case study material (Shepherd and Milne, 1999; 137) (Griffiths and Milne, 2005). The recovery of information and data is to the benefit of the investigator without any added risks of deception or errors. Potts (2005) has suggested that among many potential next stages is to use it in debriefings of covert sources, as just another type of interview.

A second strand of change came from examination and challenges to interviews where the evidence obtained both from witnesses and suspects was questioned. From 1982 onwards, Gudjonsson, Gunn, Pearse, McKeith and others explored the issues raised by Hayward and Irving (see Gudjonsson, 2003 for detailed accounts) about vulnerability to the effects of confinement and the custody environment, however innocently applied or accessed, and a resulting susceptibility to agreement with interviewers. By the late 1980s and early 1990s, a plethora of police investigator practitioners were writing Masters Degree theses on behavioural issues, the internal psychological process and contributing to the debates. Gudjonsson (2003), meanwhile, developed measures of suggestibility for compliance and acquiescence for both clinical and operational contexts. These were useful for both investigators and defence alike. Gudjonsson's tests were eventually accepted by the Court of Appeal (see, e.g. R v. Silcott, Braithwaite, Raghhip, Times Law Report 9.12.1991) and were another important driver for change.

Another milestone was the joint work of John Pearse, a serving detective, and Gudjonsson (2003) in examining in an operational investigative setting persons at risk because of specific psychological vulnerabilities. This was published as research for the Royal Commission on Criminal Justice in 1993 (Gudjonsson *et al.*, 1993). The research examined the role of serving police officers in an observational study of custody suites, decision making and vulnerability of persons in custody for ongoing offences. A substantial step also was taken for policing and investigation, in the wider recognition of the value of behavioural science in this arena. The role of appropriate adults had dated right back to Fisher (1977) and was examined afresh and in detail by Pearse and Gudjonsson (1996) and seeking means of avoiding of false confessions (Pearse *et al.*, 1997). This writer, having studied Gudjonsson's defence work, had, with Pearse, first called Gudjonnsson and McKeith to consider a robbery suspect in 1983 and on a wet Sunday night in 1987 asked Gudjonsson to examine a suspect

---

[7] GEMAC is a mnemonic for greeting, explanation, mutual activity (monitor, assert) close. This is a conversation management model and can be used for systematic probing of resistant interviewees (Fisher and Gieselman (1992); Milne and Bull 1999; Shepherd and Milne(1999)).

who was confessing to murder. Someone else was eventually charged with the offence. This led to my subsequent sponsorship of Pearse's at-risk and appropriate adult project.

Finally, the whole body of research gave rise to a training programme for tiers of investigators of increasing and varied skills at dealing with complex interviews. At the time of writing, there were five tiers in use. This is an advanced example of investigative tools being made available for the craftsman's toolbox by the psychologists as well as providing product for, as an example, the courts of appeal. Training of specialist interviewers in tiers 3 and 5, for example, needs an in-depth understanding of complex and subtle psychological theory (Milne, 2006, personal communication).

IDENTIFICATION EVIDENCE

The prior discussion of interviewing is directly relevant to the next topic to be considered: identification. If the PEACE model had considerable impact on investigative interviewing then the case of *R* v. *Turnbull* (1976) (63 Cr App R 132) had a similar impact on identification evidence where psychologists led the way to the use of the ADVOKATE model in cases of identification. This model identifies points to be considered that may render identification evidence unreliable and needs to be included in witness technology, together with any discrepancy or anomaly. It includes the amount of time the witness had for observation, the distance from object or person, visibility to viewer, any obstructions, whether previously known to the witness – and how and when the subject had been seen before – any particular reasons to remember him or her, the time elapsed before identification or any next event, or recall and any errors or material discrepancy (Shepherd and Milne, 1999, p 138). Some of the earliest miscarriages of justice involved identification evidence that though sincerely produced were shown to be false. The psychological contribution is different here in that the important piece of law, the warning required to be given to a jury, indeed the grounds for judicial or prosecutor exclusion outlined in *R* v. *Turnbull*, 1976 predates the psychologically detailed support for the rules. Lord Devlin provided a powerful endorsement of the Shepherd *et al.* (1982) text, *Identification Evidence – A Psychological Evaluation*. Nevertheless, the Royal Commission (1981) picked up on the 'possibility of unreliability of testimony of some eyewitness' (McKenzie and Dunk, 1999, p 179) and Codes of Conduct were included in Police and Criminal Evidence Act 1986 (see Code D). McKenzie – who had been one of the first serving police officers to study psychology and to return to his profession – and Dunk (1999) conclude that the contribution that psychology can make is to explore the inherent limitations of human cognition. This is a familiar role for psychology but, like Irving (1980), they also consider the role of the investigator in extracting the information from eyewitnesses, another example of the investigative tools, or process being made available as well as evidential products.

When considering a possible investigative model that includes the behavioural sciences, Miranda Fricker (2002) argues that certain kinds of testimony are afforded more weight and power within systems than others. Who the witness is can have more importance than the evidence they actually give. She cites feminist theory and evidence of women in some jurisdictions in sexual assault cases. She calls this epistemic imbalance in that some people's knowledge is more powerful than others. This still applies, not just with expert witnesses, but also with testimony from categories of witnesses with a particular history. For example, witness 'Bromley' in the Damilola Taylor case (MPS, 2004) or the testing of eyewitnesses in the *R.* v. *Turnbull* rules (1976) in such cases as Stephen Lawrence's racist murder (1999) are relevant. The failure of the private prosecution, in the Stephen Lawrence case, was in part about such testing of eyewitnesses. The work of psychologists in strengthening the tests for the rules about eyewitness testimony, as both product and process, was, and still is, fundamental.

BIAS AND PREJUDICE

The Stephen Lawrence case (1999) leads us to other immediate developments in policing behaviour, responses and training. Questions about police prejudging and stereotypical bias had been raised by Lord Scarman (1981), Bull *et al.* (1983) and Ainsworth and Pease (1987) in the 1980s. The most publicized finding of the public inquiry was one that found institutional racism in the police. The response was an anti-racist move by the police: to start planning, to be thoughtful, knowledgeable and to deal with people sensitively according to their needs. In other words, it was the opposite of unwitting, ignorant, thoughtless and stereotypical behaviour. This can also be seen to be about power, defined by John Keane (Professor of Politics at Westminster) as 'who gets what, when and how and whether they ought to have done ...' (Keane, 1999). Mr and Mrs Lawrence clearly did not get the justice they ought to have got.

Sir William MacPherson reported to Parliament through the Home Secretary in February 1999. The Stephen Lawrence Inquiry (para 6.34) described institutional racism as:

> ... the collective failure of an organisation to provide an appropriate and professional service to people because of their colour, culture or ethnic origin. It can be seen or detected in processes, attitudes and behaviour which amount to discrimination through unwitting prejudice, ignorance, thoughtlessness and racist stereotyping which disadvantages minority ethnic people.

The police service prepared the move from the aspiration not to be racist to a practical programme of policies and operations to ensure that the actions of individual officers at all levels was consciously and actively free from any form of racism. This was called anti-racist policing or 'practical cop things to do' (Prakeh *et al.*, 2001). Leaders at immediate, tactical and operational investigative level were identified. Two of the most important roles, as change agents and leaders, were family liaison officers and intelligence officers. One-quarter of the 70 recommendations (i.e. 18) in the Stephen Lawrence Inquiry refer to families and their relationships with communities so it will be no surprise to discover that a primary tool for the crafting of behavioural solutions to critical incidents, as these continuing events came to be known in the service, was the family liaison structure.

There had always been a task in the major incident room for family liaison. What was needed was a specialist discipline like exhibit officers. The family liaison officers were trained using a variation on a programme designed originally in Avon and Somerset Police. This was modified using experiences based on the hospice learning programme, specifically that of St Christopher's founder Dame Cecily Saunders. Within three years, 700 family liaison specialist police investigators had been trained (Grieve and French, 2000). The family liaison officers themselves were praised for their roles by both British victims' families and by the Prime Minister following their deployment after the attacks on New York on 11 September 2001.

It is a tribute to Mr and Mrs Lawrence and the findings of the inquiry board that so many people have benefited from their efforts, after the failure to respond to the family's and community's concerns about the way the investigation was not progressing. In particular, their expressed concerns that the lack of success in dealing with the suspects effectively who were identified early was a major driver to improving investigative skills and resources (Foster, Newburn and Souhami, 2005). The findings of the public inquiry were endorsed by all political parties and every newspaper and media grouping in the land. Of the 70 recommendations, 51 directly related to the police and had considerable impact on policing philosophy and practice. The immediate context of government and public response was also conditioned by a number of other high profile cases involving police investigations into the deaths of BME victims around this time. They included the murder of Michael Menson and Victoria Climbie, the deaths of Errol and Jason McGowan, some police firearms incidents, the death of Ricky Reel, missing person cases and other highly informed challenges to policing responses and decisions. These cases also played a part in the scale of condemnation and the determination, not least by police themselves to reform.

The current context of policing is increasingly complex. Since the Stephen Lawrence Inquiry, diversity agendas and the policing environment, including discipline issues, have changed, but not always in continuous or complementary directions. There was considerable impact from the behavioural evidence given by scientists and others to the inquiry about the nature of prejudice and stereotyping of black youths, in fact also of all youth, leading to the alienation of parts of communities. However, as was pointed out, there was a distinctly different reality to being black and young on the streets. The evidence to Part 2 of the Stephen Lawrence Inquiry has been specifically used in community and race relations training, family liaison training and critical incident training. A number of reference points about the practical outcomes for investigators of sensitivity to minority witnesses or perceived suspects and victims can be identified and can be seen to resonnate back to Fisher in 1977 and the evidence Irving (1980) gave to the Royal Commission in 1981. These included, not least, the possibility of better evidence and a greater chance of convicting the guilty.

In chronological order there are other drivers for change in the context to the Stephen Lawrence Inquiry. The national context included the Association of Chief Police Officers (ACPO) National Police Whistleblowers Conference (1999), Her Majesty's Inspectorate of Constabulary (HMIC) Reports about diversity and hate crimes (1999), and Operation Lancet Review about police discipline cases in Cleveland (2002). The Virdi Inquiry into a police internal investigation (2001) is also relevant, including some of the learning that has emerged from Part 2 of that inquiry about discipline and prejudice experienced by black officers (July, 2004). The Morris Inquiry (2004) delved similar matters not just from the criticism of the investigation into the conduct of a BME Superintendent, but also about the wider experiences of black police officers (that enquiry also considered some other cases not least that of Sergeant Virdi), the ACPO Diversity Strategy. Recent relevant reports are the Independent Police Complaints Commission (IPCC) and Commission for Racial Equality (CRE) reports into Diversity issues following the BBC TV documentary 'The Secret Policeman' which recorded blatant racist abuse and promises of violence (Calvert-Smith, 2005; IPCC, 2005). All these touch on policing diversity, bias and prejudice. There are differences, contradictions and ambiguities in the proposals behavioural scientists have for tackling diversity. In particular about how learning from the behavioural sciences might take place (see, e.g. Pertile (2005a); Fahey, 2005) and is what Waddington (2005a, p 17) describes as remedying 'ignorance and thoughtlessness' where mutual misapprehension can avoid becoming hostility. However, the Stephen Lawrence Inquiry taught us to be aware of stereotyping and the police service itself has accepted that the alibi of 'unwitting' is no longer possible or acceptable.

What cannot be defended is a failure to apply the learning available to maintain adequate investigative standards. This includes 'unusual' investigations, characterized as a failure in:

> extended intellectual engagement at a senior level about any of the behavioural sciences and in particular about learning to counter multiple discrimination involving for example feminism, anti sexism, anti racism, anti exploitation. (Parsons, 2005, p 16)

It is a travesty for senior officers, in dealing with diversity to 'reduce one's contribution to a skeletal tabularisation of figures, measures and numerical indicators' (Parsons, 2005, p 16).

This is a complex context for twenty-first century investigators, and involves experiences and reports from a range of disciplines, contexts and countries. For example, from the Police Ombudsman for Northern Ireland and the Independent Police Complaints Commission for England and Wales come other concerns about mindsets. A number of broader concerns also emerged as a result of evidence heard by the inquiries I have listed, for example, about women's roles in the service, particularly BME women, and the potential multiple aggregate discrimination they may experience (see, e.g. Cashmore, 2004; Gittens, 2004; Puwar, 2004). There are also the continuing legal developments about behaviour where prejudice can be genuinely experienced despite there being unintentional bias. The ruling on Lord Hoffman in the Pinochet case gives guidance that good, well-meaning investigators can still leave others with the experience of bias.

These matters can achieve a very high profile and can sink an investigation. A media strategy has been devised that takes into account challenges from those who are specialists in the behavioural sciences. This is of huge importance to an investigator. I adopt the specific Recommendation 8 of Virdi Inquiry Report (December 2001) in the light of the media recommendations from Morris (2004).

> A press strategy should be adopted that:
>
> - explains how to deal effectively with race-specific and high profile cases, using the learning from critical incident training cases;
> - includes the principles contained in the National Union of Journalists Guidelines on Race Reporting;
> - does not compromise the principles of natural justice.
>
> (MPA, 2001, p 80).

This is a further example of a practical investigative outcome to the sensitivity found to have been lacking by the Stephen Lawrence Inquiry.

OFFENDER PROFILING, BEHAVIOURAL INVESTIGATIVE ADVICE, IMPACT ASSESSMENT AND ANALYSIS

Hayward (1980), Bull (1983) and Irving (1977, in Fisher, 1977) and Philips (1980) described the psychology of personality, decision making and attribution. These have combined to produce a number of aids to investigators, not least in providing questions. The answers to these may provide assistance in sorting (possibly long) lists of suspects into priority. In

1985, Professor David Canter became involved with New Scotland Yard, and subsequently Surrey and Hampshire Constabulary, over the use of psychology in policing in general and in aspects of multivariate analysis and profiling in particular (Canter, 1994) (Times, 2006). This has had a continuing series of impacts on investigations. Canter's original contribution came not directly from personality theory, but more from environmental psychology in analysing behaviour at the Bradford City football stand and Kings Cross fires. This led to some scientific rigour in UK applications of FBI Behavioural Science Unit work on psychological, later offender profiling, now called investigative psychology (Canter and Alison, 2000). More recently, this has been described as Behavioural Investigative Advice (Richards, 2005a, 2005b). The author acted as a reference for the researcher in a review conducted during the early 1990s (Copson, 1995), which concluded that offender profiling of unknown offenders was only of direct assistance to investigators in 16% of cases. However, the techniques and questions they generated were seen to be of some indirect or with other factors of cumulative value.

One of the outcomes of the Stephen Lawrence Inquiry (1999) was an increased attention to the impact and behaviour of communities reacting to police behaviours not least to what was identified as institutional racism. This was identified in the behaviour of the police where they had unwittingly, ignorantly, thoughtlessly used stereotypes in their dealings with communities, specifically those that were BME. This had been previously identified by Bull *et al*. (1983) and Ainsworth (1987). As part of a menu of solutions, a number of behavioural scientists (some of whom had been involved in profiling as postgraduate students) were introduced into the heart of the intelligence based solution. The ICAS cell (Intelligence cell analysis system) in the Racial and Violent Crime Task Force was given the leading role in responding to the Inquiry's recommendations and coming up with innovative solutions. The knowledge thus generated by the psychologists and other behavioural scientists during the Understanding and Responding to Hate Crime Project (URHC) formed the basis of strategies in respect of, not just race hate crime, but also gender and sexual orientation hatred, domestic violence and serious sexual assaults (Travis, 2001). The impact on communities continues over a wide range of policing behaviours, not least counter-terrorist strategies. The problem arises of how to turn this learning into practical investigative activity.

The Race Equality Scheme (amended) (Greater Manchester Police, 2002/2005) describes a practical tool for the toolbox: a negative impact assessment precision instrument for diversity. This process and the concepts are as relevant to investigations of any kind as to discipline investigations; this is not just for individual BME officers inside the service but is for outside groups as well.

Part 4 of the scheme reads as follows:

> ASSESS ANY LIKELY IMPACT.
> This stage lies at the heart of the impact assessment process. Your starting point will be any disparities or potential disparities you have identified during the above process. You now have to make a judgement as to whether these amount to adverse impact. This involves systematically evaluating the proposed policy against all the information and evidence you have assembled and are using as a benchmark, and making a reasonable judgement as to whether the policy is likely to have significant negative consequences for a particular diverse group or groups. Greater Manchester Police Race Equality Scheme (Amended). (Greater Manchester Police, 2002)

This is a helpful way to look at assessment and adverse impact.

CONCLUSIONS

In 1983, in his ground-clearing work removing the rubble and weeds to help introduce the building blocks of behavioural sciences to policing, Ray Bull wrote 'I am aware that some police officers and some individuals in the legal profession are indifferent or hostile towards psychology' (Bull, 1983, p ix). It took another five years for Gisli Gudjonsson to get his psychological account of susceptibility accepted by the courts (Gudjonsson, 2002). Miranda Fricker (2002) argued that certain kinds of testimony are afforded more weight and power within some systems than others. What we have experienced, since Barrie Irving's work in 1977 for the Fisher report on the 1972 fire and murder at 27 Doggett Road, has been a shift in the epistemic balance in the investigative use of behavioural sciences. This has achieved sufficient impact to suggest that policing is moving to a knowledge-led stage, in this and other sciences. This being as a result of an external pressure for change, but also driven by police officers themselves. That is not to say that the indifference and hostility that Ray Bull identified has disappeared completely. As he requested, I have sought here 'to modify a little their views' (Bull, 1983, p ix).

I have argued that Hofstadter (1980) provided a useful framework for involving behavioural sciences in policing generally and knowledge-based intelligence-led investigations specifically. The reason for my raising what may be seen by those who are indifferent or hostile as too academic an analysis is part due to the current confused postmodern democratic mixture – community impact, community/family/individual needs model. Why not just concentrate on the practicalities? Some, like Adlam and Villiers, would argue that there are no absolute ways of doing things, just a need to be clear about what knowledge underpins decisions (Adlam & Villiers, 2002). It depends which discipline you turn to, even within the behavioural sciences. What may have different weight and which Fricker and Hofstadter tests come into play?

This strengthens the arguments about behavioural sciences helping understanding about attribution, motivation and recording whatever the context and rationale for particular decision making. Lack of clarity about what disciplines or aspects of disciplines underpin investigative strategies and tactics, policing philosophy and an over-reliance on the needs of the Criminal Justice System for investigative philosophy lead to both tensions and ambiguity, not least in the postmodern blurring of roles.

I have not developed the philosophy of investigation as a subset of the philosophy of law. I have not even introduced John Rawls. As Lord Scarman said, there is more to policing than servicing the needs of the legal profession. Or rather, he wrote more elegantly '"*Fiat justitia ruat caelum*" ("Let justice be done though the heavens collapse") may be apt for a judge; but it can lead a policeman (sic) into tactics disruptive of the very fabric of society' (Scarman, 1981, para 4.57, p 63).

Laming (2003), Lancet (2002), Morris (2004) and ACPO (2005) are important because as different kinds of challenges to the investigative processes they give guidance and advice about case management and the complex role of behavioural sciences assistance to the investigators and senior officers in any serious investigation.

Critical failure points in the investigation resulting in miscarriages of justice identified as of relevance to the behavioural sciences to policing (Table 3.1) have changed over time. Police actions or inaction, incompetence, malpractice, expert evidence, interpretation, weakness in trial or appeal processes have all played a role in the chronology of challenges and miscarriages of justice. Critical success factors, however, have also been identified by the public inquiries, as have investigations with implications for witness treatment, suspect interviewing, investigations management generally, critical incidents avoidance and management, communities, family liaison and training using immersive learning. The behavioural sciences have played a major role in this evolution. Their utility to investigators is as important as any other science, as any other team member, any other orchestral contributor or any other tool in the investigator's toolbox.

To reiterate, the chronology produced here leads to the four main areas of influence for behavioural sciences: (1) interrogation and investigative interviewing, (2) identification testimony, (3) profiling and behavioural analysis and (4) bias and prejudice in decision making and behaviour. But in dealing with these I have considered aspects of confession, eyewitnesses, testimony, unreliable witnesses, family liaison, community identification, engagement, independent and lay advice and community impact. Behavioural scientists have informed analysis, intelligence-led policing and detection (in contrast, as Rob Reiner (personal communication 2002) so appositely put it – to its opposite stupidity-led policing). I have been informed by psychologists in comparative case analysis, reviewing unsolved murders; and in debriefings, I have been aided in writing decision logs and their rationales by behavioural scientists. Policy reviews have been contributed to by behavioural scientists, not least in exploring the issue of stereotyping and fixed mindsets. Behavioural science has contributed to various kinds of policing communications, in the media, internally as briefing and externally to communities. Leadership in high level 'gold' command groups, strategically managing major racist inquiries and their sub groups was informed by the work of Bowling (1999) on the psychology and criminology of racist violence. This is an example of intelligence-led approaches coming from academics.

Since the very early days until today, stress and policing has been a major research and practical topic (see, e.g. Waddington, 2005b). Other areas of the disciplines, not considered directly here, show us where psychology is currently contributing to investigations. A route map for the future was explored recently at the 8th International Investigative Psychology Conference in London (15–16 December 2005) (covering, for example, homicide prevention, serial killings, ethics, covert investigations, resources, mediation, restorative justice, other CJS issues, defence, role of families, critical incidents, intelligence-led psychology, and the role of psychology that starts and ends with victims, suspects and their relationships with communities).

In the chronology of cases I have considered, policing problems often come first and are easiest for other parts of the Criminal Justice System to hide behind when the police failures are uncovered. In the course of exploring some underlying themes, I have also touched upon the role behavioural scientists have had in uncovering nondisclosure of evidence, failures in due process, administrative compliance and the misleading role of some experts.

Behavioural science does not have the same status as physical sciences; it does not have the supposed certainties of its sisters in biology or chemistry. They do have an active role in sorting suspects into categories and priorities. For example, in the design of an intelligence-led screen, narrowing down or prioritising DNA testing of large groups of suspects.

How then do the behavioural sciences continue to encourage investigators? How do we help investigators to continue to seek more and better knowledge and understanding? How do we help them get more information as opposed to seeking to close down lines of inquiry when they think they have the answers? How do we deal with communication failures not least failure to communicate with future academics in the emerging areas of behavioural sciences? In short how do we teach an attitude of open minds to investigators and analysts? How do we introduce other perspectives? One way is through knowledge of the behavioural sciences and their intelligent use.

Therefore, I conclude that Lord Laming's (2004, para 14.38) analysis of the police investigators task is the correct one. What is needed is an investigative approach, a healthy sceptical outlook and an open mind. These are not easy to achieve. They can be informed by an intelligence-led model and are easiest when minds are opened by both the material and disciplines of behavioural scientists assisting investigative teams. This is a compartment in the box which contains some of the tools needed for constructing the evidential jigsaw puzzle. With this approach a counterfactual account of the investigation and the review conducted by Fisher into the murder of Maxwell Confait, aided by Irving an innovative behavioural scientist, would have looked very different.

ACKNOWLEDGEMENTS

The author acknowledges with thanks the contributions made to his thinking and writing by his two research partners in Miscarriages of Justice at ICJS University of Portsmouth – Sam Poyser and Professor Steve Savage and also Dr Tom Williamson, Dr Becky Milne and David Carson.

REFERENCES

ACPO (2005) *Hate Crime: Delivering a Quality Service*, Centrex. Available at http://www.acpo.police.uk/asp/policies/Data/Hate%20Crime.pdf.

ACPO (2005) Practice Advice on Core Investigative Doctrine. National Centre for Policing Excellence for ACPO, Centrex. Available at http://www.acpo.police.uk/asp/policies/Data/Core%20Investigative%20Doctrine.pdf.

Adlam, R. (1981) The police personality, in *Modern Policing* (eds D.W. Pope and N.L. Weiner) Croom Helm, London.

Adlam, R. (1985) Psychological characteristics of police officers, in *Contemporary Policing*, (ed J.R. Thackrah), Sphere, London.

Adlam, R. and Villiers, P. (2002). *Police Leadership in the Twenty-First Century*, Waterside Press, Winchester.

Ainsworth, P.B. and Pease, K. (1987) *Psychology in Action. Police Work*, BPS, London.

Bull, R., Bustin, B., Evans, P. and Gahagan, D. (1983) *Psychology for Police Officers*, Wiley, Chichester.

Bland, N., Mundy, G., Russell, J. and Tuffin, R. (1999) Career Progression of Ethnic Minority Police Officers. Policing and Reducing Crime. London Home Office. Police Research Series. Paper 107.

Bowling, B. (1998) *Violent Racism*, Clarendon Press, Oxford.

Bowling, B. and Foster, J. (2002) Policing and the police, in *The Oxford Handbook of Criminology*, 3rd edn (eds M. Maguire, R. Morgan and R. Reiner), Oxford University Press, Oxford.

Bull, R. and Milne, B. (2004) Attempts to improve the Police Interviewing of Suspects, in *Interrogations, Confessions, and Entrapment* (ed D.D. Lassiter), Kluwer Academic, New York.

Byford, Sir L. (1982) *Report into the Case of Peter Sutcliffe*, Home Office, London.

Calvert-Smith (2005) *The Police Service in England and Wales. Final Report of a Formal Investigation by the Commission for Racial Equality*, CRE, London.

Canter, D. (1994) *Criminal Shadows*, Harper Collins, London.

Canter, D. (2003) *Mapping Murder*, Virgin, London.

Canter, D. and Alison, L. (1999) *Interviewing and Deception*, Ashgate, Aldershot.

Canter, D. and Alison, L. (2000) *Profiling Property Crimes*, Ashgate, Aldershot.
Cashmore, E. (2004) *Ethnic Minority Police Officers. A Final Report Prepared for the Black Police Association*. Staffordshire University.
Cox, B., Shirley, J. and Short, M. (1977) *The Fall of Scotland Yard*, Penguin, Harmondsworth.
Crandon, L. (1997) *Intelligence Driven*. Police Review.12.12.1997.
Douce, R. (2005) *Melting the ice will take time*. Police Review 06.05.05, p. 15.
Ede, R. and Shepherd, E. (2000) *Active Defence*, 2nd edn., Law Society, London.
Fahey, P. (2005) *Celebrating Diversity*. Police Review 13.5.05, pp 38–9.
Fisher, R. and Geiselman, R. (1992) *Memory Enhancing Techniques for Investigative Interviewing: The Cognitive Interview*, Charles Thomas, Springfield (IL).
Fisher, S.Z. (2003) Convictions of innocent persons in Massachusetts: an overview, *Public Interest Law Journal*, **12**, 1.
Foster, J., Newburn, T. and Souhami, A. (2005) *Assessing the Impact of the Stephen Lawrence Inquiry*, Home Office, London. (Research Study 294).
Fricker, M. (2002) Power knowledge and injustice, in *New British Philosophy. The Interviews* (eds J. Baggini and J. Stangroom), Routledge, London.
Geberth, V. J. (1996) *Practical Homicide Investigation: Tactics, Procedures, and Forensic Techniques*, CRC Press, New York.
GMP (2002/2005) *Greater Manchester Police* Race Equality Scheme (Amended), GM Police Authority, Manchester.
Grieve, J. (1998). Intelligence as education for all, in *Drugs: Partnerships for Policy, Prevention and Education* (eds L. O'Connor, D. O'Connor and R. Best), Cassell, London.
Grieve, J. and French, J. (2000) Does institutional racism exist in the police? in *Institutional Racism and the Police* (ed D. Green) (Institute for the Study of Civil Society), Cromwell Press, Trowbridge.
Grieve, J. (2003) The mask of police command, in *Police Leadership in the Twenty-First Century* (eds R. Adlam and P. Villiers), Waterside Press, Winchester.
Grieve J. (2003) From medical contagion to police corruption, in *Police Corruption – Paradigms, Models and Concepts. International Comparisons* (eds S. Einstein and M. Amir), Houston University, Huntsville (TX).
Grieve, J. (2004) Developments in criminal intelligence, in *Strategic Thinking in Criminal Intelligence* (ed J. Ratcliffe), Federation Press, Sydney.
Grieve, J. (2004) The investigation of hate crimes: Art science or philosophy? in *Hate Crimes* (ed N. Hall) Portsmouth University. Institute of Criminal Justice Studies.
Griffiths, A. and Milne, B. (2005) Will it all end in tiers? Police interviews with suspects in Britain, in *Investigative Interviewing. Rights, Research, Regulation* (ed T. Williamson) Willan, Cullompton (Devon).
Gross, H. (1934) Criminal investigation, in *Criminal Investigation: A Practical Textbook for Magistrates, Police Officers, and Lawyers Adapted from the System der Kriminalistik of Hans Gross*, Sweet & Maxwell, London.
Gudjonsson, G.H. (2003) *The Psychology of Interrogations and Confessions. A Handbook*, Wiley, Chichester.
Hall, N. (2005) *Hate Crime*, Willan, Cullompton (Devon).
Harrison, J. and Cuneen, M. (2000) *An Independent Police Complaints Commission*, Liberty, London.
Hayward, L.R.C. (1981) *Forensic Psychology*, Batsford, Bristol.
Heaton-Armstrong, A., Shepherd, E. and Wolchover, D. (1999) *Analysing Witness Testimony. A Guide for Legal Practitioners and Other Professionals*, Blackstone Press, London.
HMIC (1997) *Policing With Intelligence, Criminal Intelligence – A Thematic Inspection of Good Practice*, Home Office, London.
HMIC (1997) Her Majesty's Inspectorate of Constabulary. *Policing With Intelligence, Criminal Intelligence – A Thematic Inspection of Good Practice*, Home Office, London.
Hofstadter, D.F. (1980) *Godel, Escher, Bach. An Eternal Golden Braid*, Penquin, London.
Home Office (2002). *Operation Lancet. A Case Study Review Report*, Home Office, London.
Honeycombe, G. (1974) *Adam's Tale*, Hutchison, London.
Independent Police Complaints Commision (2005) *Secret Policeman*, (Press release), March 2005.

Innes, M. (2003) *Investigating Murder*, Oxford: University Press.
Irving, B. and Hilgendorf, L. (1980) *Police Interrogation. The Psychological Approach. (Research Study No. 1.) Royal Commission on Criminal Procedure*, HMSO, London.
Irving, B. (1980) *Police Interrogation. A Case Study of Current Practice. Royal Commission on Criminal Procedure*, HMSO, London.
Irving, B. and Dunnigham, C. (1993) *Human Factors in the Quality Control of CID Investigations. Research Study no 21. Royal Commission on Criminal Justice*, HMSO, London.
Keane, J. (1999) *Vaclav Havel. A Political Tragedy in Six Acts*, Bloomsbury, London.
Kennedy, L. (1961) *10 Rillington Place*, Victor Gollancz, London.
Kennedy, L. (2002) *36 Murders and Two Immoral Earnings*, Profile Books, London.
KPMG for Home Office (2000) *Feasibility of an Independent System for Investigating Complaints against the Police*.
Laming (2003) *The Victoria Climbie Inquiry*. Lord Laming. Cmnd.5730. TSO.
Lassiter, G.D. *Interrogations, Confessions, and Entrapment*, Kluwer Academic, New York.
Lloyd-Bostock, S. (1981) *Psychology in Legal Contexts. Applications and Limitations*, Socio-Legal Studies, Oxford.
Maguire, M., Morgan, R. and Reiner, R. (2002) *The Oxford Handbook of Criminology*, 3rd edn., Oxford.
May, Sir J. (1994) *Report of the inquiry into the circumstances surrounding the convictions arising out of the bomb attacks in Guildford and Woolwich in 1974*. Sir John May. HMSO, UK. 30.06.94.
Metropolitan Police Authority (2001a) *The Virdi Inquiry Report*. Chairman R. David Muir. *The Damilola Taylor Murder Investigation Review*.
Metropolitan Police Authority (2002a) *Informant Working Group Report. Informing the Community: Developing Informant Risk Assessment to Reflect Community Concerns*. MPS.
Metropolitan Police Authority (2002b) *The Investigation of Racist, Domestic Violence and Homophobic Incidents. A Guide to Minimum Standards*. MPS.
Metropolitan Police Authority (2001b) *Athena Spectrum. A menu of Tactical Options for combating hate crime*. MPS.
Metropolitan Police Authority (2002c) *Guide to the Management and Prevention of Critical Incidents*. MPS.
Metropolitan Police Service (2002) *Guide to the Management and Prevention of Critical Incidents*.
Morris, P. (1980) *Police Interrogation. A Review of the Literature. Research Study No. 3. Royal Commission on Criminal Procedure*. HMSO, London.
Morris, P. (2004) *The Case for Change. The Report of the Morris Inquiry*. An independent inquiry into professional standards and employment matters in the Metropolitan Police. Metropolitan Police Authority. December 2004.
National Centre for Policing Excellence (2005) see ACPO 2005.
NCIS (2000) *The National Intelligence Model*, NCIS, London.
NCIS (2002) *Annual Report. A Year in the Fight Against Serious and Organised Crime*, NCIS, London.
Neyroud, P. and Beckley, A. (2001) *Policing, Ethics and Human Rights*, Willan.
Parsons, T. (2005) *Race and diversity*. Police Review 03.06.05. (p16).
Patten, C. (1999) *A New Beginning: Report of the Independent Commission on Policing for Northern Ireland (the Patten Report)*.
Pertile, E. (2005a) Support officers who make honest mistakes about race. *Police Review* 03.06.05. (p4).
Pertile, E. (2005b) Operation Sculpture. Interview with DCI Simon Humphreys. *Police Review* 19.08.05. (p24).
Police Ombudsman for Northern Ireland (2002) (1). *First Annual Report*.
Police Ombudsman for Northern Ireland (2003) *A study of complaints involving the use of batons by the police in Nortrhern Ireland*. March 2003.
Police Ombusman for Northern I reland (2002) (2) Research Report 1/2002 Baton Rounds Report. A summary of seven reports by PON1.
Potts, J. (2005) *The use of enhanced cognitive interview techniques to debrief police informants and agents*. Paper presented to 8th Investigative Psychology Conference London, 2005.

Prakeh et al. (2001)

Puwar, N. (2004) *Summary of Pilot Research Project on the Barriers facing BME Female Police Personnel.* NBA 2005.

Richards, L. (2003) *Risk Assessment a model for Domestic Violence.* Metropolitan Police and Home Office.

Richards, L. (2005a) *An assessment of the processes involved in compiling a behavioural profile of an unknown offender.* Paper presented to 8th Investigative Psychology Conference, London 2005.

Richards, L. (2005b) *Assessing the nature of domestic violence, rape and its relationship to safety and danger.* Paper presented to 8th Investigative Psychology Conference, London 2005.

Royal Commission on Criminal Procedure (1981) Sir Cyril Philips. HMSO, UK.

Royal Commission on Criminal Justice (1993).

Rowe, W. and Garland, J. (2003) Have you been diversified yet? Developments in police – community race relations training in England and Wales. *Policing and Society*, **13**, 399–412.

Scarman (1981) *The Brixton Disorders 10–12 April 1981.* Report of an Inquiry by the Rt Hon. The Lord Scarman. OBE. HMSO. Cmnd 8427.

Scruton, R. (2002) in Adlam and Villiers (2002). *A Kantian Approach to Policing.*

Sentamu, B. J. (2002) *After Stephen Lawrence.* Toynbee Journal. No 3.

Shepherd, E. (1993) Resistance in Police Interviews; the contribution of police perceptions and behaviour, in *Aspects of Police Interviewing: Issues in Criminological and Legal Psychology, No 18* (ed. E. Shepherd), Leicester, UK, pp 5–12.

Shepherd, E. and Milne, R. (1999) *Full and Faithful: ensuring quality practice and integrity in outcome in witness interviews*, in (eds Heaton-Armstrong et al.).

Sims, J. (1993) "What is intelligence?", in *What is Intelligence? Working Group on Intelligence Reform. Consortium for the Study of Intelligence* (eds A. Shulsky and J. Sims), Georgetown University, Washington.

Stockdale, J. and Gresham, P. (1995) *Presentation of Police Evidence in Court.* Home Office PRG. Paper 15.

Thackrah, J.R. (1985) *Contemporary Policing*, Sphere, London.

Townley, L. and Ede, R. (2004). *Forensic Practice in Criminal Cases*, Law Society, London.

Travis, A. (2001) *Partners in Crime. Policemen (sic) and Academics. The Edge.* Journal of Economic and Social Research Council and Policy Forum for Executive Action. Issue 8.

TSO (1999) *Stephen Lawrence Inquiry* TSO (2003) V*ictoria Climbie Inquiry.* Command 4262.

TSO (2003) *The Victoria Climbie Inquiry.* Command 5730.

Turnbull (1976) (R- v- Turnbull 63 Cr App R 132).

Waddington, P.A.J. (2005a) Understanding the theatre of diversity. *Police Review.* 29.04.05. (pp. 16–17).

Waddington, P.A.J. (2005b) Firearms officers owed duty of care. *Police Review*, 26.08.05. (pp. 12–13).

Williamson, T. (1993) Review and prospect, in *Aspects of Police Interviewing (Issues in Criminological and Legal Psychology, No 18*, (ed. E. Shepherd), Leicester, UK, pp. 5–12.

Watts, Pope, D. and Weiner, N.L. (1981) *Modern Policing*, Croom Helm, London.

Williamson, T. (2005) *Investigative Interviewing. Rights, Research, Regulation*, Willan, Cullompton.

Wright, A. (2002) *Policing. An Introduction to Concepts and Practice*, Willan, Cullompton.

CHAPTER 4

Investigative Interviewing: The Role of Research

Becky Milne[1]
University of Portsmouth
Gary Shaw
Northumbria Police, NCPE Operations
and
Ray Bull
University of Leicester

INTRODUCTION

Interviewing is at the heart of any police investigation and thus is the root of achieving justice in society. This is because there are two key aims underpinning any investigation and these are to (1) find out what happened, and if anything did happen (2) to discover who did what (Milne and Bull, 2006). In order to answer these two primary investigative questions investigators need to gather information and invariably the source of the information is a person (e.g. witness, victim, suspect, complainant, first officer at the scene of a crime, emergency services, experts, etc.). Thus, one of the most important tools in an investigator's tool box is the interview (Milne and Bull, 2006). As a result, since the mid-1980s, practitioners and researchers have sought, and in some countries have substantially succeeded, in developing procedures that improve the quality of interviews of witnesses, victims and suspects of crime. These new procedures have been the outcome of the interplay between academic research and practical policing.

Police interviewing in the UK has seen great advances since the 1980s. Undoubtedly, the most influential piece of legislation which forced the police service to examine its interviewing practices was the Police and Criminal Evidence Act 1984. This groundbreaking piece of legislation dictated that all interviews with those suspected of crime be recorded and thus for the first time allowed the mystery that was the police interview to

---

[1] Contact address: Institute of Criminal Justice Studies, Ravelin House, Ravelin Park, Museum Road, Portsmouth, PO1 2UP, United Kingdom. E-mail: becky.milne@port.ac.uk

come into the limelight and be examined in all its glory by senior police officers, academics and courts alike.

This chapter aims to outline these developments regarding investigative interviewing and the role research has had within them.

The Police and Criminal Evidence Act (PACE)

The introduction of the Police and Criminal Evidence Act in 1984, together with a Code of Practice in relation to the interviewing of suspects (Code C, D and F),[2] was a milestone in driving through changes in England and Wales that have led to the professionalising of the investigative interviewing process. Prior to this, how custodial questioning was conducted and the accuracy of what was recorded had become a matter of great public concern and these concerns were reflected in the recommendations of the Royal Commission on Criminal Procedure (1980), which led to the new legislation. Prior to 1984, the interviewing by police officers was considered to be an inherent skill that all officers possessed and which could be developed merely by learning from more experienced colleagues. The yardstick of a good interviewer was whether they obtained a confession or damaging admission from the suspect (e.g. Plimmer, 1997). Also, there was no formal system for developing their interviewing skills.

The rules governing the admissibility of evidence obtained through custodial questioning prior to PACE had been laid down by the Judges in 1912 and were supplemented by guidance from the Home Office. Although suspects could have access to a lawyer who could be present during an interview, there was no formalized system. Hence, in practice some suspects would not have the necessary advice before or during the interview. The interview process was not tape-recorded and a summary of the interview was prepared later by the interviewing officer(s) relying on their recollection of sometimes quite lengthy and complex interviews. This would be recorded in the officers' note-books and presented to the court in evidence as direct speech. To provide an accurate account in this way was, however, a feat beyond the ability of human memory. It may be possible to provide the gist of the conversation (Campos and Alonso Quecoty, in press), but the system was open to abuse with suggestions that suspects had been 'verballed' and confessions had been fabricated and embellished. Interviewers found that they could not refute such suggestions in court and many responded to this problem by recording the questions and answers contemporaneously in long hand and getting the suspect to read and sign the record. As a result of this archaic process, challenges regarding what was actually said during the interview and whether it had been said freely were a regular occurrence. Interviewers were often accused of being untruthful, unfair, overbearing, misleading, mistaken or misrepresenting the entire picture. Irrespective of whether such allegations were true or not, the procedure was always open to challenge as it was not a transparent process. With the advent of PACE and the regulating of police practices within the interview room, including the actual tape-recording of the interviewing process, the working practices became much more transparent. For the first time police interviews were open to public scrutiny on a grand scale.

It is little wonder that due to the uncoordinated approach that existed prior to PACE, including a lack of training, a very rude awakening for the police occurred. In 1991, the

---

[2] See Code C, D and F at appendix XXX.

Home Office (i.e. the relevant Government ministry) sponsored research that assessed tape-recorded interviews with suspects. Perhaps not surprisingly due to the lack of structure, investment and the haphazard approach to interview training, the findings revealed severe shortcomings in the skills demonstrated by the police during interviews with suspects (Baldwin, 1992). The main weaknesses identified were a lack of preparation, a general ineptitude, poor technique, an assumption of guilt, undue repetitiveness, a persistent or laboured questioning, a failure to establish relevant facts, and an exertion of too much psychological pressure. There was no reason to think that the interviewing of victims and witnesses was of a consistently high standard either, with the interviewers' ultimate goal being the compilation of a detailed written statement rather than allowing the person to provide their best account and best evidence in an uninterrupted and free flowing manner (McLean, 1995).

As a direct result of Baldwin's work and pressures that emanated from the widely politicized miscarriage of justice cases (e.g. 'the Guildford 4' and 'the Birmingham 6'), where the interviews with suspects were central to the appeal case and the subsequent quashing of the conviction, a national review of investigative interviewing was instituted (see Gudjonsson, 2003; Milne and Bull, 1999, 2003; see Savage and Milne, 2007 for more on miscarriages of justice cases). This in turn led, in 1992, to the formulation and promulgation through the Home Office of the seven Principles of Investigative Interviewing (the most recent production being in the current Practical Guide to Investigative Interviewing: Centrex, 2004):

1. The role of investigative interviewing is to obtain accurate and reliable information from suspects, witnesses or victims in order to discover the truth about matters under police investigation.
2. Investigative interviewing should be approached with an open mind. Information obtained from the person who is being interviewed should always be tested against what the interviewing officer already knows or what can reasonably be established.
3. When questioning anyone, a police officer must act fairly in the circumstances of each individual case.
4. The police interviewer is not bound to accept the first answer given. Questioning is not unfair merely because it is persistent.
5. Even when the right of silence is exercised by a suspect, the police still have a right to put questions.
6. When conducting an interview, police officers are free to ask questions in order to establish the truth; except for interviews with child victims of sexual or violent abuse, which are to be used in criminal proceedings, they are not constrained by the rules applied to lawyers in court.
7. Vulnerable people, whether victims, witnesses, or suspects, must be treated with particular consideration at all times.

Having established these principles, a project team devised a training programme so that officers would be provided with the skills necessary to conduct effective and ethical interviews with victims, witnesses and suspects, with integrity and in accordance with the law (Ord and Shaw, 1999). The PEACE interviewing model was born, where PEACE is a mnemonic outlining the structure to be applied to all types of interviews; *Planning* and *Preparation* of the interview, *Engage* the interviewee and *Explaining* the ground rules of the interview process, obtaining an *Account*, clarifying and challenging the interviewee (if necessary), and appropriate *Closure* of the interview. Finally, the interview process is to be *Evaluated*, where the key question is to ask what was achieved during the interview and how this fits into the whole investigation. Evaluation also includes the development of an interviewer's skill level, through assessment (self, peer and manager) (Centrex, 2004). In 1993, during the initial stages of the development of the PEACE model, a training programme was designed that outlined the core skills and techniques thought to be required for appropriate investigative interviewing and a week-long course was established consisting of intensive practical inputs and exercises.

Alongside the development of PEACE, but independent of it, the Government in England and Wales published in 1992 the *Memorandum of Good Practice for Video Recorded Interviews with Child Witnesses for Criminal Proceedings* (Home Office and Department of Health, 1992). This substantial document was produced to assist those police officers and social workers whose interviews with child witnesses/victims would now be (as a result of the *Criminal Justice Act 1991*) routinely video recorded. This *Memorandum* was drafted by a lawyer and the third author of this present chapter (a psychologist) and its guidance on interviewing was firmly based on psychological research (Bull, 1992, 1996). Its 2002 update (now called *Achieving Best Evidence in Criminal Proceedings: Guidance for Vulnerable and Intimidated Witnesses, Including Children*) also relied heavily on relevant psychological research and included a new section regarding witnesses who are especially vulnerable. The 'phased approach' recommended in these two official publications has striking similarities with the components of PEACE (see also Yuille, 1984).

What has occurred since the early 1990s is an amazing testament to the commitment of the British Police Service to improving its interviewing standards across the board. In 1993, a large-scale operation began in England and Wales to train all officers (i.e. over 120 000 personnel) in the PEACE framework of interviewing. In addition, the initial working party, when examining what PEACE training should consist of, looked at what academia had to offer. Indeed, two models of interviewing emerged as best practice: (1) conversation management (CM; Shepherd, 1993), which was deemed useful for interviewing the more to resistant interviewee; and (2) the cognitive interview (CI) (Fisher and Geiselman, 1992), which was more useful for interviewing the more co-operative interviewee, an interviewee who is willing to speak (however truthful). Both models were developed by psychologists (see Milne and Bull, 1999). Hence, not only did research help identify the skills gap in the first place, but it helped to create a solution to the problem of how to improve interviewing performance. The PEACE course was divided into two stages covering the two models (see above) that underpin the PEACE framework. We will now briefly describe each model. (For a fuller description, see Milne and Bull, 1999).

COGNITIVE INTERVIEW

Traditionally it has been found (e.g. McLean, 1992; Fisher, Geiselman and Raymond 1987) that while officers began interviews by asking victims and witnesses (and some suspects) for their version of events, this was usually soon interrupted by the interviewers asking too many questions. Officers probably felt that they should control the interview and achieved this by doing most of the talking. Due to this interviewing style, interviewees were not encouraged to search their memory in order to give their complete version of events. Use

Table 4.1 The phases of ECI

Phase 1:	Greet and personalize the interviewee and establish rapport
Phase 2:	Explain the aims of the interview
	≈ Focused retrieval and concentrate hard
	≈ Report everything
	≈ Transfer control
Phase 3:	Initiate a free report
	≈ Context reinstatement
Phase 4:	Questioning
	≈ Report everything
	≈ Interviewee-compatible questioning
	≈ OK to say 'don't know'
	≈ Activate and probe an image
	≈ Open and appropriate closed questions
Phase 5:	Varied and extensive retrieval
	≈ Change the temporal order
	≈ Change perspectives
	≈ Focus on all senses
Phase 6:	Investigatively important questions
Phase 7	Summary
Phase 8	Closure
Phase 9	Evaluation

(Taken from Milne and Bull (1999) and Milne (2004)).

of such 'closed' interviewer-driven techniques tends to reduce the amount of information obtained and thus the subsequent evidence is likely to be an impoverished version of what the interviewee could provide. The subsequent evidence is also likely to be shaped by the account presented in the written statement which, in effect, is the officer's version of what transpired, written in police terminology (see Wolchover and Heaton-Armstrong, 1997; Milne and Shaw, 1999; Rock, 2001; Milne and Bull, 2006 for problems with the statement taking process). However, there is a truism to the axiom 'less is more' with regard witness/victim interviewing where the fewer questions asked and the less the interviewer has to say, the better the interview (Davies, Westcott and Horan, 2000; Lamb *et al.*, 2003; in press).

The cognitive interview (CI) and enhanced cognitive interview (ECI) (later version see Milne and Bull, 1999) in contrast, are interviewee led and aim to maximize the recall by the interviewee. The CI/ECI was developed by two American psychologists (Fisher and Geiselman, 1992) and it lends itself ideally to the cooperative victim or witness but can also be used for the cooperative suspect. The concept behind this approach is that it allows the interviewee to remember in their own way and at their own pace and it utilizes unbiased memory enhancing tools or mnemonics in an attempt to retrieve the maximum quality and quantity of information from an interviewee. The mnemonics being directly developed from what psychologists know about how human memory works. The ECI is composed of a number of phases as outlined in Table 4.1.

The phases of the ECI will now be briefly described (see Fisher and Geiselman, 1992; Milne and Bull, 1999, in prep. for more detailed accounts).

Personalizing the interview and establishing rapport is a core skill that is essential in setting the tone for the forthcoming interview. Not only can the experience of the incident in question be quite stressful or traumatic for a victim or witness, but the interview process itself and the simple fact of dealing with the police can also cause concern for many. Unfortunately, people's perceptions of what typically happens in police interviews are rather negative and thus expectations may be low and include stereotypical views of stark, bare rooms and light bulbs swinging (Milne and Scott, 2005). The interviewee may also have concerns about court appearances, being intimidated not to give evidence, or any countless number of personal issues. Psychological research has repeatedly found that stress/anxiety/worry reduces what people can recall. It is therefore essential that the effects of such issues be reduced at the beginning of the interview, thereby allowing the interviewee to concentrate on the task in hand which is to remember in as much detail as possible. Furthermore, free recall is a difficult task and so interviewees need to be motivated to work hard at it.

Brief Narrative: on speaking to an interviewee for the first time an interviewer may need to obtain a brief version of events first. For example, it may be that the person has already been concentrating on remembering a particular item (e.g. a vehicle registration number, a physical description, or an overheard conversation) and is keen to tell the interviewer whilst it is fresh in their memory. It may affect the interview process if they are not allowed to say what they want to say at the earliest opportunity. In the event of the interviewee immediately going into a more in-depth account of what happened, it is advisable to allow them to continue rather than interrupting the flow.

Aims of the interview: the interviewer should first explain the approach, that is to be adopted. That is what is to be expected of the interviewee and interviewer, their roles.

The interviewee should be told that detail is important, not to edit anything out as every little piece of information may be important, even details they think may not be important or can only remember partially. This is known as the 'report everything' instruction (one of the original CI mnemonics, Fisher and Geiselman, 1992). The transfer of control CI instruction is used to inform the interviewee that they will have an active role in the interview process; that they will be doing most of the talking and that the interviewer's role is to help them if they have difficulty remembering something. The cognitive interviewer is a memory facilitator, with the interviewee being in control of the information flowing from the interview (Milne, 2004).

Initiating a free recall or narrative account can be aided through using context reinstatement (one of the original CI mnemonics). Research has shown (Eich, Macauley and Ryan, 1994) that context can have a powerful effect on memory and thus trying to recreate the context, both environmental context (e.g. location) and emotional context (e.g. personal feelings) that existed at the time of the event may well assist memory. The use of sketch plans and asking the interviewee to describe what they are drawing also help context reinstatement and the recall process (Milne, 2004; Dando, Wilcock and Milne, in press).

People remember in different ways and not in a strict chronological sequence (see Milne and Bull, 1999 for more on memory). Interviewers, therefore, should allow the interviewee to recall the event in their own order without the distraction of interruptions or any questions. It is vital that during this stage the interviewer actively listens to exactly what is being said, taking brief notes where appropriate, to assist in identifying areas that may need to be probed further, later in the interview, if insufficient detail has been obtained. (Taking copious notes can be as disruptive as asking streams of questions.) The free recall or narrative account also allows an insight into the interviewee's mental representation of the event and the order in which they have stored the information, which should help the interviewer to plan for the questioning stage of the interview (i.e. interviewee compatible questioning, Milne, 2004).

Questioning: after obtaining the free recall of the event, the interviewer should then start questioning the interviewee to obtain more detailed information. This is achieved by selecting a topic or theme, in the *order* the interviewee seems to have stored the information (i.e. witness compatible questioning). The interviewee is then asked to mentally reinstate the context (again) surrounding (this time) the particular topic or theme (i.e. molecular context or mini context) and this is then extensively probed with primarily open-ended questions (Tell, Describe, Explain) and a few probing questions (e.g. 'Wh' questions) to obtain detail not elicited by open-ended questions. This continues with each topic area being covered in turn. It has been demonstrated by research (e.g. see Powell and Snow, in press) that in order to obtain detailed information of good quality the majority of questions that should be asked of co-operative interviewees should be open-ended questions. Indeed, it is believed that the interviewers' ability to maintain the use of open-ended questions is the best predictor of a good investigative interview and the most defining characteristic of an expert interviewer (Poole and Lamb, 1998). 'Forced-choice' questions (especially 'yes'/'no' questions) and leading questions should not be used unless absolutely necessary. (See Milne and Bull, 1999 for more on question types.)

Varied and extensive retrieval: the use of the senses in context reinstatement can also be used to facilitate retrieval of information stored in memory. For example, asking the interviewee to concentrate on what they heard, felt, touched or even smelt at the time of the original event can prompt further recollection of significant (potentially evidential) points. The interviewer can attempt as many recalls as they feel is appropriate in the individual circumstances and use a variety of retrieval strategies. (In certain serious cases these recall attempts may take place over several days as the tiredness of the interviewee and interviewer needs to be taken into account.) The CI techniques of 'change the temporal order of recall' and 'change of perspective' could also be used at this stage if the interviewer feels they are appropriate. The former of these involves the interviewee being asked to either go through the event backwards or from the most memorable aspect of the event and go backwards and forwards in time. This technique is to be used when the interviewee is trying to access details that are unusual, atypical. The latter, change perspective, technique asks interviewees to report the event from a perspective that they have not yet used. This technique is sometimes mis-applied (see Fisher and Geiselman, 1992; Milne and Bull, 1999 for more on these mnemonics).

Investigatively important questions: relevant areas/topics (i.e. to the investigation) that have not yet been mentioned by the interviewee can now be introduced here in an appropriate manner. It may be that, in certain circumstances, mildly leading questions may need to be used (e.g. Did you see a van?) when all other possibilities such as more neutral prompts (e.g. Did you see any vehicles?) had been exhausted. However, such questions if they prompt an answer from the interviewee, need to be immediately developed/extended through using open-ended questions.

Summary: having completed the recall and probing stages, a verbal review of what the interviewee has said is provided by the interviewer. This allows the interviewer to check that they have understood the interviewee who is encouraged to correct the interviewer if necessary. This should be completed in the interviewee's own words wherever possible. This process may also act as a further memory prompt for the interviewee. It may also be useful, depending on the length of the interview and manner in which it is conducted (i.e.

nonchallenging), to conduct periodic summaries during the interview process (if the event is a complex one and/or the interviewer is becoming confused: Milne, 2004).

Closure: the interview should be appropriately closed by thanking the interviewee and asking if there is anything further they wish to add, and if they have any questions. The functional life of the interview should also be extended (e.g. giving them a business card with contact details) in case the interviewee remembers anything at a later date.

It is advocated that best practice is for interviews to be recorded digitally (audio or video) so that (1) full attention can by paid to the interviewee and interview process (instead of writing notes or a formal report) and (2) a record of the questions put to the interviewee is made to ensure integrity to the interviewing process (see Milne and Bull, 2006; Milne and Shaw, 1999 for more on benefits of video-recording witness/victim interviews). Nevertheless, once the interview has been completed, sometimes the information that has been obtained may then have to be transferred into a written format. It is best practice to use a verbatim transcription of the interview as psychological research and theory has made it clear that obtaining an objective and accurate written record of an interview is otherwise almost impossible. This is because such summaries are based on interviewers' interpretations of the interview and will be biased by their pre-existing views of the case, prior knowledge of similar cases, and so on (Milne and Bull, 2006).

CONVERSATION MANAGEMENT

For a variety of reasons certain interviewees may not be suitable for the CI (e.g. those who are not forthcoming within the interview, those who have not directly experienced an event), interviewers should then use the Conversation Management (CM) style of interview. One of the primary differences between CI and CM is the amount of control the interviewer has over the interview. In a CI the interview control is explicitly handed over to the interviewee (transfer control instruction) whereas in a CM style of interview the control is the hands of the interviewer, who manages the conversation. CM can be neatly divided into three stages; (1) the suspect account, (2) the police agenda and (3) the challenge stage.

Suspect account: it is important to afford the suspect an opportunity to establish their position and it is vital to listen to what the suspect has to say, in response to the allegation, that is being put to them. During this, the interviewer should be noting down key areas that they may wish to explore further during the interview. Having obtained an account, if one has been offered, will assist the interviewer to break down what has been said into topics to enable further questions to be put, in a structured way. The interviewer should then verbally review the suspect's account in order to check comprehension and understanding. Appropriate questions then should be used in order to expand what is being said. After questioning on a particular area the interviewer can then again summarize that topic before moving onto the next one. This process of probing, summarizing then linking to the next topic should be repeated until the interviewer feels that they have fully explored the account. At this point, if a second interviewer is present they should be given the opportunity to ask any questions they feel may have been missed. If it is a lengthy or protracted interview, the second interviewer may be invited to contribute earlier in the proceedings. However, throughout this stage it is important that the interviewer(s) do not interrupt or introduce new areas to the interviewee. Even though the interviewer may have a completely different account of what has happened (e.g. from that gleaned from other aspects of the investigation), they should not challenge what is being said at this stage.

The police agenda: prior to the actual interview commencing, the interviewer(s) should have produced a plan which would have included the topics that they think would be relevant to discuss during the interview, such as facts they know, points to prove the offence, facts they need to establish, and also where appropriate, possible lines of defence. Thus, within the interview, after the suspect's account, there may still be areas that have not been discussed which need questions and answers. The same process conducted earlier (of identifying topics on which to question, probe, summarize, then move onto the next topic area) applies to the police agenda section too.

The challenge stage: when moving onto the identifying of topics that need challenging, the same structure as conducted in the earlier two phases still applies. If, after having heard the initial account and the answers to the probing questions, the interviewer is in possession of contradictory facts or information then the interviewee should be challenged as to the differences that exist. This phase should not be conducted in an aggressive way but should be viewed more as a presentation of information that the interviewer has in their possession. The object of this section is to afford the interviewee an opportunity to comment on the information presented which challenges their account.

It is essential to follow the three stages in the order given, and it does not always follow that they will all be concluded in a single interview.

If an interviewee is resistant or decides to remain silent during the interview then the pre-planned topics (see police agenda section earlier) still need to be covered and put to the interviewee. The suspect may well then decide to answer certain questions. Also, if the suspect is subsequently charged with an offence and decides to give an account in court, under certain circumstances, courts in England and Wales may decide to draw an adverse inference from their failure to have mentioned these facts within their prior interview. In the interview this process of putting topics and evidence (e.g. CCTV footage) to the interviewee for them to comment on if they so wish continues until all the topics have been covered. If at any time in the interview the interviewee decides to give a comprehensive account then the skilful interviewer can revert to a cognitive interview style of approach to gain as much information from them as possible.

The above accounts (e.g. of CI and CM) indicate that psychological research has helped to develop appropriate interviewing techniques for both the interviewing of co-operative and resistant interviewees.

PEACE TRAINING

PEACE training started to be rolled out to forces in England and Wales in 1993 as a week-long course for interviewers. In order to support the implementation within the workplace, a supervisor's package was also produced, as workplace supervision is key to ensuring continued high standards (Stockdale, 1993; Clarke and Milne, 2001). Time went on and the focus of PEACE training turned, in 1997, to being primarily implemented at the recruit level. (Some forces did maintain the week-long course for all in an attempt to train some experienced officers that were still left to train). In addition, some forces did realize that a more advanced level of training was required for officers interviewing in more complex and more serious cases and thus 'advanced' interview courses, which incorporated the psychology of communication and memory retrieval, were developed (see Griffiths and Milne, 2005; Bull and Milne, 2004) and training was created for interview co-ordination in serious cases (see Tier 5 later). Nevertheless, this was not a standard across the country and increasingly in-house evaluations and supervisors started to question the impact basic PEACE training was having in the workplace. This led to a National evaluation of PEACE, funded by the Home Office (Clarke and Milne, 2001). This large-scale study revealed what was already being mooted in that skills being trained on the week-long PEACE course were not being fully integrated into practice. With regard the interviews of those suspected of crime, there was some transference of skills with officers, compared to the post-PACE pre-PEACE days, being seen as more confident and being able to communicate more effectively within the interview room. However, the interviewers took a rather rigid approach and lacked flexibility.

A study of officers' use of tactics when interviewing suspects was undertaken by Soukara *et al.* (in prep.). They found that the tactics used in most interviews included open-ended questions, repetitive questioning, disclosure of evidence and leading questions. Tactics that were used in at least half the interviews included positive confrontation, challenging the suspect's account, and emphasizing contradictions. The tactics used in less than half of the interviews included concern, silences, gentle prods, suggest scenario, handling the suspect's mood, and interrupting. The tactics that were never or almost never used included minimization, maximization, situational futility and intimidation, which is in accordance with the ethos of PEACE. In addition, this sits well with the outcome of research that has demonstrated that use of such inappropriate tactics (i.e. minimization, maximization, situational futility and intimidation) are likely to result in false confessions (see Memon, Vrij and Bull, 1998; Gudjonsson, 2003).

The Clarke and Milne (2001) research project also examined officers' ability to interview witnesses to and victims of crime. Officers from across the country were asked to tape-record their interviews over a period of time. The sample included all offence types. What was revealed was a disturbing state of affairs with interviews being mainly police led, dominated by poor questioning, and the interview being mainly focused on the statement-taking process as opposed to trying to gain as much information from the interviewee about what had happened. Indeed, Clarke and Milne concluded that the standard of interviews of witnesses and victims of crime was far worse than the interviews of those suspected of crime. The Clarke and Milne report concluded with a number of recommendations to improve interviewing standards, which have subsequently been taken up by the Association of Chief Police Officers (ACPO) and developed further into the ACPO Investigative Interviewing Strategy, a national initiative. As a result, a five-tiered approach to investigative interviewing, that aims to provide a developmental approach to interview training across a police officer's career dependent on their ability, was born. This strategy is underpinned by assessment and competency levels within a National Occupational Standards framework (which include a set of statements concerning what constitutes a competent interviewer).

ACPO NATIONAL INVESTIGATIVE INTERVIEWING STRATEGY

The principles of investigative interviewing and the PEACE framework continue to be the basis for the interviewing of victims, witnesses and suspects in England and Wales. Training is now to be provided to cater for five needs identified during the Clarke and Milne (2001) research study. Tier 1 is for probationers/police recruits. Tier 2 is for uniform investigators and all detectives. Tier 3 is for specialist interviewers (i.e. child protection, homicide). Tier 4 is for investigative interview managers, and Tier 5 is for specialist interview management and co-ordination. This tiered structure (and accompanying guidance) aims to assist forces in their training and delivery of interview skills in an attempt to increase professionalism and provide an ethical foundation for all investigations. This structured and developmental approach to training officers' interviewing skills across their career is underpinned by assessment and competency levels, as only when officers reach a certain level of ability can they move onto a more advanced tier. The five tiers are an attempt to develop the right skills at the appropriate levels, together with an ability to manage interviews, supervise interviewers and provide feedback on interview performance.

Each of the five Tiers will now be briefly described.

TIER 1 – Initial Training/Recruit Training

Tier 1 training serves as an introduction to investigative interviewing. Whilst it is principally aimed at new recruits, it can also serve as refresher training for those officers who have been away from the field and who have not conducted an interview for a while. This level of training could also be for civilian investigators and members of the wider police family (e.g. special constables and community support officers). The foundation training is aimed at all personnel and aims to enable them to prepare, plan, conduct and record interviews which relate to volume crime (e.g. theft, criminal damage, public order offences), that is those offences that relate to general operational policing. The interviews concern those of victims, witnesses or suspects where there appear to be no unique or complicating features. What is trained at this level is the basic psychology of communication, interpersonal skills and the use of good questioning (i.e. open-ended questions) (see Hargie and Dickson, 2004).

TIER 2 – Uniform Investigators and Detectives

Tier 2 is aimed at officers routinely engaged in interviewing victims, witnesses or suspects. It builds on the foundation blocks of tier 1, and deals with some more complicated and technical areas surrounding interviewing (e.g. interacting with defence lawyers and developing interview strategies). The training is aimed at ensuring that interviewers are able to prepare, plan, conduct and record interviews which relate to volume crime where there is a unique or complicating feature and for those more serious crimes which do not of themselves require specialist (tier 3) training (e.g. robbery, aggravated burglary and deception). The training should also include an introduction to conducting visually recorded interviews with vulnerable, intimidated or significant victims and witnesses (and suspects) where there is no evidence of trauma or serious communication difficulty. The training is aimed at officers who have completed their probation (and who have achieved competence at this level), and are either newly appointed detectives, or police staff whose role involves them in interviewing interviewees involved in more complex cases. What is trained at this level is a development on the psychology of communication taught at tier 1, but also included are more complex retrieval strategies/mnemonics developed from cognitive psychology and specifically memory theory and research (Fisher and Geiselman, 1992).

TIER 3 – Specialist Interviewer

This tier is aimed at officers who have achieved competence at Tier 2 and who are from child protection units, family liaison officers, homicide/major investigation teams, accident investigation, fraud, serious sexual offences units, and so on. Thus, the training at this level is aimed to ensure that interviewers are able to prepare, plan, conduct and record interviews of suspects, and victims/witnesses in specialist/organized crime cases, and those cases where there is a traumatized victim/witness. Specialist is defined by the serious nature of the type of crime and characteristics of the suspect. The training is aimed at detective and specialist interviewers whose role involves serious or complex categories of crime or other incidents (e.g. murder/manslaughter, corporate manslaughter, child sexual abuse, serious sexual assault, terrorism, fatal road traffic accidents). Officers who conduct national Achieving Best Evidence (ABE) interviews (see above) primarily should be tier 3 trained. This training should take note of what is found in a study of skills gaps in specialist interviewer performance. Bull and Cherryman (1996) found that of 28 skills mentioned by experienced police interviewers and the relevant literature as being important, some were not even evident in the better interviews (e.g. flexibility, empathy/compassion and avoidance of use of closed questions). Some skills were, however, evident even in the poorer interviews (e.g. few (1) interruptions; and (2) long/complex questions; little (3) overtalking; and (4) undue pressure), suggesting that such skills might be easier to train. The skills that were found to discriminate significantly between (1) the better and (2) the poorer specialist interviews relate to PEACE and included open-mindedness, use of open-ended questions, communication, use of pauses/silences and responding to what the interviewee says.

Training at this level incorporates a number of areas of psychology including: the psychology of communication; the Enhanced Cognitive Interview (see above); resistance management (Shepherd, 1993); and the interviewing of vulnerable groups, including children. This latter area, therefore, heavily relies on research and theory within psychology that concerns how best to interview those more vulnerable in society (see Milne, 1999; Bull, 1995a,b; Wilson and Powell, 2001).

TIER 4 – Management and Development of Investigative Interviewers

Tier 4 has been created to provide a robust and professional approach to managing investigative interviewing. It aims to train managers and those whose role provides an overview of interviewing to identify good practice and areas of weakness. In turn, good practice should be then promulgated, and development needs addressed. As mentioned above, supervision has been found to be pivotal in maintaining interviewing standards within any organization (see also Walsh and Milne, 2007). This tier relates to the management, supervision, monitoring and the evaluation of interviews (witness, victims and suspect) at tiers 1, 2 and 3, to ensure that service standards are maintained and appropriate actions taken if not. The training is aimed at anyone who may help in the role of assessment, and this is not just determined by rank of appraiser, but should be based on the knowledge level of interviewing the assessor has. Indeed, research has shown that who (e.g. academic, trainer, or manager) actually assesses the interview can determine the outcome of the assessment more than the actual interviewer skill level (Cherryman, Bull and Vrij, 1998a,b).

TIER 5 – Specialist Interview Management and Co-ordination (Expert Consultant)

Tier 5 is aimed at those providing management for specialist interviews. This management and supervision for specialist interviews differs from the supervision at tier 4 because it also provides an expert consultancy role to the organization on matters relating to interview policy strategy. Tier 5 officers also can act as interview advisers to Senior Investigating Officers on difficult matters relating to individual cases. Thus, this tier encompasses three primary areas: (1) being a tactical interview adviser to act as a consultant to Senior Investigating Officers in charge of the most serious investigations, (2) co-ordinating interviews in complex cases across all interview specialisms and (3) developing interview strategies and tactics in particular cases or operations. The tier 5 training is aimed at experienced practitioners at tier three who have demonstrated the necessary qualities to work to the highest standard of interviewing. It is deemed necessary that individuals working at this level should hold a vast body of knowledge concerning the psychology of interviewing, so that they can develop strategies based on sound theoretical principals based on published academic work. Often psychologists (e.g. the first and third authors of this chapter) themselves act as interview advisors working directly with the police developing interview strategies, giving advice to interviewers and sometimes even participating at the interview itself.

For each Tier, there exists National Occupational Standards (NOS) that detail the skills levels that are to be covered and the performance criteria that are to be measured, including knowledge and evidence requirements that are needed to demonstrate interviewer competence at the relevant tier. A key element in ensuring that the NOS are met in the workplace is the assessment of interviewing officers. These NOS have already been agreed and endorsed by the police service. They were developed by the Sector Skills Council for the Justice Sector on behalf of the Police Service and detail the areas in which an officer is to achieve competence.

Tiers 1–3 concentrate on three distinct areas; (1) planning and preparing the interview, (2) conducting the interview and (3) evaluating the interview. Tier 4 details how to make the best use of teams and their members in order to achieve set objectives. The skills levels here focus on (1) planning the work of teams and individuals, (2) assessing the product and (3) the provision of feedback at the conclusion. Tier 5 is about the advising and coordination of all interviews within complex and major investigations. Here the competencies centre on (1) the provision of strategic advice, (2) coordination and monitoring of the interview and (3) the evaluation processes.

A national strategic steering group headed by a high ranking Senior Officer has responsibility for oversight of the programme across the UK, and academics and practitioners from across the criminal justice system (not only police personnel) sit on the National Steering Committee. The committee has responsibility to ensure that a consistent and professional approach is adopted by the service, which is able to withstand judicial and academic scrutiny, and has the ability to instill public confidence. What is interesting is the fact that the police now see research and academia as integral to the process of improvement. For example, one of the key roles of the National Academic Interview Advisor (the first author of this chapter), is to provide a link between academic research and national policing implications. Not only does this help with providing a link for researchers to gain access to the material they need, but it also allows the police service access to relevant research findings. They can then act on the implications of the research at a national level. Sometimes, the research has such a direct impact that it helps change national policy and subsequent practice.

It therefore follows that psychology and practical policing go hand-in-hand, with academics being involved in research that aims to identify areas in need of improvement within the interviewing arena. Psychological research also helps to develop interviewing strategies that intend to help interviewees (be they witnesses, victims or suspects; be they adult, child or a person with a specific vulnerability) gain full and faithful accounts. In addition, psychologists often train police officers at the more advanced levels of the five-tiered approach (i.e. 3 and 5) and psychologists also provide advice at the coal face within the interview and investigation itself. However, this joined-up way of thinking will only work if organizations are willing to work together. It is a testament to the professionalism of the British Police Service that it has now embraced psychological research and academia and has let so-called 'outsiders' assist in its venture of seeking to provide opportunities for best practice with regard investigative interviewing. Indeed, research presentations are always given a voice at the ACPO led National Investigative Interviewing conference held each year. This ideology is now being disseminated within Europe where the first European Investigative Interviewing conference took place in Paris in January 2006, organized by the Gendarmerie, under the auspices of the EU AGIS initiative. Officers and academics from across Europe met to discuss developments in investigative interviewing and strived to reach common terms with regard best practice. This joint approach is being taken to the world-wide level, for example at the second International Conference on Investigative Interviewing, which was held (in Portsmouth) in the UK in the summer of 2006.

REFERENCES

Baldwin, J. (1992) Videotaping of police interviews with suspects – An evaluation. *Police Research Series Paper No 1*, Home Office, London.

Bull, R. (1992) Obtaining information expertly. *Expert Evidence*, 1, 5–12.

Bull, R. (1995a) Interviewing children in legal contexts, in *Handbook of Psychology in Legal Contexts* (eds R. Bull and D. Carson), Wiley, Chichester.

Bull, R. (1995b) Interviewing witnesses with communicative disability, in *Handbook of Psychology in Legal Contexts* (eds R. Bull and D. Carson), Wiley, Chichester.

Bull, R. (1996) Good practice for video-recorded interviews with child witnesses for use in criminal proceedings, in *Psychology, Law and Criminal Justice* (eds G. Davies, S. Lloyd-Bostock, M. McMurran and C. Wilson), de Gruyter, Berlin.

Bull, R. and Cherryman, J. (1996) *Helping to Identify Skills Gaps in Specialist Investigative Interviewing: Enhancement of Professional Skills*, Home Office, London.

Bull, R. and Milne, R. (2004) Attempts to improve the police interviewing of suspects, in *Interrogations, Confessions, and Entrapment* (ed. D. Lassiter), Kluwer Academic, New York.

Campos, L. and Alonso-Quecuty, M. (in press) *Remembering a criminal conversation: Beyond eyewitness testimony. Memory.*

Cherryman, J., Bull, R. and Vrij, A. (1998a) Investigative interviewing: British police officers' evaluations of real life interviews with suspects. Paper presented at the Annual Conference of the European Association of Psychology and Law, Krakow.

Cherryman, J., Bull, R. and Vrij, A. (1998b) British police officers' evaluations of real life interviews with suspects. Poster presented at the 24th International Congress of Applied Psychology, San Francisco.

Clarke, C. and Milne, R. (2001) *National Evaluation of the PEACE Investigative Interviewing Course, Police Research Award Scheme, PRAS/149*, Home Office, London.

Dando, C., Wilcock, R. and Milne, R. (in preparation) The use of sketch plans as an aid to memory recall. Unpublished manuscript.

Davies, G.M., Westcott, H. and Horan, N. (2000) The impact of questioning style of the content of investigative interviews with suspected child sexual abuse victims. *Psychology, Crime, and Law*, **6**, 81–97.

Eich, E., Macauley, D. and Ryan, L. (1994) Mood dependent memory for events of the personal past. *Journal of Experimental Psychology: General*, **123**, 201–15.

Fisher, R. and Geiselman, R. (1992) *Memory-Enhancing Techniques for Investigative Interviewing: The Cognitive Interview*, Thomas, Springfield (IL).

Fisher, R., Geiselman, R. and Raymond, D. (1987) Critical analysis of police interviewing techniques. *Journal of Police Science and Administration*, **15**, 177–85.

Griffiths, A. and Milne, R. (2005) Will it all end in tiers: Police interviews with suspects in Britain, in *Investigative Interviewing: Rights, Research, Regulation* (ed. T. Williamson), Willan, Cullompton.

Gudjonsson, G.H. (2003) *The Psychology of Interrogations and Confessions*, Wiley, Chichester.

Hargie, O. and Dickson, D. (2004) *Skilled Interpersonal Communication: Research, Theory and Practice*, Routledge, London.

Home Office and Department of Health (1992) *Memorandum of Good Practice on Video Recorded Interviews with Child Witnesses for Criminal Proceedings*, HMSO, London.

Lamb, M. E, Sternberg, K.J., Orbach, Y. et al. (2003) Age differences in young children's responses to open-ended invitations in the course of forensic interviews. *Journal of Consulting and Clinical Psychology*, **71**, 926–34.

McLean, M. (1992). Identifying patterns in witness interviews. Unpublished BA (Hons) dissertation, University of Hull.

McLean, M. (1995) Quality investigation? Police interviewing of witnesses. *Medicine, Science and the Law*, **35**, 116–22.

Memon, A., Vrij, A. and Bull, R. (1998) *Psychology and Law: Truthfulness, Accuracy and Credibility*, McGraw Hill, Maidenhead.

Milne, R. (1999). Interviewing children with learning disability, in *Handbook of the Psychology of Interviewing* (eds A. Memon and R. Bull), Wiley, Chichester.

Milne, R. (2004) *The Cognitive Interview: A Step-by-Step Guide*. Unpublished training manual.

Milne, R. and Bull, R. (in preparation) *Investigative Interviewing: Psychology and Practice*, 2nd edn, Wiley, Chichester.

Milne, R. and Bull, R. (2006) Interviewing victims of crime, including children and people with intellectual difficulties, in *Practical Psychology for Forensic Investigations* (eds M.R. Kebbell and G.M. Davies), Wiley, Chichester.

Milne, R. and Bull, R. (2003) Interviewing by the police, in *Handbook of Psychology in Legal Contexts* (eds D. Carson and R. Bull), Wiley, Chichester.

Milne, R. and Bull, R. (1999) *Investigative Interviewing: Psychology and Practice*, Wiley, Chichester.

Milne, R. and Scott, S. (2005) Public perception of police interviewing. Paper presented at the 15th European Conference of Psychology and Law, Vilnius (June).

Milne, R. and Shaw, G. (1999) Obtaining witness statements: Best practice and proposals for innovation. *Medicine, Science and the Law*, **39**, 127–38.

Ord, B. and Shaw, G. (1999) *Investigative Interviewing Explained*, The New Police Bookshop, Surrey.

Plimmer, J. (1997) Confession rate. *Police Review*, **7** February, 16–18.

Poole, D. and Lamb, M. (1998) *Investigative Interviews of Children: A Guide for Helping Professionals*, American Psychological Association, Washington, DC.

Powell, M. and Snow, P.C. (in press) A guide to questioning children during the free-narrative phase of an interview about abuse. *Australian Psychologist*.

Rock, F. (2001) The genesis of a witness statement. *Forensic Linguistics*, **8**, 44–72.

Savage, S. and Milne, R. (in press) Miscarriages of justice – the role of the investigative process, A chapter to appear in *Handbook of Criminal Investigation* (eds T. Newburn, T. Williamson and A. Wright), Willan, Cullompton.

Shepherd, E. (1993) Resistance in interviews: The contribution of police perception and behaviour, in *Aspects of police interviewing. Issues in Criminological and Legal Psychology, No. 18* (ed. E. Shepherd), The British Psychological Society, Leicester.

Soukara, S., Bull, R., Vrij, A. et al. (in preparation) *What really happens in police interviews of suspects? Tactics and confessions*.

Stockdale, J.E. (1993) *Management and Supervision of Police Interviews*. Police Research Group, Paper No. 5, Home Office, London.

Walsh, D. and Milne, R. (2007) Giving PEACE a chance. *Public Administration* **25**, 525–540.

Wilson, C. and Powell, M. (2001) *A Guide to Interviewing Children. Essential Skills for Counsellors, Police, Lawyers and Social Workers*, Allen and Unwin, Crows Nest.

Wolchover, D. and Heaton-Armstrong, A. (1997) Tape-recording witness statements. *New Law Journal*, June 13, 894–96.

Yuille, J. (1984) Research and teaching with police; A Canadian example. *International Review of Applied Psychology*, **33**, 5–24.

CHAPTER 5

Credibility Assessments in a Legal Context

Aldert Vrij[1]
University of Portsmouth

INTRODUCTION

Lie detection is sometimes an easy task. A suspect who assures police officers that he has not spoken to his friend for several weeks, is definitely lying when CCTV footage caught him chatting with this friend just a few hours earlier. Detecting deceit is considerably more difficult when there is no physical or third-party evidence to rely on. In those situations, lie detectors have three options: (1) they can observe someone's behaviour, (2) analyse someone's speech, or (3) measure someone's physiological responses. Several credibility assessment tools designed to analyse speech and physiological responses have been developed, and the most well-known tools, Statement Validity Assessment (a verbal lie detection tool), the Control Question Test (a physiological lie detection test), and the Guilty Knowledge Test (another physiological lie detection test) will be introduced. I will briefly discuss how they work, how accurate they are, and to what extent they meet the criteria that are required for admitting expert scientific evidence in criminal courts according to the United States Supreme Court *Daubert* decision. Other verbal and physiological tools that are sometimes mentioned in the lie detection literature (Scientific Content Analysis technique (SCAN), Reality Monitoring (RM), Voice Stress Analysers (VSA), Relevant-Irrelevant Polygraph Test, and Directed Lie Polygraph Test), will also, albeit briefly, be touched on.

I will also discuss nonverbal lie detection, despite the fact that nonverbal lie detection tools are virtually nonexistent. My main motive for discussing this is that nonverbal communication is a powerful source of information that can easily influence people's judgements, including those of solicitors, judges and jurors.

A main issue in this chapter is how accurate the decisions are that lie detectors make (see Vrij in press for more information on all the lie detection tools mentioned in this chapter). Some comments about accuracy are therefore appropriate before discussing in detail the accuracy of several lie detection tests. I will begin with a definition of deception.

---

[1] Correspondence concerning this article should be addressed to: Aldert Vrij, University of Portsmouth, Psychology Department, King Henry Building, King Henry 1 Street, Portsmouth, PO1 2DY, United Kingdom or via E-mail: aldert.vrij@port.ac.uk.

Applying Psychology to Criminal Justice. Edited by David Carson, Rebecca Milne, Francis Pakes, Karen Shalev and Andrea Shawyer. © 2007 John Wiley & Sons, Ltd

DEFINITION

Deception is 'a successful or unsuccessful deliberate attempt, without forewarning, to create in another a belief which the communicator considers to be untrue' (Vrij, 2000, p. 6). Several features are worth discussing. First, deception is an intentional act. A boy who misremembers the colour of a car and therefore states the wrong colour is not lying, whereas a boy who actually remembers the colour of the car but deliberately states the wrong colour, is. Second, deception is defined solely from the perspective of the deceiver and not from the factuality of the statement. Thus, an untruthful statement is not necessarily a lie (e.g. the boy mentioned above who misremembers the colour of a car is not lying), and, also, an actual truth could be a lie. Suppose that a suspect, who believes that his friend is hiding in his apartment, tells the police that his friend is abroad. This statement is a lie, even when, unknown to the suspect, his friend has actually fled the country. A third aspect of deception is that people are only lying when they do not inform others in advance about their intentions to lie. A suspect who, by means of protest, indicates that he will fabricate his answers, is not lying when he actually starts fabricating.

ACCURACY

When a deception tool is 70 % accurate, what does this actually mean? Very little as long as no distinction is made between truth accuracy and lie accuracy. Truth accuracy is the ability to correctly classify truthful statements as truths, and lie accuracy refers to the ability to correctly classify deceptive statements as lies. As I will demonstrate below, several lie detection tools have biases. Some tools tend to classify a person as guilty (lie-bias), resulting in relatively high accuracy in detecting lies and relatively low accuracy in detecting truths; other tools tend to classify someone as being innocent (truth-bias), resulting in relatively high truth accuracy and relatively low lie accuracy scores. The importance of this difference depends on the context. In situations where only a few lies are told and where the lies that are told are minor, a truth-bias is probably beneficial. In situations where many lies are told or where undetected lies will have serious consequences, a lie-bias may be preferable. Legal systems that strive to protect innocent defendants may be better off with lie detection tools that have a truth-bias.

NONVERBAL LIE DETECTION

A review of 37 lie detection studies (Vrij, 2000) has demonstrated that laypersons are more accurate at detecting truths (67 % accuracy) than at detecting lies (44 % accuracy), which is the result of a truth-bias: Laypersons are more likely to consider that statements are truthful than deceptive. A truth-bias pays off in everyday life, because people tell on a daily basis more truths than lies, whereas the lies they tell are often minor (DePaulo et al., 1996). Lie detection studies further demonstrated that professional lie catchers, such as police officers, are often more suspicious, resulting, compared with laypersons, in a higher accuracy rate for detecting lies (55 %) and a lower accuracy rate for detecting truths (55 %) (Vrij and Mann, 2003). However, these accuracy rates are far from perfect. There are numerous reasons why people, both laypersons and professional lie catchers, have difficulty in distinguishing liars from truth tellers when they observe someone's behaviour. I have discussed these reasons in detail elsewhere (Vrij, 2004), and will only give here some of the more important reasons. First, there is not a single nonverbal cue (akin to Pinocchio's growing nose) uniquely related to deception. (Neither is a there a single verbal or physiological cue uniquely related to deception, see below.) This makes nonverbal lie detection, and lie detection in general, difficult, because there is no cue that the lie detector can rely on. Second, liars' conscious, and sometimes successful, attempts to fool lie detectors hamper nonverbal lie detection (and lie detection in general). Third, both laypersons and professional lie catchers have strong, but often inaccurate, views about how liars behave. For example, both strongly believe that liars look away and fidget (Strömwall, Granhag and Hartwig, 2004; Vrij, Akehurst and Knight, 2006), and these views are also expressed in police manuals (Granhag and Vrij, 2005). Yet, deception research has found no clear relationships between deception and gaze or fidgeting (DePaulo et al., 2003). Fourth, people have the tendency to interpret signs of nervousness too readily as signs of deception.

There is evidence that people can become more accurate at distinguishing between truths and lies by observing someone's behaviour. For example, after being taught to pay attention to more valid cues to deceit (Frank and Feeley, 2003), or after being trained in interview techniques aimed at nonverbal lie detection, like the Strategic Use of Evidence technique (Hartwig et al., 2006; Vrij and Granhag, 2007).

VERBAL LIE DETECTION

Statement Validity Assessment

To my knowledge, Statement Validity Assessment (SVA) is the only verbal lie detection tool used as evidence in criminal courts. The technique was developed in Sweden and Germany and is used as evidence in criminal court in both of those two countries, and also in other European countries, such as Austria, the Netherlands and Switzerland (Köhnken, 2004). SVA was developed to evaluate statements from *children* who are *witnesses* or *alleged victims* in sexual abuse cases, and this is how the method is used in court. Some scholars advocate expanding the use of the technique to evaluate the testimonies of adults who talk about issues other than sexual abuse, but, to my knowledge, SVA assessments are not used as evidence in court in such cases. Elsewhere, I have discussed in detail how this method works, including its accuracy Vrij, (2005, in press). I restrict myself here to presenting a brief overview. The core component of SVA is Criteria-Based Content Analysis (CBCA). CBCA comprises 19 different criteria, each of which CBCA-trained evaluators judge the presence or absence in an interview transcript. The presence of each criterion strengthens the hypothesis that the account is based on genuine personal experience. In other words, truthful statements will have more of the elements measured by CBCA than false statements.

Both cognitive and motivational factors explain why truth tellers will have higher CBCA scores than liars (Köhnken, 1996). It is assumed that the presence of several criteria is likely to indicate a genuine experience as they are typically too difficult to fabricate. Therefore, statements which are coherent and consistent (*logical structure*), whereby the information is not provided in a chronological time sequence (*unstructured production*) and which contain a significant amount of detail (*quantity of detail*) are more likely to be true. The method further distinguishes between different types of detail (see Vrij (2005, in press), for a description). Moreover, possible indicators of truthfulness are if the child reports details which are not part of the allegation but are related to it (*related external associations*, e.g. a witness who describes that the perpetrator talked about various women he had slept with and the differences between them), when the witness describes their feelings or thoughts experienced at the time of the incident (*accounts of subjective mental state*), or describes their interpretation of the perpetrator's feelings, thoughts or motives during the incident (*attribution of perpetrator's mental state*).

Other criteria are more likely to occur in truthful statements for motivational reasons. Truthful persons will not be as concerned with impression management as deceivers. Compared to truth tellers, deceivers will be keener to try to construct a report which they believe will make a credible impression on others, and will leave out information which, in their view, will damage their image of being a sincere person (Köhnken, 1996). As a result, a truthful statement is more likely to contain information that is inconsistent with the stereotypes of truthfulness. The CBCA list includes five of these so-called 'contrary-to-truthfulness-stereotype' criteria (Ruby and Brigham, 1998), including: *spontaneous corrections* (corrections made without prompting from the interviewer), and *admitting lack of memory* (expressing concern that some parts of the statement might be incorrect: 'I think', 'Maybe', 'I am not sure', etc.).

CBCA scores may be affected by factors other than the veracity of the statement. For example, cognitive ability and command of language develop throughout childhood, making it gradually easier to give detailed accounts of what has been witnessed (Davies, 1991). Therefore, all sorts of details are less likely to occur in the statements of young children, and, consequently, CBCA scores of older children are likely to be higher compared with CBCA scores of younger children.

A Validity Checklist has been developed consisting of issues that are thought to be relevant when examining interview transcripts, because they may affect CBCA scores. SVA evaluators consider eleven issues (Steller, 1989; Steller and Boychuk, 1992), including: the mental capability/age of the child; the appropriateness of affect shown by the interviewee; the interviewee's susceptibility to suggestion; the evidence of suggestive, leading or coercive questioning; and the possibility that the witness has been coached in telling their story. In another stage of the SVA procedure, *evaluation of the* CBCA *outcome*, the evaluator systematically addresses each of the external factors mentioned in the Validity Checklist, and explores and considers alternative interpretations of the CBCA outcomes.

To date, Validity Checklist research has concentrated on the impact of three external factors included in the Validity Checklist (age of the interviewee, interviewer's style and coaching of the interviewee) on CBCA scores. Research has convincingly demonstrated that, as predicted, CBCA scores are positively correlated with age Vrij (2005, in press). CBCA scores are also related to the interview style of the interviewer. For example, open-ended questions and facilitators (nonsuggestive words of encouragement) yielded more CBCA criteria than other more direct forms of questioning Vrij (2005, in press). Finally, examinees who were given some guidelines on 'how to tell a convincing story' (in fact, they were taught several CBCA criteria in such experiments) obtained higher CBCA scores than untrained participants Vrij (2005, in press). Given that some external factors influence CBCA scores, do SVA experts take these factors into account when making their final judgements? With the exception of Gumpert and Lindblad's (1999) study with SVA experts in Sweden, no research has addressed this important issue. Gumpert and Lindblad (1999) found that SVA experts sometimes highlighted the influence of external factors on children's statements in general, but then failed to discuss how this factor may have influenced the statement of the particular child they were asked to assess. Moreover, although experts sometimes indicated possible external influence on statements, they tended to rely on the CBCA outcome, and tended to judge high-quality statements as truthful and low-quality statements as fabricated. Gumpert and Lindblad (1999) only examined a limited number of cases, and to draw concrete conclusions is perhaps premature, but their findings are worrying. It implies that SVA decisions are no more likely to be accurate than CBCA assessments, as the final decision based on CBCA outcomes, together with the Validity Checklist procedure, will often be the same as the decision based on CBCA outcomes alone. It also implies that interviewees who will naturally produce low-quality statements and therefore are likely to obtain low CBCA scores (i.e. young children, interviewees with poor verbal skills, etc.) may well be in a disadvantageous position and could be judged as untruthful even when they are telling the truth.

Accuracy of SVA Assessments

Testing the accuracy of SVA assessments and other lie detection tools may sound straightforward, but, in fact, is difficult. Accuracy can easily be determined in controlled laboratory based experiments. In such experiments, participants (typically college students) are asked to tell a truth or lie for the sake of the experiment, and lie detectors attempt to distinguish between these truths and lies by using their lie detection tools. The main limitation of this procedure is the lack of ecological validity. What does the ability of an SVA expert to distinguish between lies and truths told by college students in controlled settings say about his/her ability to accurately determine the veracity of a child's statement in an alleged sexual abuse case? Very little according to many SVA experts, because the situations are very different. The same applies to polygraph tests. Being able to detect lies and truths with a polygraph test in a laboratory experiment may well be completely different from being able to detect lies and truths told by suspects in criminal cases. Psychologists therefore agree that in order to evaluate the accuracy of lie detection tools, field studies need to be carried out in which assessments are examined that were made in real life cases.

The difficulty in field studies is determining the ground truth, that is, to establish the truth/innocence status of the examinee beyond doubt. SVA assessments take place in sexual abuse cases. It is often difficult to determine the facts of a sexual abuse case, since often there is no medical or physical evidence. Frequently the alleged victim and the defendant give contradictory testimonies and often there are no independent witnesses to give an objective version of events. Therefore, in SVA field studies confessions are often used as a criterion. This is problematic, as confessions are not independent from SVA veracity judgements. For example, if the only evidence against the guilty defendant is the incriminating statement of the child, which is often the situation in sexual abuse cases, it is unlikely that the perpetrator will confess to the crime if the incriminating statement is of poor quality. On the other hand, if a false incriminating statement is persuasive and judged to be truthful by a SVA expert, the chances for the innocent defendant obtaining an acquittal decrease dramatically (at least in Germany), and it thus may be beneficial to plead guilty in order to obtain a reduced penalty (Steller and Köhnken, 1989). In summary, poor quality (e.g. unconvincing) statements decrease the likelihood of obtaining a confession and high quality (e.g. convincing) statements increase the likelihood of obtaining a confession, regardless of whether a statement is truthful or fabricated.

The same reasoning applies to polygraph tests, which are typically conducted when the veracity of the suspect's statement cannot be determined in other ways. Suspects who are found guilty in the test may well believe that they cannot demonstrate their innocence anymore, which may result in a false confession. On the other hand, guilty examinees who pass the polygraph test have no reason to confess.

The interdependence between SVA and polygraph outcomes and confessions may result in inflated accuracy figures in field studies. Incorrect assumptions of guilt that subsequently lead to false confessions will be classified as 'hits' according to the 'confession equals guilt' rule. No confessions from guilty examinees who pass the test will also be classified as 'hits' when the 'no confession of the examinee equals innocence' rule is used. However, most studies use a somewhat different rule regarding innocence. An examinee is only classified as innocent if someone else confesses to the crime. This rule still causes trouble. Many cases where the guilty examinee passes the test will remain unsolved, because it is unlikely that an innocent person will confess in this case. Cases without confessions will not be included in the field study because of a lack of ground truth. Consequently, the mistake made by the examiner will remain unnoticed.

A known error rate in CBCA field research therefore does not exist. Accuracy rates of CBCA field studies have been calculated in two CBCA field studies (Esplin, Boychuk and Raskin, 1988; Parker and Brown, 2000) but both studies were flawed. Amongst other obstacles, there were problems with how the ground truth was established Vrij (2005, in press). Error rates regarding the Validity Checklist and the SVA method as a whole only have been reported in the flawed Parker and Brown (2000) study Vrij (2005, in press). Laboratory CBCA research has revealed that, on average, 73 % of the truths and 72 % of the lies were correctly classified, resulting in a known error rate of just below 30 % for both truths and lies Vrij (2005, in press). However, the vast majority of experimental studies used undergraduate students as participants. The few studies with children as participants revealed similar accuracy rates.

SVA Assessments and the Daubert Test

In *Daubert* v. *Merrel Dow Pharmaceuticals*, Inc. (1993), the United States Supreme Court set out guidelines for admitting expert scientific evidence in the federal (American) courts. The following guidelines are provided by the Supreme Court (Honts, 1994): (1) Is the scientific hypothesis testable?, (2) Has the proposition been tested?, (3) Is there a known error rate?, (4) Has the hypothesis and/or technique been subjected to peer review and publication? and (5) Is the theory upon which the hypothesis and/or technique based generally accepted in the appropriate scientific community? Table 5.1 summarizes my answers to these questions for SVA assessments.

The prediction that truthful statements will obtain higher CBCA scores than false statements can be tested in scientific research, although this is not an easy task in field research given the problems with establishing the ground truth. The answer to the first *Daubert* question is therefore 'yes' for CBCA laboratory research but 'problematic' for CBCA in field studies. Some underlying assumptions of the Validity Checklist are also difficult to test

Table 5.1 Answers to the five Daubert questions for CBCA and SVA assessments

	CBCA laboratory	CBCA field	Validity Checklist	SVA
(1) Is the scientific hypothesis testable?	yes	problematic	problematic	problematic
(2) Has the proposition been tested?	yes	no	no	no
(3) Is there a known error rate?	yes, too high	no	no	no
(4) Has the hypothesis and/or technique been subjected to peer review and publication?	yes	yes	no	no
(5) Is the theory on which the hypothesis and/or technique is based generally accepted in the appropriate scientific community?	no	no	no	no

in real life. For example, it is already difficult to determine that a child has been coached, but, in case coaching has been established, how then can the extent to which this coaching has influenced the statement be determined? The answers are therefore 'problematic' for the Validity Checklist and for SVA as a whole.

The answer to the second *Daubert* question (has the proposition been tested) is affirmative for CBCA laboratory research, but 'no' for CBCA field research, the Validity Checklist and SVA research as a whole.

There is a known error rate (third *Daubert* question) of CBCA judgements made in experimental laboratory research, and this is discussed above. The known error rate is almost 30% for both truths and lies, indicating that truths and lies can be detected above the level of chance by using the CBCA tool (at least in experimental studies), but that errors are frequently made. It also implies that CBCA assessments are not made 'beyond reasonable doubt', which is the standard of proof regularly set in criminal courts. As reported above, reliable error rates for CBCA field research, the Validity Checklist and SVA as a whole do not exist.

A growing number of CBCA laboratory and field studies have now been published in peer reviewed journals, but most studies were laboratory based studies where the participants were often adults rather than children. Validity Checklist studies and SVA studies are lacking. The answer to the fourth *Daubert* question is thus 'yes' regarding CBCA laboratory and field research, but 'no' regarding Validity Checklist research and SVA research.

Several authors have expressed serious doubts about both the CBCA method and the Validity Checklist (see Vrij, 2005, in press), implying that the method is not generally accepted in the scientific community.

Other Verbal Lie Detection Tools

The two alternative verbal lie detection tools, Reality Monitoring (RM) and the Scientific Content Analysis technique (SCAN), that I will discuss in this section have yet to be widely tested, and therefore play only a minor role in this chapter. To my knowledge, RM is not used by professional lie detectors, but only used in scientific research. It is based on memory theory and research. The core of RM is that memories of experienced events differ in quality from memories of imagined events (Johnson and Raye, 1981). Memories of real experiences are obtained through perceptual processes and are therefore likely to contain, amongst other things, *perceptual information*: details of sound, smell, taste, touch, or visual details and *contextual information*: spatial details (details about where the event took place, and details about how objects and people were situated in relation to each other, e.g. 'He stood behind me'), and temporal details (details about time order of the events, e.g. 'First he switched on the video-recorder and then the TV', and details about duration of events). These memories are usually clear, sharp and vivid. Accounts of imagined events are derived from an internal source and are therefore likely to contain *cognitive operations*, such as thoughts and reasoning ('I must have had my coat on, as it was very cold that night'). They are usually vaguer and less concrete.

This may be relevant for detecting deception. It could be argued that 'experienced events' reflect truth telling whereas 'imagined events' reflect deception. Obviously, this is not always the case. A person who gives a false alibi by describing something he truly experienced albeit at a different time than he claims is also describing an experienced event when he lies. Nevertheless, when Masip *et al.* (2005) reviewed the RM deception research (all laboratory studies), they found lie and truth accuracy rates that were similar to those obtained with CBCA research.

SCAN is used by practitioners in the USA (Adams, 1996) and in Belgium. Its rationale 'The deceptive person builds the story out of his/her imagination, while the truthful one builds the story out of memory' (Driscoll, 1994, p. 79) is very similar to the principle underlying RM. However, SCAN examines different criteria to RM, and it is not always clear how they are linked to this principle (e.g. one criterion looks at whether truthful suspects will deny more directly the allegations than liars). In fact, the SCAN criteria resemble the CBCA criteria more. The difference is that SCAN is used with adult suspects and that it analyses statements written by these suspects. (CBCA analyses are carried out on the basis of transcripts of oral statements made by alleged child abuse victims.)

Driscoll (1994) examined written statements in real life cases and obtained considerable success. However, as he reported himself, the ground truth of any of the statements in his study was uncertain. In another study using real life cases (the ground truth was not always certain), Smith (2001) found that SCAN trained officers were reasonably successful in distinguishing between truths and lies, but so were experienced detectives who were not trained in using SCAN, and both groups did not differ from each other.

PHYSIOLOGICAL LIE DETECTION

Control Question Test (CQT)

Physiological indices are measured with a machine called a polygraph. The physiological responses typically measured are skin conductance response, heart rate and blood pressure. A polygraph is often called a 'lie detector', but that label is misleading. It does not measure lies, but examinee's arousal. Polygraph examiners believe that arousal is associated with deception. Examiners have no choice other than to measure arousal because a physiological response uniquely linked to deception does not exist. CQT polygraph outcomes have been admitted as evidence in court cases in the USA, albeit very occasionally, this to great dissatisfaction of some polygraph supporters (Daniels, 2002).

The CQT (also labelled the Comparison Question Test) is the most popular polygraph test in the USA. It compares responses to relevant questions with responses to control questions. Relevant questions (e.g. 'Did you kill Chris Smith?') are specific questions about the crime. Control questions deal with acts that are indirectly related to the crime under investigation, and do not refer to the crime in question. They are meant to embarrass the suspects (both guilty and innocent) and evoke arousal. This is facilitated by giving the suspect no choice but to lie when answering the control questions. Examiners formulate control questions for which, in their view, denials are deceptive. The exact formulation of these questions will depend on the examinee's circumstances, but a control question in a murder examination could be: 'Have you ever tried to hurt someone to get revenge?', where the examiner believes, or even better, knows that the examinee has indeed hurt someone, for such a reason, at some point in their life. Under normal circumstances, some examinees might admit to this (control) wrongdoing. However, during a polygraph examination they will not do so because the examiner will give the examinee the impression that to admit to this would cause the examiner to conclude that the examinee is the type of person who would commit the crime in question. Thus, the examinee has no choice other than to deny this (earlier) wrongdoing and thus be untruthful in answering the control questions. In case the examinee does admit this earlier wrongdoing, the question will be reformulated. This means that the questions (both control and relevant) will be discussed with the examinee prior to the examination. The examination starts when the examinee makes clear that they are happy to answer 'no' to all control and relevant questions. See Raskin and Honts (2002) for a detailed description of the CQT procedure.

The CQT is based on the assumption that in innocent suspects control questions will generate more arousal than relevant questions, because they will be more concerned about their answers to the control questions, and because they are lying to the control questions. However, the same control questions are expected to elicit less arousal in guilty suspects than the relevant questions. Guilty suspects give deceptive responses to both types of question, but relevant questions represent the most immediate and serious threat to the examinee, and are expected to lead to a stronger physiological response than the control questions.

This assumption is theoretically weak (National Research Council, 2003). Liars do not necessarily show more arousal during the key questions. They may not be as concerned about the key questions as lie detectors believe them to be; they may naturally be low responders in term of arousal, or they may have trained themselves not to show arousal to these questions (Honts and Amato, 2002). Also, truth tellers do not necessarily react calmly when answering these key questions. The mere fact that they are accused of wrongdoing could make them aroused, or their concern that they cannot convince the examiner of their innocence could make them aroused. The latter concern is probably intensified by the fact that polygraph examinations are typically carried out in situations where there is no other evidence available. This means for the innocent suspect that he cannot prove his innocence. As a result, the innocent suspect is still not exonerated from the accusations or suspicions that have surrounded them, and this could have serious negative consequences, such as continuing to be investigated and interviewed about the crime by the police, fear that the truth about their innocence may never be believed, and perhaps negative reactions from family members, colleagues, neighbours, and so on.

Accuracy of Control Question Tests

Control questions tests have been carried out in both controlled laboratory settings and in field studies. Laboratory based studies generally show favourable results for CQT polygraph testing. For example, in a review of this type of research, error rates of 9 % for guilty participants and 13 % for innocent participants were found (Vrij, 2000, in press). Raskin and Honts (2002) reported even higher accuracy rates. However, as I have argued before, laboratory studies may not be a good test for measuring accuracy due to the lack of ecological validity. Numerous field studies have been published to date, but they are subject to debate. The problem is that the quality of these published polygraph field studies is low (National Research Council, 2003), and most problems are related to establishing a ground truth that meets scientific standards.

The British Psychological Society Working Party (2004) Vrig (in press) analysed the seven reviews regarding the accuracy of CQT tests of which they were aware. Different reviews showed different outcomes because different researchers included different field studies in their reviews. There was agreement amongst the seven reviews regarding guilty suspects. Correct guilty classifications were made in 83–89 % of the cases, and incorrect innocent classifications were made in 1–17 % of the cases. (Percentages do not necessarily add up to 100 % due to the existence of an 'inconclusive' category.) There is less agreement regarding innocent suspects. Also, the findings for innocent suspects are less positive than for guilty suspects. Depending on the review, between 53 and 78 % of innocent suspects were correctly classified as innocent, and between 12 and 47 % of innocent suspects were incorrectly classified as guilty. It thus appears that CQT outcomes reveal a lie-bias. The relatively high error rates for innocent suspects imply that, despite being innocent, they nevertheless may have been aroused when answering the relevant questions (this problem has already been identified above).

CQT Assessments and the Daubert Test

My answers to the *Daubert* test for CQT assessments are summarized in Table 5.2. Regarding the first question (is the hypothesis testable?), the underlying CQT rationale could be tested in laboratory studies. Conducting CQT field studies is as equally problematic as conducting CBCA field studies, due to the difficulty in obtaining ground truth.[2] The answer to the second *Daubert* question (has the proposition been tested?) is 'yes' regarding CQT laboratory tests. My preferred answer is 'possibly' for field studies due to the low quality of most of these studies (see above). Regarding the third *Daubert* question (is there a known error rate?), the CQT field studies accuracy rates, reported above, raise some concerns, particularly for innocent suspects. Depending on the review, 12–47 % of innocent suspects

---

[2] My verdict could easily have been more negative, due to the fact that CQT testing is not based on a valid theoretical premise (see above). The question than arises, as phrased by Gallai (1999, p. 96): 'How can the underlying science be tested when it has been conceded that no adequate explanation exists as to how the underlying science operates?'

Table 5.2 Answers to the five Daubert questions for CQT assessments

	CQT laboratory	CQT field
(1) Is the scientific hypothesis testable?	yes	problematic
(2) Has the proposition been tested?	yes	possibly
(3) Is there a known error rate?	yes	yes, too high
(4) Has the hypothesis and/or technique been subjected to peer review and publication?	yes	yes
(5) Is the theory on which the hypothesis and/or technique is based generally accepted in the appropriate scientific community?	no	no

were incorrectly classified as guilty. The accuracy scores thus reveal that also CQT polygraph examiners are not able to present the accuracy of their CQT assessments as being 'beyond reasonable doubt'.

The answer to the fourth *Daubert* question (has the test been subjected to peer review?) is 'yes' for both CQT laboratory and field research, although the number of high quality CQT field studies is relatively low.

Iacono and Lykken (1997) published a survey where the scientific opinion concerning the polygraph was examined. They asked members of the American Society of Psychophysiological Research (who can be considered as experts) and fellows of the American Psychological Association (Division 1, General Psychology) for their opinions regarding CQT polygraph tests. Both groups of psychologists expressed similar opinions. A minority of interviewees (about 33 %) considered the CQT test to be based on scientifically sound psychological principles, and only 22 % would advocate that courts admit into evidence the outcome of CQT tests. The answer to the final *Daubert* question (is the test widely accepted?) is thus 'no' for CQT polygraph testing.

Guilty Knowledge Test (GKT)

Like the CQT test, during a GKT polygraph examination, the examinees' skin conductance responses, heart rate and blood pressure are measured. The GKT test, often used in Japan and Israel, is based on the premise that an orienting response occurs in response to personally significant stimuli. Thus, people can be unaware of the conversations around them, yet notice when their name is mentioned in one of these conversations. This principle can be applied to lie detection. When a body was found in the living room, but the suspect denies any knowledge of the crime, the suspect could be asked the following question: Where did we find the body, was that: In the kitchen? In the bedroom? In the living room? In the dining room? In case the suspect has actually committed the crime, he is now likely to show an orienting response when the correct alternative is mentioned. Orienting responses are associated with increased arousal (Lykken, 1998).

This orienting response premise is theoretically more plausible than the premise underlying the CQT polygraph test (National Research Council, 2003; Fiedler, Schmidt and Stahl, 2002). However, interview protocols designed to demonstrate orienting responses are not easily applicable. Obviously, the test requires that the examiner possesses knowledge about the crime (e.g. where the body was found, how the person was murdered, etc.), otherwise the questions cannot be formulated. In addition, questions should be asked about main aspects of the crime in order to make sure that the guilty examinee does know the correct answer to the question. Finally, the innocent suspect should not know the correct answer or should not be able to guess what the correct answer is, otherwise they will also reveal 'guilty knowledge'. In many cases, the salient details of the crime are made available by investigators during the interviews, but also by the media or attorneys (Ben-Shakhar, Bar-Hillel and Kremnitzer, 2002).

Accuracy of Guilty Knowledge Test

Numerous GKT laboratory tests have been conducted (see Ben-Shakhar and Elaad, 2003, MacLaren, 2001 and Vrij, 2000, in press for reviews) showing favourable results, particularly regarding innocent examinees. My own review showed that only 4% of innocent people were incorrectly classified and that 18% of guilty examinees were classified as innocent (Vrij, 2000).

Only two GKT field studies have been published (Elaad, 1990; Elaad, Ginton and Jungman, 1992) and their findings differed considerably. Both tests revealed very good results regarding the classification of innocent suspects (94% and 98% of innocent suspects were correctly classified) but rather poor results regarding the classification of guilty suspects (76% and 42% of guilty suspects were correctly classified). In other words, it appears that GKT tests reveal a truth-bias. One explanation for the poor results regarding guilty suspects is a lack of guilty knowledge. Perhaps questions were asked about minor details which the guilty suspect simply has forgotten or perhaps has never known (e.g. The culprit stole the laptop from a room where a TV was also located. Where exactly was the TV located? Next to the door? Next to the window? Next to the bed?, etc.).

GKT Assessments and the Daubert Test

My answers regarding the *Daubert* test for GKT assessments are summarized in Table 5.3. The underlying rationale of GKT, the orienting response, is easily testable in laboratory studies but more problematic in field studies for the reason already mentioned above: Difficulty in obtaining ground truth. The proposition has been tested in laboratory research (the second *Daubert* question) but rarely in field research. The error rate (third *Daubert*

Table 5.3 Answers to the five Daubert questions for GKT assessments

	GKT laboratory	GKT field
(1) Is the scientific hypothesis testable?	yes	problematic
(2) Has the proposition been tested?	yes	rarely
(3) Is there a known error rate?	yes	yes, too high
(4) Has the hypothesis and/or technique been subjected to peer review and publication?	yes	yes
(5) Is the theory on which the hypothesis and/or technique is based generally accepted in the appropriate scientific community?	yes	yes

question) is known in laboratory research and is acceptable, particularly for innocent examinees. However, the known error rate for guilty examinees is too high for field research, and does not pass the 'beyond reasonable doubt' criterion. GKT polygraph testing has been subjected to peer review (fourth *Daubert* question), although the number of published field studies ($N = 2$) is very low. Iacono and Lykken's (1997) survey, introduced above, revealed that the respondents favoured the Guilty Knowledge Test. Seventy-five percent of interviewees considered the GKT test to be based on scientifically sound psychological principles or theory (33 % thought that this was the case for the CQT test). In other words, GKT polygraph examinations are generally accepted by the relevant scientific community.

Other Physiological Lie Detection Tests

Two more polygraph tests are worth mentioning. First, the Relevant-Irrelevant Test. This test is based upon the same principle as the CQT test (only liars will be more aroused when answering the relevant questions due to their heightened fear of not being believed), but it differs in the control questions that are used. Rather than asking questions that are related to the crime under investigation, which would raise concern amongst examinees (CQT test), neutral questions such as 'Is today Tuesday?' are asked. This response is then compared to the answer to relevant questions such as 'Did you take the money?' One of the criticisms of the CQT test was that truth tellers could also be more aroused when answering the relevant questions. It is obvious that this criticism also applies to this test, and it is therefore widely criticized, even amongst those who favour CQT polygraph testing.

Another polygraph test is called the Directed Lie Test (DLT). In CQT tests, the control questions that are formulated depend on (1) the type of crime and (2) the examinee's history. Thus, the control question 'Have you ever tried to hurt someone to get revenge?' is asked in crime investigations concerning physical assault where the examiner believes or knows that the examinee has actually hurt someone in his life before. This implies that the examiner needs to design a bespoke test for virtually every examination (it should match both the type of crime and history of the examinee), and the quality of these questions will depend, amongst other factors, on the examiner's skills. This lack of standardisation/subjectivity issue is addressed in the DLT test. The control questions used in DLT tests can be asked in all situations. Typical examples are: 'During the first 27 years of your life, did you ever tell even one lie?' and 'Before age 27, did you ever break even one rule or regulation?' (Raskin and Honts, 2002). Examinees will be instructed to answer 'No' to these questions. They will also be instructed to think about particular situations in which they did tell a lie or did break a rule during these (control) denials. As was the case with the CQT, guilty suspects are thought to be most concerned with the relevant questions and are expected to show the strongest responses to these questions. Innocent suspects, however, are thought to be more concerned with the control questions since they will wish to make sure that their responses while lying to these control questions differ from their responses when telling the truth to the relevant questions. Because the underlying principles of DLT and CQT are similar, the problems related to CQT also apply to DLT. Thus, the problems that guilty suspects are not necessarily more aroused while answering the relevant questions, and that innocent suspects are not necessarily more aroused while answering the control questions remains. To date, not enough studies have been carried out to assess the accuracy of DLT (Raskin and Honts, 2002).

Voice Stress Analysers (VSA) differ from traditional polygraph tests because arousal is measured differently. VSA measures arousal nonintrusively by measuring people's pitch of voice (another indicator of arousal) with a microphone. A possible benefit is that lie detection tests can be carried out without the examinees' awareness. This is how I suspect VSA tests are typically conducted, for example, by insurance companies when they assess claims made via the telephone. The most appropriate method to use in order to do this would be the Relevant-Irrelevant Test, discussed above, because this is the test that could most easily be carried out without the examinee being aware of being tested. In a Control Question Test examinees must be subtly guided to lie to the control questions. It is difficult to see how this could be achieved without raising their suspicions. A further complication of CQT tests is that background information about the examinees is required when formulating the control questions. As already noted, the irrelevant-relevant polygraph test has been criticized even by academics who support polygraph testing. Given the problems with this simplistic way of testing, it is not surprising that the National Research Council (2003, p. 167) concluded that 'although proponents of voice stress analysis claim high levels of accuracy, empirical research on the validity of the technique has been far from encouraging'.

FINAL REMARKS

CQT tests and SVA evaluations do not meet the *Daubert* guidelines for admitting expert scientific evidence in criminal courts. The error rate is unknown for SVA assessments and too high for CQT polygraph testing, and the two methods are not undisputed in the relevant scientific community. I also raised doubts about whether the scientific hypotheses underlying both methods are actually testable.

I therefore believe that both methods should not be allowed as evidence in criminal courts. I am aware that this firm standpoint will be challenged by those who propose to allow CQT and SVA analyses as evidence in criminal court. Their main argument is that these methods need to be compared with other methods used in court procedures that yield even lower accuracy rates (Daniels, 2002; Köhnken, 2004). I expect that more people working in the criminal justice system will be sensitive to this argument. If it is decided to allow CQT and SVA assessments as evidence in criminal courts then, at the very least, SVA and CQT experts should present the problems and limitations of their assessments when giving their evidence, so that judges, jurors, prosecutors and solicitors can make a considered decision about the validity of their decisions. In addition, because of the subjective nature of both assessments (i.e. involving human interpretation rather than fact finding), more than one expert should judge each statement in order to establish interrater reliability between evaluators.

The Guilty Knowledge Test (GKT) yielded the most favourable outcome in the *Daubert* test. My main concern with this test is that it has rarely been tested in real life situations, and in the incidental cases where it has been tested, it resulted in relatively high error rates that do not satisfy *Daubert* standards. However, these low accuracy rates may have been caused by an inappropriate use of the test (i.e. using inappropriate questions). This indicates that proper training of examiners in conducting a GKT test may improve its accuracy in the future.

Truths and lies can be detected above the level of chance with CBCA and properly conducted GKT assessments, and hence one could argue that using such tests are acceptable in civil courts that have a lower standard of proof than criminal courts. I don't think that

CQT assessments should be allowed in such courts, due to the fact that CQT testing is not based on sound theoretical assumptions.

REFERENCES

Adams, S.H. (1996) Statement analysis: What do suspects words really reveal? *FBI Law Enforcement Bulletin*, October, 13–20.

Ben-Shakhar, G., Bar-Hillel, M. and Kremnitzer, M. (2002) Trial by polygraph: Reconsidering the use of the guilty knowledge technique in court. *Law and Human Behaviour*, **26**, 527–41.

Ben-Shakhar, G. and Elaad, E. (2003) The validity of psychophysiological detection of information with the guilty knowledge test: A meta-analytic review. *Journal of Applied Psychology*, **88**, 131–51.

BPS Working Party (2004) *A Review of the Current Scientific Status and Fields of Application of Polygraphic Deception Detection*, BPS, Leicester.

Daniels, C.W. (2002) Legal aspects of polygraph admissibility in the United States, in *Handbook of Polygraph Testing* (ed. M. Kleiner), Academic Press, London, pp. 327–38.

Daubert v Merrell Dow Pharmacurticals, Inc. 113 S. Ct. 2786, 1993.

Davies, G.M. (1991) Research on children's testimony: Implications for interviewing practice, in *Clinical Approaches to Sex Offenders and Their Victims* (eds C.R. Hollin and K. Howells), Wiley, New York, pp. 177–191.

DePaulo, B.M., Kashy, D.A., Kirkendol, S.E. et al. (1996) Lying in everyday life. *Journal of Personality and Social Psychology*, **70**, 979–95.

DePaulo, B.M., Lindsay, J.L., Malone, B.E. et al. (2003) Cues to deception. *Psychological Bulletin*, **129**, 74–118.

Driscoll, L.N. (1994) A validity assessment of written statements from suspects in criminal investigations using the SCAN technique. *Police Studies*, **17**, 77–88.

Elaad, E. (1990) Detection of guilty knowledge in real-life criminal investigations. *Journal of Applied Psychology*, **75**, 521–29.

Elaad, E., Ginton, A. and Jungman, N. (1992) Detection measures in real-life criminal guilty knowledge tests. *Journal of Applied Psychology*, **77**, 757–67.

Esplin, P.W., Boychuk, T. and Raskin, D.C. (1988, June) *A field validity study of Criteria-Based Content Analysis of children's statements in sexual abuse cases*. Paper presented at the NATO Advanced Study Institute on Credibility Assessment in Maratea, Italy.

Fiedler, K., Schmidt, J. and Stahl, T. (2002) What is the current truth about polygraph lie detection? *Basic and Applied Social Psychology*, **24**, 313–24.

Frank, M.G. and Feeley, T.H. (2003) To catch a liar: Challenges for research in lie detection. *Journal of Applied Communication Research*, **31**, 58–75.

Granhag, P.A. and Vrij, A. (2005) Deception detection, in *Psychology and Law: An Empirical Perspective* (eds N. Brewer and K. Williams), Guilford Press, New York (NJ), pp. 43–92.

Gumpert, C.H. and Lindblad, F. (1999) Expert testimony on child sexual abuse: A qualitative study of the Swedish approach to statement analysis. *Expert Evidence*, **7**, 279–314.

Hartwig, M., Granhag, P.A., Strömwall, L.A. and Kronkvist, O. (2006) Strategic use of evidence during police interrogations: When training to detect deception works. *Law and Human Behavior*, **30**, 603–619.

Honts, C.R. (1994) Assessing children's credibility: Scientific and legal issues in 1994. *North Dakota Law Review*, **70**, 879–903.

Honts, C.R. and Amato, S.L. (2002) Countermeasures, in *Handbook of Polygraph Testing* (ed. M. Kleiner), Academic Press, London, pp. 251–64.

Johnson, M.K. and Raye, C.L. (1981) Reality monitoring. *Psychological Review*, **88**, 67–85.

Köhnken, G. (1996) Social psychology and the law, in *Applied Social Psychology* (eds G.R. Semin and K. Fiedler), Sage, London, pp. 257–82.

Köhnken, G. (2004) Statement validity analysis and the "detection of the truth", in *The Detection of Deception in Forensic Contexts* (eds P.A. Granhag and L.A. Strömwall), Cambridge University Press, Cambridge, pp. 41–63.

Lykken, D.T. (1998) *A Tremor in the Blood: Use and Abuses of lie Detection*, Plenum Trade, New York.

MacLaren, V.V. (2001) A quantitative review of the guilty knowledge test. *Journal of Applied Psychology*, **86**, 674–83.

Masip, J., Sporer, S.L., Garrido, E. and Herrero, C. (2005) The detection of deception with the Reality Monitoring approach: A review of the empirical evidence. *Psychology, Crime, & Law*, **11**, 99–122.

National Research Council (2003) *The Polygraph and Lie Detection*. Committee to Review the Scientific Evidence on the Polygraph (2003) The National Academic Press, Washington, DC.

Parker, A.D. and Brown, J. (2000) Detection of deception: Statement validity analysis as a means of determining truthfulness or falsity of rape allegations. *Legal and Criminological Psychology*, **5**, 237–59.

Raskin, D.C. and Honts, C.R. (2002) The comparison question test, in *Handbook of Polygraph Testing* (ed. M. Kleiner), Academic Press, London, pp. 1–47.

Ruby, C.L. and Brigham, J.C. (1998) Can Criteria-Based Content Analysis distinguish between true and false statements of African-American speakers? *Law and Human Behavior*, **22**, 369–88.

Smith, N. (2001) *Reading between the lines: An evaluation of the Scientific Content Analysis technique (SCAN)*. Home Office: Police Research Series, paper 135.

Steller, M. (1989) Recent developments in statement analysis, in *Credibility Assessment* (ed. J.C. Yuille), Kluwer, Deventer, The Netherlands, pp. 135–54.

Steller, M. and Boychuk, T. (1992) Children as witnesses in sexual abuse cases: Investigative interview and assessment techniques, in *Children as Witnesses* (eds H. Dent and R. Flin), John Wiley & Sons, New York, pp. 47–73.

Steller, M. and Köhnken, G. (1989) Criteria-based content analysis, in *Psychological Methods in Criminal Investigation and Evidence* (ed. D.C. Raskin), Springer-Verlag, New York, pp. 217–245.

Strömwall, L.A., Granhag, P.A. and Hartwig, M. (2004) Practitioners' beliefs about deception, in *Deception Detection in Forensic Contexts* (eds P.A. Granhag and L.A. Strömwall), Cambridge University Press, Cambridge, pp. 229–50.

Vrij, A. (2000) *Detecting Lies and Deceit: The Psychology of Lying and its Implications for Professional Practice*, John Wiley and Sons, Chichester.

Vrij, A. (in press) *Detecting Lies and Deceit: Pitfalls and Opportunities* (Second Edition), John Wiley and Sons, Chichester.

Vrij, A. (2004) Why professionals fail to catch liars and how they can improve. *Legal and Criminological Psychology*, **9**, 159–81.

Vrij, A. (2005) Criteria-Based Content Analysis: A qualitative review of the first 37 studies. *Psychology, Public Policy, and Law*, **11**, 3–41.

Vrij, A., Akehurst, L. and Knight, S. (2006). Police officers', social workers', teachers' and the general public's beliefs about deception in children, adolescents and adults. *Legal and Criminological Psychology*, **11**, 297–312.

Vrij, A. and Granhag, P.A. (2007) Interviewing to detect deception, in *Offenders Memories of Violent Crimes* (ed. S.A. Christianson) Wiley & Sons, Chichester, England, pp. 279–304.

Vrij, A. and Mann, S. (2003) Deceptive responses and detecting deceit, in *Malingering and Illness Deception: Clinical and Theoretical Perspectives* (eds P.W. Halligan, C. Bass and D. Oakley), University Press, Oxford, pp. 347–61.

CHAPTER 6

Fact Finding and Evidence

Jenny McEwan
Exeter University

In adversarial systems, the finders of fact (magistrates, jurors or, on some issues, single judges) hear an 'edited' version of the facts, since exclusionary rules of evidence cause some pieces of information to be withheld from their consideration. Although there are many theories to explain this phenomenon, part of the rationale clearly lies in what Damaska calls the 'lay disability rationale', that is, that laypeople are not capable of ascribing proper value to individual items of evidence (Damaska, 1997). The exclusionary system may be contrasted with the Continental principle of Free Proof, which developed in the belief that the probative weight of evidence is 'a matter too unruly to obey the lawgiver's rein, too contextual to be captured in a web of categorical legal norms' (Damaska, 1997, p. 20). Since every exclusionary rule of evidence, be it hearsay or evidence of the accused's bad character, carries with it a multitude of exceptions of bewildering complexity, jurors are characteristically regaled with complex directions as to the proper meaning and weight to be attached to evidence. Occasionally they are instructed to disregard entirely something they have heard. In some cases, a jury should be told to regard a witness or piece of evidence as potentially unreliable, as in the case of identification evidence, discussed below, and of the now abolished requirement for a corroboration warning in relation to sexual complainants, children and accomplices (Criminal Justice Act, 1994 s32(1)). In order to be effective, this judicial instruction must be comprehensible to the finders of fact; psychologists have investigated to what extent, if at all, this is the case. Of course, comprehensibility does not guarantee compliance.

JUDICIAL INSTRUCTIONS

Investigations into the question whether juries obey judicial instructions to disregard certain evidence have produced mixed results. Data indicating that mock jurors do apply judicial directions (Carretta and Moreland, 1983) are contradicted by studies that suggest that directions are ineffective (e.g. Casper, Benedict and Perry, 1988). Other research suggests that it depends on at what point in the trial the directions are given, possibly because to include the warning in the judge's final summing-up simply reminds the jury of evidence hitherto less prominent in their memory (Sue, Smith and Caldwell, 1973; Wolf and Montgomery,

---

Applying Psychology to Criminal Justice. Edited by David Carson, Rebecca Milne, Francis Pakes, Karen Shalev and Andrea Shawyer. © 2007 John Wiley & Sons, Ltd

1977a). Warning the jury to disregard evidence they heard about some time ago, and may have partly forgotten about until reminded, may backfire (Walker, Thibaut and Andreoli, 1972). Research supports the possibility of a recent effect (Sue, Smith and Caldwell, 1973; Sealy, 1988). There is some evidence that an instruction to disregard media coverage is effective (Simon, 1966); on the other hand, some researchers found the opposite (Constantini and King, 1980; Kramer, Kerr and Carroll, 1990).

Where evidence of the defendant's bad character is admitted, it seems that mock jurors and magistrates are slightly more likely to convict where a similar offence has been committed in the past, but if the previous offence was dissimilar to the current charge, less likely to convict than if they are not told of any criminal record at all (Sealy and Cornish, 1973; Lloyd-Bostock, 2000; Lloyd-Bostock, 2001). A study of real jurors in New Zealand showed that they tended to distrust a prosecution case relying on evidence of previous convictions (Young, Cameron and Tinsley, 1999). Here, lay opinion appeared to echo the legal view that a criminal record is normally of limited significance. Certain offences, however, do appear to have a particularly prejudicial effect. Mock jurors are far more likely to convict where they are told of a previous conviction for indecent assault on a child, and magistrates are similarly affected by the revelation that the defendant has been convicted of wounding with intent (Lloyd-Bostock, 2000; Lloyd-Bostock, 2001). Both these effects are recorded irrespective of the nature of the charge in the current case. Accordingly, the statutory instrument that represents the Government's initial foray into classifications of relevant propensity attempts to prevent undue prejudice by allowing evidence of a criminal record for indecency with a child only where the current charge is within the same category of offence (Criminal Justice Act 2003 (Commencement No 6 and Transitional Provisions) Order 2004 SI 2004/3033/17 November 2004). To retain the traditional barrier (albeit riddled with exceptions) against evidence of the accused's bad character may backfire. Post-trial interviews in New Zealand indicate that where jurors guessed that evidence was being withheld, they either construed this as counsel trying to stop damaging evidence coming in, or began to speculate on what was missing, defeating the purpose of the exclusion (Young *et al.*, 1999; see also Darbyshire, 1997).

Although many lawyers seem convinced that laypeople will not understand the weaknesses of hearsay as compared with direct testimony, Pickel's mock jurors (students of psychology) successfully ignored hearsay evidence when instructed to do so (Pickel, 1995). Given that hearsay evidence is regularly admitted because of the large number of exceptions to the rule against hearsay, this is just as well. The reality is that jurors and magistrates frequently have to assess the reliability of hearsay evidence. The exceptions themselves appear to be based on a lawyerly version of armchair psychology. For example, under the *res gestae* exception, a hearsay statement is admissible if made by a person so emotionally overpowered by an event that the possibility of concoction or distortion can be disregarded (Criminal Justice Act, 2003 s 118(1)4, enacting *Andrews*, 1987). This exception was retained in the absence of any serious analysis of the reliability of statements made in the heat of the moment, the Law Commission apparently being content simply that 'nobody was aware of miscarriages of justice caused by the admission of *res gestae*' (Law Commission, 1997, 8.119; but see Clifford and Hollin, 1981; Contra, Thompson, Morton and Fraser, 1997; Cutshall and Yuille, 1989; Loftus and Burns, 1982; Loftus, Loftus and Messo, 1987; Steblay, 1992). The Commission appear similarly unconcerned by the prospect of the lay finder of fact being required without guidance to assess the level of emotional engagement of the absent witness, and whether it is such as to dispel any risk of dishonesty.

Research into the effect of judicial instructions on jurors has tended to concentrate on identification evidence. In the wake of psychological research demonstrating the unreliability of identification evidence, fact finders in many jurisdictions are warned that they should treat it with caution. Nevertheless, juror faith in the eyewitness appears to survive a judicial warning of the weaknesses of identification evidence (Wagenaar, van Koppen and Crombag, 1993; Williams, Loftus and Deffenbacher, 1992). The decision of the Court of Appeal for England and Wales in *Turnbull* (1977) requires that the jury be told of the need for caution in relation to eyewitness evidence, even where the witness knows the suspect. Where the prosecution case consists of nothing more than poor quality identification evidence, such as a 'fleeting glimpse', the judge should withdraw the case from the jury unless there is evidence that goes to support the correctness of the identification. These guidelines are insufficient to protect defendants from miscarriages of justice founded on mistaken identity. They take no account of the increased likelihood of mistakes where identifications take place across races (Shepherd, Deregoswski and Ellis, 1974; but see Lindsay and Wells, 1983; Cross, Cross and Daly, 1971) and across genders and age groups (Jalbert and Getting, 1992; Shapiro and Penrod, 1986). Courts should be far more robust in applying the No Case to Answer test at close of the prosecution case. Although in *Turnbull* it was stated that a case must be stopped if it rests on nothing more than poor quality identification evidence, it seems that two poor quality identifications can support each other and ultimately lead to a conviction (*Weeder*, 1980). Yet it is clear from the *Turnbull* judgement that the Court of Appeal is aware of the huge quantity of empirical work on identification that shows that several apparently confident eyewitnesses can be mistaken. In the trial of Barry George, accused of the murder of Jill Dando (*George, Barry Michael*, 2002) a number of 'fleeting glimpse' identifications supported each other, even though they may not all have referred to the same person and some were several hours apart. Also, the Court's concern about the reliability of eyewitnesses is not carried across to other kinds of recognition, such as voice recognition (Ormerod, 2001). Although there are detailed guidelines on visual identifications in the provisions of Code D of the Police and Criminal Evidence Act 1984, there is no obligation to hold a voice identification parade in an appropriate case, nor any guidance as to its conduct, even though voice recognition may be more difficult than face recognition (Yarmey and Matthys, 1992). Given that in any event warnings of the *Turnbull* variety appear to have little effect on finders of fact, there is a case for allowing expert evidence on the dangers of erroneous identification. Experts should also explain what kind of physical conditions reduce the accuracy of identification evidence (Cutler and Penrod, 1995). Expert testimony of this kind seems to reduce fact finders' reliance on eyewitness testimony, although jurors may nevertheless be unable to distinguish between accurate and inaccurate identifications (Wells, Lindsay and Tousignant, 1980).

Juries may decide completely to disregard instructions in an act of defiance (nullification). This is seen by some theorists as a protection for the citizen against oppression by public authorities but by others as antidemocratic, defeating the will of the legislature (Horovitz, 1985; Weiner *et al.*, 1991; Arce, 1995; Wolf and Montgomery, 1977b; Weinstein, 1993; Auld, 2001, 5.10). In the main, however, it seems that juries conscientiously try to follow instructions (Steele and Thornburg, 1988) but, if they cannot understand them, they use some form of common-sense justice, or what ordinary people think the law should be (Finkel, 1995). Most juries appear to be considerably at sea on the legal issues (Reifman, Gusick and Ellsworth, 1992; Elwork, Sales and Alfini, 1982; Hastie, Penrod and Pennington, 1983; Severance and Loftus, 1982). In his study, Ellsworth found that although mock jurors spent a considerable time discussing the law, only about half of their statements were correct and a fifth were seriously wrong (Ellsworth, 1989). Yet the same jurors were quite competent in their grasp of the facts. The New Zealand study recorded high levels of misunderstanding of the trial judge's directions. Although they did their best, jurors went astray in all but 13 of the 48 trials involved in the research (Young *et al.*, 1999 7.14). Tanford sent questionnaires to persons who had actually served on juries and also to people who had been selected for jury service but did not ultimately serve on a jury. Those who had acted as jurors and therefore had heard a judicial summing up had a significantly better awareness of jurors' duties and of procedural rules. However, on matters such as the burden of proof or the substantive criminal law, levels of comprehension were alarmingly low amongst those who had sat in real criminal cases, frequently knowing no more about the legal issues that arose in the cases they had actually heard than did those who had never sat as jurors (Tanford, 1990).

There is empirical evidence to suggest that if lawyers could express themselves more simply, lay finders of fact would be more able to do as instructed (Sales, Elwork and Alfini, 1977; Charrow and Charrow, 1979). Penny Darbyshire has shown that American courts are worse offenders than British ones in the complexity of language used in 'specimen' directions (Darbyshire, Maugham and Steward, 2001). All judicial instructions, however, present problems of comprehension and recall. If they are comprised in an oral speech which jurors may not even be in a position or have the time accurately to commit to paper, the problems are exacerbated. Any jury that returns to the judge to ask to explain the direction further is unlikely to find itself much assisted. The trial judge, mindful of the risk of appeal if he deviates from the standard direction, will generally do no more than repeat what was said in the first place (Severance and Loftus, 1982). The New Zealand Law Commission recommended that flow charts be provided to jurors (Law Commission of New Zealand, 2001, 6.12) In his review of the Criminal Courts in England and Wales, Sir Robin Auld suggests that judges produce guidance in the form of a series of questions and answers to facilitate structured jury discussion (Auld, 2001, 8.24). The recommendation has not met with universal judicial enthusiasm. Judge LJ has warned that it is not to be assumed that 'the judiciary as a whole' supported it. 'The proposal overlooks the principle that although each member of the jury participates in the verdict, each must arrive at his or her conclusion by a conscientious personal examination of the evidence in the context of legal principles which have been defined by the trial judge' (*Cannings*, 2004, p. 767). Yet one may wonder why, on the issue of the application of the relevant law to the facts in the case, his Lordship is untroubled by a situation where one member of the jury 'may be convinced of guilt for reasons which are different to those of each of the other members who nevertheless, for their own conscientious reasons, are agreed on the result.'

THE END OF THE TRIAL: TIMING OF INSTRUCTIONS AND RECALLING EVIDENCE

Jurors are traditionally not told the relevance of evidence at the time they are listening to it (See Kassin and Wrightsman, 1988). This has been compared with 'telling jurors to watch a baseball game and decide who won without telling them what the rules are until the end of the game' (Grove, 2000). At a trial for rape observed by Jackson and

Doran, the jury listened to the medical evidence and then passed a note to the judge to ask whether rape could be committed in the absence of violence. They were told that the judge would explain the definition of rape at the end of the trial (Jackson and Doran, 1995). There seems no good reason to put the jury in this difficulty. In Heuer and Penrod's experiment, more accurate verdicts (as measured against the opinion of the trial judge) were achieved where the law was explained to the jury at the beginning of the case (Heuer and Penrod, 1989). Scottish juries are given a copy of the charge at the beginning of the trial. It would be sensible to adopt Auld's suggestion that juries should also have, at the beginning of the trial, a summary of the case and issues arising (as agreed by counsel) so that there would be no need for a long summing up on the law at the end (Auld, 2001, 11.22).

In New Zealand, there have been changes of practice following the publication of the jury survey. These centre on making the information provided to juries accessible and manageable. Comprehension and memory are assisted by much greater reliance on visual and written aids (Tinsley, 2002). Informing and assisting jurors may be a more constructive way forward than abandoning jury trials altogether. There have been attempts in England and Wales to provide juries with a more structured approach to both the law and the evidence, but this approach seems confined to complicated fraud trials, where it is assumed that the jury will struggle to understand the case. In serious fraud cases, counsel for the prosecution may be required to supply any explanatory material which would aid comprehension by the jury (Criminal Justice Act, 1987, s.9). Thus, the jury in the Maxwell fraud trial was given an outline of relevant company law at the beginning. In a mirror-image experimental trial of the case, mock jurors showed a reasonably high level of understanding (Honess, Levi and Charman, 1998). Fraud trials are frequently singled out as being beyond the intellectual powers of lay finders of fact. In such trials, in fact, technology has made navigation through mountains of papers far easier. Trials of commercial fraud may involve computer screens on which the movement of money can be illustrated and transcripts can appear simultaneously (Miskin, 1995). The New Zealand researchers found that fraud was not in itself necessarily problematic. Jurors were far more likely to go astray when dealing with legal complexities such as several counts against one or more defendants with a number of possible alternative verdicts. Lempert similarly argues that the law is more confusing to jurors than a great number of complicated facts (Lempert, 1981).

Adversarial systems traditionally do not make it easy for jurors to recall the facts at the end of the trial. Note taking is not encouraged by lawyers for the very reason that the jurors interviewed by Darbyshire apparently abandoned their attempts to take notes; they wanted to watch the reactions of witnesses, but could not do that and make notes at the same time (Darbyshire, 1971). Psychological research suggests that jurors who take notes do not reach more accurate verdicts (Heuer and Penrod, 1994; Heuer and Penrod, 1995). Most people cannot take accurate notes at speed. In the New Zealand survey, 16 out of the 48 juries studied came back to the courtroom, during consideration of their verdicts, to ask that the transcript of some of the testimony be read back to them (Young *et al.*, 1999, 3.9). Why should they not have access to a transcript throughout their deliberations? The New Zealand jurors relied heavily on those amongst them who had made notes, although many of the most detailed notes were inaccurate records. However, the more detailed they were, the more the jurors tended to believe they were a true reflection of what was said. Without such notes being available, they were often unable to remember which witness had testified to a particular fact.

THE JURY IN THE DARK: CONSTRUCTING STORIES

The procedural and evidential rules affecting the order in which witnesses are called and the way they give their evidence ensure that facts are not presented in a chronological or coherent way (Hansen, Schaefer and Lawless, 1993). The task for the jury is to impose structure on what they have heard and fill in any gaps where no relevant facts have been supplied. The New Zealand Jury Project confirms that the order of presentation of evidence made it difficult for jurors to construct a narrative. Indeed, their assumption that they were going to listen to a story caused some jurors to take inadequate notes of a witness's testimony because they assumed that the witness would come back again later in the trial. Many jurors found that the order of presentation of evidence militated against their understanding of the story (Young *et al.*, 1999, 5.30).

We have seen that the criminal justice system seems designed to minimize accurate recall of facts. This heightens the risk that holes will appear in the story and be filled with material which may be irrelevant or misleading or both. Much has been written of the desire of both jurors and judges to construct a meaningful narrative out of the hotchpotch of evidence they have heard (Bennett and Feldman, 1981; Wagenaar, van Koppen and Crombag, 1993; Pennington and Hastie, 1988; Young *et al.*, 1999; Jackson and Doran, 1995). The 'story model' of decision making suggests that facts are selected to make a plausible story, which then itself fills any gaps in the evidence. The more blank spots in the jurors' memory, the more influence these inferences will have (Schank and Abelson, 1977). The New Zealand Jury Project also found some confirmation of Lempert's theory that jurors prefer to embellish a story with details (Lempert, 2002). These additional facts may be of marginal relevance from a legal point of view, but give colour and texture to the narrative. A richly textured story might be even more likely to fill evidential gaps than a plain one. The New Zealand jurors said they found maps and photographs useful and wished that they had more of these to give them a picture of the events in question. However, where exhibits were taken with them into the jury room, jurors frequently were not sure of their relevance (Young *et al.*, 1999).

According to the theory of anchored narratives, a story must be tied to reality by means of evidence. This may itself be another narrative, but the ultimate anchor is 'common sense', allowing misleading heuristics or stereotypes to influence the outcome (Wagenaar, van Koppen and Crombag, 1993). Would an innocent man joke to his second wife that he had murdered his first (*Kay*, 2001)? Is it likely that a ship's First Officer would, in front of the family of a crewman he does not know, announce his intention to run the ship aground so that he can earn extra overtime payment (Bingham, 2000)?

DRAWING INFERENCES

The criminal justice system, in fact, encourages the use of heuristics insofar as it requires fact finders to draw inferences from established facts. It is well documented, for example, that advocates are aware of, and where advantageous will appeal to, cultural assumptions that affect the drawing of inferences. For example, in sexual cases, defence lawyers typically attempt to paint a picture of a female complainant, not merely in terms of her previous sexual relationships, but also her efforts to look attractive, her style of dress and social habits. The purpose is to appeal to a rape script with which this behaviour is inconsistent (McEwan, 2005). Another area heavily reliant on inferences from fact is that of *mens rea* (guilty mind) in criminal law. Most serious crimes require that the prosecution prove, in addition to showing that the defendant performed the relevant act, that he or she possessed *mens rea* in terms of some level of subjective awareness of risk. Thus, although there are crimes that do not require subjective awareness, as with gross negligence manslaughter, offences of recklessness and malice (*G*, 2003; *Mowatt*, 1968) do. This state of mind is to be inferred partly from circumstances and partly through the application of 'common sense' – the field of operation of scripts and heuristics.

Intention is the highest form of subjective *mens rea*. It includes where a person desires that a particular consequence flow from his or her action. Inference of this kind of intention will often depend on circumstances. It has been found, for example, that jurors are willing to convict of murder even where death was caused through driving if there is evidence that the defendant used the vehicle as a weapon, where they are told that the car mounted the pavement, or where there was evidence that the defendant knew, and had quarrelled with, the victim (Cunningham, 2001). However, in law, an undesired consequence may also be intended, if the actor was aware of a high degree or risk that it would occur. To find subjective awareness of the risk, jurors are directed to make inferences by analogy, effectively having placed themselves in the shoes of the defendant. Lord Bridge explained how one finds intention, in *Moloney* ([1985] 1 All ER 1025, 1039),

> First, was death or really serious injury in a murder case (or whatever relevant consequence must be proved to have been intended in any other case) a natural consequence of the defendant's voluntary act? Second, did the defendant foresee that consequence as being a natural consequence of his act?

The answer to the second question is determined by the answer to the first. If any reasonable person would have realized that there was a substantial risk attached to the act, why would the defendant not have been aware of it? He might be able to supply a plausible explanation, but, in the absence of that, the answer will be that if the juror in those circumstances would have perceived the nature of the risk, the defendant will similarly be taken to have done so. The language in which this reasoning process is to take place has been amended by the courts since *Moloney's* case; jurors are now asked to consider whether the outcome was virtually certain, and whether therefore they believe that the defendant also foresaw it as a 'virtual certainty' (*Woollin*, 1999)

Jurors in New Zealand found it difficult to distinguish purpose (or motive) from intent. They also tended to think intention and premeditation were the same thing (Young *et al.*, 1999, 7.14), Even lawyers are not immune to the effect of motive in the blaming process. Lawyers' efforts to accommodate praiseworthy risk-taking have from time to time obscured the meaning of legal concepts, such as intention and recklessness, as in the House of Lords case, *Hyam* v *DPP* (1974). Here Lord Hailsham attempted to refine his own test for the *mens rea* of murder to exclude a hypothetical surgeon who attempts to save life by performing a procedure, known to be very high risk, that in the event causes the patient's death. Perhaps because of the difficulty of devising workable definitions that serve all these purposes at once, criminal lawyers have developed a tendency to leave concepts borderless, throwing the responsibility for formulating a coherent link between legitimacy of risk taking and criminal responsibility on to the jury. Hence, in the leading case on the meaning of intention in the criminal law (*Woollin*, 1999), we are told that if the jury find that a reasonable person would have considered an outcome virtually certain to occur, and therefore conclude that the defendant believed an undesired outcome was virtually certain, that conclusion supplies only evidence from which the jury is *entitled*, but not *obliged*, to infer intention. There are no judicial guidelines to suggest when it would be appropriate not to infer intention where such a high degree of foresight exists. This leaves jurors free to take account of laudable motive, such as attempting to save a life. Foresight of a high degree of risk may not amount to evidence of intention to kill in such a case, but, that is a matter for them. It is perhaps unsurprising to discover that jurors in New Zealand were confused as to the meaning of intention.

Some defendants will deny *mens rea* whilst at the same time accepting that the risk of harm would have been obvious had they stopped to think at the time of the alleged offence. It appears to be difficult, however, to convince jurors that someone who is not medically unconscious is unaware of his or her actions. According to Gauld and Shotter (1977), they interpret behaviour as action unless there is a reason not to do so. A person is assumed to be a 'conscious, purposeful and rational agent' not as a series of inferences, from what he or she is seen to do, but on the basis of 'inference by analogy'– how the observers' own behaviour has been linked with a particular intention in the past, and on their interaction, from infancy, with others (Gauld and Shotter, 1977, p. 166). Indeed, inference from analogy is the very basis on which judges are to direct juries when searching for subjective foresight.

In that light, it is noteworthy that juries tend to reject claims by defendants that the effect of extreme rage was to prevent them from appreciating the probable consequences of their acts. In *Woollin* (1999), the defendant killed his three-month-old son by throwing him onto a hard surface, so that his skull was fractured. The defendant denied desiring either death or injury for his son; he had lost control through irritation with him. In *Doughty*, a 'conscientious father' who had sole care of his wife and new-born baby son during his wife's confinement to bed, became exhausted and unable to cope with the baby's constant crying. After all attempts to placate the baby failed, Doughty covered his face with cushions and knelt on them. The child suffocated and died. Both these men were convicted of murder despite their claim not to have realized what would be the likely outcome of their behaviour. There is some psychological research into the impact of strong emotions on human behaviour, although little consensus as to whether emotional arousal might prevent or hinder the mental processes that control action (Kahan and Nussbaum, 1986). Were the legal system to recognize the kind of defence raised in these cases, a great deal of violent behaviour would fall outside its control. Most crimes of violence are committed in 'hot blood' (Gibson, 1975; Daly and Wilson, 1988).

We know that emotions may affect motor activity such as heart rate. They may not entirely negate consciousness, but they do affect its operation, influencing perceptions (Taylor, 1999). To psychologists, the distinction between voluntary and involuntary conduct is far more elusive than the legal approach suggests. Benjamin Libet argues that decisions to move can originate unconsciously, a conscious wish appearing later. Libet, for example, would ask subjects to make hand movements whenever they chose, while he measured the electrical activity in their brains. They had to indicate when they were doing this. He found that the brain impulses connected with the subjects' movements began about a third of a second before they reported any conscious intention to make the movement. His conclusion has been criticized, partly on the ground that he depended on subjects to report at what stage they became aware of intention (Libet, 1985 and replies; Hoffman and Kravitz, 1987). An obvious weakness in his argument is that awareness of having an intention is not necessarily the same thing as, nor necessarily contemporaneous with, intending the action.

There are other studies, however, that suggest that consciousness evolves gradually, from completely unconscious to preconscious, and, finally, to a settled state of consciousness. In task-switching experiments, subjects may be asked to perform a task, but then to switch to a different task at regular intervals or on a signal. The task set might be naming the colour a word is written in or naming the word itself (Allport, Styles and Hsieh, 1994); subtracting from a list of numbers; switching the number to be subtracted, or switching to adding (Jersild, 1927); and identifying a vowel or consonant (Rogers and Monsell, 1995). Irrespective of the nature of the task, there is an increased reaction time (or switch cost) and increased error rate whenever the task is switched. This may indicate the control processes involved in reconnecting and reconfiguring the brain. Contamination amongst the impulses directing different tasks may explain well-known phenomena such as: going upstairs and, at the top, wondering what the reason for the action was; or driving off to the shops and finding oneself on the route to work instead (Monsell, 1996). Although there is a difference between deeds carried out during a period of heightened emotion and those carried out 'automatically', such as driving (Gauld and Shotter, 1977), the absolute dichotomy the law imposes between willed movement or action and involuntariness ignores the very real possibility that there are degrees of awareness between consciousness and unconsciousness. Lawyers prefer to assume the existence of a controlling 'executive computer system' (Monsell and Driver, 2000) or seat of consciousness. Yet, it is clear that much remains to be discovered about human control processes.

The inference of intention, based as it must be on the everyday experience of the finder of fact, is a process highly susceptible to the influence of heuristics, and, in particular, to the effect of common errors in the assessment of risk. Tversky and Kahneman have shown heuristics to be reasoning mechanisms useful to those who for some reason are obliged to interpret the behaviour of other people (Tversky and Kahneman, 1974; see also Einhorn and Hogarth, 1981). Where fact finders are asked to judge the probability of an outcome, the operation of heuristics is likely to be acute and may lead to mistakes. The 'availability heuristic' and 'representative heuristic' both involve dangerous oversimplification. The availability heuristic is employed where the frequency and therefore the probability of events are measured by the ease with which instances or associations are recalled (Tversky and Kahneman, 1973; Kahneman, Slovic and Tversky, 1982). The easier it is to bring instances of it to mind, the more probable, or frequent, it is thought to be. This does not create major problems in most cases, since frequent, rather than rare, events are more easily imagined or remembered. However, if the process is distorted, for example, by selective media coverage of particular kinds of event, predictions are likely to become inaccurate. Thus, media focus on major catastrophes such as flood or rail crashes may cause a general perception that these events are more frequent than they are. Psychology has shown that frequency judgements of causes of death, for example, by cancer, fire, or motor vehicles, can be wildly inaccurate, even if they are firmly believed (Lichtenstein *et al.*, 1978).

The *mens rea* judgement forces fact finders in the first place to assess how probable it was that x would cause y. Once they are satisfied that it was highly likely, they may proceed to the conclusion that the defendant knew that it was highly probable that x would cause y. According to Tversky and Kahnemann, estimations of probability often depend on the employment of the 'representativeness heuristic', finding a 'comparable known event' and assuming that this one will be similar (Kahneman and Tversky, 1972). The number of known events may be very small, and yet we are likely to believe it to be typical of events in its category. Thus, if I meet three people from Australia who are extravert and drink beer, I am likely to assume that all Australians are like this. Such reasoning, however, ignores the base rate (how often x does *not* cause y, or the number of Australians who are not like this), which means that these events may not be typical at all. It seems that lay finders of fact are not alone in paying insufficient heed to base-rate information. According to Saks and Kidd, courts in the USA tend to overestimate risk in scientific and technological cases such as antitrust, product liability and pollution (Saks and Kidd, 1980–1981). In England and Wales, some notorious miscarriage of justice cases can also to some extent be attributed to the operation of the representativeness heuristic. It occurred, for example, in the evidence of the expert witness in the trials of Angela Cannings, in 1991, and Sally Clark, in 1999. Both were convicted of murdering their children. In Cannings's case, the alleged victims were seven-week-old J and 18-week-old M. She had also lost a child aged 12 weeks in 1989 (*Cannings*, 2004). Clark's two sons, C and H, died at the ages of 11 weeks and eight weeks respectively. In her case, the Crown put forward statistical evidence that the probability of two 'cot deaths' in one family with this profile was one in 73 million. At her first appeal it was accepted that the Royal Statistical Society had demonstrated the statistic of 1 in 73 million to be wrong. However, the Court of Appeal thought the error was of minimal significance and would not have affected the jury verdict. It was considered that it is, in any event, very rare for two natural deaths of this kind to occur within the same family (*Clark* (No 1) 2000). In neither the prosecutions of Sally Clark nor Angela Cannings did the trial court appear to recognize the uncertainty surrounding the base rate, the number of infant deaths that do occur through natural causes.

FACT AND OPINION

Ordinary witnesses are required to give evidence only of facts, not their opinion, although they are permitted to use descriptive terms if the facts and their conclusions from those facts cannot realistically be separated. Thus the witness may say that someone was 'fat' or 'young' (*Davies*, 1962). Expert opinion will be received in England and Wales if the court is satisfied that the particular expert is a specialist in their field. There is no specific test, as long as the field of expertise falls outside the everyday experience of members of the general public (*Silverlock*, 1894) Courts are generally hostile to expert evidence on matters upon which the finders of fact are to adjudicate, such as the credibility of witnesses. Thus, psychiatrists may not explain what the effect of provocative acts would be on a 'normal' person, nor may they give an opinion on whether the defendant intended the harm he caused (*Chard*, 1971).

The nature of adversarial proceedings inevitably requires each side to call their own expert witnesses, so that conflicting scientific opinions have to be resolved by the finders of fact. Courts traditionally have managed to cope with uncertainty in science by pretending that it does not exist, preferring to treat conflicts of opinion as matters of rival levels of expertise (Jones, 1994). It seems that courts assume that the resolution of a conflict of opinion between scientists amounts to the discovery of who is 'right' (Wagenaar, van Koppen and Crombag, 1993). The finders of fact thus are required to judge where the correct scientific answer lies.

However, some recent cases in England have shown that simply to devolve all responsibility for resolving conflicting expert testimony to the jury is highly dangerous. In *Cannings* (2004, p. 768), the Court of Appeal acknowledged that the conviction had to be quashed, remarking:

> With unexplained infant deaths...in many important respects we are still at the frontiers of knowledge. For the time being, where a full investigation into two or more sudden unexplained deaths in the same family is followed by a serious disagreement between reputable experts about the cause of death, and a body of such expert opinion concludes that internal causes, whether explained or unexplained, cannot be excluded, as a reasonable...possibility, the prosecution of a parent or parents for murder should not be started, or continued, unless there is additional, cogent, evidence...In cases like the present, if the outcome of the trial depends exclusively or almost exclusively on a serious disagreement between distinguished and reputable experts, it will often be unwise, and therefore unsafe, to proceed.

It is rare for the Court of Appeal in this way to describe a particular area of expertise as suspect and deserving of particularly cautious treatment. However, the guidance offered in this passage is relatively unhelpful to prosecutors and trial judges. The case should be discontinued if the disagreement exists among 'distinguished and reputable experts'. Presumably, if the only dissenting voice belongs to someone whose expertise is considered inferior, the case may proceed. Hence, the court will be obliged to make a judgement on that expert's standing within their field of expertise. Meanwhile, other areas of scientific uncertainty are to be battled over in courts in the traditional way, with the tribunal of fact as ultimate arbiter.

Psychology and Expert Evidence

Although there are fields of psychology endowed with very obvious scientific credentials, other areas of specialism may struggle to 'pass the judge'. The *Frye* v *US* (1923) test of 'general acceptability to the scientific community' has been referred to with approval in English cases, for example to exclude 'psychological autopsy' evidence on the likelihood of the deceased wishing to commit suicide (*Gilfoyle*, 2001). The court also made the point, however, that there were no criteria by reference to which the quality of the opinion could be tested. Sociology and psychology do not fit comfortably either into the newer American test for scientific respectability that, in theory, was designed to allow more flexibility particularly in relation to new areas of science. From *Daubert* v *Merrell Dow Pharmaceuticals* (1993), the trial court should enquire whether a technique has been subjected to peer review, whether it has been generally accepted, and whether the theory or technique can be or has been tested. Economics, sociology and psychology sit uneasily in a model that requires a set of propositions demonstrated to hold in all circumstances. There is, within the disciplines, extensive disagreement about questions of central importance, such as methodology (Richardson *et al.*, 1995). The requirement for study of the ability to falsify is not appropriate to social sciences: 'we correctly refuse to abuse a child for the sake of research' (Graham, 1998). Controlled experiments are virtually impossible. Aware of this, many American judges have in consequence sidestepped *Daubert* (Slovenko, 1998). Thus, evidence of false confessions and suggestible personalities, post-traumatic stress disorder and repressed memory syndrome has been admitted.

The reception of 'syndrome evidence' has not met with universal approval. For instance, controversy surrounds the reception in sexual assault trials of Rape Trauma Syndrome or Child Sexual Abuse Accommodation Syndrome evidence. Complainants in such cases must overcome a 'culture of scepticism' if they are to be believed (Harris and Grace, 1999). There is considerable resistance amongst the legal professions of the USA and the UK to the use of such syndrome evidence for diagnostic purposes in relation to the particular complainant, or to supply a 'profile' suggesting that behaviour which fits the model indicates that the complainant has indeed been sexually assaulted (Ellison, 2005). However, the judicial response is not consistent. The Louisiana Supreme Court has been flexible on the issue of child sexual abuse accommodation syndrome, since the inability to test it arises from its 'very nature as an opinion as to the causes of human behaviour' (*State* v *Foret*, 1993). In contrast, evidence of rape trauma syndrome was rejected by the Supreme Court of New Hampshire, which considered that it dealt almost exclusively with vague psychological profiles and symptoms, and unquantifiable evaluation results (*State* v *Cressey*, 1993). In *Borawick* v *Shay* (1994), the controversy surrounding repressed memory theory, in terms of reliability and of general acceptance, was discussed at length. The testimony was disallowed. There was no discussion of the ability to falsify issue.

There is nothing in law to prevent the use of syndrome evidence to overcome the impression created amongst jurors where the complainant's behaviour after the alleged assault contradicts intuitive notions of likely reactions. The expert here is able to indicate that the behaviour is not unusual in genuine victims and not inconsistent with having been sexually assaulted. In this context, there is a much less stringent test of scientific validity; the expert witness may speak from experience, without having to attest to the existence of a particular syndrome associated with victims of rape and sexual abuse (Frazier and Borgida, 1992). With this legal possibility in mind, the Crown Prosecution Service of England and Wales recently recommended greater use of expert witness testimony in the prosecution of domestic violence cases. Here the purpose of the evidence would be to explain any behaviour from the alleged victim of the violence that appears counter-intuitive but which is not in fact uncommon (Dempsey, 2004).

Assessing Expert Evidence

Rightly or wrongly, jurors seem confident that they have understood expert testimony placed before them in court. According to the theory of anchored narratives, where conflicting expert evidence is evenly balanced the court will accept whatever opinion fits its purpose best, anchoring its choice on the authority of the preferred expert (Wagenaar, van Koppen and Crombag, 1993). Thus, the outcome depends on the plausibility of the narrative offered by each of the parties to the litigation. Even where the scientific evidence is complex, detailed and expensive, common sense is seen to be the arbiter of choice. For example, in a test case against British Nuclear Fuels, 50 experts in genetics, epidemiology and radiation damage gave evidence, and 100 leading scientists in several countries submitted reports. It was alleged that exposure to radiation had caused leukaemia in the child of a worker at a nuclear processing plant (*Reay and Hope* v *British Nuclear Fuels*, 1994). The trier of fact was to be the trial judge sitting alone. Leading counsel explained to the Press: 'Mr Justice French will come to a common sense conclusion. He is not likely to be bogged down by the scientific refinements. One cannot have judges spending their time analysing what scientists say and forgetting about ordinary people' (Dan Brennan QC, *The Times*, October 27 1992).

If a narrative is very strong, the trier of fact may become contemptuous of scientific evidence. Thus, in the Canadian case, *Farrell v Snell* (1990), the defence argued that there was insufficient evidence that a surgical operation on the plaintiff's eye had caused him to lose sight in that eye. This was rejected, since it was known that the surgeon had continued to operate despite noticing a haemorrhage in the eye. The suggestion that blindness could have arisen independently of the procedure lacked plausibility. 'Causation need not be determined by scientific precision. It is...essentially a practical question of fact which can best be answered by ordinary common sense' (at 306). In *Cherry v Borsman* (1991), also from Canada, the plaintiff could not supply clear scientific evidence of causation, but the court was similarly unpersuaded of the possibility of coincidence. Here the defendant negligently failed to carry out an abortion. The baby born in consequence was severely disabled. It was held that common sense indicated the cause despite doubts expressed by expert witnesses called by the defendant.

Some notorious British miscarriage of justice cases lend support to Wagenaar's theory that fact finders assume extra scientific expertise in the testimony of expert witnesses called by the prosecution, particularly if they are employed by government scientific facilities (Jones, 1994; Wagenaar, van Koppen and Crombag, 1993). The impact of expert evidence may also, to some extent, depend on the reaction of the finder of fact to the personality of the expert witness, particularly where the scientific content is intellectually challenging (Cooper, Barnett and Sukel, 1996). Judges appear content to allow the impression displayed by the expert witness during the course of giving evidence to dictate the ultimate verdict if the jury cannot understand the science, For example, Bridge J directed the jury at the trial of the Birmingham Six as follows (quoted in Nobles and Schiff, 1995):

> Members of the jury, the resolution of scientific argument of this sort is difficult, particularly difficult for a jury of laypeople. The only way you can resolve these differences is by your impression of the witnesses. Use any technological knowledge that you have, but in the end you will judge it primarily by your impression of the witnesses, and secondly, perhaps by a comparison of their relevant experience.

Although advocates tend to prefer expert witnesses who can communicate effectively with juries, experts who succumb to pressure to explain scientific content in terms the jury can understand may regret it later. Professor Sir Roy Meadow, an expert paediatrician, not a statistician, testified in *Clarke* that the chance of two cot deaths occurring without human intervention in one family in the social group occupied by the defendant's family was 1 in 73 million. To make this more vivid, he went on:

> It's the chance of backing that long odds outsider at the Grand National, you know: let's say it's an 80 to 1 chance, you back the winner last year, then the next year there's another horse at 80 to 1...you back it again and it wins...So it's the same with cot deaths. You have to say two unlikely events have happened and together it's very, very, very, unlikely.

This 'graphic reference by Professor Meadow to the chances of backing long odds winners of the Grand National year after year' was, in the opinion of Judge LJ, likely to have been uppermost in the minds of the jury when considering Sally Clarke's guilt. As a result her conviction was quashed at her second appeal (*Clark (No 2)* 2003). Professor Meadow, who had also given evidence at the trial of Angela Cannings, was struck off the medical register in 2005 by the General Medical Council for giving misleading evidence at Sally Clarke's trial. His conduct was described as 'fundamentally unacceptable in that he had strayed into areas not within his remit of expertise.' Although the GMC order was subsequently reversed by the Administrative Court and the Court of Appeal (*Meadow* v *GMC*, 2006), it seems that the expert who collaborates with lawyers in their own domain, the adversarial trial, does so at his peril. The fate of Professor Meadow supports the argument made by Carole Jones some years previously (Jones, 1994, 269): 'The legal process encourages selectivity amongst experts in their man of law role, whilst at the same time punishing them for such selections when they fail to live up to an idealized vision of the man of science'.

REFERENCES

Allport, D.A., Styles, E.A. and Hsieh, S. (1994) Shifting intentional set: exploring the dynamic control of tasks, in *Attention and Performance XV: Conscious and Nonconscious Information Processing* (eds C. Umiltà and M. Moscovitch), MIT Press, Cambridge, MA.

Arce, R. (1995) Evidence evaluation in jury decision-making, in *Handbook of Psychology in Legal Contexts* (eds R. Bull and D. Carson), Wiley, Chichester.

Auld, Sir Robin (2001) *Criminal Courts Review*, HMSO, London, www.criminal-courts-review.org.uk.

Bennett, W.L. and Feldman, M.S. (1981) *Reconstructing Reality in the Courtroom*, Tavistock, London.

Bingham, T. (2000) *The Business of Judging: Selected Essays and Speeches*, Oxford University Press, Oxford, p 14.

Carretta, T.R. and Moreland, R.L. (1983) The direct and indirect effects of inadmissible evidence. *Journal of Applied Social Psychology*, **13**, 291.

Casper, J.D., Benedict, K. and Perry, J.L. (1988) The tort remedy in search and seizure cases: a case study in juror decision making. *Law and Social Inquiry*, **13**, 279.

Charrow, R.P. and Charrow, V.R. (1979) Making legal language understandable: a psycholinguistic study of jury instructions. *Colombian Law Review*, **79**, 306.

Clifford, B.R. and Hollin, C. (1981) Effects of type of incident and the number of perpetrators in eyewitness testimony. *Journal of Applied Psychology*, **66**, 352.

Constantini, E. and King, J. (1980) The potential juror: Correlate causes of judgement. *Law and Society Review*, **15**, 9.

Cooper, J.L., Barnett, E.A. and Sukel, H.L. (1996) Complex scientific testimony: how do jurors make decisions? *Law and Human Behavior*, **70**, 379.

Cross, J., Cross, J. and Daly, J. (1971) Sex, race, age and beauty as factors in the recognition of faces. *Perception and Psychophysics*, **10**, 393.

Cunningham, S. (2001) The reality of vehicular homicides; convictions for murder, manslaughter and causing death by dangerous driving. *Criminal Law Review*, 679.

Cutler, B.L. and Penrod, S.D. (1995) *Mistaken Identification: the Eyewitness, Psychology and the Law*, Cambridge University Press, Cambridge.

Cutshall, J.C. and Yuille, J.C. (1989) Field studies of eyewitness memory of actual crimes, in *Psychological Methods in Criminal Investigation and Evidence* (ed. D. Raskin), Springer-Verlag, New York.

Daly, M. and Wilson, M. (1988) *Homicide*, De Gruyter, New York.

Damaska, M.R. (1997) *Evidence Law Adrift*, Yale University Press, New Haven.

Darbyshire, P. (1971) The lamp that shows that freedom lives: Is it worth the candle? *Criminal Law Review*, 740.

Darbyshire, P. (1997) Previous misconduct and magistrates' courts: some tales from the real world. *Criminal Law Review*, 105.

Darbyshire, P., Maugham, A. and Steward, A. (2001) *What Can the English Legal System Learn from Jury Research Published Up to 2001? Criminal Courts Review*, www.criminal-courts-review.org.uk/.

Dempsey, M. (2004) *The Use of Expert Testimony in the Prosecution of Domestic Violence*, CPS, London.
Einhorn, H.J. and Hogarth, R.M. (1981) Behavioral decision theory: processes of judgement and choice. *Annual Review of Psychology*, **32**, 53.
Ellison, L. (2005) Prosecutorial use of expert witness testimony in sexual assault cases. *International Journal of Evidence and Proof*, **9**, 239.
Ellsworth, P.C. (1989) Are twelve heads better than one? *Law and Contemporary Problems*, **52**, 205.
Elwork, A., Sales, B. and Alfini, J.J. (1982) *Making Jury Instructions Understandable*, Mitchie, Charlottesville, VA.
Finkel, N.J. (1995) *Commonsense Justice: Jurors' Notions of the Law*, Harvard University Press, Cambridge, MA.
Frazier, P.A. and Borgida, E. (1992) Rape trauma syndrome; a review of case law and psychological research. *Law and Human Behavior*, **16**, 293.
Gauld, A. and Shotter, J. (1977) *Human Action and its Psychological Investigation*, Routledge & Kegan Paul, London.
Gibson, E. (1975) *Homicide in England and Wales 1967–71*, Home Office Research Study 31, HMSO, London.
Graham, M.H. (1998) The *Daubert* dilemma: at last a viable solution. *International Journal of Evidence and Proof*, **2**, 211.
Grove, T. (2000) *The Juryman's Tale*, Bloomsbury, London.
Hansen, K.L., Schaefer, E.G. and Lawless, J.J. (1993) Temporal patterns of normative, informational and procedural-legal discussion in jury deliberations. *Basic and Applied Social Psychology*, **14**, 33.
Harris, J. and Grace, S. (1999) *A Question of Evidence? Investigating and Prosecution Rape in the 1990s*, Home Office Research Study 196, HMSO, London.
Hastie, R., Penrod, S.D. and Pennington, N. (1983) *Inside the Jury*, Harvard University Press, Cambridge, MA.
Heuer, L. and Penrod, S.D. (1989) Instructing jurors: a field experiment with written and preliminary instructions. *Law and Human Behavior*, **13**, 409.
Heuer, L. and Penrod, S. (1994) Trial complexity: a field investigation of its meaning and its effects. *Law and Human Behavior*, **18**, 29.
Heuer, L. and Penrod, S. (1995) Jury decision-making in complex trials, in (eds Bull R. and Carson D.) *Handbook of Psychology in Legal Contexts*, Wiley, Chichester, p. 171.
Hoffman, R.E. and Kravitz, R.E. (1987) Feedforward action regulation and the experience of will. *Behavioral and Brain Sciences*, **10**, 782.
Honess, T.M., Levi, M. and Charman, E.A. (1998) Juror competence in processing complex information: implications from a simulation of the maxwell trial. *Criminal Law Review*, 763.
Horovitz, I.A. (1985) The impact of jury nullification instruction on verdicts and jury functioning in criminal trials. *Law and Human Behavior*, **9**, 23.
Jackson, J. and Doran, S. (1995) *Judge Without Jury: Diplock Trials and the Adversary System*, Clarendon, Oxford.
Jalbert, N.L. and Getting, J. (1992) Race and gender issues in facial recognition, in *Psychology and Law: International Perspective* (eds L. Lösel, D. Bender and T. Bleisener), de Gruyter, New York.
Jersild, A.T. (1927) Mental set and shift. *Archives of Psychology*, **89**, 5.
Jones, C.A. (1994) *Expert Witnesses: Science, Medicine and the Practice of Law*, Clarendon, Oxford.
Kahan, D.M. and Nussbaum, M.C. (1986) Two conceptions of emotion in criminal law. *Columbia Law Review*, **96**, 270–374.
Kahneman, D. and Tversky, A. (1972) Subjective probability: a judgement of representativeness. *Cognitive Psychology*, **3**, 430.
Kahneman, D., Slovic, P. and Tversky, A. (1982) *Judgement Under Uncertainty*, Cambridge University Press, Cambridge.
Kassin, S.M. and Wrightsman, L.S. (1988) *The American Jury on Trial*, Hemisphere, New York, p. 144.
Kramer, G.P., Kerr, N.L. and Carroll, J.S. (1990) Pre-trial publicity, judicial remedies and jury bias. *Law and Human Behavior*, **14**, 409.

Law Commission (1997) *Evidence in Criminal Proceedings: Hearsay and Related Topics,* Report, The Stationery Office, London.
Law Commission of New Zealand (2001) *Juries in Criminal Trials,* Report 69, Law Commission of New Zealand, Wellington.
Lempert, R.O. (1981) Civil juries and complex cases: Let's not rush to judgement. *Michigan Law Review,* **80,** 68.
Lempert, R.O. (2002) Narrative relevance, imagined juries and a supreme court inspired agenda for jury research. *St Louis University Public Law Review,* **21,** 15.
Libet, B. (1985) Unconscious cerebral intitiative and the role of conscious will in voluntary action. *Behavioral and Brain Sciences,* **8,** 529; Replies, ibid., 539–566.
Lichtenstein, S., Slovic, P. and Fischhoff, B., *et al.* (1978) Judged frequency of lethal events. *Journal of Experimental Psychology, Human Learning and Memory,* **4,** 551.
Lindsay, R.C.L. and Wells, G.L. (1983) What do we really know about cross-race identification evidence? in *Evaluating Witness Evidence* (eds S. Lloyd-Bostock and B.R. Clifford), Wiley, Chichester.
Lloyd-Bostock, S. (2000) The effects on jurors of hearing about the defendant's previous convictions: a simulation study. *Criminal Law Review,* 734.
Lloyd-Bostock, S. (2001) The effect on magistrates of knowing a Defendant's criminal record, in law commission. *Evidence of Bad Character in Criminal Proceedings* Law Com No 273 Cm 5257, London HMSO) Appendix A.
Loftus, E.F. and Burns, H.J. (1982) Mental shock can produce retrograde amnesia. *Memory and Cognition,* **10,** 318.
Loftus, E.F., Loftus, G.R. and Messo, J. (1987) Some facts about weapon focus. *Law and Human Behavior,* **11,** 55.
McEwan, J. (2005) Proving consent in sexual cases: Legislative change and cultural evolution. *International Journal of Evidence and Proof,* **9,** 1.
Miskin, C. (1995) Watch his honour's light pen. *New Law Journal,* 648.
Monsell, S. (1996) Control of mental processes, in *Unsolved Mysteries of the Mind: Tutorial Essays in Cognition* (ed. V. Bruce), Taylor & Francis, Hove, p. 109.
Monsell, S. and Driver, J. (2000) Banishing the control homunculus, in *Control of Cognitive Processes: Attention and Performance, XVIII* (eds S. Monsell and J. Driver), MIT Press, Cambridge, MA.
Nobles, R. and Schiff, D. (1995), Miscarriages of justice: A systems approach. *Modern Law Review,* **58,** 299.
Ormerod, D. (2001) Sounds familiar? Voice identification evidence. *Criminal Law Review,* 595.
Pennington, N. and Hastie, R. (1988) Explanation-based decision making: effects of memory structure on judgement. *Journal of Experimental Psychology: Learning, Memory and Recognition,* **14,** 521.
Pickel, K.L. (1995) Inducing jurors to disregard inadmissible evidence: a legal explanation does not help. *Law and Human Behavior,* **19,** 407.
Reifman, A., Gusick, S.M. and Ellsworth, P.C. (1992) Real Jurors' understanding of the law in real cases. *Law and Human Behavior,* **16,** 539.
Richardson, J.T., Ginsburg, G.P., Gatowski, S. and Dobbin, S. (1995) The problem of applying *Daubert* to psychological syndrome evidence. *Judicature,* **79** (1), 10.
Rogers, R.D. and Monsell, S. (1995) The cost of a predictable switch between simple cognitive tasks. *Journal of Experimental Psychology,* 207.
Saks, M.J. and Kidd, R.F. (1980–1981) Human information processing and adjudication: trial by Heuristics. *Law and Society Review,* **15,** 123.
Sales, B.D., Elwork, A. and Alfini, J. (1977) Improving comprehension for jury instruction in *Perspectives in Law and Psychology Vol 1, The Criminal Justice System* (ed. B.D. Sales), Plenum, New York.
Schank, R.C. and Abelson, R.P. (1977) *Scripts, Plans, Goals and Understanding: an Inquiry into Human Knowledge Structures,* Erlbaum, Hillsdale, NJ.
Sealy, A.P. and Cornish, W.R. (1973) Juries and their verdicts. *Modern Law Review,* **36,** 496.
Sealy, A.P. (1988) Instructional sets in trials of rape, in *Lawyers on Psychology, and Psychologists on Law* (eds P.J. van Koppen and G. van den Heuvel), Swets and Zeitlinger, Amsterdam.

Severance, L. and Loftus, E.F. (1982) Improving the ability of jurors to comprehend and apply jury instructions. *Law and Society Review*, **17**, 153.
Shapiro, P.N. and Penrod, S.D. (1986) Meta-analysis of facial identification studies. *Psychological Bulletin*, **100**, 139.
Shepherd, J.W., Deregowski, J.B. and Ellis, M.D. (1974) A cross-cultural study of recognition memory for faces. *International Journal of Psychology*, **9**, 205.
Simon, R.J. (1966) Murders, juries and the press – does sensational reporting lead to verdicts of guilty? *Trans-Action*, **3**, 40.
Slovenko, R. (1998) The *Daubert* sequelae. *International Journal of Evidence and Proof*, **2**, 190.
Steblay, N.M. (1992) A meta-analysistic review of the weapon focus effect. *Law and Human Behavior*, **16**, 4.
Steele, W.W. and Thornburg, E.G. (1988) Jury instructions: a persistent failure to communicate. *North Carolina Law Review*, **67**, 77.
Sue, S., Smith, R.E. and Caldwell, C. (1973) Effects of inadmissible evidence and decisions of simulated jurors: a moral dilemma. *Journal of Applied Psychology*, **3**, 345.
Tanford, J.A. (1990) The law and psychology of jury instructions. *Nebraska Law Review*, **69**, 71.
Taylor, J.G. (1999) *The Race for Consciousness*, MIT Press, Cambridge, MA.
Thompson, J., Morton, T. and Fraser, L. (1997) Memories for the marchioness. *Memory*, **5**, 615.
Tinsley, Y. (September 2002) *Paper presented to the Criminal Law Group, SLS Conference*, deMontfort University, Leicester.
Tversky, A. and Kahneman, D. (1973) Availability: a heuristic for judging frequency and probability. *Cognitive Psychology*, **5**, 207.
Tversky, A. and Kahneman, D. (1974) Judgement under uncertainty; Heuristics and Biases. *Science*, **185**, 1124.
Wagenaar, W.A., van Koppen, P.J. and Crombag, H.M. (1993) *Anchored Narratives: the Psychology of Criminal Evidence*, Harvester Wheatsheaf, Hemel Hempstead.
Walker, L., Thibaut, J. and Andreoli, V. (1972) Order of presentation at trial. *Yale Law Journal*, 216.
Wells, G.L., Lindsay, R.C.L. and Tousignant, J.P. (1980) Effects of expert psychiatric advice on human performance in judging the validity of eyewitness testimony. *Law and Human Behavior*, **4**, 275.
Weiner, R., Habert, K., Shkodriani, G. and Staebler, C. (1991) The social psychology of jury nullification: predicting when jurors disobey the law. *Journal of Applied Social Psychology*, **21**, 379.
Weinstein, J.B. (1993) Considering jury nullification: When may and should a jury reject the law to do justice? *American Criminal Law Review*, **30**, 239.
Williams, K.D., Loftus, E.F. and Deffenbacher, K.A. (1992) Eyewitness testimony in (eds D.K. Kagehiro and W.S. Laufer), *Handbook of Psychology and Law*, Springer-Verlag, New York.
Wolf, S., Montgomery, D.A. (1977a) Effect of inadmissible evidence and level of judicial admonishment to disregard on the judgements of mock jurors. *Journal of Applied Social Psychology*, **7**, 205.
Wolf, S. and Montgomery, D.A. (1977b) Effect of inadmissable evidence on the decisions of simulated jurors: a moral dilemma. *Journal of Applied Social Psychology*, **3**, 213.
Yarmey, A.D. and Matthys, E. (1992) Voice evidence of an abductor. *Applied Cognitive Psychology*, **6**, 367–77.
Young, W., Cameron, N. and Tinsley, Y. (1999) *Juries in Criminal Trials: Part II*, New Zealand Law Commission Preliminary Paper 37, Wellington, New Zealand.

CASES

Andrews [1987] 1 All ER 513.
Borawick v Shay (1994) 842 F Supp 1501 (D Conn 1994).
Cannings [2004] 1 All ER 725, 768.
Chard (1971) 56 Cr App R 268.
Cherry v Borsman (1991) 75 DLR 4th 668.

Clark (No 1) 2 (October 2000) www.lexis-nexis.com/professional. Court of Appeal (CD).
Clark (No 2) [2003] 2 FCR 44.
Davies [1962] 3 All ER 97.
Daubert v Merrell Dow Pharmaceuticals (1993) 113 S Ct 2786.
Farrell v Snell (1990) 72 DLR 4th 289.
Frye v US (1923) 293 F 1013 (DC Cir 1923).
G [2003] 4 All ER 765.
George (Barry Michael) (2002) *The Times* August 30.
Gilfoyle [2001] Crim LR 312.
Kay (2001) *The Daily Telegraph*, October 6.
Meadow v General Medical Council [2006] 1 WLR 1452 (HC); [2006] EWCA Civ 1390 (CA).
Mowatt [1968] 1 QB 421.
Reay and Hope v British Nuclear Fuels (1994) 5 Med LR 1.
Silverlock [1894] 2 QB 766.
State v Cressey 628 A 2d 696, 700 (NH 1993).
State v Foret 628 So 2d 1116 (La) 1993.
Turnbull [1977] 2 QB 871.
Weeder (1980) 71 Cr App R 228.
Woollin [1999] 1 AC 82.

CHAPTER 7

A Psychology and Law of Fact finding?

David Carson
University of Portsmouth

The field of evidence is no other than the field of knowledge. (Jeremy Bentham, 1810).

[P]sychology ... is a study of how we do think and is irrelevant to logic, which is a study of how we *ought* to think. (Burks, 1946, at 302, referring to the work of Charles Sanders Peirce (1839–1914)).

This chapter will examine the possibility, and discuss the desirability, of developing an explicit psychology and law of fact finding. A New Evidence Scholarship (NES) has developed within academic law circles, and psychology has made substantial contributions to fact finding (e.g. identification, memory, interviewing). However, there have been relatively few attempts to pull these developments together. There have been even fewer attempts to generalize, or theorize, towards a psychology and law of fact finding. This chapter will, diffidently, suggest that such developments are both possible and long overdue.

INTRODUCTION: LAW

Lawyers, who work in trial courts, spend a much higher proportion of their time investigating facts than in discovering the law. Yet very little, in their academic training, will have prepared them for this. (This statement is less true in the USA where it is possible to work in a law clinic whilst, and as part of, studying for a law degree.) Academic legal study focuses on substantive rules, for example the analysis of legislation or precedent decisions of the appellate courts. The study or 'science' of fact finding is not part of most academic law curricula. Assessment for law degrees regularly includes 'problem solving'. This requires the student to identify, and then to analyse, the legal issues involved in a written problem. This will have been invented by the examiner to test students' analytical skills as well as knowledge. The examiner will regularly ensure that some of the facts are ambiguous to test the students' ability to identify alternative interpretations and signify their significance for legal issues. Some issues will be 'buried' to test the prowess of the better students. (Can they 'see' that if Y is like X, rather than W, then Z might apply?) But, other than identifying ambiguities and omissions (where further information could significantly alter the legal issues), the student must take the facts as given. Whether and how those facts may be proved is irrelevant to the intellectual endeavour; the student must assume that they can or will be – even with crimes it is exceptionally difficult to prove when contested.

Some law students will choose to study the law of evidence, or evidence and procedure. (In England and Wales, at least, it remains an optional course, however central it may be to the work of litigators and to the processes of fact finding.) They may expect to study the processes whereby the facts of past disputed events are identified, declared, assessed and proved, on a balance of probabilities for civil claims but beyond reasonable doubts where a criminal charge is preferred. If so, they will be disappointed. The law of evidence is, parallel to other substantive law subjects, taught as the analysis of the rules governing the admission, processing and weighing of information to be presented to trial courts. It is concerned, for example with when hearsay evidence may be given, when a witness's prior convictions may be mentioned in court or when evidence, however relevant and accurate, may be excluded because of impropriety in its collection.

The substantive law of evidence, which law students usually learn and which is reflected in leading textbooks, on both sides of the Atlantic Ocean (e.g. Tapper, 2004; Dennis, 2002; Fisher, 2002) focuses on procedures and exceptions to the principle of free proof. Leading philosophers, such as Jeremy Bentham (quoted in Twining, 1994), and evidence scholars such as Cross (said, by Twining (1972) to be working for the day his subject was abolished) in the UK and Thayer (1898) in the USA, have advocated free proof, where the jury, or other fact finder, is allowed to hear and consider any relevant information. The law of evidence, in both those and many other countries, however, is concerned with what juries and other fact finders must not be told, and procedurally how not. Murphy (2001) has argued that law is the only discipline that artificially restricts the application of logic and other systems of proof. Some textbooks and courses do make reference to psychological research and insights into fact finding and proof (e.g. Roberts and Zuckerman, 2004), but the legal hegemony is manifestly dominant.

A New Evidence Scholarship (NES) has developed, since the 1990s, as a reaction to this narrow conception of 'evidence'. The term was coined by Richard Lempert in 1986, but the domain is also known as Evidence, Proof and Facts (EPF), which is also the title of a book of sources edited by Murphy (2003). NES adopts a much wider conception of evidence, with a focus on process (Jackson, 1996).

> The broader conception of the subject includes inferential reasoning, probabilities, narrative, and the practical and theoretical implications of developments in forensic science, forensic psychology, and information technology. Insofar as such topics find a modest place in some orthodox courses on the Law of Evidence, the focus is distorted, the intellectual framework is incoherent, and many important aspects are marginalized, especially when the contested jury trial is treated as the prototypical arena in which such topics are important. (Twining, 2003, p. 96)

Whilst the NES is a relatively recent development it has a substantial intellectual history (Twining, 1994). Important transitions, for example from proof by ordeal (where the fact that a confession was extracted by torture did not seem to worry anyone about its reliability), to proof by procedure (e.g. where it was the number, rather than the quality of the witnesses that mattered), to our more (relatively) empirical and rational current position (Jackson, 1988; Twining, 1994). (Note that, even in the 'developed' world, we still rely on evidence that has been obtained by torture. Even if it is inadmissible in the courts of some countries it can still, perfectly legitimately, be used by the police and related services as 'intelligence' to prevent or disrupt other crimes (*A (FC) and* others (FC) (Appellants) *v. Secretary of State for the Home Department (Respondent) (2004), [2005] UKHL 71*). Intriguingly, some of the most important current work in the New Evidence Scholarship has involved the rediscovery of work undertaken at the turn of the twentieth, not the twenty-first, century. Anderson and Twining (1991) have 'rediscovered' the work of American legal academic John Henry Wigmore (1863–1943). His 'traditional' work on the law of evidence (1904–5) has continued to be popular, but his more interdisciplinary studies on fact finding and proof (1913) had been largely lost. Now NES is finding its way into law courses (Anderson, Schum and Twining, 2005; Murphy, 2001, 2003), but it is, with some critical exceptions (e.g. Schum, 1994), dominated by law academics. As recently as 2003, Twining has had to argue for sustained attention to be paid to evidence as a multidisciplinary subject. Whilst identifying forensic psychology (see quote above) as a critical topic for consideration, he did not identify developments in psychology and law as pointing the way to valuable collaboration.

INTRODUCTION: PSYCHOLOGY

Psychology has contributed both to the science of fact finding and to the analysis of substantive rules, such as the nature of incapacity to make certain decisions (e.g. Grisso and Appelbaum, 1998). Indeed much, if not most of the developed research corpus of psychology and law, has been focused on making the determination and proof of facts more productive and reliable. Consider, for example, eyewitness identification, memory, interviewing, detection of deceit, offender profiling, and so on. Some of these topics have developed out of interaction with practitioners (e.g. the cognitive interview arose out of requests from police officers for a more effective method of undertaking interviews (Fisher and Geiselman, 1992), or with policy makers (e.g. interviewing vulnerable witnesses (Home Office, 1992). Some have been applications, to legal contexts, of research on core psychological processes such as memory, leading to valuable work on identification evidence (e.g. Wells *et al.*, 1998). Whilst there have been attempts to generalize this into an investigative psychology (e.g. see Canter and Youngs, 2003), however, there has not been, it is submitted, an overt attempt to develop a psychology and law of fact finding (but see Saks and Thompson, 2003).

Psychologists have tended to adopt the legal hegemony and limited their critiques to the particular rules or processes that they have studied. The legal manner of doing things, for example showing witnesses pictures of possible offenders simultaneously rather than sequentially, may have been challenged (Wells *et al.*, 1998), but not the appropriateness of concentrating on the similarity of foils rather than differences. (The argument is that the 'physical' forensic sciences, such as DNA and finger-printing, concentrate on identifying differences between samples, whilst psychological research has focused on ensuring that the foils are similar to the suspect. The legal assumption, that it is the fairness of the procedure which matters most, has been co-opted.) Very important work, enabling more vulnerable witnesses to be heard in the courts of England and Wales, has been undertaken. But, perhaps, the vulnerable witness (whose weakness has been officially recognized and reinforced in legislation) should not have been seen as the problem. Rather, the way in which legal processes can make all witnesses vulnerable, and their evidence dubious, could have been the target (Carson, 2003a).

Fact Finding

Twining has argued that the common theme for multidisciplinary work related to fact finding and evidence is inductive reasoning (2003). However, doesn't that presuppose the existence of facts and their nature? Ted may say that he saw Sam enter Vera's house at 6.00 p.m. and emerge, half an hour later, in an agitated state and with blood dripping from his hands. That information could be used to infer that Sam killed Vera between 6.00 and 6.30 p.m. It should not be treated as sufficient information to justify a conviction for murder, but it is certainly significant. It may be made more credible, or more appropriate to infer from, if Ted identifies Sam at an identification parade, more so if the parade complies with procedures recognized, by research, as likely to minimize errors. Certainly it would be less credible if the identification parade was improperly organized. More contentiously it could be more appropriate to infer that Ted's evidence is reliable if it was obtained during an interview where, scrupulously, no leading questions were asked and Ted felt that he was in charge and was able to say anything, in his own words, that he wished. That would be consistent with the principles of conversation management (Shepherd and Milne, 1999; Holmberg, 2004). Expert witnesses could inform the court about the greater suitability and greater veracity, other things being equal, of inferring from information produced by such an interview over other types, particularly oppressive (Gudjonsson, 2003). That would demonstrate the relevance and value of recent developments in psychology and law. But does that not start too late in the process?

Consider case construction, a popular explanation given for miscarriages of justice (McConville, Sanders and Leng, 1991; Maguire and Norris, 1992). The argument is that once the police identify a suspect for a crime they stop investigating the crime and, instead, concentrate on proving the suspect guilty. So, in the above simple example, the criminal investigation would quickly move from an inquiry into how and why Vera died, to how to show that Sam is guilty of her death. However, case construction is not a very useful theory. It has been conceded (Maguire, 2003) that there have to be some reasons why the particular suspect is identified. Case construction does not allow for the legal requirement that the police are supposed to move from investigating the crime, to nominating a suspect, whom they must then demonstrate is likely to be guilty. They would not be performing their jobs properly if they did not identify suspects and seek to demonstrate their guilt. It would be more appropriate, and less judgemental, to identify the problem as premature decision making. Further, case construction does not allow for the contribution of the criminal justice system (e.g. adversarial or investigatory) applying in the particular jurisdiction and the significance of the relationship between the police, prosecutors and courts (Jackson, 2004). It is not a predictive theory; it does not help us to identify the cases where the wrong suspect has been, or will be, identified, recalling that most suspects who reach the stage of being prosecuted are found, or plead, guilty and are not subject to claims of wrongful conviction. It also explains little as it can only be 'verified' in cases where wrongful conviction – which includes cases where the suspect is guilty but there was insufficient valid evidence to prove that – is declared. It is submitted that it would be more appropriate to focus on the decision-making process, including the rationalization for the decisions made. We need to look at the whole process, which does not begin with the evidence being given. Evidence construction, rather than case construction, is the problem.

Our problems begin with the nature and existence of facts, not from inferring *from* them but inferring *about* them. We live in a world of sensory experiences; we see, hear, smell, touch things. In order to communicate, or even just think about them, we turn those experiences into words. Immediately we are constrained by the finite limits of that language (often cultural), and our skills in utilizing it. We may describe something as 'red' because we could not, then or at all, think of, or did not know, a more appropriate expression. We have one word for 'snow,' other cultures may have many more. Life is not experienced as if a foreign language film or an opera with sub- or surtitles telling us what is happening. Yet once facts are described in language the words used seem to become 'concrete,' to represent or to be the actual facts, rather than one imperfect attempt at using language to summarize an experience. This is particularly explicit and powerful in legal contexts. The words can be recorded in the dossier of evidence as the facts found, or they can be analysed as if independent of the past event: that is "What do you mean by 'agitated'?" We seem to share understandings, for pragmatic reasons, about the degree of description necessary. No limits are given for the degree of detail necessary to describe something or an event. However, we learn roughly appropriate limits, for example we are not expected to provide the detail associated with charts for wall paint when asked the colour of someone's tie. Lawyers have confused some expert witnesses by challenging this assumption. They have, unexpectedly, required more information than the witness was expecting to provide (Wynne, 1989).

Indeed, it can be tempting to claim that facts do not exist, that everything is an interpretation. But that can lead to inappropriate relativism. Whether it was, or was not, blood on Sam's hands, should be capable of resolution to a sufficient degree of certainty for practical purposes, including proof beyond reasonable doubt. But the reality of other 'facts,' such as that Sam was 'agitated,' is much more questionable. What may be interpreted as 'agitated' by one person may not be by another. It is not just the ambiguity of the behaviour and the vagueness of the language. It is also the way in which we construct boundaries around events and rely on pragmatic understandings. Events do not have beginnings or endings, until we decide to ascribe them. We adopt a start and end point that satisfies the needs of the immediate purpose. Asked about our holidays we do not begin by describing how we came to choose the destination or all the anticipatory pleasures. We know that that was not meant. We – well most of us anyway – know when to stop, when we have given more than enough information. Stories, to be such, need to have beginnings and ends. But life is not a story, particularly if you accept that our behaviour and much more, is biologically, as well as in many other ways, influenced by our parents, and their parents. Before we infer, or utilize inductive reasoning about the facts, we need to find them. Or is it entirely an inferential process?

DEDUCTION, INDUCTION, ABDUCTION

Three stages, with regard to how we have approached the problems of identifying and using facts as evidence, can be identified. Jackson (1988) has noted that, before the dominance of science, proof involved reliance on adherence to a rule provided by an authoritative source. Thus conviction was possible if there was a confession, even if it was produced by violence, or two identifications. This may be associated with deductive reasoning. The conclusion, the verdict, was correct just because a preprescribed rule was followed. But, as empiricism developed as the *modus operandi* of science, so investigation to satisfy a fact-finder became necessary in courts. It was no longer, for example, the number of witnesses but rather the quality of their evidence that mattered. This may be associated with inductive reasoning because, instead of deducing from given rules, courts have to induce from experiences of the world as related by witnesses. But then, just as science has increasingly recognized that observation is tainted by interpretation, that entirely value-free science is impossible and that induction may describe events but does not explain them, Jackson suggests we are moving towards an emphasis on evidence as interpretation. Instead of demonstrating that the facts (free from observation bias) match those specified in the criminal charge, we examine whether our interpretation is coherent and consistent with the indictment. From focusing on whether the evidence corresponds with the allegations in the indictment laid against the suspect, we move to examining whether the indictment provides a coherent explanation for the facts found (Jackson, 1988). Indeed, practicing lawyers already refer to whether a case 'stands up', meaning whether it makes sense within the context of the facts.

> This involves rejecting the dichotomy between discovery and justification, and recognising that there is a kind of logic in discovery, which involves justification, which has been called abduction. (p. 561)

Jackson argues for judges to have a creative, not just a declaratory role in the evidence gathering, decision-making and justifying process.

Whilst deduction and induction may be considered to be in opposition, as claims to being appropriate methodologies, abduction is not in competition with either. Abduction was identified and developed by the American nineteenth century philosopher, Charles S. Peirce. Co-incidentally this was at the same time as Arthur Conan Doyle's fictional detective, Sherlock Holmes, was demonstrating it (Schum, 2001). Peirce presented them as three kinds of inquiry.

> Abduction is the process of forming an explanatory hypothesis. It is the only logical operation which introduces any new idea; for induction does nothing but determine a value, and deduction merely evolves the necessary consequences of a pure hypothesis. (Quoted in Burks, 1946, at 303).

Abduction describes the process whereby, when we observe some information, facts, events, we automatically impose an explanation for, or understanding of, them. We see marks on a road. They appear to be tyre marks. We infer that a vehicle skidded, as they are not in a line parallel to the road. We observe the corpse of a cat by the side of the road. We conclude that the vehicle skidded when trying to stop or to avoid killing the cat.

> *Abduction*, or *inference to the best explanation*, is a form of inference that goes from data describing something to a hypothesis that best explains or accounts for the data. Thus abduction is a kind of theory-forming or interpretive inference. (Josephson and Josephson, 1966, p. 1.)

It can only be to the best, current, explanation; the cat's death may have nothing to do with the car. So abduction fits within Twining's argument (2003) that the common theme to interest in fact finding, evidence and proof, is inferential reasoning. The point being made, in this chapter, is that we need to study the abductive process whereby facts are identified and declared. This occurs at a much earlier stage in the process, of fact finding, than identifying a suspect. Abduction 'is really an appeal to instinct' (Pierce, quoted by Burks, 1946, at 302). However, it is a continuous process whereby new information can lead to a revision of our theory.

Is, or could there be, a 'psychology of abduction'? (A search on Google Scholar for 'psychology' and 'abduction,' revealed many references to the psychology of belief in abduction by alien beings.) Most of the psychologists involved in psychology and law relate to the subdisciplines of forensic (legal) or clinical psychology. Perhaps other subdisciplines, for example developmental and Gestalt psychology, have much to offer. Gestalt psychology, for example reveals that 'people automatically focus on some objects in the perceptual field to the exclusion of others' (Kassin, 1998, p. 107). Apparently, for example, the closer together physical articles are the more we perceive them as a unit. Things, which are similar in shape, size or colour, get grouped together, and so on. This shapes *what* we see, not just *how* we interpret it, and thus has clear relevance to fact finding and its reliability.

Research into the heuristics that influence our decision making would also be relevant (see Chapter 6 and Chapter 11, this volume). For example, there may be so much information for us to observe that we find it easier to summarize it and make a generalization. That then becomes 'the fact' that we recall and report to the investigators. We may use the frequency with which we obtain certain information as indicating the likelihood of an event, or the reliability of an interpretation, when it simply happens to be the case that such information is more available, or more likely to be repeated. An explicit forensic psychology of abduction could examine the processes involved in the initial perception of past events, as well as assess the direction and significance of those processes for the quality of subsequent decision making, such as when choosing a story, a suspect or, eventually, a verdict. Opportunities for theorizing, or generalizing, might be greater with such a generic approach than with our current specialist, and rather separate, psychologies of memory, identification, recall through interviewing, and so on.

Abduction is a key interest of New Evidence Scholars (NES) and within developments in policing. For example, practical advice prepared by the National Centre for Policing Excellence, and endorsed by the Association of Chief Police Officers in England, Wales and Northern Ireland (ACPO, 2005), lists several of the heuristics that can taint evidence gathering as factors to be considered by investigators (see pages 58–60). They state, over optimistically: 'Whilst no one can rid their mind of these ingrained flaws anyone can learn to understand the traps and compensate for them (p. 59).' Twining recognizes that some more modern legal textbooks on the law of evidence are addressing issues about fact finding and inference to proof (identifying Roberts and Zuckerman, 2004), but notes it is instruction, or information about – rather than training in – new methods of reasoning, and so on (Twining, 2003, p. 96). It is education by osmosis rather than immersion.

BEST DESCRIPTION: BEST EXPLANATION

Any forensic psychology of abduction will need to recognize that the legal context is liable to distort the process for witnesses. We experience many sensations throughout the day. We only attend to a few. Some of those will force their way into our conscious consideration because of their relevance to what we are doing (e.g. our actions at a particular time when conscious of an upcoming appointment), or because of their 'drama,' such as their distinctiveness.

> Every inquiry whatsoever takes its rise in the observation ... of some surprising phenomenon, some experience which either disappoints an expectation, or breaks in upon some habit of expectation ... (Peirce, quoted by Burks, 1946, at 303).

The law and criminal justice processes will provide many of these 'breakages,' and in the process distort them. A witness may have turned and looked more deliberatively at a bank, because they hear what sounded like gun shots from that direction, before seeing three or more individuals jump into a greenish sort of car and drive off at some speed. The witness will draw inferences, will make best sense of what they observed, utilizing any schemas or mental representations available to them (Kassin, 1998). The attendance of the police, soon after, will provide another breakage in the individual's normal life and lead to further abductive processes and uses of schemas to make best sense of what happened and is now happening. The police will bring legal and investigative categories of relevance with them. They will want to know enough to be able to demonstrate it was one or more types of crime. They will want to know the colour of the car, even though it is legally irrelevant, to help them find it and, thereby, the presumed offenders. Many of the witness's objectives, needs to understand, and conceptions of relevance will be effectively ignored. It is inference to the best explanation, which depends on purpose (Abimbola, 2001), and the legal purposes take over.

Anderson, Schum and Twining (2005) have developed techniques for demonstrating how conclusions can, most appropriately, be inferred from the evidence collected. In particular, they have refined Wigmore's (1913) charting method. What needs to be proved, for legal purposes, is broken down into its constituent parts, for example that Sam entered a house, at 6.00 p.m., emerged about 6.30 p.m., that Vera died in the house between 6.00 p.m. and 6.30 p.m., and that Sam emerged with Vera's blood on his hands. Ted's evidence will be able (assuming he is willing to be a witness) to support some of these inferences. But the quality of the inferential links between the evidence of facts observed, and that which has to be proved, will vary considerably. The Wigmorean charting method draws attention to the quality of these links.

Anderson, Schum and Twining (2005) have also begun to identify the detail involved in forensic abduction. For example, we can start with 'facts', in the abstract sense of something, capable of perception, which happened, by virtue of our being alive. As Pierce (see above) stressed, something has to make this distinctive, in the senses of a breach from the norm and capable of being severed from 'background reality'. This could be the perceived gun shot leading the witness to turn and look at where they thought it originated (which could be wrong). It could also be Sam emerging from the house, at 6.30 p.m., with blood on his hands. (Was the blood 'dripping' then, or only later when Ted tried to make sense of what he believes he observed, and/or because has now seen drip marks on the ground?) Some of those facts/observations will be potential evidence, because relevant to the legal theory developed by the investigators.

There is now a 'cause for suspicion,' which will lead to hypotheses being generated. The quantity and quality of these will depend on the investigator's and witness's qualities of insight, imagination and creativity. (These competencies could help or hinder, in relation to the final decision.) The hypotheses will have different degrees of relevance, credibility, ability to be proved. They will relate back to the evidence, which will depend on its form, for example whether physical and still available for observation and test. To the extent that they are dependant on observation, they will bring in issues relating to the skills of the observer, for example memory, objectivity, motivation, ability to differentiate between what the witness actually observed and what they might have expected to see. (Note that identifying the observer's schemas is part, but only part, of this process.) Issues also arise from the absence of evidence. A witness might have failed to see something, which could be a forgivable human error, but it might also be the case that they did not see it because it did not happen and the hypothesis being worked on is incorrect (Anderson, Schum and Twining, 2005, particularly Chapter 2). The significance of different hypotheses needs to be assessed as, with each additional piece of information, the number of possible hypotheses increases incrementally.

ARGUING ABOUT ARGUMENTS

Defeasible reasoning, based on the work of Pollock (e.g. 1987) provides a means of assessing, rating and eliminating, these hypotheses. It relates to nonmonotonic or nondeductive reasoning. This is appropriate to investigations where the factual premises are not given. We may be able to reason, deductively, on the law that all intentional killings of another human being are murder (conveniently ignoring defences for explanatory purposes) and, since the case of *R. v. Sam*, outlined above, is such, Sam is guilty of murder. But our problem is that we do not know that the case of *R. v. Sam* fits within those factual terms. We have to discover the 'facts' which arise as inferences from our and others' perceptions of events.

> The full picture can be summarised as follows. First *perception* is applied to sense data, yielding specific beliefs, and *memory* is used to record and retrieve these data. Then *induction* infers general rules from them, after which the *statistical syllogism* derives new specific beliefs from these rules. Finally, beliefs thus derived *persist* over time. (Bex *et al.*, 2003, p. 134.)

These beliefs and inferences can be stated as arguments and assessed as such.

> Reasoning proceeds by arguments, and arguments are constructed by starting from perceptual and memory states, moving from them to beliefs, from those beliefs to new beliefs and so on. (Pollock, 1987, p. 490.)

Arguing about arguments reflects legal practice. It also provides a useful alternative to probabilistic reasoning since there are rarely sufficiently relevant and robust statistics, let alone agreed between the parties, for use in legal disputes (Prakken, 2004). (Robertson and Vignaux 1993 have sought to combine probability theory and Wigmorean charts.) Each argument is contingent; it can be refuted or undercut to challenge its reliability in the particular case.

Argumentation systems can be applied to defeasible reasoning.

> They tell us how arguments can be constructed, when arguments are in conflict, how conflicting arguments can be compared, and which arguments survive the competition between all conflicting arguments. (Prakken, 2004, p. 37.)

They are also very appropriate for use with Wigmorean charts (e.g. see Bex *et al.*, 2003). The reliability of inferences can be examined. 'Argumentation schemes' have been developed which identify key questions to be asked to test an argument. For example arguments concerned with the credibility of a witness's testimony can be investigated by considering his or her veracity, objectivity and observational competence, all of which may be give rise to further questions (Schum, 1994, p. 325; Tillers and Schum, 1991). Here are clear linkages with research in psychology and law which should be able to enrich these discussions. Unfortunately whilst work on abduction and defeasible arguments is exciting the interest of computational scientists interested in artificial intelligence (e.g. (Bex *et al.*, 2003; Pollock, 2001) it has provoked less interest amongst psychologists, with exceptions in The Netherlands (Malsch and Nijboer, 1999; Wagenaar, van Koppen and Crombag, 1993).

A possible application, of these ideas, relates to the extant work on the detection of deception, in particular Criteria Based Content Analysis, part of Statement Validity Analysis (SVA) (Vrij, 2000, 2003). This involves examining a witness's statement for the presence or absence of 19 criteria, compiled by Steller and Köhnken (1989), as indicative of truth-telling (which is not necessarily synonymous with accuracy). The criteria include examples of 'unstructured production,' 'descriptions of interactions' 'reproduction of speech' and 'descriptions of interactions.' It has been hypothesized that these criteria indicate that the truth is being told (although that may be false because based on inaccurate observations, etc.), because it would be too complex to invent such details, recalling that consistency and coherence of account are also critical criteria (Steller, 1989; Vrij, 2003). Might an additional explanation, for these theories and research findings, lie in abduction? Is it not highly likely that witnesses' initial descriptions, particularly if there has been limited time to contemplate richer explanations, would take this form? Is it not entirely reasonable, for example to expect a witness to an event to provide an unstructured description? He or she will be searching his or her memory which, if the event was not long past, may not be well structured or have been rehearsed. So it is liable to ignore chronological order and involve recall of details with little relevance (now defined by the legal context), because the witness is responding in an unpractised, immediate and unmediated fashion. Inclusion of speech samples may also be expected because they too involve a more immediate response. The witness is able to 'quote' (although it may not be accurate, because it is recalled as 'an act,' before effort has been expended on reviewing its 'correct' interpretation.

An alleged rape victim, in a fly-on-the-wall documentary in England and Wales (which was controversial because the police interviewing was so aggressive that it led fewer women to report victimisation but, in due course to major improvements in police practice), reported that, after the event, she wiped herself with a blue and white tea towel and, in her haste to leave, put her tights on back to front. This was of no interest to the interviewing police officers, as it had nothing to do with what they would have to prove in court, but it was what the woman recalled. (The woman withdrew her allegation. The police convinced her that her story, and her affect, was not credible. Several of the police officers involved were severely criticized, and some disciplined, although others admitted it reflected practice elsewhere. Nobody noted that similar questions would be asked, and points made, in the formal setting of a court.) Adopting an abductive or interpretative understanding of the alleged victim's position, her account, what and how she gave it was, it is submitted, understandable. Her lack of verbal dexterity, the lack of organisational structure in her statement, her focus on what was seemingly important to her rather than to the requirements of the law of rape, and so on were, it is submitted indicative of an attempt and to recall and interpret the best understanding of what happened to her a few hours earlier, after her boyfriend insisted she reported the case to the police. Might a forensic psychology of abduction be developed to test how 'unstructured,' and so on a witness's account is, and relate that to the individual's linguistic and other skills plus his or her opportunities to prepare a different account. For fact finding we need both descriptions and interpretations of the past, plus ways of assessing their reliability.

Defeasible reasoning might also be used to assess the reliability of descriptions/interpretations of facts as evidence. SVA is only admissible, in legal proceedings, in some countries (Vrij, 2003). That is a consequence of conceiving the issues as relating to expert, or scientific, evidence where the focus is upon the reliability of the theory. SVA is not admissible in certain countries, such as the UK, because it is not, at least yet, considered sufficiently reliable. But, that is not the only approach possible. People knowledgeable in SVA, such as forensic psychologists, could show lawyers how they can persuasively (inferentially) argue that a witness's statement of recall is, or is not, appropriate. For example an individual witness's evidence is likely to be truthful (from which further inferences might be built that it is also accurate), because it is consistent with what and how we should expect people, in those circumstances, with those abilities and with that history, to say. They could argue that it is both understandable, and to be expected, that witnesses to a traumatic event, who have not rehearsed their story or evidence several times and who have not become compliant with the expectations of his or her interviewers, would incorporate snatches of speech from the event. That is easier (involves less cognitive effort), and is more natural than summarising what the witness heard. Judges and jurors could be encouraged to think about how the evidence was 'created' through an interview. Is this what and how a person in this position should be expected to behave, including speak? Instead of trying to convince the court that the witness's statement is likely to be true, because of an expert's analysis of the witness's statement and inferences from research on other witnesses' behaviour, the presenting lawyer could argue persuasively about this unique case. This approach and emphasis would correspond with the move to a coherence rather than correspondence theory of proof which Jackson (1988), amongst others, maintains has or is becoming the dominant theory of legal proof.

It would also tend to highlight the role of generalisations, and inferences from them, within defeasible reasoning (Prakken, 2004). Twining (1999) has highlighted their role in producing errors.

> Generalizations are dangerous in argumentation about doubtful or disputed questions of fact because they tend to provide invalid, illegitimate, or false reasons for accepting conclusions based on inference. They are especially dangerous when they are implicit or unexpressed. (p. 78)

However this points to psychology's paradigm role in challenging allegedly commonsense assumptions about human behaviour. This role, tackling 'fireside inductions' (Meehl, 1989), needs further development and would demonstrate the importance of psychology's contribution as a partner, rather than servant of law who is only permitted a voice when invited. A more explicit interest and role in developing our understanding of abductive processes and defeasible reasoning could give psychologists a critical role in challenging inappropriate inferences, not least when established by empirical research.

TO BE OR OUGHT TO BE?

However a core issue, which permeates psychology and law but which is rarely made explicit, needs resolution. Should our interest and work in relation to fact finding and proof be descriptive or normative? Should we focus on researching and analysing how fact finding and proof are, actually, undertaken in practice or should we be concerned with how it ought to be? It is, of course, perfectly proper and very useful for research to identify how we determine what happened. At the very least it will help to identify errors and other problems, such as inefficiencies. Insofar as legal psychology merely seeks to reflect contemporary society, and service the needs of the laws, systems and professionals of particular jurisdictions, it is appropriate to simply describe what happens. But if psychology and law recognizes that it is – necessarily – part of a 'reform project' (Carson 2003b), because of the internationalism of science and inherent value structures and issues (e.g. the natures of 'justice' and 'science') involved in the practice of law, then description should be the servant of prescription. For example it is important to know that we use schemas and that these influence our perception and interpretation of events observed (Pennington and Hastie, 1992). But we need to put that knowledge at the service of improving the accuracy of witnessing.

Several papers on how judges and juries actually make decisions reflect on the gap between the ideal and the real. Van Koppen (1995), for example reviewed arguments about the use of 'Bayes' Theorem in court. 'Bayes' Rule is a logical theorem – there can be no doubt about its truth. It tells us how to upgrade our knowledge by incorporating new evidence.' (Robertson and Vignaux, 1993, p. 17.) Van Koppen concluded that the problems, with the theory, are overwhelming.

> The most important argument against the use of models of hypothesis testing for decision-making in criminal cases, however, is that judges and juries do not argue and decide in that way. In fact hypothesis testing is so far off what actually happens in court that it is not only unsuccessful as a descriptive model, but also too alien to the legal tradition to be of use as a prescriptive model either. (Van Koppen, 1995, p. 592.)

Should this neatly expressed conclusion, and it is implicitly adopted by many other psychologists, be accepted? Judges and juries may not make their decisions in the manner in which Bayes' or other rules indicate that they should. But should those rules, particularly given their power in producing deductively correct inferences, be dismissed? Is it too improper an analogy to point out that many, if not most, people ignore speed limits on roads, but we do not, or at least most of us do not, conclude that those limits should be abolished? Psychology regularly and rightly reveals when our behaviour, including decisions, is often inappropriate against certain standards. For example it has demonstrated that we often reason improperly about likelihood (Tversky and Kahneman, 1974). But we do not accept that that finding of fact should justify our continuing to make those mistakes in risk-taking, especially when the consequences could be dire.

We need to work, dialectically, towards the best methods of making the largest number of best decisions we can manage. Issues of principle are important, not least for establishing the direction of reforms and case for investment. Pragmatic considerations, such as the absence of training in psychology in legal education, must be recognized. But recognition that the implications of an appropriate theory are 'alien' should relate to the enormity of the task and not to its inappropriateness. Resolution, of such disputes, does not have to involve a conflict over who is right and who is wrong. Smaller steps can be taken to work towards a reconciliation of principle and practice. For example judges and jurors could be given decision-aids to aid their inferences about the effects of different pieces of evidence on the overall likelihood of guilt. They could be required to articulate the reasons for their decisions both to assure everyone as to the effort they made and to facilitate appeals by identifying poor reasoning or poor inferential networks.

We need a marriage, or at least a significant relationship, between 'is' and 'ought.' It is submitted that the 'is' corner (to mix metaphors, although boxing may not be too inappropriate), may be represented by 'anchored narratives.' This theory seeks to explain how judges make their decisions on the evidence (Wagenaar, van Koppen and Crombag, 1993; Van Koppen, 1995). It is based upon research into story-telling (e.g. Bennett and Feldman, 1981; Pennington and Hastie, 1986). This indicates that the credibility of evidence, and hence the likelihood of its being accepted by judges and juries, depends upon its qualities as a story, for example the availability of an easy to believe motivation for behaviour. Anchored narratives add to this the importance of the parts of the evidence being 'anchored' within generally accepted knowledge. For example it is generally accepted that someone who recognizes, not just sees, a known neighbour, in good lighting, at close proximity, with time to be sure, is likely to be accurate. The argument for anchored narratives is that it is a good description, as a statement, of how judges and jurors actually decide. However it has also been used as a tood for identifying when and how judges have made mistakes. So it is unfair to characterize it as purely descriptive of current decision-making processes.

In the other corner may be placed the Wigmorean chart method as amended by Anderson, Schum and Twining (2005). Here the emphasis is upon analysing what needs to be proved in order to make the legal decision which provides the context. So an allegation of murder will be broken down into the evidence that must be proved in order to satisfy the legal requirement that it be shown that the defendant intentionally caused the death of the victim without a legal defence. The evidential reasons, for accepting each part of the evidence, are then analysed. The Wigmorean chart method may be regarded as more of a top-down approach because it focuses upon the quality of the inferential links involved in accepting interpretations of and conclusions from the evidence. By contrast the narratives approach focuses on how well the references to generally accepted knowledge are anchored. Twining, who emphasizes that he agrees with much more of anchored narrative theory than he disagrees, notes the problems that arise in accepting generalisations. He identifies them as useful vehicles for bias, and notes that they are:

> ... often indeterminate in respect of frequency, level of abstraction, empirical reliability, defeasibility, identity (which generalization?), and power (whose generalization?). (1999, p. 72.)

The difference, it is submitted, arises from the differential focus on 'is' and 'ought.'

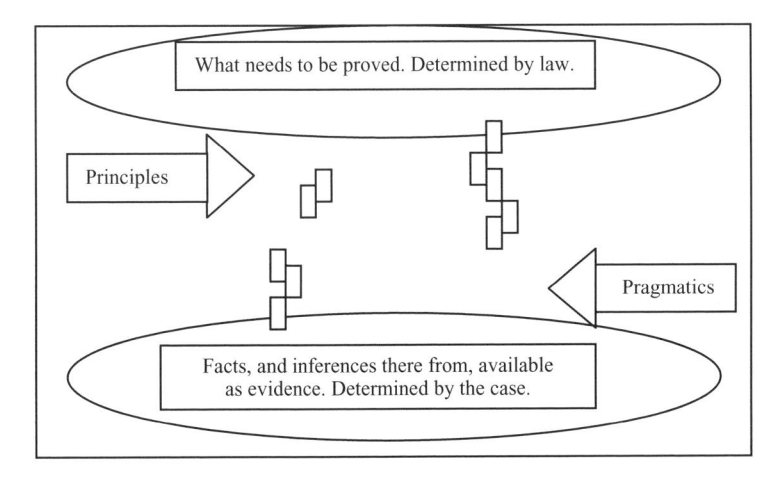

A 'marriage' between the two approaches might be represented by the diagram. The task is to link two 'islands,' one being what has to be proved and the other the evidence as collated for that purpose. The legal requirements might be represented as 'pontoons' connected to each other but affixed to the logical certainty, deduced from the law, of what must be proved. The facts, and inferences from them, might be represented as 'pontoons' mainly connected to each other and anchored to the sea bed by 'cables' of different strength and weight. (Some 'pontoons' may not be harnessed together, although anchored. However they remain part of the potential link because the inference for their existence and reliability is circumstantial.) This approach should favour judgements, about the reliability of the evidence and conclusions drawn from them, being based upon coherence rather than conformity.

The diagram is also offered as a means of emphasising the importance of principles or ideals and pragmatics or reality. It is, for example only too easy to forget that fact finding (investigations) is undertaken, if at all, within an economic context (Carson, 2007). There are insufficient resources to undertake all inquiries theoretically possible, let alone in response to all reports of crime. Simultaneously there are also concerns, which seem to vary with media attention, with miscarriages of justice and 'attacks' upon perceived ideal systems of proof, for example proposals to restrict jury trial (e.g. Kennedy, 2005).

CONCLUSION

Hopefully, this chapter has made a case for psychology paying more attention to fact finding and to the inferential processes of abductive reasoning in particular. Fact finding is logically prior to applying the law and very much a human process. Thus, it is suggested, it should be surprising that it has attracted so relatively little attention from psychologists.

REFERENCES

Abimbola, K. (2001) Abductive reasoning in law: Taxonomy and inference to the best explanation. *Cardozo Law Review*, **22**, 1682–89.

ACPO (Association of Chief Police Officers) (2005) *Practice Advice on Core Investigative Doctrine*, National Centre for Policing Excellence, Cambourne.

Anderson, T. and Twining, W. (1991) *Analysis of Evidence: How to Do Things with Facts*, Weidenfield and Nicolson, London.

Anderson, T., Schum, D. and Twining, W. (2005) *Analysis of Evidence*, 2nd edn, Cambridge University Press, Cambridge.

Bennett, W.L. and Feldman, M.S. (1981) *Reconstructing Reality in the Courtroom*, Tavistock, London.

Bentham, J. (1810) *An Introductory View of the Rationale of the Law of Evidence for use by Non-Lawyers as well as Lawyers* (ed. J. Mill), vi-works 187, Bowring Edition, 1837–43).

Bex, F., Prakken, H., Reed, C. and Walton, D. (2003) Towards a formal account of Reasoning about Evidence: Argument Schemes and Generalisations. *Artificial Intelligence & Law*, **11** (2–3), 125–65.

Burks, A.W. (1946) Peirce's theory of abduction. *Philosophy of Science*, **13** (4), 301–6.

Canter, D. and Youngs, D. (2003) Beyond 'offender profiling:' The need for an investigative psychology, in *Handbook of Psychology in Legal Contexts* (eds D. Carson and R. Bull), Wiley, Chichester.

Carson, D. (2003a) Therapeutic jurisprudence and adversarial injustice: Questioning questions. *Western Criminology Review*, **4** (2), 34–43.

Carson, D. (2003b) Psychology and law: A subdiscipline, an interdisciplinary collaboration or a project? in *Handbook of Psychology in Legal Contexts* (eds D. Carson and R. Bull), Wiley, Chichester, pp. 1–27.
Carson, D. (2007) Investigating investigations: Models of investigation, in *Handbook of Criminal Investigation* (eds T. Newburn, T. Williamson and A. Wright), Willan, Cullompton.
Dennis, I.H. (2002) *The Law of Evidence*, 2nd edn. Sweet & Maxwell, London.
Fisher, G. (2002) *Evidence*, Foundation Press.
Fisher, R.P. and Geiselman, R.E. (1992) *Memory-Enhancing Techniques for Investigative Interviewing*, Charles C. Thompson, Springfield.
Grisso, T. and Appelbaum, P.S. (1998) *Assessing Competence to Consent to Treatment: A Guide for Physicians and Other Health Professionals*, Oxford University Press, New York.
Gudjonsson, G. (2003) *The Psychology of Interrogations and Confessions*, Wiley, Chichester.
Holmberg, U. (2004) Crime victims' experiences of police interviews and their inclination to provide or omit information. *International Journal of Police Science and Management*, **6** (3), 155–70.
Home Office (1992) *Memorandum of Good Practice for Video Recorded Interviews with Child Witnesses for Criminal Proceedings*, HMSO, London.
Jackson, J.D. (1988) Two methods of proof in criminal procedure. *Modern Law Review*, **51** (5), 549–68.
Jackson, J.D. (1996) Analysing the new evidence scholarship: Towards a new conception of the law of evidence. *Oxford Journal of Legal Studies*, **16** (2), 309–28.
Jackson, J.D. (2004) The effect of legal culture and proof in decisions to prosecute. *Law, Probability and Risk*, **3**, 109–31.
Kassin, S. (1998) *Psychology*, Prentice-Hall, Upper Saddle River (NJ).
Kennedy, H. (2005) *Just Law: The Changing Face of Justice – and Why it Matters to Us All*, Vintage, London.
Lempert, R. (1986) The new evidence scholarship: analyzing the process of proof. *Boston University Law Review*, **66**, 439–77.
Maguire, M. (2003) Criminal investigation and crime control, in *Handbook of Policing*, (ed. T. Newburn), Willan, Cullompton, pp. 363–93.
Maguire, M. and Norris, C. (1992) The Conduct and Supervision of Criminal Investigations. *(Royal Commission on Criminal Justice, Research Study No. 5)*. HMSO, London.
Malsch, M. and Nijboer, J.F. (eds) (1999) *Complex Cases. Perspectives on the Netherlands Criminal Justice System*, Thela Thesis, Amsterdam.
McConville, M., Sanders, A. and Leng, R. (1991) *The Case for the Prosecution*, Routledge, London.
Meehl, P.E. (1989) Law and the fireside inductions (with Postscript): Some reflections of a clinical psychologist. *Behavioral Sciences and the Law*, **7**, 521–50.
Murphy, P.W. (2001) Teaching evidence, proof, and facts: Providing a background in factual analysis and case evaluation. *Journal of Legal Education*, **51** (4), 568–98.
Murphy, P. (2003) *Evidence, Proof, and Facts: A Book of Sources*, Oxford University Press, Oxford.
Pennington, N. and Hastie, R. (1986) Evidence evaluation in complex decision making. *Journal of Personality and Social Psychology*, **51**, 242–58.
Pennington, N. and Hastie, R. (1992) Explaining the evidence: Tests of the story model for juror decision making. *Journal of Personality and Social Psychology*, **62** (2), 189–206.
Pollock, J.L. (1987) Defeasible reasoning. *Cognitive Science*, **11**, 481–518.
Pollock, J.L. (2001) Evaluative cognition. *Nous*, **35**, 325–64.
Prakken, H. (2004) Analysing reasoning about evidence with formal models of argumentation. *Law, Probability and Risk*, **3**, 33–50.
Roberts, P. and Zuckerman, A. (2004). *Criminal Evidence*, Oxford University Press, Oxford.
Robertson, B. and Vignaux, G.A. (1993) Taking fact analysis seriously. *Michigan Law Review*, **91**, 1442–64.
Saks, M.J. and Thomson, W.C. (2003) Assessing evidence: Proving facts, in *Handbook of Psychology in Legal Contexts* (eds D. Carson and R. Bull), Wiley, Chichester.
Schum, D.A. (1994) *Evidential Foundations of Probabilistic Reasoning*, Wiley, New York.
Schum, D.A. (2001) Species of abductive reasoning in fact investigation in law. *Cardozo Law Review*, **22**, 1644–81.

Shepherd, E. and Milne, R. (1999) Full and faithful: ensuring quality practice and integrity of outcome in witness interviews, in *Analysing Witness Testimony: A Guide for Legal Practitioners and Other Professionals* (eds A. Heaton-Armstrong, E. Shepherd and D. Wolchover), Blackstone Press, London.

Steller, M. (1989) Recent Developments in statement analysis, in *Credibility Assessment* (ed. J.C. Yuille), Kluwer, Deventer, The Netherlands, pp. 135–54.

Steller, M. and Köhnken, G. (1989) Criteria-based content analysis, in *Psychological Methods in Criminal Investigation and Evidence* (ed. D.C. Rankin), Springer-Verlag, New York, pp. 217–45.

Tapper, C. (2004) *Cross and Tapper on Evidence*, 10th edn, Oxford University Press, Oxford.

Thayer, J.B. (1898) *A Preliminary Treatise on Evidence at the Common Law*, Little, Brown, Boston.

Tillers, P. and Schum, D. (1991) A theory of preliminary fact investigation. *University of California Davis Law Review*, 1329.

Tversky, A. and Kahneman, D. (1974) Judgment under uncertainty: Heuristics and biases. *Science*, **185**, 1124–30.

Twining, W. (1994) The rationalist tradition of evidence scholarship, in *Rethinking Evidence: Exploratory Essays* (ed. W. Twining), Northwestern University Press, Evanston (IL).

Twining, W. (1999) Necessary but dangerous: Generalizations and narrative in argumentation about 'facts' in criminal process, in (eds M. Malsch and J.F. Nijboer), *Complex Cases: Perspectives on the Netherlands Criminal Justice System*, Thela Thesis, Amsterdam, pp. 69–98.

Twining, W. (2003) Evidence as a multidisciplinary subject. *Law Probability and Risk*, **2**, 91–107.

Van Koppen, P.J. (1995) Judges' decision-making, in (eds D. Carson and R. Bull) *Handbook of Psychology in Legal Contexts*, Wiley, Chichester, pp 581–610.

Vrij, A. (2000) *Detecting Lies and Deceit: The Psychology of Lying and the Implications for Professional Practice*, Wiley, Chichester.

Vrij, A. (2003) The assessment and detection of deceit, in *Handbook of Psychology in Legal Contexts* (eds D. Carson and R. Bull), Wiley, Chichester.

Wagenaar, W.A., van Koppen, P.J. and Crombag, H. (1993) *Anchored Narratives. The Psychology of Criminal Evidence*, Harvester Wheatsheaf, New York.

Wells, G.L., Small, M., Malpass, R.S. et al. (1998) Eyewitness identification procedures: Recommendations for lineups and photospreads. *Law and Human Behavior*, **22** (6), 1–39.

Wigmore, J.H. (1904–5) *A Treatise on the System of Evidence in Trials at Common Law*, Boston.

Wigmore, J.H. (1913) *The Principles of Judicial Proof: As Given by Logic, Psychology and General Experience, and Illustrated in Judicial Trials*, F.B. Rothman, Littleton (CO).

Wynne, B. (1989) Establishing the rules of laws: Constructing expert authority, in *Expert Evidence: Interpreting Science in the Law* (eds R. Smith and B. Wynne), Routledge, London.

A (FC) and others (FC) (Appellants) v. Secretary of State for the Home Department (Respondent) (2004), [2005] UKHL 71.

CHAPTER 8

Criminal Responsibility

Susan Dennison
Griffith University

INTRODUCTION

Psychology and law are at a crossroads regarding the underlying premise of criminal responsibility. The law typically regards individuals as having complete ability to control and affect their futures, thus having the free will to choose among an endless array of life options. In contrast, most psychologists would argue that behaviour is determined by natural laws. That is, whilst individuals do have the capacity to plan behaviour and make choices, such choices and the way they are expressed are based on both the biological make-up of the individual and their interaction with the environment. These differing assumptions about human behaviour exemplify the free will versus determinism debate that polarizes psychology and law. Nevertheless, it is the law's assumption of free will that characterizes the legal requirements for criminal responsibility. In this chapter, I will identify where psychological and other scientific research poses particular challenges to the assumption of free will and assignment of criminal responsibility. I will argue that the law is heavily influenced by moral beliefs about responsibility and contrast this with the utilitarian approach to offending, that is characteristic of psychology. However, the goals underpinning the moral emphasis in the law and the utilitarian approach within psychology are not dissimilar. Suggestions will be made for revising the principles of criminal responsibility by taking a functional approach to community safety. Such an approach would account for what we know about voluntary behaviour, control and intentions, in a way that still meets the aims and responsibilities of the legal system.

Overview

This chapter will identify challenges to our current method of assessing criminal responsibility that arise out of psychological research. It will also address the question of whether the legal system could benefit by using knowledge from psychological research to revise the application of, or the principles of, criminal responsibility. For example, how would an acceptance of determinism change our understanding of *mens rea*, its associated assumptions (i.e. voluntariness), and its application in the criminal law setting? In order to examine whether

---

Applying Psychology to Criminal Justice. Edited by David Carson, Rebecca Milne, Francis Pakes, Karen Shalev and Andrea Shawyer. © 2007 John Wiley & Sons, Ltd

psychology can assist our understanding and assessment of criminal responsibility, this chapter will focus primarily on the concepts of *mens rea*, causation and voluntary behaviour.

The following sections take a critical look at the psychological research pertaining to criminal responsibility. Two specific challenges to the concept of criminal responsibility will be examined. These challenges are: (1) understandings of intention and foresight, which addresses questions about common-sense understanding of legal concepts and the expansion of relevant terms as a way of holding individuals responsible for their actions; and (2) the assumption of free will, with a focus on cognitive neuroscience, consciousness and automatism, and behavioural genetics. Suggestions will then be provided for reconciling the disciplines by taking a utilitarian approach to criminal responsibility. This approach would involve recognizing relevant psychological research and thereby restricting the scope of criminal responsibility, whilst at the same time providing an additional mechanism to address community safety needs. The potential consequences and limitations of such revisions are discussed.

Definitions of Criminal Responsibility

Four elements generally need to be satisfied for a person to be held criminally responsible for their actions (Carson and Felthous, 2003). The first is *actus reus*, which requires that the defendant committed the illegal act. The second requirement is that the defendant committed the act with the requisite intent. That is the 'state of mind' or *mens rea* of the defendant was such that they intended to bring about particular consequences (except for strict liability offences). Third, the actions of the defendant must have caused the particular proscribed consequences. Finally, the defendant must not have an acceptable legal defence for their behaviour, such as insanity, self-defence or intoxication in some jurisdictions (Carson and Felthous, 2003).

Whilst it might seem reasonably straightforward to establish that the defendant committed the proscribed act, unless the identity of the perpetrator is under question, establishing *actus reus* can still be problematic. This is because the element also requires that the person engaged in the act voluntarily (McSherry, 2003). The issue of free will aside, a number of psychological deficits or environmental conditions call into question the capacity of an individual to act voluntarily. These will be discussed later in the chapter.

The *mens rea* requirement also presents a number of challenges. In the absence of the defendant truthfully disclosing what their intentions were and this being able to be verified, the intentions of the defendant must be deduced from what they said and did prior to, during, and after committing the proscribed act (McCall Smith, 2004). Therefore, establishing the intent to affect an outcome can often be difficult. However, the 'state of mind' of the defendant can also be interpreted more broadly to hold a person criminally responsible for their behaviour. Whether they were negligent or reckless in their actions, failing to foresee the dire consequences that a reasonable person could anticipate in the same situation, may be enough to establish the requisite *mens rea* in some jurisdictions (McSherry, 2003). It will be argued that these lesser forms of intent have been developed to meet a societal need to hold someone responsible when a wrong is committed (McCall Smith, 2004). They are driven by moral values rather than a practical understanding of human behaviour. The problem with the constructs used to establish *mens rea*, such as intent, negligence, recklessness and foresight, is that they are ill-defined legal concepts that may be used and understood differently in the social environment where the behaviour took place (Malle and Nelson, 2003).

A similar problem in interpretation may also arise with the element of causation of consequences. The extent that a person is held to be solely and directly accountable for bringing about certain proscribed consequences may be more a result of a judge or jury believing that the individual *should* be held morally responsible for the outcome rather than because their behaviour directly caused harm. Therefore, the term 'causation' as it is constructed within a legal setting may differ markedly from causation as it is known within science, including the behavioural sciences (McEwan, 2003).

Defences to criminal responsibility usually centre on some defect of reasoning that rendered the defendant incapable of forming the requisite intent (McSherry, 2003). For example, the presence of a mental disorder can be used to invoke the insanity defence or establish diminished responsibility (Morse, 2000). Similarly, becoming intoxicated against one's will may be used as a defence in some jurisdictions to demonstrate lack of intent or inability to foresee the potential consequences of one's actions. Such defences will not be a focus here. However, one potential defence to criminal responsibility that has arisen over the past decade, and which squarely challenges the law's assumption of free will, is a so-called 'genetic defence'. This research will be discussed later in the chapter.

There is a potential for psychological research, and that of related disciplines like neuroscience and behavioural genetics, to find its way into the legal system in the near future. The questions that such research raises for concepts such as intentions, voluntary behaviour and moral responsibility justify a reanalysis of the assumptions made by the legal system. The research also sends a challenge to psychologists to offer a new way of assessing and understanding criminal responsibility. Any reform to the assignment of criminal responsibility must address three issues. First, it must meet the demand by the community to hold individuals to a particular standard of behaviour. Second, it needs to use tangible and broadly understood concepts to define criminal responsibility. Third, it must have the capacity to respond to emerging research in the behavioural and related sciences.

SPECIFIC CHALLENGES TO DEFINING CRIMINAL RESPONSIBILITY

Understanding Intentions and Foresight

Mens rea refers to whether the accused had a 'guilty mind' at the time of committing the offence (McCall Smith, 2004). Most criminal offences require that that the requisite *mens rea* be proved in order for the accused to be held criminally responsible, except where the offence is defined as 'strict' or 'absolute' liability (Morse, 2000). An example of laws applying strict liability are traffic offences, where the acts of violating speed restrictions, driving through a red light or driving with a blood-alcohol level in excess of the law are sufficient to hold a person criminally responsible, regardless of their intentions. However, for the majority of criminal offences the defendant must satisfy the *mens rea* requirement, which is usually defined in relation to whether the defendant 'intended' to bring about particular consequences (Morse, 2000). In the case of murder, the requisite intent would be that the accused intended to cause the death of the victim.

The rationale for requiring that a person intended to act in a particular way in order to hold them criminally responsible is a moral one (McCall Smith, 2004; McEwan, 2003). It stems from the 'fault principle' that 'only those agents who are sufficiently at fault (culpable) for committing the requisite harms deserve to be blamed and punished' (Morse, 2000, p. 351). Therefore, if a person intended to kill another and acted in such a way that they brought about this result they are culpable for the death. However, culpability is seen more broadly than the relatively narrow requirement of intent. Thus, the concept of 'knowing' is also important in assessing culpability and assigning punishment. If a person acted in such a way, knowing that their behaviour was likely to bring about harm to another (although not necessarily intending it to do so), then they can also be seen as at fault. The concept of knowing implies the conscious awareness of the individual in acting in a particular way and with anticipation of potential consequences (Barrat and Felthous, 2003; Morse 2000). A person acting in this way can be seen to be 'reckless' or 'negligent' in their actions. To the extent that a person was reckless or negligent is usually determined by the reasonable person test, by considering what a reasonable person could have foreseen as a consequence of their behaviour in a similar situation (McCall Smith, 2004). Therefore, the mental element of criminal responsibility can be satisfied by the presence of a range of concepts including intent, recklessness, negligence and 'foreseeability'.

The extensions to the concept of *mens rea* appear to be moral in their origin. Society shares certain moral values about standards of behaviour and these are reflected in our criminal laws. If a person drives recklessly on the road, causing an accident and killing a passenger or the occupant of another vehicle, they are held to be morally responsible for that death even though did not intend it. The fact that they had such little regard for other road users, or should have foreseen that an accident might arise that could potentially cause serious harm or death, is sufficient to hold a person blameworthy for the outcome. In contrast, if a pedestrian unexpectedly ran across a road and is hit and killed by an oncoming car, that driver can be seen as accidentally causing the death and would not be culpable since they neither intended the consequences, were reckless or negligent in their actions, or could foresee the event and its outcome. They were not morally responsible for the accident.

Whilst there is general agreement on the circumstances under which a person should be held culpable or blameworthy for their actions, it has been argued that the mental elements of intent, recklessness, negligence and foreseeability are ill-defined and often poorly understood (Malle and Nelson, 2003). The concepts have become muddled and extended to include negligent or reckless behaviour as a way of holding individuals responsible for actions or outcomes they did not intend. The challenge to psychologists is whether research in the behavioural sciences can help to illuminate or reshape these concepts such that the gaps between mental state elements of criminal responsibility and the blameworthiness of an individual can be identified and reconciled.

Common-sense Understanding of Intention

The potential problem with using a myriad of ways to fulfill a requirement of intention is that intention is a large part of assigning criminal responsibility and such responsibility results in punishment. Therefore, it is possible that an individual may be punished as if they intended to bring about a particular consequence, even though they did not really intend the result (Carson and Felthous, 2003). For example, the person may have acted recklessly and without forethought, rather than with specific intent. The law's willingness and ability to make inferences about the mental states of intention and foreseeability has been questioned on the basis of the validity and precision of these legal constructs (Malle and Nelson, 2003). Rather, it is argued that an empirically-based strategy using common-sense definitions of mens rea would better support jury decision making and perceptions of justice (Malle and Nelson, 2003).

Malle and Knobe (1997) examined the definition of acting intentionally in a study on 159 undergraduate students. They reported that the definitions provided reflected four separate components of intentionality. These were '(i) a desire for an outcome; (ii) beliefs about an action that leads to an outcome; (iii) an intention to perform the action; and (iv) awareness of fulfilling the intention whilst performing the act' (Malle and Nelson, 2003, p. 567). The authors subsequently added a fifth component of 'skill' to the model, based on additional research that revealed the relevance of skill information to participant's judgements of intentionality (Malle and Knobe, 1997; Malle and Nelson, 2003). Their model suggests that both desire and belief are necessary in the identification of intention (which relates to trying or planning to achieve an outcome). Intention, awareness and skill are then essential for making judgements of intentionality, that is that a person performed an act intentionally (Malle and Nelson, 2003).

The model proposed by Malle and Knobe (1997) raises particular questions about legal definitions of intention and the resulting blame attributed to an actor. Malle and Nelson (2003) argue that intention and intentionality are often treated the same under the law, whereas the constructs are conceptually different. A person may intend to act in a particular way but may in fact act differently and without the intentionality to bring about the actual outcome. To what extent can and should the law differentiate these constructs? Malle and Nelson (2003) suggest that where a person formed an intention to perform an illegal act, but accidentally performed a separate illegal act, this should result in two separate charges. By adding sentences together, the authors argue that common-sense intuitions of human behaviour would be upheld whilst also providing for appropriate sentencing for offences (Malle and Nelson, 2003).

The problem with the concept of separating charges where intentions, actions and outcomes differ is that a person cannot (and should not) be charged for forming an intention. The problem of proving intention without behaviour is likely to be even more difficult than inferring intentions from behaviour. It also contradicts the notion that individuals should not be punished for their thoughts alone (Denno, 2003). Therefore, the person would have to act with intent, rather than just form an intention without any resulting action. Presumably the authors mean that the person acted with a particular intent (such as to moderately injure an individual), but accidentally brought about a different outcome (i.e. killed the individual). Nevertheless, the point of the authors is that lay persons have ordinary meanings for intentions and intentionality but these meanings are often ignored by the use of technical and ill-defined legal concepts. These legal terms may lead to misunderstandings and confusion not only in relation to distinctions between the terms, but also the overlap between intentions and culpability (Malle and Nelson, 2003). The authors suggest the adoption of ordinary meanings and terms into the law and a separation of mental state concepts from culpability and punishment (Malle and Nelson, 2003).

Common-sense Understandings of Causation

Whilst causation might seem like a straightforward concept to define (i.e. did the actions of the accused cause the harm to the victim?), in reality the legal definition of causation bears little resemblance to scientific explanations of causation (McEwan, 2003). In a legal setting there is a strong overlap in the way that both intentions and causation are determined. That is, the question of causation is largely dependent on whether the accused could have reasonably foreseen the consequences of their actions (McEwan, 2003). If the consequences were foreseeable, then a defendant is said to have caused that outcome, often regardless of whether there were any intervening events that might have broken the chain of causation (such as in a civil case of negligence) (McEwan, 2003). For example, imagine a person is driving along a highway and notices a large billboard displaying a catchy slogan and something exotic. They may momentarily look away from the road to glance at the billboard and by the time they look back the traffic has stopped and there is insufficient time to break. The driver crashes into the car in front. Did the driver cause the crash? In determining an answer to this question it might be useful to consider whether the accident would have occurred if the billboard contained an advertisement for washing detergent, or if the billboard had not been placed so close to a set of traffic lights. Did the billboard cause the crash instead? In this example, the driver would no doubt be held responsible for the accident, merely for the reason that it is a reasonably foreseeable consequence that you might have an accident if you take your eyes off the road, even for a second or two. That, however, is a slightly different from saying that the driver caused the accident.

It is clear that causation is interpreted broadly in a legal setting and more often reflects a mechanism to hold someone responsible for an outcome when they are seen to be morally blameworthy (McEwan, 2003). The above example also illustrates the presumptions of free will and voluntariness in the concept of causation. Assigning responsibility to the driver assumes that the driver freely chose to look at the billboard instead of concentrating on the road, rather than that the billboard was designed to be eye-catching. In this case, the driver neither intended the accident, drove recklessly so as to endanger the lives of other road users (since this would assume that the driver anticipated the potential consequences but had little regard for them), or was likely to have foreseen the likelihood of the accident (since this would assume that the driver was consciously aware of what they were doing and made a calculated decision as to whether to look at the billboard or not). It is also debatable whether the driver was the sole cause of the accident. Yet when an accident occurs and property is damaged or a person is harmed, there is a need to assign blame to an individual. In both this example and the previous example of the driver hitting a pedestrian who ran across the road, the collisions could both be seen as 'accidents', neither intended nor foreseen. Yet in one situation the pedestrian would be responsible for the accident but no one would be culpable, whilst in the other the placement of the billboard might be seen to be partly the cause, but the driver would be both blamed and held responsible for the accident. This raises the question as to whether mixing the concepts of causation and blame, or any of the mental states and blame, is the best method of determining criminal responsibility. That is, should the issue of who is responsible and who is to blame be determined separately? This question will be addressed later in the chapter.

Psychopathy and Moral Knowing

Challenges to concepts of criminal responsibility are not only made in relation to the definitions of legal constructs, but are also directed to the central role of moral knowing and moral responsibility in justifying the breadth of criminal responsibility. A recent case in point can be found in debates as to whether psychopathy mitigates criminal responsibility (e.g. Ciocchetti, 2003a; Fine and Kennett, 2004; McCall Smith, 2004). As better knowledge of the psychological features of psychopathy emerges, it brings with it questions about the moral understanding of individuals diagnosed with psychopathy. In particular, it challenges whether criminal responsibility should be assigned in the absence of an understanding as to why behaviour was morally wrong (Ciocchetti, 2003a; Fine and Kennett, 2004).

In their recent paper, Fine and Kennett (2004) argue that individuals with a psychopathy diagnosis who commit an offence cannot legitimately be held criminally responsible for that act since they lack the moral capacity to understand that the act was wrong. They utilize McSherry's (1997) interpretation of mental impairment and criminal responsibility, derived from the draft Australian *Criminal Code Act 1995 (Cth)* Section 7.3(1), to posit that psychopathy falls under the defence of mental impairment. McSherry (1997) suggested that under common law 'wrong' means something more than knowing that an act is contrary to law. That is, it requires the capacity to distinguish right from wrong in a moral sense. According to Fine and Kennett (2004), it is precisely this moral capacity to know right from wrong, that is lacking in psychopathic offenders, due to incomplete moral development.

Research on the moral development of psychopathic offenders aside, the implications of a lack of moral knowing on the part of the offender may mean that they would not fulfill requirements of criminal responsibility. These somewhat radical views would therefore lead to the untenable outcome that a psychopathic offender could escape accountability and punishment for their crime. Meanwhile, Ciocchetti (2003a) argues that an inability in individuals with psychopathy to interpret their actions as part of relationships renders punishment inappropriate. He suggests that psychopathic offenders have diminished responsibility and should not be punished because they do not understand the wrongfulness of their actions (Ciocchetti, 2003a). Rather, he argues that they could be detained to receive treatment and to prevent further harm to the community (Ciocchetti, 2003b; see Shuman, 2003, for a legal critique of this paper). This approach would essentially have the same effect as sentencing due to culpability, but may avoid the need to extend principles of criminal responsibility.

In addressing the problem of detention and the link between moral knowing and punishment, Fine and Kennett (2004) adopt an approach put forward by Ellis (2003) that argues that force against another is only justified when it is in self-defence. This force includes punishment as deterrence and other legislation aimed to protect the community. Therefore, when an offender might otherwise be judged as blameless, the right to self-defence can be used by the community to justify the punishment or containment of the offender to prevent future offending (Fine and Kennett, 2004). The authors thereby argue that the misapplication of criminal responsibility to psychopathic offenders can be avoided without compromising the safety of the community or societal desires to see an offender punished for a serious crime (Fine and Kennett, 2004). However, it must be noted that detention on the grounds of the likelihood of future offending contains its own problems, most notably in regards to the accuracy of risk prediction and constraints on civil liberties.

Assumption of Free Will

At the cornerstone of criminal responsibility is the assumption of free will. This assumption presupposes that individuals are able to form intentions and be held responsible for their behaviour because they are able to freely choose their actions (Alper, 1998; Halwani and Krupp, 2004). Whilst notions of free will appear to be in direct contrast with determinism, the incompatibility of these two constructs is debatable (Brock and Buchanan, 1999). Alper 1998, p. 1601) suggests that 'the legal system implicitly assumes that determinism is true. However, it operates "as if" human beings enjoy free will and are responsible for their actions'. The *actus reus* element of criminal responsibility not only requires that the accused person committed the criminal act, but that they did so voluntarily (McCall Smith, 2004). A person is acquitted if the prosecution cannot satisfy this legal burden (McSherry, 2003, 2004). In recent years, the concept of free will and voluntary action has been directly challenged by research in psychology, the neurosciences and behavioural genetics. Whilst still controversial, these scientific advances directly challenge the law's capacity to continue to administer the law 'as if' free will exists. The purpose of this section is not to conclude whether or not free will exists, but rather to consider the implications of the research for determining criminal responsibility.

Cognitive Neuroscience – Implications for Voluntary Behaviour

Prior to the seminal research of Kornhuber and Deecke (1965, cited in Libet, 1999), it was assumed that brain electrical activity coincided with the voluntary actions of an individual. However, Kornhuber and Deecke's (1965) discovered that voluntary movements are preceded by a slow negative cortical potential that occurs half a second or more before movement. This electrical activity has become known as the 'readiness potential'. The implication stemming from this research was that a readiness for action may occur without an individual's consciousness or awareness (Gomes, 1999). Libet, Gleason, Wright and Pearl (1983a, cited in Libet, 1999) investigated this proposition further and, after a series of experiments, concluded that participants became aware of an intention to act after the readiness potential began, but before the actual movement. Whilst the timings of the intention to act and the awareness of the intention in Libet's research have been critiqued (e.g. Gomes, 1998), there is some agreement that voluntary acts are initiated without an awareness of this initiation (Gomes, 1999).

On the basis of his findings, Libet (1999) suggested that the initiation of volitional processes occurs unconsciously. However, because of the window of opportunity that exists between awareness of an intention to act and the act itself (approximately 200 milliseconds), he argued that an individual could still control whether or not to veto the act. Therefore he suggested that an individual still has control over whether to perform the act, even if they did not initiate the intention to act of their own free will (Libet, 1999). He went further to conclude, 'Since it is the performance of an act that can be consciously controlled, it should be legitimate to hold individuals guilty of and responsible for their acts' (Libet, 1999, p. 55). Although, one might assume that the ability to veto an act is similarly determined.

The implication from Libet's (1999) conclusion is that everyone has the ability to veto their actions in the short time in which they become conscious of their intention to act.

It is unclear how statements such as these fit alongside neuropsychological research that has examined the relationship between executive functions and antisocial or offending behaviour. Executive functions include anticipation and planning of behaviour, initiation of sequences of motor behaviour, self-monitoring and inhibition of inappropriate or impulsive behaviour (Kolb and Wishaw, 1985). In an examination of the executive functions of self-reported delinquents, Moffitt and Henry (1989) found that deficits in the executive functions of the adolescents were related to the development of delinquent behaviour. The authors hypothesized that deficits in self-control may increase the likelihood of a young person engaging in impulsive aggressive behaviour in social situations. Therefore, if motor actions are initiated unconsciously in the first instance and if it is possible for individuals to veto those actions before they occur, it is plausible that individuals with executive deficits will have greater difficulty overriding an action once it has been cortically initiated (see also Barrat and Felthous, 2003, for a related discussion impulsivity). Similarly, in the case of automatism, as described in the next section, the awareness of an intention to act may never occur, thus removing the option to veto the action. The implications of this research for the determination of criminal responsibility will be discussed later in this chapter.

Consciousness, Automatism and Dissociation

Whilst the voluntary state of the accused can be challenged when the accused has a mental disorder, their inability to act rationally and voluntarily can also be used to raise the insanity defence or to demonstrate that the accused did not possess the requisite *mens rea* (Denno, 2003; McSherry, 2003). Therefore involuntary or unconscious behaviours can feasibly be used to argue for an acquittal on the basis of a failure to prove *actus reus* or *mens rea*, or instead used as the basis for an insanity defence (McCall Smith, 2004). McSherry (2003) has argued that these options for addressing involuntary conduct create unnecessary complexity in the law.

The concept of voluntary conduct is not legally defined, although impaired consciousness is one form that has developed in case law. This category is also referred to as *automatism* and includes a range of impairments, including sleep disorders, drug induced states, head injuries, epilepsy, neurological disorders and dissociation (McSherry, 2003, 2004; Bronitt and McSherry, 2001). Automatism has been further divided into 'sane' (nonmental disorder) automatism and 'insane' (mental disorder) automatism depending on whether the impairment arises from a recognised mental disorder (*R v Stone* (1999); Glancy, Bradford and Fedak, 2002; McSherry, 2003). However, there is some confusion regarding this distinction, with sleepwalking alternatively being identified as 'sane' automatism in Canada (*R v Parks*) but as 'insane' automatism in England (*R v Burgess* (1991)). Dissociation can also fall under 'sane' automatism, despite dissociation being recognized in the fourth edition of the Diagnostic and Statistical Manual for Mental Disorders (DSM-IV-TR; American Psychiatric Association, 2000). Furthermore, McLeod, Byrne and Aitken (2004) note that a diagnosis of dissociation is not necessarily indicative of automatism or lack of responsibility. Generally speaking, mental disorder automatism should be produced by a disease of the mind, whilst nonmental disorder includes other automatic states arising from external causes (Glancy, Bradford and Fedak, 2002).

The Canadian case of *R v Parks* (1992) is frequently used as an example of automatism. After having fallen asleep on the couch in the living room in the late evening, Mr Parks partially dressed and drove 23 kilometres to his parents-in-law's house. He entered the house using his key, taking with him a tyre iron, hatchet, two knives and other tools from his car. On going inside he supposedly killed his mother-in-law and caused serious injuries to his father-in-law. He then went to the local police station and turned himself in, confessing to having killed two people. During the trial it was revealed that Mr Parks had been sleepwalking at the time of the offence and indeed had a history of sleepwalking (Glancy, Bradford and Fedak, 2002). Sleepwalking was described to the court as a disorder of sleep, rather than a neurological, psychiatric or other form of mental disorder. On the basis of this information the jury rendered a finding of noninsane automatism (legally referred to as 'non-not criminally responsible due to mental disorder [non-NCR-MD] automatism') and Mr Parks was subsequently acquitted (Glancy, Bradford and Fedak, 2002).

The use of evidence of mental disease to determine whether an accused person acted voluntarily has been criticized in the Australian case of *Hawkins* v *The Queen* (1994). In this case, the High Court indicated such evidence should be excluded from the issue of voluntary conduct, but that it could be used to address the fault element of intent when the insanity defence is not applicable (McSherry, 2003). However, criticisms have also been made regarding the use of mental disorder to negate the requisite intention. This criticism is based on concerns that a complete acquittal would be available to the accused, as it would if the conduct element of voluntariness could not be established. An acquittal would return the accused to the community, when some form of detention for psychiatric care might be more appropriate to reduce the likelihood of further dangerous behaviour (McSherry, 2003). Similar concerns were raised following the acquittal of Mr Parks (*R* v *Parks*; see also McCall Smith, 2004). These dilemmas highlight the distinction between the need to hold someone morally responsible for serious harm in order to protect society versus a utilitarian focus on community safety that operates outside of moral beliefs.

In order to avoid the potential circumstances of a person with a mental disorder being acquitted on the basis of not meeting the voluntary or intentional conduct elements, McSherry (2003) suggests that a separate defence of mental disorder should be created. Such a defence would include a range of mental disorders and should be used as the only means of addressing involuntary conduct arising from a disorder affecting consciousness (McSherry, 2003). The purpose of this argument is to provide a mechanism for recognizing that a person is not criminally responsible, whilst at the same time providing an array of dispositional options to maximize the safety of the defendant and the community (McSherry, 2003).

In proposing a new defence, McSherry (2003, 2004) argues that the problem of existing processes in dealing with issues of consciousness may stem from the legal dichotomies used to describe behaviour as either intentional or unintentional, or voluntary or involuntary (see also Denno, 2002; Denno 2003; McCall Smith, 2004). In contrast, psychologists and neuroscientists would more likely see control over behaviour as existing on a continuum (Denno, 2002; McSherry, 2003, 2004). For this reason, Denno (2003) proposes a revision of the voluntary act requirement, so that it allows for semivoluntary acts as well as voluntary and involuntary acts. She suggests that by using this three-tiered approach, behaviour such as that of Mr Parks could be classified as semivoluntary and be informed by psychological and medical research. This classification would preclude a complete acquittal but also avoid placing the individual in a forensic mental health institution (Denno, 2003). However, Denno (2003) does not go so far as to suggest what procedures should be in place for 'semivoluntary' findings.

McSherry (2003) proposes a broad definition for mental disorder that could include recognized mental disorders, as well as intellectual disability and impaired states of consciousness. These could include dissociative states, somnambulism and epilepsy, among others. Such a defence would recognize the varying levels of consciousness and control that the defendant possessed. The dispositional stage of the court proceedings could then be used to determine whether the defendant required treatment or whether it is safe for the individual to be discharged into the community (McSherry, 2003). A similar process is used in Ontario, Canada, if a verdict of automatism is reached (Glancy, Bradford and Fedak, 2002). McSherry (2004) suggests that the real issue is whether individuals that suffer fleeting mental states, such as that recognized in forms of automatism, should be held criminally responsible for their acts. Where some goal-directed behaviour exists, even if it is not completely willed, total acquittal should not be possible for such individuals. Rather, for public policy reasons, a defence of mental disorder should be used (McSherry, 2004).

Genetics and Human Behaviour

Although to date there are no successful attempts of the use of a genetic defence in court, recent scientific evidence based on genetic research provides the most convincing argument yet to challenge the existence of free will and diminish or eliminate criminal responsibility. A defence based on the XYY syndrome has previously been unsuccessful in the USA (Appelbaum, 2005; Halwani and Krupp, 2004). This defence was based on the presence of an extra Y chromosome in some men which, it was argued, made them more aggressive (Halwani and Krupp, 2004). More commonly however, a history of criminality or violence in the family is used in an attempt to mitigate a crime and obtain a reduced sentence (Halwani and Krupp, 2004). The recent discovery of a relationship between the enzyme monoamine oxidase A (MAOA) and antisocial behaviour has once again challenged the scope of criminal responsibility.

The potential role of MAOA in aggressive or antisocial behaviour was first reported in a Dutch study whereby several male relatives who had borderline mental retardation and displayed impulsive aggression were found to have an absence of the MAOA enzyme (Brunner *et al.*, 1993). MAO regulates the concentration of neurotransmitters, whereby low MAO activity leads to high levels of dopamine and norepinephrine (Halwani and Krupp, 2004). High levels of these neurotransmitters have been linked to increased aggression and low self-control (Halwani and Krupp, 2004). The Dutch study caused little stir in the legal community considering that an absence of MAOA is considered to be rare (Appelbaum, 2005). However, a clearer relationship between MAOA and offending emerged in a longitudinal study of a birth cohort in Dunedin, New Zealand and also indicated that low MAOA, rather than a complete absence of MAOA activity, might exert its effects through an interaction with other developmental risk factors (Caspi *et al.*, 2002).

Using a subsample of males from the Dunedin study, Caspi *et al.* (2002) examined the interactions between the strength of MAOA expression in individuals and their environment. In particular, they compared children who had either high or low MAOA activity and tested the effects of child maltreatment that occurred between the ages 3–11 and subsequent antisocial behaviour. The authors found significant increases in each of the four measures of antisocial behaviour (official and unofficial reports) for children who had low MAOA activity and a history of severe child maltreatment. In contrast, children with the same histories of child maltreatment but who had high MAOA activity did not exhibit increased levels of antisocial behaviour (Caspi et al., 2002). Somewhat disturbingly, the study found that 85 % of males with both a history of child maltreatment and low MAOA exhibited some form of antisocial behaviour in later adolescence or adulthood (Caspi et al., 2002).

Although extensive research is required to replicate and examine these findings further, the study demonstrated an increased likelihood for individuals to engage in antisocial behaviour, including violent crime, depending on interactions between their genetic composition and environmental risk factors. Given that the majority of males with the detrimental combination of low MAOA and maltreatment did behave in antisocial ways, the findings call into question the capacity for these individuals to freely choose whether or not to engage in criminal behaviour. Halwani and Krupp (2004) argue that punishment for a crime must be directly proportionate to the blameworthiness of the offender and that such blameworthiness must be based on actions exercised through choice. The issue then is the extent to which low or nonexistent MAOA limits an individual's capacity to choose their actions, including whether they behave aggressively. Further research is required to explore these possibilities, but the existing research certainly challenges the legal system's assumption of free will and the voluntary element of *actus reus*.

Limitations in research aside, some commentators suggest that a genetics defence is unlikely to be successful because of difficulties in establishing a causal link between the genetic deficit and the criminal act or because of rules of evidence regarding propensity (Appelbaum, 2005; Alper, 1998). Arguments for a causal link are further diminished due to the fact that not all individuals with low MAOA activity who have been maltreated commit offences, nor do those who commit offences necessarily commit the same type of offence (Alper, 1998). Nevertheless, the issue remains as to whether a person with low MAOA and adverse environmental conditions during development, such as maltreatment, should be held responsible for their actions to the same extent as someone without the genetic effect of poor regulation over aggression. Brock and Buchanan (1999) ask whether it is fair to hold people responsible and to punish them for their behaviour if their behaviour has a considerable genetic basis. The same argument could be made for individuals whose behaviour is largely a product of a poor environment characterized by violence, maltreatment or poor parenting, or more likely, some interaction between genetics and the environment (Baron, 2001). It is this issue that will likely challenge the courts in the near future, which is why the roles of blameworthiness, moral knowing, causation, intention and free will in criminal responsibility require examination and potentially revision.

A related implication of the findings of Caspi et al. (2002) is that the research might be used as a mitigating factor in the sentencing process by arguing that a genetic predisposition reduces the accused person's moral responsibility (Appelbaum, 2005). A similar argument might arise regarding the psychopathic offender, since it is unlikely that an individual can control whether they develop this personality disposition (McCall Smith, 2004). The problem with these arguments is that a person considered to be a higher risk of reoffending is unlikely to be given a more lenient sentence (Appelbaum, 2005). In the absence of treatment that modifies a genetic influence on criminal behaviour, it is possible that offenders with low MAOA could receive longer sentences (Appelbaum, 2005; see also McCall Smith, 2004). Halwani and Krupp (2004) and Appelbaum (2005) suggest that courts and policy makers should begin to consider the implications of these and other emerging behavioural genetics research before such a genetic defence or request for reduced sentences is used in court. Essentially, assignment of responsibility for one's actions relies not only on whether an individual was aware that what they were doing was wrong or whether it was foreseeable that the actions were likely to cause harm, but whether the individual was able to control or regulate their behaviour (see Schopp, 1999, e.g.). As Schopp (1999, p. 90) argues, 'personal responsibility depends primarily on the capacities one possesses rather than on the presence or absence of causal influences'. The challenge to the law is whether a theory of criminal responsibility can accommodate changes to our understanding of free will, moral knowing and capacity for behavioural control.

RECONCILING THE DISCIPLINES

In considering the challenges that arise when deciding how criminal responsibility should be assigned, two competing themes emerge. The first theme centres on the need to hold individuals responsible for their actions, even if they are not technically at fault. This need might stem from recognition that someone's actions were at odds with the law, or it might be due to a crime being so abhorrent or creating so much harm that someone needs to be held accountable. Therefore there is a moral component to this theme. It may be seen to be morally unjust not to blame and punish someone for harming another person. The problem with this approach is that it ignores psychological research on common-sense understandings of intention and intentionality and what we know about causation, self-control, genes and the impact of the environment on behaviour. So a problem arises in trying to fit the law and legal terminology, which is heavily shaped by moral beliefs, to complex events and individuals.

The second theme that emerges is the functionality of the law. One function might be to meet the moral standards of the community, by punishing those that have acted contrary to the law. In this way the moral values of the community are upheld, and the punishment of wrongdoers acts in an exclamatory way to convey the standards of behaviour. Another function might be to protect the community from further harm. This may be achieved by detaining individuals who pose a tangible risk to the community, by supervising individuals within the community, or by providing treatment to individuals to lessen the likelihood of similar behaviour occurring in the future.

Events such as committing murder whilst in a state of automatism or having poor executive control over impulsive behaviour raise particular problems for the law in meeting moral standards. In attempting to hold individuals responsible for their behaviour, the law has expanded the ways that the elements of criminal responsibility can be fulfilled. One way to overcome the problems inherent in this approach might be instead to focus on the functions that can be served by the law. By taking a utilitarian approach to the law a system could be developed that recognizes a lack of moral blameworthiness in individuals. Yet it could also allow for the protection of the community if the risk of an individual reoffending was high. Such a shift in focus is not completely at odds with how the law currently operates, yet it may require some reconsideration of how the elements of criminal responsibility operate.

The suggestions for change are based on the current flaws with the assumption of free will and the fact that the law operates as if it exists (Alper, 1998). To operate in this way and still aim to protect the community, the law has found ways to extend the elements of criminal responsibility so that a verdict can be rendered and a sentence dispensed. Even when a defence is successfully established, there may still be options for treatment and detention. It is proposed that an alternative approach to criminal responsibility exists. This approach would involve recognizing the lack of moral blameworthiness of an individual at the verdict or disposition stage. It would make sense to recognize the lack of moral blameworthiness of an individual at the verdict stage, since this would indicate that one of the elements of criminal responsibility had not be satisfied. However, it is possible that the individual suffers from some particular neurological, cognitive or genetic deficit that means that they are likely to engage in similar behaviour again. Therefore detention, treatment or supervision options must be available to the judge to allow for the protection of the community even in the absence of criminal responsibility (see, e.g. McCall Smith, 2004). Alternatively, a defence could be constructed, similar to the defence for mental disorder proposed by McSherry (2003, 2004) in relation to cases of automatism, which would recognize a lack of criminal responsibility whilst allowing for disposition options. These approaches would also allow for the revision of the constructs used to define criminal responsibility, bringing them more in line with their common-sense usage.

One of the limitations that exist with the proposal to recognize a lack of criminal responsibility at the verdict stage, in the absence of a defence, is the danger that new laws allowing for detainment will go too far. That is, a revision of the law could lead to the excessive detainment of individuals who were found not guilty due to being unable to control their behaviour or form the requisite intent. Furthermore, in the case of genetic influences on behaviour, it is possible that the risks could not be minimized by any existing treatment. Clearly, the success of any revision to criminal responsibility and detention laws would also reside on the ability to produce valid risk assessments. There are likely to be other limitations to the above suggestions as well. However, these suggestions are not intended to be a comprehensive map of the way forward. They are only an attempt to condense some of the key issues as identified by psychological and related research. Any solution requires thorough consideration and debate. It is argued that such debate should include not only legal professionals, but researchers and practitioners in the fields of psychology and psychiatry, neuroscience, behavioural genetics and other related disciplines.

CONCLUSION

This chapter sought to identify the current advances in psychological research that challenge definitions of criminal responsibility. It was demonstrated that particular situations may arise where an individual lacks voluntary control, moral knowledge, intention or awareness regarding their actions, and yet their behaviour has detrimental consequences. Scientific understanding of the underlying causes of such mental state elements may be ignored in an attempt to uphold the premise of free will. In order to uphold this premise, some researchers have argued that the elements of criminal responsibility have been expanded to the extent that they are muddled, imprecise and lacking any common understanding. However, in this way it has been possible, at least to a certain extent, to assign blameworthiness and punishment and meet the expectations of community members. Related court findings serve an exclamatory function regarding acceptable standards of behaviour.

Whilst the law can continue to expand notions of responsibility to ensure that all individuals who society believes should be punished are punished or detained for the safety of the community, it may be an opportune time to reconsider the topic of criminal responsibility. It may be possible to develop the law in a utilitarian fashion that acknowledges psychological research and attempts to tease apart the elements necessary for responsibility with some precision. It has been suggested that complimentary law could be developed to address the kinds of cases that may fall outside the scope of criminal responsibility, so that protection of the community would still be possible. It is likely that this chapter only serves as a basic starting point for debating the ways in which criminal responsibility can be understood and operationalized. The challenge will be to accommodate knowledge from psychological research into the law without compromising the essence of criminal law or the moral values that underpin it. Nevertheless, it is argued that psychological research has much to offer this endeavour.

REFERENCES

Alper, J.S. (1998) Genes, free will and criminal responsibility. *Social Science & Medicine*, **46** (12), 1599–611.

American Psychiatric Association (2000) *Diagnostic and Statistical Manual of Mental Disorders: DSM-IV-TR*, 4th edn, text revision, American Psychiatric Association, Washington, DC.

Appelbaum, P.S. (2005) Behavioral genetics and the punishment of crime. *Psychiatric Services*, **56** (1), 25–7.

Baron, M. (2001) Crime, genes, and responsibility, in *Genetics and Criminal Behavior* (eds D. Wasserman and R. Wachbroit), Cambridge University Press, Cambridge, pp. 201–23.

Barrat, E.S. and Felthous, A.R. (2003) Impulsive versus premeditated aggression: Implications for *mens reas* decisions. *Behavioral Sciences and the Law*, **21**, 619–30.

Brock, D.W. and Buchanan, A.E. (1999) The genetics of behavior and concepts of free will and determinism, in *Genetics and Criminality: The Potential Misuse of Scientific Information in Court* (eds J.R. Botkin, W.M. McMahon and L. Pickeringdr Francis), American Psychological Association, Washington, DC, pp. 67–98.

Bronitt, S. and McSherry, B. (2001) *Principles of Criminal Law*, Law Book Company, Sydney.

Brunner, H.G., Nelen, M., Breakefield, X.O. *et al.* (1993) Abnormal behavior associated with a point mutation in the structural gene for monoamine oxidase A. *Science*, **262**, 578–80.

Caspi, A., McClay, J., Moffitt, T. *et al.* (2002) Evidence that the cycle of violence in maltreated children depends on genotype. *Science*, **297**, 851–54.

Carson, D.C. and Felthous, A.R. (2003) Introduction to this issue: Mens rea. *Behavioral Sciences and the Law*, **21** (5), 559–62.

Ciocchetti, C. (2003a) The responsibility of the psychopathic offender. *Philosophy, Psychiatry, & Psychology*, **10** (2), 175–83.

Ciocchetti, C. (2003b) Some thoughts on diverse psychopathic offenders and legal responsibility. *Philosophy, Psychiatry, & Psychology*, **10** (2), 195–98.

Denno, D. (2002) Crime and consciousness: Science and involuntary acts. *Minnesota Law Review*, **87**, 269–399.

Denno, D. (2003) A mind to blame: New views on involuntary acts. *Behavioral Sciences and the Law*, **21**, 601–18.

Ellis, A. (2003) A deterrence theory of punishment. *The Philosophical Quarterly*, **53** (212), 337–51.

Fine, C. and Kennett, J. (2004) Mental impairment, moral understanding and criminal responsibility: Psychopathy and the purposes of punishment. *International Journal of Law and Psychiatry*, **27** (5), 425–43.

Glancy, G.D., Bradford, J.M. and Fedak, L. (2002) A comparison of R. v. Stone with R. v. Parks: Two cases of automatism. *Journal of the American Academy of Psychiatry & the Law*, **30** (4), 541–47.

Gomes, G. (1998) The timing of conscious experience: A critical review and reinterpretation of Libet's research. *Consciousness and Cognition*, **7**, 559–95.

Gomes, G. (1999) Volition and the readiness potential, in *The Volitional Brain: Towards a Neuroscience of Free Will* (eds B. Libet, A. Freeman and K. Sutherland), Imprint Academic, Thorverton, pp. 59–76.

Halwani, S. and Krupp, D.B. (2004) The genetic defence: The impact of genetics on the concept of criminal responsibility. *Health Law Journal*, **12**, 35–70.

Hawkins v The Queen [1994] 179 CLR 500.

Kolb, B. and Wishaw, I.Q. (1985) *Fundamentals of Human Neuropsychology*, 2nd edn, W.H. Freeman, New York.

Kornhuber, H.H. and Deecke, L. (1965) [Changes in the brain potential in voluntary movements and passive movements in man: Readiness potential and reafferent potentials.] Pflugers Arch Gesamte Physiol Menschen Tiere, **284**, 1–17.

Libet, B. (1999) Do we have free will? in *The Volitional Brain: Towards a Neuroscience of Free Will* (eds B. Libet, A. Freeman and K. Sutherland), Imprint Academic, Thorverton, pp. 47–57.

Malle, B.F. and Knobe, J. (1997) The folk concept of intentionality. *Journal of Experimental Social Psychology*, **33**, 101–21.

Malle, B.F. and Nelson, S.E. (2003) Judging mens rea: The tension between folk concepts and legal concepts of intentionality. *Behavioral Sciences & the Law*, **21** (5), 563–80.

McCall Smith, A. (2004) Human action, neuroscience and the law, in *The New Brain Sciences: Perils and Prospects* (eds D. Rees and S. Rose), Cambridge University Press, Cambridge, pp. 103–22.

McEwan, J. (2003) *The Verdict of the Court: Passing Judgment in Law and Psychology*, Hart Publishing, Portland, OR.

McLeod, H.J., Byrne, M.K. and Aitken, R. (2004) Automatism and dissociation: Disturbances of consciousness and volition from a psychological perspective. *International Journal of Law & Psychiatry*, **27** (5), 471–87.

McSherry, B. (1997) The reformulated defence of insanity in the Australian Criminal Code Act 1995 (Cth). *International Journal of Law and Psychiatry*, **20** (2), 183–97.

McSherry, B. (2003) Voluntariness, intention, and the defence of mental disorder: Toward a rational approach. *Behavioral Sciences and the Law*, **21** (5), 581–99.

McSherry, B. (2004) Criminal responsibility, "fleeting" states of mental impairment, and the power of self-control. *International Journal of Law & Psychiatry*, **27** (5), 445–57.

Moffitt, T.E. and Henry, B. (1989) Neuropsychological assessment of executive functions in self-reported delinquents. *Development and Psychopathology*, **1**, 105–18.

Morse, S.J. (2000) Criminal responsibility, in *Encyclopedia of Psychology* (ed. A.E. Kazdin), American Psychological Association, Oxford University Press, Washington, DC.

R v Burgess [1991] 2 All ER 769.

R v Parks [1992] 2 SCR 871.

R v Stone [1999] 2 SCR 290.

Schopp, R.F. (1999) Natural-born defense attorneys, in *Genetics and Criminality: The Potential Misuse of Scientific Information in Court* (eds J.R. Botkin, W.M. McMahon and L. Pickering Francis), American Psychological Association, Washington, DC.

Shuman, D.W. (2003) A comment on Christopher Ciocchetti: "The responsibility of the psychopathic offender". *Philosophy, Psychiatry, & Psychology*, **10** (2), 193–94.

CHAPTER 9

Criminal Thinking

Emma J. Palmer
University of Leicester

INTRODUCTION

The literature relating to criminal thinking styles and patterns often makes reference to the term *cognition*. Within psychology, the term cognition is defined in many ways, ranging from perception, memory, and intelligence through to the interpersonal skills used in dealing with social situations. Ross and Fabiano (1985) made the distinction between *impersonal* cognition and *interpersonal* cognition. Impersonal cognition refers to the skills used to perceive and understand the physical world (e.g. visual perception, memory). In contrast interpersonal cognition represents those interpersonal skills used in social situations to understand other people and to solve interpersonal problems (e.g. social perspective-taking, means-end thinking). Although there is research examining the relationship between offending and impersonal cognition, such as the role of intelligence in offending (e.g. Fergusson, Horwood and Ridder, 2005), of more pertinence to the current discussion is the link between interpersonal cognition and offending.

This chapter, therefore, has three objectives. First, the evidence examining the link between interpersonal cognition and criminal behaviour will be reviewed, paying attention to both the content and processes of cognition, and placing these factors into a developmental context. Second, interventions aimed at changing offenders' cognition, and therefore reducing their reoffending will be considered, along with the literature relating to their effectiveness. Finally, this chapter will reflect on the implications of the literature on criminal thinking for the law, paying specific attention to issues such as mitigation and sentencing.

THINKING STYLES

One of the first studies to examine offenders' thinking styles was carried out by Yochelson and Samenow 1976. Based on interviews with 240 male offenders referred to hospital for mental state assessment, they concluded there to be distinct 'criminal thinking patterns' among the offenders. Among the patterns observed were poor decision making, lack of empathy, perception of the self as a victim, and irresponsibility. However, a number of criticisms have been made of this study, notably the lack of a control group, the extreme

---

Applying Psychology to Criminal Justice. Edited by David Carson, Rebecca Milne, Francis Pakes, Karen Shalev and Andrea Shawyer. © 2007 John Wiley & Sons, Ltd

nature of the offenders (the majority of the sample had been found 'Not guilty by reason of insanity'), and the reliability and validity of the measures used to assess cognition.

Other research has focused on examining the differences between offenders and nonoffenders on various dimensions of social cognition. A review of this research by Ross and Fabiano (1985, and recently updated by Antonowicz, 2005) showed various patterns of social cognition to characterize offenders, although they were careful to note that these were general group differences and were not necessarily present in all offenders. The characteristics found to be present among the offender groups included:

- Lack of self-control and high levels of impulsivity
- An external locus of control, whereby the causes of their behaviour are attributed to factors that are beyond their control (e.g. other people or chance), rather than to themselves (an internal locus of control)
- A tendency to use a concrete, rather than an abstract, style of thinking
- Poor social perspective-taking and empathy
- Poor social problem-solving, and
- Less mature moral reasoning.

Overall, the research showed offenders to have a number of social cognitive deficits as compared with nonoffenders, and led Ross and Fabiano (1985) to propose a *cognitive model of offender rehabilitation*. However, the early research in this area tended to be disparate in nature, with studies focusing only on one or two variables, and there were gaps in the theoretical framework proposed by Ross and Fabiano. Despite this, the available evidence suggested cognition to be a useful area to explore with respect to offending behaviour, and one that would also provide a basis for interventions to remedy the identified deficits. More recently, evidence from a range of studies has pointed to a link between cognition and offending (e.g. Greening, 1997; Whitton and McGuire, 2002, as cited in McGuire, 2002). This research base now includes not only comparisons of offender and nonoffender groups on psychometric measures, but also studies using self-report and interview methodologies covering a range of offence types (McGuire, 2004). This has been further corroborated by research showing sexual offenders and domestic violence offenders to hold specific cognitive distortions supportive of their offending (Russell, 2002; Ward, Hudson and Keenan, 2001).

More recently, attention has also turned to a consideration of social information-processing as a way of conceptualizing the cognitive distortions and social problem-solving patterns that are associated with antisocial and offending behaviour. Although much of this research has been carried out with children and adolescents (including juvenile delinquents), it provides a useful framework through which to consider the role of cognition in offending behaviour.

SOCIAL INFORMATION-PROCESSING

An influential model of social information-processing that has been used to explain antisocial and offending behaviour is described by Crick and Dodge (1994). This six-step model outlines how individuals perceive and interpret the social world around them, and the impact of previous experiences and emotions on these processes (Lemerise and Arsenio,

2000). Within this model, therefore, account is taken of the role of both cognitions (social perceptions and social problem solving) and affect (emotions, motivations and goals). The six steps of the model are:

1. Encoding of social cues
2. Interpretation and mental representation of the social situation
3. Clarification of goals and outcomes for the situation
4. Accessing or construction of potential responses to the situation
5. Evaluation and choice of a response for the situation, and
6. Performance of the chosen response.

Steps 1 and 2: Encoding and Interpretation of Cues

The first two steps of the model outline how individuals use internal schema and external social cues to build up a mental representation of a given situation. This is achieved through encoding and then interpreting the cues from the environment. The types of external cues typically attended to is selective and varies between individuals. Various cognitive procedures are involved in this process, including making attributions about other people's intent (e.g. if someone knocks into you, is this accidental or intentional?); making attributions about causality (e.g. if you get into a fight, is this because the other person provoked you and so caused by something not in your control, or is it because you could not control your aggression and so caused by yourself); making evaluations about how you have behaved in previous interactions with the individual(s) in this situation (e.g. if you have a history of aggressive behaviour with a peer, you might expect similar behaviour to occur); and making evaluations about the meaning of the situation for yourself and the other people involved in it (e.g. if a situation involves a rival peer, both individuals are likely to rate it as of high importance due to issues of maintaining status within the wider peer group).

An individual's previous experience informs these processes, through the influence of internal schemas and scripts (Schank and Abelson, 1977). These allow social information from the environment to be dealt with more quickly, acting as cognitive shortcuts.

Step 3: Clarification of Goals

Once a situation has been mentally represented, a preferred outcome or goal can be identified for that situation (Crick and Dodge, 1994). Individuals are likely to bring pre-existing goal orientations to situations, which may be amended in response to the ongoing current situation. For example, in a peer conflict situation an individual might have a general goal of establishing dominance, which includes a specific outcome of winning a fight with the other person.

Step 4: Construction of Responses

Crick and Dodge (1994) propose that the fourth step involves the accessing of responses from an individual's memory or the construction of new responses. Accessing of responses involves searching of social scripts for similar situations from which responses can be drawn. An example of this is where an individual's goal is to establish superiority over a peer could elicit various potential responses (e.g. verbal aggression, physical aggression, fair competition, or negotiation). However, if the individual had a specific goal of using physical force to achieve superiority, then only physically aggressive responses would be accessed and therefore considered for use.

Step 5: Response Evaluation and Choice

Step 5 involves evaluation of the responses generated at the previous step to inform the decision as to which one will be performed (Crick and Dodge, 1994). The potential responses are evaluated against a range of criteria, including perceived outcome of the response and how this corresponds to the preferred outcome for the situation, perceived efficacy, likelihood of success, ease of execution, appropriateness of the responses, what has worked in previous similar situations, and the individual's belief systems. Going back to the situation used in the previous example, involving establishment of social superiority, the individual might evaluate whether verbal aggression or physical aggression would achieve the desired outcome. This decision would be likely to be informed by their opinion as to how effective verbal aggression would be on its own, the likelihood of winning the fight, their attitudes towards use of violence to achieve goals, as well as the individual's memories of previous interactions with the other person or similar people.

Step 6: Performance of Response

Performance of the chosen response is the final step of the model, something that requires the individual to have competency in a range of social skills.

For a specific situational stimulus these six steps are passed through sequentially. However, it is proposed that the different processing steps can be performed simultaneously (Crick and Dodge, 1994). Therefore, responses may be accessed whilst new social cues are being processed, allowing for feedback to occur between steps. As a result, Crick and Dodge (1994) conceptualize their social information-processing model as circular, rather than a linear sequence that proceeds from step one to step six in a situation. This interactivity is further emphasized by the importance that is placed on the influence of social knowledge structures, such as social schemas and scripts, at all six steps.

SOCIAL INFORMATION-PROCESSING AND ANTI-SOCIAL BEHAVIOUR

Research has revealed there to be a number of patterns of social information-processing and cognitive distortions associated with antisocial and aggressive behaviour in children and adolescents, including adolescent offenders (for a fuller review, see Crick and Dodge, 1994; Palmer, 2003b). This research will be reviewed next, again examining the evidence at each step of the model.

Steps 1 and 2: Encoding and Interpretation of Cues

Differences exist at both the encoding and interpretation stages of forming a representation of a situation. Compared with their peers, aggressive and antisocial children and adolescents use fewer external cues when interpreting situations (Dodge and Newman, 1981). Those cues that are used tend to be more likely to have occurred towards the end of an interaction (Dodge and Tomlin, 1987) and be aggressive in nature (Gouze, 1987). It has also been shown that aggressive and antisocial children and adolescents rely more on internal schema and scripts than external cues when interpreting a situation (known as top-down processing) (Dodge and Tomlin, 1987), and that these schema tend to be aggressive in nature (Strassberg and Dodge, 1987).

Various studies have shown the existence of a hostile attributional bias among aggressive children and adolescents (Crick, Grotpeter and Bigbee, 2002; Palmer and Hollin, 2000; Slaby and Guerra, 1988), meaning that ambiguous situations are often misinterpreted as being hostile. This bias has been found to be exacerbated when aggressive children feel threatened (Dodge and Somberg, 1987) or react impulsively (Dodge and Newman, 1981). Whilst there are mixed findings as to differences in attribution of blame between different samples, aggressive children and adolescents do appear more likely to blame external factors for events (Fondacaro and Heller, 1990). Overall, it can be seen that aggressive children and adolescents experience a range of problems in encoding and interpreting social cues that may result in an inaccurate representation of the situation.

Step 3: Clarification of Goals

Both the pre-existing goals brought to a situation and the generation of new goals will be influenced by various factors. These include cultural norms, temperament and emotions, as well as short-term circumstantial factors (e.g. anger, tiredness) and stable traits (e.g. aggression) (Crick and Dodge, 1994). Goals that are aggressive, dominant and revenge-based in nature are predominant among aggressive children and adolescent offenders (Crick and Dodge, 1989; Lochman, Wayland and White, 1993; Slaby and Guerra, 1988), in contrast to the prosocial goals preferred by their prosocial peers (e.g. forming new friendships, enhancing relationships).

Step 4: Construction of Responses

The quantity and quality of responses generated are key areas of difference at this step. Aggressive children and adolescents generate far fewer responses overall than nonaggressive children and adolescents (Dodge *et al.*, 1986; Slaby and Guerra, 1988), suggesting they have a limited repertoire on which to draw. Furthermore, the content of responses is far more antisocial among aggressive children and adolescents, as compared with the more prosocial responses (e.g. forming new friendships, enhancing relationships) elicited from nonaggressive individuals (Dodge *et al.*, 1986; Pettit, Dodge and Brown, 1988; Quiggle *et al.*, 1992).

Step 5: Response Evaluation and Choice

Research has found the criteria by which responses are evaluated differ between aggressive and nonaggressive individuals. Amongst aggressive children and adolescents, aggressive responses are rated more positively than prosocial responses (Crick and Ladd, 1990; Quiggle *et al.*, 1992). This is supported by the more positive outcome expectancies and perceptions of self-efficacy this group have for aggression (Hart, Ladd and Burleson, 1990; Crick and Dodge, 1989), in which aggression is viewed as being more likely to be effective in achieving desired social goals.

Step 6: Performance of Response

At this step, the consequences of using the chosen response will enter the individual's database of past experiences and may lead to amendments in their social schema. In turn, these can impact on the social information-processing steps through self-evaluation. Therefore, if the chosen response is successful, it will be positively evaluated and reinforced. In contrast, unsuccessful responses will be evaluated negatively and will be less likely to be used in future situations. Therefore, individuals with poor social skills who find it difficult to use novel responses may come to rely on a limited repertoire of responses.

Although the vast majority of research examining this social information-processing model has been with children, research with adolescent nonoffender and offender samples has found similar results. Furthermore, the distinctive patterns of processing associated with antisocial and aggressive behaviour in these studies reflects the social cognitive deficits found in the earlier research with adolescent and adult offenders. This has led to the proposal that social information-processing and associated social cognitions are influential in the development of adolescent delinquency and adult offending (Palmer, 2000, 2003b), and that they mediate the relationship between early experiences and later behavioural adjustment. This suggestion is supported by research examining the acquisition and maintenance of the social information-processing patterns outlined above. As research has consistently shown these patterns in even quite young children (4–5 years old), it would appear that socialization practices such as child-rearing styles play an important role in their acquisition.

To date, disciplinary practices have received most attention in the literature. Dodge *et al.* (1995) found that children's experiences of discipline and punishment practices influenced the encoding of cues and interpretation of situations. This study is supported by findings that high levels of aggression in young children are associated with harsh maternal discipline (Strassberg *et al.*, 1994; Weiss *et al.*, 1992). Amongst adolescent offenders and nonoffenders, high levels of perceived parental rejection and low levels of perceived parental warmth have been found to correlate with having a hostile attributional bias (Palmer and Hollin, 2000). This research led Palmer (2000) to suggest the overattribution of hostility to others may represent a learned defensive response to a perceived threat, based on negative previous experiences.

Parental attitudes towards aggression have also been linked to children's social information-processing patterns and use of aggression, which has implications for the types of goal orientation brought to situations. For example, Pettit *et al.* (1988) reported an association between children's aggressive behaviour and their mother's endorsement of aggression and use of aggression. Parental attitudes and discipline practices can also impact on the evaluation of social strategies for dealing with situations. Maternal discipline that involves high levels of power assertion was shown by Hart *et al.* (1990) to be associated with an expectation of success for aggression among children.

MORAL REASONING

A further area of social cognition that has attracted attention in the offending literature is that of moral reasoning (for recent reviews, see Palmer, 2003a, 2003b). Moral reasoning refers to how individuals reason about and justify their behaviour, and was first conceptualized by Piaget (1932) in his work examining young children's understanding of the world. This work was later expanded by Kohlberg (1969, 1984) into a theory proposing moral reasoning to involve active construction of moral judgements based on individuals' social experiences. The emphasis this theory placed on the structure and process of moral reasoning (i.e. why something is right or wrong) placed it in contrast to approaches that are more concerned with the content of moral beliefs (i.e. what is right or wrong). Kohlberg's proposed a six-stage theory of moral reasoning through which individuals progress, with reasoning becoming more abstract and complex over time. Progression through these stages is linked to individual's general cognitive development, particularly social perspective-taking.

Gibbs (2003) has recently revised Kohlberg's theory to form a four-stage theory of 'sociomoral' reasoning, placing a greater importance on the role of social perspective-taking (see Table 9.1). The first two stages represent immature moral reasoning, which is superficial and egocentric in nature. Individuals using reasoning at these stages beyond adolescence are considered to show a developmental delay. Stages 3 and 4 represent mature moral reasoning, and involve understanding of interpersonal relationships (Stage 3) and the needs of society (Stage 4). Mature moral reasoning is seen as reflecting 'the cognitive-structural norm for any culture' (Gibbs, Potter and Goldstein, 1995, p. 44), including the

Table 9.1 Gibbs's stages of sociomoral reasoning

Immature moral reasoning
   Stage 1: Unilateral and physicalistic
     Reasoning refers to powerful authority figures (e.g. parents) and the physical consequences of behaviour. Individuals show little or no perspective-taking.
   Stage 2: Exchanging and instrumental
     Reasoning incorporates a basic understanding of social interaction. However, this is typically in terms of cost/benefit deals, with the benefits to the individual being of most importance.
Mature moral reasoning
   Stage 3: Mutual and prosocial
     Reasoning reflects an understanding of interpersonal relationship and the norms/expectations associated with these. Empathy and social perspective taking are apparent, along with ideas appeals to one's own conscience.
   Stage 4: Systemic and standard
     Reasoning reflects an understanding of complex social systems, with appeals to societal requirements, basic rights and values and character/integrity.

formal laws and informal values of a society. The affective aspects of moral reasoning, such as social perspective-taking and empathy are seen as prerequisites for these stages.

Gibbs (2003) also considers how the content of social cognitions relates to the process of moral reasoning, with specific reference to cognitive distortions that contribute to the persistence of immature moral reasoning beyond childhood. The primary distortion is proposed to be egocentric bias in which individuals hold attitudes and values placing their own interests above those of other people. Although an egocentric bias is typical of young children's thinking (Flavell, Miller and Miller, 2002), there is normally a shift towards 'decentration' as individuals move towards adolescence. This is reflected in an increasing ability to take the perspective of other people. The immature stages of moral reasoning are also underpinned by an egocentric bias, as seen in the limited social perspective-taking and emphasis on one's own wishes at these two stages.

Egocentric bias is supported by a number of secondary cognitive distortions that are used to justify behaviour resulting from this bias (Gibbs, 2003). First is 'assumption of the worst', or holding a hostile attributional bias, where individuals tend to interpret ambiguous events as hostile. Second is a tendency to blame other people or external causes (e.g. being drunk) for their behaviour, rather than taking responsibility for themselves, their actions and the consequences. Finally is mislabelling of one's behaviour/minimization of consequences to reduce feelings of anger and regret.

By applying moral reasoning theory to offending, it can be seen that offending can be justified at each of the stages:

- Stage 1 – offending is justified if punishment can be avoided
- Stage 2 – offending is justified if the benefits outweigh the costs
- Stage 3 – offending is justified if it maintains personal relationships
- Stage 4 – offending is justified if it maintains society or is sanctioned by a social institution.

However, the circumstances in which offending would be seen as morally justified are more likely to occur at the less mature stages of the theory. Research supports the prediction that offenders are likely to have less mature moral reasoning than nonoffenders (for reviews, see Blasi, 1980; Nelson, Smith and Dodd, 1990; Palmer, 2003b), although the majority of studies have been with adolescent samples. With regard to the cognitive distortions considered by Gibbs (2003), egocentric bias is common among offenders (Antonowicz, 2005; Ross and Fabiano, 1985), and a number of studies have shown use of the secondary cognitive distortions by adolescent delinquents to justify their offending behaviour (Barriga and Gibbs, 1996; Liau, Barriga and Gibbs, 1998; Palmer and Hollin, 2000; Slaby and Guerra, 1988). As such, offending is seen as a result of moral (or sociomoral) developmental delay beyond childhood, accompanied by a persistent egocentric bias. The self-serving secondary cognitive distortions then allow offenders to justify their behaviour and so contribute to its continuation.

The development of moral reasoning has been examined with reference to both parental child-rearing styles and peer relationships. This research shows progression through the stages to be facilitated by a child-rearing style that is warm (Palmer and Hollin, 1996, 1997) and uses inductive discipline (Boyes and Allen, 1993; Janssens and Deković, 1997), with moral issues discussed in a supportive, yet challenging environment in which all family members participate (Walker, Hennig and Krettenauer, 2000; Walker and Taylor, 1991).

The importance of peers in moral development is in providing role-taking opportunities that will allow for the development of social perspective-taking (Kohlberg, 1984). The key aspect of peer relationships is seen to be the equality of interactions between peers as opposed to those between children and adults (Kruger, 1992).

As has been shown, similar child-rearing styles are implicated in the development of both social information-processing patterns and moral reasoning. Further, the cognitive distortions outlined by Gibbs (2003) parallel those found among aggressive children/adolescents and young offenders in the social information-processing research. Parental child-rearing styles also have a well established association with later delinquency and offending (for reviews, see Farrington, 2002; Patterson, Reid and Dishion, 1992). Research shows delinquency to be associated with lax, erratic, and harsh discipline; poor parental supervision; and a lack of warmth in parent–child interactions. Thus it appears that social cognition (including social information-processing, moral reasoning and the content of cognitive distortions) mediates the relationship between child-rearing styles and later delinquency and offending (Palmer, 2000, 2003b). From a developmental perspective, children who receive harsh and neglectful parenting are at risk of moral developmental delay and developing hostile schemas relating to relationships and the social world. New experiences are filtered through these hostile schemas, making aggressive and antisocial responses more likely. In turn, this behaviour will influence how other people perceive and react to them, which can lead to a self-perpetuating cycle of aggressive and antisocial behaviour, which may escalate into juvenile delinquency and adult offending.

INTERVENTION PROGRAMMES TO IMPROVE THINKING SKILLS

A number of intervention programmes have been designed to improve individual's functioning in these areas, and thereby reduce reoffending. Early work in this area focused on changing single components of social problem-solving, such as generating alternative solutions or means-end thinking (see McGuire, 2005a). Evaluations of these types of interventions showed positive results with respect to individual's social problem-solving skills.

Interventions addressing more complex aspects of social problem solving and cognition were also reported. For example, Chandler (1973) evaluated the impact of role-taking training on young offenders. In comparison with an attention placebo group and no-treatment group, the treated group showed post-training gains in their role-playing and social perspective-taking skills, as well as significantly lower recidivism at 18-month follow-up.

The first study examining a comprehensive intervention aimed at addressing cognitive skills deficits with offenders was the *Wharton Tract Program* (Platt, Perry and Metzger, 1980). This programme was delivered to adult male offenders with a history of heroin abuse in an open unit supporting offenders in the transition from prison to the community. The intervention provided structured training in communication and social problem-solving skills, including recognizing problems, generating alternative solutions, means-end thinking, consequential thinking, decision making and social perspective-taking. This training used a *guided group interaction* format in which participants were encouraged to take responsibility for change in themselves and others. At a two-year follow-up, participants in the intervention group had significantly better outcomes as compared with a comparison sample on a number of measures, including rearrest rate (49 % vs. 66 %), rate of reimprisonment, and time to first rearrest.

Whilst the programme described above focused on the skills, or *structure*, of cognition, other interventions focus on changing the *content* of cognition, such as attitudes or beliefs. The latter approach is typically used in interventions designed to address offending where distorted cognitions are seen to play a role in the commission of offences, such as sexual offending, domestic violence and responsible driving (McGuire, 2006). A consideration of the effectiveness of such interventions in reducing offenders' criminal behaviour is provided later in this chapter.

In recent years, interventions with offenders have become subject to more stringent criteria to ensure quality of both content and delivery, with many criminal justice systems introducing accreditation criteria and related processes (for a review, see Hollin and Palmer, 2006a). A number of programmes focusing on offenders' cognitive skills and the content of their cognitions have been developed within this framework, and these will be reviewed next.

General Offending Behaviour Programmes

General offending behaviour programmes refer to interventions that were designed for use with offenders who have committed various offence types, and are assessed as having problems in their thinking patterns and styles that are associated with their offending behaviour. By addressing cognitive skills deficits and cognitions supportive of offending, these programmes aim to effect a reduction in reoffending amongst participants.

One of the first, and subsequently most widely used, of these programmes is the *Reasoning and Rehabilitation* programme. Originally developed in Canada during the 1980s by Ross and Fabiano (Ross, Fabiano and Ewles, 1988; Ross, Fabiano and Ross, 1989), the *Reasoning and Rehabilitation (R & R)* programme aims to replace offenders' problematic thinking patterns with thinking skills more likely to promote prosocial behaviour. Specific targets of the programme include offenders' social problem-solving skills, social perspective-taking, self-control, critical reasoning and cognitions that support offending (e.g. attitudes and beliefs). Techniques, including role-playing, modelling, rehearsal, reinforcement and cognitive exercises, are used to promote reflective, rather than reactive, thinking. Throughout, an emphasis is placed on the practicing of skills (Goldstein, 1988) and linking them to offenders' everyday lives.

The R & R programme was designed to be delivered by a range of criminal justice professionals, including probation and prison staff, prison officers and psychologists. Tutors are required to attend intensive training, and video monitoring of sessions is used throughout programme delivery to provide formal feedback to staff to ensure integrity of delivery. The programme itself consists of 36 two-hour sessions that are delivered by tutors to groups of offenders. To date, the R & R programme has been used in institutional and community settings in a number of jurisdictions, including Canada, North America, England and Wales, Scotland, Germany, Scandinavia, Spain, Australia and New Zealand.

An adaptation of the R & R programme is the *Enhanced Thinking Skills (ETS)* programme, developed in England and Wales to provide a shorter, 20 session alternative to the R & R programme (Clark, 2000). As such, ETS has the same targets as R & R and uses similar techniques to bring about changes in offenders' cognitive style, as well as having parallel procedures in place for staff training and ensuring treatment integrity.

The third major intervention for general offending behaviour is the *Think First* programme (McGuire, 2000). As well as covering similar topics using the same techniques as R & R and ETS, Think First also focuses specifically on the offender's offending behaviour and requires participants to complete an analysis of crime events. Therefore, unlike the other two programmes Think First makes a direct link between an individual's offending behaviour and cognitive skills. The prison version of Think First consists of 30 two-hour group sessions, whilst the community setting version involves four pregroup sessions of an hour (three on an individual basis and one introductory group meeting), 22 two-hour group sessions, and six individual postgroup sessions lasting one hour. More details of Think First can be found in McGuire (2005b).

Of these three programmes, R & R has been subject to the most evaluations across a number of settings and jurisdictions. Large-scale evaluations have shown generally positive results for the R & R programme with respect to reoffending rates amongst male adult offenders who complete the programme. However, participants who fail to complete the programme tend to fare less well than comparison groups (for reviews, see Antonowicz, 2005; Robinson and Porporino, 2001; Tong and Farrington, 2006). Less evidence of effectiveness is available, however, amongst other offender populations such as female offenders, offenders from ethnic minorities and young offenders (e.g. Mitchell and Palmer, 2004).

Within England and Wales, most evaluations of R & R and ETS in the Prison Service have examined the effectiveness of the two programmes together. The first study was reported by Friendship *et al.* (2003), comparing adult male offenders who had participated in the programmes between 1992 and 1996 ($n=667$) with a matched comparison group ($n=1081$) using a retrospective, quasi-experimental design. At two-year follow-up, reductions in reconviction were found among both medium–low risk offenders (14%) and medium–high risk offenders (11%). Offenders' chances of being reconvicted within two years also dropped after participation in both the programmes (55% reduction for the R & R programme and 52% reduction for the ETS programme). However, in this study no differentiation was made between those participants who completed the programme and those who dropped-out during the programme ($n=66$). Therefore, it is not possible to know the true effect on reconviction of completing the programmes.

Falshaw and colleagues (2003, 2004) presented the results of a second evaluation of R & R and ETS in the English and Welsh Prison Service, carried out between 1996 and 1998 with adult males. Again, a retrospective quasi-experimental design was used, with participants ($n=649$) matched to a comparison group of offenders ($n=1947$). When participants who had not completed the programmes were excluded from analyses, no significant differences were reported in the two-year reconviction rates of the two groups. One possible explanation for this finding proposed by the authors was the rapid expansion of use of the two programmes within the prison service during the study period. This is in line with recent suggestions by experts that small-scale interventions have a greater effect than those implemented on a wider scale due to compromised treatment integrity (e.g. Gendreau, Goggin and Smith, 2002).

The final prison study using the same design as the previous two studies included male adult offenders ($n=2195$) and male young offenders ($n=1534$) who participated in R & R and ETS, who were matched to comparison groups of offenders ($n=2195$ and $n=1534$ respectively) (Cann *et al.*, 2003). At one-year follow-up the reconviction rates were significantly lower for programme completers than for the comparison groups for both young and adult offenders (4.1% for young offenders and 2.5% for adult offenders), although these positive results were not maintained at two-year follow-up. Of the two programmes, ETS had the greater effect on reconviction, with Cann *et al.* (2003) suggesting this might be due to ETS being developed specifically for the English and Welsh prison population.

Since 2001, all three general offending behaviour programmes have been implemented on a national basis within the English and Welsh Probation Service as part of the *Pathfinder* programmes policy. Previous to this date versions of both R & R and Think First had been used in some areas for a number of years. An early Pathfinder evaluation of Think First in the three probation areas that originally piloted the programme reported a two-year reconviction follow-up study (Roberts, 2004). Among medium and higher risk offenders, programme completers had significantly lower reconviction rates than those offenders who did not start the programme, and those offenders who started the programme but did not complete it. However, no effect of programme completion was found among lower risk offenders.

A larger evaluation of the three general offending behaviour programmes in the Probation Service in England and Wales has been reported in two inter-related studies of over 4,500 offenders participating in the programmes between 2000 and 2002 (Hollin *et al.*, 2004; Hollin *et al.*, 2005; Palmer *et al.*, in press). In both studies, once differences between the groups had been statistically controlled, completers had significantly lower reconviction rates than noncompleters and the comparison group. This finding held across all three programmes separately, as well as for the whole sample. An issue that was highlighted in these studies was the low completion rate. In the first study these were 21.2, 28.9 and 38.0% for R & R, ETS, and Think First respectively, and in the second study, 35.0, 42.6 and 37.4% respectively. Furthermore, in the second study it was possible to break down the noncompletion group into those who did not start the programme and those who started the programme but did not complete. This revealed alarmingly high rates of 'nonstarters' across all three programmes: 62.3, 55.9 and 43.2% respectively.

Offence-specific Programmes

As well as the programmes outlined above, interventions have also been developed based on research examining the cognitive styles and patterns of offenders who have committed specific types of offences. The most numerous of these are directed at sexual offenders, although programmes also exist for violent offenders, domestic violence offenders and motoring offenders (e.g. drink-driving offences). More recently, programmes have been developed for specific groups of offenders, including women offenders, substance using offenders, racially motivated offenders and high-risk offenders. Further discussion of these specific programmes is precluded by space constraints, but for further details see Hollin and Palmer (2006b).

Delivery and Management of Programmes

A key issue in the effectiveness of programmes is the manner of their delivery and management, with many jurisdictions drawing up formal guidelines and procedures for running programmes. Much of the pioneering work in this area was undertaken by the English and Welsh Prison Service in the mid-1990s, leading to the development of Accreditation

Criteria, the establishment of Accreditation Panels, and a system of auditing programme sites. In 1999, programmes delivered in the Probation Service were brought within the remit of this process. The formal body charged with overseeing this process is the Correctional Services Accreditation Panel (CSAP), an advisory nondepartmental public body with formal independence from the Home Office. CSAP's formal remit includes reviewing the criteria for accreditation of programmes; accrediting of programmes; authorizing procedures for auditing programme delivery; authorizing the annual assessment of delivery quality; conducting an annual review of the interventions evidence base that will allow advice to be given relating to programme design; providing advice on training; and receiving reports on the effectiveness of programmes and giving advice on the implications of these reports (Prison Service Order 4360, 2004).

When programmes are considered for accreditation in England and Wales, they are judged against 10 criteria drawn from the literature on effective interventions with offenders. These criteria cover issues relating to the underlying model of change, selection of offenders, targets and methods of programmes, dosage, engagement and motivation of offenders, continuity of services, monitoring of treatment integrity and ongoing evaluation. Programmes are also required to be fully manualised (for a fuller discussion, see Hollin and Polmer, 2006a).

The audit procedures overseen by CSAP concern the process and appropriateness of implementation of programmes. One of the key issues here is the need to monitor programme integrity, that is whether programmes are delivered as intended (Hollin, 1995). The annual audit system within the prison service has been running for a number of years now, and covers four areas (Blud *et al.*, 2003). First, *institutional support* examines the management and running of the programme; second, *treatment support* examines staff selection, supervision and support procedures, and whether the selection criteria for prisoners onto programmes are being used appropriately; third, *throughcare* considers the continuity of rehabilitative work across different services; and fourth, *quality of delivery* refers to programme delivery issues such as completion and drop-out rates, and uses video-monitoring to ensure tutors' adhere to the programme manual when delivering the programme. A similar set of audit procedures is in place within the Probation Service.

Similar procedures for accrediting programmes with offenders are also in place in Scottish Prison Service (SPS, 2003). Canada is another country whose Correctional Service is advanced in terms of the quality assurance procedures for offending behaviour programmes. For example *The Correctional Program Assessment Inventory* (CPAI; Gendreau *et al.*, 2002; Goggin and Gendreau, 2006) uses 75 items to collect programme management information across six domains of programme implementation: client preservice assessment, programme characteristics, staff characteristics, evaluation and other relevant issues.

IMPLICATIONS FOR THE LAW

The research suggesting that offenders may have distinctive criminal thinking styles, and the corresponding implementation on such a large scale of offending behaviour programmes designed to change these criminal thinking styles raises various issues for the law and legal system. First, is mitigation and whether it would be possible to cite the thinking patterns and styles highlighted in the research as mitigation for offending? As it can be argued that many individuals might show problematic thinking patterns (e.g. being impulsive) without offending, it is difficult to put forward a strong argument here. However, the research showing the presence of these thinking styles among offenders *and* that interventions designed to address these problematic thinking styles can be effective, does offer the law a means to divert offenders towards more appropriate sentences.

The provision of offending behaviour programmes designed to reduce recidivism is a *key performance indicator* within the Prison and Probation Service in England and Wales. In prisons, only structured offending behaviour programmes are available, but within the Probation Service there are also resettlement projects designed to address the needs of short-term prisoners (Lewis *et al.*, 2003) and interventions within Community Punishment projects (Rex *et al.*, 2004). Attending offending behaviour programmes is voluntary within prisons, although it is often recommended as part of a prisoner's Sentence Plan. In contrast, in the Probation Service attendance is a requirement of the offender's sentence (either a Community Rehabilitation Order or Community Rehabilitation and Punishment Order) under the Powers of Criminal Courts (Sentencing) Act 2000. Therefore, if an offender does not attend the programme, they can be sent back to court for breach of their Order and resentencing.

The advent of policies whereby attendance at rehabilitative programmes is linked to sentencing is an interesting development, and links in with the notion of therapeutic jurisprudence. Therapeutic jurisprudence refers to using the law as a therapeutic agent (Petrucci, Winick and Wexler, 2003; Stolle, Wexler and Winick, 2000; Wexler and Winick, 1991, 1996), and Wexler (1998) has noted the potential of research about psychologically based interventions with offenders for improving sentencing. He argued that if courts understood the evidence in this area it could be used to help in the rehabilitation of offenders. In practice, this would mean putting the defendant central to proceedings, and making courts more active agents of motivating offenders to change (i.e. stop offending). This could be achieved by engaging defendants in the preparation of presentence reports, supervision or parole reports; ensuring the involvement of significant other people in decisions (both from other agencies and the offender's life); and setting conditions for the implementation of sentence plans and providing support to enable this to occur. Courts could also make use of the research evidence relating to relapse prevention in order to make recommendations and/or conditions when sentencing offenders. Referring back to the recent evaluations of the Probation Service's Pathfinder programmes (Hollin *et al.*, 2004, 2005), it is possible that more informed sentencing and sentence planning by all agencies would reduce the high nonstarter and noncompletion rates noted.

Other writers have noted alternative ways in which the law could become more therapeutic. Simon (2003) describes the concept of proactive judging in the USA in which judges do not passively react to crime but seek to make links with other agencies and communities to reduce crime through the way courts work. One result of this has been the development of specialized courts for domestic violence, substance abuse, young offenders and mentally disordered offenders, which are better able to take account of the complexities of cases (e.g. Fritzler and Simon, 2000). Although not reviewed in depth in the current chapter, research clearly shows offences such as sexual offences and domestic violence to be associated with specific distortions in thinking (e.g. Russell, 2002; Ward *et al.*, 2001). Therefore, the introduction of specialized courts based on a better understanding of these offenders and their offending is clearly a step forward. Where these types of courts have been put into practice initial evaluations have shown positive results both in terms of participation by clients and recidivism outcome (Minor *et al.*, 1999; Peters and Murrin, 2000; Springer, McNeece and Arnold, 2002).

CONCLUSIONS

The extent to which offending behaviour programmes aimed at changing offenders' thinking styles have been implemented on both a national and international basis is an indication of the faith that many jurisdictions are placing in them. Whether they can deliver – and should be expected to deliver – large-scale reductions in crime remains to be seen. As noted by Ogloff and Davis (2004), if these reductions are not achieved or are less than expected, rehabilitative interventions may be replaced by more punitive sanctions. It is, therefore, of great importance that rehabilitative interventions of all types, not just those relating to thinking styles, are implemented properly and with integrity. This includes the need for the law to have a full understanding of the evidence in this area, so as to play its role in this sphere.

REFERENCES

Antonowicz, D.H. (2005) The Reasoning and rehabilitation program: Outcome evaluations with offenders, in *Social Problem-solving and Offending: Evidence, Evaluation and Evolution* (eds M. McMurran and J. McGuire), Wiley, Chichester, pp. 163–81.

Barriga, A.Q. and Gibbs, J.C. (1996) Measuring cognitive distortion in antisocial youth: Development and preliminary validation of the "How I Think" questionnaire. *Aggressive Behavior*, **22**, 333–43.

Blasi, A. (1980) Bridging moral cognition and moral action: A critical review of the literature. *Psychological Bulletin*, **88**, 1–45.

Blud, L., Travers, R., Nugent, F. and Thornton, D.M. (2003). Accreditation of offending behaviour programmes in HM Prison Service: 'What Works' in practice. *Legal and Criminological Psychology*, **8**, 69–81.

Boyes, M.C. and Allen, S.G. (1993) Styles of parent-child interaction and moral reasoning in adolescence. *Merrill-Palmer Quarterly*, **39**, 551–70.

Cann, J., Falshaw, L., Nugent, F. and Friendship, C. (2003) *Understanding what works: Accredited cognitive skills programmes for adult men and young offenders*. Home Office Research Findings No. 226. London: Home Office.

Chandler, M. (1973) Egocentrism and antisocial behavior: The assessment and training of social perspective-taking skills. *Developmental Psychology*, **9**, 326–32.

Clark, D.A. (2000) *Theory manual for Enhanced Thinking Skills*. Prepared for the Joint Prison Probation Accreditation Panel.

Crick, N.R. and Dodge, K.A. (1989) Children's perceptions of peer entry and conflict situations: Social strategies, goals, and outcome expectancies, in *Social Competence in Developmental Perspective* (eds B. Schneider, J. Nadel, G. Attili and R. Weissberg), Kluwer, Dordrecht, pp. 396–9).

Crick, N.R. and Dodge, K.A. (1994) A review and reformulation of social information-processing mechanisms in children's social adjustment. *Psychological Bulletin*, **115**, 74–101.

Crick, N.R., Grotpeter, J.K. and Bigbee, M.A. (2002) Relationally and physically aggressive children's intent attributions and feelings of distress for relational and instrumental peer provocations. *Child Development*, **73**, 1134–42.

Crick, N.R. and Ladd, G.W. (1990) Children's perceptions of the outcomes of aggressive strategies: Do the ends justify being mean? *Developmental Psychology*, **26**, 612–20.

Dodge, K.A. and Newman, J.P. (1981) Biased decision-making processes in aggressive boys. *Journal of Abnormal Psychology*, **90**, 375–9.

Dodge, K.A., Pettit, G.S., Bates, J.E. and Valente, E. (1995) Social information processing patterns partially mediate the effect of early physical abuse on later conduct problems. *Journal of Abnormal Psychology*, **104**, 632–43.

Dodge, K.A., Pettit, G.S., McClaskey, C.L. and Brown, M.M. (1986) Social competence in children. *Monographs of the Society for Research in Child Development*, **51** (2, Serial No. 213).

Dodge, K.A. and Somberg, D.R. (1987) Hostile attributional biases among aggressive boys are exacerbated under conditions of threat to the self. *Child Development*, **58**, 213–24.

Dodge, K.A. and Tomlin, A.M. (1987) Utilization of self-schemas as a mechanism of interpersonal bias in aggressive children. *Social Cognition*, **5**, 280–300.

Falshaw, L., Friendship, C., Travers, L. and Nugent, F. (2003) *Searching for what works: An evaluation of cognitive skills programmes*. Home Office Research Findings No. 206. London: Home Office.

Falshaw, L., Friendship, C., Travers, L. and Nugent, F. (2004) Searching for 'what works': HM Prison Service accredited cognitive skills programmes. *British Journal of Forensic Practice*, **6**, 3–13.

Farrington, D.P. (2002) Developmental criminology and risk-focused prevention, in *Oxford Handbook of Criminology* (eds M. Maguire, R. Morgan and R. Reiner), Oxford University Press, Oxford, pp. 657–701.

Fergusson, D.M., Horwood, L.J. and Ridder, E.M. (2005) Show me the child at seven II: Childhood intelligence and later outcomes in adolescence and young adulthood. *Journal of Child Psychology and Psychiatry*, **46**, 850–8.

Flavell, J.H., Miller, P.H. and Miller, S.A. (2002) *Cognitive development*, 4th edn, Prentice Hall, Upper Saddle River, NJ.

Fondacaro, M.R. and Heller, K. (1990) Attributional style in aggressive adolescent boys. *Journal of Abnormal Child Psychology*, **18**, 75–89.

Friendship, C., Blud, L., Erikson, M. *et al*. (2003) Cognitive-behavioural treatment for imprisoned offenders: An evaluation of HM Prison Service's cognitive skills programmes. *Legal and Criminological Psychology*, **8**, 103–14.

Fritzler, R.B. and Simon, L.M.J. (2000) Creating a domestic violence court: Combat in the trenches. *Court Review*, **37**, 28–39.

Gendreau, P., Goggin, C. and Smith, P. (2002) Implementation guidelines for correctional programs in the "real world", in *Offender Rehabilitation in Practice: Implementing and Evaluating Effective Programmes* (eds G.A. Bernfeld, D.P. Farrington and A.W. Leschied), Wiley, Chichester, pp. 228–68.

Gibbs, J.C. (2003) *Moral Development and Reality: Beyond the Theories of Kohlberg and Hoffman*, Sage Publications, Thousand Oaks, CA.

Gibbs, J.C., Potter, G.B. and Goldstein, A.P. (1995) *The EQUIP Program: Teaching Youth to Think and Act Responsibly Through a Peer-helping Approach*, Research Press, Champaign, IL.

Goggin, C. and Gendreau, P. (2006) The implementation and maintenance of quality services in offender rehabilitation programmes, in *Offending Behaviour Programmes: Development, Application, and Controversies* (eds C.R. Hollin and E.J. Palmer), Wiley, Chichester, pp. 209–46.

Goldstein, A.P. (1988) *The Prepare Curriculum*, Research Press, Champaign, IL.

Gouze, K.R. (1987) Attention and problem solving as correlates of aggression in preschool males. *Journal of Abnormal Psychology*, **15**, 181–97.

Greening, L. (1997) Adolescent stealers' and nonstealers' social problem-solving skills. *Adolescence*, **32**, 51–5.

Hart, C.H., Ladd, G.W. and Burleson, B.R. (1990) Children's expectations of the outcomes of social strategies: Relations with sociometric status and maternal disciplinary styles. *Chid Development*, **61**, 127–37.

Hollin, C.R. (1995) The meaning and implications of "programme integrity", in *What Works: Reducing Reoffending* (ed. J. McGuire), Wiley, Chichester, pp. 195–208.

Hollin, C.R. and Palmer, E.J. (2006a) Offending behaviour programmes: History and development, in *Offending Behaviour Programmes: Development, Application, and Controversies* (eds C.R. Hollin and E.J. Palmer), Wiley, Chichester, pp. 1–32.

Hollin, C.R. and Palmer, E.J. (eds) (2006b) *Offending Behaviour Programmes: Development, Application, and Controversies*, Wiley, Chichester.

Hollin, C.R., Palmer, E.J., McGuire, J. *et al*. (2004) *Pathfinder Programmes in the Probation Service: A Retrospective Analysis*. Home Office Online Report 66/04.

Hollin, C.R., Palmer, E.J., McGuire, J. et al. (2005) *An evaluation of pathfinder programmes in the Probation Service*. Grant Report for the Home Office, Research Development and Statistics Directorate.

Janssens, J.M.A.M. and Deković, M. (1997) Child rearing, prosocial moral reasoning, and prosocial behaviour. *International Journal of Behavioral Development*, **20**, 509–27.

Kohlberg, L. (1969) Stage and sequence: The cognitive-developmental approach to socialization, in *Handbook of Socialization Theory and Research* (ed. D.A. Goslin), Rand McNally, Chicago, IL, pp. 347–480.

Kohlberg, L. (1984) *Essays on Moral Development: The Psychology of Moral Development*, Harper and Row, San Francisco, CA.

Kruger, A.C. (1992) The effect of peer and adult-child transactive discussions on moral reasoning. *Merrill-Palmer Quarterly*, **38**, 191–211.

Lemerise, E.A. and Arsenio, W.E. (2000) An integrated model of emotion processes and cognition in social information processing. *Child Development*, **71**, 107–18.

Lewis, S., Maguire, M., Raynor, P., et al. (2003) *The resettlement of short-term offenders: An evaluation of seven Pathfinder programmes*. Home Office Research Findings No. 200. London: Home Office.

Liau, A.K., Barriga, A.Q. and Gibbs, J.C. (1998) Relations between self-serving cognitive distortions and overt vs. covert antisocial behavior in adolescents. *Aggressive Behavior*, **24**, 335–46.

Lochman, J.E., Wayland, K.K. and White, K.J. (1993) Social goals: Relationship to adolescent adjustment and to social problem solving. *Journal of Abnormal Child Psychology*, **21**, 135–51.

McGuire, J. (2000) *Theory manual for Think First*. Prepared for the Joint Prison Probation Accreditation Panel.

McGuire, J. (2002) What is problem-solving? A review of theory, research and applications. *Criminal Behaviour and Mental Health*, **11**, 210–35.

McGuire, J. (2004) *Understanding Psychology and Crime: Perspectives on Theory and Action*, Open University Press/McGraw-Hill Education, Maidenhead.

McGuire, J. (2005a) Social problem solving: Basic concepts, research, and applications, in *Social Problem Solving and Offending: Evidence, Evaluation and Evolution* (eds M. McMurran and J. McGuire), Wiley, Chichester, pp. 3–29.

McGuire, J. (2005b) The Think First programme, in *Social Problem Solving and Offending: Evidence, Evaluation and Evolution* (eds M. McMurran and J. McGuire), Wiley, Chichester, pp. 183–206.

McGuire, J. (2006) General offending behaviour programmes: Concept, theory and practice, in *Offending Behaviour Programmes: Development, Application, and Controversies* (eds C.R. Hollin and E.J. Palmer), Wiley, Chichester, pp. 69–111.

Minor, K.I., Wells, J.B., Soderstrom, I.R., Bingham, R. and Williamson, D. (1999) Sentence completion and recidivism among juveniles referred to teen courts. *Crime and Delinquency*, **45**, 467–80.

Mitchell, J. and Palmer, E.J. (2004) An evaluation of the Reasoning and Rehabilitation program with incarcerated juvenile offenders. *Journal of Offender Rehabilitation*, **39** (4), 31–45.

Nelson, J.R., Smith, D.J. and Dodd, J. (1990) The moral reasoning of juvenile delinquents: A meta-analysis. *Journal of Abnormal Child Psychology*, **18**, 231–9.

Ogloff, J.R.P. and Davis, M.R. (2004) Advances in offender assessment and rehabilitation: Contributions of the risk-needs-responsivity approach. *Psychology, Crime and Law*, **10**, 229–42.

Palmer, E.J. (2000) Perceptions of parenting, social cognition and delinquency. *Clinical Psychology and Psychotherapy*, **7**, 303–9.

Palmer, E.J. (2003a) An overview of the relationship between moral reasoning and offending. *Australian Psychologist*, **38**, 165–74.

Palmer, E.J. (2003b) *Offending Behaviour: Moral Reasoning, Criminal Conduct and the Rehabilitation of Offenders*, Willan Publishing, Cullompton.

Palmer, E.J. and Hollin, C.R. (1996) Sociomoral reasoning, perceptions of own parenting and self-reported delinquency. *Personality and Individual Differences*, **21**, 175–82.

Palmer, E.J. and Hollin, C.R. (1997) The influence of perceptions of own parenting on sociomoral reasoning, attributions for criminal behaviour, and self-reported delinquency. *Personality and Individual Differences*, **23**, 193–7.

Palmer, E.J. and Hollin, C.R. (2000) The inter-relations of sociomoral reasoning, perceptions of own parenting, and attribution of intent with self-reported delinquency. *Legal and Criminological Psychology*, **5**, 201–18.

Palmer, E.J., McGuire, J., Hounsome, J.C., *et al.* (in press) Offending behaviour programmes in the community: The effects on reconviction of three programmes with adult male offenders. *Legal and Criminological Psychology*.

Patterson, G.R., Reid, J. and Dishion, T.J. (1992) *Antisocial Boys*, Castalia Press, Eugene, OR.

Peters, R.H. and Murrin, M.R. (2000) Effectiveness of treatment-based drug courts in reducing criminal recidivism. *Criminal Justice and Behavior*, **27**, 72–96.

Petrucci, C.J., Winick, B.J. and Wexler, D.B. (2003) Therapeutic jurisprudence: An invitation to social scientists, in *Handbook of Psychology in Legal Contexts* (eds D. Carson and R. Bull), Wiley, Chichester, pp. 579–601.

Pettit, G.S., Dodge, K.A. and Brown, M.M. (1988) Early family experience, social problem solving patterns and children's social competence. *Child Development*, **59**, 107–20.

Piaget, J. (1932) *The Moral Judgment of the Child*, Routledge and Kegan Paul, London.

Platt, J.J., Perry, G. and Metzger, D. (1980) The evaluation of a heroin addiction treatment program within a correctional environment, in *Effective Correctional Treatment* (eds R.R. Ross and P. Gendreau), Butterworths, Toronto.

Prison Service Order 4360 (2004) London, UK: HM Prison Service. http://www.hmprisonservice.gov.uk/resourcecentre/psispsos/listpsos/

Quiggle, N.L., Garber, J., Panak, W.F. and Dodge, K.A. (1992) Social information processing in aggressive and depressed children. *Child Development*, **63**, 1305–20.

Rex, S., Gelsthorpe, L., Roberts, C. and Jordan, P. (2004) *What's promising in Community Service: Implementation of seven Pathfinder projects*. Home Office Research Findings No. 231. London: Home Office.

Roberts, C. (2004) An early evaluation of a cognitive offending behaviour programme ('Think First') in probation areas. *Vista: Perspectives on Probation*, **8**, 130–6.

Robinson, D. and Porporino, F.J. (2001) Programming in cognitive skills: The Reasoning and Rehabilitation programme, in *Handbook of Offender Assessment and Treatment* (ed. C.R. Hollin), Wiley, Chichester, pp. 179–93.

Ross, R.R. and Fabiano, E.A. (1985) *Time to Think: A Cognitive Model of Delinquency Prevention and Offender Rehabilitation*, Institute of Social Sciences and Arts, Johnson City, TN.

Ross, R.R., Fabiano, E.A. and Ewles, C.D. (1988) Reasoning and Rehabilitation. *International Journal of Offender Therapy and Comparative Criminology*, **32**, 29–35.

Ross, R.R., Fabiano, E.A. and Ross, B. (1989) *Reasoning and Rehabilitation: A Handbook for Teaching Cognitive Skills*, The Cognitive Centre, Ottawa.

Russell, M.N. (2002) Changing beliefs of spouse abusers, in *Offender Rehabilitation and Treatment: Effective Programmes and Policies to Reduce Re-offending* (ed. J. McGuire), Wiley, Chichester, pp. 243–58.

Schank, R.C. and Abelson, R.P. (1977) *Scripts, Plans, Goals and Understanding*, Erlbaum, Hillsdale, NJ.

Scottish Prison Service (2003) *Manual of Standards and Guidelines for the Design Accreditation of Prisoner Programmes and the Implementation of Programmes in Establishments*, Scottish Prison Service, Edinburgh.

Simon, L.M.J. (2003) Proactive judges: Solving problems and transforming communities, in *Handbook of Psychology in Legal Contexts*, 2nd edn (eds D. Carson and R. Bull), Wiley, Chichester, pp. 449–72.

Slaby, R.G. and Guerra, N.G. (1988) Cognitive mediators of aggression in adolescent offenders: Part 1. Assessment. *Development Psychology*, **24**, 580–8.

Springer, D.W., McNeece, C.A. and Arnold, E.M. (2002) *Substance Abuse Treatment for Criminal Offenders: An Evidence-based Guide for Practitioners*, American Psychological Association, Washington, DC.

Stolle, D.P., Wexler, D.B. and Winick, B.J. (Eds.) (2000) *Practicing Therapeutic Jurisprudence: Law as a Helping Profession*, Carolina Academic Press, Durham, NC.

Strassberg, Z. and Dodge, K.A. (1987) *Focus of social attention among children varying in peer status*. Paper presented at the annual meeting of the Association for the Advancement of Behavior Therapy, Boston, MA.

Strassberg, Z., Dodge, K.A., Bates, J.E. and Pettit, G.S. (1994) Spanking in the home and children's subsequent aggression towards kindergarten peers. *Development and Psychopathology*, **6**, 445–61.

Tong, L.S.J. and Farrington, D.P. (2006) How effective is the "Reasoning and Rehabilitation" programme in reducing reoffending? A meta-analysis of evaluations in four countries. *Psychology, Crime and Law*, **12**, 3–24.

Walker, L.J., Hennig, K.H. and Krettenauer, T. (2000) Parent and peer contexts for children's moral reasoning. *Child Development*, **71**, 1033–48.

Walker, L.J. and Taylor, J.H. (1991) Family interactions and the development of moral reasoning. *Child Development*, **62**, 264–83.

Ward, T., Hudson, S.M. and Keenan, T.R. (2001) The assessment and treatment of sexual offenders against children, in *Handbook of Offender Assessment and Treatment* (ed. C.R. Hollin), Wiley, Chichester, pp. 349–61.

Weiss, B., Dodge, K.A., Bates, J.E. and Pettit, G.S. (1992) Some consequences of early harsh discipline: Chid aggression and a maladaptive social information processing system. *Child Development*, **63**, 1321–35.

Wexler, D.B. (1998) How the law can use *What Works*: A therapeutic jurisprudence look at recent research on rehabilitation. *Behavioral Sciences and the Law*, **15**, 368–9.

Wexler, D.B. and Winick, B.J. (1991) *Essays in Therapeutic Jurisprudence*, Carolina Academic Press, Durham, NC.

Wexler, D.B. and Winick, B.J. (eds) (1996) *Law in a Therapeutic Key: Developments in Therapeutic Jurisprudence*, Carolina Academic Press, Durham, NC.

Yochelson, S. and Samenow, S.E. (1976) *The Criminal Personality, Volume 1. A Profile for Change*, Jason Aronson, New York.

CHAPTER 10

The Mentally Disordered Offender: Disenablers for the Delivery of Justice

Jane Winstone and Francis Pakes
University of Portsmouth

INTRODUCTION

Mental disorder intersects with the criminal justice system in complex and changing relationships (Morris, 2001, p. 595). It affects all agencies and criminal justice processes (see Stone, 2003) and it is no overstatement to say that offenders with mental health problems offer a particular challenge to the criminal justice system (Stone, 2003; Peay, 2002; Laing, 1999; Winstone and Pakes, 2005). The term reserved for these individuals is mentally disordered offenders (MDO), but the way in which this group is defined is far from straightforward. A narrow perspective would limit the application of the term MDO exclusively to those sentenced under the *Mental Health Act 1983*. That presumes the presence of mental disorder (itself a complex issue, Laing, 1999), as well as the establishment of a certain relevance of the disorder to offending, or reoffending. Those contained and treated under the *Mental Health Act 1983* are an identifiable group of individuals and are subject to close scrutiny (e.g. Ly and Howard, 2004). Under such a definition, MDOs will concern only a small subset of the criminal justice population.

However, there is a more inclusive way of looking at mental health within the criminal justice population. The perspective that might better serve to identify mental health needs for the sentenced population and which might facilitate access to services is if offenders with any mental health need are included.

To demonstrate our point, we will present data on the probable numbers of individuals with mental health needs passing through the criminal justice system in Britain, after which we will identify a number of obstacles, or 'disenablers', to an effective way of managing and treating these individuals. We argue that sustaining an artificial division that distinguishes between those sentenced under the *Mental Health Act* and those with a range of mental health issues from the minor to the significant, who are sentenced through usual provisions, creates resource and management difficulties for those responsible for

---

Applying Psychology to Criminal Justice. Edited by David Carson, Rebecca Milne, Francis Pakes, Karen Shalev and Andrea Shawyer. © 2007 John Wiley & Sons, Ltd

the administration of justice, both in the community and in the prison setting. From this discussion, the areas where psychological research is of relevance can readily be identified. The potential involvement of psychology might vary from systems analysis in order to chart the actual provisions in place for those with mental health needs, to addressing what might be called the 64,000 dollar question: 'What Works' with mentally disordered offenders?

The data and issues discussed in this chapter particularly apply to the fate of mentally disordered offenders in Britain, but it should be acknowledged that the problems faced in relation to this group are in no way unique to Britain (e.g. Fazel and Danesh, 2002).

THE SIZE OF THE PROBLEM

The first issue to be established is the size of the problem; that is, what are the likely numbers of individuals passing through the criminal justice system with a mental disorder and what is the nature of the disorder?

It is relatively easy to establish the numbers of individuals detained under the *Mental Health Act 1983*. The 2003 Home Office Statistics of Mentally Disorder Offenders, compiled by Ly and Howard (2004), provide information on restricted patients (those who cannot be discharged without the consent of the Secretary of State or a Mental Health Review Tribunal). It documents the number of patients admitted to, detained in or discharged from hospital. On 31 December 2003 there were 3118 restricted patients detained in hospitals. Of those, 1103 (35%) were held in High Security Hospitals (Ashworth, Broadmoor and Rampton), with the remaining 2015 (65%) patients treated in other hospitals. The number of female patients detained has risen to an unprecedented 398. That comprises 13% of the total population (Ly and Howard, 2004).

Among these restricted patients detained in hospital at the end of 2003, 50% (1554) had been convicted of, or charged with, acts of violence against the person. In 241 cases the offence was murder and in 411 it was 'other homicide'. Thirteen per cent of the restricted population had been convicted of, or charged with, sexual offences and a further 13% with arson. Amongst the sentenced population, violent offences were the most common offences amongst patients suffering from mental illness, especially where there was a diagnosis of psychopathy, whilst sexual offences accounted for the highest proportion of offences amongst those with mental impairment and severe mental impairment (Ly and Howard, 2004).

By comparison, establishing the numbers of other individuals passing through the criminal justice system who are not sentenced under the *Mental Health Act 1983* is far more problematic. To begin with the police, the first observation must be that nationwide data on undetected or neglected mental health problems in police stations do not exist. James (2000) looked at police station diversion schemes in three areas in London and found that 1.1% of those in police custody were suspected of suffering from an 'overt' mental disorder. Of these, 42.1% were diagnosed with schizophrenia or allied states, 9.0% with substance dependence, 8.5% with a personality disorder, 7% with depression, 6.6% were manic, whereas 1.3% had a mental handicap. The arrest at issue involved summary offences (33.0%); theft and handling (27.2%); violence to others involved in charges (23.1%); violence against the person (8.9%); or no offence (8.7%). Similarly, Bucke and Brown (1997) found an overall prevalence of mental disorder of 2 % within those kept in a police cell. It is assumed that prevalence in large urban areas is substantially higher than in rural areas (Greenberg and Haines, 2003).

One key difficulty for dealing with mental disorder in police stations is that it requires police officers to make an initial 'lay diagnosis' and only when that suggests presence of mental health problems will a Forensic Medical Examiner be called. Stone argues that police officers are likely to underdetect mental health problems, partly due to their lack of formal psychiatric training and partly because psychiatric problems easily become obscured by more acute manifestations of alcohol and drug abuse, for example based on analysis of 1575 custody records, a third of all arrests involved an arrestee who had been drinking (Man et al., 2002).

Many individuals with mental health problems enter the police station via usage of section 136 of the *Mental Health Act 1983*. If it appears to a police officer that a person in a public place is suffering from mental disorder and is in immediate need of care or control, they can take that person to a place of safety, usually a hospital, but it can be a police station using the provision under Section 136. Many of those taken to a police station do end up eventually in hospital.

For levels of mental illness of those on remand, Singleton, Meltzer and Gatward's (1998) data from 1997 are taken as authoritative on the incidence of mental illness in remand prisons. Commissioned by the Department of Health, under the umbrella of the Office of National Statistics, Singleton, Meltzer and Gatward carried out no less than 3142 interviews and 505 follow-up interviews among male and female sentenced and remand prisoners in order to assess their mental health needs. Their data show very high levels of mental health problems, particularly with those on remand. Women prisoners suffer especially from psychotic and neurotic mental health problems, but less often from personality disorders, than men (see Table 10.1).

The Singleton et al. data show high prevalence of personality disorders, psychosis (experienced within the previous 12 months), as well as neurotic disorders such as depressive episodes, generalized anxiety disorder, mixed anxiety and depressive disorder, phobia, obsessive-compulsive disorder and panic. As a point of comparison, prevalence data in the general population (from a sample under adults living in private households) are shown in Table 10.2, data from Singleton et al. (2000).

It is clear that the prevalence of mental illness amongst the offender population is significantly higher than in private households and from this the conclusion can be drawn that, even where mental illness is not a factor in the offending behaviour, it is a significant issue for those with responsibility for the management of offenders in the Secure Estate and in Community settings.

Table 10.1 Morbidity of mental health problems amongst prisoners

	% Remand (males)	% Prison (males)	% Remand (females)	% Prison (females)
Psychosis	10	7	14 (combined)	
Personality disorders	78	64	50	
Neurotic disorders	59	40	76	63

Source: Singleton, N., Meltzer, H. and Gatward, R. (1998) Psychiatric Morbidity among Prisoners in England and Wales, Office for National Statistics, London.

Table 10.2 Prevalence of mental illness: adults living in private households

Illness	Males (%)	Females (%)
Personality disorders	5.4	3.4
Psychosis	0.5	0.6
Neurosis	14.4	20.2

Source: Singleton, N.B., O'Brien, M., Lee, A. and Meltzer, H. (2000) Psychiatric morbidity among adults living in single households. International Review of Psychiatry, 15, 63–73.

In terms of Community Sentences, under the provisions of the *Criminal Justice Act (2003)*, which came into force in April 2005, a Community Order or Suspended Sentence Order with a mental health treatment requirement may be imposed. This is a requirement that the offender must submit, during a period or periods specified in the order, to treatment by or under the direction of a registered medical practitioner or a chartered psychologist (or both, for different periods) with a view to the improvement of the offender's mental condition. The condition must be susceptible to treatment (*Sentencing Guidelines 2004*). Information on numbers of orders made under this provision is not yet available. Prior to the *Criminal Justice Act (2003)* information is available on the numbers of offenders starting probation supervision with a mental health requirement as extracted in Table 10.3.

From other data presented here, it would appear that numbers receiving a community sentence under Mental Health justice provisions are unlikely to accurately represent the actual numbers sentenced who have mental health problems. This is further illustrated when we look at young offenders.

Young offenders can be sentenced under the provisions of a Psychiatric Supervision Order. Only 25 such orders were made in the five years 1996–2000, out of a total of 10,873 where the probation service was the nominated supervising agency (Harrington *et al.*, 2005). The Youth Justice Board has not been able to identify the number of Psychiatric Supervision Orders imposed since the Youth Offending Teams took responsibility for youth justice because their statistical returns do not require that specific information (Stone, 2003).

In contrast to these rather low figures Laden, Singleton and Meltzer (2000, 2003) demonstrated that over 80% of young offenders suffered from a personality disorder (usually antisocial personality disorder), which is even higher than amongst the prison population as a whole, whilst psychotic and neurotic mental health problems were at a comparable level to imprisoned adults.

Table 10.3 Persons starting Probation Service supervision by type of requirement, in 2002

Community Rehabilitation Order	
Nonresidential mental treatment	319
Residential mental treatment	30
Residence in institution	35
Mental treatment by/under qualified medical person	172
With additional requirement: total	556
No additional MH requirement: total	58 184

Source: Home Office (2004) Probation Statistics for England and Wales. http://www.homeoffice.gov.uk.

Table 10.4 Number of mental disorders by prisoner type and gender (percentages)

Number of disorders	Males remand N=1250	Males sentenced N=1121	Females remand N=187	Females sentenced N=584
0	5	8	4	10
1	14	20	13	19
2	28	28	22	28
3	32	30	34	24
4	19	12	21	15
5	3	2	6	3

Source: Singleton, N., Meltzer, H. and Gatward, R. (1998) Psychiatric Morbidity among Prisoners in England and Wales, Office for National Statistics, London.

From the data generated by Singleton, Meltzer and Gatward (1998) and Laden, Singleton and Meltzer (2000), the conclusion must be that mental health problems within the criminal justice population are rife. This is most acutely the case for youngsters and for those on remand. Although the data are hardly new and coherent with what we know from prison populations abroad (Fazel and Danesh, 2002), it is nevertheless worth a moment of reflection: mental health problems amongst the sentenced population within and outside the secure estate are not a trivial or occasional matter, mental health problems sadly are not the exception but the norm.

The situation is exacerbated by the fact that whereas it is only 1 in 10 prison inmates who do not suffer from a mental health problem, it is still only a minority who 'only' suffer from one identifiable mental health issue. In other words, comorbidity is highly frequent, as Table 10.4 shows.

Despite these figures which have been around for some eight years, it is equally unquestionable that there is a dearth of reliable, current, statistical information on which to base an informed debate when it comes to provision, resourcing, staffing, training and so on. That is of obvious importance in relation to rehabilitation and reoffending but also simply because these data indicate that a great deal of suffering takes place within the secure estate. There is a moral obligation to seek to reduce that. The reasons for the limited statistical data probably lie in the complexity of diagnosis and assessment of mental health problems, the contribution that a mental illness makes (or does not make) to offending behaviour in establishing future risk of harm to self and others and the difficulty of undertaking robust, empirically reliable research in an area fraught with ethical and methodological difficulties. These issues will be discussed in terms of 'disenablers'.

DISENABLERS

Disenablers is a term we use to denote difficulty in obtaining access to accurate diagnosis and appropriate intervention for an offender with mental health problems. In addition to lack of statistical information, these include inadequate definitions, weak risk assessment tools and lack of resources, effective interventions and trained personnel in the criminal justice system.

Definitions

One of the main disenablers to the delivery of justice for mentally disordered offenders is inadequate definitions. Winstone and Pakes (2005) established the lack of an agreed definition across services and professions that have an input to the justice process. Firstly, there is no widely accepted definition of mental disorder. This makes it difficult to decide exactly what distinguishes it from 'normal' or healthy mental states. Legal definitions (*Mental Health Act 1983*) have given rise to a series of commentaries for guidance under the heading of mental disorder. For example, mental disorder is any illness with significant psychological or behavioural manifestations; that is, associated with either a painful or distressing symptom or impairment in one or more areas of functioning (see Davison, Neale and Kring, 2004). It is immediately obvious that such a definition of mental disorder requires interpretation. Legal categories include psychopathic disorder, mental impairment and 'arrested or incomplete development of mind'. Finally, newly established is the term Dangerous and Severe Personality Disorder, strictly a legal term, not a psychiatric category. The government is in the process of providing 300 highly secure places for those with Dangerous and Severe Personality Disorder (DSPD), in HMP Whitemoor, HMP Frankland and the High Security Hospitals Broadmoor and Rampton (Home Office, 2005).

On the other hand, the term 'mental illness' (as opposed to mental disorder) is the working tool of the health professions (but also a term used in the *Mental Health Act 1983*, but is left undefined there). Medical definitions of mental illness are also not absolute and the diagnosis of mental illness can be as much of an art as a science with all the attendant diagnostic issues of differences between professional expertise and opinion. Diagnosis is usually based on symptoms and not necessarily on causation, which is useful when considering how to manage those symptoms but not necessarily helpful when seeking to deal with the underlying causes. Thus, both the legal and the psychiatric professions work with troublesome, and separates definitions. In addition, within both legal and professional bodies there is tension within and between regarding interpretation.

Labelling an individual as a mentally disordered offender for criminal justice disposal purposes requires both a psychiatric determination of disorder as well as a demonstration by a multi-agency panel that the disorder has contributed to the offending behaviour before the court can make a decision to sentence under the provisions of the *Mental Health Act 1983* (with provision for management as set out under the *Criminal Justice Act 1991*).

Such a range of professional perspectives, with the additional issue of competing multi-agency philosophies and aims, brings about a situation in which the needs assessment for mentally disordered offenders rests on less than firm foundations. Within this context there are various ways in which unconscious stereotyping and bias in assessment can occur. This can lead to false positives in diagnosis resulting in an untenable situation that black and minority ethnic groups are over-represented as mentally disordered offenders in the criminal justice system (Badger *et al.*, 1999).

Equally untenable is the situation that many people with mental health problems go undetected in the sentencing and postconviction period. It is for this reason that we propose that a definition more appropriate to the emerging evidence around mental health and offenders be adopted, that of 'individuals within the criminal justice system with mental health needs'. This more inclusive definition should emphasize that it is desirable to both consider and support mental health needs in the offender population without the requirement for an offender to be labelled with the heavy stigma of being 'mentally disordered'. For this situation to come about, we need accurate diagnosis and good risk assessment tools in order for appropriate resources to be provided and accessed.

Detection and Assessment

We have already discussed the difficulties related to medical diagnosis but, that said, there seems to be consistent evidence that those entering the criminal justice system already under the mantel of the Care Programme Approach (CPA) fare better in terms of ongoing assessment and provision of appropriate care (DOH, 2005a).

The Care Programme Approach (CPA) was revised and integrated with Care Management in 1999 to form a single care co-ordination approach for adults of working age with mental health needs, to be used as the format for assessment, care planning and review of care by health and social care staff in all settings, including inpatient care (Warner, 2005). Two tiers of CPA were established nationally. Standard CPA is for those people whose needs can be met by one agency or professional or who need only low key support from more than one agency or professional, who are more able to self-manage their mental health problem, who pose little danger to self or others and who are more likely to maintain contact with services. People on the Enhanced CPA level are likely to have multiple care needs, which require interagency co-ordination to require more frequent and intensive interventions, to be at risk of harming themselves or others and to be more likely to disengage with services.

Adult offenders who are not on an existing CPA can be identified as possibly requiring mental health service provision through the initial use of OASYs, an actuarial risk assessment tool used by the Probation Service and Youth Offenders through ASSET and the preliminary stages of assessment are available to all at the point of charge. Standard forms will indicate whether presenting problems indicate whether further action needs to be taken. The aim is to facilitate the early detection of offenders with mental health problems and divert them out of the criminal justice system into the regular National Health Service for care and treatment (DOH 2005b; Anderson, 2003).

For those without an existing CPA, there is a not inconsiderable body of evidence to suggest that once an offender is being processed through the justice system that assessment tools are both inadequate and poorly used and that this accounts for the failure to detect many individuals with mental health problems, for example at the Police Station where 'intervening at this early stage might have a preventive impact in terms of further offending' (James, 2000, p. 553).

Birmingham *et al.* (2000) argue that many mental disorders remain undetected by prison reception health screening. Their study, supported recently by the Department of Health (DOH 2005b) suggests that diagnostic problems are frequent and serious, as psychotic problems were no less likely to be overlooked than milder mental health problems. Singleton *et al.*'s Office for National Statistics survey found that of over three-quarters of the men on remand, nearly two-thirds of the males sentenced and half of the women sentenced fitted a diagnosis of personality disorder (Singleton, Meltzer and Gatward, 1998), but it seems that often these are not detected, if present, on entering prison. As OASYS is used also by the Probation Service it seems an inevitable conclusion that mental health screening is no less inadequate at detecting mental health problems in determining appropriate community sentences and subsequent mental health provision.

The situation is no less problematic in relation to young offenders. The Youth Justice Board commissioned a report, published in 2005, entitled *Mental Health Needs and Effectiveness of Provision for Young Offenders in Custody and in the Community* (Harrington et al., 2005). The brief of this report is to identify the gaps in provision in the delivery of mental health to young offenders. It concluded that over secure and community sites there were several shortcomings. It identified significant evidence of unmet mental health needs and for these the single most important factor appeared to be inadequate screening (assessment) and, therefore, under-recognition of these needs. It concluded that this causes severe problems at all point of delivery and resourcing.

It would therefore appear that inadequate screening and risk assessment tools exacerbate the issues already identified by problematic definitions and diagnosis in the management of offenders with mental health problems in the criminal justice system.

Resources

The literature suggests that there are systemic shortcomings in what to do about meeting mental health needs once mental health problems have been identified (Gunn, 2000). There are shortages of community residential places, high secure and medium secure beds, as well as beds in local hospitals and an apparent 'gulf between the policy aim of moving the mentally disordered from prison and the means of achieving it' (Grounds, 2002, p. S35). In addition, the unstable clinical nature of mental disorder means that it is not possible to state categorically who the services are targeted at in terms of offence type, because this will be dependant on mental health need at any given time. That is, an individual with significant mental health needs may have committed a minor offence and vice versa, an individual with minor mental health needs may nevertheless commit a serious violent or sexual offence.

At present there is no national scoping of provision versus take up versus offence type and mental health need. This severely hampers any conclusions which can be drawn about resourcing and provision in the criminal justice system, other than that it appears to be patchy and limited. Unsurprising, since neither the prison nor community sector have any idea of the numbers sentenced or on remand that are likely to be requiring mental health support.

Despite this limitation, a major potential as both an enabler and disenabler to access resources is multi-agency work. When multi-agency work is effective, it is the best way to support offenders with mental health problems (Stone, 2003). However, once again we have to say that it is difficult to ascertain the coherence and effectiveness of multi-agency collaboration in through-care, community settings and prisons (DOH 2005b; Harrington et al., 2005). To cite an example, the Department of Health (2005b) recognizes that the arrangements detailed for the access of offenders in prison to mental health care is the ideal. The review of such provisions state that there are a number of pertinent questions that should be resolved in order to ensure that access is seamless and appropriate to needs. These include assessment, training and liaison, protocols, networking with relevant agencies; access to local support groups to provide additional support, as well as the availability of doctors to prescribe medication and of safe cell accommodation.

In summary, all aspects of provision to support multi-agency work require further professional scrutiny.

Similar problems are identified in provision and resourcing for young offenders. Harrington et al. (2005) identified gaps in mental health services for 16–18-year-olds and continuity of care overall posed frequent problems (Harrington et al., 2005).

It will come as no surprise that the literature continues to suggest that interagency and multi-agency processes work best where the personnel involved have developed good working relationships (Stone, 2003). It remains to be seen whether the National Offender Management Service for adult offenders will be able to improve the multi-agency practices and training, which underpin access to resources. However, it would appear that significant funding of new resources will need to take place at the same time as any multi-agency initiatives in order to provide the type of community, hospital and secure accommodation appropriate to mental health needs in which interventions can be implemented.

Intervention, Effectiveness and Research

Forensic mental health services around the world have the dual mandate of treating the patient and containing the offender (Mullen, 2002). This sets up a blurring of distinction between the goals of treatment and rehabilitation on the one hand and on the other, the goal of social control (Blackburn, 2004).

Blackburn (2004) states that 'outcome research for services to mentally disordered offenders has changed little since Quinsey (1998) remarked that treatment programmes for this group were noteworthy primarily by their absence, poor implementation, unevaluated status, lack of conceptual sophistication and incomplete description'. McGuire (2000, 2002) and Blackburn (2004) attribute this in part to the unstable clinical nature of mental disorder that impedes robust evaluation and the focus of research on the management of risk factors rather than the intervention with risk factors. However, the paucity of well-controlled treatment trials in this area does not mean that there is no evidence that might indicate the interventions that could be usefully pursued (McGuire, 2000; Heilbrun and Peters, 2000).

Pharmacological treatment for psychotic disorder is the most widely used intervention in secure settings. However, these alone do not appear to address the issues as patients exhibit a wide range of psychological problems and most psychological treatment methods developed in mental health services have been employed in secure hospitals alongside pharmacological treatments (Rice and Harris, 1997 in Blackburn, 2004). A combination of interventions is therefore seen as most promising and effective, which includes social skills training for problems of social withdrawal, psychodynamic and cognitive therapy for depression, anger management and training in problem-solving and moral reasoning to deal with criminal thinking. Common problems targeted include social and motivational deficits associated with chronic mental disorder. However, it should be noted that problems of poor self-esteem, inappropriately expressed anger, or dysfunctional personality traits are as common among the mentally ill as among the nonpsychotic (Blackburn et al., 2003).

Neuroleptic medication can ameliorate positive symptoms of schizophrenia but many patients remain treatment resistant because of associated behaviour problems of social interaction (Blackburn, 2004). These may often be amenable to skills training interventions aimed at conversational skills, emotional recognition and coping strategies (Rice and Harris, 1997 in Blackburn, 2004). The application of cognitive-behavioural methods to positive symptoms (these are the acute symptoms of the disease such as hallucinations and delusions) of schizophrenia has also been reported, although their use in secure setting so far seems to be limited. Some interventions have short-term goals of reducing problems of institutional management of patients, such as aggressive behaviours, impulsive outbursts and property destruction (Blackburn, 2004). Applied behaviour analysis has been used to deal with such problems. Anger management has been used on both an individual and group basis in several High Security Hospitals. Renwick *et al.* (1997 in Blackburn, 2004) carried out a small pilot study, which indicated that positive changes in anger and aggression had been achieved. However, there was no controlled evaluation and efficacy in reducing self-harming behaviour has not been reported.

Long-term follow-up of mentally disordered offenders released from high security in Britain and North America have generally focused on recidivism as an indication of the effectiveness of intervention (Murray, 1989, Quinsey *et al.*, 1998 in Blackburn, 2004). The most common findings have been that the overall rate of reoffending is lower than that usually reported for released prisoners. Ly and Howard's (2004) data confirms this, as only a minority of patients go on to commit a further serious violent or sexual offence. It is generally accepted that psychotic patients reoffend at a lower rate than nonpsychotic, personality-disordered patients and that there is some evidence that patients discharged with a condition of supervision are less likely to reoffend than those discharged directly to the community (Blackburn, 2004, Ly and Howard, 2004).

None of the studies involved controlled comparisons and Blackburn (2004) concludes that these studies and follow-ups do not permit conclusions about the effects of specific programmes on long-term clinical functioning or in reducing risk. Given the exposure of patients to a variety of treatment agents and environmental influences, rigorous controlled studies of the efficacy of specific treatments may not be feasible.

One of the alternatives to a traditional secure setting is the use of so-called therapeutic communities. These are dedicated to promoting intrapsychic forms of behaviour change intervention. There are two main types, democratic and concept-based/hierarchical. Democratic communities describe a holistic approach that defines an entire setting, whilst concept-based/hierarchical therapeutic communities usually describe a unit developed within a prison or secure hospital setting. The majority of secure therapeutic communities admit male offenders only. Secure therapeutic communities are located mainly within prison and correctional services. Of these, only HMP Grendon is an entirely therapeutic community prison. Other therapeutic communities comprise small units inside larger mainstream prisons.

Most democratic prison therapeutic communities specialize in personality disorders and recidivism, whilst concept-based therapeutic communities are directed specifically at substance abuse, which usually refers to drug rather than alcohol use. However, there are overlaps here and Lees, Manning and Rawlings (1999) pointed out that concept-based therapeutic communities in the community are required to deal with a high level of comorbidity between drug abuse and personality disorder and between drug abuse and mental illnesses.

Non-secure therapeutic communities, such as Henderson Hospital, might typically include psychopaths, sociopaths, personality disorders and character disorders. For example, Lees, Manning and Rawlings (1999) report that in the Henderson Hospital, the majority are young people, with a lower age limit of 18 and that 87 % of residents meet DSM-IV-R criteria for borderline personality disorder and 95 % met the criteria for at least one Cluster B Axis II diagnoses.

Treatment is usually voluntary. In secure therapeutic communities, inmates are generally selected by staff. In other therapeutic communities, selection is by the community, or by staff–patient assessment group. Inmates can leave if they choose to do so, or be expelled from the community for their behaviour. All units offer a regime of group activities, daily or community meeting, democracy or patient participation in decision making and running the therapeutic community (Association of Therapeutic Communities, 1999).

Lees, Manning and Rawlings (1999) conducted a systematic international review of therapeutic community treatment for people with personality disorders and mentally disordered offenders. They concluded that there is meta-analytical and clinical evidence that therapeutic communities produce changes in people's mental health and functioning but this needs to be further complemented by qualitative and quantitative research. In the absence of conclusive evidence of the effectiveness of any alternative treatment it was concluded that there should be a focus on those therapies that can demonstrate some efficacy in treating personality disorder. It was suggested that a review of concept-based therapeutic community literature should be commissioned to complement the current (1999) review with a concomitant meta-analysis based on the studies found (Lees, Manning and Rawlings, 1999). However, this piece of research, useful as it would be, has not been undertaken. Blackburn (2004) concludes that a therapeutic community may not be a suitable environment for psychopaths, but nonpsychopathic offenders may benefit.

The 'What Works' structured programmes of intervention arising out of cognitive behaviour studies and meta-analysis in the 1990s are the bedrock upon which prison and community interventions are developed. The guidance offered by the Offending Behaviour Programme Board (2004) concludes that it is inappropriate ethically and possibly counterproductive in terms of outcomes, to expose offenders with mental health problems to accredited programmes as run by the probation and prison service, even where the mental health problem is of a low order status, for example depression or anxiety. It is inevitable, however, with the numbers of offenders with mental health problems who are not identified by screening processes, that postsentencing they are very likely to be attending accredited programmes.

The question of effective interventions in community settings is mainly addressed around the effectiveness of different statutory or professional arrangements in minimizing harmful behaviour and promoting autonomous living. As in secure services, there is a paucity of evaluation studies (Blackburn, 2004; McGuire, 2000; Heilbrun and Peters, 2000; Hodgins and Muller-Isberner, 2000).

Reviewing this area, Heilbrun and Peters (2000) found too few studies allowing the calculation of effect sizes to permit a meta-analysis and only limited empirical generalizations on the impact of specific programmes were possible. However, they conclude that the most effective and cost-effective influences on minimizing harmful (reoffending) behaviour in the community include:

- conditional release
- intensive case management
- skills-based training
- the delivery of a range of services that include housing support and vocational training
- specialized treatment for substance abuse.

McGuire 2000 states that given consistent linkages found with adjacent fields of treatment in which there are sizeable volumes of positive evidence (e.g. cognitive behavioural intervention and evidence-based practice based on the What Works initiative), there are no reasons why those interventions that have proved beneficial with other groups should not be *appropriately adapted* and offered to offenders with mental health problems. There would appear to be some merit in this recommendation but lack of research continues to hamper developments in this area.

Personality disorders are of particular concern to those passing sentence and practitioners alike, as it is the condition that most frequently comes before the court as a factor to be taken into account in determining the most appropriate disposal. In addition, much of the provision of the proposed reforms to the Mental Health Act have been directed towards identifying a perceived loophole in current provision where the mental health condition must be amenable to treatment if sentencing is to take place under mental health provisions. Although many clinicians believe that psychopaths are untreatable, the treatment literature provides no clear support for this view (Blackburn, 2000). Blackburn (2004) notes that few programmes are designed for these disorders and those that are take place are in secure settings. Too few reports contain controlled evaluations or follow-ups to permit definitive conclusions about what methods of intervention are effective for this group (Blackburn, 2004; Blackburn, 2000; Rice and Harris, 1997). What evidence there is supports the possibility that interventions can achieve short-term clinical goals, even though it is not possible to determine which specific procedures were responsible. Blackburn 2004 comments that, in this respect, what we know about interventions to date suggests that they are probably no less effective than comparable procedures employed in mental health services more widely.

The focus on risk management through Public Protection Units and the introduction of tiered offender management under the National Probation Service (NPS) offender-management arrangements has placed a particular emphasis on dangerous and severe personality disordered offenders and the NPS has launched the Dangerous and Severe Personality Disorder (DSPD) programme. As we have already stated, the term itself is contentious amongst the medical fraternity, but the Home Office regards those with DSPD as a group hitherto poorly served by criminal justice or mental health services and contends that the serious nature of the crimes they typically commit has a disproportionate impact on the public's fear of crime. Much of the impetus for the DSPD programme has therefore come from high-profile cases such as that of Michael Stone, who in 1996 attacked Josie Russell and killed her mother and sister several years after his personality disorder was deemed untreatable.

The NPS claims that the DSPD is a new approach to assessing, managing and treating offenders who are dangerous as a result of a severe personality disorder. The DSPD is based on three factors: risk of serious harm, personality disorder and the existence of a functional link between the two. This programme brings together the Home Office, National Offender Management Service, Department of Health, Probation and Prison Services and the NHS to deliver a mental health service for this group of offenders. High priority is being given to those who are serving determinate sentences who are assessed as high or very high risk of serious harm and likely to require management through the MAPPA level 2 or 3.

Those assessed as suitable will receive a psychological therapy called dialectical behavioural therapy (DBT), which aims to help them respond to everyday situations in a problem-solving manner rather than emotionally and aggressively. This more positive mindset is intended to enable them to take part in rehabilitation programmes, such as re-offending reduction courses. However, as with other intervention initiatives, the research evidence remains thin for the potential effectiveness of this programme. DBT has predominantly been used to treat women with borderline personality disorder who deliberately harm themselves and there is little evidence it will prove effective in helping those with DSPD.

With regard to young offenders, two literature reviews, Hagell (2002) and Harrington et al. (2005) concur that there are significant problems with provision of mental health services to young offenders. Harrington et al. (2005) looked at four different areas of intervention: psychological treatments, pharmacotherapy, family therapy and multi-modal treatments. The study did not evaluate educational or youth justice approaches to reduce offending.

Psychological treatments include parent management training, which is one of the best-researched therapy techniques for the treatment of antisocial behaviour in young people. The available evidence, however, suggests that parent management training is not particularly effective for adolescents with behaviour problems, unlike with younger children. Overall, cognitive-behavioural and skills-orientated methods are likely to be more effective. Pharmacological treatments are rarely effective in isolation and any short-term benefits will need to be balanced against potential short- and long-term side effects. There is limited evidence to suggest that pharmacological treatments (mood stabilizers and neuroleptics) may reduce aggressive behaviour in adolescents with learning difficulties in the short term. Functional family therapy is a promising treatment for antisocial behaviour in young people, with several studies producing consistent beneficial effects. However, whereas family therapy skills and training are widely available within Child and Adolescent Mental Health Service settings, they are not, as yet, widely available within youth justice settings. Multi-systemic therapy is a multi-modal intervention. There have been a number of trials of multi-systemic therapy that look promising in reducing offending behaviour.

Harrington et al. (2005) state that the reporting of many of these interventions fell short of CONSORT (Consolidated Standards for Reporting Trials) and few were found to be effective when evaluated independently. They recommend that interventions should include evaluation for effectiveness with young offenders accredited by the Youth Justice Board, adaptation to the young person's individual circumstances, using a cognitive behavioural and problem-solving skills training approach based on assessment of needs, severity, motivation and ability. Furthermore, a multi-modal approach focusing on the individual, family and peer group, motivational work to engage young people in interventions, delivery by trained staff, identification and referral of those with moderate and severe mental health problems to the appropriate professional or agency.

Clearly a disenabler to managing mental health and offending behaviour is the problem of rigorous research to inform the subject area that is made more complex by the unstable nature of the condition and the ethical imperative to treat as and when required. In 2007, the *Mental Capacity Act* will come into force. The Act, which is supported by a *Code of Practice*, makes new law governing the way in which decisions are made on behalf of people who lack mental capacity. The Act imposes some additional conditions on the researcher who wants to enrol 'incompetent' adults into a study (Wilkinson, 2005) and a lack of coherence with formal ethical requirements will constitute unlawful research activity. On the one hand, this can only be for the good, as it will further ensure the protection of vulnerable people with mental health conditions. On the other hand, as McGuire (2002), amongst others, has already noted, research in this area already tends to be focused on easier targets, such as organizational roles and responsibilities, which do little to actually address the pressing need for knowledge of effective intervention strategies and further researcher restrictions is unlikely to encourage the gathering of this data.

CONCLUSION

This chapter has explored a range of disenablers in the provision of justice to those who offend and have mental health problems. People with lower level mental health disorders are usually managed with a distinctively different approach from those with higher order mental health problems. This may not be the most fruitful way to proceed. It appears to lead to confusion as to how many people with mental health problems are sentenced offenders in the criminal justice system and this exacerbates issues of how many professionals should receive appropriate training and the demand on resources. We already know that definitions are not coherent across professions and are contestable within professions, that current diagnostic and screening tools are inadequate, multi-agency provision is fraught with a range of problems and current resourcing can not even meet current demand. Knowledge generation in this area, whilst appearing to be paramount to inform policy and practice, is limited and hedged around by methodological difficulties – the fact being we know more about what we do not know that what we do. There is much to do and much that can be done to ensure that offenders with mental health problems receive justice, even if the start point is to recognize the limitations of the current modus operandi.

REFERENCES

Anderson, J. (2003) Mental Health Criminal Justice Liaison Service. Presentation. Avon and Wiltshire Mental Health Partnership NHS Trust.

Association of Therapeutic Communities (1999) Briefing Paper. Available at http://www.therapeutic communities.org. Accessed 3 March 2006.

Badger, D., Nursten, J., Williams, P. and Woodward, M. (1999) CRD Report 15 – Systematic Review of the Internation Literature on the Epidemiology of Mentally Disordered Offenders. Available at http://www.york.ac.uk/inst/crd/report15.htm

Birmingham, L., Gray, J., Mason, D. and Grubin, D. (2000) Mental illness at reception into prison. *Criminal Behaviour and Mental Health*, **10**, 77–87.

Blackburn, R. (2000) Treatment or incapacitation? Implications of research on personality disorders for the management of dangerous offenders. *Legal and Criminological Psychology*, **5**, 1–21.

Blackburn, R. (2004) "What Works" with mentally disordered offenders. *Psychology, Crime and Law*, **10**, 297–308.

Blackburn, R., Logan, C., Donnelly, J. and Renwick, S. (2003) Personality disorder, psychopathy and other mental disorders: Comborbidity Among patients at English and Scottish high security hospitals. *Journal of Forensic Psychiatry and Psychology*, **14**, 111–37.

Bucke, T. and Brown, D. (1997) In police custody: Police powers and suspects' rights under the revised PACE code of practice. Research study 174, Home Office.

Davison, G.C., Neale, J.M. and Kring, A.M. (2004) *Abnormal Psychology*, 9th edn, Wiley, Hoboken, NJ.

Department of Health (DOH) (2005a) *Mental Health Care Pathway*, DOH, London.

Department of Health (2005b) *Delivering Race Equality in Mental Health Care: An Action Plan for*

Reform Inside and Outside Services and the Government's Response to the Independent Inquiry into the Death of David Bennett, DOH, London.

Fazel, S. and Danesh, J. (2002) Serious mental disorder in 23 000 prisoners: A systematic review of 62 surveys. *Lancet*, **359**, 545–50.

Greenberg, N and Haines, N. (2003) The use of Section 136 of the Mental Health Act 1983 in a family of rural English police forces. *Medicine, Science and Law*, **43**, 75–9.

Grounds, A. (2002) Prisons and prisoners. *Criminal Behaviour and Mental Health*, **12**, S24-34.

Gunn, J. (2000) Future directions for treatment in forensic psychiatry. *British Journal of Psychiatry*, **176**, 332–8.

Hagell, A. (2002) *The Mental Health of Young Offenders, Bright Futures: Working with Vulnerable Young People*, Mental Health Foundation, London.

Harrington, R., Bailey, S., Chitsabesan, P. et al. (2005) *Mental Health Needs and Effectiveness of Provision for Young Offenders in Custody and in the Community*, Youth Justice Board for England and Wales, London.

Heilbrun, K. and Peters, L. (2000) Community-based treatment programmes, in *Violence, Crime and Mentally Disordered Offenders: Concepts and Methods for Effective Treatment and Prevention* (eds S. Hodgins and R. Muller-Isberner). Wiley, Chichester.

Hodgins, S. and Muller-Isberner R. (2000) Evidence-based treatment for mentally disordered offenders, in *Violence, Crime and Mentally Disordered Offenders: Concepts and Methods for Effective Treatment and Prevention* (eds S. Hodgins and R. Muller-Isberner). Wiley, Chichester.

Home Office (2004) Probation Statistics for England and Wales. http://www.homeoffice.gov.uk.

Home Office (2005) *Dangerous and Severe Personality Disorder (DSPD): High Secure Services for Men, Planning and Delivery Guide*, HMSO, London.

James, D. (2000) Police station diversion: Role and efficacy in central London. *The Journal of Forensic Psychiatry*, **11**, 532–55.

Laden, D, Singleton, N. and Meltzer, H. (2000) *Psychiatric Morbidity among Young Offenders in England and Wales*, Office of National Statistics, London.

Laden, D, Singleton, N. and Meltzer, H. (2003) Psychiatric morbidity among young offenders in England and Wales. *International Review of Psychiatry*, **15**, 144–7.

Laing, J.M. (1999) *Care or Custody? Mentally Disordered Offenders in the Criminal Justice System*, Oxford University Press, Oxford.

Lees, J., Manning, N. and Rawlings, B. (1999) A systematic International review of therapeutic community treatment for people with personality disorders and mentally disordered offenders in CRD Report 17, Therapeutic Community Effectiveness: Centre for Reviews and Dissemination. Available at http://www.york.ac.uk.

Ly, L, and Howard, D. (2004) Statistics of Mentally Disordered Offenders 2003, England and Wales. *Home Office Statistical Bulletin*, HMSO, London.

McGuire, J. (2000) Treatment Approaches for Offenders with Mental Disorder. *Correction Services Canada*. Available at http://www.csc-scc.gc.ca.

McGuire, J. (ed) (2002) *Offender Rehabilitation and Treatment: Effective Programmes and Policies to Reduce Re-offending*, Wiley & Sons, Chichester.

Man, L.H., Best, D, Marshalll, J. et al. (2002) Dealing with alcohol-related detainees in the custody suite. *Home Office Research Development and Statistics Directorate*, paper no 178, Home Office, London.

Mullen, P. (2002) Serious mental disorder and offending behaviours, in *Offender Rehabilitation and Treatment: Effective Programmes and Policies to Reduce Re-offending* (ed. J. McGuire), Wiley & Sons, Chichester.

Murray, D.J. (1989) Review of research on reoffending of mentally disordered offenders. Research and Planning Unit Paper, 55, London, Home Office.

Peay, J. (2002) Mentally disordered offenders, mental health, and crime, in *Oxford Handbook of Criminology* (eds R. Maguire, R. Morgan and R. Reiner), Oxford University Press, Oxford, pp. 746–91.

Quinsey, V.L. (1988) Assessment of the treatability of forensic patients. *Behavioural Sciences and the Law*, **6**, 443–52.

Quinsey, V. L. (1998) Assessment of the treatability of forensic patients. *Behavioural Sciences and the Law*, **6**, 443–52.

Renwick, S.J., Black, L., Ramm, M. and Novaco, R.W. (1997) Anger treatment with forensic hospital patients. *Legal and Criminological Psychology*, **2**, 103–16.

Rice, M.E. and Harris, G.T. (1997) The treatment of mentally disordered offenders. *Psychology, Public Policy and Law*, **3**, 126–83.

Sentencing Guidelines Council (2004) Guidelines: Criminal Justice Act 2003. Available at http://www.sentencing-guidelines.gov.uk.

Singleton, N., Meltzer, H. and Gatward, R. (1998) *Psychiatric Morbidity among Prisoners in England and Wales*, Office for National Statistics, London.

Singleton, N.B., O'Brien, M., Lee, A. and Meltzer, H. (2000) Psychiatric morbidity among adults living in single households. *International Review of Psychiatry*, **15**, 63–73.

Stone, N. (2003) *A Companion Guide to Mentally Disordered Offenders*, 2nd edn, Shaw and Sons, Crayford.

Warner, L. (2005) *Review of the Literature on the Care Programme Approach*. The Sainsbury Centre for Mental Health.

Winstone, J. and Pakes, F. (2005) Marginalised and disenfranchised: community justice and mentally disordered offenders, in *Community Justice: Issues for Probation and Criminal Justice* (eds J. Winstone and F. Pakes), Willan, Cullompton.

Wilkinson, R. (2005) Reviewing research with mentally incapacitated adults: what RECs need to consider under the Mental Capacity Act 2005. *Research Ethics Review*, **a** (4), 127–31.

CHAPTER 11

Decision Making in Criminal Justice

Edie Greene[1]
University of Colorado at Colorado Springs
and
Leslie Ellis
TrialGraphix, Inc.

The criminal justice system involves a complicated set of rules, roles and procedures, and professionals and laypeople alike can be overwhelmed by its enormity and complexity. In particular, individuals who make decisions in the context of the criminal law – judges, magistrates, attorneys and jurors – can be inundated with vast amounts of information they must consider in reaching the desired judgements, including complicated legal rules, ambiguous facts and contradictory arguments about the application of the rules to the facts. Furthermore, many of the questions asked in the realm of criminal law (e.g. 'Did the defendant intend to kill the victim?') require judgements based on probabilities and likelihoods, rather than certainties, further complicating the decision task.

Our intent in this chapter is to describe what psychologists and other behavioural scientists have learned about the ways that people make decisions in the context of the criminal law and, in particular, to detail how decision makers wade through the vast amount of information that could potentially inform their judgements. We explore ways in which the complexity of the decision-making task can lead, sometimes, to biases and errors in the reasoning process and describe how those errors can affect legal decisions. In particular, we show that legal decisions are often informed by patterns of short-cut, heuristical thinking and describe decision makers' reliance on six cognitive heuristics: the availability heuristic, the representativeness heuristic, hindsight bias, overconfidence, anchoring-and-adjustment and the simulation heuristic. We detail psychological theories about the role of these heuristics in legal judgements and apply theories and empirical findings to the real-world context of criminal courtrooms and tribunals. Most of this review will focus on laypeople as decision makers (i.e. jurors and juries) because psychologists have devoted most of their

---

[1] To whom correspondence should be addressed. Department of Psychology, University of Colorado, Colorado Springs, CO 80933, USA. e-mail: egreene@uccs.edu

Applying Psychology to Criminal Justice. Edited by David Carson, Rebecca Milne, Francis Pakes, Karen Shalev and Andrea Shawyer. © 2007 John Wiley & Sons, Ltd

research efforts to this group. There exist a few empirical studies of judges' and magistrates' decisional abilities and fewer still that look at judgements made by attorneys, and those studies will be described as well.

BIASES IN LEGAL DECISIONS: THE USE OF JUDGEMENT HEURISTICS

When people encounter vast quantities of information, their cognitive processing systems must exert some selectivity in determining what information is attended to and what information is essentially ignored. Similarly, when people rely on information stored in memory in order to facilitate decision making, they must also exercise selectivity in bringing to mind only information relevant to the task at hand. Ideally, once information has been attended to and made accessible in memory, the decision maker will use these sources as bases for judgements that reflect deliberative thought, careful weighing of alternatives and accurate consideration of all relevant evidence. However, given the complexity and uncertainty of many decisions (including those assigned to legal decision makers), the multiple sources of arguably relevant information, and the ambiguous nature of many judgement tasks, decision makers do not always use systematic and rational thought processes.

One of the ways in which they stray from rationality is by relying on cognitive shortcuts that ease the judgement task. These shortcuts are referred to as judgement heuristics and generally defined as simple rules of thumb or strategies that make the decision or judgement task simpler. They are often relied on in situations, including the criminal law, where the decision maker must make a judgement based on complicated, probabilistic, or ambiguous information and may be under time pressure to do so.

Although heuristics are most often used in situations that require a difficult decision to be made in the face of uncertain information, other factors influence how likely one is to use a heuristic. For example, when the decision maker is under a high cognitive load (needing to attend to and remember a large amount of information or to comprehend complicated and confusing evidence), they are more likely to use a heuristic than if not under a high cognitive load (Fiske and Taylor, 1991). In addition, a person who is distracted will be more likely to rely on heuristical reasoning when making a decision than one who is not. When an individual lacks the cognitive capabilities necessary to make a particular decision because they are being applied elsewhere, heuristics are sometimes used to simplify the task.

The use of heuristics in decision tasks does not *necessarily* result in the selection of invalid or inappropriate choices, but because it involves shortcut procedures rather than optimal strategies for making decisions, heuristical reasoning often leads to biased and erroneous conclusions (Tversky and Kahneman, 1982b). So, for example, jurors using the so-called availability heuristic (described in more detail below) are likely to rely on irrelevant or inadmissible evidence in reaching their verdicts if that information is highly accessible in memory or especially vivid or memorable (Kelman, Rottenstreich and Tversky, 1996). As another example, jurors who rely on the representativeness heuristic (also described below) may ignore relevant evidence presented during the trial in favour of irrelevant, but more characteristic information (Moore, 1989). Another type of reasoning strategy, hindsight bias, can affect people's beliefs that litigants should have been able to predict the outcomes of events that *no one* could have predicted (Kamin and Rachlinski, 1995).

Jurors are certainly not the only legal decision makers to employ short-cut reasoning strategies; even experienced legal thinkers sometimes show biased judgement processes. For example, when judges misperceive the likelihood that their decisions would be overturned on appeal or prefer less useful anecdotal evidence over more useful statistical evidence, they too, may be relying on heuristics (Guthrie, Rachlinski and Wistrich, 2001). Finally, attorneys who misperceive the probability of a particular outcome at trial may be using heuristical reasoning processes (Goodman-Delahunty, Granhag and Loftus, 1998).

The use of heuristics is sometimes seen as irrational. Indeed, if one could sense when a heuristic was being used and either terminate its use or consider a wider range of information in reaching a decision, the end result might well be a more rational choice. (We ponder these possibilities later in the chapter when we discuss implications of these research findings for legal judgements and the attempts that have been made to minimize biased reasoning.) In most people, the use of heuristics goes largely undetected, however, and most heuristics are used unconsciously (Tversky and Kahneman, 1974, 1982). The largely automatic operation of heuristics corroborates recent findings on automaticity that suggest that many of our thoughts do not result from deliberative contemplation, but rather from quicker, more reflexive processes that are less available for conscious control (Bargh and Chartrand, 1999). Although the label of 'heuristic' has historically referred to these unconscious thought processes, it has recently been expanded to include conscious decisions that make cognitive tasks easier, as well as conscious and unconscious social inferences about one's self and other people.

Many of the conditions that result in reliance on heuristics are present in the context of jury decision making, and jurors' use of heuristics has been well documented (Moore, 1989; Wiener et al., 1994). In fact, jurors may be especially likely to rely on cognitive heuristics because their task invariably involves a complex set of judgements about the weight, relationship and probative value of discrete pieces of information and because they often lack the legal background needed to make sense of this information (Saks and Kidd, 1980). In some cases, the evidence concerns issues with which jurors have little familiarity and no expertise. In addition, by the time jurors are sent to deliberate, they are under a very high cognitive load. They have heard several hours, days, or weeks of witness testimony, listened to a set of complex judicial instructions, and observed the testimony of several witnesses. They may feel that they are under time pressure (or may actually be working under a self-imposed deadline), and must make very important decisions with potentially profound consequences for other human beings. Further, as jury trials have begun to receive more publicity than in the past (in print, on television and over the internet) and as several high-profile juries have been criticized in recent years for seemingly indefensible verdicts, the pressure to arrive at a decision that is both legally and socially acceptable may also contribute to jurors' stress. Thus, the resulting decision-making task can be very difficult indeed, and cognitive shortcuts can make that task somewhat more manageable.

Jurors may use heuristics at any of several points during their encoding of the evidence and discussion of it during deliberations: to better understand the attorneys' opening and closing arguments, when evaluating lay and expert witnesses and the merits of their testimony, when trying to decipher the legal instructions, and when determining guilt. Judges and magistrates may rely on heuristics when making pretrial rulings about the admissibility of evidence, evaluating challenges made by attorneys during jury selection, responding to objections raised during trial, instructing the jury on the law and sentencing offenders. In this chapter, we describe a number of heuristics that may affect legal judgements and cite research findings in psychology and law that document their use. Finally, we describe how these research findings can be applied in real-life settings of courtrooms and tribunals. Although many of the studies we rely on were conducted in the USA using American trial procedures and rules of evidence, we are confident that the thinking processes that they uncover are universal. Though legal rules and roles may differ across countries and cultures, the underlying influences on legal decision making are similar.

AVAILABILITY HEURISTIC

Many decisions require assessments of probabilities that events occurred as claimed (e.g. how likely it is that the defendant's version of the facts is true), and of the frequency with which particular events occur (e.g. how frequently a certain type of crime is committed). Relying on a heuristic in these situations is often simpler and less taxing than attempting to use all available and relevant information to make the assessment. For example, jurors making judgements about the likelihood of the defendant's version of the facts and, by extension, about his guilt are likely to rely on a short-cut strategy termed the availability heuristic (see, e.g. Moore, 1989; Saks and Kidd, 1980).

The availability heuristic is used when one has to estimate the frequency or probability of some event (Fiske and Taylor, 1991; Markus and Zajonc, 1985; Tversky and Kahneman, 1974, 1982a). One way in which a person might estimate the frequency or probability of an event is to rely on the ease with which examples of that event can be retrieved from memory or imagined. Rather than methodically thinking through or researching every possible instance of the event's occurrences, the decision maker often chooses to use, or is only cognitively capable of using, what is available in memory to estimate the frequency or probability. If there are many instances of the event that are easily accessible in memory, then it is reasonable to infer that the event happens with some regularity.

The disadvantage of using recall to estimate or judge the frequency of occurrence is that memory is notoriously selective: not all possible instances or examples of a particular situation will be committed to memory, and irrelevant or unusual examples may achieve a position of undue prominence in memory. In other words, variables other than *actual* frequency can affect accessibility. Thus, when the mental availability of an event is the basis for the frequency estimate of that event, the estimate will often be biased (Nisbett and Ross, 1980; Tversky and Kahneman, 1982a).

The availability heuristic can be used by jurors at any time during a trial. As they are listening to the evidence and deliberating with other jurors they may need to determine whether a particular event did, in fact, occur and, if so, how often it occurred. But if the juror had been exposed to some kind of pretrial information about the event in question, it may be highly accessible in memory and thus, seem particularly memorable. Hence, the ease with which this event (or precise details about the event that may be important in assessing guilt) can be recalled from memory may be completely unrelated to its likelihood. In other words, jurors' decisions may be based more on access to pretrial information than on any evidence related to this topic that was presented at trial.

An example of the impact of pretrial publicity and its role in making some case facts highly available in memory comes from data reported by Vidmar (2002). Louise Reynolds was charged with murder in connection with the death of her 7-year-old daughter in Kingston, Ontario in 1997. In the two year period that followed this incident, the local newspaper, the *Kingston Whig Standard*, printed 48 articles about the case, including many lengthy features, and provided extensive coverage of the prosecution's allegations against Mrs Reynolds, including its belief that she stabbed her daughter 84 times in the head. The paper also described the child's tragic and abuse-filled life in some detail. The defendant's alternate theory – that the child was killed by a pit-bull found near the crime scene and covered in blood – was corroborated by two forensic scientists, although this information was never printed in the local paper. According to Vidmar,

> [C]ommunity emotions were initially inflamed against the mother when news accounts reported that the child had been brutally killed, that the mother had fathered (sic) all five of her children by different men, and that at the time of her daughter's death she was under investigation by the Children's Aid Society. . . and community emotions were fanned again a year later when the local newspaper published a tribute poem that the mother had written for her deceased daughter to commemorate the first anniversary of the girl's death. The public emotions were so high that an official police report expressed concern for the safety of the mother when she was held in detention. (p. 78)

Professor Vidmar was hired in 2000 to conduct a public opinion survey of the community in order to assess whether attitudes had dissipated or whether they were still inflamed. He used open-ended questions and recorded respondents' answers verbatim. A majority of respondents knew about the case and many were able to provide detailed factual knowledge. Although this case never went to trial (charges against Mrs Reynolds were dismissed after a forensic scientist hired by the prosecution admitted errors and changed his opinion), one would suspect that jurors exposed to this kind of pretrial information (including those who swore to be fair and impartial) would have a very hard time setting it aside and evaluating the trial testimony on its own merits. If pretrial information is accessible and available in memory, it can change the way that other evidence is interpreted and remembered.

Information that is readily available to jurors can also affect a category of defendants as well as a particular defendant. Consider the vast amounts of air time and print lines devoted to alleged instances of corporate misconduct over the past few years – the Enron, WorldCom and Martha Stewart cases in the USA come to mind. Jurors' perceptions of American blue-chip executives has likely evolved with the coverage – in many jurors' minds, corporate executives are all conspirators and crooks, out to steal from the little guy to line their own pockets. When an individual is accused of similar conduct it is possible, and perhaps likely, that jurors will have a readily-available stereotype of how corporate executives behave, and categorize any particular defendant with those who have been widely discussed in the popular media.

Personal experiences obviously affect the ease with which certain events can be brought to mind, and by extension, the likelihood that availability-based judgement biases will be present. Colwell (2005) recounts the story of a judge's sentencing decision that was influenced by his personal experiences with the issues before him in court. This small town Pennsylvania judge sentenced a defendant charged with cruelty to animals to the maximum term of two years in prison, whereas the defendant in the following case, guilty of robbery for a second time, received probation. The discrepancy was apparently related to the fact that the judge had buried his pet of 14 years earlier that morning; this experience, highly salient and vivid in his memory, affected (some would say, biased) his sentencing decision.

REPRESENTATIVENESS HEURISTIC

The representativeness heuristic is also used to assess the likelihood or probability of an event (Fiske and Taylor, 1991; Kahneman and Tversky, 1982b; Nisbett and Ross, 1980;

Tversky and Kahneman, 1974). When estimating the likelihood of some event (e.g. that a child had been sexually abused), people tend to base their decisions on the extent to which the exemplar (e.g. the child in question) resembles or is representative of a broader class or category (e.g. all victims of child sexual abuse). If there is a good match – for example if the child appears to be frightened and evasive in the presence of the defendant in the courtroom (traits found to be representative of sexually abused children) – then observers will decide that the exemplar is a member of the category. If there is not a good match (e.g. the child witness appears to be calm or confrontational in the presence of the alleged offender), then observers will decide that the exemplar is not a member of the category. Representativeness is deemed a heuristical strategy because decision makers who use it do not thoroughly examine the evidence available to them (in our example, evidence regarding the allegedly illegal actions of the defendant). Rather, they make a 'goodness of fit' judgement, asking whether the exemplar fits the category.

Although estimating an event's probability by relying on representativeness of the evidence will often produce fairly accurate judgements, it can sometimes lead to errors (Fiske and Taylor, 1991). In particular, it can lead people to discount relevant statistical information. For example, the probability of the event actually occurring (the so-called 'base rate') may be ignored in favour of information about the similarity of the exemplar to a particular category. Modifying the above example slightly, consider a case involving alleged ritualistic sexual abuse, a very rare crime. People who are asked if an alleged child victim was subjected to ritualistic sexual abuse may ignore the fact that few such crimes occur and instead consider how similar the targeted behaviour (the child's nervous, evasive demeanor in the courtroom) is to their notions of how victims react to ritualistic abuse. This error is called the base rate fallacy – people often fail to consider the base rate of the event's occurrence when estimating the likelihood of that event, perhaps because the relevant statistical evidence is unknown and it is simply easier for people to focus on vivid, individuating evidence (Gigerenzer and Goldstein, 1996).

In fact, there is empirical evidence that a child witness's demeanour in the courtroom can affect perceptions of the child and of the defendant's guilt. Regan and Baker (1998) asked men and women to provide a listing of the affective and behavioural responses they would expect a child victim of sexual assault to show when first confronting the defendant in a courtroom. Respondents apparently had little difficulty generating this list of representative behaviours. The researchers then manipulated the presence or absence of one of these expected responses (e.g. crying) in a jury analogue study and found that the child who cried on seeing the defendant (i.e. who demonstrated the behaviour representative of the category of child sexual abuse victims) was deemed more honest, credible and reliable than a child who did not. Further, mock jurors were more likely to convict the defendant when the child demonstrated representative behaviours than when the child did not. Subsequent research has shown that too little or too much emotion from an alleged child victim can reduce his or her credibility (Golding et al., 2003). Apparently, there is a narrow range of emotional responding that mock jurors deem prototypical of child sexual abuse victims.

Use of the representativeness heuristic is also apparent in situations where people use their prior knowledge about crimes and criminal activity to filter incoming information and reach verdicts in a criminal case. Smith (1991, 1993) determined that people can readily list the prototypical or representative features of various crimes, based on their naïve beliefs about these crimes (e.g. that burglaries happen only at night). Importantly, when matched against legal requirements, the features they list tend to be incomplete, incorrect or irrelevant. Nonetheless, people have been shown to use these features in their judgements of a defendant's guilt in a jury analogue setting.

When Smith varied the nature of the evidence in her jury simulations, including either many participant-generated features of the crime or few such features, she found that scenarios containing many characteristic features were rated as more representative of the crime category and produced more guilty verdicts than scenarios containing few prototypic features, despite the fact that all scenarios met the legal requirements for the crime in question. In other words, events that fit jurors' expectations of what those crimes are like were more apt to be categorized as crimes than events that did not fit their expectations. Jurors' prior knowledge of crime categories, though often erroneous, influences their verdict choices.

Further research showed that prior knowledge of crime features influences not just jurors' verdicts but other stages of the decision task as well. When people rely on their prior knowledge during a trial, their expectations about what is typical or representative for the type of crime charged can influence the inferences they make about the evidence. Smith and Studebaker (1996) showed that mock jurors misremembered evidence (i.e. made memory intrusions) in line with their expectations of that evidence. In other words, jurors will make inferences about the trial evidence and judge the defendant's guilt in light of their notions of representativeness; if the evidence is representative of their preconceived notions of a particular category of crime, it is given credence and factored into their decision-making process.

Expectations about who might commit a particular crime can also influence jurors' readiness to convict. Although jurors often refer to the standard of proof during their deliberations (the burden of proof in criminal litigation is 'beyond a reasonable doubt' or some version of that language), those definitions are to some extent subjective. Further, jurors may have their own 'psychological burdens' or standards of proof that are influenced by how much convincing they need given a particular set of facts. Consider a scenario in which a defendant is charged with dealing drugs, and the venue is a mostly middle-class, conservative, white neighbourhood. In one instance the defendant is a poor, urban, young, immigrant male and in another instance the defendant is a middle-aged, middle-class, suburban white male. Jurors have stereotypes of who commits what types of crimes, and so they are likely to find the first defendant more representative of drug dealers than the second. Therefore, they will need more convincing that the second defendant committed the crime. Their sense of what a defendant is supposed to 'seem like' influences their psychological burden of proof when judging an actual defendant.

Judges are experienced and legally-astute decision makers. One might surmise that they would be less prone to heuristical reasoning than laypeople. Are they? Guthrie, Rachlinski and Wistrich (2001) examined the possibility that judges also fall prey to a variety of cognitive heuristics, including the representativeness heuristic. (Their experimental materials involved a fact pattern from a civil lawsuit, but we have no reason to suspect that findings would be different in a criminal case.) They asked 167 federal magistrates in the USA to read a brief description of a case based on the classic English case, *Byrne* v. *Boadle* (1863). The plaintiff, passing the defendant's warehouse, was struck by a barrel that was being hoisted into the warehouse. Government safety inspectors investigating the warehouse determined that: (1) when barrels are negligently secured, there is a 90 % chance that they will break loose; (2) when barrels are safely secured, they break loose only 1 % of the time; and (3) workers negligently secure barrels only 1 in 1,000 times. Judges were asked how likely it was that the barrel fell due to negligence of the defendant's workers. The probability that the defendant was negligent is actually only 8.3 %, although most people assume the likelihood of negligence is high because they fail to attend to the base rate (that workers negligently secure barrels only 1 time in 1000 attempts). Approximately 40 % of judges selected a response in the correct range (0–25 % probability of negligence) but 60 % selected an erroneous response that suggested reliance on the representativeness heuristic. Guthrie *et al.* suspect that judges' apparent preference for individuating evidence (e.g. eyewitness testimony) over statistical evidence (e.g. base rate information) is caused by over-reliance on the representativeness heuristic. In other words, because the evidence presented in the case seemed to represent a situation in which the defendant had acted negligently, judges assessed a higher level of liability against the defendant than was warranted; they ignored the fact that workers rarely mishandle barrels.

HINDSIGHT BIAS

Once the outcome of an event is known to people, they overestimate the likelihood that the event would have transpired in just that way. This well-known phenomenon, termed 'hindsight bias', was originally described by Fischhoff (1975). In his original studies of the hindsight bias, Fischhoff found that when people were told how an event turned out, they perceived that outcome as far more likely than did people not told of the outcome. Apparently, people find it difficult to disregard information that they already possess and to reproduce the judgements they would have made without that information. According to Guthrie, Rachlinski and Wistrich (2001), '[l]earning the outcome has such profound and subtle effects on people's beliefs that recreating a past prediction is like trying to cross the same river twice – upon learning the outcome the brain has developed a new set of beliefs and can never really return to its previous state' (p. 825). In addition, people tend to remember more information that is consistent with a known outcome than information that is inconsistent with that outcome (Hawkins and Hastie, 1990).

Although few judgements in life require people to disregard information they acquired previously, legal judgements frequently require this mental gymnastic. Hindsight biases have been demonstrated in cases in which jurors have to assess a defendant's liability after they have learned the outcome of the defendant's actions. For example, Kamin and Rachlinski (1995) compared participants' evaluations of whether a municipality should take (foresight condition), or have taken (hindsight condition), precautions to protect property from flood damage. Participants in the hindsight condition had outcome knowledge about the occurrence of a flood; foresight participants did not. Although three-quarters of foresight participants concluded that a flood was too improbable to justify precautions by the municipality, a majority of hindsight participants determined that this decision was negligent. They had difficulty disregarding their knowledge of the flood.

Casper, Benedict and Perry (1989) examined the influence of the outcome of a police search on mock jurors' judgements of liability of the police officers alleged to have conducted the illegal search. After seeing a videotaped trial simulation of an illegal search and seizure civil suit brought against two police officers, jurors learned about the outcome of the search: In the 'guilty outcome', police had found evidence of illegal conduct. In the 'innocent outcome', they did not find any incriminating evidence against the suspect and later arrested a different person for the offence. There was also a 'no outcome' version.

Mock jurors then heard jury instructions that defined the criteria for a legal search and included an admonition to disregard outcome information in making a decision about damages. However, when jurors learned that the subject of the search was guilty of a crime, they were less likely to find the police officers liable for compensatory damages than when they learned that the suspect was not guilty. Jurors were unable to follow the admonition to disregard evidence related to the outcome of the search.

Jurors are occasionally asked to ignore information that they became aware of prior to or during trial. How effective are these admonitions on focusing jurors' attention solely on the evidence adduced at trial, rather than information acquired elsewhere? Although some early research indicated that admonitions can successfully overcome effects of pretrial publicity (e.g. Kline and Jess, 1966; Simon, 1966), more recent studies using improved methodology suggest that the prejudicial impact of pretrial publicity is difficult to undo. Once jurors know some details about a case, it is hard for them to return to a preknowledge state and to judge the defendant based only on the information they learn at trial (Fein, McCloskey and Tomlinson, 1997; Kramer, Kerr and Carroll, 1990).

On occasion, jurors are also instructed to disregard evidence that is introduced during the trial. This situation arises whenever an attorney objects to the inclusion of certain evidence, the judge sustains the objection, and then instructs or admonishes the jury to disregard the material. Hindsight biases cause jurors to have difficulty ignoring or disregarding information they are aware of, but have been instructed not to use. For example, Pickel (1995) presented mock jurors with information that a defendant in a theft trial had a prior conviction. That information was (1) admitted as evidence, (2) ruled inadmissible with a simple admonition for the jury to disregard it, or (3) ruled inadmissible and accompanied by an explanation of this ruling by the judge. Results showed that when the judge gave a legal explanation as to why the jurors were to disregard information about the defendant's prior conviction, they were actually *more* likely to convict him. When mock jurors in a different study were told to disregard certain evidence because of a legal technicality, they still allowed that evidence to influence their verdicts when they thought that it enhanced the accuracy of their decisions (Sommers and Kassin, 2001). After a very thorough review of the experimental evidence, Tanford (1990) concluded, 'the empirical research clearly demonstrates that instructions to disregard are ineffective in reducing the harm caused by inadmissible evidence and improper arguments' (p. 95). Jurors have difficulty ignoring relevant information when asked to do so and a harder time basing a judgement only on a subset of relevant (i.e. admissible) information. Some recent work suggests, however, that the biasing effects of exposure to inadmissible evidence may be tempered by the process of deliberating (London and Nunez, 2000).

Defendants might demonstrate hindsight biases in their beliefs about the effectiveness of their attorneys. After being convicted, a criminal defendant might second-guess the decisions made by the attorney during the course of the trial and imagine a different outcome had the attorney used a different trial strategy (Guthrie, Rachlinski and Wistrich, 2001). One wonders how many appeals based on ineffective assistance of counsel actually represent the effects of hindsight biases.

Judges are also vulnerable to the influence of the hindsight bias. For example, Guthrie *et al.* asked the same set of magistrates to read a hypothetical fact pattern about a state prisoner who filed an action against the Director of the Department of Criminal Justice in his state, claiming that the prison had provided him with negligent medical treatment. The judge described in the scenario dismissed the complaint, finding that the prisoner knew his claims were not actionable because they had been dismissed in the past, and sanctioned him. The plaintiff-prisoner appealed. Guthrie and his colleagues varied the outcome of the appeal: one-third of participant-magistrates learned that the court of appeals affirmed the lower court's decision, one-third learned that the court of appeals ruled that the lower court had abused its discretion and remanded the case for imposition of a less onerous sanction, and one-third learned that the court of appeals found that the lower court abused its discretion and vacated the sanction against the plaintiff. All respondents were asked 'In light of the facts of the case, which of the following possible outcomes of the appeal was the most likely to have occurred?' The three possible outcomes were provided. Knowing the outcome of the appeal significantly influenced the judges' assessments of which outcome was most likely: after learning that the court of appeals had affirmed the lower court, fully 82 % of judges indicated that they would have predicted this result, whereas only 28 % of those told that the court of appeals had vacated the decision predicted affirmance.

It is troubling (though not terribly surprising) that judges fall prey to the same biases as laypeople because judges must make many evidentiary rulings in light of information learned in hindsight. If judges are as susceptible as laypeople to the influence of hindsight, they will have difficulty ignoring that information and making rulings in a fair and even-handed manner (Guthrie, Rachlinski and Wistrich, 2001).

OVERCONFIDENCE

Legal decision makers are routinely called on to evaluate evidence and assess confidence – both in themselves and in others (e.g. defendants, witnesses). In terms of evaluating confidence in one's self, consider the dilemmas facing a criminal defence attorney when he or she advises a client about pleading guilty to a lesser charge, negotiates a plea bargain, and develops a trial strategy. Consider the situation facing a plaintiff's attorney who must decide whether to take a case, sue, or settle out of court. Clearly, those choices cannot be determined by the application of scientific formulas. Rather, they are informed by the lawyers' own perspectives on the probabilities of success in the courtroom. How able are we to predict our own successes and anticipate our own failures? Some recent research has shown that attorneys often overestimate their abilities and the relative merits of their case. As a result, they place far more confidence in their judgements about how to proceed (and in the likelihood of success) than is warranted by the facts.

In studies that have measured lawyers' judgements about the likelihood of winning their cases, American lawyers showed very poor accuracy (Goodman-Delahunty, Granhag and Loftus, 1998), and Dutch attorneys were only somewhat better calibrated (Malsch, 1989). Base rates in both studies were approximately 50 % but both sets of attorneys were overconfident of success for high probability events. Not surprisingly, American attorneys who were surveyed close to the time of trial showed better discrimination than attorneys who were questioned farther from the trial date, perhaps because the reality of a looming court date forced attorneys to become better prepared and therefore, more realistic about their chances.

Often, overconfidence results from the egocentric, or self-serving ways that people make judgements about themselves and issues that are meaningful to them. For example, when Goodman-Delahunty *et al.* (1998) questioned a subset of attorneys working on a contingency fee arrangement for a plaintiff (a situation with heightened personal relevance to the attorney), they found evidence of significant overconfidence: these lawyers were generally about 65 % confident – as were attorneys working on noncontingency fee bases – but won their cases much less often (42 % versus 56 % overall).

Egocentric biases affect the ways that people evaluate evidence. For example, laypeople who were asked to play the role of either the plaintiff or defendant in a personal injury case involving an automobile-motorcycle collision and to assess the value of the case interpreted the evidence in ways that were self-serving: although all participants had the same information, those who evaluated the case from the perspective of the plaintiff predicted that the judge would award approximately $14,500 more than the role-playing defendants predicted (Loewenstein et al., 1993). When asked what they believed to be a fair settlement in the case, the number offered by the 'plaintiffs' was, on average, nearly $18,000 more than the amount suggested by the 'defence'.

Judges are also likely to interpret evidence in self-serving ways and attribute more confidence to their decisions than is warranted. Guthrie, Rachlinski and Wistrich (2001) demonstrated this phenomenon by asking magistrates to respond to a simple question about the reversal of their decisions on appeal. Specifically, judges were asked to rank themselves in relation to other judges by placing themselves into the quartile corresponding to their reversal rates: highest (>75 %), second highest (>50 %), third highest (>25 %) or lowest (<25 %). More than half of the judges (56 %) placed themselves in the lowest quartile and nearly a third (31.5 %) placed themselves in the second highest quartile. In other words, nearly 90 % believed that half of their peers had higher reversal rates than they did – a statistical impossibility apparently caused by egocentric biases. (Although these findings may simply show that judges are unwilling to admit they had high reversal rates, people believe themselves to be better than average across a range of tasks and domains and judges are probably no different.) Garrison Keillor, story-telling host of a popular weekly radio broadcast in the USA, describes a fictitious town where 'all the men are strong, all the women are good-looking, and all the children are above-average'. Keillor's tongue-in-cheek description is an apt assessment of people's self-serving beliefs about themselves (and their children).

Jurors are swayed by others' confidence as well as their own. Decision makers have been shown to rely more heavily on confidently asserted statements than modestly asserted ones (e.g. Narby, Cutler and Penrod, 1996). The basic concept underlying this form of bias is that a confidently-made statement is perceived as more accurate than a timidly-made statement. However, the relationship between accuracy and confidence has been shown to be rather low (see, e.g. Penrod and Cutler, 1995).

This bias can be particularly damaging when jurors are evaluating the veracity of eyewitness testimony: eyewitness confidence in the accuracy of the identification is not strongly correlated with the accuracy of the identification (Narby, Cutler and Penrod, 1996; Smith, Kassin and Ellsworth, 1989). This is especially troubling in the light of the fact that many judges instruct jurors that they can use a witness's confidence as an indicator of their accuracy (*Neil* v. *Biggers*, 1972; Smith, Kassin and Ellsworth, 1989).

ANCHORING AND ADJUSTMENT

When making quantitative judgements in situations that involve uncertainty, people often begin with some tentative initial estimate. This initial value is sometimes suggested by a salient numerical reference point that serves as an anchor for the subsequent judgement. Even if new information causes people to adjust their judgements, these adjustments tend to be insufficient. Thus, a low anchor keeps a judgement too low and a high anchor keeps a judgement too high. Individuals who reason in this way are invoking an anchoring-and-adjustment heuristic (Tversky and Kahneman, 1974). This bias is quite pervasive, and even wildly extreme anchors can influence judgements. People provided higher estimates of the average temperature in San Francisco when first asked whether it was higher or lower than 558 degrees, a number that may have induced people to consider the very unlikely possibility that San Francisco temperatures are actually warm (cited by Guthrie, Rachlinski and Wistrich, 2001).

Anchors are influential in decisions about damage awards because jurors typically lack confidence in their own abilities to assign dollar values to various injuries. People who are not confident of their judgements are more susceptible to being influenced by an anchor (Jacowitz and Kahneman, 1995). Hinsz and Indahl (1995) assessed the impact of a quantitative anchor on mock jury damage awards. They re-enacted a civil trial in which the defendant was being sued for wrongful death by the parents of two children killed in an automobile accident. In one version, the plaintiff's lawyer requested $2 million, and in another, $20 million. When jurors were asked to fairly and reasonably compensate the plaintiffs for their losses, they assessed damages of $1,053,000 in the former condition and $9,062,000 in the latter.

Data from Chapman and Bornstein (1996) support the contention that even extreme anchors have some residual affect on a subsequent judgement. In one version of their mock personal injury trial in which the plaintiff claimed that her birth control pills led to her ovarian cancer, she requested $1 billion in compensation. Although she was perceived as more selfish and less honorable than a hypothetical plaintiff who asked for only $5 million, still jurors awarded more to her than to the more reasonable plaintiff. Hastie, Schkade and Payne (1999) have shown dramatic effects of the plaintiff's request for punitive damages on the resulting award.

Jurors are not unique in their susceptibility to anchoring effects; attorneys can be influenced by anchoring effects in plea bargaining negotiations and decision making (Bibas, 2004). In observational analysis of the bail-setting decisions in two London courts, Dhami (2003) found that the best predictor of judicial behaviour on the bail question was the prosecutor's request (the anchor) and that a model based on only three cues – the prosecutor's request, the position of the police and actions of the previous court – was a better predictor of judicial behaviour than a model incorporating various factors thought to be relevant to the bail-setting decision (e.g. defendant's record, seriousness of offence). In the context of a persuasive anchor, judges are unlikely to search through all information relevant to bail-setting and weigh it according to reliability and validity, despite the fact that bail decisions may influence subsequent judgements about a defendant's guilt and sentencing (Davies, 1971).

Judges apparently also invoke the anchoring-and-adjustment heuristic when making decisions about sentencing. Biased or misleading sentencing recommendations can come from both prosecutor and defence attorney and can apparently influence judicial decisions about sentencing. Englich and Mussweiler (2001) demonstrated that trial judges' sentencing decisions are assimilated to the sentences demanded by the prosecutor, that this influence is independent of the perceived legitimacy of the demands, and that even experienced judges fall prey to their effects. Mandatory sentencing guidelines, like those in place (or in an advisory capacity) in federal courts and many state courts in the USA, can constrain the range of available sentencing options and serve as a sort of neutral anchor, reducing judges' reliance on recommendations from the parties.

SIMULATION HEURISTIC AND COUNTERFACTUAL THINKING

Jurors and judges evaluate events that have already taken place, but their reactions to these events depend on more than the facts alone. Psychologists have examined the kind of thought processes that this situation engenders in observers (e.g. jurors and judges) and have identified a cognitive heuristic, termed the simulation heuristic, that concerns the ease with which people construct simulations (or scenarios) that fit a particular event (Kahneman and Tversky, 1982). Because most of this work has concerned simulations that lead to alternative outcomes (so-called 'counterfactuals'), the research has been categorized as an investigation of counterfactual thinking. Counterfactual thinking arises in situations where people ponder what *might* have happened differently so that an alternative – typically better – outcome would have occurred. Decision makers' judgements of responsibility, guilt, harm and compensation can all be influenced by counterfactual thinking.

Observers tend to react to negative events (e.g. crimes and accidents) by construing events that can be imagined otherwise to be events that ought not to have happened (Kahneman and Miller, 1986). Events that ought not to have happened tend to evoke strong reactions towards both perpetrators and victims. Consider the real-life example of a New York City police officer who was killed by a drug dealer during the search of a housing project. At the time of the shooting, the police officer was searching for a young girl who had been reported missing. The day after the killing, the New York City police commissioner noted the especially tragic nature of the officer's death by announcing that the girl had not actually been lost at all. Rather, she had been playing at a neighbour's home. People hearing these facts can easily engage in counterfactual 'if only' thinking (e.g. if only the child's parents had checked the neighbour's home before calling police, if only the officer had checked the neighbour's home before encountering the drug dealer). These sentiments can affect their judgements of blame to the perpetrator and sympathy to the victim.

Of further relevance to the legal system are studies showing that to the extent it is easy to mentally undo some event, the perpetrator of that event is deemed blameworthy and the victims of harm are seen as deserving of sympathy and compensation (Macrae, 1992; Miller and McFarland, 1986). For example, mock civil jurors who could mentally mutate the defendant's behaviour to undo an injurious act tended to find the defendant's behaviour unreasonable and award the victim more compensation (Wiener *et al.*, 1994).

Complementary findings should arise in a criminal case. Consider a case of sexual assault. Obviously, when construing the circumstances of a sexual assault, jurors and judges can focus on the actions of both the assailant and the victim and ponder how easy it is imagine different actions on both parts that would have resulted in an alternative outcome (i.e. no sexual assault). The ease with which decision makers can generate different outcomes should affect their assignments of blame.

Although it is usually hard to justify the notion that crime victims are responsible for their own fate, a victim's actions are often perceived as more mutable than those of a perpetrator

(Kahneman and Miller, 1986). Fact finders may ask 'Why didn't the victim do X?', or say 'If only the victim had done X and not done Y'. Counterfactual scenarios that modify the victim's actions can result in the impression that the victim is responsible for being victimized. In fact, some research has shown that if mock jurors perceive that different behaviours on the part of a rape victim would have produced an alternative outcome, blame to that victim is greater and blame to the alleged rapist is lower. However, in situations where it is difficult to generate changes to the victim's behaviour that could effectively undo the event, blame to the victim is lower and blame to the assailant is higher (Branscombe et al., 1996).

Obviously, some imagined outcomes are better than the actual event and some are worse. The term 'upward counterfactual' refers to alternatives that improve on reality. Upward counterfactuals tend to take the form of 'if only' statements. The term 'downward counterfactual' describes alternatives that worsen reality. Although people are generally more likely to engage in upward counterfactual thinking (to imagine a better alternative to a bad outcome) than to generate downward counterfactuals (to imagine a less favourable reality), some data suggest that downward counterfactuals are generated when people perceive their situations to be satisfying and have a desire to enjoy, or be comforted by that outcome (Markman et al., 1993).

What happens when legal decision makers imagine an alternative outcome that is even worse than the original outcome (i.e. engage in downward counterfactual thinking)? This question was addressed in a mock jury study in which perceivers considered what else the assailant could have done to the victim and how the rape event could have been worse for her (Nario-Redmond and Branscombe, 1996). In this situation, their perceptions of the severity of the actual rape and the injustice committed on the victim were reduced and the alleged perpetrator was deemed less blameworthy than in situations in which they did not imagine a worse alternative. In a separate condition of the study, mock jurors pondered an alternative outcome that was better for the victim than the original rape event. In comparison with that alternative, perceptions of the severity of the original rape increased and the perpetrator was deemed more blameworthy.

Finally, counterfactual thoughts tend to be about actions that are controllable by a person involved, rather than about uncontrollable actions. For example, researchers who interviewed individuals who lost a spouse or child in a car accident found that, although many of them generated counterfactual thoughts, these 'if-only...' thoughts focused on what the interviewee or the victim could have done differently, and not on what the offender might have otherwise done (Davis et al., 1995). The former possibilities were controllable and the latter were not.

APPLIED IMPLICATIONS OF RESEARCH FINDINGS

Heuristical reasoning is likely to occur under the conditions of uncertainty that characterize many decisions within the criminal justice system. Just as likely, the quality of justice will be compromised. What can be done to avoid or minimize these judgemental biases? If lawyers and judges were to become educated about the likelihood of judgemental errors, would that be sufficient protection? Is it appropriate to expect that experienced legal thinkers could learn to avoid these errors in their own decisions? Could they effectively instruct laypeople to do the same? Alternatively, should legislators and policy-makers consider changing legal rules or procedures to minimize the adverse effects of biased reasoning?

As we noted above, the use of heuristics in judgement is primarily an automatic process, not something that decision makers can easily avoid. Hence, simply informing jurors of the possibility of distortions in their reasoning processes will probably have little effect; people are not likely to be able to refrain from using heuristics. In fact, understanding the hindsight bias does nothing to diminish its impact (Rachlinski, 1998) and attempts at instructing jurors to be careful of the biasing effects of hindsight have been largely ineffective (e.g. Kamin and Rachlinski, 1995; Smith and Greene, 2005). However, one jury analogue study showed a reduction in reliance on hindsight when defence attorneys incorporated a warning about it in their closing arguments (Stallard and Worthington, 1998). An appeal from defence attorneys to jurors' sense of justice and a reminder about the possibility of 20/20 hindsight reduced the effects of hindsight by over 70%.

Attempts at informing judges about the biasing effects of heuristics in their reasoning may be somewhat more effective. These experienced decision makers have some control over the information that is presented to them, so perhaps can learn to limit their exposure to anchors, temper their confidence in the correctness of their thinking, understand that reliance on representativeness can lead to erroneous evidentiary rulings, and be suspicious of potentially misleading evidence (Guthrie, Rachlinski and Wistrich, 2001). To our knowledge, however, no empirical studies have evaluated the effectiveness of debiasing techniques on judges.

Even if professional decision makers (e.g. attorneys and judges) have difficulty noting and curtailing their own use of heuristics, it would be useful for them to become knowledgeable about the errors that heuristics tend to produce in *others* (i.e. jurors). In that way, attorneys could craft arguments and present evidence in a manner that fits with jurors' natural inclinations and judges could make rulings (e.g. about the admissibility of eyewitness identifications, confessions, expert testimony and scientific evidence) in light of this knowledge.

Finally, some thought could be given to the possibility of revising the legal rules and procedures that give rise to biased decision processes. Some success in this realm has been shown in studies of mock civil juries. In negligence cases, jurors' knowledge of a plaintiff's injuries can retroactively influence their beliefs about the defendant's liability – a hindsight bias effect. Yet, when the format of the evidence presentation is varied so that rather than hearing evidence about the defendant's conduct *and* the plaintiff's injuries, jurors hear one or the other but not both, reliance on legally-irrelevant information can be reduced. When evidence was limited in this way in a jury analogue study, decisions about liability and compensation were both more favorable to the defence because evidence concerning the plaintiff's serious injuries was not a factor in liability judgements and evidence concerning the defendant's errant conduct was not a factor in assessing damages (Horowitz and Bordens, 1990; Smith and Greene, 2005).

In criminal cases, access to pretrial publicity can cause irrelevant and inadmissible information to achieve a place of prominence in jurors' memory. The availability of this information can result in biased judgements about the defendant's guilt. This bias could be reduced by granting a continuance (an extension of time prior to trial) to allow the publicity effects to dissipate or by granting a change of venue so the case could be tried in a jurisdiction where pretrial publicity (and hence availability) effects are not an issue.

Similarly, in cases where a defendant is charged with multiple offences, jurors may perceive a pattern of criminality in his actions, deem him dangerous and determine that his actions, taken in total, are representative of those of a felon (Greene and Loftus, 1985). From this perspective, jurors may have difficulty weighing the facts objectively and reaching a decision on any one charge without relying on evidence they learned about another. To reduce reliance on the representativeness heuristic, judges should carefully consider the possibility of severing the charges so that any particular jury would hear only the evidence relevant to one charge and reach a verdict based on that evidence exclusively.

CONCLUSION

Most victims and witnesses to crimes and accidents attempt to provide reliable details about their experiences. In similar fashion, most legal decision makers – jurors, judges, magistrates and attorneys – try to set their personal biases and preconceived notions aside and make rational and fair-minded judgements about information relevant to criminal justice. However, just as victims and witnesses are sometimes hampered by their biased perspectives and by the frailties of human memory, so too, are legal decision makers sometimes stymied by fallibilities inherent in the judgement process. We have described several ways that the complexity of their decisional task can lead to intuitive, illusory thinking and ultimately, to biased decision making. We have shown how legal judgements, in particular, are influenced by short-cut, heuristical reasoning processes. We believe that by elucidating the psychological underpinnings of complex legal decisions we learn something very valuable about the ways that people really think about criminal justice and the law. From a base of understanding, we can begin to structure decision tasks to yield fairer, more predictable choices.

REFERENCES

Bargh, J. and Chartrand, T. (1999) The unbearable automaticity of being. *American Psychologist*, **54**, 462–79.

Bibas, S. (2004) Plea bargaining outside the shadow of trial. *Harvard Law Review*, **117**, 2463–547.

Branscombe, N., Owen, S., Gartska, T. and Coleman, J. (1996) Rape and accident counterfactuals: Who might have done otherwise and would it have changed the outcome? *Journal of Applied Social Psychology*, **26**, 1042–67.

Byrne v. Boadle (1863), 159 Eng. Rep. 299 (Ex.Ch.).

Casper, J.D., Benedict & Perry (1989) Juror decision making, attitudes, and the hindsight bias. *Law and Human Behaviour*, **13**, 291–310.

Chapman, G.B. and Bornstein, B.H. (1996) The more you ask for, the more you get: Anchoring in personal injury verdicts. *Applied Cognitive Psychology*, **10**, 519–40.

Colwell, L. (2005) Cognitive heuristics in the context of legal decision making. *American Journal of Forensic Psychology*, **23**, 17–41.

Davies, C. (1971) Pre-trial imprisonment: A Liverpool study. *British Journal of Criminology*, **11**, 32–48.

Davis, C., Lehman, D., Wortman, C. and Silver, R. (1995) The undoing of traumatic life events. *Personality and Social Psychology Bulletin*, **21**. 109–24.

Dhami, M. (2003) Psychological models of professional decision making. *Psychological Science*, **14**, 175–80.

Englich, B. and Mussweiler, T. (2001) Sentencing under uncertainty: Anchoring effects in the courtroom. *Journal of Applied Social Psychology*, **31**, 1535–51.

Fein, S., McCloskey, A. and Tomlinson, T. (1997) Can the jury disregard that information? The use of suspicion to reduce the prejudicial effects of pretrial publicity and inadmissible evidence. *Personality and Social Psychology Bulletin*, **23**, 1215–26.

Fischhoff, B. (1975) Hindsight ≠ foresight: The effect of outcome knowledge on judgement under uncertainty. *Journal of Experimental Psychology: Human Perception and Performance*, **1**, 288–99.

Fiske, S.T. and Taylor, S.E. (1991) *Social Cognition*, 2nd edn, McGraw-Hill, New York.

Gigerenzer, G. and Goldstein, D. (1996) Reasoning the fast and frugal way: Models of bounded rationality. *Psychological Review*, **103**, 650–69.

Golding, J., Fryman, H., Marsil, D. and Yozwiak, J. (2003) Big girls don't cry: The effect of child witness demeanor on juror decisions in a child sexual abuse trial. *Child Abuse and Neglect*, **27**, 1311–21.

Goodman-Delahunty, J., Granhag, P. and Loftus, E. (1998) *How Well Can Lawyers Predict Their Chances of Success?* Unpublished manuscript, University of Washington.

Greene, E. and Loftus, E.F. (1985) When crimes are joined at trial. *Law and Human Behaviour*, **9**, 193–207.

Guthrie, C., Rachlinski, J. and Wistrich, A. (2001) Inside the judicial mind. *Cornell Law Review*, **86**, 777–830.

Hastie, R., Schkade, D. and Payne, J. (1999) Juror judgements in civil cases: Effects of plaintiff's request and plaintiff's identity on punitive damage awards. *Law and Human Behaviour*, **23**, 445–70.

Hawkins, S. and Hastie, R. (1990) Hindsight: Biased judgements of past events after the outcomes are known. *Psychological Bulletin*, **107**, 311–27.

Hinsz, V. and Indahl, K. (1995) Assimilation to anchors for damage awards in a mock civil trial. *Journal of Applied Social Psychology*, **25**, 991–1026.

Horowitz, I. and Bordens, K. (1990) An experimental investigation of procedural issues in complex tort trials. *Law and Human Behaviour*, **14**, 269–85.

Jacowitz, K. and Kahneman, D. (1995) Measures of anchoring in estimation tasks. *Personality and Social Psychology Bulletin*, **21**, 1161–6.

Kahneman, D. and Miller, D. (1986) Norm theory: Comparing reality to its alternatives. *Psychological Review*, **93**, 237–51.

Kahneman, D. and Tversky, A. (1982) Subjective probability: A judgement of representativeness, in *Judgments Under Uncertainty: Heuristics and Biases* (eds D. Kahneman, P. Slovic and A. Tversky), Cambridge University Press, Cambridge.

Kamin, K. and Rachlinski, J. (1995) Ex post ≠ ex ante: Determining liability in hindsight. *Law and Human Behaviour*, **19**, 89–104.

Kelman, M., Rottenstreich, Y. and Tversky, A. (1996) Context-dependence in legal decision making. *Journal of Legal Studies*, **25**, 287–97.

Kline, F. and Jess, P. (1966) Pretrial publicity: Its effect on law school mock juries. *Journalism Quarterly*, **43**, 113.

Kramer, G., Kerr, N. and Carroll, J. (1990) Pretrial publicity, judicial remedies, and jury bias. *Law and Human Behaviour*, **14**, 409–38.

Loewenstein, G., Issacharoff, S., Camerer, C. and Babcock, L. (1993) Self-serving assessments of fairness and pretrial bargaining. *Journal of Legal Studies*, **22**, 135–59.

London, K. and Nunez, N. (2000) The effect of jury deliberations on jurors' propensity to disregard inadmissible evidence. *Journal of Applied Psychology*, **85**, 932–9.

Macrae, C.N. (1992) A tale of two curries: Counterfactual thinking and accident-related judgements. *Personality and Social Psychology Bulletin*, **18**, 84–7.

Malsch, M. (1989) *Lawyers' predictions of judicial decisions*. Doctoral thesis, University of Leiden, The Netherlands.

Markman, K., Gavanski, I., Sherman, S. and McMullen, M. (1993) The mental simulation of better and worse possible worlds. *Journal of Experimental Social Psychology*, **29**, 87–109.

Markus, H. and Zajonc, R.B. (1985) The cognitive perspective in social psychology, in *The Handbook of Social Psychology*, **vol. 1**, 3rd edn, (eds G. Lindzey and E. Aronson), Random House, New York.

Miller, D. and McFarland, C. (1986) Counterfactual thinking and victim compensation: A test of norm theory. *Personality and Social Psychology Bulletin*, **12**, 513–9.

Moore, A.J. (1989) Trial by schema: Cognitive filters in the courtroom. *UCLA Law Review*, **37**, 273–341.
Narby, D.J., Cutler, B.L. and Penrod, S.D. (1996) The effects of witness, target, and situational factors on eyewitness identifications, in *Psychological Issues in Eyewitness Identification* (eds S. Sporer et al.), Lawrence Erlbaum, Mahwah, NJ.
Nario-Redmond, M. and Branscombe, N. (1996) It could have been better or it might have been worse: Implications for blame assignment in rape cases. *Basic and Applied Social Psychology*, **18**, 347–66.
Neil v. Biggers, 409 U.S. 188. (1972).
Nisbett, R. and Ross, L. (1980) *Human Inference: Strategies and Shortcomings of Social Judgement*, Prentice-Hall, Inc., Englewood Cliffs, NJ.
Penrod, S. and Cutler, B. (1995) Witness confidence and witness accuracy: Assessing their forensic relation. *Psychology, Public Policy, & Law*, **1**, 817–45.
Pickel, K. (1995) Inducing jurors to disregard inadmissible evidence: A legal explanation does not help. *Law and Human Behaviour*, **19**, 407–24.
Rachlinski, J. (1998) A positive psychological theory of judging in hindsight. *University of Chicago Law Review*, **65**, 571–625.
Regan, P. and Baker, S. (1998) The impact of child witness demeanor on perceived credibility and trial outcome in sexual abuse cases. *Journal of Family Violence*, **13**, 187–95.
Saks, M.J. and Kidd, R.F. (1980) Human information processing and adjudication: Trial by heuristics. *Law & Society*, **15**, 123–60.
Simon, R. (1966) Murder, juries, and the press. *Trans-action*, 64–65.
Smith, A. and Greene, E. (2005) Conduct and its consequences: Attempts at debiasing jury judgements. *Law and Human Behaviour*, **29**, 505–26.
Smith, V. (1991) Prototypes in the courtroom: Lay representations of legal concepts. *Journal of Personality and Social Psychology*, **61**, 857–72.
Smith, V. (1993) When prior knowledge and the law collide: Helping jurors use the law. *Law and Human Behaviour*, **17**, 507–36.
Smith, V., Kassin, S. and Ellsworth, P. (1989) Eyewitness accuracy and confidence: Within versus between subject correlations. *Journal of Applied Psychology*, **74**, 356–9.
Smith, V. and Studebaker, C. (1996) What do you expect?: The influence of people's prior knowledge of crime categories on fact-finding. *Law and Human Behaviour*, **20**, 517–32.
Sommers, S. and Kassin, S. (2001) On the many impacts of inadmissible testimony: Selective compliance, need for cognition, and the overcorrection bias. *Personality and Social Psychology Bulletin*, **27**, 1368–77.
Stallard, M. and Worthington, D. (1998) Reducing the hindsight bias utilizing attorney closing arguments. *Law and Human Behaviour*, **22**, 671–82.
Tanford, J.A. (1990) Law reforms by courts, legislatures, and commissions following empirical research on jury instructions. *Law and Society Review*, **25**, 155–75.
Tversky, A. and Kahneman, D. (1974) Judgement under uncertainty: Heuristics and biases. *Science*, **27**, 1124–31.
Tversky, A. and Kahneman, D. (1982a) Availability: A heuristic for judging frequency and probability, in *Judgments Under Uncertainty: Heuristics and Biases* (eds D. Kahneman, P. Slovic and A. Tversky), Cambridge University Press, Cambridge.
Tversky, A. and Kahneman, D. (1982b) Judgement under uncertainty: Heuristics and biases, in *Judgments Under Uncertainty: Heuristics and Biases* (eds D. Kahneman, P. Slovic and A. Tversky), Cambridge University Press, Cambridge.
Vidmar, N. (2002) Case studies of pre-and midtrial prejudice in criminal and civil litigation. *Law and Human Behaviour*, **26**, 73–106.
Wiener, R., Gaborit, M., Pritchard, C. et al. (1994) Counterfactual thinking in mock juror assessments of negligence: A preliminary investigation. *Behavioural Sciences and the Law*, **12**, 89–102.

CHAPTER 12

A Behavioural Science Perspective on Identifying and Managing Hindsight Bias and Unstructured Judgement: Implications for Legal Decision Making

Kirk Heilbrun[1] and Jacey Erickson[2]
Drexel University Villanova School of Law

The question of how the accuracy of human judgement and decision making can be enhanced is of great interest to both law and the behavioural sciences. If the answer were as straightforward as simply developing comparable strategies to improve the accuracy of decision making in both domains, there would undoubtedly be more judges subscribing to behavioural science journals. However, the differing contexts of decisions made in legal realms versus those made in medical, scientific and societal domains make the generalization of the results of research on human decision making to legal arenas a difficult one. Scholars who attempt to bridge this chasm (e.g. Monahan and Walker, 2002; Wrightsman, 1999) must consider these contextual differences carefully.

However, much of the focus in the interdisciplinary field of psychology and law since the mid-1970s has been on providing relevant information that has the potential to better inform judicial decision making. The translation of scientific research results to judicial decision making has been a particularly important aspect of US evidentiary law for over a decade (*Daubert* v. *Merrell Dow Pharmaceuticals, Inc.*,), and the expansion of the professional literature to include interdisciplinary journals and books such as this one has provided a

---

[1] Kirk Heilbrun is Professor and Head, Department of Psychology, Drexel University.
[2] Jacey Erickson is a fourth-year graduate student in the Law-Psychology program at Villanova School of Law and Drexel University.

Applying Psychology to Criminal Justice. Edited by David Carson, Rebecca Milne, Francis Pakes, Karen Shalev and Andrea Shawyer. © 2007 John Wiley & Sons, Ltd

means for researchers and scholars to describe aspects of behavioural science research that are relevant to legal decision making.

The present chapter will offer such a description, drawing on research in the area of cognitive psychology and human decision making. There are a variety of influences that systematically reduce the accuracy of certain kinds of human decisions. Two such influences will be described: (1) actuarial versus clinical judgement, and (2) hindsight bias. Each was selected on the basis of being well-established in the scientific literature, applicable to at least several instances of legal decision making, and amenable to being limited through the application of 'debiasing strategy'. In the discussion of each influence, following the definition and examples of manifestation in the legal decision-making process, we will offer a description of one or more 'debiasing strategies' – approaches that could be used by a judge or jury to limit the impact of the particular biasing influence discussed in this particular section.

ACTUARIAL VERSUS CLINICAL JUDGEMENT

It has been over 50 years since Paul Meehl, a psychologist who studied the area of clinical judgement and decision making, published a, now classic, book on the topic of 'clinical versus statistical prediction' (Meehl, 1955). In it, he reviewed the research on the accuracy of two kinds of human judgement. 'Clinical prediction' involves the application of the judgement of experts (in the context of clinical prediction, such experts are often psychiatrists and psychologists) to a question such as diagnosis or prognosis, but without the assistance of any established 'formula' using clearly-defined predictor variables. Statistical (or 'actuarial') prediction, by contrast, employs such predictors, which are combined in a way that maximizes their predictive accuracy, usually guided by previous research that has derived and applied predictors to similar populations. Meehl's conclusion in 1955 was that statistical prediction is consistently more accurate than clinical prediction, assuming that the decision maker has a choice between using variables that are empirically derived and actuarially combined versus using unaided human judgement (even the judgement of those with considerable expertise). This conclusion has received continued support from the behavioural science literature over the intervening decades (Dawes, Faust and Meehl, 1989; Monahan, 1981; Monahan et al., 2001; Quinsey et al., 2005), suggesting that the application of actuarial approaches to predictive questions is one of the best-supported procedures that can be drawn from behavioural science.

What questions addressed by legal decision makers are in the form of a prediction, as framed by Meehl and other behavioural science researchers over the past 50 years? There is a wide range of such questions. Perhaps the most straightforward illustration involves the application of risk assessment, when an expert before the court (and ultimately the judge) must gauge the likelihood of a certain kind of behaviour occurring some time in the future. Under US law, this behaviour of interest is often something that would cause harm to others. The area of violence risk assessment thus has a very large number of legal decisions that are made at least partly by considering the likelihood that the litigant will harm others: (1) involuntary civil commitment; (2) pretrial detention versus release on bail; (3) criminal sentencing and juvenile commitment; (4) commitment to secure hospital for defendants who are Incompetent to Stand Trial or Not Guilty by Reason of Insanity; (5) transfer of pretrial defendants (from jail) or sentenced inmates (from prison) to a secure hospital; (6) the postsentence commitment of sexual offenders; (7) the release or transfer back of individuals described in numbers 3–6, above; and (8) the determination of parenting fitness in divorce/child custody litigation.

There are two ways in which a judge could use these findings to make more accurate prediction-based decisions. The first involves how they use the testimony of experts who provide such information; the second would apply these findings directly to their own deliberations. Each will be considered.

When a court hears testimony from an expert witness regarding a litigant's likelihood of committing future violence, there are sometimes actuarial tools available to help shape the expert's opinion. When such tools are available, it is far preferable to incorporate them into the information provided by the expert. There are appropriate measures for violence prediction in the areas of civil commitment (Classification of Violence Risk, or COVR; Monahan *et al.*, 2005), criminal sentencing (Level of Service Inventory-Revised, or LSI-R; Andrews and Bonta, 1995), and commitment and release of individuals found Not Guilty by Reason of Insanity (Violence Risk Appraisal Guide, or VRAG; Harris, Rice and Quinsey, 1993; Historic, Clinical and Risk Management-20, or HCR-20; Webster *et al.*, 1997). However, there are other tools that have not been appropriately derived, fully validated, or adequately documented and therefore should not be used in legal proceedings to address predictive questions.

When might it be appropriate to conclude that such a tool is ready for use in a legal context? Some guidelines have been proposed to assist courts in making this discrimination:

- *Commercial publication of the test.* Tests used by experts in forensic evaluations should be commercially published and distributed, which promotes available and uniform test materials. Occasionally, noncommercial publication and distribution might be workable if relevant information regarding the test (see 'test manual,' next) can be provided to test users and others.
- *Available test manual.* Test manuals describe the user qualifications, and the development, standardization, administration, scoring and psychometric properties of the instrument. When a test or measure does not have a manual, this increases the likelihood of inappropriate application, administration, scoring and interpretation.
- *Demonstrated levels of reliability.* Test reliability (the extent to which the test is free of measurement error) limits test validity (the extent to which the test measures what it is intended to measure). Experts should use instruments with known and adequate levels of reliability, which usually include more than one of the following: internal consistency, inter-rater reliability, test-retest reliability and reliability of parallel forms.
- *Demonstrated levels of validity.* Tests used by experts in legal contexts should also have established validity. Such validity has different forms – for instance, discriminant validity, predictive validity, concurrent validity, construct validity and face validity – and should be established using different forms and in different studies before it is used by an expert in a legal proceeding.
- *Validity for the specific purpose at hand.* A test should be valid for the purpose for which it will be used: for a particular application, when used in a particular way, and with a particular population. For example, a measure such as the VRAG, developed using individuals who had been charged with a criminal offence and validated over a multi-year outcome period, would not be appropriate for use in a context such as civil commitment, in which the outcome period of interest is relatively short and the individuals being considered for commitment have typically not been charged with a criminal offence.

- *Successful peer review.* Tests and measures used in forensic contexts have typically been subject to peer review. Such review involves the publication of studies on reliability and validity in journals in which the submissions are reviewed by experts. Judges should be sceptical of tests that have not undergone peer review, and whose investigation has been performed only by the test author(s).
- *Decision-making formulae are known to the examiners.* Experts in legal proceedings are required by law and ethics to describe fully the data that provide the basis for their opinions. Forensic experts should avoid tests that offer predictions based on formulae with which the expert is unfamiliar (Heilbrun, Rogers and Otto, 2002).

The general basis for the superior accuracy of actuarial over clinical prediction involves minimizing the error in measuring predictors (reliability), and choosing the most accurate predictors for the purpose at hand (validity). This is not straightforward and sometimes simply impossible in legal contexts, given the value on individualized justice that is characteristic of the law in various societies. However, there are three steps that a judge might take to reduce predictive error in the context of their own decision making. The first involves increased structuring of the factors considered in a predictive decision. Human decision makers are invariably helped to consider all relevant influences by a 'memory aid', in the form of a detailed checklist, which also serves to document the factors that were considered in making the prediction. The second step involves obtaining outcomes in cases in which predictions are made. Third and finally, recording the relationship between predictive factors, final predictive decision, and outcome will allow the decision maker to gauge the general accuracy with which predictions are made, and to determine which of the predictors seem most strongly related to outcome.

HINDSIGHT BIAS

Hindsight bias, or the 'I knew it all along' effect, is the tendency for individuals with outcome knowledge (obtained from learning the outcome after it has occurred and looking back at what preceded it) to overestimate the predictability of the reported outcome. The impact of hindsight bias on human judgement has been widely investigated by cognitive psychologists and decision-theory researchers for over 30 years (Villejoubert, 2005). Some of the most relevant of this research will be described in this section.

Hindsight bias can affect any legal decision in which the court must determine whether a given outcome could reasonably have been predicted and possibly prevented. Under US law, this question often arises in the course of personal injury litigation, particularly when (as in professional malpractice) the defendant owed a duty to the plaintiff that involved anticipating the consequences of a professional intervention or the probability of a client's harmful behaviour toward an identifiable third party. It is particularly tempting to conclude that events were predictable when the damages are severe, when there is an associated societal interest in punishing the responsible parties. Such determinations are fairer, however, when a potential influence such as hindsight bias is identified and managed through specific steps. We will now turn towards a description of particularly relevant studies of hindsight bias, and conclude with recommendations for managing its impact.

Hindsight bias has been described as pervasive, not only in laboratory settings (where it can be observed, manipulated and measured with more precision), but in natural environments as well (Villejoubert, 2005). It has been investigated at length and over nearly three decades, but the factors that influence it are not yet fully understood by investigators. Nonetheless, there is certainly enough known about hindsight bias to discuss its applicability in both the research context and a 'natural environment', such as the courtroom.

Mental health law scholars have considered how hindsight bias applies in the context of mental health malpractice litigation (Wexler and Schopp, 1989). They discussed possible 'debiasing mechanisms' to reduce the impact of such bias, including specific jury instructions, bifurcation and testimony from an expert researcher regarding hindsight bias. These will be discussed at greater length later in this section.

Some investigators (Hertwig, Faneslow and Hoffrage, 2003) have reported that the impact of hindsight bias is more limited when considered by those with expertise in the area. Having more 'foresight knowledge' (awareness of the facts and circumstances that precede a given outcome) tends to reduce the impact of hindsight bias, even when the foresight is not accurate in a specific case. This may reflect awareness by those with more expertise of the complexity of a given question, which in turn may limit the tendency to reduce the perceived ease in predicting such phenomena.

In research using jury-eligible individuals (although not in the context of an actual jury), the impact of hindsight bias has been clearly demonstrated. Researchers focused on civil liability for punitive damages (Hastie, Schkade and Payne, 1999), with jury-eligible citizens shown a video-taped summary of the circumstances surrounding an environmental damage lawsuit. Some participants were presented a foresight perspective and asked to determine whether a railroad should comply with an order to stop operations on a section of track that had been declared hazardous. Others were asked to decide whether the railroad was liable for punitive damages after an accident occurred. Almost all measures of participants' judgements and thoughts about the case showed very substantial differences between foresight and hindsight, with damages awarded in hindsight significantly higher.

Another demonstration of the impact of hindsight bias may be seen in a study focusing on drug courier profiles and illegal search and seizure (Robbennolt and Sobus, 1997). A total of 178 participants were given fictional vignettes of a warrant-less search and seizure based on a drug courier profile, under one of three conditions. In the first condition, participants were told nothing about the outcome; in the second condition, they were informed that the search had uncovered evidence of criminal activity; and in the third, they were told that the search failed to reveal any evidence of illegal activity. Participants were clearly influenced by hindsight bias, providing the highest compensatory and punitive damages to the plaintiff under the condition in which they were told that the search revealed evidence of criminal activity, and the lowest damages when they were informed that no evidence of criminal activity had been obtained from this search.

Hindsight bias is not the only source of potential error that can affect judges and jurors, nor does it operate in isolation. In another study on jury decision making in civil suits against police officers alleged to have engaged in illegal searches (Casper, Benedict and Perry, 1989), investigators used simulated case materials and mock jurors, including 253 adults called for jury service and 283 university undergraduates. They reported that both hindsight bias and individual attitudes regarding awards affected participants' responses.

Some investigators have reported a more limited impact of hindsight bias than the studies just cited. Cannon and Quinsey (1995) studied the effects of variations in base rate information and temporal context on predictions of violence and hindsight bias. A total of 270 university undergraduates estimated the probability that violent offenders would commit another violent offence based on case history information (which the investigators varied systematically). Participants were told that the population base rate applicable to a given offender was either 30 % (the lower risk condition) or 70 % (the higher risk condition). Further, participants were asked to estimate this probability either before the reoffence/no reoffence outcome, or after this outcome was known. The investigators determined that neither the given base rate (30 % versus 70 %) nor the time at which participants estimated the probability made much of a difference, so the impact of hindsight bias in this study was described as 'weak and inconsistent'.

This should not be interpreted to suggest that hindsight bias is not an active or generalized phenomenon in legal contexts. It may be that the particular focus of this study, or the questions that they investigated, affected their minimal findings. It should be added that this study, like much of the research on hindsight bias in legal contexts, was carried out using individuals who might be eligible for juries (as most university undergraduates would be), but who may be called less frequently for jury service than are older adults. It is also important to note that actual jury deliberations or judicial decisions may be done under considerably different circumstances than investigators studying participants' behaviour individually (rather than in the context of jury deliberations, where social as well as individual influences are present) can provide.

One of the more powerful tools available to behavioural science researchers is meta-analysis, in which the results of a number of studies on a similar question are combined to form a single 'effect size', overcoming the problem created when a number of smaller studies (with fewer participants) may yield findings in one direction, but larger studies yield opposing findings. To determine whether there is an overall 'effect' for a scientific phenomenon, researchers can use meta-analysis – but must also be careful to avoid the 'file drawer problem' (research with findings of no significant differences is often rejected by journals and hence relegated to the 'file drawer') by actively seeking to include unpublished studies as well as those that have been included in journals.

Such a meta-analysis on hindsight bias has been conducted. Guilbault et al. (2004) incorporated a total of 95 studies (83 published and 12 unpublished). When excluding missing effect sizes, the authors reported that the overall average effect size for hindsight bias, as demonstrated across all included studies, was quite substantial ($d = 0.39$, with a 95 % confidence interval of .36 to .42.) Additional important findings indicated that (1) studies that included manipulations to increase hindsight bias resulted in significantly larger effect sizes than studies without experimental manipulation to reduce or increase hindsight bias; but (2) studies that included manipulations to reduce hindsight bias did not produce lower effect sizes. The latter should serve a cautionary note: after 30 years of research, identifying hindsight bias as a potential source of error in decision making is straightforward, but implementing ways to reduce it is less so.

Nonetheless, several investigators have proposed 'debiasing strategies' that are relevant to litigation. These will now be discussed, and comment aspects identified.

The most detailed set of recommendations (Kamin and Rachlinski, 1995) includes six recommendations, each of which is relevant for judges:

- Trials could be bifurcated to avoid possible bias from knowing the outcome when evaluating there is negligence. Under this suggested procedure, jurors would not be informed about the actual harm, and the details of the harm, whilst considering the question of negligence.

- Jury instructions addressing hindsight bias (and other sources of decision-making bias) could be presented before any evidence. Jurors who are aware of such influences on decision making may be in a better position to guard against the unfettered impact of hindsight bias.
- Using an expert witness to explain how such cognitive biases operate could also help to limit their impact. Such an expert would not testify about case-specific questions, but would rather describe the state of the applicable science and the implications of research findings in this area.
- Defence attorneys should attempt to reconstruct the case and ask jurors to imagine knowing the preceding details without knowing the outcome.
- Jury instructions asking jurors to consider 'alternative outcomes' might be effective in counteracting hindsight bias, but this has not been consistently demonstrated in laboratory studies – so 'more intrusive procedures' might be necessary.
- Judges, attorneys and mediators have a better understanding of negligence than laypersons (jurors and university undergraduates), and may thus be less susceptible to hindsight bias because of this greater expertise. In this respect, a bench trial may be an effective way to control for hindsight bias.

Hindsight bias is clearest when the decision maker is considering negative events (consistently the case in litigation) and when the outcome is inconsistent with a priori expectations, resulting in a sense of surprise (LaBine and Labine, 1996). They noted that the use of an expert witness, a remedy suggested by other commentators, may backfire if the result of such testimony involves having jurors focus more weight on information consistent with their knowledge of the outcome. The preferable strategy, by contrast, involves having jurors focus on the information available to the defendant at the time and imagine that they do not know the outcome. Since it may be ineffective simply to ask jurors to imagine that they do not know the outcome, it is possible that additional testimony concerning the meaning of such circumstances in other cases – along with the known outcomes in such cases – may be helpful. The authors also suggest the use of bifurcated trials as a debiasing mechanism.

The 'alternative outcomes' approach to managing hindsight bias has been discussed in some detail (Sanna, Schwatz and Stocker, 2002). Asking jurors (or a judge) to imagine different outcomes to the one that actually occurred, and reasons why such outcomes might have occurred, has been recommended by a number of commentators. The number of such imagined alternatives may affect the overall usefulness of this debiasing strategy. When participants were asked to imagine a large number of alternative outcomes (10), they were less likely to be affected by this procedure than when they were asked for a small number of alternatives (2). It seems quite likely that participants asked to generate 10 alternative outcomes were including some that were unrealistic or inconsistent with existing evidence. Perhaps those imagining only two alternative outcomes were envisioning possibilities that occurred to them readily – and were more likely to be realistic, under the circumstances.

The use of defence attorney language in closing arguments has also been considered for its potential impact on hindsight debiasing (Stallard and Worthington, 1998). The closing argument in question contained two particular elements. First, the defence attorney noted that the plaintiff's strategy was to ask jurors to be 'Monday morning quarterbacks' (a phenomenon well known to fans of the American version of professional football played on Sundays, but perhaps less so to European citizens, who might prefer an analogy involving day-after goal-tending decisions made in a World Cup competition). Second, the closing argument appealed to jurors to avoid automatically second-guessing the defendant's decisions. Such a strategy might be effective because it is both vivid (as any sporting fan can attest) and linked to a human activity in which some decisions, which appear reasonable and appropriate under the circumstances, invariably are 'wrong' when viewed through the retrospective lens of a lost game. At least in the context of a single experiment, with individuals rather than jurors in a group, this strategy indeed appears effective – the investigators reported that those receiving this particular debiasing strategy judged the plaintiff to be significantly less negligent than those who did not.

DISCUSSION

The potential for the introduction of error into legal decision making from two sources – unstructured judgement and hindsight bias – appears significant. These are clearly not the only sources of such error. However, the presence of each is well established in the scientific literature, and there are multiple ways in which each may affect litigation.

Any recommendations made that are applicable to legal decision making are at some risk of being irrelevant (because of applicable evidentiary law) or, worse, intrusive. The issue of the limits on the expertise of mental health professionals in legal contexts has received longstanding attention (see, e.g. Grisso, 1986), and recommendations on the applications of behavioural science to the law ought to be made with comparable discretion. However, the application of the research findings of behavioural science – particularly when they are as clear and longstanding as in the areas of actuarial judgement and hindsight bias – hopefully have sufficient potential to reduce systematic bias in decision-making to justify the comments in this chapter.

Judges can increase the accuracy of predictive decisions through greater use of expert testimony involving actuarial prediction, and also through systematically obtaining information regarding the factors associated with their predictions, the predicted outcomes, and the actual outcomes. Courts can reduce the impact of hindsight bias through a variety of mechanisms, including expert testimony on hindsight bias, envisioning a small number of alternative outcomes that might be reasonable under the defendant's circumstances, and asking experts to describe outcomes in cases under circumstances comparable to the case at hand. The bifurcation of the trial, the specificity of jury instructions, the vividness of a defence attorney's closing argument, and the issue of bench versus jury trial may be outside the judge's immediate discretion, but it is useful to consider these as additional approaches to the reduction of hindsight bias.

REFERENCES

Andrews, D. and Bonta, J. (1995) *Level of Service Inventory-Revised*, Multi-Health Systems, Toronto.
Cannon, C. and Quinsey, V. (1995) The likelihood of violent behaviour: Predictions, postdictions, and hindsight bias. *Canadian Journal of Behavioural Science*, **27**, 92–106.
Casper, J., Benedict, K. and Perry, J. (1989) Juror decision making, attitudes, and the hindsight bias. *Law & Human Behaviour*, **13**, 291–310.
Daubert v. Merrell Dow Pharmaceuticals, Inc., 113 S.Ct. 2786 (1993).
Dawes, R. Faust, D. and Meehl, P. (1989) Clinical versus actuarial judgement. *Science*, **243**, 1668–74.
Grisso, T. (1986) *Evaluating Competencies: Forensic Assessments and Instruments*, Plenum Press, New York.

Guilbault, R., Bryant, F., Brockway, J.H. and Posavac, E. (2004) A meta-analysis of research on hindsight bias. *Basic & Applied Social Psychology*, **26**, 103–17.

Harris, G., Rice, M. and Quinsey, V. (1993) Violent recidivism of mentally disordered offenders: The development of a statistical prediction instrument. *Criminal Justice and Behaviour*, **20**, 315–35.

Hastie, R., Schkade, D. and Payne, J. (1999) Juror judgements in civil cases: Hindsight effects on judgements of liability for punitive damages. *Law & Human Behaviour*, **23**, 597–614.

Heilbrun, K., Rogers, R. and Otto, R. (2002) Forensic assessment: Current status and future directions, in *Psychology and Law: Reviewing the Discipline* (ed J. Ogloff), Kluwer Academic/Plenum Press, New York, pp. 120–47.

Hertwig, R., Fanselow, C. and Hoffrage, U. (2003) Hindsight bias: How knowledge and heuristics affect our reconstruction of the past. *Memory*, **11**, 357–77.

Kamin, K. and Rachlinski, J. (1995) Ex post ≠ ex ante: Determining liability in hindsight. *Law & Human Behaviour*, **19**, 89–104.

LaBine, S. and LaBine, G. (1996) Determinations of negligence and the hindsight bias. *Law & Human Behaviour*, **20**, 501–16.

Monahan, J. (1981) *Predicting Violent Behaviour: An Assessment of Clinical Techniques*, Sage Publications, Beverly Hills, CA.

Monahan, J. and Walker, L. (2002) *Social Science in Law: Cases and Materials*, 5th edn, Foundation Press, Westbury, New York.

Monahan, J., Steadman, H., Silver, E. et al. (2001) *Rethinking Risk Assessment: The MacArthur Study of Mental Disorder and Violence*, Oxford University Press, New York.

Monahan, J., Steadman, H., Appelbaum, P. et al. (2005) *Classification of Violence Risk (COVR)*, Psychological Assessment Resources, Lutz, FL.

Quinsey, V., Harris, G., Rice, M. and Cormier, C. (2005) *Violent Offenders: Appraising and Managing Risk*, 2nd edn, American Psychological Association Press, Washington, DC.

Robbennolt, J. and Sobus, M. (1997) An integration of hindsight bias and counterfactual thinking: Decision-making and drug courier profiles. *Law & Human Behaviour*, **21**, 539–60.

Sanna, L., Schwarz, N. and Stocker, S. (2002) When debiasing backfires: Accessible content and accessibility experiences in debiasing hindsight. *Journal of Experimental Psychology: Learning, Memory, & Cognition*, **28**, 497–502.

Stallard, M. and Worthington, D. (1998) Reducing the hindsight bias utilizing attorney closing arguments. *Law & Human Behaviour*, **22**, 671–83.

Villejoubert, G. (2005) Could they have known better? *Applied Cognitive Psychology*, **19**, 140–3.

Webster, C., Douglas, K., Eaves, D. and Hart, S. (1997) *HCR-20: Assessing Risk for Violence (Version 2)*, Mental Health, Law, and Policy Institute, Simon Fraser University, Burnaby, BC.

Wexler, D. and Schopp, R. (1989) How and when to correct for juror hindsight bias in mental health malpractice litigation: Some preliminary observations. *Behavioural Sciences & the Law*, **7**, 485–504.

Wrightsman, L. (1999) *Judicial Decision-Making: Is Psychology Relevant?* Kluwer Academic Press, Dordrecht.

CHAPTER 13

To Decide or not to Decide: Decision Making and Decision Avoidance in Critical Incidents

Marie Eyre and Laurence Alison
University of Liverpool

The authors' research area concerns the specialist domain of police decision making and leadership. It is firmly rooted within a criminal justice context; in particular, it focuses on police responses to and investigation of critical incidents. Despite the specialist focus, generic literature on decision making has much to offer and some of the findings we discuss in this chapter are as relevant to lawyers as any other professional or lay person. On the other hand, a criminal justice context has distinct features and we argue that context has an overwhelming impact on decision making so factors that are specific to a criminal justice context must be considered. Both police officers and barristers may claim that they prepare a case for prosecution. Even though each is ostensibly carrying out the same task, their different environments, aims, procedures and constraints will have different influences on their decision making.

In this chapter, we shall first review different decision-making theories and their relative merits and weaknesses; next we shall outline some of the factors that can have an impact on decision making[1] from those factors that can influence an individual (e.g. how emotion can affect decision making), to a consideration of the organizational and political culture in which professionals work and how this broader context can also affect decision making in critical incidents. Examples throughout this chapter will be criminal justice related and they mostly refer to decision making in critical incidents. There are some examples indicating the application and relevance of a particular point to the field of law but, limited by space we invite, indeed encourage, the reader to consider throughout how the issues we discuss in this chapter might apply to their own particular field of expertise.

---

[1] To avoid unwieldy repetition, the term 'decision making' is sometimes used interchangeably with 'decision avoidance'.

Applying Psychology to Criminal Justice. Edited by David Carson, Rebecca Milne, Francis Pakes, Karen Shalev and Andrea Shawyer. © 2007 John Wiley & Sons, Ltd

INTRODUCTION – THE ALL-IMPORTANT CONTEXT

> To be or not to be. That is the question: Whether 'tis nobler in the mind to suffer The slings and arrows of outrageous fortune, Or to take arms against a sea of troubles, And by opposing end them? (*Hamlet*)

'To be or not to be. That is the question' – perhaps the most famous quotation of all and for anyone who has read or seen Shakespeare's play, Hamlet takes a pretty long time to make his mind up. The consequences of his decision or nondecision will have an impact on Hamlet and other sundry characters, but all the actors can wash off the greasepaint and go home after he has finally made a decision.

By contrast, professionals involved in managing critical incidents are often under intense time pressure to make decisions and the consequences of getting it wrong can mean life or death for others, sometimes great numbers of ordinary members of the public. Critical incidents constitute a very particular context where immense pressure is brought to bear upon the professionals involved, both pressure of time and the magnitude of the potential consequences if they make the wrong decision.

As we have moved into the twenty-first century, cultural change has altered the broader context in which critical incident managers work. For example in a policing context, the government white paper, *Policing a New Century: A Blueprint for Reform* (2001) states that relations with communities are an integral part of the current government's agenda for change. The police as a whole will need to adapt their policies and procedures in response to political demands; in turn, there are implications for decision making in critical incidents.

Relations with communities are increasingly filtered through the lens of the media. The new century has seen the advent of 24-hour news media with a voracious appetite for immediate stories. Managers of critical incidents have to respond to the media and be aware of the very real fact that the common thrust of such news gathering is 'Who's to Blame?' Equally real is the prospect of a public inquiry that may well have the same 'Who's to Blame?' agenda, should things go wrong. Beyond that, an increasingly litigious culture awaits with at least a widespread perception that more claims for negligence are being made.

How, then, are decisions made in such daunting circumstances? Decision making has been studied by psychologists for decades. However, the influence of organizations and the broader cultural context surrounding critical incidents is under-researched. Equally important (but much neglected in the literature) is how and when people fail to make decisions at all. Now they are the interesting questions.

TRADITIONAL, NATURALISTIC AND PRAGMATIC APPROACHES TO DECISION MAKING

Traditional Decision-Making Theory

Traditional Decision-Making Theory (TDM) cast humans as principally rational beings. Faced with several alternative choices, decision makers conduct a thorough search for information and calculate the subjective expected utility (SEU) of each option. The option with the highest SEU is then chosen – decision made. Based largely on traditional experimental studies in the laboratory, TDM has contributed a good deal to the understanding of the cognitive processes involved when decision makers are faced with choices. Careful consideration of options may obtain in some situations but decision making is a much more complex process than the early models suggested.

Heuristics and Biases

Seminal work by Kahneman and Tversky (1973) indicated that humans are not always so rational and an exhaustive search for information is not always conducted. Rather, individuals rely on heuristics as cognitive short cuts to reduce the time taken to explore endless alternatives. These two authors also identified several biases that influence decision making, particularly in conditions of uncertainty. For example, decision makers may make judgements on the basis of how easily they can call to mind other examples they deem to be relevant to the decision in question. Termed the 'Availability Bias', decision makers will incorporate the most salient, 'available' information into the decision-making process and neglect other information that may be relevant or even crucial. (See Kahneman and Tversky (1973) for a fuller discussion of biases and heuristics.) In decision making, heuristics are important in reducing cognitive load and processing time, but there is potential for decision errors because individuals' judgements are susceptible to well-documented biases and an individual's heuristics may be idiosyncratic. A legal issue, arising from this, has not received the attention it deserves. To avoid being negligent, a professional must, amongst other requirements, make decisions consistent with those that a responsible body of coprofessionals would make (*Bolam* v. *Friern HMC* ([1957] 4 All ER 118)). Is the test normative, how those professionals ought to have decided (i.e. unaffected by availability and other biases), or descriptive, how those professionals, being human and fallible, would have decided? Fortunately, or otherwise, lawyers have not paid sufficient attention to decision research, for the manner in which decisions are taken, not just their content, might provide fruitful pickings for compensation claims.

Researchers learned, then, that decision makers are not entirely rational and are affected by a lifetime's baggage of experiences and biases. These biases and heuristics were understood to exist but the focus was still very much on the individual decision maker in the here and now, rather than an exploration of the social context in which all humans exist and the ways in which it comes to influence decision makers over the long term.

Thus, one of the limitations of TDM is that it did not consider context. Important though it is to understand cognitive processes, humans do not exist in a social vacuum and context necessarily influences the way that decisions are made, from different situations, through the context, that is, the group or team of people who make decisions together to the organizational context that imposes constraints on decision makers.

A second, related limitation of TDM was methodological. The methodological strength of laboratory studies is the control the researcher has over the experiment. The weakness is that laboratory studies can have limited ecological validity; that is, their applicability beyond the lab to the 'real-world' that is far more complex and far less controllable. TDM offers us only a limited and imperfect idea about how decisions are made. For example, university students in a laboratory study take their time to decide which hypothetical car dealer has the best offer. A critical incident manager must decide in moments whether or which workers to send to the scene of a shooting. The consequences of that decision will be the lead news story before they arrive home from work. The two situations are simply not comparable. TDM was not invalid, just incomplete and decision-making theory required further development.

Naturalistic Decision Making Theory

Naturalistic decision-making theory (NDM) addressed some of the limitations of TDM with a greater focus on what decision makers actually do in 'natural' conditions in the real-world. It advocates the study of practitioners making decisions in real-life, familiar contexts. In essence, NDM researchers argue that the starting point for research is to investigate what *is* done rather than what *ought* to be done. There are disagreements between different researchers with claims that TDM research actually does investigate 'what is' done by experts and there is also debate about whether 'what is' can be divorced from 'what ought'. Similarly, other researchers argue that such distinctions are somewhat contrived. In a bid to draw distinctions between different schools of thought in decision-making theory, it is possible that a false dichotomy has been created.

No matter what the starting point for decision-making research (traditional laboratory or naturalistic experts in the field), ultimately all research can uncover systematic weaknesses. Therefore, there must be a normative framework within which to operate, one that includes optimal solutions or at the very least, the framework should include satisfactory solutions. Prescription, thereafter, is unavoidable if the research is to have any practical value; in other words, what *ought* to be done necessarily follows from what *is* done. NDM researchers may criticize TDM researchers because they prefer the creation of 'ideal world' conditions in a laboratory instead of looking at 'what *is* done' by expert decision makers, but NDM researchers must at some point embrace the goal of an 'ideal world' if they are to improve the decision making they find practitioners using in their day-to-day professional lives. In this respect, to avoid prescription is to relegate one's research to the merely descriptive; description can be an extremely useful starting point, but it not a useful end point for research. (See LeBoeuf and Shafir, 2001; Lipshitz *et al.*, 2001.)

Detailed distinctions and different emphases are beyond the scope of this chapter, but some substantive points hold. NDM research gives a greater emphasis to expertise and how decisions are made in familiar, real-world contexts. These contexts are dynamic and multi-faceted and typically occur under great time constraints; indeed, it can be difficult even to define with any great precision what the decision problem is. TDM, on the other hand, deals with well-defined decision-making problems, focuses on the individual decision maker in a fairly stable unchanging context and is not usually subject to time constraints. Although the decision making under investigation may be mundane by comparison, researchers can be sure which variables they are investigating and controlling. The issues are also reflected in the key legal distinction between subjective and objective *mens rea*. The defendant's behaviour may be adjudged as, objectively, very dangerous. If the legal test is objective then they will be guilty of a crime that can be committed recklessly, for example manslaughter. However, if the law requires the defendant to have been subjectively aware of wrong-doing, their misperceptions, misunderstandings and general confusion at the time of making the decision leading to harm, could allow them to escape liability (see Chapter 9, this volume.). Such issues are at the heart of the review of the law of homicide, in England and Wales, being undertaken, at the time of writing, by the Law Commission (2005).

An NDM perspective, then, recognized the context to a greater degree in that it did not view decision making as a discrete event uninfluenced by other factors. It took greater account of the situation in which decision makers made their choices and what it lacked in controllability found in lab-based studies, it compensated for in the greater ecological validity of field based work.

Recognition Primed Decision Making

A prototypical model within NDM is Recognition Primed Decision Making (RPDM) (Klein, 1993). Expertise in the field was used as a starting point for research and the subsequent development of Klein's model where he analysed the decision-making processes employed by experienced fire-fighting commanders. The model was devised from self-reports of the strategies used by commanders.

It transpired that expert decision makers can assess the situation and, far from considering and weighing alternative options (as predicted by SEU theory), they can simply decide to take action based on the first option they generate. Based on experience, they can assess the typicality of a situation and act appropriately.

Where a situation is not typical and there is some uncertainty, decision makers often rely on a story building strategy and generate a narrative about the events that might have led up to the situation. They can also use forward based reasoning and construct mental simulations to consider hypothetically how a specific action might unfold.

RPDM sheds light on 'what *is* done' by expert commanders dealing with fire-fighting incidents and indicated how decision makers can cope with extreme time pressure in emergency situations. The model has since had empirical support in other arenas. For example, Randal and Pugh (1996) compared expert and novice electronic warfare technicians from US navy ships, whose tasks include monitoring the number of hostile ships that appear on radar screens. They found that experts placed greater emphasis on assessing the situation whereas novices spent more time considering different courses of action. In accordance with the RPDM model, having assessed the situation thoroughly, the experts generated one option only; that option usually became their course of action. RPDM can be thought of as pattern matching using 'If > then' rules (sometimes referred to as 'productions') – *If* (situation) A, *then* (action) X. Unsurprisingly, the experts also made more correct decisions than novices. Kobus, Proctor and Holste (2001) also found that experts take longer to assess situation but are faster than novices at choosing a course of action.

Like anyone, experts store memories of different situations they've experienced but expertise lies in the development of a complex memory model that assists in assessing the situation at hand and contains knowledge of how rules should be applied (Lipshitz *et al.*, 2001). Decision making for experts who have developed these complex memory structures is less cognitively demanding; it is analogous to a learner driver who has to think consciously to decide when to cross a junction, change gear, brake, indicate, and so on whereas an experienced 'expert' driver finds these decisions so undemanding, they can hold a conversation and light a cigarette at the same time.

Of course, this type of multiple decision making relies on expertise and wide ranging experience. Less experienced managers of critical incidents who do not have a complex memory structure containing a broad repertoire of typical situations from which to generate first and best options are more likely to be prone to error. Expertise is clearly crucially important when managing critical incidents.[2] Whitfield and Alison (2005) highlighted the many cognitive and interpersonal skills required by police critical incident managers, from making good decisions that will drive an inquiry forward, through managing the team and all the roles and responsibilities of each member, to managing relationships with communities and the media. Crego and Alison (2004) note the concerns of the Policing Skills and Standards Organization regarding the lack of such expertise. It is predicted that by 2010, 80 % of officers running major enquiries will have fewer than five years' experience.

However, experts can also be prone to error if the heuristics they rely on are too rigid and inflexible – in other words, if their situation assessment is wrong. To use a more concrete example, it is possible that the tragic events at Hillsborough in which 97 Liverpool football fans were crushed to death in an overcrowded pen, could have been compounded by RPDM. If officers were primed from past experience to recognize the unfolding but still uncertain situation such as a pitch invasion, they would have assessed the situation as a public order problem; in this case, the first option generated would have been to contain and control the crowd, which was the reported experience of many of those trapped in the pens. Recognized as situation A (public order problem), action X (contain the crowd) followed. Once the situation became clearer and it was recognized as a situation in which people were being injured, it was recognized as a situation of public safety rather than public order and police took action accordingly. Fortunately, the civil law recognizes that acting in an emergency, or crisis, is different. The standard of care expected is not so high, but that depends on the now past situation being acknowledged as having been an emergency. After the event, with the alleged benefits of hindsight, it may be difficult to understand how the police officers could have thought it was a public order event. This difficulty in understanding neatly reveals another cognitive bias that is empirically well established in the decision-making literature – the hindsight bias. Once we know the outcome of an event, we are more likely to regard it as having been foreseeable (Fischoff, 1975). When making a judgement, individuals tend not to discount information that could only have been known after the event; as a result, antecedent decisions are more likely to be judged as decision errors *because* the outcome is known.

Decision making in critical incidents is a complex, dynamic and uncertain world with high stakes; of course, this complexity makes it particularly difficult to research. By retaining the factors that exist in the real-world beyond the lab (time pressure, uncertainty, stress generated by the situation, etc.), NDM has offered insights into what actually happens, though the relative contribution of each of these factors also needs to be understood. A balance needs to be drawn between preserving the rich, real context in which decisions are made and a more detailed, specific analysis of the relevant contributory factors. In the classic example used by gestalt theorists, we may wish to take the watch apart to understand how it works but all we are left with is a heap of wheels and cogs; it is no longer a watch.

Pragmatism

Pragmatism (Fishman, 1999) is an eclectic approach that can draw on the strengths of different decision-making theories. In line with NDM, it follows the principle of looking to

---

[2] This may be expected to transfer to other domains. For example, faced with unexpected evidence under time pressure, an experienced advocate could draw on a repertoire of typical cases and immediately generate a best option.

experts in a particular context as a starting point for research. Pragmatism is unlike TDM in this respect. TDM research begins with a theory from which testable hypotheses are derived whereas pragmatism views theory building as a secondary activity. Note, it does not eschew theory or model building completely. Its focus is on applied goals rather than theory for its own sake.

Having identified key issues of concern to practitioners in the field, and conducted qualitative research to identify themes relevant to the decision-making process, more traditional empirical studies can then be undertaken. In this respect, pragmatism retains the strengths of TDM and can isolate and control specific variables that may have an influence on decision making in the field. In a final process of triangulation, research results can then be fed back into the specific context from which the research question originated. This approach offers the opportunity for new learning to take place, for research to have a genuine applied value and retain scientific rigour.

The fact that pragmatic research remains rooted in the domain from which it emerged may be at the cost of generalizability. However, this is not regarded as a weakness. Decision making in critical incidents is a complex process in a dynamic environment and decision consequences can be profound. It is doubtful that a theory broad enough to transfer across domains would be rich or detailed enough to capture the specific and often unique nature of this domain. Lord and Hall (2005) argue that expert knowledge is organized around general principles (rather than surface features), it is domain specific and should not be expected to transfer at all to domains that do not build on the same principles. One size does not fit all and to attempt to impose more general theories on critical incidents may be to miss crucial and specific detail in the process (akin to building a theory of how *all* watches work). It is equally important not to narrow the focus to the other extreme. Crego and Alison (2004) warn against the danger of an atomistic approach whereby the complexity and interplay between different influences in a critical incident are lost (akin to focusing only on the heap of separate wheels and cogs).

In this respect, the eclectic nature of pragmatism can bring the flexibility required to accommodate the specialist nature of critical incident management without missing the sometimes unique detail, whilst preserving the 'big picture' that is meaningful to professionals. Critical incidents are powerful enough events that they inform changes in future policy making and can radically reshape political agendas (e.g. Macpherson, 1999; Bichard, 2004) so rigorous research in this area is crucial. Pragmatism's ability to embrace and incorporate more traditional experimental research work might also help to avoid the criticism sometimes levelled at NDM; namely, that NDM can be perceived as a poor relation if it does not embrace rigorous empirical work.

PRAGMATISM AND 10 000 VOLTS (10 kV)

A representative method of investigation within the pragmatic paradigm is Crego's (2002) ten thousand volts (10 kV) method (so called because the impact of a critical incident on professionals and the community has been likened to experiencing a 10 000 volt shock). The 10 kV is an electronic focus group originally modelled on learning systems within the aviation industry. Such systems provide a means of nonattributable reporting (to ensure full, frank and blameless reporting of incidents that endangered public safety). They also accumulate into a rich database of expert knowledge that can be accessed for research purposes or future training needs; in short, such resources provide a practical means to ensure that the clichéd phrase 'Lessons will be learned' actually becomes a reality rather than just a media briefing soundbite.

Used as a debriefing method for senior police officers and other professionals, 10 kV elicits and stores the decision-making experiences from a wide range of enquiries, including critical incidents. In NDM terms, 10 kV begins by capturing 'what *was* done' and overcomes the prescriptive 'what *ought* to be done' emphasis of TDM. Participants record information on a laptop and their anonymized comments are shared with the whole group. Thus, a group discussion can be captured without the usual disadvantages of a public arena (where 'loud voices' dominate discussion and time limitations mean many views go unheard). The simultaneous recording in 10 kV sessions facilitates rapid and fully inclusive sharing of information whilst preserving the dynamic interactions of group discussion.

Example 10 kV Session

Crego and Alison (2004) conducted a 10 kV session involving 28 critical incident managers who had worked on cases ranging from sieges to child murders and the group generated over 250 statements in the first 20 minutes. Officers in the session indicated that one of the most significant issues for them in managing a critical incident was the way the police service would be judged by the wider community, victims and the media. It was also perceived as one of the most difficult aspects of an inquiry to manage. For example, delegates in that session commented on the difficulty of 'satisfying the insatiable appetite of the media and preventing their intrusion when they hold little to no respect for their voluntary regulatory authorities and attendant rules' (Crego and Alison, 2004, p. 11)

The issues that have an impact on decision making have been identified by the professionals themselves; not only does this have ecological validity, it also ensures that professionals regard any ensuing research as meaningful and credible. Having identified the research agenda, models and even theories may be developed thereafter but pragmatism's principle of utility means that a specific end goal always takes precedence over theory building.

FACTORS THAT INFLUENCE AN INDIVIDUAL'S DECISION MAKING

There has been much research into factors that affect decision making, both from TDM and NDM. Earlier research focused on cognitive processes of the individual decision maker and the heuristics and biases that influence the individual are well established empirically. Given that TDM regarded human decision makers as rational beings, emotion was not considered to affect decision making (these are also known as consequentialist theories). The impact of emotion on decision making emerged more from NDM research, along with other factors that influence decision making such as stress or time pressure.

In the real life situation of a critical incident, these factors will interact with each other. Time pressure often means that information is incomplete, ambiguous and uncertain; these factors can create or add to stress. In turn, stress may mean that information is ignored and thus incomplete. Given limited space, this section only looks very briefly at these factors and how they can influence decision making or cause decision errors, but we shall return to the idea of emotion in the later section on decision avoidance.

Emotion

TDM models that focused exclusively on rationality neglected to consider the influence of emotions on decision making. Mellers, Schwartz and Cook (1998) offer a substantial review of the factors that can affect decision making and the interested reader may find it a useful source for further study. Some of the major findings are outlined below. Isen (1993, cited in Mellers, Schwartz and Cook, 1998) established that positive emotions increase creative problem solving. Estrada, Isen and Young (1994) found that decision makers with positive emotions integrate information more efficiently than controls. On the other hand, Luce, Bettman and Payne (1997) found that negative emotions can lead to faster use of available information and this can lead to increased choice accuracy in some situations. However, increased accuracy only obtains in situations where the task is easy. If the task is hard, accuracy is decreased when the decision maker experiences negative emotions. Critical incident situations might be intuitively characterized as situations where the task is hard, but, again, experts' perceptions of the task need to be considered so experience may moderate the effect here.

The emotions of anticipated regret or blame can also influence decision choices in different situations (See Bar-Hillel and Neter, 1996, on gambles; Simonson, 1992, on consumer products; Richard, van der Pligt and de Vries, 1996, on sexual practices). These emotions will be discussed further in the section on decision avoidance.

The empirical findings above are largely from lab studies and may or may not transfer to the domain of critical incidents though they give a general flavour of how emotion can affect decision making. In addition, the focus is on individual processes and although Josephs et al. (1992) found that feedback on decision outcomes can influence anticipated regret, the research does not fully address the influence of broader contexts.

Stress

Stress is a ubiquitous everyday term and we must make some distinctions; a feature of the situation that may cause stress is termed the stressor and stress is the individual's response. It may be physiological (pounding heart, sweating, etc.) or psychological (fear, worry, etc.) or behavioural (e.g. reactive depression, post-traumatic stress disorder). Individual differences exist so an objective measure of stress is unhelpful. Some may enjoy the thrill of a roller coaster whilst others will find it stressful and frightening, so definitions must incorporate the individual's cognitive interpretation. Jones and Bright (2001) define stress in terms of the relationship between an individual and the environment, which is perceived by the individual as taxing or exceeding their resources to cope and endangering their well-being.

Stress can impair cognitive processing. Research on attention shows a decline in cognitive performance even when simple dual tasks are undertaken (Pashler and Johnston, 1998) and critical incident management entails many simultaneous complex tasks. Stress can further narrow attention (Kahneman, 1973). More generally, Fiedler (1988, cited in Mellers,

Schwartz and Cook, 1998) found that any negative affect narrows attention and can result in a failure to search for new alternatives. So it may be ironic that decision makers, anxious about doing a good job in order to avoid legal liability, perform less well.

Thus, decision makers under stress can miss or ignore vital information, a condition termed premature closure. A practical remedy might therefore be to make decision makers aware of and guard against such possibilities by being vigilant. Janis, (1982, cited in Keinan and Friedland, 1987) argued that vigilance could contribute to rational decision making by ensuring a complete and thorough search for information so that all options are generated. However, in stressful situations, this can be replaced by hypervigilance where the individual may consider information in a very disorganized fashion and make poor decisions.[3]

Of course, these findings are interpreted within the paradigm of TDM whereby a failure to conduct a complete information search is regarded as a negative decision strategy and it is not necessarily relevant in naturalistic situations. Klein's (1993) RPDM model showed how experts use a very different decision strategy that does not rely on generation of all options and explains how stressful situations are managed. However, this focus is very much on the here and now of the decision situation.

In the broader context, role conflict and role ambiguity have been identified as significant causes of work-related stress; role conflict refers to the difficulty in managing competing demands from different individuals or groups, and role ambiguity is caused by uncertainty about what the job entails. Work overload is also a significant factor (Wastell and Newman, 1993). We can see the relevance of all these factors to decision making in critical incidents. Many groups demand different information (e.g. the media, senior managers, other agencies). A less experienced professional may well be uncertain about what the job entails and, moreover, has less recourse to RPDM decision strategies that rely on expertise and may buffer against the effects of stress.

Certainly, stress is an important area of research for professionals involved in critical incidents as repeated exposure to stressful situations puts these workers at greater risk of suffering stress responses or even being diagnosed with post-traumatic stress disorder (Everly and Mitchell, 1992, cited in Kowalski, 1995). Doran and Alison (2005) argue that more emphasis is needed on the relationship between stressors and stress moderators. Patterson (2003) found that seeking social support helped to buffer the effects of work-related stress amongst police officers but worryingly, Pogrebin and Poole (1991) found that US police officers regard the discussion of emotions and stress responses as taboo because they may be viewed as a personal inadequacy; it is therefore rarely discussed. This is an example of how organizational norms can affect individuals (of which more later) and in a reciprocal fashion, how negative emotions that are unresolved may affect future decision making.

Ambiguity

Information and knowledge in critical incidents is typically uncertain. It may be incomplete, or overwhelming in quantity and subsequent impact. Both can lead to ambiguity. Frisch and

---

[3] A practical application of decision-making research can be made here. An individual is innocently caught up in an affray; a third party offers assistance; stress narrows attention so not all available information is processed; the individual perceives the helper as a threat and *decides* to defend themselves. Thus, the erstwhile 'victim' ends up facing an assault charge.

Baron define ambiguity as 'The subjective experience of missing information relevant to a prediction' (1988, p. 152), so missing pieces of vital information can make the situation ambiguous. Information overload means reliance on selection and interpretation, which can also constitute ambiguity if the relevant information is not selected or not understood. TDM studies have shown that decision makers are averse to ambiguity and prefer unambiguous options (Ellsberg, 1961, cited in van Dijk and Zeelenberg, 2003). However, in naturalistic environments, an unambiguous option is often not available and decision makers must contend with uncertainty. Van Dijk and Zeelenberg (2003) found that decision makers simply discount ambiguous information. In the context of a real time and still unfolding situation, the discounted information may transpire to be crucial.

Aversion to ambiguity may drive a decision maker in the opposite direction; rather than discount ambiguous information, they may embellish it. Decision makers may generate a narrative or story to explain causes and then base subsequent decisions on their explanations (Pennington and Hastie, 1992). Further, decision makers are likely to infer meaning in the absence of solid information (Innes, 2002). For example, the absence of information or an explanation can make evidence, in court, difficult to believe. Evidence in court can also be difficult for lay jurors to understand and, hence, a story 'template' assists them in categorizing, organizing and understanding complex evidence. Such templates also have disadvantages. Mock jurors were found to infer details that had not actually been contained in direct testimony; they also systematically deleted evidence that was unrelated to their preconstructed narrative of events. The decision-making concern here is that jurors are thought to use the stories they have constructed to decide on verdicts (Pennington and Hastie, 1986).

Decision makers, then, may extrapolate from what is certain (known as assumption based reasoning) to reduce uncertainty (Lipshitz and Strauss, 1997). They may also forestall, which is a form of decision avoidance. Whilst such strategies for dealing with uncertainty may be helpful, without ongoing review, the strategies may result in decision errors.

In naturalistic situations, this potential for decision errors may be compounded by other factors. Morrison *et al.* (n.d) studied tactical decision making in the navy, where participants had to track visual computer generated displays (known as geo-plots) and identify weapon threats. They found increased hypervigilance (and the attendant attentional narrowing) and increased confirmation bias when information was ambiguous.

Time Pressure

Ariely and Zakay (2001) argue that decision makers can and do adapt to time pressure. They may respond by being more selective about which information to consider when weighing options but under intense time pressure, they are likely to switch decision strategies. Klein (1993) found that RPDM decision strategies can be used to good effect under time pressure, but Kahneman and Tversky (1973) found that a greater reliance on heuristics may lead to greater confirmation biases. Decision making may even become dysfunctional. Dorner (1987, cited in Wastell and Newman, 1993) proposed the term 'Intellectual Emergency Reaction' whereby individuals in critical incidents became more and more rigid in their thinking and decision making, focusing on narrower issues and selecting only options that confirm their rigid heuristics. The dangers of simplistic pattern matching coupled with a lack of evaluation and review of actions and the contribution to decision errors are clear.

Although considered separately here, factors that influence decision making may be co-present and, moreover, interact in a critical incident situation to influence decision making. Whilst experience can help decision makers to deal with situations, expertise is no simple panacea that will ensure good decision making. Indeed, greater experience means greater exposure to the broad context; that is, the organization, which may be a significant factor in decision avoidance. We shall discuss both in the next section.

DECISION AVOIDANCE

Everyone can readily call to mind examples where failure to make a decision and take subsequent action has resulted in tragedy. Anyone who has read a newspaper or watched television knows that the one of the first questions asked by news journalists is: 'Why did the relevant authorities not act sooner?' when an abused child has not been taken into care or a murderer turns out to have had a lengthy history of preconvictions for violence. The failure to make decisions has also been a cause for criticism in public inquiries into critical incident management (e.g. Laming, 2003). Yet despite the ubiquity of such tragic stories and the prominence of awareness amongst the general public about the failure to make decisions and take subsequent action, there has been surprisingly little psychological research into why people fail to make decisions. The focus is overwhelmingly on how and why decisions *are* made.

A similar position may be noted with regard to the law. People can be prosecuted or sued for harm caused by their omission to act, not just for acts of commission. There has to be a special duty of care (e.g. a very close family relationship or the individual was responsible for the danger which they failed to avert) for criminal liability. However, the focus, both in civil and criminal law and practice, is overwhelmingly on positive acts. A partial explanation is that we do not as readily 'see' the consequences of an omission to act as we do a commission; that is, they are not as salient. We know the consequences if a doctor gives us the wrong medication (well sometimes), but we are unlikely, without special skills and knowledge, to know the consequences of the doctor's failure to provide us with a different treatment.

Anderson (2003) attributes some of this failure to focus on decision avoidance to the many subdisciplines within psychology and the constraints of particular paradigms used by researchers. If Anderson's claim is true that 'decision avoidance is the dominant attitude of human decision makers within certain boundary conditions' (2003, p. 140), this is an extremely important omission in the literature; pragmatism's eclecticism may provide some opportunity to redress this narrow focus and investigate the phenomenon of decision avoidance.

Anderson defines decision avoidance thus: 'A tendency to avoid making a choice by postponing it or by seeking an easy way out that involves no action or no change' (2003, p. 139). It is distinguished from procrastination whereby an individual has a specific intention. We are all familiar with our decisions to write the essay, pay the bills, visit an ageing relative; we have, in effect, *decided* on a particular action but don't carry it through usually because we'd rather watch television or go to the pub.

Anderson's (2003) Model of Decision Avoidance

Anderson proposes an integrated model of decision avoidance that incorporates both rational and emotional influences on decision avoidance and he cites selection difficulty as the major contributor to decision avoidance. There are many factors under the umbrella of selection difficulty in Anderson's model; we shall consider two here – blame and regret as contributors to decision avoidance. Anticipated blame or regret are construed as mental simulations of future outcomes. Anticipatory blame or regret are felt during the decision-making process and individuals may seek, in various ways, to reduce these uncomfortable feelings. Indeed, for Anderson, managing emotions underpins decision avoidance.

Laboratory studies show support for the idea that anticipated regret leads to decision avoidance in the form of omission bias (discussed below). Ritov and Baron (1990) argued that anticipated regret explained the result that participants refused a (hypothetical) vaccination despite the fact that the fatal side effects of the vaccine were a fraction of the death rate posed by the disease. This is clearly not rational in the strict terms of TDM theory. One *ought* to consider all the information and choose the option that offers a substantially lower chance of dying. However, the regret anticipated by positively, proactively choosing the vaccine option was far greater than omitting to choose it and thereby avoiding responsibility for the decision. (See also Baron, 1991; Baron and Ritov, 1994; Spranca, Minsk and Baron, 1991.)

Anderson identifies four effects as follows: (1) status quo bias, (2) omission bias, (3) choice deferral and (4) inaction inertia (although inaction inertia is seen to overlap with the other three factors).

Status quo bias – whereby an individual prefers the status quo and will tend to avoid decisions that may change it: The status quo is the normal state of affairs and deviation from the status quo is, therefore, seen as abnormal. Norms are highly salient and considering deviation from them will give rise to uncomfortable emotions that must be managed. For example, if a social worker considers the decision to take a child at risk into care, they might anticipate the blame and regret that that will ensue if they make the wrong decision (by imagining or mentally simulating the outcome). These uncomfortable feelings of anticipatory regret or blame may increase their propensity to retain the status quo; that is, leave the child at home where they are at risk of significant harm. Organizational context can also have an influence (this will be discussed in more detail in a later section). If the social worker works in an organization that has a policy of keeping children with their families wherever possible, these organizational norms will also be highly salient and a deviation from the organizational status quo will also be perceived as abnormal and may contribute to decision avoidance. On this view, retaining the status quo can reduce an uncomfortable regret for the decision maker. (Of course, this obtains *during* the decision-making process. Regret would be severe in the event of a tragic outcome.)

Omission bias – whereby individuals prefer options that entail no action: There is empirical evidence from decision-making literature that acts of commission are perceived as more culpable than acts of omission (Spranca, Minsk and Baron, 1991) and Kahneman (1995, cited in Mellers, Schwartz and Cook, 1998) showed that action is perceived as leading to more regret than inaction. This too may contribute to decision avoidance; less blame or regret will accrue from doing nothing than doing something, so if outcomes are uncertain, it is better to err on the side of caution in a bid to avoid a decision error.

Choice deferral – here individuals choose to delay making a decision: From a TDM perspective, this may be construed as a positive decision strategy to wait for more information and conduct a thorough search but if time pressure of the situational context dictates that a decision must be made quickly, it is construed here as decision avoidance.

Incidentally, this highlights the importance of considering context in decision making and some of the difficulty in interpreting decision strategies. What is positive in a context of unlimited time (waiting for more information to clarify the options) is negative in a different context (harm may have resulted by deferral).

Dhar (1997) found that choice deferral decreased under time pressure. A possible explanation for this effect lies in the decision-making strategy adopted. Recall that Klein (1993) found support for his RPDM model amongst fire commanders under time pressure. If only one option is generated, selection difficulty is absent; if a decision maker does not weigh the values of different options, anticipatory regret or blame will not be elicited and a decision can readily be made rather than avoided.

However, this ignores the impact of organizational context and culture; it is also possible that the mental models employed during RPDM contain prior experience of blame or regret that can affect the decision-making process in either direction – to decide and act or to avoid. For example, recent experience of a public enquiry that named and shamed individuals within one's own organization or profession might well elicit mental simulations of anticipated blame or regret and evoke anticipatory blame or regret that might lead to decision avoidance; in the pattern matching terms of the RPDM model – if situation A, then action 0 (nothing at all if you want to avoid blame). There may be long-term implications here for the decision-making abilities of people whose organizational context is one where a blame culture is chronic and/or endemic.

Essentially, there are two different but relevant trajectories here, the immediate (proximal) context and the long-term (distal) context. If time pressure is a feature in the proximal context of a critical incident, less decision avoidance should be predicted. If a name, shame and blame culture is a feature of the distal context, more decision avoidance may be predicted. Both proximal and distal contexts can influence decision making and the next section will focus on theories that might offer ways to determine the relative impact of each.

ORGANIZATIONAL CONTEXT AND CULTURE: IMPACT ON DECISION MAKING AND DECISION AVOIDANCE

Social Identity Theory and Self-Categorization Theory

Social identity theory (SIT) (Tajfel and Turner, 1986) and its subsequent development, self-categorization theory (SCT) (Turner *et al.*, 1987) may offer valuable insights into the impact of organizations on the behaviour of individuals, including decision-making behaviour. Social identity is defined as 'An individual's knowledge that he or she belongs to certain social groups together with some emotional and value significance to him or her of this group membership' (Tajfel, 1972, p. 31, cited in Haslam, Postmes and Ellemers, 2003), for example one may belong to the social groups, student, Manchester United fan, and so on. Self-categorization theory extended the idea of social identity and is concerned with an individual's subjective sense of self; SCT offers a continuum between individual and collective identities that become increasingly inclusive. At one end of the continuum, any one person has a sense of themselves as an individual with their own unique identity; at the other extreme, we all share a collective identity as a human being.

For our purposes here (in the middle of the continuum), individuals will self-categorize and may have a social identity relating to their work organization. An individual knows they belong to a particular professional group and it is meaningful to the individual to define themselves as a police officer, a lawyer or a social worker. Importantly, social identity has an impact on behaviour. It would be unremarkable to find that a police officer is less likely than a career criminal to rob banks regularly. Moreover, the theory predicts that people with the same social identities will perceive their views as interchangeable. A Liverpool fan would expect another Liverpool fan to dislike Manchester United supporters because it is one of the defining features of the social identity 'Liverpool Fan' that they do not like (and, crucially, are not like) Manchester United fans. There are, of course, many individual fans that are not so extreme in their personal views and herein lies the influence of groups and social identity.

Social groups have norms and any individual must negotiate conflict between individual identity (e.g. uncomfortable prejudging all Manchester United fans) and a particular social identity (e.g. pressure to conform to group norm of rivalry with Manchester United fans). Strong identification with the group should predict behaviour in accordance with group norms.

Group norms may also underpin the idea of shared mental models (defined as individuals who possess a similar cognitive representation of a situation or phenomenon) (Langan-Fox et al., 2001). A shared mental model is thought to enhance effectiveness of teams working towards a shared aim or goal. Discussion of teams is precluded here (see Flin, 1996, on teams in critical incident management), but an individual's social identity and self-categorization as part of a team will be mediated through identification with the larger group; that is, the organization, and we may look to those organizational norms to identify the derivation of mental models or a 'team mind'.

Organizational Identity

Social identity and self-categorization theories, then, offer an explanation for the influence of group norms on behavioural outcomes. This relates to the individual decision maker, thus: the stronger the identification with the organization, the more the decisions will be influenced by the prevailing organizational culture. Haslam, Postmes and Ellemers (2003) identify three factors that are likely to strengthen an individual's organizational identity as follows: (1) the length of time they have worked there; (2) whether the organization is in competition with another organization; and (3) if they feel proud of the organization.

We can consider our earlier hypothetical example, the social worker who does not take the child into care although they are at risk of significant harm. Anderson's (2003) model of decision avoidance is helpful in explaining these processes in the individual: the worker displays a status quo bias. The worker may experience anticipatory regret in the decision situation. In order to manage this uncomfortable anticipatory regret they feel, the worker avoids a decision and sticks with the status quo. The worker may also experience anticipated blame or regret whereby they construct mental simulations of future outcomes.

These contributory factors are features of the proximal context but, crucially, they do not emerge from nowhere. Such ideas and feelings must have an earlier source.

In SIT/SCT terms, the distal context influences the proximal context; put simply, the past will influence the present and the decision maker's mental simulations of future outcomes will be based on prior experience (a factor also identified by Klein and incorporated into his RPDM model). SIT/SCT can help to explain the mechanisms through which these earlier sources (the distal context) can evoke such uncomfortable emotions in the decision-making situation (the proximal context).

Consider the recent political culture that promotes accountability in public sector organizations such as the police service. This generates a focus on accountability in each force (often framed in terms of audited targets and performance indicators). This context will have a cumulative impact on the organization's identity. Accountability is high on the agenda, is increasingly salient and becomes one of the norms of the organization. This will have an impact on the organizational identity of its employees; to self-categorize and identify yourself as a police officer, you will be aware that you are a public servant and conform to the organizational norm of public accountability. If this accountability has manifested as an experience of public blaming and shaming, an individual decision maker will carry that experience forward; it is an integral part of their organizational identity and can influence their decision making. This is the route through which heuristics and biases may be formed. Decision makers will anticipate blame or regret for decisions made (proximal context) if that is the history of the organization with which they identify (distal context).

Recall that earlier we mentioned that delegates in Crego and Alison's (2004) 10 kV session identified such public accountability as one of the most significant issues in managing critical incidents (i.e. how they would be perceived by the community, victims and the media). They also found it one of the most difficult aspects to manage. It is easy to see the potential for long-term damage to decision-making skills in an organization that has experienced public blaming and shaming. In terms of Anderson's (2003) model, anticipated blame or regret is a major contributor to decision avoidance.

Recall too that an individual's organizational identity will be strengthened if they feel proud of the organization and/or perceive it to be in competition with others (Haslam, Postmes and Ellemers, 2003). We can see how a defensive culture emerges when an organizational identity contains (very salient) notions of anticipated blame for decisions made. Decision makers are likely to be more concerned with sticking together (if they are proud of and identify with their organization) and watching their backs (if outsiders are regarded as the competition) than they are about making decisions.

Again, illustrated with the earlier example from Crego and Alison's (2004) study where critical incident managers found the media difficult to manage, particularly given that the intrusion was perceived as contravening regulatory codes of practice. The media represent outside organizations (with different identities from the police). Moreover, they may be perceived as competing (for access to and control of information). This will strengthen the organizational identity of individuals in both the police and the media and a concomitant effect in the long term may be to increase the difference in identities between the two organizations. For the individual, it is extremely difficult to manage someone who is adhering to organizational norms that are very different from your own. They are unfamiliar or even unknown (the police's only reference point may be regulatory codes of practice for the media; they may not be organizational norms in reality). The ensuing uncertainty may cause anxiety and affect decision making or tend towards decision avoidance if blame or regret is anticipated. People are entitled to complain; indeed complaints can be a valuable source of information, but many complaints procedures then provide for the person complained against to be suspended from work. However technically proper such procedures may be, and however often it may be stressed that the complaint is not being prejudged, they rarely convince, especially when the person criticized finds it more difficult to mount a defence to the accusation.

Abstract Communication Systems Theory

There are some parallels between SIT/SCT and abstract communication systems theory (Luhmann 1996, cited in Andras and Charlton, 2005). Communication systems theory may offer insight into the processes of how organizational identity becomes established. A detailed exploration is precluded here but, essentially, the management of an organization has three main functions, all of which relate to organizational identity. They are: (1) to define the organizational identity, (2) to check the organizational identity and (3) to enforce the organizational identity. The communications or rules of the organization serve as the conduit and act as a reference point against which identity can be checked and confirmed or disconfirmed. Thus, a department that does not comply with the rules as communicated by the management would be closed down (and individuals would be absolutely aware that they are not conforming to the norms of the organizational identity).

In an applied sense, one can see the propensity for decision makers to stick closely to policies and procedures because they will act as a reference point that a decision maker is adhering to organizational norms. Existing policies and procedures are powerful communicators of the organizational identity; as such, they exert influence on decision makers not to stray from them. To do so would be to stray from the individual's own organizational identity and potentially evoke uncomfortable and dissonant feelings of, say, anticipatory or anticipated blame or regret.

MULTI-AGENCY PARTNERSHIPS AND INACTION INERTIA

Different (or worse still, competing) organizational identities may also militate against successful multi-agency partnerships. Smith and Dowell (2000) highlight the difficulties engendered by a lack of shared mental models across agencies. Hallett (1995, cited in McClean and Alison, 2005) commented that one of the most persistent findings of child abuse inquiries is the recurrent failures and weaknesses in interagency co-ordination. Sinclair and Bullock (2002, cited in McClean and Alison, 2005) analysed 40 UK child abuse case reviews and found inadequate sharing of information as one of the most common shortcomings.

In terms of communication systems theory, each organization will have different systems of communication or rules and the language of such communications is unlikely to translate readily across agencies. For example, a request to a police officer to 'Check the history of the case' is likely to result in a search of the Police National Computer (PNC) database for previous convictions; the same request verbatim to a social worker is likely to elicit sociological details of family background, living arrangements, and so on; a health worker may report past medical conditions. Murphy (2004, cited in McClean and Alison, 2005) found evidence to support this idea of different languages and systems between agencies as a contributing factor to problems in multi-agency co-operation.

From a SIT/SCT perspective, individuals will be adhering to very different organizational norms. Reder and Duncan (2003, cited in McClean and Alison, 2005) found that a lack of trust between agencies posed a major difficulty. McClean and Alison (2005) analysed a 10 kV debrief following a multi-agency critical incident exercise (MACIE), involving professionals from health, education, social services and the police service who had collaborated on four simulated child abuse inquiries. Again, accountability emerged as a major concern for these public sector professionals. Decision avoidance was prominent in the form of omission bias. Having identified child protection concerns, little action ensued (in Anderson's terminology – inaction inertia). Moreover, this was often attributed to a failure of other agencies. Sample comments were:

> Police and Social Services did not carry through the decision to do a home visit
>
> Why did health not follow through decisions of strategy meeting? (2005, p. 12).

SIT/SCT and communication systems theory (through aspects of competing organizational identities and different communication systems manifested as different procedural priorities) can contribute to our understanding of how blame came to be a common feature in this study and help to explain the defensive stance assumed by several delegates.

In the private sector, competition is expected and regarded as healthy. One burger company does not expect its employees to collaborate with those of a different fast food organization so strengthening organizational identity via competition poses few practical problems. However, in the public sector, 'joined up thinking' is a stated aim of the government and multi-agency partnerships are an increasing reality in the current political climate. The chair of the public inquiry into the death of Victoria Climbié, Lord Laming, stated, 'The future lies with those managers who can demonstrate the capacity to work effectively across organizational boundaries (because) such boundaries will always exist... those who persist in making decisions alone... must either change or be replaced' (2003, p. 9). This constitutes a significant, powerful context for (and subsequent influence on decision making in) public sector organizations in the long term. We can also see some of the factors that make it difficult to achieve the aim of working together; that is, how different organizational identities between agencies that are expected to collaborate may affect decision making and increase decision avoidance.

Even for a single agency, policies and procedures may be unlikely to encompass enough information to assist decision makers in critical incidents because they are, by definition, atypical or even unique events. In the uncertain and complex situation of a critical incident, a decision maker may be 'creative' enough to generate a solution to a problem but we can also see some of the very powerful organizational influences that militate against an individual thinking and making decisions creatively and more importantly, taking action based on the decision. It would require a singularly robust individual to do so. In 2002, it was acknowledged that, 'there are very few experienced senior investigators within the police service who could easily manage challenges at this level' (Metropolitan Police Service, 2002, p. 14).

There is, then, pressure from organizational norms mediated through the individual's own social/organizational identity to stick to the rules, policies, procedures and keep to the status quo. It is unsurprising, in typically stressful, uncertain situations that strong emotions are elicited and decision avoidance occurs.

Where decisions are made, decision errors may occur because options generated may not fit the unique features of a critical incident. Pressure to adhere to policies and procedures leaves little scope for an individual decision maker to reject their organizational identity and act as an individual who is (1) creative enough to generate a bespoke solution and (2) brave enough to act on that decision. It may be no coincidence that it is the rare or even unique incidents that ultimately result in public inquiries.

CONCLUSION

We have reviewed different theories of decision making and considered their strengths and weaknesses. We have given a necessarily brief outline of some of the factors that can influence decision making in different situations and begun to explore some of the broader theories that may help us to understand the context behind the complex nature of decision making in critical incidents.

In this chapter, the emphasis has been on problems that can occur (decision errors and decision avoidance) to the detriment of exploring solutions. As mentioned earlier, description is a useful start point but not the end point for research. In the absence of complete information in this chapter, the reader should not infer that psychologists have limited their research to identifying and describing the difficulties in decision making. Vigorous research is ongoing; solutions and models, theories and practical tools have been designed to support decision making. For example, Crego (2002) designed Hydra, a sophisticated high fidelity immersive system that simulates critical incidents in real time over hours and days. Devised for and used by the police service in the UK, Hydra is an unparalleled resource and is leading the world in training and preparing practitioners for response to crises. (See also Crego and Alison, 2004; Hutchins, 1996; Schraagen et al., 2005; McCann et al., 2000; Kontogiannis, 1996.)

It is also crucial to investigate success and not focus exclusively on failure in decision making. Such research has much to contribute in supporting critical incident managers who repeatedly deal with chaotic, complex and life-threatening situations. They continue to do so despite an ever intensifying blame culture and they are often overwhelmingly successful in their efforts. We should be wary of our own availability and hindsight biases; news stories of failure and tragedy are salient to us all.

A topical example is the London bombings in July 2005. Comparatively little attention has been paid to the professionals in the emergency services who managed and co-ordinated an enormously complex response to the tragedy as they rescued, treated and continue to treat scores of injured and distressed people. In the face of 'outrageous fortune', they decided to act 'against a sea of troubles' on behalf of us all.

POSTSCRIPT

The London Assembly report into the 2005 London bombings, prepared by Richard Barnes, has been published since this chapter was written. It contains a finding that may be pertinent to future decision avoidance.

At the end of the chapter, we mention that, in the midst of chaos and uncertainty in a critical incident, a very robust individual would be required to decide and act on a creative 'bespoke' solution if the decision deviates from policy and procedural norms. Just such a decision was made by James Hart, the Commissioner of the City of London Police.

The context was this: Under Access Overload Control arrangements (ACCOC), network providers can render the mobile phone system inaccessible to the vast majority of users, meaning that only selected individuals can use their mobile phones. Strategic 'gold' commanders in charge of the incident had decided not to activate ACCOC for fear of panicking the public and also because most Metropolitan police personnel did not possess ACCOC-enabled mobile phones.

Mid morning on July 7th, as mobile phone networks struggled under the volume of calls, James Hart was still unaware of the strategic decision *not* to activate ACCOC. He made a solo decision to activate ACCOC. In collaboration with a network provider, James Hart established a one kilometre 'exclusion zone' around Aldgate tube station. The Barnes report found that,

> The City of London Police acted outside the [command and control] framework. This should not be allowed to happen again (2006, p. 48).

Thus, Hart may be seen to have been publicly censured for deviating from policy and procedure despite the important practical benefits of his decision; namely, he reported that, as communications deteriorated, his decision/action had effectively freed up the airwaves for emergency workers to communicate via mobiles between the scene at Aldgate and casualty reception at hospitals receiving the injured and, rather ironically, that a press liaison officer of the Metropolitan Police had borrowed ACCOC-enabled mobiles to communicate what was happening at the scene. Some of the difficulties inherent in multi-agency working are highlighted as well as the long-term implications. If Hart's colleagues were to find themselves in a similar situation in the future, the potential for decision avoidance is clear.

REFERENCES

Anderson, C.J. (2003) The psychology of doing nothing: forms of decision avoidance result from reason and emotion. *Psychological Bulletin*, **129**, 139–67.

Andras, P. and Charlton, B. (2005) A systems theoretic analysis of structures in organizations. Available: [Online] http://www.liv.ac.uk/ccr/2005 [Accessed March 2006].

Ariely, D. and Zakay, D. (2001) A timely account of the role of duration in decision making. *Acta Psychologia*, **108**, 187–207.

Bar-Hillel, M. and Neter, E. (1996) Why are people reluctant to exchange lottery tickets? *Journal of Personality and Social Psychology*, **70**, 17–27.

Barnes, R. (Chair) (2006) Report of the 7th July Review Committee. Greater London Authoirty, London. Available: [Online] http://news.bbc.co.uk/1/shared/bsp/hi/pdfs/05_06_06_london_bombing.pdf [Accessed February 2007].

Baron, J. (1991) Nonconsequentialist decisions. *Behavioural and Brain Sciences*, **17**, 1–42.

Baron, J. and Ritov, I. (1994) Reference points and omission bias. *Organizational Behaviour and Human Decision Processes*, **59**, 475–98.

Bichard, M. (2004) The Bichard Inquiry Report. The Stationery Office, London, UK. Available: [Online] http://www.bichardinquiry.org.uk/report [Accessed February 2006].

Crego, J. (2002) *10 000 Volts for Critical Incident Managers*. Police Training College, November, 2002.

Crego, J. and Alison, L. (2004) Control and legacy as functions of perceived criticality in major incidents. *Journal of Investigative Psychology and Offender Profiling*, **1**, 207–25.

Dhar, R. (1997) Consumer Preference for a No-choice Option. *Journal of Consumer Research*, **24**, 215–31.

Doran, B. and Alison, A. (2005, December) Stressors and stress moderators in critical incident management. Paper presented at 8th International Investigative Psychology Conference, London, UK.

Estrada, C.A., Isen, A.M. and Young, M.J. (1994) Positive affect improves creative problem solving and influences reported source of practice satisfaction in physicians. *Motivation and Emotion*, **18**, 285–99.

Flin, R. (1996) *Sitting in the Hot Seat: Leaders and Teams for Critical Incident Management*, Wiley, Chichester.

Fischhoff, B. (1975) Hindsight does not equal foresight: The effect of outcome knowledge on judgment under uncertainty. *Journal of Experimental Psychology: Human Perform and Perception*, (1), 288–99.

Fishman, D.B. (1999) *The Case for Pragmatic Psychology*, New York University Press, New York, NY.

Frisch, D. and Baron, J. (1988) Ambiguity and rationality. *Journal of Behavioural Decision Making*, **1**, 149–57.

Haslam, S.A., Postmes, T. and Ellemers, N. (2003) More than a Metaphor: Organizational identity makes organizational life possible. *British Journal of Management*, **14**, 357–69.

Hutchins, S. (1996) Principles for intelligent decision aiding. Technical Report 1718. Available [Online]: http://www.spawar.navy.mil/sti/publications/pubs/tr1718/pr1718.pdf [Accessed March 2006].

Innes, M. (2002) The 'process structures' of police homicide investigations. *British Journal of Criminology*, **42**, 669–88.

Jones, F. and Bright, J. (2001) *Stress: Myth, Theory and Research*, Prentice Hall, Essex.

Josephs, R.A., Larrick, R.P., Steele, C.M. and Nisbett, R.E. (1992) Protecting the self from the negative consequences of risky decisions. *Journal of Personality and Social Psychology*, **62**, 26–37.

Kahneman, D. (1973) *Attention and Effort*, Prentice Hall, New York.

Kahneman, D. and Tversky, A. (1973) *Judgement Under Uncertainty: Heuristics and Biases*, Cambridge University Press, Cambridge.

Keinan, G. and Friedland, N. (1987) Decision making under stress: Scanning of physical alternatives under physical threat. *Acta Psychologica*, **64**, 219–28.

Klein, G. (1993) A recognition primed decision (RPD) model of rapid decision making, in *Decision Making in Action: Models and Methods* (eds G.A. Klein, J. Orasanu, R. Calderwood and C.E. Zsambok), Ablex, Norwood, CT.

Kobus, D.A., Proctor, S. and Holste, S. (2001) Effects of experience and uncertainty during dynamic decision making. *International Journal of Industrial Ergonomics*, **28**, 275–90.

Kontogiannis, T. (1996) Stress and operator decision making in coping with emergencies. *International Journal of Human Computer Studies*, **45**, 75–104.

Kowalski, K.M. (1995) A human component to consider in your emergency management plans: The critical incident stress factor. *Safety Science*, **20**, 115–23.

Laming, H. (2003) The Victoria Climbié Inquiry. Report of an Inquiry by Lord Laming. The Stationery Office, London, UK. Available [online]: http://www.victoria-climbie-inquiry.org.uk/finreport/finreport.htm [Accessed March 2006].

Langan-Fox, J., Wirth, A. and Code, S. *et al.* (2001) Analysing shared and team mental models. *International Journal of Industrial Ergonomics*, **28**, 99–112.

LeBeouf, R.A. and Shafir, E. (2001) Problems and methods in naturalistic decision making. *Journal of Behavioural Decision Making*, **14**, 353–84.

Lipshitz, R., Klein, G., Orasanu, J. and Salas, E. (2001) Taking stock of naturalistic decision making. *Journal of Behavioural Decision Making*, **14**, 331–52.

Lipshitz, R. and Strauss, O. (1997) Coping with uncertainty: A naturalistic decision making analysis. *Organizational Behaviour and Human Decision Processes*, **69**, 149–63.

Lord, R.G. and Hall, R.J. (2005) Identity, deep structure and the development of leadership skill. *The Leadership Quarterly*, **16**, 591–615.

Luce, M., Bettman, J. and Payne, J.W. (1997) Choice processing in emotionally difficult decisions. *Journal of Experimental Psychology: Learning, Memory and Cognition*, **23**, 384–405.

Macpherson, W. (1999) The Stephen Lawrence Inquiry. Report of an Inquiry by Sir William Macpherson of Cluny. Available [Online]: http://www.archive.official-documents.co.uk/document/cm42/4262/4262/htm [Accessed March 2006].

McCann, C., Baranski, J.V., Thompson, M.M. and Pigeau, R.A. (2000) On the utility of experiential cross-training for team decision making under time stress. *Ergonomics*, **43** (8), 1095–110.

McClean, C. and Alison, L. (2005) Difficulties and decision-making in multi-agency child abuse enquiries. Internal Working Report for The Metropolitan Police Service.

Mellers, B.A., Schwartz, A. and Cooke, A.D.J. (1998) Judgment and decision making. *Annual Review of Psychology*, **49**, 447–77.

Morrison, J.G., Kelly, R.T., Moore, R.A. and Hutchins, S. (n.d) Tactical decision making under Stress (TADMUS) Decision Support System. Available: [Online] http://www.pacific_science.com/fmds/TADMUS_DSS.pdf [Accessed March 2006].

Patterson, G.T. (2003) Examining the effects of coping and social support on work and life stress amongst police officers. *Journal of Criminal Justice*, **31**, 215–26.

Pashler, H. and Johnston, J.C. (1998) Attentional limitations on dual-task performance, in *Attention* (ed. H. Pashler), Psychology Press, Hove.

Pennington, N. and Hastie, R. (1986) Evidence evaluation in complex decision making. *Journal of Personality and Social Psychology*, **51**, 242–58.

Pennington, N. and Hastie, R. (1992) Explaining the evidence: Tests of the story model for juror decision making. *Journal of Personality and Social Psychology*, **62** (2), 189–206.

Pogrebin, M. and Poole, E.D. (1991) Police and tragic events: The management of emotions. *Journal of Criminal Justice*, **19**, 395–403.

Randal, J.M. and Pugh, H.L. (1996) Differences in expert and novice situation awareness in naturalistic decision making. *International Journal of Human-Computer Studies*, **45**, 579–97.

Richard, R., Van Der Pligt, J. and de Vries, N. (1996) Anticipated regret and time perspective: changing sexual risk-taking behaviour. *Journal of Behavioural Decision Making*, **9**, 185–99.

Ritov, I. and Baron, J. (1990) Reluctance to vaccinate: Omission bias and ambiguity. *Journal of Behavioural Decision Making*, **3**, 263–77.

Schraagen, J.M., Eikelboom, A., van Dongen, K. and te Brake, G. (2005) Experimental evaluation of a critical thinking tool to support decision making in crisis situations. Available: [online]. http://www.combined.decis.nl/tiki-download_file.php?fileId=53 [Accessed March 2006].

Smith, W. and Dowell, J. (2000) A case study of co-ordinative decision making in disaster management. *Ergonomics*, **43** (8), 1153–66.

Simonson, I. (1992) The influence of anticipating regret and responsibility on purchase decisions. *Journal of Consumer Research*, **19**, 105–18.

Spranca, M., Minsk, E. and Baron, J. (1991) Omission and commission in judgment and choice. *Journal of Experimental Social Psychology*, **27**, 76–105.

Tajfel, H. and Turner, J.C. (1986) The social identity theory of intergroup behaviour, in *Psychology of Intergroup Relations* (eds S. Worchel and L.W. Austin), Nelson-Hall, Chigago.

Turner, J.C., Hogg, M.A., Oakes, P.J. *et al.* (1987) *Re-discovering the Social Group: A Self-categorization Theory*, Blackwell, Oxford.

Van Dijk, E. and Zeelenberg, M. (2003) The discounting of information in economic decision making. *Journal of Behavioural Decision Making*, **16**, 341–52.

Wastell, D. and Newman, M. (1993) The behavioural dynamics of information system devlopment: A stress perspective. *Accounting Management and Information Technology*, **3** (2), 121–48.

Whitfield, K. and Alison, L. (2005, December) *Cognitive and Interpersonal Skills of Police Leaders*. Paper presented at 8th International Investigative Psychology Conference, London, UK.

CHAPTER 14

Processes: Proving Guilt, Disproving Innocence

David Carson
University of Portsmouth

INTRODUCTION

This chapter considers some issues about 'guilt' and 'innocence,' and their proof within criminal justice systems. By elaborating on a number of legal issues it invites psychologists to consider whether they might develop appropriate research studies to take the ideas further. In particular, the chapter invites readers to suspend their insistence that things, laws and procedures, must be as they currently are, just because they are. It invites reconsideration of some key issues.

PROOF: ACCORDING TO LAW

The object of a criminal trial is to decide whether the defendant is guilty, 'according to law.' Those last three words are important. The act of finding someone guilty, or not guilty, provides the legal justification for imposing a punishment, or releasing the defendant from temporary detention in court or prison. It authorizes, and for most people justifies, considering the defendant guilty or not guilty, but it does not prove guilt, or non guilt, in any complete (scientific?) sense. That is beyond our courts. Ground truth, knowing *for certain* what actually happened, is beyond trials and courts. It is also beyond science. That much law and science share. A finding of 'not guilty' is not a finding of not being guilty – let alone innocence. Our courts do not 'do innocence.' It is a finding that the defendant has been declared not guilty, according to law, and is not a claim that they are actually – in all moral, factual, scientific and other senses – not (factually) guilty. The court has decided that – according to law – it cannot, properly, find the defendant guilty. There are only two alternatives, guilty or not guilty. A verdict of 'not proven', as possible in Scotland, is not really a third option for it has the same consequences, the same meaning in practice, as a declaration of 'not guilty' (Shiels, 1999).

This is an example of dichotomous thinking, beloved of lawyers (Campbell, 1974). It is tempting to believe that it is, indeed, a categorical distinction. But, in real life, we

---

Applying Psychology to Criminal Justice. Edited by David Carson, Rebecca Milne, Francis Pakes, Karen Shalev and Andrea Shawyer. © 2007 John Wiley & Sons, Ltd

recognize that it is much more complex. Parents, for example, soon discover that neat categorizations of the wrongness of their children's behaviour are very difficult – although pretence otherwise can come easily. The defendant has not been proven, as opposed to declared, guilty. Defendants have to be proven guilty, 'according to law', 'beyond reasonable doubt'. We are not entitled, on that level of proof, to conclude that they 'really are' guilty, (1) because we cannot know ground truth and (2) because we know (perhaps better to say 'accept') that errors (miscarriages of justice) have been made in the past. Therefore, how can we be entitled to conclude that someone is innocent just because there has been a reasonable doubt about guilt? Our courts take a risk, although it is called making a judgement, that the defendant actually is guilty. They rely on the nature and quality of the processes involved in getting a judge (e.g. a magistrate) or a jury to conclude, 'beyond reasonable doubt', that the defendant 'is' guilty. It is considered, at the end of the process, to be 'worth the risk' of error.

To make these points is not – necessarily – to approve of the current position. It will, for example, be argued below that our courts could, and should, 'do innocence' – to an extent and after a fashion. These proposals should not be considered dreadfully dramatic, radical or upsetting. Most of us accept, intellectually and emotionally, that most of the time, in most cases, that most trials get it right, according to law.

Well, not entirely. We might accept that most findings of guilt are correct, but that is not the only decision possible. Four, not two, outcomes are possible. The defendant may be:

1. Correctly found guilty,
2. Incorrectly found guilty,
3. Correctly found not guilty, and
4. Incorrectly found not guilty.

Only one of those outcomes can be entirely proper. Being incorrectly found guilty – position 2 – is incontrovertibly wrong. It is the paradigm form of miscarriage of justice. Being incorrectly found not guilty – position 4 – is also wrong. It is also a miscarriage of justice, particularly from the perspective of victims. Being correctly found not guilty may appear to be a correct outcome, and is regularly so regarded, but it is also wrong; it is another miscarriage of justice. The error was in the defendant being charged and prosecuted and proceeded against to the stage – with a significant risk – of a court possibly finding the defendant guilty – wrongly. Being found not guilty is certainly preferable to being found guilty, wrongly. But the correct decision would have involved no prosecution, no interference with civil liberties (such as arrest and possible pretrial detention), and no lingering suspicion because they have been found 'not guilty,' rather than innocent. The defendant may have been found and declared 'not guilty,' by the court, but the public do not know, cannot know, whether that was because they actually are innocent or because the prosecution could not, or did not, present enough evidence.

Imagine we have 100 criminal court verdicts. How (1) should they be, and then (2) how are they likely to be, distributed around the four alternative decisions identified above? Wanting all 100 cases to be in category 1, all defendants correctly found guilty, may appear to be a perfect system. It could be a state of paradise on earth for Ministers of the Interior, and comparable government officials; but it cannot be. It could only be achieved if lots of guilty, but liable to be found not guilty, people are never prosecuted. It might constitute a 'fail-safe', due process, position in court, but it could not be in the broader context of crime control. Many guilty people would wrongly not be convicted, because they were not prosecuted. Equally it would be inappropriate to want all 100 cases to appear in category 3, to be correctly found not guilty. That outcome would be the consequence of only innocent people being prosecuted or guilty people prosecuted without sufficient evidence to demonstrate guilt, according to law, or a combination thereof. Whatever the reasons, and despite the correctness of the outcome, according to law, they would involve poor processes. We should also not want anyone to fall into category 2, incorrectly found guilty, or category 4, incorrectly found not guilty, because they are incorrect.

As we are likely to consider category 2 errors to be more serious than category 4 errors, we may, reluctantly, agree that *if* there must be people in each of these categories, then there ought to be a clear differential (van Koppen, 1995). That value is clearly expressed in such statements as: 'It is better that 19 guilty men should go free (category 4) than that one innocent man should be convicted (category 2)'. Such statements are often used, rhetorically, to demonstrate the values implicit in a criminal justice legal system. However, such statements also demonstrate remarkably sloppy thinking. Where are the controls? Nineteen men guilty of what; rape? One man innocent of what; theft? Is that still better? Lord Denning (a senior and often unorthodox judge in England), claimed that 'beyond reasonable doubt' involved a sliding scale, requiring a higher level of proof as the crimes charged became more serious (*Bater v. Bater*, [1951] P 35). An acceptable error rate of 5 %, when applied to 100 000 trials, produces an 'acceptable' 5000 people (or 1 % produces 1000) people wrongly convicted. Quite simply our system accepts, is predicated on and relies on causing miscarriages of justice (Nobles and Schiff, 2000).

PROOF: BEFORE AND AFTER

To this point, as is traditional, the focus has been on decision making at the verdict stage. But trials are part of a decision making process. Before the trial begins evidence must have been acquired and processed. This often includes arrest, detention, and search of person and property. 'Errors', albeit invariably authorized by the law, can also be made at these stages. After the trial, assuming a conviction, a sentence has to be passed. That may be inappropriate or mistaken, not just in the sense that it is altered on legal appeal. Further decisions may be taken by parole boards, or similar, bodies like the Criminal Cases Review Commission, for England and Wales, with power to have the Court of Appeal review the correctness of the conviction. Where defendants have been acquitted, at trial, there can be such issues (if the legal system in question admits them), as payment of compensation for wrongful prosecution and/or repayment of legal expenses. So the two-by-two table suggested above, by the four possible decisions at the verdict stage, may be better represented by the following table (Table 14.1). This table identifies three time periods: investigation of a crime, trial and reaching a verdict on the charges resulting from the investigation, and decision making about the appropriate disposal. This is a summary of the criminal justice process. Many more stages, because many decisions are involved both before and after a verdict is reached, could have been devised but the primary objective, here, is to suggest points and issues. (The numbers allocated in the two-by-two above, about decision making on the verdict, are replicated here for convenience. Thus, the first column does not begin with 1.)

Most of us should spend most of our time in box 7, because we have not committed an offence. There is always a risk, however, as Kafka (1925) liked to remind us, that we

Table 14.1 Potential for miscarriages of justice taking a 'process' perspective.

Investigation		Verdict		Sentence	
5. Correctly proceeded against as guilty.	6. Incorrectly proceeded against as not guilty.	1. Correctly found guilty	2. Incorrectly found guilty.	9. Correct and appropriate sentence.	10. Incorrect sentence although appropriate.
7. Correctly not proceeded against as not guilty.	8. Incorrectly not proceeded against because guilty.	3. Correctly found not guilty	4. Incorrectly found not guilty.	11. Correct but inappropriate sentence.	12. Incorrect and inappropriate sentence.

will appear in box 6, because of a misidentification, a misinterpretation of a fingerprint, a mistake or a lie told by another person. The fear of such errors largely explains our ambiguous attitudes towards the police and other authority figures. Again we would like everyone, who is charged with an offence, to appear in box 5. However, that is both unrealistic and, in order to achieve it, we would have to increase the number appearing in box 8. If prosecutors are to achieve a record of only prosecuting people who are actually guilty, that is achieve box 5, they will need to take fewer risks, be more conservative in their policies, and only prosecute where they are certain of success. To achieve that they will have to decide not to prosecute people, who are actually guilty, because they do not have enough quality evidence and risk a not guilty finding, which is inconsistent with box 5. Box 8 is already very large. Not only does it include all those cases where the prosecutors decide there is not enough quality evidence to justify prosecuting (Crown Prosecution Service, 2004), but all those cases which are not reported, let alone any action taken leading to a prosecution or even a conviction.

Correction: most of us do not spend our time in box 7 but, especially if drivers and 'borrowers' of office stationery, and so on in box 8. It may be tempting to dismiss our appearances in box 8 with references to our behaviour being 'not really criminal,' and similar. But useful information to recall is that, for example, there are around 3500 deaths in road accidents in England and Wales (which has a relatively good record compared with other countries), of which a third are related to speeding (Department of Transport, 2004). The resulting calculations could cause some damage to the notion that the same country has only about 800 homicides per annum (Cotton, 2003).

Boxes 1–4 and 5–8

Is there, or should there be, a relationship between boxes 1–4 and 5–8? There is a legal relationship in the sense that only cases where, for example in England and Wales, there is a 'realistic prospect of conviction', should proceed to trial (e.g. Crown Prosecution Service, 2004, para. 5.2). 'Correctly proceeded against' refers to the likelihood of conviction rather than to guilt. In turn, it involves interpretations of experience and the practice of trial courts. That can vary over time and place and type of case. For example, many offenders, particularly serial, will become forensically aware so as not to leave highly credible evidence that may be traced to them. Successful prosecutions are regularly the consequence of offender incompetence which, unfortunately, they can rectify. So box 5 may be over-represented, and Box 8 under-represented, by incompetent offenders.

In at least one sense there is no relationship between 1–4 and 5–8, or between investigation and trial. It is entirely unrealistic to expect all crimes to be prosecuted, let alone to correct conviction, even if they were reported. Most will never be (Carson, 2007). The police, and other investigators, well know that they will not be able to successfully prosecute most crimes (except most murders). Even if there were the resources of skilled people, time and funding, to undertake all the inquiries and evidence collecting necessary, there will regularly be insufficient evidence to make a finding of 'guilt', at trial, possible. Nevertheless, the police will still be expected to prevent, and act on, actual and potential crimes by disruption and deterrence. It will regularly be wiser, not just in terms of public safety, for them to disrupt or to prevent planned crimes. That will make it more difficult to prove guilt. For example, to convict someone for an attempted crime in England and Wales the prosecution must prove that the defendants committed acts 'more than merely preparatory' towards completing the offence (*Criminal Attempts Act 1981*, s. 1(1); Ormerod, 2005). That requires the police to wait until the crime is almost completed, which could endanger members of the public and themselves. They must also prove an intention to commit the full crime. Intent is the only *mens rea* possible for an attempted crime (to attempt anything involves intending to achieve it), irrespective of what it may be for the completed crime (Ormerod, 2005). Many crimes, for example causing criminal damage, can be committed recklessly (*Criminal Damage Act 1971* in England and Wales) and others negligently. For a conviction for attempted criminal damage, or a crime which can be committed negligently, there must be proof that it was intended. If the police disrupt behaviour, because they believe that a crime is about to be committed, they will find it more difficult to prove intention if they intervene at an early stage, in terms of steps towards completing the crime. For example, they will find it difficult to prove the defendant intended to rob a bank, let alone commit murder of a bank teller, when they arrested him, with a gun in his pocket, several streets away. They are likely to be confined to charging him with carrying a weapon in a public place – which seems to be a constitutional entitlement in certain countries.

Particularly with forensically aware offenders, police officers will have to use what Choong (1997, 1998) calls 'social discipline', and Hillyard and Gordon (1999) call 'informal methods', in order to control and discourage people believed to be (but without sufficient evidence to convince a criminal court), serial or prolific offenders, planning or attempting crimes. As Hillyard and Gordon 1999 point out, arrest rates have gone up although convictions are down. Investigatory powers, designed to access and to obtain evidence leading to trial, are used as a means of controlling and disciplining these believed offenders. This may be called an 'informal' system but it is a necessary product of our criminal justice trial systems. It must also be expected to grow in significance as the police find it more difficult, whether for lack of resources or legal difficulties, for example with forms of admissible evidence, to obtain convictions. The number of people in box 6, people incorrectly proceeded against because duly found not guilty according to law, must be expected to grow the more difficult it is to get cases into box 1. There is a symbiotic relationship between boxes 1–4 and 5–8.

It may appear inappropriate, or unnecessary, to worry about 'erroneous' pretrial decisions, such as arresting and detaining but subsequently releasing suspects, provided the police and prosecutors do not exceed their powers. It is an unfortunate but necessary evil, many are likely to argue, that the police will suspect, investigate and possibly arrest and detain, people who are not only erroneously proceeded against, because of an absence of sufficient evidence, but whom they later acknowledge were wrongly, even if understandably, suspected. Their powers are legally constrained, in a democratic society. But those views are, disproportionately, likely to be held by those of us who have not been suspected, arrested, had their homes suddenly invaded by overwhelming force. Those who do experience these unfortunate consequences of living in a democratic society, governed by the rule of law, may experience it as harassment, as prejudice. Shouldn't they? Are they wrong to do so, particularly as the police have to move, increasingly, to using the so-called informal and social control methods of deterring and preventing crime because it is so difficult to prosecute completed crimes? The more difficult (including expensive) it is to obtain proper convictions the more we must expect, if the police are 'doing their job', 'informal justice' and associated complaints of harassment, and so on. The more we reduce miscarriages of justice inside court the more we seem to increase them outside of court (Nobles and Schiff, 1997, 2000).

Should we complain if the police acknowledge that past behaviour (e.g. criminal convictions for a particular offence) is one of the best predictors of future behaviour and consequently respond to a crime by – crudely expressed – 'rounding up the usual suspects?' It is an appropriate, actuarial, decision-making strategy. If they wish to deter, disrupt or prevent crime – which it is already arguably preferable to letting it occur – should we not expect them to do things which could be interpreted as 'harassment', particularly when and where they anticipate problems in collecting sufficient evidence for a conviction, according to law. The expression 'noble cause corruption' was coined (Kleinig, 2002) to describe the behaviour of police officers who invented, or falsified, evidence in order to ensure the conviction of people they believed, but could not prove to a court's satisfaction, were guilty of offences. It was corrupt, but argued to be noble, because it was achieving appropriate consequences which the law and legal system prevented. Noble corruption, of that form, may have been eradicated. Should we not expect it to live on in the form of disruptive and intrusive action, but not prosecution, against persons believed to be offenders? The people disrupted, or harassed, may actually be past offenders. They may be planning and beginning acts which would lead to a crime. But this sort of police action is undertaken before a crime is committed, before even an attempt or other inchoate offence (e.g. conspiracy) has been committed (Ormerod, 2005). Once again our law and legal system generate this form of 'noble misuse of investigative powers' because of the difficulties in securing sufficient evidence for a conviction, and the narrowness of the laws of attempt. Difficulties in obtaining sufficient evidence will regularly be a consequence of limited resources, which will always be a problem relating to miscarriages of justice (Nobles and Schiff, 1997, 2000).

Boxes 1–4 and 9–12

Is, or should there be, a relationship between boxes 1–4 and 9–12? Boxes 9–12 are concerned with whether the sentence, decided by the court, is both correct and appropriate. Here 'correct' means in line with current sentencing law, policy and practice. Whilst judges have considerable discretion, when sentencing, their decisions are often appealed and sometimes changed by the Court of Appeal. (Even a 'mandatory' life sentence, in England and Wales, involves considerable discretion. The judge has to decide the minimum period

PROCESSES: PROVING GUILT, DISPROVING INNOCENCE

of imprisonment to be served before eligibility for parole may be considered, regularly from eight to over 20 years.)

'Appropriately' sentenced, in this context, could have many meanings but let it first, here, refer to the practical value of the sentence in terms of tackling the offending behaviour. Thus, in this context, a sentence would be 'correct' because it was consistent with sentencing law, guidelines and practice, but it could be 'inappropriate' because it failed to tackle, insofar as a sentence can, the offender's behaviour. For example, a prison sentence could be 'inappropriate' because it was too long and lost the offender's motivation to change, too short to have any future deterrent effect, ineffective because it failed to provide the correct skills or support that the offender needed to sustain changes effected in prison, or failed for some other reason other than simple reoffending. With these meanings of 'correct' and 'appropriate' we would hope that all cases fell in box 9. This is not technically impossible, although it is expecting considerable finesse (and/or interaction with parole boards or equivalent), on behalf of judges (including magistrates where appropriate). Box 10 would contain people who received the wrong sentence, according to contemporary rules and tariffs, but the sentence had the desired effect. It would be very difficult to 'prove' this category. We cannot know that the sentence was effective until some time after its completion, perhaps not before the offender's death where the concern is another serious offence, such as homicide or rape. There are also causal issues; how are we to know that it was the sentence rather than, for example, family members who caused the result. But we can still use the box for discussion purposes. Box 11 would involve cases where the correct rules about sentencing were followed but they were not appropriate because ineffective. That could be the consequence of the sentencing rules being inappropriate or the offender not being amenable to change. Many people might appear to be in box 11, because they reoffend. However, the later offence may be unrelated to the objectives of the sentence for the last offence.

Spending time on such ideas may seem wasteful. Sentencing goals include retribution, not just rehabilitation. They may be 'correct' and 'appropriate' in those terms, although fail because they do not reduce future offending other than during incarceration. It will regularly be impossible to discover the root cause of offending and nonoffending. However, key considerations of this chapter are (1) to encourage a focus on the criminal justice system as a decision-making system, and (2) to identify the extent to which that system seeks to learn about its processes. It is as if we, systematically, fail to learn about the success or failure of the sentencing stage.

According to law there is no relationship between boxes 1–4 and 9–12. Decision-making about verdict, and decision-making about sentence, are separate and unrelated. One decision, guilt or innocence is, within the British system at least, exclusively for the jury and the other, the sentence if found guilty, is for the judge. (Magistrates, within the British system, decide both verdict and sentence.) But could, and should, there be a relationship? Could and should the risk of error, in the verdict, be reflected in the sentence? An increased risk of error, in terms of box 2, might be reflected by a reduction in the sentence. For example, in a different criminal justice legal system, a judge might decide that a doubt about the correctness of the verdict could be offset by a corresponding reduction in the sentence. That suggestion may appear 'crazy' and fundamentally misconceived because of the categorical distinction between decisions on the verdicts and decisions on the sentence. It makes sense if such decision-making is conceived of in terms of risk taking.

When a judge, jury or magistrate decides whether someone is guilty or not, according to law, they take a risk. Calling it a 'judgement' adds nothing, although it may carry associations about the difficulty of the decision and the conscientiousness of the decision makers. The degree of risk is assessed in terms of the seriousness of the outcomes and the likelihood of error. A murder trial is more serious than a parking violation because of the level of punishment likely to be imposed (required in England and Wales) on conviction. (There are other factors, e.g. the impact on victims who do not see someone convicted, but we will ignore those for the moment to simplify the argument.) The likelihood factor, however, is supposed to be the same in both instances, proof beyond reasonable doubt. If we are concerned about the risk of erroneous convictions, miscarriages of justice, then we can seek to mitigate the outcomes or alter the likelihood requirements.

The risk 'costs' of a possible erroneous verdict could be mitigated by a reduced sentence. But this approach is not adopted (even contemplated) by most, at least western, legal systems. Decisions on verdict, boxes 1–4, are entirely separate, from decisions on sentence, boxes 9–12. Should this be challenged? Many, especially lawyers, would argue that it is grossly inappropriate to change this bifurcation, this dichotomy, between decisions on verdict and decisions on sentence. The defendant, actually since the verdict, the offender, is guilty, according to law. There are opportunities and procedures for challenging the verdict, particularly by appeal and, if that is not successful, by seeking a review if that country allows such a procedure (in England and Wales the Criminal Cases Review Commission). Courts can reduce the punishment for a guilty plea (see below), even though that can increase the number of innocent people wrongly pleading guilty, but we do not reduce the sentence to take into account the risk of error. We do not distribute the risk.

Another potential link between boxes 1–4 and 9–12 relates to the objectives of trials. We have trials to determine guilt. If guilt is established then there are further proceedings where an appropriate sentence is discussed. The trial focuses on 'who' 'what' and 'whether' a crime was committed. It does not focus on 'why' it was committed, beyond the extent to which motive (why) is valuable for explaining *mens rea*, (e.g. intention). Only 'relevant' evidence is admissible. That is any fact which makes it more, or less, likely that other facts, those which have to be satisfactorily proved if the legal requirements of the offence charged are to be proved, are true (Roberts and Zuckerman, 2004). Evidence, for example that the defendant was easily led, could be highly relevant to explaining why the crime was committed but would be ruled irrelevant to the trial. However, an understanding of 'why' is critical to determining what would be the most suitable punishment, at least for the rehabilitative goal (see Palmer, Chapter 9, this volume).

Lawyers are interested in *mens rea*, the mental element of the crime, in order to determine whether and which crime was committed. *Mens rea* should also be relevant to psychologists, and others responding to criminal or antisocial behaviour. They could learn what the offender knew (and arguably as important did not know), intended, how they made the decisions involved, how they reflected on the risks involved, learn, or do not learn, from experience. There is a difference in that lawyers are interested in the category of *mens rea* (e.g. intention or foresight), and just the slice of time when the *actus reus* of the crime was committed; did the defendant intend or just anticipate injury when throwing the brick? Psychologists are more likely to be interested in the defendant's thinking processes over a longer period of time. The rich seam of individualistic information, about why the offence was committed, is not mined in trials, beyond that strictly relevant to the guilty or not guilty 'according to law' dichotomy. The policy question is whether it would be appropriate to make a formal link, between these sets of boxes, by investing some trial time, albeit after a finding of guilt, to understand better why the crime was committed? This not only has the potential for making more appropriate decisions on interventions to discourage reoffending, with considerable potential financial and other savings, but also opportunities to provide information and reassurance to victims and communities, as in restorative justice senses. An investigation of why a particular rape was committed may reveal that the victim was 'chosen' at random. That is significant information for those designing intervention programmes, and for the victim.

Initially any direct links between boxes 5–8 and 9–12 would appear very inappropriate; it seems wrong to 'jump' from crime investigation straight to crime punishment. But consider reality, rather than ideal states. The reality, in an adversary system, is that most people plead guilty; they do not have a trial of the evidence. Some suspects plead guilty, even when not guilty, because they fear that their not guilty plea would be disbelieved and they would miss out on the sentence reduction for a guilty plea (*R. v. Goodyear*, [2005] EWCA Crim 888) (Gudjonsson, 2003; Dell, 1971). Decisions about whether to plead guilty, and to which charges, will appropriately include consideration of the likely sentence as well as the likely verdict. Changes to the rules of evidence, such as more frequent admission of information about defendants' prior criminal convictions, will also increase the proportion in this group. (Perhaps Table 14.1 should have one or more 2 by 2s, between boxes 7 and 8 and 1 and 2. These would reflect the stage(s) when the prosecution reviews the evidence and decides whether to go to trial, and when the defendant decides whether to force a full trial.)

There is also a relationship between boxes 5–8 and 9–12, in relation to the growing phenomenon of problem-solving courts (e.g. Winick and Wexler, 2003). The distinctive goal of a drug court, for example, is to use the extra powers and prestige of a court to help get offenders off their drug, and thereby criminal, habits. They reflect a concern with being effective, and involve a reaction against simply processing offenders through the system. Their regimes are, or should be, limited to those who admit their offences, and are motivated to change. Those who dispute their guilt should go to trial. But if access to treatment and support regimes is limited or delayed, and courts can surmount such problems, then there will be incentives to ignore boxes 1–4 and jump from 5–8 to 9–12. The due process ideology of criminal justice, with its emphasis on individual responsibility and culpability, can appear rather irrelevant when contrasted with the daily reality of first instance courts processing serial offenders who have great difficulties in living their lives differently.

Does examining decision making, in criminal justice systems in this manner, and Table 14.1, help? The table certainly under-represents, and thereby misrepresents, the complexity of criminal justice system. But, as a model, it begins to represent it as a system and as a sequence of processes. As such, it is easy to identify ways in which the parts operate against, or independent of, each other when they ought to work sequentially and co-operatively. This approach also, it is suggested, highlights the contribution of other disciplines, particularly psychology. For example, it highlights the importance of understanding why offenders commit crimes and, thereby, the importance of psychologists working with lawyers (defence and prosecution) and investigators to ensure that appropriate information is obtained and secured in order to inform post-conviction interventions. Yes, it is critical to focus on whether the offender is guilty, but it should also be possible to collate information to inform decisions at later stages. It is also appropriate to study processes and systems and whether they interact appropriately and effectively.

PROOF: GUILT AND INNOCENCE

An emphasis on process, it is submitted, is also valuable for considering what we mean by 'proof', and how we might reach more reliable decisions about guilt and 'innocence'. An emphasis on how the evidence was obtained, collated, processed, assessed and presented, not just its contents or nature, could – rightly – increase or decrease the trust placed in it. Indeed, we might be able to go beyond current standards of proof and protections against error.

Currently the prosecution must prove the defendant guilty, beyond reasonable doubt. Technically, the defence need introduce no evidence, need prove nothing. It is the prosecution's duty to demonstrate guilt. Indeed the case may be dismissed, before the defence produces any evidence, if the judge is satisfied that insufficient evidence has been adduced for a jury to safely convict (Roberts and Zuckerman, 2004). Intuitively, however, it is wise for the defence both to attack the quality and quantity of the prosecution's evidence and to produce further evidence suggesting lack of guilt. The emphasis on the prosecution proving guilt is long-standing, although some 'challenges' can be observed. First, the defence can have an 'evidentiary burden.' This requires them to produce sufficient evidence, for example that the defendant was drunk, to make it appropriate to require the prosecution to disprove that assertion, where it would be legally relevant. But this rule can be explained as simply preventing the defence from complaining that every possible defence was not disproved, even when there was no evidence even to suggest it might be relevant (Ormerod, 2005). The prosecution will still have to disprove the defence, beyond reasonable doubt. (There are a few special cases, e.g. the defence of insanity, where the rules are different (Ormerod, 2005). For reasons of space, and because they do not really challenge the argument to be developed, these will not be discussed here.) Second, there are the limits on 'the right to silence'. In England and Wales, for example, when suspects are arrested they are warned that failure to give investigators relevant information, which they could provide, may be adversely commented on in court, if they rely on it later. The practice is, however, complicated when suspects do not provide the information – on the advice of their lawyers (see Roberts and Zuckerman, 2004).

However, despite all the history of, and international consensus on this core rule about proof, would it be possible and appropriate to recast the prosecution's duty? This section will argue that the prosecution, and thereby the police, should be obliged both (1) to prove guilt and (2) to disprove innocence, beyond reasonable doubt. This, it will be argued, would improve the quality of decision making, appropriately increase trust in that decision making, and reduce the number of miscarriages of justice.

But what would the prosecution, and police, have to do in order to disprove innocence? Guilt can be presented as a 'positive' state, the presence of certain facts. The defendant caused the proscribed behaviour or result, with the specified mens rea for that crime, and without any defence that could apply. Even though ground truth cannot be discovered a jury could be satisfied, beyond reasonable doubt, of that. In this sense 'innocence' is a negative state. It is one thing to 'prove' a positive, entirely different to prove a negative. Disproving innocence would seem to require demonstration that every possible alternative (e.g. considering every other person to be a potential defendant) is incompatible with guilt. That would be an incredibly onerous task, even if possible, and prove exceptionally wasteful of resources. So, in this context, 'disproving innocence' needs to be given a working definition. This, it is suggested, should include disproving (1) any reasonable alternative explanation for who committed the offence, when, where or how, arising out of the evidence found or implicit in the allegation of guilt; (2) any alternative explanation or hypothesis – reasonably – suggested by the defence (with disputes about 'reasonableness' determined by a pretrial judge); and (3) any alternative explanation or hypothesis regularly associated with that type of offence.

Changing the duty of the police and prosecution in this way would involve adopting a scientific paradigm. That should lead to a greater use of scientific methodologies, skills and standards. The benefits of the change might be greater in practice, for example in terms of change in working culture, in training and self-regard, than in theory. The case for change would need to be made in terms of 'concrete results'; for example, if police investigators come to be perceived as more neutral investigators of the truth, rather than partial instruments of the state, judges and jurors could become more willing to trust their evidence. It should encourage a focus on the decision-making processes as well as on concrete or 'real' (Roberts and Zuckerman, 2004) evidence. That would facilitate a greater contribution by psychologists, by other behavioural scientists and decision theorists.

For example, it ought to be able to attack problems arising from precipitous police and prosecutor decision-making (Smith and Flanaghan, 2000) tunnel vision and case construction (Maguire and Norris, 1992; Maguire, 2003). They argue that, when the police have a suspect in mind, they move too quickly to seeking evidence of the suspect's guilt rather than further evidence about the crime, which might suggest alternative hypotheses, in particular suspects. Once the emphasis is on demonstrating the suspect's guilt, opportunities for further errors are magnified such as through interviews (Gudjonsson, 2003) and identifications, the science of which is far from perfect. The authors argue that each of these three decision-making errors lead to false positive mistakes, and thereby miscarriages of justice. Whilst the three criticisms differ in degree and detail they all suggest that police investigators can identify a suspect too early. But the criticisms are largely circuitous. They are responding to cases where a miscarriage of justice has been demonstrated, for example where further evidence shows the defendant could not be guilty or introduces a reasonable doubt. That finding demonstrates that the investigators reached an erroneous conclusion. By definition they must have decided on whom they thought was guilty too early, did not investigate sufficiently to discover the new facts which have led to the appeal, and focused on finding evidence of the suspect's guilt rather than considering other possible suspects. Those theories explain those cases. They do not, on their own, however, help us to identify which cases were precipitously decided, constructed or involved tunnel vision. They help to explain, or judge, some cases; they do not help us to predict which cases will, subsequently, be shown to be erroneous for those reasons.

The authors are right to identify these decision-making problems because they are very important errors. However, the problem is not simply one of overeager investigators but also our adversarial trial system, in which they must operate (Carson, 2007). The police and prosecutors are tasked to present suspects to the courts where the issue will not be an examination of the crime, or how it was investigated, but whether the suspect is guilty as charged. The adversarial legal system invites investigators to act in the way criticized, particularly when issues of cost are included. So, it is submitted, the legislative changes, such as the Criminal Procedure and Investigations Act 1996, s. 23, are insufficient. That Act, for England and Wales, requires the police to consider evidence which points away from the suspect as well as towards (Secretary of State for the Home Department, 2005). We need an explicit change in the role of prosecutors, and in the test for proof at trial.

Psychological research might substantiate the suggestion that the proposed change would reduce the likelihood of erroneous decisions. If investigators know that they will have to be able to demonstrate, in court, that they considered a range of alternative hypotheses or stories, then they are more likely to seek and examine all the relevant evidence and its implications, and not just seek the 'usual suspects'. Indeed this practice, of being able to demonstrate that alternative theories are improbable is, to a considerable extent, already good practice in England and Wales (ACPO, 2005). It is suggested that investigators should go further than just demonstrate they have investigated alternative and null hypotheses; they should also be able to show that they analysed and assessed the evidence for and against the preferred and alternate stories. The change in the requirements for proof would also provide an opportunity to introduce ideas and mechanisms being developed within New Evidence Scholarship, for example Wigmorean Chart Analysis, as amended by Anderson, Schum and Twining (2005).

Proof of guilt and disproof of innocence should, it is submitted, lead to a greater emphasis on the 'rationality' of the evidence produced, not just its content. Juries would be required to contrast stories and the evidence for them. Prosecutors would need to explain how and why juries could and should rely on the evidence presented. The emphasis, it is suggested, would move to the 'intellectual' rationale for conviction, or nonconviction, from the present position, which can be 'emotional' in that jurors are invited to consider the magnitude of their doubts, how 'happy' they are to convict on the evidence presented, with a guess as to the subsequent likely sentence.

Investigators ought to become more neutral and objective. They should be encouraged to adopt an ethic of truth-finding rather than crime-fighting. Indeed, a case could be developed for a distinct cadre of investigators who relate to (other) forensic scientists and are informed and served by law-enforcement police officers. The commonalities and interrelations between investigators across a wide spectrum, for example revenue, customs, social security fraud, and so on, might be emphasized rather than their differences. The sciences of fact finding, inference drawing and decision making, alongside critical awareness and skill to assess a range of forms of forensic science, could become the core of investigation rather than policing practices and procedures. (Compare Anderson, Schum and Twining 2005 with ACPO (2005) and Hutton, Johnston and Sampson 2004.)

No diminution of the requirement to prove guilt 'beyond reasonable doubt', is suggested. It would be an additional duty to disprove innocence, again 'beyond reasonable doubt'. This might appear an onerous duty, but emphasis must be placed on the requirement of 'reasonableness'. Trial judges could be empowered to decide that certain defence claims, suggesting innocence, should be dismissed because the supporting evidence, because of its quantity and/or quality, makes any claim based on it unreasonable. This would be similar to their current practice when deciding whether the evidentiary burden, to make it the prosecution's duty to disprove a proffered defence, has been satisfied. The jury would still have to decide whether any remaining hypothesis was reasonable, but the focus would be on the reasonableness (i.e. its nature and quality) rather than an overall sense of concern about convicting or acquitting the defendant. They would be encouraged to concentrate on analysing the evidence, its credibility, the appropriateness of the inferences drawn and the overarching degree of confidence that can be placed in the allegations being true, rather than assessing the quality of the story, as researchers have suggested is what happens (e.g. Pennington and Hastie, 1986).

If this change was enacted, it would make it more appropriate to require the courts to give an account of their decision-making processes. The European Court of Human Rights is said to be developing a case law on the need, and desirability, of courts explaining their decisions (Cheney *et al.*, 2001, p. 122). In the future, judges could help a jury by identifying the hypotheses and evidence supporting innocence (or nonguilt) as well as of guilt. Particularly if these aids were presented in a skilful, written and perhaps diagrammatic manner, then juries could be required to answer questions about which evidence and inferences they accepted and rejected. This would both allow the judge to test the coherence and rationality of the jury's decision as well as facilitate appeal courts and review bodies if and when fresh evidence is submitted. It would be possible to discover what the implications for the jury's decision would be if the new evidence is accepted (Jackson and Doran, 1995).

Implementing such a change is liable to make trials less adversary and more investigatory. That should not be grounds for criticism as it would retain the essential rationale for the adversarial system. As Lord Devlin (1981) expressed it, the adversarial system is based on the hypothesis that the best way of getting at the truth is to give two motivated parties the maximum opportunity to put their case. The adversarial system can be criticized. For example, the prosecution is not, primarily, supposed to seek to prove guilt but rather to ensure that all appropriate evidence is presented to the courts (Roberts and Zuckerman, 2004). Secondly there is, regularly, a gross imbalance of resources available to support investigation, in favour of the prosecution. The changes proposed would reinforce the primary ethic for the prosecution to be truth finding, and would ensure that resources are available to investigate any evidence or hypotheses about the crime which the defence reasonably suggest. There might be a case, particularly for certain crimes, for different teams of investigators to seek to prove guilt and disprove innocence. That could reinforce the neutrality of investigators and, perhaps, encourage skills in looking both for guilt and innocence.

A major consequence, of the proposed changes in the requirements for proof, would relate to 'the right to silence.' The defence would, if they wished to have a line of enquiry undertaken, need to explain this to the investigators, for them to undertake it. It would be much more difficult for the defence not to inform the prosecution of their approach before the trial. This could be criticized for further weakening the defendant's position. They could not rely on saying nothing, requiring the prosecution to make its case. Would this involve much change, in practice? In England and Wales, at least, the defence already has duties to disclose the nature of its defence after the prosecution has identified the evidence it intends to rely on (Criminal Procedure and Investigations Act 1996, s. 5; Sprack, 2004). The defendant's unjustified failure to give information on arrest (exercise of the 'right to silence'), which they later seek to rely on in court, can now lead to a critical comment from the judge, to the jury. Relatively few suspects, at least in England and Wales, provide no information during police interviews (McConville and Hodgson, 1993), and when used it can be a bargaining device for information from the police (Dixon, 1997). Nevertheless, such changes would be controversial, in England and Wales. The current legislative position has arisen, over many years, through a dialectical process of alternative emphasis on crime control and due process, on protecting suspects from miscarriages and then preventing criminals from 'getting away with it' (Roberts and Zuckerman, 2004). A rigorous review of what is necessary to produce a fair system of investigations, taking into account many developments such as trends towards more ethical policing (ACPO, 2005), is necessary, rather than more piecemeal changes.

Such restrictions on 'the right to silence' are designed to ensure both that jurors will be influenced by the judge's comments on its exercise, to the extent and only when he or she makes them. However, we do not know whether the jury would be influenced, when it learns that a defendant responded 'no comment' to every question asked by the police, irrespective of any judicial guidance. The judicial warning may be redundant as jurors may draw inferences even in cases where the judge makes no comment. They may also, implicitly or explicitly, reason against the defence when and because they do not offer an alternative version of events to that of the prosecution. The judge may tell the jury, several times, that it is the prosecution's job to find the defendant guilty, not the defence's job to prove themselves not guilty, but the jury may infer (also known as 'jump to conclusions') because the defence does not offer evidence. In this sense, we know that juries may draw impermissible or inappropriate conclusions and yet do not act to prevent it, current practice is irrational. The changes proposed would make the position explicit. The implications of a failure to provide a defence, or evidence, would be at issue between the parties. Perhaps, given the features of the case, it is not possible for the defence to provide certain information. They cannot, for example, be expected to suggest whom the perpetrator really was if they contend that they were not present. The key point is that the judge and jury can hear an explicit discussion of the reasonably possible alternative hypotheses and inferences as to how the crime was committed, both from the presence and unreasonably absent evidence.

PROOF: FINDING GUILTY AND INNOCENT

The implications, of requiring the prosecution both to prove guilt and to disprove innocence, would not be limited to the trial. Whilst it should reduce the number of false positive convictions, people wrongly convicted, it should also reduce the number of false negative decisions, which is people who would fall into boxes 4 and 8 above, those wrongly found not guilty and those wrongly not proceeded against because actually guilty. It is suspected both that more defendants would be proceeded against and that more would plead guilty. Defendants, and their legal advisors, would know that jurors would know both (1) that they had been given opportunities to have their defence investigated and (2) that any failure, on their part, to provide relevant information available to them would be debated in front of the jury. This, it is suggested, would lead to more pleas of guilty, and at earlier stages than might be the position at present. The lottery character of trials would be reduced. Reducing the types of error represented by boxes 2, 4 and 8 would be an extension of justice, but that should not be sufficient.

There remains a risk that defendants will wrongly plead guilty. They may confess improperly (Gudjonsson, 2003). They may also decide that they are unlikely to be believed, by the jury, and wish to benefit from any reduction in sentence that is available for pleading guilty (even if they are not) at an early stage. Intuitively, the changes proposed should not increase the likelihood of these errors, but it is actual defendants' decision making that matters. The changes should promise defendants that their defence will be thoroughly investigated, but many defendants, particularly where legal advice is wanting in quantity or quality, may be unable to make an informed or skilful decision. The circumstances of their case, for example an inability to remember people or circumstances which could inform their defence, in circumstances where that inability to remember is liable to make a jury suspicious, could be against them. Protections against the creation of systemic problems should be adopted. That could include a duty, where there are any grounds to suspect, to investigate the defendant's capacity.

A consequence, of the proposed change in the duty of proving, should be a more rational system. There should be more emphasis on proof than on persuasion. To reinforce this change, a number of precepts could be made explicit and adopted in practice. For example, current practice provides more intellectual and other resources for more serous cases, such as murder, even though they can be much easier to investigate and prove (Carson, 2007). A change in the rules about proof would provide an excellent opportunity for addressing such 'irrationalities' in the existing system. The degree of resources invested should reflect, directly, the difficulties involved in investigating the allegations and testing the evidence and conclusions drawn in a trial. The proposed changes are likely to produce a more investigatory trial system, at least up to the beginning of the trial, particularly during preliminary proceedings where the core issues in dispute are identified. Others have already suggested that the British system is moving towards an investigatory system (Jorg, Field and Brants, 1995). Pre-trial judges would be more active in deciding, for example, which defences the defence is entitled to have investigated, and to which standards. Whilst this may appear to suggest a more expensive and resource intensive system, which would have implications for the total number of cases that could be processed, there should be savings in terms of a higher proportion of cases leading to guilty pleas at an earlier stage.

To guard against such system failures as more, or even as many people wrongly admit guilt, it is suggested that judges should have, at least before anyone is imprisoned, a duty to review the quantity and quality of evidence against them. They should provide an independent safeguard of the quality of the investigation and be prepared to direct that further investigations be undertaken, or that proceedings be dropped, even where the defendant has confessed. This could, in practice, produce a position where judges check that the police have, at least, followed the basic steps recommended by their procedure and policy guides (e.g. ACPO, 2005). This would guarantee, at least, non-negligent standards. The more faith that jurors, witnesses and the public can have in the quality of investigations then the more likely they are to provide evidence and serve as witnesses in other cases, and as jurors have faith in the quality of evidence presented. Lack of confidence in 'the system' is a critical problem for current criminal justice systems.

PROVING: CRIMINAL AND CIVIL

It is much more difficult, than might intuitively be assumed, to distinguish the 'criminal' from the 'civil' (Ormerod, 2005). One practical consequence, however, with exceptions that need not detain us here, is that criminal cases must be proved beyond reasonable doubt whilst civil cases are proved on a balance of probabilities (Roberts and Zuckerman, 2004), without any requirement for a minimum base-line quantity or quality of evidence. Yet, despite this major difference, most, if not all, crimes are also civil wrongs. Victims of both personal injury and property damage can sue as well as seek to prosecute the perpetrators. Yet it is relatively rare for victims to take civil proceedings. Victims of property damage will regularly rely on their insurance policies, spreading their losses amongst other premium payers. Victims of physical injury may be compensated by a criminal injuries compensation scheme if, as with the UK, their country has such a scheme. They might wish to sue those who offended against them for a range of reasons. These are as likely to be associated with restorative justice goals (such as gaining more details about what happened, ascribing blame, discovering why they were victimized, ensuring learning and action by the offender, etc.), as with retributive objects.

Even with a change to a system where the prosecution must disprove innocence as well as prove guilt, there will still be many cases where there is insufficient evidence to justify a conviction, even to take the case to trial. Two further reforms should be considered. First, there may be insufficient evidence to find the defendant guilty beyond reasonable doubt. They should not be found guilty, but there could be sufficient evidence to find that the defendant committed a civil wrong, for example trespass to the person or negligent injury (Rogers, 2006). If this is the case then the court, whether the judge or the jury, could make a finding that a civil wrong (e.g. a tort) had been committed and award compensation and any other appropriate civil remedy. It is highly likely that many defendants would be unable to pay the compensation awarded, certainly as a lump sum. As the amount would be calculated on the basis of trying to put the victim back into the position, as far as money can, that they were in before the injury or loss, it would regularly exceed what a court could impose as a punishment. So there would be problems in ensuring payment. A state agency might pay some or all of the compensation awarded and become responsible for collecting payments over time, such as through the tax system, but that would have many disincentives for rehabilitation. The key goals of such a change would be to ensure that more people, in boxes 4 and 8, and their victims, received some justice, including explanation. The latter goal, explanation, might have to be valued over compensation.

A second reform could be to allow – or require – police and comparable investigators to pass to victims of crimes, or their families, the evidence that they have collected but which a court has decided, or they have concluded, is insufficient to prove a defendant guilty, and/or disprove innocent, beyond reasonable doubt. This would empower the victims to bring a civil action, if they wished. Hopefully, it would not automatically lead to litigation, not least because it is expensive and time and other resource intensive. Rather it would give the victim some power with which to negotiate for restorative remedies. The victim could require, as a possible alternative to going to court for compensation, that the perpetrator provide an explanation an apology for the crime, or ensure that they discover and appreciate the harm caused.

CONCLUSION

These suggestions for reform could maximize the quality and quantity of justice. They could both reduce the number of incorrect decisions whilst ensuring that more victims get a remedy, albeit not all they might wish for. Nevertheless, there would still be many people left without any remedy. Given our (correct) insistence on high standards of proof there will always be many cases where criminal convictions cannot be achieved. However, that cannot justify us in not improving the quality of proof decisions and allowing more victims in particular to get some justice without changing standards of what has to be proved, or how.

Psychology and psychologists could make a considerable contribution to the testing of the hypotheses involved in these arguments. They could also contribute to drawing out more benefits from change. Their expertise, albeit not unique, in analysing and predicting human decision-making behaviour could inform techniques for identifying and assessing relevant evidence.

REFERENCES

ACPO (Association of Chief Police Officers) (2005) *Practice Advice on Core Investigative Doctrine*, National Centre for Policing Excellence, Cambourne.
Anderson, T., Schum, D. and Twining, W. (2005) *Analysis of Evidence*, 2nd edn, Cambridge University Press, Cambridge.
Campbell, C. (1974) Legal thoughts and juristic values. *British Journal of Law and Society*, **1** (1), 13–31.
Carson, D. (2007) Investigating investigations: models of investigation, in *Handbook of Criminal Investigation* (eds T. Newburn, T. Williamson and A. Wright), Willan, Cullompton.
Cheney, D., Dickson, L., Skilbeck, R. et al. (2001) *Criminal Justice and the Human Rights Act 1998*, Jordans, Bristol.
Crown Prosecution Service (2004) *The Code*, Crown Prosecution Service, London.
Choong, S. (1997) *Policing as Social Discipline*, Clarendon Press, Oxford.
Choong, S. (1998) Policing the dross. *British Journal of Criminology*, **38**, 623–634.
Cotton, J. (2003) Homicide, in *Crime in England and Wales, 2001/2002: Supplementary Volume* (eds C. Flood-Page and J. Taylor), Home Office, London.
Dell, S. (1971) *Silent in Court: The Legal Representation of Women Who Went to Prison*. Bell, London.
Department of Transport (2004) *Tomorrow's Roads – Safer for Everyone*, Department for Transport, London.
Devlin, P. (1981) *The Judge*, Oxford University Press, Oxford.
Dixon, D. (1997) *Law in Policing: Legal Regulation and Police Practices*, Clarendon Press, Oxford.
Kafka, F. (1925) *The Trial*, Kurt Wolff Verlag, Munich.
Gudjonsson, G. (2003) *The Psychology of Interrogations and Confessions: A Handbook*, Wiley, Chichester.
Hillyard, P. and Gordon, D. (1999) Arresting statistics: The drift to informal justice in England and Wales. *Journal of Law and Society*, **26** (4), 502–22.
Hutton, G., Johnston, D. and Sampson, F. (2004) *Blackstone's Police Investigator's Manual*, Oxford University Press, Oxford.
Jackson, J. and Doran, S. (1995) *Judge without Jury*, Oxford University Press, Oxford.
Jorg, N., Field, S. and Brants, C. (1995) Are inquisitorial and adversarial systems converging?, in *Criminal Justice in Europe: A Comparative Study* (eds P. Fennell, C. Harding, N. Jorg and B. Swart), Oxford University Press, Oxford.
Kleinig, J. (2002) Rethinking noble cause corruption. *International Journal of Police Science & Management*, **4** (4), 287–324.
Maguire, M. (2003) Criminal investigation and crime control, in *Handbook of Policing* (ed T. Newburn), Willan, Cullompton, pp. 363–93.
Maguire, M. and Norris, C. (1992) *The Conduct and Supervision of Criminal Investigations* (Royal Commission on Criminal Justice, Research Study No. 5), HMSO, London.
McConville, M. and Hodgson, J. (1993) *Custodial Legal Advice and the Right to Silence* (Royal Commission on Criminal Justice Research Study No. 16), HMSO, London.
Nobles, R. and Schiff, D. (1997) The never ending story: Disguising tragic choices in criminal justice. *Modern Law Review*, **60** (2), 293–304.
Nobles, R. and Schiff, D. (2000) *Understanding Miscarriages of Justice*, Oxford University Press, Oxford.
Ormerod, D. (2005) *Smith and Hogan Criminal Law*, Oxford University Press, Oxford.
Pennington, N. and Hastie, R. (1986) Evidence evaluation in complex decision making. *Journal of Personality and Social Psychology* **51**, 242–58.
Roberts, P. and Zuckerman, A. (2004) *Criminal Evidence*, Oxford University Press, Oxford.

Rogers, W.V.H. (2006) *Winfield & Jolowicz on Tort*, 17th edn, Sweet & Maxwell, London.

Secretary of State for the Home Department (2005) *Criminal Procedure and Investigations Act 1966: Code of Practice Under Part II*, Home Office, London.

Shiels, R.S. (1999) *Scottish Legal System*. W. Green/Sweet & Maxwell, Edinburgh.

Smith, N. and Flanaghan, C. (2000) *The Effective Detective: Identifying the Skills of an Effective Detective*, Home Office, London.

Sprack, J. (2004) *A Practical Guide to Criminal Procedure*, 10th edn, Oxford University Press, Oxford.

Van Koppen, P.J. (1995) Judges' decision-making, in *Psychology in Legal Contexts* (eds R. Bull and D. Carson), Wiley, Chichester, pp. 581–610.

Winick, B.J. and Wexler, D.B. (2003) *Judging in a Therapeutic Key: Therapeutic Jurisprudence in the Courts*, Carolina Academic Press, Durham (NC).

CHAPTER 15

The Changing Nature of Adversarial, Inquisitorial and Islamic Trials

Francis Pakes
University of Portsmouth

Trials are decision-making forums. Despite that seeming unity of purpose Damaška (1986) identified a truly bewildering variety in arrangements surrounding the trial process, and more than twenty years on that variety has not subsided but, if anything, increased. In particular, when taking arrangements at International criminal tribunals (e.g. Pakes, 2003) and so-called internationalized criminal courts (Romano, Nollkeamper and Kleffner, 2004) into account, the ways in which courts are run continues to diversity. Classification systems commonly identify three 'families' of trial systems that exist in the inquisitorial (common on the European continent), adversarial (such as in the USA and the UK) and the Islamic or Sharia legal tradition which is widespread in, but not limited to, the Middle East. Their differences have been explained by referring to the role of state in society, public levels of trust in official bodies, the role of religion and the extent to which crime is considered a major social problem.

It has been identified that these systems seek to achieve the same ultimate goal (justice), but strive to attain this via different means (Crombag, 2003). Inquisitorial systems are based on the assumption that a state-instigated objective inquiry is most likely to uncover the truth; the adversarial foundation is that of getting at the truth via partisan contest between opposing parties, whereas in Sharia law, the substantive and procedural law is derived from the Koran, so that religious purity is the instrument for achieving justice. However, the differences between the three are not fixed and all are subject to continuing change. What King calls an 'unfettered public discourse' (King, 2001, p. 93) about trial procedures in the USA probably occurs in many jurisdictions, and indeed trial arrangements anywhere seem to be perennially reformed, enhanced, rationalized and overhauled. The question then is to what extent does (or could) psychology inform those changes, and can we say that such changes, generally, serve to improve the conditions under which decision making occurs? These questions are arguably too broad to answer in a single chapter. I will,

---

Applying Psychology to Criminal Justice. Edited by David Carson, Rebecca Milne, Francis Pakes, Karen Shalev and Andrea Shawyer. © 2007 John Wiley & Sons, Ltd

however, discuss developments in adversarial, inquisitorial and Sharia law to suggest what the possible answers might be.

INTRODUCTION: THE CHANGING NATURE OF CRIMINAL TRIALS

Establishing the exact purpose of trials might seem a straightforward proposition but closer scrutiny reveals that it is not so. Lord Justice Auld, in his influential report from 2001 argues that, 'it is obvious that their purpose and function are not confined to the forensic practicalities of convicting and sentencing the guilty and acquitting others' (Auld, 2001, Chapter 1, para 1.4). These aims that are intrinsic to the goings on inside the courtroom are well rehearsed and relate to the objective of achieving fair outcomes, convicting the 'truly guilty', whilst not interfering in the life of the 'truly innocent'. We should look beyond the confines of the courtroom, however, and take the wider context in which trials take place into account. Lord Justice Auld relates those to the aims of the criminal justice as a whole, reframed by the New Labour Government as reducing crime and the fear of crime and their social and economic costs as well as dispensing justice fairly and efficiently, and promoting confidence in the law (Home Office, 1999, para 1.3). That is a tall order as these aims are not easily achieving in conjunction. Balancing conflicting aims and priorities is of course part and parcel of the criminal justice enterprise, nowhere more so than in sentencing where there is a long tradition of socio-legal research on the goals of punishment, and an abundance of empirical psychological research into whether such goals are, or even can be, achieved. 'What works?' is the common denominator of this research (McGuire, 1995).

The situation for trials is different. The objectives of criminal trials are more the stuff of undercurrents. Debates on reform tend to focus on what is wrong with the way they are run rather than what they are for: invariably trials are too costly, too protracted, or too erratic (e.g. Stevens, 2002). A glimpse of insight into what trials are for might be gained by considering the seemingly widespread desire to do the criminal justice system's business without them. That rather puts the position of the trial as the 'showpiece' of the criminal justice process into question. Diversion, a variety of processes of avoiding trial can be summarized, as can of course be done for the most noble as well as for the most sinister of motives. Restorative justice, certainly within youth justice, is widely regarded to be a constructive way of dispensing justice, for instance by means of family group conferences (McKenzie, 2005; Braithwaite, 1989). Other ways to avoid the criminal trial occur via plea-bargaining and the use of civil measures in order to control undesirable behaviour, for instance via Anti-Social Behaviour Orders (see Hatcher and Hollin, 2005; Burney, 2005). More unsavoury is the use of long-term detention without trial of suspected terrorists, such as on Guantanamo Bay, Cuba or in Belmarsh Prison in the UK. Social control via freedom-restricting measures on specific individuals is routinely done without trial, or, strictly, without the criminal justice involvement altogether.

So for whom are trials staged in the first place? The traditional answer to decide on the guilt of the defendant and possibly from there on their punishment does not suffice. Trials increasingly serve a function beyond the courtroom: trials cannot be understood simply be looking at the trial itself. We must examine the criminal justice process of which it forms a part, the philosophy that underlies the concept of justice per se, and we must look at the wider context: a perspective that is too, as it were, inward looking is unlikely to uncover their true meaning. In this chapter, I will look at developments in the adversarial legal tradition first, and identify an area that is subject to 'inquisitorialization', the role of the judge. Subsequently, I will examine inquisitorial justice and scrutinize a development that we can call 'adversarialization': the enhancement of its trial function as the dramatic 'day in court'. Finally, we look at court arrangements in the Islamic tradition, and identify where resistance to change, but coupled with a desire to 'purify' proceedings in accordance with religious sources, comes from. We will see that psychology's influence on these processes of change rather differs from one system to the next, with possibly the adversarial mode of justice most receptive to its body of knowledge and the Islamic legal tradition least so.

ADVERSARIAL TRANSITIONS: LESS SPECTACLE, MORE PROBLEM SOLVING

The adversarial trial tradition, originating in England and exported to a good number of former colonies, assigns prime importance to the trial. Damaška (1986) refers to this as 'the day in court':

> The day-in-court trial can be packed with excitement and drama: the vivacity of first impressions is not adversely affected by a documentary curtain over the trial. Surprises and unpredictable turns are commonplace, but coordinate officials are accustomed to deciding on the basis of what might be called 'astonished reflection'. The dramatic courtroom atmosphere is enhanced by the possible finality of the trial court's judgement: no punches can be pulled in reliance on a next procedural round before a higher authority. [...] Under favorable conditions, trials can thus truly become events where, in the setting of a public performance, social norms are articulated, or those already articulated are solemnly confirmed. (Damaška, 1986, p. 62).

It highlights a number of adversarial characteristics. The fact that, in principle, all evidence is presented orally in open court is one such characteristic. The fact that an adversarial trial is a 'grande finale': a showdown after which it will be clear who won and who lost. It also emphasizes its norm setting or affirming function, whereas of course the oral presentation of evidence is particularly suited to lay participation in the form of a jury. It also hints at the problems associated with the day in court. Oral evidence produces problems of memory and presentation, and the risk of jurors swayed by testimony that sounds persuasive, rather than by evidence of a high standard. No wonder that adversarial laws of evidence are extensive, as compared with those in the inquisitorial tradition where the law of evidence often fits on the back of an envelop (e.g. Nijboer, 1997). The jury, impressionable as it is assumed to be, needs to be protected from improper evidence so that the judge is armed with ways in which evidence can be forbidden, or sanitized before it is fit for the eyes and ears of the jury.

However, in Damaška's analysis, these elements, notably 'courtroom drama', are only the 'naturalia' rather than the 'essentialia' (Damaška, 1973, p. 564) of adversarial systems. Drama is particularly associated with adversarial justice but is possible in inquisitorial courtrooms as well. Similarly, the jury is not exclusive to adversarial systems either, nor is the fact that the proceedings are public. In fact, most cases in adversarial systems are disposed of without trial, further to a guilty plea by the defendant. Similarly, most minor offences are tried at lower court where the jury is not an option. Thus, the day in court, essential to how the adversarial system is viewed by opponents and proponents alike, is rather the exception than rule. However, because of the ideological love affair with the 'day in court' (Damaška, 1986; Lloyd-Bostock and Thomas, 2001), the full blown adversarial trial remains at the centre of any debate of this nature. When it comes to adversarial trials in their pure essence, Damaška argues that we need to look outside the courtroom and examine the role of the state in dispensing justice.

Adversarial justice as an archetype (its pure and idealized version) fits the passive state that befits a society where crime and order are not part of the 'governmentality' project: crimes occur and need to be dealt with but the state has not embraced crime as a major social problem. In this philosophy, crimes are merely disputes between individuals rather than offences against the state, public order or morality. All the state seeks to do is to provide a platform on which these disputes can be fairly decided. That platform is the adversarial trial: a fair fight between two parties in conflict. The fact that the state, allegedly, is indifferent to the outcome is symbolized by the jury: the decision regarding guilt or innocence is left to amateurs who bear no relation to those in power. Adversarial justice, in its purest form, therefore is suited to a society in which the state does not engage in law and order politics. It feels no need to instigate matters itself, and has no desire to make policy through court action. All it provides is a level playing field.

Realistically, though, many strands of reform have served to dilute any adversarial system away from the archetype. Most trials, after all do not involve a jury, whereas other measures involve steering key issues away from the trial to the pretrial phase. The defendant's 'day in court' is under pressure, and this is partly due to the fact that the states in which adversarial trials operate are no longer without substantive interest in the outcome of criminal cases. There is increased reluctance to have the 'hit and miss' element of jury justice wreak havoc on terrorism, sex offending or complex fraud cases. Where the state has an interest, that interest is poorly served by the jury or even the adversarial mode of justice altogether. That, of course, enhances its value from a due process perspective but it also puts its existence in jeopardy.

Other criticisms against the traditional adversarial trial, relate to the treatment of victims and witnesses should the adversarial process be left to its own devices. In England and Wales, as elsewhere, a plethora of measures have been taken to make cross-examinations for vulnerable witnesses (including children) and victims less traumatic. Further to the implementations of the interdepartmental working group Speaking up for Justice (Home Office, 1998) various allowances have been made: for video-recorded statements to replace the evidence-in-chief; video-recorded pretrial cross-examination; live TV links; screens around the witnesses box so that the witness does not need to face the defendant in court; removal of wigs and gowns; power for the judge to clear the public gallery in cases involving sexual offences or intimidation so the witness can give evidence in private. In addition, limitations on the defendant conducting their own cross-examination have been enhanced: it was already in place for sexual offences, but the judge has acquired the discretionary power to extend that ban to other types of cases as well (Home Office, 2001). It seems that in England and Wales these measures have produced a positive effect in terms of witness satisfaction (Hamlyn *et al.*, 2004), but convictions for rape remain notoriously low (Kelly, Lovett and Regan, 2005).

Generally, within the USA and the UK, when a certain arrangement is called 'non-adversarial', it is meant as an endorsement, as is the case with drug courts in the USA. The same is true for New York City's community courts (Gebelein, 2000; Simon, 2003). Bernan and Feinblatt (2000) go as far as saying that such courts have altered the dynamics of the courtroom and the adversarial system. Judges are becoming proactive case managers and problem solvers rather than passive referees (Simon, 2003). Simon mentions increasingly nonadversarial proceedings in various specialized courts, including Mental Health Courts, Family Courts, Drug Courts, Community Courts and Domestic Violence Courts (Simon, 2003). The nonadversarial and restorative way of doing justice seems to be making headway.

This trend fits a more therapeutic fashion of solving disputes. It is an example of how psychological research into victimization and conflict resolution has informed and continues to inform a transformation of the legal process (Berman and Feinblatt, 2000). The classic passive judge, merely refereeing whilst influencing proceeding as little as possible has made way for a judge who is active, seeks consensus or compromise and is driven towards achieving outcomes.

THE INQUISITORIAL SHIFT TOWARDS EXPRESSIVE JUSTICE

Meanwhile, it seems as if a certain degree of 'adversarialization' within inquisitorial courtrooms occurs as well (see Jörg, Field and Brandts, 1995). In these days of politics of law and order (Garland, 2001) and the new punitiveness (Pratt *et al.*, 2005), doing justice is increasingly expressive. Inquisitorial trials have trouble emulating the 'spectacle' element commonly found in traditional adversarial courtrooms in order to articulate that expressive element. There are a few ingredients that can provide it but they require the defendant to 'play ball', to conduct themselves in a way to enhance the spectacle element of the trial. Defendants in many inquisitorial systems are free to speak and are not put under any oath. Indeed the trial, certainly in France (Hodgson, 2002) and the Netherlands (Pakes, 2004), tends to unfold via a largely unscripted conversation between presiding judge and defendant. As the judge normally is aware of the facts of the case before trial due to their familiarity with the dossier, this conversation rarely serves a real fact-finding purpose. Rather, it seeks to confirm that the impression gained from the accumulation of paperwork, interview transcripts and so on, is accurate. Although the defendant can decide to paint a different picture of events at trial, it is invariably an uphill struggle to get any sort of credibility assigned to that: so-called 'ambush defences' (i.e. the submission of evidence at the eleventh hour so as to make it difficult for the prosecution to rebut it) are ill-suited to the inquisitorial tradition. On occasion, however, a defendant may opt to exercise their right to have the final word, to, ill-advisedly or not, indulge in a speech.

A recent example in the Netherlands was the trial of Mohammed B., tried for the murder of film maker and broadcaster Theo van Gogh. Van Gogh, distant relative of painter Vincent van Gogh, was murdered when cycling in the East of Amsterdam on November 2, 2004. He was both stabbed and shot, after which the offender proceeded to pin a note to his body with a knife. Mohammed B. was arrested almost immediately, following a police shoot-out near the scene of the crime. Widely regarded as an act of Islamist extremist terrorism (Van Gogh had recently made a film called Submission examining the treatment of women in Islamic societies, which caused furore. It was Hirsi Ali who had scripted the film. She is a former Somali refugee, ex-Muslim and Member of the Netherlands's Parliament. The note on Van Gogh's body comprised a death threat to her. There was considerable media build up to the trial, which consequently attracted a great deal of attention (Pakes, 2006). It took place in the Amsterdam suburb of Osdorp over two days in September 2005. However, as Mohammed B. was seemingly intent on remaining silent, and the evidence against him was overwhelming, the trial was set to be a nondramatic affair, as inquisitorial trials frequently are. In a turn of events, the defendant did decide to speak. In particular, he addressed the victim's mother who was present in the courtroom.

> The reason for me to speak now is not because I feel obliged to speak before this court. The only person to whom possibly I have that obligation is Mister van Gogh's mother. But I have to be honest and say that I do not feel sorry for you. I do not feel your pain. I can't. I do not know what it is to lose a child that you with pain and tears have brought into this world. This is partly because I am not a woman. It is also because you are a non-believer.

He later on was equally clear on his lack of remorse:

> I take full responsibility for my actions. You (referring to the prosecutor) have outlined what my motivations may have been. Well, it is my faith that has driven me. And I can assure you, should I ever regain my freedom, I shall do the same thing. Exactly the same thing.

He was subsequently convicted and sentenced to life imprisonment.

The above example is only meant to show that drama can and does occur in the inquisitorial courtroom: it can on occasion be a vehicle to vividly depict the evil nature of the offence or offender, and norms can be affirmed in an emphatic fashion, but it is the exception, not the rule: most defendants do not utilize their right to have the final word, and if they do, their remarks tend not to be noteworthy. Whilst no policy maker would explicitly encourage the development of inquisitorial trials as dramatic events, some movement in that direction may nevertheless be identified as part of many systems' commitment to more meaningfully engage victims into the process.

In 2004, in the Netherlands, victims acquired the right to have a written statement considered at trial. It enhances the importance of the trial although the statement is in fact included in the dossier. A judge may decide to read it out, in full or in part or simply mention the fact that the letter has been considered (Kool and Moerings, 2004). A more telling augmentation of that right was introduced in 2005. Victims of certain crimes have the right to appear in court and have their say. That right, however is only reserved for victims of serious offences, the time to speak is limited, their statement should only concern the consequences of the crime to them, and not concern the crime itself or the defendant; and in the interests of due process, the defence can respond to the statement, the judge can ask questions for clarification, and, when the victim is dead, only one relative can exercise this right (Dutch Ministry of Justice, 2005). Member of Parliament Boris Dittrich, when advocating the measure back in 2001 argued that, apart from benefits for the victim, there was an increased realization of the effects of the wrongdoing on behalf of the offender and a better perspective on the crime and its effects on behalf of the judge. However, all those things would traditionally have been conducted on paper, and if that would be not possible, privately in judges' chambers. The final, and arguably crucial, aim of this measure is its public function (Dittrich, 2001). It helps reshape the trial towards Damaška's day in court. In conjunction with another recent development, the admission of TV cameras in court to broadcast parts of a trial, this is an important departure from tradition: the trial as the 'day in court' is enhanced and so does, potentially, its function of spectacle – inquisitorial justice emulating adversarial proceedings.

In addition, there also is the tendency by a small proportion of Dutch defence lawyers of almost celebrity status to stretch the goings on at trial so as to conduct it in as adversarial style as possible. One of the results is that victims of sex offences are more regularly questioned in open court than they used to, as private chambers is often the nonadversarial locus for such events, which is another example of the adversarialization of what in essence is quite a pure inquisitorial legal tradition (see also Jörg, Field and Brandts, 1995).

Currently, there is upheaval regarding the performance of court-appointed expert witnesses. It transpired that the National Forensic Institute, a government funding body that routinely performs forensic tests of all sorts on behalf of the court, had withheld evidence in a murder case that has led to a wrongful conviction, the so-called Schiedam Park murder case (Posthumus, 2005; Van Koppen, in submission). A 10-year-old girl was killed, and her 11-year-old friend wounded, in a park in the town of Schiedam. Kees B. was convicted, largely on the basis of a false confession. Years later it transpired that another person had confessed to the crime and suppressed DNA evidence strongly linked this latter suspect, Wik H., to the crime.

This is a serious systemic failure: when, in an inquisitorial system, a court-appointed expert actually takes on a partisan, proprosecution attitude, the truth finding element of the system of proof is deprived of a safety net. Exonerating evidence should be brought forward without hesitation. If it is not the integrity, as well as the quality, of decision making is in jeopardy (Van Koppen, in submission).

There are, of course, inquisitorial systems in which the victim's role at trial can stretch much further, such as in Germany and Sweden where they can, in certain cases, assist the prosecutor throughout the trial process (Brienen and Hoegen, 2001). Nevertheless, the victim statement in the Netherlands is a small but telling example of the adversarialization of an essentially inquisitorial trial process. A call for the introduction of the jury though, has yet to be made, apart from one or two political fringe parties.

Thus, separate developments in the Netherlands and the USA seem to suggest that, on the one hand, adversarial systems are looking to import the cooperative and active position of the judge into their way of administering justice. Conversely, inquisitorial systems appear to seek ways of having trials meet the need to dispense expressive justice. It is in those two distinct spheres where, as it were, cross-fertilization takes place. The process is not so much one of policy transfer: the ways in which these convergences take place is at the level of 'naturalia', importing orientations, rather than actual practices: after all, victim impact statements and victim statements of opinion are almost as novel in many adversarial systems as they are in inquisitorial ones. Rather, it is the fact that victims should have their say in open court, rather than be a muted spectator from the sidelines and this is introduced to make trials become more meaningful, to the victims at least, and, by implication, to 'the public' as well.

At this stage it is too early to tell whether the victims' right to speak is part of a fundamental shift towards more victim-oriented justice or is not much more than a gimmick. It is questionable to what extent this provision for victims will improve the quality of judgements rendered. Evaluative research is taking place at present. However, it must be feared that the provision particularly will satisfy the need for more expressive justice, which carries the risk of it becoming increasingly based on emotions (as Buruma warned as early as 1994). Vindictive victims fit this development well. We shall have to await the arrival of victims who argue for forgiveness, to see the actual value of the new measures.

BETWEEN PURITY AND CONTROL: THE ISLAMIZATION PROCESS OF TRIALS IN THE MIDDLE EAST

The essential characteristic of Islamic law is, as the name obviously suggests, its religious foundation. Nevertheless, it would be oversimplifying matters to suggest that the operation of Islamic, or Sharia, law in various countries is essentially the same in any 'Muslim' country. The organization of justice in Saudi Arabia, for instance, is different to that in Afghanistan (Wardak, 2004, 2005). The inspiration of law might be identical but the social and cultural structures in which they are set are very different. Sharia law is usually not transplanted wholesale but is reconciled with pre-existing, less formal mechanisms of justice.

It is also important to note that despite the fact that the sources of law are highly dogmatic and therefore resistant to change, Islamic criminal justice systems seem as ever changing as their western counterparts. A pivotal event in this regard has been the revolution in Iran in 1979, after which the country developed a revolutionary system to incorporate and uphold Sharia law (Rezeai, 2002). After 1979 we see increased in zeal in the 'purification' of justice in the Middle East towards what is considered Islamic law proper.

Courts in most Islamic jurisdictions involve the *qadi*, or judge administering Sharia law (Sharia is defined as 'the collection of legal provisions divinely revealed to the Prophet' (Rezeai, 2002, p. 54). These judges are usually men, although there are instances and places where the role of women in criminal proceedings, even as judge, can be possible. The legal decision or ruling is called a *fatwa*. Juries do not exist; minor cases are dealt with by one *qadi* and by three in case of more serious offences. Wardak (2005) explains that in Saudi Arabia a panel of five *qadis* deal with cases of appeal. The paramount position of the *qadi* as both principal fact finder and as decider on guilt has been criticized but it must be remembered that the magistrate in an inquisitorial courtroom in say, France or the Netherlands is by and large in a similar position. Principles such as the right to silence, and the right to an impartial tribunal apply as elsewhere. In Iran, the presumption of innocence is even guaranteed in the constitution, but qualified with reference to Islamic criteria. It shows the dual nature of the Iranian justice system, at once 'republican' and Islamic (Rezeai, 2002).

Islamic courts recognize three types of evidence. The first is witness testimony (Rezeai, 2002). It depends on the type of crime how many witnesses are required in order to be sufficient proof. It also differs between the various Middle Eastern jurisdictions whether women are allowed as witnesses at all, and what weight their evidence is given. Often witnesses need to be of the Muslim faith, and when non-Muslims testify their testimony might carry less weight. A key role for the *qadi* is their ability to ensure that only 'proper', that is credible, witnesses of a high moral standard appear in court. The second type of proof is the defendant's admission. The third is the one that puzzles (or enrages) people not familiar with Islamic justice most: it is the oath on behalf of the defendant. When the evidence is inconclusive (as decided by the *qadi*) he can then offer the accuser to, as it were, put the defendant on the spot and require that they take an oath; to solemnly and truthfully declare that they are innocent. If the defendant does this, they shall be acquitted. When refused, that should swing the case towards a conviction (Rezeai, 2002; Souryal, 1987).

Thus, religious sources determine the credibility of key evidence. The cultural assumption is that lying under oath in court is unthinkable, as true devotion to Allah would prevent that from even being considered an option, which is why a statement under oath has such power. It highlights the fact that administration of justice in Sharia law is an activity that is of profound religious significance as it is in essence a religious activity. The law of evidence can be said to be both strict and archaic, as usually evidence relies on eyewitnesses, rather than on documentary, forensic or circumstantial evidence. On the other hand, much in practice depends on how the *qadi* use their discretion in the admission of witnesses. It must of course be realized that the by and large exclusion of forensic and documentary evidence will hamper the prosecution of certain types of cases more than others. A fight in a public place will be straightforward, but sexual offending in the absence of any witnesses apart from the victim will be very unlikely to lead to convictions unless the defendant were compelled to confess. It is therefore possible that certain victims (possibly women suffering abuse in the private sphere) will find it much more difficult to find the system works for them than others. That is obviously true in many societies and systems of law, but at least forensic evidence may enhance the chances of convictions in some of these cases, whereas in Sharia law that option simply is not there.

Furthermore, it is important to consider four types of crimes as the way they are dealt with differs remarkably when it comes to discretion, mediation in sentencing. *Hudud* crimes are crimes against Islam, Allah and the Islamic community as a whole. The penalties it attracts are fixed and often brutal, as *Hudud* refers to 'maximum punishment'. The classic example is stoning for adultery, another is the amputation of the hand for theft. Conversely, there is more room for manoeuvring in cases of so-called *Quesas* crimes, offences regarded as private wrongdoings. They can be severe crimes but the commission of this type of crime does not involve offending against Islam. Although the essential orientation for the sentencing of crimes can be summarized as 'an eye for an eye', informally there is often room for restitution, charity and forgiveness. Cases that involve 'buying off' a victim of a serious offence or their family would fall under this category. But the grim reality is that 'an eye for an eye' can apply literally: an Egyptian national was sentenced to having one eye removed, as punishment for a crime in which the victim lost an eye as well, in August 2000 (Amnesty International, 2002). The two other types of crime offer further leeway in deciding on punishment, compensation and restitution. They are *Diyat* (crimes of compensation for unintentional homicide and battery and as alternative for retaliation) and *Tazirat* (crimes of discretionary punishments) (Rezeai, 2002; see also Ghodsi, 2004).

Criticisms of the application of Sharia law are numerous, and often made by organizations such as Amnesty International (2002) and the United Nations (e.g. United Nations 2002a, 2002b). They relate to the principle of corporal and capital punishment, whereas many a case is documented in which defendants have been denied basic rights such as to know the allegations against them, to legal representation, and to have documents and proceedings translated to them. There are also frequent allegations of police brutality, torture, of unnecessary custody, and instances of bias against foreigners, women and non-Muslims. In 2001, Amnesty International recorded 172 instances of the flogging of youths in Saudi Arabia. It also recorded 33 amputations and nine so-called cross-amputations (involving the amputation of the right hand and the left foot, the prescribed *Hudud* punishment for highway robbery) (Amnesty International, 2002). An important point of criticism is that the law fails to provide safeguards and that, due to their position in society and the way in which justice operates in Saudi Arabia, it is particularly foreigners and women who suffer the brunt of it. Crystal observes similarly that Sharia law fails to protect citizens against the state in Qatar (Crystal, 2004)

In Nigeria, Sharia law in criminal justice matters has only been adopted in a number of states. It is also said to be applicable only to Muslims. The impression gained by UN Commission of Human Rights observers (UNCHR, 2005) is that the practice is used against non-Muslim women and that harsh punishments are particularly undergone by women (of any faith) as well. The treatment received by foreigners under Sharia law in Saudi Arabia is explained by Amnesty International, (2002, para 2.3.1.) as follows:

> The social make-up of the Saudi Arabian society: families, tribes, friendship and traditions of solidarity, plays a highly valuable role against abuse by the authorities of the state. These social institutions come into action when Saudi Arabian nationals confront the criminal justice system, with families, friends, heads of tribes or persons of authority engaging in inquiries about them. Such actions can, albeit not always, result in the effective protection from torture of those detained. Foreign nationals are deprived of such valuable social protection against torture.

What is true for torture is probably true for other forms of injustice as well. On the other hand, there is a documented case of an American national working for an oil company standing trial for assaulting and slandering a coworker in Saudi Arabia. This accuser was unable to provide sufficient evidence due to an insufficient number of witnesses to the event so that the defendant was instructed to deny the offences under oath. Being a Christian, an oath tailored to that faith was taken, the defendant denied the charge and walked free. It does show that on occasion it is possible to have the system work in favour of a non-Muslim foreigner as well (Baroody, 1966). It, of course, should also be mentioned that both western inquisitorial and adversarial systems are commonly accused, and sometimes rightly so, for particularly coming down hard on foreigners and on ethnic minorities as well. After all, problems of language and cultural expectations may work against foreigners in any legal setting.

Theoretically, trials in the Islamic tradition serve the purpose of dealing with dispute in the way prescribed by the main religious sources. Whereas adversarial trials are arguably the spectacle that shows that those in power mean business when addressing the fears of the people (which is an interesting historical u-turn as originally adversarial justice, particularly the jury, was in place to demonstrate the opposite), Sharia law starts from the premise that it is the offence against Islam that cannot be tolerated. It is a faith-affirming rather than a law and order-affirming exercise. Saudi Arabia's notoriously low crime rate is regularly attributed to it (Souryal, 1987; Ali, 1985). However, Adler (1983) emphasized the role of informal social control, whereas Wardak (2005) describes five, interrelating and overlapping forms of social control that together explain the low rate of crime. Most important is the extended family, but schools (with substantial time devoted to religious teachings) and the Mosque are potent instruments of social control as well. In addition to the judicial system, there is an approximately 20 000 men-strong body of 'enforcers' of Islamic values. These *Motawwa'in* tend to police attendance at prayers, and any form of public indecency or immorality. They do not have police powers apart from the power to detain for 24 hours. Wardak acknowledges a lack of research into the actual practice of these people who regularly behave rather autonomously and their effect on crime rates. They do seem to be valued by the 'traditional' criminal justice system, which is the fifth system of social control. There is little doubt that the criminal justice process is part of a patriarchal, familiar and tribal system of power that serves to keep the powerful on top and those on the receiving end with few formal powers to be protected from it (Crystal, 2001).

Sharia trials cannot be faulted for their internal logic. You would expect them to work best in a culture that is homogeneous in its faith. When the culture supports the substantive laws in place (including those that criminalize use of alcohol and adultery, and those that restrict the freedom of movement and expression of women), when there is trust in the *qadi* and the system of religious education that produces them, and when the oath as a proof-producing measure is seen to work and be immune to abuse, the system's internal checks and balances are all in order. What is more, as the foundation of the process lies in its religious sources, 'reform' for pragmatic reasons is by and large an anathema. There is no need for annual statistics, performance indicators, drives, initiatives, focus groups or surveys to determine the quality of the justice provided. How well the system operates is nothing to do with consumer satisfaction. Its proximate goal is that of Islamic purity and reform, in Iran, Afghanistan and Nigeria, is aimed at that. However, as Crystal (1999) argues, Sharia law also serves the more down-to-earth purpose of serving those in power as an instrument to suppress dissent. That may well serve as a drive for change away from the pure Sharia ideal, as documented by Rezeai (2002). In addition, it might require spectacular miscarriages of justice of the 'failure to convict' kind to consider the allowance of modern-day technological types of evidence, such as DNA evidence.

Adopting Damaška's terminology, Islamic law's 'essentiala' might be the derivation of substantive law from the *Koran* and other religious sources, whereas the oath to Allah would serve as the ultimate truth-finding instrument. The question about inequality and breaches of human rights that do occur in many countries where Sharia law is in operation are, of course, cause for concern. However, where Wardak argues that the Mosque and the family are more potent shapers of social control as well as custom and tradition, Sharia law in all likelihood reflects the dominant values of many Muslim societies. In its pure form, void of state-serving strategies and pragmatics, psychology will often be of no relevance. For example, much psychological research has gone into working with offenders in order to reduce reoffending. It requires empirical research of the typical pretest, intervention, evaluation format and it underlies the assumption that 'good' justice, in both inquisitorial and adversarial systems, reduces social harm, and one of the ways in which that can be achieved is to reduce the extent of future victimization. Sharia law also, of course, aims to do the same, but as its pillar is dogma rather than pragmatics, such research is not of any interest. It would nevertheless be very welcome if there were empirical research into the law-in-practice of the Sharia courtroom. There is little in the way of aggregate data; we do not know how often amputations and mutilations take place; we have little insight into processes of diversion, review or pardon. Such knowledge would be vital in establishing whether certain styles of justice might be preferable to others, and might therefore come to serve as examples to drive change in the region. With a foot in the door, psychology can be of immense utility there.

CONCLUSION

In summary, and as sketchy as this chapter inevitably is, whereas ultimately the legal systems covered in the chapter seek to achieve the same thing, justice, the road that they have embarked on to achieve it differs. That has important repercussions for the trial function and hence its format. Moreover, the societal context in which these trials operate is changing. Inquisitorial trials are changing not least due to the fact that crime and justice are increasingly emotive issues, so that the state seeks ways to expressively flex its muscles, and what better venue than the trial. The Dutch case of victim statements (coupled with the introduction of TV cameras in the court room) serves as such an example.

In adversarial trials it is the lack of restorative power that is addressed with the emerging trend of nonadversarial justice: rather than a contest the trial becomes a problem-solving medium in which the judge actively seeks solutions and consensus to support those solutions. That makes it interesting to borrow from the inquisitorial tradition where the active judge within a coordinate system of interaction (Damaška, 1986) is part of the set up.

Zest for change in the Islamic legal tradition seems to come from two desiderata: one is the purification of Sharia law but the other is to do with the politics of power and control. As is the case elsewhere, the need for control may often receive precedent over any sort of due process orientation but empirical research that established if, and, if so, how, a balance might be struck between the two is lacking.

Psychology has certainly assisted in advancing the process of change in many adversarial type of court, at least in the USA. Victimology and the increased awareness of the victim experience certainly played a part in advancing the recent developments in the Netherlands, although at present it is too early to tell whether real change has been achieved. Psychological research would be vital in establishing the exact everyday operation of the law in action in Islamic legal systems, but even if that were feasible, the extent to which that research might serve as impetus for change is, given the strongly dogmatic nature of the legal orientation, questionable.

REFERENCES

Adler, F. (1983) *Nations Not Obsessed with Crime*, Rotham, Littleton, CO.
Ali, B. (1985) Islamic law and crime: The case of Saudi Arabia. *International Journal of Comparative and Applied Criminal Justice*, **9**, 4–57.
Amnesty International (2002) *SAUDI ARABIA Remains a Fertile Ground for Torture with Impunity.* Available at http://web.amnesty.org/library/index/engmde230042002.
Auld, L.J. (2001) *Review of the Criminal Courts*. Available at www.criminal-courts-review.org.uk.
Baroody, G.M. (1966) Shar'iah: Law of Islam. Saudi AramcoWorld, 17, issue 6 (November/December). Available at www.saudiaramcoworld.com/issue/196606/shari.ah-law.of.islam.htm.
Berman, G. and Feinblatt, J. (2000). Problem-solving courts: A brief primer. *Law and Policy*, **23**, 125–40.
Braithwaite, J. (1989) *Crime, Shame and Reintegration*, Cambridge University Press, Cambridge.
Brienen, M.E.I. and Hoegen, E.H. (2001) Het Nederlandse slachtofferbeleid: Een rechtsvergelijkend perspectief. *Justitiele Verkenningen*, **27** (3), 43–57.
Burney, E. (2005) *Making People Behave: Anti-Social Behaviour, Politics and Policy*, Willan, Cullompton.
Buruma, Y. (1994) Victimalisering van het strafrecht, in *Hoe Punitief is Nederland?* (ed. M. Moerings), Gouda Quint, Arnhem, pp. 211–33.
Crombag, H.F.M. (2003) Adversarial or inquisitorial: Do we have a choice? in *Adversarial Versus Inquisitorial Justice: Psychological Perspectives on Criminal Justice Systems* (eds P.J. van Koppen and S.D. Penrod), Kluwer, New York, pp. 21–5.
Crystal, J. (2001) Criminal justice in the Middle East. *Journal of Criminal Justice*, **29**, 469–82.
Crystal, J. (2004) *Countries at the Crossroads: Country Profile of Qatar*, Available at http://unpan1.un.org/intradoc/groups/public/documents/nispacee/unpan016205.pdf.
Damaška, M.R (1986). *The Faces of Justice and State Authority: A Comparative Approach to the Legal Process*, Yale University Press, New Haven.
Damaška, M.R. (1973) Evidentiary barriers to conviction and two models of criminal procedure: A comparative study. *University of Pennsylvania Law Review*, **121**, 506–89.
Damaška, M.R. (1997) The uncertain fate of evidentiary transplants: Anglo-American and Continental experiments. *American Journal of Comparative Law*, **55**, 839–49.
Damaška, M.R. (2003) Epistemology and legal regulation of proof. *Law, Probability and Risk*, **2**, 117–30.

Dittrich, B. (2001) Voorstel van wet van het lid Dittricht to wijziging van enige bepalingen van het Wetboek van Strafvordering (invoering van spreekrecht voor slachtoffers en nabestaanden). Memorie van Toelichting. The Hague, Tweede Kamer, 28 September 2001 no. 27632.

Dutch Ministry of Justice (2005) Spreekrecht en schriftelijke slachtofferverklaring. Available at www.justitie.nl/themas/slachtofferzorg/rechten_van_slachtoffers/schriftelijke_slachtofferverklaring/index.asp.

Gebelein, R.S. (2000). *The Rebirth of Rehabilitation: Promise and Perils of Drug Courts*, US Department of Justice, Washington, DC.

Ghodsi, E. (2004) Murder in the criminal law of Iran and Islam. *Journal of Criminal Law*, **68**, 160–9.

Hamlyn, B., Phelps, A., Turtle, J. and Sattar, G. (2004) Are special measures working? Evidence from surveys of vulnerable and intimidated witnesses. Home Office Research Study no. 283. HMSO, London.

Hatcher, R.M. and Hollin, C.E. (2005) The identification and management of antisocial and offending behaviour, in *Community Justice: Issues for Probation and Criminal Justice* (eds J. Winstone and F. Pakes), Willan, Cullompton, pp. 165–82.

Hodgson, J. (2002) Suspects, defendants and victims in the French criminal justice process: The context of recent reform. *International and Comparative Law Quarterly*, **51**, 781–816.

Home Office (1998) Speaking up for justice: Report of the interdepartmental working group on the treatment of vulnerable or intimidated witnesses in the criminal justice system, HMSO, London.

Home Office (1999) *Criminal Justice Strategic Plan 1999–2002*, Home Office, London.

Home Office (2001) Measures to assist vulnerable or intimidated witnesses in the criminal justice system: Implementing the Speaking up for Justice Report, Home Office, London.

Garland, D. (2001) *The Culture of Control*, Chicago University Press, Chicago, IL.

Jörg, N., Field, S. and Brandts, C. (1995) Are inquisitorial and adversarial systems converging? in *Criminal Justice in Europe: A Comparative Study* (eds P. Fennel, C. Harding, N. Jörg and B. Swart), Clarendon Press, Oxford, pp. 41–56.

Kelly, L., Lovett, J. and Regan, L. (2005) *A Gap or a Chasm? Attrition in Reported Rape cases*, Home Office Research, Development and Statistics Directorate, London.

King, N.J. (2001) The American criminal jury, in *World Jury Systems* (ed. N. Vidmar), Oxford University Press, Oxford, pp. 53–91.

Kool, R. and Moerings, M. (2004) The victim has the floor: The victim's right to be heard in writing or orally in the Dutch courtroom. *European Journal of Crime, Criminal and Criminal Justice*, **12**, 46–60.

Lloyd-Bostock, S. and Thomas, C. (2001) The continuing decline of the English jury, in *World Jury Systems* (ed. N. Vidmar), Oxford University Press, Oxford, pp. 53–91.

McGuire, J. (1995) (Ed.) *What Works: Reducing Re-offending*, Wiley, Chichester.

McKenzie, N. (2005) Community youth justice: Policy, practices and public perception, in *Community Justice: Issues for Probation And Criminal Justice* (eds J. Winstone and F. Pakes), Willan, Cullompton, pp. 183–197.

Nijboer, J.F. (1997) *Strafrechtelijk Bewijsrecht*, Ars Aequi, Nijmegen.

Office of the United Nations High Commissioner on Human Rights (OHUNCHR) (2005) Mission to Nigeria: Report of the Special Rapporteur on freedom of religion or belief, Asma Jahangir. OHUNCHR, 10 August 2005.

Pakes, F. (2003) Styles of trial procedure at the International Criminal Tribunal for the Former Yugoslavia, in *Adversarial Versus Inquisitorial Justice: Psychological Perspectives on Criminal Justice Systems* (eds P.J. van Koppen and S.D. Penrod), Kluwer, New York.

Pakes, F. (2004) *Comparative Criminal Justice*, Willan Publishing, Cullompton.

Pakes, F. (2006) The ebb and flow of criminal justice in the Netherlands. *International Journal of the Sociology of Law*, **34**, 141–156.

Posthumus, F. (2005) *Evaluatieonderzoek in de Schiedammer Parkmoord*, Openbaar Ministerie, The Hague.

Pratt, J., Brown, D., Brown, M. et al. (2005) *The New Punitiveness: Trends, Theories, Perspectives*, Willan Publishing, Cullompton.

Rezeai, H. (2002) The Iranian criminal justice under the Islamization project. *European Journal of Crime, Criminal Law and Criminal Justice*, **10**, 54–69.

Romano, C.P.R., Nollkaemper, A. and Kleffner, J.K. (eds) (2004) *Internationalized Criminal Courts: Sierra Leone, East Timor, Kosovo and Cambodia*, Cambridge University Press, Cambridge.

Simon, L.M.J. (2003) Proactive judges: Solving problems and transforming communties, in *Handbook of Psychology in Legal Contexts*, 2nd edn (eds D. Carson and R. Bull), Wiley, Chichester, pp. 449–72.

Souryal, S.S. (1987) The religionization of a society: The continuing application of Shariah law in Saudi Arabia. *Journal for the Scientific Study of Religion*, **26**, 429–49.

Stevens, J. (2002) *The Search for Truth in the Criminal Justice System*, Lecture delivered at the University of Leicester, 6 March.

Tamadonfar, M. (2001) Islam, Law, and Political Control in Contemporary Iran. *Journal for the Scientific Study of Religion*, **40**, 205–20.

United Nations (2002a) *Human Rights Committee Concludes Seventy-Sixth Session: Adopts Final Conclusions and Recommendations on Reports of Egypt and Togo*, UN press release HR/CT 626, New York.

United Nations (2002b) *The Twenty-Seventh Special Session of The General Assembly On Children*, UN, New York, 8–10 May.

Van Koppen, P.J. (in submission) De Fluwelen Handschoen van Posthumus: Over Hetgeen Ontbreekt in het Rapport over de Schiedammer Parkmoord.

Wardak, A. (2004) Building a postwar justice system in Afghanistan. *Crime Law and Social Change*, **41**, 319–41.

Wardak, A. (2005) Crime and social control in Saudi Arabia, in *Transnational and Comparative Criminology* (eds J. Sheptycki and A. Wardak), Glasshouse, London.

CHAPTER 16

Misapplication of Psychology in Court

Peter J. van Koppen
Netherlands Institute for the Study of Crime and Law Enforcement

Expert witnesses exist to help the fact finder – be it judge or jury – with the decisions that have to be made. That seems to be a simple and quite obvious statement, but in this chapter I will try to demonstrate that this may have various implications; some of the paradoxical kind. I start with the bottom line of this Chapter: in many cases the expert can only be of any help if they assume the role of fact finder in the case. Many of the issues discussed below also apply to expertise in other fields than psychology, but I limit myself to psychological issues.

THE COURT AND THE SCIENTIST

In most criminal trials two main decisions have to be made. It has to be decided whether or not the defendant committed the crime he is accused of and then it has to be decided what to do with him. These are not scientific decisions of any kind, but practical judgements to solve a practical matter in society. Nevertheless, these decisions have to be based as much as possible on what happened in the past in relation to the crime and also as much as possible on what we know about the accused. To serve that purpose, criminal trials are designed to reduce uncertainty to an extent that a decision can be based on more or less solid grounds.

Most criminal cases are relatively routine matters in this respect. A reasonable estimation is that these routine cases comprise some 88% of the serious cases that are handled by courts (Crombag, van Koppen and Wagenaar, 1994, pp. 20 ff). However, a non-negligible number of cases pose problems of decision making. The problems more often than not fall outside the domain of the law. Then, the defence, the prosecution or the court can turn to an expert to shed some light on the matter.

An expert is usually a scientifically trained individual who is expected to give an 'objective' judgement on the matter put before him that would lead to an uncontested true fact. That is a paradox, because scientists are not the kind of people who are in the habit of producing certainty. In days of old, the idea that scientists produced certainty was indeed

Applying Psychology to Criminal Justice. Edited by David Carson, Rebecca Milne, Francis Pakes, Karen Shalev and Andrea Shawyer. © 2007 John Wiley & Sons, Ltd.

entertained, but philosopher Karl Popper showed us that the scientific endeavour is in fact quite different (Popper, 1934, 1968). Popper learned that we only have hypotheses and theories that are verified or falsified by sound empirical research. A hypothesis or theory that is supported with empirical research is only true temporarily and forms no more than a proposition for continued discussions amongst peers. On logical grounds a hypothesis can only be supported or falsified, but never be proven right. Scientific 'facts', then, are no more than interpretations of observations on which there is a certain agreement amongst the participants in the relevant scientific field. One step further, the scientific industry can be regarded as a social field (Hofstee, 1980) where scientific 'facts' are not more than issues on which the peers agree on at a certain point in time, until somebody comes up with a better theory. Contrarily, in criminal trials a judgement has to be made based on the available evidence. That judgement should be final and uncontested. Terminating social conflicts with a court ruling is in the interest of victims, society at large, but also in the interest of the accused. Final court verdicts should end discussions once and for all. Thus, the scientific endeavour is not aimed at producing the kind of certainty the judge or jury requires.

ASSESSING ALLEGATIONS OF SEXUAL ABUSE

In criminal cases, not only is a higher level of certainty required than the scientist often can provide, but it should also concern the specific case. Scientists, however, are in the habit of producing statements on general states of affairs.

Let me give an example: the experiment in psychology. We want to know whether sexually abused children display distinctively different behaviour, when playing with anatomically correct dolls, than children that have not been abused (see for instance Cohn, 1991; Faller, 2005; White *et al.*, 1986). Indeed, we find that between the experimental group, the abused children, and the control group, the nonabused children, a difference is found: the abused children, on average, display more behaviour with the dolls that can be interpreted as sexual. The difference is such that we conclude it cannot be attributed to chance, so we call the difference significant. That is a sound conclusion in the domain of psychology; the study is ready to be published in an academic journal.

Is all this useful for the fact finder in a criminal trial? No, and for various reasons. First, the difference in playing between the two groups may be significant, but that does not mean it is a great or even a meaningful difference. Second, the fact finder is not interested in differences between group means, but in something completely different. The judge or jury wants to know, with as much certainty as possible, whether alleged victim Claudia has been abused by her uncle Bert. Not: does sexual abuse cause different playing behaviour with dolls, but: can we deduce from Claudia's playing behaviour that she was abused sexually (see on this problem also Rassin and Merckelbach, 1999). For that forensic use, anatomically correct dolls fail dramatically, for instance because many nonabused children are curious and also put their finger in the doll's vagina.[1] An expert should discuss this matter in his report or testimony at trial, but he can only do so if he is sensitive enough for the differences between psychological research and the problems faced by the fact finder.

---

[1] The Dutch Supreme Court (Hoge Raad) saw this problem and banned the use of these dolls from forensic use. See Hoge Raad 28 February 1989, *Nederlandse Jurisprudentie* 1989, 748 (*Anatomically Correct Dolls*).

Experts are often asked to apply scientific insights to the specific case (see the taxonomy by Gross and Mnookin, 2003). That could be more helpful to the fact finder in many more cases. Popper argued that his principle of falsification – that a hypothesis is never proven, but can only be falsified – only holds for general statements. It would not hold for specific statements. He was right, in the sense that many simple phenomena – such as the height of someone or their hair colour – can be established with little or no doubt. But as soon as things become somewhat more complicated, one is confronted with the same problems. Assessing whether a child has been sexually abused certainly falls into the more complicated category.

A better method than anatomically correct dolls, for establishing whether a child has been sexually abused or not, seems to be Statement Validity Analysis (SVA) (see Horowitz, 1991; Lamb and Sternberg, 1997; Undeutsch, 1983; Yuille and Cutshall, 1989). I write 'seems' because psychologists who use this method typically overstate their case. SVA consists of two parts: first Criteria Based Content Analysis (CBCA) (see Rassin, 1999; Vrij, 2005) to assess the interview of the alleged victim and, second, the Validity Check List (VCL) to assess characteristics of the child and the rest of the case. With CBCA the interview is analysed using 19 criteria to draw conclusions on the believability and validity of the statement (see for a fuller description Sporer, 1997; Vrij, 2005). The method, however, has been much criticized (see for instance Horowitz *et al.*, 1997; van Koppen and Saks, 2003; Lamb and Sternberg, 1998; Rassin and Van Koppen, 2002; Ruby and Brigham, 1997). The gist of the argument is that CBCA has some scientific potential but has too low a diagnostic value to be used in a forensic setting. Ruby and Brigham summarize the state of affairs as follows:

> The CBCA may have the potential to enhance the objectivity of the investigation and prosecution of allegations of child sexual abuse. It might also aid in protecting those who are unfortunate enough to be at the receiving end of an unfounded child sexual abuse allegation. But much more empirical validation work is necessary before it can adequately fulfil such a role. (Ruby and Brigham, 1997, p. 729)

Again, the CBCA is a valid method in the psychological domain, because it can be used to discriminate between the statements of sexually abused children and nonabused children. Some argue that CBCA is valid enough only if it is supplemented with the VCL. Raskin and Esplin (1991a) propose that a useful statement assessment should be more than just scoring a statement of the 19 criteria on the CBCA (see also McGough, 1991; Raskin and Esplin 1991b; Wells and Loftus, 1991). In addition, information must be gathered outside the interview. Since children differ in their cognitive abilities and these differences influence the scoring of the criteria, information must be collected on these abilities and other personality characteristics of the interviewee. Also alternative hypotheses, on the genesis of the story as told by the child, must be investigated. The story may be in error because of earlier suggestive interviews by parents or others, by deficient memory of the child, or by other pressures on the child. For evaluating the latter elements, the VCL has been developed. The VCL consists of four clusters:

A. Psychological characteristics of the child
B. Interview characteristics of the child and the examiner
C. Motivational factors relevant to the child and others involved in the allegations
D. Investigative questions regarding the consistency and realism of the entire body of data.

The usefulness of the VCL, however, is currently unsupported; studies are very scarce and do not exceed casuistic illustrations (see Endres, 1997). Thus, it is not clear which role should be assigned to the psychological characteristics or motivational factors of the child in evaluating the veracity of the statements made. The VCL is neither based on sound empirical research (see Horowitz *et al.*, 1997), nor is it limited to psychological insights. This is particularly troublesome because, since no clear-cut scoring scheme exists for the CBCA or the VCL. This leaves ample room for idiosyncratic interpretations by the expert psychologist and for other unwarranted influences in the expert's opinion (see for instance Merckelbach, Crombag and van Koppen, 2003; Risinger *et al.*, 2002).

FACT FINDERS AS SCIENTISTS

Evaluating the meaning of expert testimony is not a straightforward task for the judge or jury. They are confronted with a paradoxical situation. The expert was hired, in the first place, because the fact finder does not know enough of the subject matter. After an expert has given testimony, however, the same fact finder has to evaluate whether the testimony is strong enough to serve as evidence. This problem is even enhanced, when two or more experts produce conflicting testimony. An extreme example was given by Fisher and Whiting 1998. A mother reported that her ex-husband had sexually abused their three-year-old son. The grandmother and aunt were present when the boy told this, and they confirmed the mother's story. Several experts gave their learned opinion on the case. One expert said no firm conclusions were possible on the veracity of the boy's statement. A second concluded that the boy was a victim of oral genital contact and masturbation. A third expert said that the account, by the boy, was implanted and advised that he be protected from his mother. Finally, the fourth expert was of the opinion that the boy could not have been abused by his father, because daddy did not fit into the profile of a paedophile. There is no way a fact finder could choose between these expert opinions, without a thorough knowledge of the field.

In its decision on the CBCA, the Dutch Supreme Court ruled that, in these kinds of situations, the court has to explain why it follows the testimony of one expert and rejects the testimony of another (*Hoge Raad 30th March 1999, Nederlandse Jurisprudentie 1999, 451, CBCA*).[2] Experts sometimes differ, in their opinions, because one is a good scientist whilst the other is a quack. More often, however, differences of opinion are inherent in the operations of the scientific community. That community lives by differences of opinion; it is current and future debate and discussion that drives progress in the field. Hence, the experts are asked to generate certainty but subsequently confront the fact finder with differences in opinion and a scientific discussion. My experience in cases, where other experts were also consulted, is that we soon have interesting discussions that, also soon, are hardly relevant to the case at hand. Then the fact finder has to choose between these conflicting opinions. The fact finder is, in principle as a nonexpert, not able to make that judgement.

The judge or jury nevertheless bears the sad fate that a choice has to be made. Lacking subject knowledge, the evaluations has to be done in an indirect manner. In the USA for

---

[2] See, for a comparable American case: *New Jersey v. Cavallo*, 88 N.J. 508, 443 A.2d. 1020 (1982), in which the courts are given the task – in cases of doubt about a statement by an expert – to ask for a second expert or, in cases where experts differ, to consult scientific literature of legal precedents. Of course this does not solve anything.

many decades, the precedent for this evaluation was the so-called Frye-criterion (*Frye* v. *United States*, 293 F. 1013, D.C. Cir., 1923):

> Just when a scientific principle or discovery crosses the line between experimental and the demonstrable stages is difficult to define. [...] [W]hile the courts go a long way in admitting expert testimony deduced from a well-recognized scientific principle or discovery, the thing from which the deduction is made must be sufficiently established to have general acceptance in the particular field in which it belongs.

This appears to give a solution: do not decide yourself, but go by the judgements of the peers. But general acceptance does not solve anything at all since, for instance, a lot of nonsense is generally accepted in a field like astrology. The judge needs another criterion (see also Van Kampen, 1998).

The US Supreme Court gave the judges a helping hand with its decision in *Daubert* (*Daubert* v. *Merrell Dow Pharmaceuticals Inc.*, 509 U.S. 579, 113 S.Ct. 2795, 1993). In that decision it gave five criteria to the judges for assessing the admissibility of expert testimony: (1) the theory or technique is testable; (2) it has been subjected to peer review or published; (3) there are maintainable standards controlling the use of the technique; (4) scientists generally accept it works; and (5) there is a known error rate. By now, there has been a large flow of discussion in the scientific community on this decision (see, for instance recently, Brodin, 2005; Dahir *et al.*, 2005; Groscup *et al.*, 2002; Kovera, Russano and McAuliff, 2002; Owen, 2002). In the literature on Daubert one generally assumes that the Supreme Court gave an exhaustive list of criteria. It did not, because just prior to giving the list I quoted, the Supreme Court wrote:

> Faced with a proffer of expert scientific testimony, then, the trial judge must determine at the outset [...] whether the expert is proposing to testify to (1) scientific knowledge that (2) will assist the trier of fact to understand or determine a fact in issue. This entails a preliminary assessment of whether the reasoning or methodology underlying the testimony is scientifically valid and of whether that reasoning or methodology properly can be applied to the facts in issue. We are confident that federal judges possess the capacity to undertake this review. Many factors will bear on the inquiry, and we do not presume to set out a definitive checklist or test. But some general observations are appropriate.

In fact, in *Daubert* and subsequent decisions (*General Electric Co.* v. *Joiner*, 522 U.S. 136, 118 S.Ct. 512, 39 L.Ed.2d 508 (1997) and *Kumho Tire Co.* v. *Carmichael*, 119 S.Ct. 1167 (1999)) the Supreme Court ordered the American judge to evaluate expert testimony himself. Apparently the Supreme Court considers the judge capable of doing so. In that sense, the *Daubert* decision is the same as a recent landmark decision by the Dutch Supreme Court (*Hoge Raad 27 January 1998, Nederlandse Jurisprudentie* 1998, 404, *Shoemaker*). This case concerns the work of a shoemaker in a murder committed during the Helmond carnival. The police engaged a shoemaker to compare the soles of the suspect's shoes with sole traces found at the scene of the crime. The Appellate Court used the shoemaker's report as evidence. The Supreme Court sensed that being a shoemaker is something different from being a sole trace expert and held that the Appellate Court should have explained in its decision: (1) why this particular expert could be considered an expert in sole marks; (2) if so, what method the expert used; (3) why this method could be considered reliable; and (4) why this expert could have applied the method competently.

Are these requirements necessary? Yes, and a lot more are too (see Knörnschild and Van Koppen, 2003; Van Koppen, 2000; Van Koppen and Penrod, 2003; van Koppen and

Saks, 2003; Saks, 2003). These requirements are not necessary because experts do not do their best or would pull the court's leg. They are necessary because many experts do not understand their role in the criminal trial and are not sensitive to differences between their own science and the application of their science in the forensic context.

At the same time, these and other possible requirements do not solve the paradox for the court. The paradox can partly be considered a problem of communication. The typical lawyer who serves as judge does not have any training in scientific methods or thought during his university education (Crombag, 2000). More training of lawyers would help, but it should be noted that even in psychology alone the subdisciplines are quite diverse: perception by witnesses, the quality of interrogations (Gudjonsson, 2003; Vrij, 2002), the validity of confessions (Gudjonsson, 2003), identification procedures (Cutler and Penrod, 1995; Wells and Seelau, 1995; Wells *et al.*, 1998), the scent line-up (Schoon and Van Koppen, 2002), but also reports related to the insanity defence and future dangerousness of the defendant (De Ruiter, 2000, 2004). To bridge the gap between judges and experts, legal training could be filled with courses on a large range of subjects that should also include basic training in medicine, DNA, finger prints, accountancy, and so on. Little room would remain to teach law students any law.

High demands on experts do not solve the paradox either, but it may help. Of course the court is not concerned with the track record of the expert, but hiring someone with an impeccable curriculum vitae at least raises the probability that the expert opinion in a specific case is of good quality. Still, the court has to evaluate whether the expert opinion in this particular case is any good. That judgement can only be based on an evaluation of the content of the opinion. I do not see how lawyers could perform that task, let alone lay jurors.

TRANSFERRING FROM ONE FIELD TO ANOTHER

What may be a valid line of reasoning in psychology may be far off in the forensic field. I give three examples; one on post-traumatic stress disorder (PTSD), one on child sexual abuse and one on amnesia.

Take the following, unfortunately all too common, case. A grown woman files a complaint against her stepfather. She claims he has been abusing her for many years. The stepfather denies the accusations. Without any additional evidence, fact finders are hesitant to go along with the complaint. In fact, under Dutch law, judges cannot convict on a single witness or victim statement alone. However, help may be available from psychologists.

We know that long-term sexual abuse is related to PTSD in later life (Beitchman *et al.*, 1992; Cahill, Llewellyn and Pearson, 1991; Feerick and Snow, 2005; Neumann *et al.*, 1996). So prosecutors hope that her accusations can be validated in some way or another, for instance by a psychologist who diagnoses PTSD in the complainant. A psychologist is asked to assess the psychological state of the complainant and give a report. In several cases, which I have come across, these reports (see, for instance, the case described in Van Koppen and Merckelbach, 1998) typically conclude: this woman suffers from PTSD, this is an indication of a trauma in childhood, probably of a sexual nature.

Please note that the court – or one of the parties involved – asked the psychologist to validate the trauma with a possible PTSD. The psychologist, in making the diagnosis, then follows the DSM-IV-TR (American Psychiatric Association, 2000). This lists the criteria for a diagnosis. For PTSD, the first one reads as follows:

> A. The person has been exposed to a traumatic event in which both of the following were present: (1) the person experienced, witnessed, or was confronted with an event or events that involved actual or threatened death or serious injury, or a threat to the physical integrity of self or others (2) the person's response involved intense fear, helplessness, or horror. Note: In children, this may be expressed instead by disorganized or agitated behavior (American Psychiatric Association, 2000, no 309.81).

In order to make a diagnosis, the first task of the psychologist is to establish whether a trauma occurred. That can only be done by asking the complainant: 'Did you suffer a trauma?' This is common practice in intakes for psychotherapy, where the word of the future patient is taken for granted. For forensic purposes this manner of working has a consequence that in fact the psychologist says to the fact finder: She suffered a trauma, because she says so. In practice, this circular reasoning remains completely hidden to the fact finder, because the criteria for the diagnosis are not revealed in court.

Apart from this problem, inferring sexual abuse in the past, from a present syndrome, is also for other reasons less straightforward than it seems. First, not everybody who has a traumatic past develops psychiatric symptoms. It is estimated that 20–50 % of trauma victims do (Kendall-Tackett, Williams and Finkelhorn, 1993). Second, the reverse relation is neither evident, because less than 10 % of individuals with psychiatric symptoms has a traumatic history in their youth (Rind, Tromovitch and Bauserman, 1998). Third, the individuals with both psychiatric symptoms and a traumatic youth cannot readily be identified, because they suffer from a wide range of syndromes and symptoms (Figueroa et al., 1997). Indeed, the causal relation between PTSD and any other psychiatric symptoms is so weak that experts can never validly testify on this subject. Some seem to try to circumvent this problem by using a rhetorical trick: they testify that the psychiatric symptoms are 'consistent' with a traumatic past (Rassin and Merckelbach, 1999). Formally this statement is usually not wrong, but it lacks any relevant content. For instance, having leukaemia is consistent with exposure to radioactive fall-out, but leukaemia can have a host of other causes and thus having leukaemia does not imply, in any way, that the patient has been exposed to fall-out. Nevertheless, the 'consistency' trick leaves the impression with judges and jurors that there is a relevant relation (see the discussion by Miller and Allen, 1998).

A comparable problem occurs in some expert evidence on sexual abuse of children. In many such cases there is no physical evidence, and there are no eyewitnesses. With very young alleged victims a police interview is hardly useful; many older children are not able to make a clear-cut statement. Experts are sometimes called to give an assessment of the behaviour of the child. Indeed many child victims of sexual abuse demonstrate behavioural problems. These behavioural problems are seen as a sign of sexual abuse. This has even been given a name: Child Sexual Abuse Accommodation Syndrome (Summit, 1983).

It is then concluded that because a child suffers from behavioural problems there must have been sexual abuse. This is again a misapplication of psychology in court. Children may suffer from behavioural problems for many other reasons than just sexual abuse. Even if the child has been abused, the behavioural consequences are far from evident. One reason is that sexual abuse can involve a wide range of behaviours by the perpetrator, varying from a single act of masturbation in the presence of the child to repeated rapes. It can be expected that this range of forms of abuse do not have the same effects. Indeed, children's reactions are quite heterogeneous (Fisher and Whiting, 1998; London et al., 2005). Thus there is no more or less fixed pattern of behavioural symptoms that would allow a conclusion of sexual abuse of a particular child (Sbraga and O'Donohue, 2003). This supports the argument that this kind of expert evidence should not be permitted (Freckelton, 1997) or at least be considered very carefully (Miller and Allen, 1998).

THE AMNESIC KILLER

The third example of misapplication of psychological reasoning occurs in cases where the accused claims amnesia for the crime. This is not an uncommon phenomenon. A considerable minority of defendants claims that they suffer from amnesia for the crime they supposedly committed (Gudjonsson, Kopelman and MacKeith, 1999; Leitch, 1948; Taylor and Kopelman, 1984). A fair estimate seems to be that some 25 % of people accused of serious violent offences claim amnesia for the offence (Cima et al., 2004; Pyszora, Barker and Kopelman, 2003).

Amnesia could have an organic source, such as, for instance, dementia (Savla and Palmer, 2005), sleeping problems that cause sleep walking (Fenwick, 1993; Jacobs, 1993; Oswald and Evans, 1985), or closed head injury (Ahmed et al., 2000; Ellenberg, Levin and Saydjari, 1996). Some contend that crime-related amnesia could also come from a so-called psychological trauma: strong emotions could lead to memory loss (Kopelman, 1995; Porter et al., 2001; Swihart, Yuille and Porter, 1999). It is assumed than a psychological 'blow' may cause neurological dysfunction, but it remains difficult to establish how this would work (McNally, 2003; Parkin, 1997, p. 147; Schacter, 1996). Of course, the accused can feign his amnesia. Suspects can do so, because it seems to present them with some advantages. For instance, during interrogation they need not call in their right to silence, but can keep quiet on the basis of 'I am sorry, but I cannot remember what happened'. That discharges them from explaining often very grim details of the crime and their own life. They may also hope that the case will be dealt with more favourable if everybody believes they just forgot. In that, the amnesic killer from Drenthe was successful.

In the Dutch province of Drenthe a man was accused of strangling his wife (see on this case also Merckelbach et al., 2005; Wagenaar and Crombag, 2005, Chapter 12). He tells the police they were in the middle of a nasty divorce. One night they had a row in their living room and his wife announced that she would do anything to get him into trouble. She promised to go to the police the next day to accuse him of sexually molesting their daughter. The man's story continues as follows. He got very angry, he turned hot, started to sweat and his ears began to buzz. The light went out in his eyes. He came to in the garden with his hands loosely around the neck of his wife. She did not move any more and he realized she was dead. He then drove to the police station and turned himself in. He cannot remember anything between the moment his light went out in the living room and the moment he came to in the garden.

This is the story he maintained with the police, the psychologist and two psychiatrists who examined him, and during the trial. The prosecution asked these psychologist and psychiatrists to examine the suspect. All three described him as a physical and psychological healthy man. In addition, all three came to the conclusion that he suffered from an acute dissociative disorder. One of them wrote, for instance:

> He had an acute dissociative disorder with a breakthrough of aggression. [...] This was to an extent that he, if it is proven that he committed the facts, cannot be held accountable. The deed occurred while the defendant could not influence it. He only came to himself after he strangled his wife. During an acute dissociative disorder any logical thinking is out of the question and one acts automatically.

The court followed the psychiatrists and psychologist, the man was not held accountable. Since he appeared to be of sound body and mind at the time of the trial and thus the chance of recidivism was considered low, he was not committed to a hospital for the treatment of mental disorders and was acquitted altogether (Rechtbank (District Court) Assen, 12th June 2002, *LJN-AE* 3911).

The psychologist and psychiatrists, who served as experts in this case, not only accepted a psychological trauma as an explanation for the accused's amnesia, but also gave the diagnosis 'dissociative amnesia'. 'The essential feature of dissociative disorders [is a] disruption of the usually integrated functions of consciousness, memory, identity, or perception of the environment' (see American Psychiatric Association, 2000, pp. 392). However, it is quite uncertain 'whether dissociation means anything more than a score on a questionnaire of uncertain meaning, a phenomenon that exists in the world of *some* psychiatrists and psychologists rather than in the world of psychiatry' (Wagenaar and Crombag, 2005, p. 199, emphasis in original).

Whether or not such psychogenetic amnesia exists, is doubtful. For instance, concentration camp survivors make all kinds of errors in their recollections, but do not show amnesia for the time they were incarcerated in the concentration camp (Yehuda *et al.*, 1996). A psychological originating amnesia is at least very rare and short lived, if it exists at all (McNally, 2003, p. 210; Schacter, 1996, p. 225). It is a fair estimate that the number of defendants of violent crime who feign amnesia considerably outnumber those with genuine amnesia, be it of the organic or psychogenetic type (Christianson and Merckelbach, 2004).

So the experts in the Drenthe case made three errors. First they accepted the existence of dissociative amnesia, while its existence is at least doubtful or the likelihood of feigned amnesia is much higher than any psychogenetic form. Second, they accepted the dissociative amnesia as a sign that the defendant was not in control during the crime. Please note that loss of control is not part of the definition of dissociative amnesia in the DSM-IV-TR (American Psychiatric Association, 2000). For the question whether he was in control during the crime, his later amnesia is immaterial (in that sense, *United States Court of Military Appeals*, 4 U.S.C.M.A. 134, 1954 CMA Lexis 572, 15 C.M.R. 134, April 9, 1954 *(United States* v. *Olvera)*. See also Wagenaar and Crombag, 2005, Chapter 12).

The third problem is the same as the one I discussed in the case of PTSD. The experts knew that the man lost his memory from one source: the man told them. The psychologist tested him with a battery of tests, but the only validation of his amnesia came from himself during the interviews. The experts did not test the veracity of his amnesia, while they could have done so. There are several possibilities for distinguishing genuine from feigned amnesia. Organic amnesia, from a physical trauma, seems to follow a fixed pattern (Hodges, 1991; Meeter and Murre, 2004). Amnesia, because of sleeping problems, can be traced using neuropsychological tests and measures like the electro encephalogram (EEG). Since most faking amnesiacs are not aware of the typical patterns by which amnesia develops and the symptoms that go along with it, they have a tendency to exaggerate their symptoms (Christianson and Merckelbach, 2004; Iverson, 1995). The Structured Inventory of Malingered Symptomatology (SIMS, see Smith, 1997; Smith and Burger, 1997) is based on the idea that many malingerers tend to exaggerate their symptoms. A second test could be the Symptom Validity Testing (SVT, see Denney, 1996; Frederick, Carter and Powel, 1995; Merckelbach, Hauer and Rassin, 2002). That is a questionnaire especially developed for each crime in which, in a yes/no format, the defendant is asked about details of the crime (for instance the murder weapon or the shawl the victim was wearing). The accused has to answer all questions. If the amnesia is genuine, the number of right answers will be around chance. If the amnesia is faked, the accused will try to evade the right alternatives and thus will score well below chance. Even if the defendant knows how the test works – and tries to give about 50 % right answers if a yes/no format is presented – he still has to take care that the sequential pattern of correct and incorrect answers is random. That is a difficult task. Whether or not the sequential pattern is random can be checked using the so-called runs test (see Cliffe, 1992).

If the experts in the Drenthe case had not made so many errors, the accused would probably not have been home free.

ANSWERING THE WRONG QUESTION

Fact finders want experts to answer questions in the form: given symptoms A we can observe now, what does it tell us about the likelihood of phenomenon B that may have occurred in the past? An example of this is: now we observe behaviour of the alleged victim (A); what does this tell us about the occurrence of sexual abuse against that child (B)? Psychologists are not used to answering this type of question. First, their diagnosis is always aimed at predicting the future, rather than explaining the past. Second, they usually start from a known situation – the story told by the prospective client during intake – and investigate whether certain symptoms are in accordance with that state of affairs. Taking this typical psychological attitude can cause the psychologist to answer the wrong question, as can be demonstrated by the case of the pimp and his two prostitutes.

In a case in the south of The Netherlands a pimp was accused of molesting two of his prostitutes and raping one of them. Although the police knew of the violent character of the pimp, the case confronted them with a problem: the prostitutes had also accused the pimp of forcing them to sell their bodies but, after the pimp was arrested and detained in custody, both women continued to work in that trade all the same. Were they just making up their whole story, or was it typical for women who had been forced into prostitution to continue in the trade even after the force has been removed? To answer these questions, the prosecution called in a psychologist the very day before the case was scheduled for trial in the district court.

The prosecution chose this psychologist because she had done some research on molested prostitutes. She read the police reports of the prostitutes' statements, and spoke to each of them for an hour. The following day she testified in court on the results of her short investigation. She told the court that she recognized the pattern of behaviour of both girls – they were quite young prostitutes – from her studies of prostitute behaviour: 'The story they told tallied with the behaviour of pimps I encountered before.... I was not surprised by the things I heard and read.'

The psychologist did not give the answer the court needed. That would have been the answer to the question: 'What can we infer from the continuation of being a prostitute about what the pimp did to the two women?' The psychologist answered the reversed question: 'Do maltreated prostitutes commonly show this kind of behaviour?' The answer to that question is of little relevance, but the major problem is that this is often not detected by the court.

A more hidden version of the answering-the-wrong-question problem was described by Rassin and Merckelbach (1999). The extent to which an accused is sensitive to suggestion by the interrogators can play a role in making false confessions (Gudjonsson, 2003). Gudjonsson developed an instrument to measure the level of suggestibility of individuals, the Gudjonsson Suggestibility Scale (GSS) (Gudjonsson, 1984, 1987, 1992; Merckelbach *et al.*, 1998). Assume we administer the GSS to an accused who allegedly made a false confession. Does that give the fact finder relevant information as to the veracity of the confession? It is assumed that confessions by individuals who score high on the GSS should be accepted with caution, because these individuals are prone to making false confessions (Kassin, 1997; Kassin and Norwick, 2004; McCann, 1998). A GSS score, then, would be relevant for the evaluation of the confession, but it remains unclear how relevant and in what manner. False confessions are generated by a number of factors; amongst others, pressure in and out of the interrogation room, the circumstances of the accused's detention, and the psychological demeanour of the accused. Possible motives of the accused to make a false confession – even in the absence of any pressure to do so – may be relevant. Only part of the psychological demeanour of the suspect can be measured with the GSS. However, the other relevant factors can be so powerful that even someone with the lowest GSS score would make a false confession. The confession of someone with a particularly high GSS score may be true. GSS scores, then, seem to be relevant only in the context of all the other relevant factors. It can contribute to an explanation of what happened during the interrogations, but in itself it is not relevant.

STAYING WITHIN YOUR DOMAIN

This shows that it is naïve to expect that an expert's opinion, on one topic, can ascertain the truth of past events. Facts do not exist; only interpreted facts exist. Facts can only be assessed in the context of an interpretation by a particular individual for a particular purpose. This always takes the form of a narrative or story (Bennett, 1992; Bennett and Feldman, 1981; Crombag, van Koppen and Wagenaar, 1992; Pennington and Hastie, 1986, 1993; Wagenaar, van Koppen and Crombag, 1993):

> Narratives are the only conceivable means for ordinary people to use in organizing, recalling, comparing, and testing the vast amounts of information that go into American-style legal judgements (Bennett, 1992, p. 153).

The context given in the story is vital to the interpretation. 'Science without context ... is meaningless at best and dangerous at worst', (Gallop and Stockdale, 1998, p. 70). This context seems to be at odds with the requirement that experts should not step outside their domain and limit themselves to what is subjected to their opinion (Dwyer, 2003). To be of any use to the fact finder, however, experts at least should be sensitive to the decisions the fact finder is facing in criminal cases, but that is not enough. They should also take the context of their expertise into account. In many, if not most, cases the expert's opinion is only of use if a wider context, a wider narrative, is discussed than just the very narrow aspect that is subjected to the expert. For instance, an expert who is asked to evaluate a child's statement in a sexual abuse case can only do so effectively and meaningful when he also assesses, amongst others, the family interaction, possible preparations to the interview of the child by the parents, the manner in which the allegations were first disclosed, possible other perpetrators and possible reasons why the child would make false accusations or could have been induced to do so.

I draw a second example from the type of psychological expertise that is very common: on identity parades (see in general Cutler and Penrod, 1995; Wells et al., 1998). Much is known of how a proper identification procedure should be conducted, and in the Netherlands there are clear-cut rules about how the police should conduct such procedures (Van Amelsvoort, 2005; Werkgroep Identificatie, 1992). Still they are frequently performed improperly by the police. The most common error made is that a one-person show-up is used instead of a proper multi-person identity parade with a witness who knows the perpetrator just from the crime scene.

An identity parade is used to assess whether the appearance of the suspect corresponds to the memory the witness has of the appearance of the perpetrator. A good identity parade, live, with photographs or on video, seeks to accomplish two purposes simultaneously: to try to learn from an eyewitness who perpetrated a crime and, at the same time, to test the accuracy of that eyewitness's memory of the offender. This dual objective is achieved by confronting the witness with a line-up of people, all of whom conform to the general description of the perpetrator. One of these is the suspect; the others are innocent foils unknown to the witness. The witness's task is to indicate the one person in the parade they recognize, if they recognize anyone at all.

The result of a properly conducted identity parade has a very high diagnostic value (Wagenaar, van Koppen and Crombag, 1993). It is essential, however, that the procedures minimize the likelihood that an identification is the result of judgements of the relative similarity of a member of the line-up to the witness's memory (i.e. that the witness chooses the suspect who looks most like the memory of the perpetrator rather than the one who is the perpetrator), or that subtle or not so subtle cues suggest to the witness who is the 'right' suspect to choose. There are many more requirements, however (Van Amelsvoort, 2005; Cutler and Penrod, 1995; Wells et al., 1998). All these requirements boil down to the same thing: if the witness pointed out the suspect, we can conclude that the suspect is recognized as the offender only if all other cues by which the witness could know who the suspect in the line is, apart from his own memory of the offender.

The one-person show-up should be used in one situation and one situation only: when the witness already knew the perpetrator before the crime took place. The identification then takes place at the scene of the crime and showing the suspect to the witness can only serve to prevent administrative errors ('Is this the neighbour you meant?'). If the witness knows the perpetrator by name, this procedure is unnecessary. If used with a witness who saw the perpetrator only at the scene of the crime, the one-person show-up is much more likely to yield false identifications than are properly constructed line-ups (see Dekle et al., 1996; Lindsay et al., 1997; Yarmey, Yarmey and Yarmey, 1996).

In Dutch police practice, most identifications are attempted using the one-person show-up. In fact, the police regularly make every conceivable error in conducting identification procedures. A good exception was the case of the Park Rapist in Drachten, in the North of the Netherlands. A man had raped a number of women in the local park. All the victims described that a young man approached then while riding a bike in a peculiar manner: he steered with his elbows. The police made an arrest. A video was made that was an almost perfect identity parade. Although the two victims who participated were instructed in writing, the video started with a repetition of the most important instructions both on screen and read aloud. Then a police officer played a probe foil showing how he rode the bike steering with his elbows and then he was shown close up. Thereafter the video was stopped to check whether the witness completely understood the procedure. Only then were the suspect and foils shown, in the same manner as the probe foil.

The two rape victims both identified the suspect. But there remained another problem: the victims and the suspect all lived in the vicinity of the park and came there regularly. Thus the possibility that the victims recalled the suspect from sight from other occasions than the rape could not be excluded; indeed they could have recognized him but not from the crime. This, of course, decreased the diagnostic value of the identifications in the otherwise impeccable identity parade. The magnitude of the decrease is unknown; only something can be said about the direction. This opinion could only be given after studying the whole case file and taking information into account that was not formally put to the expert.

I gave these examples to demonstrate that the context is important. Of course, this varies, depending on the case at hand, but it also demonstrates that an expert should always go through the whole case, looking for elements that may be relevant to their opinion. In some cases, it will result in an opinion that encompasses all or almost all of the elements in the case that are relevant to the fact finder as well. Crombag and Wagenaar (2000) argued that experts should, in their opinions, always consider the proposed scenario and rival scenarios of what may have happened. In these cases, the expert can only be of help to the fact finder if he enters the province of the fact finder. That again is a paradox. The expert can only be helpful to the fact finder by assessing alternative scenarios. That will blur the distinction between the work of the expert and the work of the fact finder. So be it.

CONCLUSIONS

Psychologists can be very helpful to fact finders in deciding criminal cases. However, serving as a psychology expert in court can pose many problems. A few of these problems I have discussed above. Part of the problem is related to the difference between decision making in science and decision making in criminal cases. Science is a different endeavour than legal decision making. Another part of the problem is that psychologists, as scientists or as therapists, do not understand the special role of forensic expertise in court. For forensic expertise there are different rules than for psychology in general. Transferring statements from one part of the field to the other can be silly or even misleading in the legal domain.

All this is not just a problem of communication between psychologist, jurists and lay jurors. Indeed, if all forensic psychologists were also lawyers and all lawyers were versed in psychology, some of the problems could be evaded, but even this is a hypothetical situation. The fact finder cannot check whether an expert opinion in a specific case is sound or not. That is not just a matter of principle, but a highly practical problem. In legal precedents, one tried to circumvent this by assessing expert opinions indirectly. That has resulted in requirements such that there is a known error rate of the method used by the expert – as if legal decision making has a known error rate. Or that the expert's theory should be testable – as if this would say anything on the validity of the theory and its application in the specific case. Or that a method has been subjected to peer review – as if the peers know anything about the forensic application and do not just apply notions that are valid only in the psychological domain. In short, the helpfulness of the psychologist to the fact finder does pose many paradoxical difficulties that leaves one to wonder: is it ever helpful and, if so, how do we know?

REFERENCES

Ahmed, S., Bierley, R., Sheikh, J.I. and Date, E.S. (2000) Post-traumatic amnesia after closed head injury: A review of the literature and some suggestions for further research. *Brain Injury*, **14**, 765–780.

American Psychiatric Association (2000) *Diagnostic and Statistical Manual of Mental Disorders (DSM-IV-TR)*, 4th edn, text revision, American Psychiatric Association, Washington, DC.

Beitchman, J.H., Zucker, K.J., Hood, J.E. *et al.* (1992) A review of the long-term effects of child sexual abuse. *Child Abuse and Neglect*, **16**, 101–118.

Bennett, W.L. (1992) Legal fictions: Telling stories and doing justice, in *Explaining One's Self to Others: Reason-Giving in a Social Context* (eds M.L. McLaughlin, M.J. Cody and S.J. Read), Erlbaum, Hillsdale, NJ, pp. 149–64.

Bennett, W.L. and Feldman, M.S. (1981) *Reconstructing Reality in the Courtroom: Justice and Judgement in American Culture*, Rutgers University Press, New Brunswick, NJ.

Brodin, M.S. (2005) Behavioral science evidence in the age of Daubert: Reflections of a skeptic. *University of Cincinnati Law Review*, **73**, 867–943.

Cahill, C., Llewellyn, S.P. and Pearson, C. (1991) Long-term effects of sexual abuse which occurred in childhood: A review. *British Journal of Clinical Psychology*, **30**, 117–30.

Christianson, S.-Å. and Merckelbach, H. (2004) Crime-related amnesia as a form of deception, in *The Detection of Deception in Forensic Contexts* (eds P.A. Granhag and L.A. Strömwall), Cambridge University Press, Cambridge, pp. 195–227.

Cima, M., Nijman, H.L.I., Merckelbach, H. *et al.* (2004) Claims of crime-related amnesia in forensic patients. *International Journal of Law and Psychiatry*, **27**, 215–21.

Cliffe, M.J. (1992) Symptom-validity testing of feigned sensory or memory deficits: A further elaboration for subjects who understand the rationale. *British Journal of Clinical Psychology*, **31**, 207–9.

Cohn, D.S. (1991) Anatomical doll play of preschoolers referred for sexual abuse and those not referred. *Child Abuse and Neglect*, **15**, 455–466.

Crombag, H.F.M. (2000) Rechters en deskundigen [Judges and experts]. *Nederlands Juristenblad*, **75**, 1659–65 (Maastricht University).

Crombag, H.F.M., van Koppen, P.J. and Wagenaar, W.A. (1992). *Dubieuze Zaken: De Psychologie Van Strafrechtelijk Bewijs* [Dubious cases: The psychology of criminal evidence]. Contact, Amsterdam.

Crombag, H.F.M., van Koppen, P.J. and Wagenaar, W.A. (1994). *Dubieuze zaken: De psychologie van strafrechtelijk bewijs* [Dubious cases: The psychology of criminal evidence], 2nd edn, Contact, Amsterdam.

Crombag, H.F.M. and Wagenaar, W.A. (2000) Audite et alteram partem. *Trema*, **23**, 93–6.

Cutler, B.L. and Penrod, S.D. (1995) *Mistaken Identification: The Eyewitness, Psychology, and the Law*, Cambridge University Press, Cambridge.

Dahir, V.B., Richardson, J.T.E., Ginsburg, G.P. *et al.* (2005) Judicial application of Daubert to psychological syndrome and profile evidence: A research note. *Psychology Public Policy and Law*, **11**, 62–82.

Dekle, D.J., Beale, C.R., Elliot, R. and Huneycutt, D. (1996). Children as witnesses: A comparison of lineup versus showup methods. *Applied Cognitive Psychology*, **10**, 1–12.

de Ruiter, C. (2000) Voor verbetering vatbaar [To improve behaviour]. *De Psycholoog*, **35**, 423–8 (inaugural lecture Amsterdam University).

de Ruiter, C. (2004). Forensisch gedragsonderzoek in strafzaken [Forensic expertise on behaviour in criminal cases]. *Justitiële Verkenningen*, **30** (1), 50–60.

Denney, R.L. (1996) Symptom validity testing of remote memory in a criminal forensic setting. *Archives of Clinical Neuropsychology*, **11**, 589–603.

Dwyer, D. (2003) The duties of expert witnesses of fact and opinion: R. v. Clark (Sally). *International Journal of Evidence and Proof*, **7**, 264–9.

Ellenberg, J.H., Levin, H.S. and Saydjari, C. (1996) Posttraumatic amnesia as a predictor of outcome after severe closed head injury: Prospective assessment. *Archives of Neurology*, **53**, 782–91.

Endres, J. (1997) The suggestibility of the child witness: The role of individual differences and their assessment. *Journal of Credibility Assessment and Witness Psychology*, **1**, 44–67.

Faller, K.C. (2005) Anatomical dolls: Their use in assessment of children who may have been sexually abused. *Journal of Child Sexual Abuse*, **14**, 1–22.

Feerick, M.M. and Snow, K.L. (2005) The relationships between childhood sexual abuse, social anxiety, and symptoms of posttraumatic stress disorder in women. *Journal of Family Violence*, **20**, 409–19.

Fenwick, P.B.C. (1993) Brain, mind, and behaviour: Some medico-legal aspects. *British Journal of Psychiatry*, **163**, 565–73.

Figueroa, E.F., Silk, K.R., Huth, A. and Lohr, N.E. (1997) History of childhood sexual abuse and general psychopathology. *Comprehensive Psychiatry*, **38**, 23–30.

Fisher, C.B. and Whiting, K.A. (1998) How valid are child sexual abuse validations? in *Expert Witnesses in Child Abuse Cases: What Can (and should) be Said in Court?* (eds S.J. Ceci and H. Hembrooke), American Psychological Association, Washington, DC, pp. 159–84.

Freckelton, I. (1997) Child sexual abuse accommodation evidence: The travails of counterintuitive evidence in Australia and New Zealand. *Behavioral Sciences and the Law*, **15**, 247–83.

Frederick, R.I., Carter, M. and Powel, J. (1995). Adapting symptom validity testing to evaluate suspicious complaints of amnesia in medicolegal evaluations. *Bulletin of the American Academy of Psychiatry and the Law*, **23**, 227–33.

Gallop, A. and Stockdale, R. (1998). Trace and contact evidence, in *Crime Scene to Court: The Essentials of Forensic Science* (ed. P. White), Royal Society of Chemistry, Cambridge.

Groscup, J.L., Penrod, S.D., Studebaker, C.A., Huss, M.T. and O'Neil, K.M. (2002) The effects of Daubert on the admissibility of expert testimony in state and federal criminal cases. *Psychology, Public Policy, and Law*, **8**, 339–72.

Gross, S.R. and Mnookin, J.L. (2003) Expert information and expert evidence: A preliminary taxonomy. *Seton Hall Law Review*, **34**, 141–89.

Gudjonsson, G.H. (1984) A new scale of interrogative suggestibility. *Personality and Individual Differences*, **5**, 303–14.

Gudjonsson, G.H. (1987) A parallel form of the Gudjonsson Suggestibility Scale. *British Journal of Clinical Psychology*, **26**, 215–21.

Gudjonsson, G.H. (1992) Interrogative suggestibility: Factor analysis of the Gudjonsson Suggestibility Scale (GSS 2). *Personality and Individual Differences*, **13**, 479–81.

Gudjonsson, G.H. (2003) *The Psychology of Interrogations and Confessions: A Handbook*, Wiley, Chichester.

Gudjonsson, G.H., Kopelman, M.D. and MacKeith, J.A.C. (1999) Unreliable admissions to homicide: A case of misdiagnosis of amnesia and misuse of abreaction technique. *British Journal of Psychiatry*, **174**, 455–9.

Hodges, J.R. (1991) *Transient Amnesia: Clinical and Neuropsychological Aspects*, Saunders, London.

Hofstee, W.K.B. (1980) *De Empirische Discussie: Theorie Van Het Sociaal-Wetenschappelijk Onderzoek* [The empirical discussion: Theory of social science research]. Boom, Meppel.

Horowitz, S.W. (1991) Empirical support for Statement Validity Analysis. *Behavioral Assessment*, **13**, 293–313.

Horowitz, S.W., Lamb, M.E., Esplin, P.W. et al. (1997) Reliability of criteria-based content analysis of child witness statements. *Legal and Criminological Psychology*, **2**, 11–22.

Iverson, G.L. (1995). Qualitative aspects of malingered memory deficits. *Brain Injury*, **9**, 35–40.

Jacobs, T. (1993). The big sleep. *Fortean Times*, **167**, 42–5.

Kassin, S.M. (1997) The psychology of confession evidence. *American Psychologist*, **52**, 221–33.

Kassin, S.M. and Norwick, R.J. (2004) Why people waive their Miranda rights: The power of innocence. *Law and Human Behavior*, **28**, 211–21.

Kendall-Tackett, K.A., Williams, L.M. and Finkelhorn, D. (1993) Impact of abuse on children: A review and synthesis of recent empirical studies. *Psychological Bulletin*, **113**, 164–80.

Knörnschild, C. and van Koppen, P.J. (2003) Psychological expert witnesses in Germany and the Netherlands, in *Adversarial Versus Inquisitorial Justice: Psychological Perspectives on Criminal Justice Systems* (eds P.J. van Koppen and S.D. Penrod), Plenum, New York, pp. 255–82.

Kopelman, M.D. (1995) The assessment of psychogenic amnesia, in *Handbook of Memory Disorders* (eds A.D. Baddeley, B.A. Wilson and F.N. Watts), Wiley, New York, pp. 427–48.

Kovera, M.B., Russano, M.B. and McAuliff, B.D. (2002) Assessment of the commonsense psychology underlying Daubert – Legal decision makers' abilities to evaluate expert evidence in hostile work environment cases. *Psychology, Public Policy, and Law*, **8**, 180–200.

Lamb, M.E. and Sternberg, K.J. (1997) Criteria-based content analysis: A field validation study. *Child Abuse and Neglect*, **21**, 255–64.

Lamb, M.E. and Sternberg, K.J. (1998) Conducting investigative interviews of alleged sexual abuse victims. *Child Abuse and Neglect*, **22**, 813–23.

Leitch, A. (1948) Notes on amnesia in crime for the general practitioner. *The Medical Press*, **26**, 459–63.

Lindsay, R.C.L., Pozzulo, J.D., Craig, W. et al. (1997) Simultaneous lineups, sequential lineups, and showups: Eyewitness identification decisions of adults and children. *Law and Human Behavior*, **21**, 391–404.

London, K., Bruck, M., Ceci, S.J. and Shuman, D.W. (2005) Disclosure of child sexual abuse: What does the research tell us about the ways that children tell? *Psychology, Public Policy and Law*, **11**, 194–226.

McCann, J.T. (1998) A conceptual framework for identifying various types of confessions. *Behavioral Sciences and the Law*, **16**, 441–53.

McGough, L.S. (1991) Commentary: Assessing the credibility of witnesses' statements, in *The Suggestibility of Children's Recollections* (ed. J.L. Doris), American Psychological Association, Washington, DC, pp. 165–7.

McNally, R.J. (2003) *Remembering Trauma*, The Belknap Press of Harvard University Press, Cambridge.

Meeter, M. and Murre, J.M.J. (2004) Consolidation of long-term memory: Evidence and alternatives. *Psychological Bulletin*, **130**, 843–57.

Merckelbach, H., Crombag, H.F.M. and van Koppen, P.J. (2003). Hoge verwachtingen: Over het corrumperend effect van verwachtingen op forensische expertise [High expectations: The corrupting effect of expectations on forensic expertise]. *Nederlands Juristenblad*, **78**, 710–6.

Merckelbach, H., Hauer, B. and Rassin, E. (2002) Symptom validity testing of feigned dissociative amnesia: A simulation study. *Psychology, Crime, and Law*, **8**, 311–8.

Merckelbach, H., Muris, P., Wessel, I. and van Koppen, P.J. (1998) The Gudjonssons Suggestibility Scale (GSS): Further data on its reliability, validity, and metacognition correlates. *Social Behavior and Personality*, **26**, 203–10.

Merckelbach, H., van Oorsouw, K.I.M., van Koppen, P.J. and Jelicic, M. (2005). Weet er niets meer van, edelachtbare: Over daderamnesie [I really cannot remember, my lord: On perpetrator amnesia]. *Delikt en Delinkwent*, **35**, 11–30.

Miller, J.S. and Allen, R.J. (1998) The expert as educator, in *Expert Witnesses in Child Abuse Cases: What can (and should) be Said in Court?* (eds S.J. Ceci and H. Hembrooke), American Psychological Association, Washington, DC, pp. 137–55.

Neumann, D.A., Houskamp, B.M., Pollock, V.E. and Briere, J. (1996) The long-term sequelae of childhood sexual abuse in women: A meta-analytic review. *Child Maltreatment*, **1**, 6–16.

Oswald, I. and Evans, J. (1985) On serious violence during sleep-walking. *British Journal of Psychiatry*, **147**, 688–91.

Owen, D.G. (2002). A decade of Daubert. *Denver University Law Review*, **80**, 345–73.

Parkin, A.J. (1997). *Memory and Amnesia: An Introduction*, 2nd edn, Blackwell, Oxford.

Pennington, N. and Hastie, R. (1986) Evidence evaluation in complex decision making. *Journal of Personality and Social Psychology*, **51**, 242–58.

Pennington, N. and Hastie, R. (1993) The story model for juror decision making, in *Inside the Jury: The Psychology of Juror Decision Making* (ed. R. Hastie), Cambridge University Press, Cambridge, pp. 192–221.

Popper, K.R. (1934) *Logik der Forschung: Zur Erkenntnistheorie der modernen Naturwissenschaft*, Springer, Wien.

Popper, K.R. (1968) *The Logic of Scientific Discovery*, Hutchinson, London.

Porter, S., Birt, A.R., Yuille, J.C. and Herve, H.F. (2001) Memory for murder: A psychological perspective on dissociative amnesia in legal contexts. *International Journal of Law and Psychiatry*, **24**, 23–42.

Pyszora, N.M., Barker, A.F. and Kopelman, M.D. (2003) Amnesia for criminal offences: A study of life sentence prisoners. *Journal of Forensic Psychiatry and Psychology*, **14**, 475–90.

Raskin, D.C. and Esplin, P.W. (1991a) Assessments of childrens' statements of sexual abuse, in *The Suggestibility of Childen's Recollections* (ed. J.L. Doris), American Psychological Association, Washington, DC, pp. 153–64.

Raskin, D.C. and Esplin, P.W. (1991b) Commentary: response to Wells, Loftus and MeGough, in *The Suggestibility of Childen's Recollections* (ed. J.L. Doris), American Psychological Association, Washington, DC, pp. 172–6.

Rassin, E. (1999) Criteria based content analysis: The less scientific road to truth. *Expert Evidence*, **7**, 265–78.

Rassin, E. and van Koppen, P.J. (2002) Het verhoren van kinderen in zedenzaken [Interrogating children in vice cases], in *Het Recht Van Binnen: Psychologie Van Het Recht* (eds P.J. van Koppen, D.J. Hessing, H. Merckelbach and H.F.M. Crombag), Kluwer, Deventer, pp. 507–30.

Rassin, E. and Merckelbach, H. (1999) The potential conflict between clinical and judicial decision making heuristics. *Behavioral Sciences and the Law*, **17**, 237–48.

Rind, B., Tromovitch, P. and Bauserman, R. (1998). A meta-analytic examination of assumed properties of child sexual abuse using college samples. *Psychological Bulletin*, **124**, 22–53.

Risinger, D.M., Saks, M.J., Thompson, C.T. and Rosenthal, R. (2002). The Daubert/Kumho implications of observer effects in forensic science: Hidden problems of expectation and suggestion. *California Law Review*, **90**, 1–56.

Ruby, C.L. and Brigham, J.C. (1997). The usefulness of the Criteria-Based-Content Analysis technique in distinguishing between truthful and fabricated allegations: A critical review. *Psychology, Public Policy, and Law*, **3**, 705–37.

Saks, M.J. (2003) Expert evidence in Europe and the United States, in *Adversarial Versus Inquisitorial Justice: Psychological Perspectives on Criminal Justice Systems* (eds P.J. van Koppen and S.D. Penrod), Plenum, New York, pp. 235–44.

Savla, G.N. and Palmer, B.W. (2005) Neuropsychology in Alzheimer's disease and other dementia research. *Current Opinion in Psychiatry*, **18**, 621–7.

Sbraga, T.P. and O'Donohue, W. (2003) Post hoc reasoning in possible cases of child sexual abuse: Symptoms of inconclusive origins. *Clinical Psychology: Science and Practice*, **10**, 320–34.

Schacter, D.L. (1996) *Searching for Memory: The Brain, the Mind, and the Past*, Basic Books, New York.

Schoon, G.A.A. and van Koppen, P.J. (2002) Identificatie door honden [Identification by dogs], in *Het recht Van Binnen: Psychologie Van Het Recht* (eds P.J. van Koppen, D.J. Hessing, H. Merckelbach and H.F.M. Crombag), Kluwer, Deventer, pp. 597–622.

Smith, G.P. (1997) Assessment of malingering with self-report instruments, in *Clinical Assessment of Malingering and Deception* (ed. R. Rogers), Guildford, New York, pp. 351–70.

Smith, G.P. and Burger, G.K. (1997) Detection of malingering: Validation of the Structured Inventory of Malingered Symptomatology (SIMS). *Journal of the Academy of Psychiatry and the Law*, **25**, 183–180.

Sporer, S.L. (1997) The less travelled road to truth: Verbal cues in deception detection in accounts of fabricated and self-experienced events. *Applied Cognitive Psychology*, **11**, 373–97.

Summit, R.C. (1983) The child sexual abuse accommodation syndrome. *Child Abuse and Neglect*, **7**, 177–93.

Swihart, G., Yuille, J.C. and Porter, S. (1999) The role of state-dependent memory in 'red-outs'. *International Journal of Law and Psychiatry*, **22**, 199–212.

Taylor, P.J. and Kopelman, M.D. (1984) Amnesia for criminal offences. *Psychological Medicine*, **14**, 581–8.

Undeutsch, U. (1983) Statement reality analysis, in *Reconstructing the Past: The Role of Psychologists in Criminal Trials* (ed. A. Trankell), Kluwer, Deventer, pp. 27–56.

van Amelsvoort, A.G. (2005) Handleiding Confrontatie *[Guidebook idenfication]*, 5th edn, Elsevier, Den Haag.

van Kampen, P.T.C. (1998). *Expert Evidence Compared: Rules and Practices in the Dutch and American Criminal Justice System*, Intersentia (diss. Leiden), Antwerpen.

van Koppen, P.J. (2000) How psychologists should help courts, in *Harmonisation in Forensic Expertise: An Inquiry into the Desirability of and Opportunities for International Standards* (eds J.F. Nijboer and W.J.J.M. Sprangers), Thela Thesis, Amsterdam, pp. 257–75.

van Koppen, P.J. and Merckelbach, H. (1998) De waarheid in therapie en in rechte: Pseudoherinneringen aan seksueel misbruik [The truth in therapy and under the law: Pseudo memories of sexual abuse]. *Nederlands Juristenblad*, **73**, 899–904.

van Koppen, P.J. and Penrod, S.D. (2003) The John Wayne and Judge Dee versions of justice, in *Adversarial Versus Inquisitorial Justice: Psychological Perspectives on Criminal Justice Systems* (eds P.J. van Koppen and S.D. Penrod), Plenum, New York, pp. 347–68.

van Koppen, P.J. and Saks, M.J. (2003) Preventing bad psychological scientific evidence in The Netherlands and The United States, in *Adversarial Versus Inquisitorial Justice: Psychological Perspectives on Criminal Justice Systems* (eds P.J. van Koppen and S.D. Penrod), Plenum, New York, pp. 283–308.

Vrij, A. (2002) Het verhoren van verdachten [Interrogating suspects], in *Het Recht Van Binnen: Psychologie Van Het Recht* (eds P.J. van Koppen, D.J. Hessing, H. Merckelbach and H.F.M. Crombag), Kluwer, Deventer, pp. 699–725.

Vrij, A. (2005) Criteria-based content analysis: A qualitative review of the first 37 studies. *Psychology, Public Policy, and Law*, **11**, 3–41.

Wagenaar, W.A. and Crombag, H.F.M. (2005) *The Popular Policeman and Other Cases: Psychological Perspectives on Legal Evidence*, Amsterdam University Press, Amsterdam.

Wagenaar, W.A., van Koppen, P.J. and Crombag, H.F.M. (1993) *Anchored Narratives: The Psychology of Criminal Evidence*, Harvester Wheatsheaf, London.

Wells, G.L. and Loftus, E.F. (1991) Commentary: is this child fabricating? Reactions to a new assessment technique, in *The Suggestibility of Childen's Recollections* (ed. J.L. Doris), American Psychological Association, Washington, DC, pp. 168–71.

Wells, G.L. and Seelau, E.P. (1995) Eyewitness identification: Psychological research and legal policy on lineups. *Psychology, Public Policy, and Law*, **1**, 765–91.

Wells, G.L., Small, M., Penrod, S.D. et al. (1998) Eyewitness identification procedures: Recommendations for lineups and photospreads. *Law and Human Behavior*, **23**, 603–647.

Werkgroep Identificatie (1992) *Rapport identificatie van personen door ooggetuigen* [Report on identification of persons by eyewitnesses]. Den Haag: Ministerie van Justitie, Recherche Advies Commissie, werkgroep Identificatie (voorzitter P. Bender; 2nd edn).

White, S.O., Strom, G.A., Santilli, G. and Halpin, B.M. (1986). Interviewing young sexual abuse victims with anatomically correct dolls. *Child Abuse and Neglect*, **10**, 519–29.

Yarmey, A.D., Yarmey, M.J. and Yarmey, A.L. (1996). Accuracy of eyewitness identifications in show-ups and lineups. *Law and Human Behavior*, **20**, 459–77.

Yehuda, R., Elkin, A., Binder-Brynes, K. et al. (1996). Dissociation in aging Holocaust survivors. *American Journal of Psychiatry*, **153**, 935–40.

Yuille, J.C. and Cutshall, J.L. (1989) Analysis of the statements of victims, witnesses and suspects, in *Credibility Assessment* (ed. J.C. Yuille), Dordrecht, pp. 175–91.

CHAPTER 17

Identifying Liability for Organizational Errors

David Carson
University of Portsmouth

Blaming individuals is emotionally more satisfying than targeting institutions (Reason, 2000, p. 768).

When things go wrong, pathological climates encourage finding a scapegoat, bureaucratic organisations seek justice, and the generative organisation tries to discover the basic problems with the system (Westrum, 2004, p. 23).

If an organisation cannot distinguish between good luck and good management, bad luck and bad management, individuals will manage risk accordingly (Chapman and Ward, 1997, p. 36).

The key goals of this volume are to identify and to promote alternative ways in which psychology might be applied to inform and improve criminal justice systems. In doing so the authors have not adopted a strict or exclusive notion of 'psychology' but, rather, they have recognized it as one of the behavioural sciences. However, there has also been an, implicit, tendency to adopt an individualistic focus. In one sense that is unsurprising since criminal justice systems are, overwhelmingly, concerned with issues relating to individuals, for example their capacity, criminality, intentions and punishment. But individuals live, work and play in groups, communities, organizations. It is, at least, artificial to ignore or to underplay the significance of social, cultural and other factors on our individual behaviour and organizations can constitute legal entities. Corporations, for example, are 'people' in legal terms; they have 'births,' can 'die,' although they merge rather than marry. As well as being able to own property and make contracts, and so on, in their corporate capacity, they can also be sued and – to a limited extent – be prosecuted. Many other organizations, public, private and voluntary, such as police forces, hospital trusts, prisons and voluntary bodies, are in a similar position, whether for profit or not.

Analysing individuals' liability, criminal and civil, is, of course, regularly appropriate. The surgeon was more concerned with flirting with a colleague than watching where the scalpel was going. However, it will, regularly, be equally or more important to consider colleagues' and others' contributions. The surgeon may be the most important person – other

Applying Psychology to Criminal Justice. Edited by David Carson, Rebecca Milne, Francis Pakes, Karen Shalev and Andrea Shawyer. © 2007 John Wiley & Sons, Ltd

than the patient – in the operating theatre, but they rely on a team effort which may, occasionally, be lacking. Actually, the surgeon will often not be the most important person since the anaesthetist is regarded as in charge of the patient although the surgeon is responsible for the treatment. In such cases it may be appropriate, although regularly impractical, to sue or prosecute every member of the team and there is a stage where it becomes improper for individual team members to follow any leaders' instructions. Team members need to think both as, or for, the group as well as themselves. At some stage it becomes more appropriate to analyse the successes, and failures, in terms of the team, the group, the organization, as an entity. The causes of success or failure will regularly be attributable, in whole or part, to the organizational context within which the individuals work.

A surgical team may have, over time, consistently poorer success rates than others, and these may not be explained by, for example a more difficult case load. For example, the success rate for paediatric cardiac surgery may have been lower, at one hospital or by one team, than at comparable hospitals, without review by the team or intervention by appropriate management teams (e.g. Kennedy, 2001). We can continue to analyse the problems in ever broader contexts. For example, the UK's (at least) medical negligence 'crisis' can, substantially, be seen in terms of the National Health Service's failure to ensure the adoption of a learning paradigm (Chief Medical Officer, 2000). Researchers, who have acted on this analysis, include psychologists such as James Reason (1990, 1997).

Decisions, and other behaviour, can be analysed in terms of what the individuals, who were involved, did. That will often be an inadequate, and thereby unfair, analysis. The role and influence of the organization will often be as or more significant a factor. Indeed, it is suggested that 'system' and 'organizational' factors are – correctly and increasingly – being identified as causes of harm. Inquiries after incidents which have attracted considerable public and media attention appear, increasingly, to identify system and/or organizational failures (e.g. the inquiry into the death of Victoria Climbie (Laming, 2003; Johnson and Petrie, 2004)). Several researchers (e.g. Borodzicz, 2005; Turner, 1978; Toft and Reynolds, 1994) have suggested that accidents are a normal by-product of systems and that disaster can arise from failures to identify failings and to design appropriate responses.

This chapter will focus on organizational, and systemic, contributions to crime and other criminal justice issues. It will seek to identify the distinctive features of systems and principal theories as to why organizational failures occur. It will identify legal problems in making organizations responsible for what would otherwise be their crimes. At the time of writing, the British Parliament is considering the Government's *Corporate Manslaughter and Corporate Homicide Bill*. This provides a neat example and focal point both for discussing the problems and alternative approaches to tackling these problems. Despite extensive consultation (Secretary of State for the Home Department, 2006; Monbiot, 2005) many regard the proposals as inadequate. For example, an expert group proposed a significantly different approach for Scotland, reflecting laws in the Australian Capital Territory. However, it has been decided that, as the devolved government in Scotland lacks legislative competence in this area, the new law will apply throughout the UK. The chapter will then consider the opportunities for applying this psychological knowledge and behavioural science to issues in criminal responsibility and justice. The chapter should help to identify some of the things which lawyers, and other investigators, could take into account when considering whether to take criminal proceedings against an organization, or its senior managers. As the prospect of that happening ought to galvanize managers into action, I hope this chapter will have a preventive value.

INDIVIDUALS V. ORGANIZATIONS

This section will make the case for distinguishing and emphasizing the role of systems and organizations against that of the individuals within them. It will identify some key ways in which organizations and systems are significantly independent of the individuals that make them up, as causes of accidents of different degrees of severity. That will emphasize the importance of considering organizational responsibilities for accidents and disasters. The following section will then summarize the legal liability for organizations, civil and criminal. That section will, in particular, highlight how difficult it is – or has been – to make major organizations criminally liable. That contrast, between the importance of organizations as causes of harm and yet the difficulty in making them criminally liable, will be used to highlight the importance of the call for fresh applications of behavioural science to criminal justice, in the rest of the chapter.

Reason, an international authority on the psychology and causation of organizational accidents (1990, 1997), emphasizes system, over individual, causes. He distinguishes the 'person' and the 'system' approaches (Reason, 2000). Those who adopt the 'person' approach analyse individuals, and their attributes (or lack thereof), as the causes of harm. Interventions are focused on reducing human variations from norms, or normal conduct.

> Followers of this approach tend to treat errors as moral issues, assuming that bad things happen to bad people – what psychologists have called the just world hypothesis. [Reason here cites Lerner, 1970.]
>
> ...
>
> People are viewed as free agents capable of choosing between safe and unsafe modes of behaviour. If something goes wrong, it seems obvious that an individual (or group of individuals) must have been responsible. Seeking as far as possible to uncouple a person's safe acts from any institutional responsibility is clearly in the interests of managers. It is also legally more convenient, at least in Britain. (p. 768)

This mirrors many attitudes, particularly of those trained in the law, towards crime. The individual offender had, and took, a choice. Institutional factors such as poor housing, upbringing, schooling, and so on, however predictive, are ignored, as legally relevant causative factors and relegated, at best, to matters for mention in mitigation after guilt has been determined. Legal analyses and assumptions regularly ignore the social determinism of crime.

For Reason, individual failure is normal behaviour (even by the best workers), and it should be expected and anticipated in well-managed organizations. In the system approach errors are the consequences of 'latent conditions' as well as 'active failures' committed by individuals (2000). He developed a Swiss cheese model of organizational accidents. The slices of cheese represent the barriers, the procedures, the safeguards and policies designed to prevent accidents occurring. Being Swiss cheese they have holes. When the holes, in a sequence of barriers or defences, are aligned it allows errors to get through. Some of these will not be caught by individual intervention at the end of the process. The holes, 'latent conditions' or 'resident pathogens', result from the work of those who designed, built, manage and maintain the system, both physical and procedural. They can also include insufficient or inappropriate resources. They can lie dormant, for many years, until particular conditions create a problem. Many potential accidents, due to these latent defects, will be prevented by the intervention of human actors at late stages.

Key and seemingly common, latent conditions include how the organization learns from, and communicates about, experience (Edmonson, 2004). For example, Tucker and Edmondson found that, despite hospitals paying greater attention to health care accidents, including system causes, 86 % of process failures were 'problems'. (Process failures were identified as averaging one per hour per nurse.) For them, 'problems' were disruptions in a healthcare worker's ability to act because something or someone was unavailable at the time, place, or in the quantity or quality necessary. In other words, the system designed to ensure integrated working, particularly prevalent and important in health care, failed. 'Errors' were defined by them as unnecessary or incorrect acts, which could have been avoided if information had been properly distributed in advance (Edmonson, 2004). They found that most 'errors' were caught and avoided before harm occurred. Whilst workers were aware of 'problems,' which should not be surprising given that they involve the multitude of frustrations which stymie smooth professional working, they were unaware of, and failed to learn from, their 'errors'. These distinctions will be highlighted, below, with regard to the law of negligence.

For Reason, the probability of an unsafe act being committed is a function of the current condition of the individuals involved, the context and the potential for error involved with the act (2004). He suggests that humans are very good at intuitive ordinal ratings of situations and could be further trained to identify potential errors. He cites a large-scale observational study of 21 surgery teams (de Leval, Carthey, Wright, Farewell and Reason, 2000). Errors and problems were relatively commonplace, on average seven for each procedure. The best teams were not those that had the least errors and problems but rather those which were most successful in compensating for them (Reason, 2004). So it might be more appropriate to consider, at least in health care and similar working environments), not just what caused the latent conditions to merge with more immediate problems and issues, but how individuals were unable to stop harm occurring. As we will see, legal liability invariably focuses on commission rather than omissions.

The studies cited above have identified how errors usually associated with, or implicating, individuals with causation and blame, can equally be understood as having organizational causes. The same point can be made with regard to the culture of the organization. Westrum, a sociologist in the USA, has identified three types of organizational culture, based on how they respond to problems and opportunities (2004). He identifies three typical patterns.

> The first is a preoccupation with personal power, needs, and glory. The second is a preoccupation with rules, positions and departmental turf. The third is a concentration on the mission itself, as opposed to a concentration on persons or positions. I call these three, respectively, pathological, bureaucratic and generative. (Edmondson, 2003, p. ii23)

Westrum relates this typology, in particular, to how information is shared and distributed around the organization. He links this to the leadership style adopted in the organization. That may be very appropriate in relation to industry, the military and the private sector, where hierarchies are manifest and regularly reinforced. Leadership in health care (Carroll and Quijada, 2004), and, it is suggested, human services such as social work and police or forensic services, is more diffuse with managers regularly not having – or not properly having – control over professionals with specialist knowledge and/or responsibilities (such as legal powers to detain certain individuals). Nevertheless, the emphasis on information exchange is important given the seeming frequency with which communication problems are cited by inquiries into accidents (e.g. Laming, 2003). Through a sequence of cases studies, Westrum associates organizational cultures with prowess in safety. The better the flow of information the better the safety record is likely to be.

> [B]y changing the culture, virtually everything can change – trust, openness, confidence, and even competence. A generative culture will make the best use of its assets, a pathological one will not. (Westrum, 2004, ii26)

ORGANIZATIONAL LIABILITY AND RESPONSIBILITY

Individual, Vicarious and Direct Liability

It is commonplace for organizations to be sued in the civil courts. However, this is invariably because they are held to be vicariously liable for the negligence of their employees. For example, a worker behaves negligently causing a colleague to be injured. The employers will be responsible for compensating the injured person. This is a consequence of their vicarious, not their 'individual', liability. To decide whether there was any negligence, the court will investigate the behaviour of the employee(s) who caused the harm. Their blame will be analysed. They could examine the quality of a manager's supervision of the employees, which would be another example of analysing individual responsibility, but the claimant only needs to show that one employee was negligent. That is enough to make their employer liable. Employers are liable, vicariously, because they are responsible for any negligence of their employees that is sufficiently related (which is interpreted quite widely) to what they were employed to do (Rogers, 2006). They are not liable because of *their* negligence but because of that of their employee. They are liable because, if they had not employed that or indeed any other person to do that job, the harm would not have occurred. If what the worker did was not sufficiently related to their job (and breach of some work instructions, and some other forms of misconduct as well as negligence is regularly regarded as sufficiently related), then the harm would not be due to the fact of employment. An employee might, for example, take too long over a work break, and might play a prank on a colleague who gets injured. The employer is likely to be held legally responsible because the harm would not have occurred but for the fact that the victim and perpetrator were employed in their jobs. The employer might have been very careful and conscientious (i.e. not negligent) in the way that rules about breaks and playing pranks were enforced. With vicarious liability, however, it is the fact of employment that creates the opportunities for harm to occur, rather than the ways in which the employers behave, that matters.

Employers, unlike most employees, have the funds or insurance to meet compensation claims. (Note that the amount of compensation awarded is related to the amount of harm caused, not to the degree of negligence.) As they can be made liable, through the vicarious liability rules, there is little or no practical need to examine the employers' liability for organizational or systemic negligence. *Bull* v. *Devon Area Health Authority* ((1989) 22 BMLR 79) was a rare case where none of those immediately involved in the delayed delivery of a baby, leading to brain damage, was negligent. Thus, it was necessary to examine the contribution of the organization. Perhaps, for example a particular organization has very poor working practices creating – at least in retrospect – a 'disaster waiting to happen'. Why should anyone, injured as a consequence of the disaster which duly occurs, spend time and effort on analysing organizational contributions to the harm when they are almost certainly going to be able to identify an individual as having been negligent? All they need to do is to demonstrate, on a balance of probabilities, that an individual was negligent, and then wait for the employers to pay compensation because they are vicariously liable. If, as in the *Bull* case, none of the individuals directly involved in the direct causation of the incident behaved negligently, it will be necessary to consider whether the employers are liable 'directly'. Yet this term adds little. Instead of focusing on the doctors and midwives it can be placed – 'directly' – on those who designed the service. In that case, it was readily foreseeable that if it would not be possible to get a second qualified obstetrician to the maternity service's delivery rooms for over 20 minutes, then harm would occur. Instead of focusing on whether a responsible body of obstetricians would, or would not do whatever, the question becomes (although the court did not investigate the factual question) whether responsible planners of maternity services would design such a service, and whether responsible managers would continue to operate it. The focus is still not on the organization as an entity, its values, culture and so on.

Corporate Criminal Liability

Whilst criminal courts can, and do, order compensation, their goals have much more to do with marking disapproval and organizing punishment. That creates immediate, major, problems for corporate criminal responsibility. For example, who should be punished and how? Individual human-beings can be executed (the barbaric practice continues in several countries), imprisoned, fined, made to undertake community work, required to attend for treatment and undertake learning programmes. The same can be said for individual directors, managers, workers, investors. The corporate entity, or organization itself, however, cannot be imprisoned, and although it could be made bankrupt and dissolved, it would not be too difficult for another organization to replace it with similar objectives, structures, values and directors, who have not been debarred from acting as such. Corporations can also be fined and required to sponsor public works and to amend their structures and practices. But who 'feels the pain'? If organizations can pay compensation awards they can also pay fines, which will regularly be less burdensome. They ought, as a normal business practice, to have insurance policies in place to meet compensation claims. What is the effective difference, to the organization, between a compensation award, a fine, or a requirement to subsidize a public activity? If a fine is substantial it is liable to endanger the business, so putting the employees at risk of unemployment, and the investors at risk of financial loss. Insurance premiums are a predictable business expense. Given that we are assuming that it is the organization which is at fault, then its employees – who may become unemployed – are blameless. The investors, for whose benefit private companies are run, will often be inanimate organizations themselves, for example pension companies. They might argue, with the employees, that it is unfair to punish them because they were not in effective, day-to-day, control of the organization and so could not have prevented the crime being committed. That may, sometimes, be true. So, even if it is possible to identify the organization as a separate entity from the people who make it up, work for it, finance it, and so on there are major difficulties in finding ways of punishing it. If you cannot punish it, is there any point in holding it criminally responsible? Would it not be more effective to focus on the senior, controlling people in the organization who, even if they did not directly commission harm, ought to have worked harder to ensure it did not occur.

A basic ingredient, of criminal liability, is *mens rea*. This is regularly interpreted as 'guilty mind', connoting active cognitive states such as paying attention to an issue or intending an outcome. In law, however, *mens rea* also covers normative descriptions of behaviour such as negligence and carelessness. This has immediate problems for corporate liability. It is easy to imagine an organization being negligent or careless, because we would be examining its behaviour and the consequences. It is much more difficult to conceive of it as having active cognitive states. These are known to lawyers as subjective *mens rea* because they relate to a particular individual's actual state of thinking, such as 'intending,' 'foreseeing,' 'planning', and so on. We can easily imagine a director or senior manager deliberately (i.e. subjectively) taking a risk, say to maximize profits despite being aware of consequential risks of injury to consumers or others, but we cannot, similarly, speak of the organization 'intending,' foreseeing' or 'planning.'

Organizations could be made criminally liable, vicariously, for the acts of their employees. As described above, the civil courts accept this. But the common law has long articulated a principle that criminal liability should be personal (e.g. Reed and Seago, 2002). The justification for punishment is that the person punished behaved badly, not just that 'he' or 'she' employed someone who behaved badly. (The person who instructs, helps or advises another to commit a crime is personally blameworthy for those acts, not vicariously.) So the person in charge of a prison was not criminally responsible for a prisoner's death through neglect, as he was unaware of the state of the prison (*Higgins,* (1730) 2 Strange 883). That argument can be limited to crimes with subjective *mens rea*, which are the ones requiring an active cognitive state. Whatever our immediate outrage that a prison governor was ignorant of the state of their prison (i.e. lacked a subjective state of mind), nobody should be found guilty of a crime which requires actual knowledge if ignorant. The governor could not 'knowingly' manage a rotten prison if he (subjectively) did not 'know' about its state. He simply would not fit the requirements for that offence. In addition, he would not know about the dangerous state of the prison just because his deputies knew. Of course, it may well be that they *ought* to have known, that their ignorance (objectively assessed) was culpable and deserving of punishment. If there is a crime where that objective state of *mens rea* would suffice then they should, and would, be liable for that offence – but as an individual rather than vicariously.

Vicarious criminal liability is recognized in some circumstances. Modern statutes can create, or judges can imply vicarious liability where the object of the legislation is to ensure high standards of supervision (Reed and Seago, 2002). Such statutes can also impose strict liability. That is where a crime is committed even though the person committing it had no *mens rea* whatsoever, subjective or objective. For example, a strict liability crime could involve selling certain products to children, irrespective of their apparent age. If, that is the crime, and the statute is written in such strict terms that it does not matter how careful the shop assistants were to avoid committing the crime, it would be inappropriate for them to be prosecuted and not the organization running, directing or owning it. Vicarious liability can also be recognized where delegation applies. For example, those who are licensed to run public houses, and other places where alcohol is sold, are obliged to follow certain rules, such as not serving drunks and children. However, they are entitled to a holiday, so they will delegate their responsibilities. It would be inappropriate for such licence holders always to escape responsibility by simply answering that they never had any *mens rea*, because they always delegated their responsibilities to their staff.

The courts have also recognized organizational, or corporate, liability in a few cases where an exceptionally senior person in the management can be shown to have had *mens rea*. The organization is criminally liable because, it can be shown, a person with the prescribed subjective *mens rea* for the offence (e.g. 'intention' or 'knowledge'), was so senior that he was or had a 'directing mind and will' of the organization (*H.L. Bolton (Engineering) Co. Ltd.* v. *T.J. Graham & Sons Ltd,* [1957] 1 QB 159 at 172). However, this is a very narrow test. For example, the European sales manager of Dunlop (Aviation) Ltd was insufficiently senior for that organization to be made criminally liable (*Redfern,* [1993] Crim L.R. 43).

The Herald of Free Enterprise was a ferry sailing between Britain and The Netherlands, but it capsized, in 1987, as it began a voyage from Zeebrugge. The bow doors had been left open – the responsible person was asleep – and the water poured in. One hundred and ninety-two people were killed. Mr Justice Sheen led an inquiry and concluded that the operational integrity of the company was rotten to the core.

> At first sight the faults which led to this disaster were the ... errors of omission on the part of the Master, the Chief Officer and the assistant bosun ... But a full investigation into the circumstances of the disaster leads inexorably to the conclusion that the underlying or ordinal faults lay higher up in the Company ... From top to bottom the body corporate was infected with the disease of sloppiness. (Sheen, 1987)

Nevertheless, the company escaped criminal liability (*P & O European Ferries (Dover) Ltd.* (1991) 93 Cr. App.R. 72). It could not be shown that a 'directing mind', at a sufficiently senior level in the organization, was actually aware of the shoddy practices. That case can be contrasted with *Kite and OLL Ltd* (unreported, 1994). Both the managing director and the company were found guilty of manslaughter. Four children drowned on a trip that should not have taken place. It was a very small firm, where the managing director was involved in all aspects of the work and was, plainly, the 'directing mind'.

The problems, of making a corporate entity criminally responsible for the harm it causes, are formidable. It appears tempting to give up the attempt and to rely on alternative strategies. Given that the law is looking for 'directing minds' who have to be individuals, would it not be more appropriate to just concentrate on making individuals liable? The requirements for *mens rea* could be restated so as to focus on behavioural criteria, for example on how badly the managers and owners were behaving rather than on anyone's active cognitive states such as 'knowing.' Or alternative legislative strategies could be utilized. For example, in England and Wales, the Health and Safety Executive (H&SE) has powers to prosecute organizations for poor safety standards, such as under the *Health and Safety at Work Act 1974.* As Sullivan (2001) emphasizes, this approach goes straight to the heart of the matter and asks whether there a safe system of work in place. The focus, of the legislation is not on the drama, or the degree of the outcome, but on the quality of the management. Indeed, should we focus on the outcome when the problem is the behaviour?

Why do we not seek corporate criminal liability for personal injuries (and then diseases and illnesses)? A partial answer could be that we should have a separate source of laws, and discrete arrangements for their enforcement, from those which specialist organizations, like the H&SE, are created to enforce. They are entitled to take their own views on the best ways of improving industrial safety, generally. They are entitled to prefer to work with industry, to cajole them and to encourage improvements and compliance indirectly, rather than to use the law as their first and principal resort. Fear of litigation, for example could encourage some employers into not keeping proper records. The Canadian Supreme Court has recognized the special feature of regulatory offences as being directed at prevention rather than at punishment (*R.* v *Wholesale Travel Group Inc* [1991] 3 SCR 154). Nevertheless, organizations are much more powerful than individuals; they kill and maim many more people than the individuals whose cases clog our courts and criminal justice systems. Their rationale, and legal duty (in company law terms), is to maximize profits. Even if more modern management philosophies are adopted, and the beneficiaries of a for-profit company are seen as including their employees, they must seek to maximize profit and minimize costs if they are to continue in existence. A corporation, faced with a risk, is duty bound to value – within limits – the maximization of their profits. There is, surely, a major role for the criminal law in articulating and enforcing those limits.

The Corporate Manslaughter and Corporate Homicide Bill

The debate, about how the criminal law on corporate liability for homicide ought to develop, is quite neatly exemplified by the Bill before the UK parliament, at the time of writing. The Labour Government had been promising a new law for several years when, in 2005, it published a consultation paper (Home Office, 2005). It recognized that the requirement to identify a 'directing mind' had led, since 1992, to only 34 prosecutions for work-related manslaughter and only six convictions of – small – corporations (Home Office, 2005, para. 9). It departed from the recommendations of its Law Commission (1996), which would have focused on management failures and the organization's responsibilities for the health and safety of employees and the public, to concentrate upon the concept of gross negligence. That is already, a basis for holding individuals and corporations liable for manslaughter in the law of England and Wales. In *Adomako* ([1995] 1 A.C.171), Lord MacKay decided, for the House of Lords:

> The essence of the matter which is supremely a jury question is whether having regard to the risk of death involved, the conduct of the defendant was so bad in all the circumstances as to amount in their judgement to a criminal act or omission ... (p. 187).

The problems are (1) that the identification principle makes it difficult to apply that law to organizations and (2) the test is exceptionally vague and gives the jury enormous discretion with which to apply their prejudices. It is submitted that, in such cases, juries are particularly likely to be affected by the appearance and demeanour of the defendant whilst in custody in court and in the witness box. Some people are more skilled at looking, whether they actually are or not, more ashamed and apologetic than others.

Under the original proposals corporations could be liable for manslaughter if there was a management failure at senior levels. That, however, would replace problems in identifying 'directing minds' with problems in identifying 'senior' managers of 'substantial' parts of the organization (see the difficulties and vagueness of such a test in paras. 25–30). Only gross failings that fell far below the management standards to be expected, would suffice.

The Home Office (2005) paper noted that separate consultation would take place in Scotland and Northern Ireland, which have different legal systems. The Scottish Executive decided to appoint an expert group, including representatives from managers' and employee organizations and academics. Their, majority, proposals differed significantly from the approach proposed for England and Wales (Scottish Executive, 2005). The Group took evidence from a number of people and organizations and considered developments in a range of countries, particularly Australia and Canada, although they noted that there was no empirical data on the effectiveness of recent legislative changes. They noted that a charge of culpable homicide (the different terminology recognizes differences in the sources of Scots Law), had been made against the major gas supply company Transco, but had failed (*Transco PLC* v. *HMA*, 2004 SCCR 1). Scots law also has problems with the identification of a controlling mind (paras. 2.2–2.7). Several argued that, since Transco had been fined £15 million under provisions of the *Health and Safety Act 1974*, there was no need for a separate corporate culpable homicide offence, especially as a fine would be the likely punishment for such an offence. The majority, of the Expert Group, disagreed.

Whilst they recognized that it was very desirable that the law, on corporate criminal responsibility for deaths, should be the same throughout the UK, a majority of the Scottish Expert Group so disagreed with the proposals for England and Wales that they proposed a distinctly different system. They wished to move away from a focus on what senior managers did know, or should have known, towards the existence, quality and enforcement of appropriate management practices (paras 10.1–10.6). (They cited, approvingly, the English and Welsh Law Commission's 1966 report. It also focused on management failures.) One example of a management failure could be an inappropriate 'corporate culture'. This idea is entirely missing from the proposals for England and Wales.

> Thus for an organization to have a written set of policies and regulations would not be sufficient in itself; the culture of the organization would have to be such that a proper emphasis was put on informing employees and contractors of the rules and ensuring their implementation and enforcement. If the organization either allowed a corporate culture to exist which directly encouraged, tolerated or led to practices which resulted in a death – or if it failed to take all reasonable steps to prevent such a culture existing – it would be liable. (para. 10.7)

The organization would escape liability if it could demonstrate due diligence by having policies, procedures and systems in place (para 11.1) – and presumably reasonably enforced – which could have prevented the death.

The Scottish Expert Group cited the Australian Criminal Code Act 1995 as a model. That Act provides that the criminal law applies to corporate bodies as well as, with necessary modifications, individuals (s. 12.1). The subjective *mens rea* required for a particular offence may be attributed to a corporation if it '... expressly, tacitly or impliedly authorized or permitted the commission of the offence' (s. 12.3(1)). Authorisation or permission can, *inter alia*, be demonstrated:

> (c) proving that a corporate culture existed within the body corporate that directed, encouraged, tolerated or led to noncompliance with the relevant provision; or
> (d) proving that the body corporate failed to create and maintain a corporate culture that required compliance with the relevant provision (S. 12.3.)

'Corporate culture' is defined as 'an attitude, policy, rule, course of conduct or practice existing within the body corporate generally or in the part of the body corporate in which the relevant activities takes place' (s. 12.6).

Similar debates have taken place in Canada. It also had narrow corporate manslaughter rules again caused by the requirement to identify a controlling mind (*Canadian Dredge and Dock Co. v. The Queen* ([1985] 1 S.C.R. 662). Their Law Commission recommended, in 1987 (cited in Bittle and Snider, 2006), that organizations be responsible, corporately, for the actions of any employee, as well as director, who was authorized to formulate or to implement policy and who was acting within their authority at the time. But there was little action on this proposal until a political party, not in government, proposed Bill C-284. The Bill was withdrawn, in 2002, when a Parliamentary Standing Committee decided to take evidence on the issues. It then proposed Bill C-45.

The earlier Bill would have considered failings in corporate culture but the Standing Committee was advised that the only proper, legal, approach to focus on the subjective *mens rea* of senior managers (Bittle and Snider, 2006). Corporations will be liable if senior managers departed, seriously, from what they should have done to stop employees committing the crime in question. Bittle and Snider (2006) analysed the Standing Committee's debates. They noted how issues of power were avoided. Many parliamentarians and witnesses stressed how work safety was everyone's responsibility – ignoring gross differences in power and other resources to identify and make changes. It eventually came to be perceived as a technical issue for existing legal machinery and concepts to solve.

> The deliberations of Committee members reveal a striking tendency to assume that law is a universal, objective measuring rod that delivers a formula for correcting legal ills. Discovering the 'correct' meaning of law is seen as basically a technical task, one that requires them to 'get the law right.' Therefore there is no need for Parliament to involve itself in messy human conflicts between employers and employees or to examine power and privilege – their job is to find the legal phrases consistent with precedent and existing understandings of *mens rea*. (p. 478/9)

Rather predictably, the UK's Labour Government, has at the time of writing, in its Corporate Manslaughter and Corporate Homicide Bill, opted for the more conservative approach. Scotland's independent approach was short-lived. It has been decided that Scotland is not, contrary to the original discussion paper (Home Office, 2005), competent to make laws on this subject. So the new legislation will apply across the United Kingdom with minor differences to take account of different criminal justice systems.

The Bill, at the time of writing, provides that it will be corporate manslaughter (or homicide in Scotland), if the manner in which an organization's activities are managed or organized, by senior managers, amounts to a gross breach of a relevant duty of care which causes a death. So the opportunity, seized in Australia, to tackle corporate liability across the board, not just for relatively rare and often atypical and accidental deaths, is being avoided. (However the Australian law only applies to offences against federal law, which will significantly inhibit its effects.)

Clarkson (2005), who particularly compares the Government's proposals with developments in Australia, argues that it would make much more sense, particularly if the law is to have a preventive and not just penal role, if there was also corporate criminal liability for personal injuries. The same degree of bad management could result in death, personal injury or nothing at all. The same push, which knocks someone over, could kill or simple graze them, depending on how the victim lands, on what, any pre-existing disabilities such as a thin skull, and the speed and quality of medical intervention. Quite simply there is no necessary correlation between the degree of blameworthy action and the nature and degree of the outcome. However, if that were conceded would it not also follow that there should be corporate liability for workplace diseases (i.e. specifically related to the workplace rather than, e.g. colds and flu caught at work).

The reference to 'senior managers' in the draft Bill, will replicate many, if not all, of the problems involved in identifying the 'controlling mind'. Providing a definition can help. Clause 2 provides a definition which requires that the individual 'plays a significant role' in making decisions about, or actually managing, how the whole or a 'substantial part' of the organization is managed or organized. But statutory definitions can compound problems where, for example one vague expression is explained by several vague words. What, for example do 'significant', 'substantial', 'managed' and 'organized' mean? 'Organized' and 'managed', presumably, are intended to connote different things. They suggest narrower meanings than everything that a manager might do; if not why use two expressions where one would do? However detailed, definitional problems, with potential for protracted litigation and government embarrassment, are avoided by adopting the legal technique of making it a jury decision. The Bill specifies that the definition of 'duty' is a matter of law (clause 3(3)); which ensures that that remains an exclusively judicial task to determine, including making findings of fact necessary for that decision. No such provision is made for 'senior manager'. The prospect of a criminal trial jury receiving instruction on the organizational structure of an international corporation, in order to decide whether a specified individual played a 'significant role' in organizing or managing a 'substantial part' of it is – well interesting.

The reference to 'duty' is designed to limit liability. Clause 3 specifies that there will only be liability for breach of a duty of care recognized by the civil law of negligence in respect of employees, occupiers of premises, suppliers of goods and services, providers of construction or maintenance operations, using or keeping vehicles or carrying on commercial activities. That should ensure that potential victims are identifiable, thus making the consequences of increased liability more predictable – and insurable. Fines are the only punishments authorized (clause 1(5)), although the prosecution may apply for specific faults to be remedied (clause 10). In determining whether there was a 'gross breach' of the duty, which the trial judge has declared to exist, the jury must consider whether health and safety legislation was breached and, if so, how seriously and with what degree of risk of death (clause 9(2)). Whilst juries 'must' consider this evidence the secrecy of jury deliberations, particularly in the UK, would make any such law entirely unenforceable. It is specified (clause 9(3)) that the jury 'may also' consider whether there were attitudes, policies, and so on which were likely to have encouraged the breach of health and safety legislation, as well as any other matter (clause 3(4)) they think relevant.

DISCUSSION

So could, and should, psychology be applied to identifying when and how organizations might be held liable, in criminal and civil law, for organizational or systemic caused of accidents? Hopefully the brief incursion, above, to just a small part of the research on accident causation and safety was sufficient to demonstrate that psychology has much to offer. The problems have more to do with the relative absence of opportunities to do so. Victims are compensated, in the civil courts, on proof of individuals' negligence. There is no need to demonstrate that the employers or their systems were, for instance, negligently designed or maintained. Vicarious liability will, almost always, be sufficient to ensure the employers pay out the compensation without any analysis of the employers' or their managers' direct contribution through systemic failures. It is also highly unlikely that identifying their contribution would increase the compensation payable. Exemplary damages have been awarded, at least within English and Welsh law, where defendants have profited from their wrong-doing. That might be demonstrated against certain employers who calculated that paying compensation was cheaper than instituting certain safety procedures. However, the courts have tended, increasingly, to limit that heading to libel awards (Rogers, 2006).

The potential of a systems analysis for understanding how services, as well as individuals, failed a young girl is demonstrated by Lord Laming's (2003) inquiry into the death of Victoria Climbié, at the hands of her carers.

> It is deeply disturbing that during the days and months following her initial contact with Ealing Housing Department's Homeless Persons' Unit, Victoria was known to no less than two further housing authorities, four social services departments, two child protection teams of the Metropolitan Police Service (MPS), a specialist centre managed by the NSPCC, and she was admitted to two different hospitals because of suspected deliberate harm. The dreadful reality was that these services knew little or nothing more about Victoria at the end of the process than they did when she was first referred to Ealing Social Services by the Homeless Persons' Unit in April 1999. The final irony was that Haringey Social Services formally closed Victoria's case on the very day she died. The extent of the failure to protect Victoria was lamentable. (Para. 1.16)

He described a 'widespread organizational malaise' (para. 1.21). Johnson and Petrie 2004 reanalysed the Inquiry Report in terms of Reason's (1990b) five stages in the development of an accident: fallible decisions made at high levels in the organization, line management problems, the preconditions for unsafe acts, the unsafe acts and weak defences against them. They demonstrate, with considerable ease, how appropriate the analysis is to what happened in that case although the organizational and system causes were, themselves, substantially due to organizational restructuring and failures to communicate adequately between services.

Such analyses, it is submitted, might be repeated across a range of accidents. They should prove more productive than debating vague 'cultural' causes. Perhaps such analyses would have identified wrongdoing at a senior level in the *Spirit of Free Enterprise* case; it is difficult to understand how an organization, described as sloppy from top to bottom, could not satisfy Reason's criteria. Any organization should be concerned about safety. Private, for profit, organizations should be concerned about the potential costs of having to pay compensation, should be interested in reducing their insurance premiums, and should be anxious about their public image. Safety is part of business, not just an add-on desirable when it can be afforded.

We need tests that can be used by the initial investigators, such as lawyers and police officers. Psychologists, amongst others, ought to be able to provide these. Investigators need to be able to apply such analyses when and where there are suggestions of possible corporate manslaughter. Later they could call in psychologists, for richer analyses, as expert witnesses. They could, for example be encouraged to compare transactional and transformative leadership styles. Transactional leaders instruct their staff, monitor and audit performance. Transformational leaders provide direction, identify values, use encouragement.

> Senior managers who provide a vision, influence middle managers and supervisors to articulate it, a devote critical decision making to an appropriate level tended to be found to be associated with the highest safety performing business units. (Flin and Yule, 2004, p. ii49)

Whether the serious management failure is perceived as an act of commission, undertaking an inadequate safety audit, or an omission, a failure to undertake an appropriate analysis of potential systemic causes of accidents, it should be possible to use expert evidence from occupational psychologists. Of course, particularly given the clear message that accidents are normal –

> What is remarkable is not that dangerous errors happen, but that they happen so rarely. (Reason 2005, p. 60)

– it would not be sufficient, for civil or criminal liability, just to demonstrate a failure. For civil liability it would have to be such a failure as would not be acceptable to a responsible body of safety system designers and/or operation managers. For criminal liability there would have to be reckless conduct, such as a failure falling far beneath professional standards or awareness of low standards (say at a civil liability standard) but inaction to remedy them.

The status quo is not good enough. It is not enough that victims are compensated. The number of future victims ought to be reduced through prevention (Chief Medical Officer, 2000). The present position is actually harmful. Reason (2004) argues that blaming individuals is often likely to prove counter-productive. A study of Norwegian doctors (Assland and Førde, 2005), and there is no apparent reason to believe the circumstances are distinctively different elsewhere, found that one in three had been responsible for at least one serious injury to a patient. Only half those doctors felt able to criticize their colleagues even though discussion was vital for understanding and important in ensuring change. But legal systems, with major sums of money – and individuals' reputations – at stake, do not encourage openness, and thereby do not encourage learning or prevention.

Legal systems need to be seen as organizations, although there may be a problem in identifying the owners and employers, which need analysis for their systemic contributions to errors and loss.

REFERENCES

Assland, O.G. and Førde, R. (2005) Impact of feeling responsible for adverse events on doctors' personal and professional lives: The importance of being open to criticism from colleagues. *Quality and Safety in Health Care*, **14**, 13–7.

Bittle, S. and Snider, L. (2006) From manslaughter to preventable accident: Shaping corporate criminal liability. *Law & Policy*, **28** (4), 470–96.

Borodzicz, E. (2005) *Risk, Crisis & Security Management*, Wiley, Chichester.

Carroll, J.S. and Quiijada, M.A. (2004) Redirecting traditional professional values to support safety: Changing organizational culture in health care. *Quality and Safety in Health Care*, **13** (Suppl. II), ii16–21.

Chapman, C. and Ward, S. (1997) *Project Risk Management: Processes, Techniques and Insights*, Wiley, Chichester.

Chief Medical Officer (2000) *An Organization with a Memory: Report of an Expert Group on Learning from Adverse Events in the NHS Chaired by the Chief Medical Officer*, Stationery Office, London.

Clarkson, C.M.V. (2005) Corporate manslaughter: Yet more government proposals. *Criminal Law Review*, 677–89.

Criminal Code Act (1995) http://www.comlaw.gov.au/ComLaw/Legislation/ActCompilation1.nsf/0/F50A71634790BDB3CA257116001525A3/$file/CriminalCode1995_WD02_Version3.pdf. (Accessed 17 October 2006)

de Leval, M.R., Carthey, J., Wright, D.J., Farewell, V.T. and Reason, J.T. (2000) Human factors and cardiac surgery: A multicenter study. *Journal of Thoracic and Cardiovascular Surgery*, **119**, 661–72.

Edmonson, A.C. (2004) Learning from failure in health care. Frequent opporuntieis, pervasive barriers. *Quality and Safety in Health Care*, **13** (Supp. 2), ii3–9.

Flin, R. and Yule, S. (2004) Leadership for safety: Industrial experience. *Quality and Safety in Health Care*, **13** (suppl. II), ii45–51.

Home Office (2005) *Corporate Manslaughter: The Government's Draft Bill for Reform*, Home Office, London.

Johnson, S. and Petrie, S. (2004) Child protection and risk-management: The death of Victoria Climbie. *Journal of Social Policy*, **33** (2), 179–202.

Kennedy, I. (2001) *Learning from Bristol: The Report of the Public Inquiry into children's Heart Surgery at the Bristol Royal Infirmary1984–1995*, HMSO, London.

Laming, Lord (2003) *The Victoria Climbié Inquiry*, HMSO, London (CM 5730).

Law Commission (1996) *Legislating the Criminal Code: Involuntary Manslaughter*, Law Commission, London (Law Com No 237).

Lerner, M.J. (1970) The desire for justice and reactions to victims, in *Altruism and Helping Behavior* (eds J. McCauley and L. Berkowitz), Academic Press, New York.

Monbiot, G. (2005) The business of killing. The Guardian, March 29th. http://www.monbiot.com/archives/2005/03/29/the-business-of-killing/ (Accessed 30 January 2007).

Reason, J. (1990a) *Human Error*, Cambridge University Press, Cambridge.

Reason, J. (1990b), The contribution of latent human failures to the breakdown of complex systems, in (eds D.E. Broadbent, A. Baddeley and J.T. Reason), *Human Factors in Hazardous Situations*, Oxford University Press, London, pp. 27–36.

Reason, J. (1997) *Managing the Risks of Organizational Accidents*, Ashgate, Aldershot.

Reason, J. (2000) Human error: Models and management. *British Medical Journal*, **320**, 768–70.

Reason, J. (2004) Beyond the organizational accident: The need for "error wisdom" on the frontline. *Quality and Safety in Health Care*, **13** (Suppl. 2), ii28–33.

Reason, J. (2005) Safety in the operating theatre – Part 2: Human error and organizational failure. *Quality and Safety in Health Care*, **14**, 56–61.

Reed, A. and Seago, P. (2002) *Criminal Law*, Sweet & Maxwell, London.

Rogers, W.V.H. (2006) *Winfield & Jolowicz on Tort*, 17th edn, Thomson Sweet & Maxwell, London.

Scottish Executive (2005) *Corporate Homicide: Expert Group Report*, Scottish Executive, Edinburgh.

Secretary of State for the Home Department (2006) *Draft Corporate Manslaughter Bill: The Government Reply to the First Joint Report from the Home Affairs and Work and Pensions Committees Session 2005–06*, HMSO, London.

Sheen, Mr Justice (1987) *MV Herald of Free Enterprise. Report of Court No 8074 Formal Investigation*, Department of Transport, London.

Sullivan, G.R. (2001) Corporate killing: Some government proposals. *Criminal Law Review*, **31**, 31–9.

Toft, B. and Reynolds, S. (1994) *Learning from Disasters: A Management Approach*, Butterworth-Heinemann, Oxford.

Turner, B. (1978) *Man-Made Disasters*, Wykeham, London.

Westrum, R. (2004) A typology of organizational cultures. *Quality, Safety and Health Care*, **13** (Suppl. ii), ii22–27.

CHAPTER 18

Applying Key Civil Law Concepts

David Carson, Becky Milne, Francis Pakes,
Karen Shalev and Andrea Shawyer

University of Portsmouth

We argued, in Chapter 1, that psychology could and should be applied to law, to legal practice and to the criminal justice legal system, in a much wider range of ways than has been the case to date. We believe, and hope readers agree, that our authors have demonstrated how this is both possible and desirable. We, and they, have in the process offered many compelling examples. In this concluding chapter we wish to argue that psychologists could, and should, address some legal concepts directly. We will address two examples, contract and negligence.

It might, immediately, be objected that these are civil law concepts and this book is concerned with the criminal justice system. However, that would involve assuming that there both is, and should be, a clear distinctive difference between what is 'civil' and what is 'criminal.' The distinction is, in reality, imprecise. For example, what is the essential difference between imposing a fine and awarding compensation? The fine will go to the state, the compensation to the victim, but in terms of the experience for the defendant (the same term is used in both civil and criminal litigation), especially as the amount of compensation awarded will regularly be larger than a fine would be, is there a significant difference? There is an extensive overlap with many civil wrongs, known as torts by lawyers in common law countries, also being crimes. We may know that A injured B, but that does not tell us whether the incident will be treated, if at all, as a crime, as a civil wrong or both. A may be convicted of causing grievous bodily harm to B but that does not stop B from suing A for compensation for those injuries. Whilst A will not have the advantage of the police collecting evidence and the state prosecution services presenting it to a criminal court, they will only have to prove their case on the civil law standard of the balance of the probabilities rather than the criminal standard of beyond reasonable doubt. This may have a particular appeal in cases of rape and sexual assault where rates of successful prosecution are exceptionally low (Kelly, 2002; Westmarland, 2004; Her Majesty's Inspectorate of Constabulary and Her Majesty's Crown Prosecution Service Inspectorate, 2002). The alleged victims would only have to prove their case on a balance of probabilities. Whilst success, in the civil courts, would not lead to the defendant

---

Applying Psychology to Criminal Justice. Edited by David Carson, Rebecca Milne, Francis Pakes, Karen Shalev and Andrea Shawyer. © 2007 John Wiley & Sons, Ltd

being imprisoned, the victims would receive some compensation (if the defendant could afford to pay it), and there would be a public declaration that they were telling the truth.

Indeed, it might be considered more appropriate to tackle certain problems in the civil rather than criminal courts. For example, the British government has created special court procedures to tackle 'antisocial' behaviour. All the associations are with criminal law but the civil law standard of proof makes it much easier for the police to prove claims and get orders. In the last resort decisions must be made and cases must be brought in either the civil or the criminal courts. Hence, issues have to be constructed to fit within with the available forms of proceedings. However, it will often be appropriate to think of a continuum, rather than dichotomy, between civil and criminal law. The growth of interest in restorative justice (e.g. Hoyle and Young, 2002; Johnstone and van Ness, 2006), including problem-solving courts (e.g. Winick and Wexler, 2003), is, substantially, a reflection of growing dissatisfaction with the narrow retributive goals and limited effectiveness of traditional criminal processes. Whilst retribution is as regularly associated with criminal processes, as restoration or reparation is with civil trials, we would suggest that restorative justice should not be limited to considerations after guilt is admitted or declared. Rather, it should be allowed to influence pretrial proceedings and even substantive criminal law. However, the goals for this chapter are more modest and relate to indicating the relevance of a few primarily civil law concepts, negligence and contract. The, necessarily, brief descriptions refer to the law in England and Wales. However, similar concepts can be found in the law of many other countries, particularly within the common law tradition, which includes most North American and many Commonwealth countries. Differences of detail, between countries, would not invalidate the main points being made.

'NEGLIGENCE': TOWARDS A PSYCHOLOGY OF REASONABLE BEHAVIOUR

Negligence: The Law

Personal injuries at work, on the road, as a consequence of professional practice, and in many other circumstances may be litigated, in the civil courts, under the rubric of the law of negligence. In practical terms the law of negligence is, by far, the most important area of the law of tort (Rogers, 2006). It is worth noting that the law of negligence was only 'invented' in the early twentieth century (*Donoghue* v. *Stephenson,* [1932] A.C 502). It was a reaction to the inadequacies of the pre-existing laws covering intentional and nonintentional injuries, such as trespass (Rogers, 2006). For a claimant to win they would have to satisfy the trial court – on a balance of probabilities as this is a civil claim – that five conditions have been satisfied. (The idea of five conditions, or tests, is an explanatory device. Just because all judges and textbooks do not use it, some conflate the last two tests, does not make it wrong.)

1. The victim, known as the claimant in England and Wales, must have been owed a *duty of care* by the person being sued, known as the defendant.
2. The defendant must be shown to have *breached* that duty of care.
3. That breach must have *caused* injuries to the claimant.
4. Those injuries must be of a nature which the courts *recognize for compensation* purposes.
5. The *injuries* must have occurred in a manner that was *reasonably foreseeable*.

All five of these requirements must be satisfied for there to be liability in the law of negligence. To avoid problems note that the word 'negligence' can be used in two distinctly different ways. When we speak or write of the 'law of negligence' (or of 'negligence' when we mean the 'law of negligence'), we are (1) using 'negligence' as a noun and (2) thereby referring to all five tests. However, when we refer to behaviour, to decisions and so on as being 'negligent' we are (1) using the word as an adjective or adverb and (2) only referring to one of the five tests stated above, the second. Confusion can and does arise because 'negligence' can be used to refer to a quality of behaviour as well as to a legal category where the quality of behaviour is only one of five tests. It is, in law, perfectly possible to make a negligent decision but not be liable for negligence.

A second confusion often arises when the first two, sometimes three, tests, which emphasize 'duty of care', are wrongly conflated. Take an easy example. We are going to be operated on by a surgeon. The surgeon owes us a duty of care; we know that surgeons get sued in the courts. Imagine something goes wrong during the operation and we are injured. He or she owed us a duty of care. Can we sue the surgeon for negligence? Yes, in terms of entitlement to do so; but will we succeed? Possibly; courts and lawyers cannot answer that question without much more information. Having a duty of care does not decide the issue. That is only the first test. The surgeon must also have broken the standard of care which attaches to that duty. Just because harm results it does not follow, even in the highly regulated circumstances of an operating theatre that it was due to the surgeon doing something wrong, or failing to do something that needed doing. That may appear obvious, here. However, it is commonplace, in practice, for people to emphasize, and to allow their behaviour and decisions to be affected by, the mere existence of a duty of care. That is never enough to establish legal liability. Practitioners need to emphasize the standard, as well as the duty, of care.

Consider two possible cases. In the first, a car driver is tired and gets distracted by hoardings at the side of the road (Susan Dennison uses the same example, for different purposes, in Chapter 8). As a consequence he fails to register a bend in the road and drives onto the adjoining pavement hitting and breaking the leg of a pedestrian. In the second case, a psychologist is asked to assess the dangerousness of a patient on a ward where she works. Unfortunately she has failed to keep up to date with the relevant literature and fails to seek information from relevant nurses. This leads her to make a risk assessment which, in due course, allows the patient access to sharp objects which the patient uses to injure a nurse and then to commit suicide. If lawyers are approached then, in both cases, they will work through the five tests. (Note that they may also have to consider the criminal law; the driver is likely to have broken criminal laws relating to quality of driving and the psychologist may be considered in relation to manslaughter laws (Ormerod, 2005).) They will decide that both defendants, the driver and the psychologist, owed their victims a duty of care. However, that is not an automatic finding. 'Duty of care' has a restricted legal meaning. It is commonplace to hear nonlawyers speaking of someone being owed a duty of care, but that is often wrong, as a statement of law, since they are only referring, whether they realize it or not, to a moral or other perceived duty.

Only certain relationships create a legal duty of care. (The criminal law also uses the concept of 'duty of care', particularly to designate when a defendant will be liable for a failure, an omission, to act to help the victim, such as a parent to his or her child (Ormerod, 2005). However, we are not referring to that kind of 'duty of care' here.) These duty relationships, for the law of negligence, have been developed by judges in the light of previous decisions. Another difference between the existence of duty of care (test 1 above), and its breach (test 2 above), is that the former is a question of law whilst the latter is an issue of fact. Using the case law that has developed, it is clear enough for lawyers to know (i.e. to predict to a sufficiently high degree of likelihood) that, in the examples outlined above, the driver owed a duty of care to the pedestrian and the psychologist both to the patient and to the coworker nurse (see Rogers, 2006). However, the driver would not owe a duty of care to the pedestrian's hairdresser, who was very upset when he heard about the injuries, nor would the psychologist owe a duty to a member of the public, even though they were attacked and killed by the patient, if the facts were that he had been discharged because of the risk assessment (*Clunis v. Camden and Islington H. A.* [1998] Q.B. 978).

Negligence: The Psychology

Psychologists might help to inform, and/or make more consistent and predictable, judges' decisions about (1) when a duty of care is and is not (dichotomously), owed and (2) when the standard of care has been breached. Judges' decisions, on whether a duty of care should exist are, in the final analysis, rationalized in terms of public policy. For example, in England and Wales, the judges have decided that police investigators (*Brooks v. Commissioner of Police for the Metropolis and Others* ([2005] 2 All ER 489) and statutory child protection risk decision-makers (*JD v. East Berkshire Community Health NHS Trust and Others* ([2005] 2 FLR 284), do not owe a duty of care to victims of negligently investigated crimes or child protection inquiries. Several other countries have decided that duties of care should be recognized in such circumstances (in Canada see *Jane Doe v. Metropolitan Police of Toronto,* (1998) 160 DLD (4th) 697; for France, Germany, South Africa see Hoyano, 1999; see also Markesinis *et al.*, 1999). A major part of the rationale, for the decisions of the English and Welsh courts, is that to decide otherwise would be counter-productive, for example standards would suffer as the police, and others involved, would spent too much time worrying about being sued. This is an assumption, or prediction, about human behaviour, which is made without reference to any empirical evidence. It may be justifiable, as an initial assumption, but only until such time as research is undertaken that confirms or contradicts it.

Psychologists are ideally placed to test judicial hypotheses about the consequences of recognizing duties of care in different circumstances. First there is the starting point of psychological research into decision making (see Chapter 11 by Greene and Ellis), albeit shared with other behavioural scientists. Then there are the criteria that judges take into account when considering both whether a duty of care should be recognized, and whether it has been breached. Key tests, for the existence of a duty are 'proximity' and 'foreseeability' (Rogers, 2006). Is the victim or outcome of a class or group which is so close to the actor's activities that the latter ought to owe a duty of care to the former? For example, it is clear law, it is sufficiently proximate and reasonably foreseeable, that a patient regarded as being dangerous and being treated for a mental disorder could attack and injure a nurse, or other carer, in the unit where being treated. In terms of opportunity, which explains so many injuries or losses, members of staff are more predictable as victims and as individual victims because they are known to work there. However, members of the public are not in a similar category. Mr C was discharged from a mental illness unit in London. He did not injure a member of staff but rather a member of public, Mr Z, who just happened to be in the wrong place, a station platform, at the wrong time (*Clunis* v. *Camden and Islington H. A.* [1998] Q.B. 978). Even if we assume that the discharge decisions were negligent (adjective), it did not make the professionals concerned liable to Mr Z's family, because they did not owe him a duty of care in negligence (noun). There was nothing in the relationship, between those professionals and Mr Z, which made it distinctive, which made it compelling for a duty to be recognized. It is true that if the potential victim was not a member of the hospital staff or a family member, then it would have to be a member of the public. That is perfectly predictable, especially if no other category is recognized. However, if members of the public are recognized as being a category to whom a duty of care is owed, then the effect would be to conclude that everyone is owed a duty of care. There would be no point in having a duty of care; it would be logically superfluous, as only a breach of the standard of care would have to be proved.

The requirement of a *duty* of care, in the law of negligence, is there in order to restrict the remedy to certain people in recognized relationships. Could psychology help to identify, to provide better rules and criteria for *rationalizing* the existence, or nonexistence of such relationships? When lawyers use the test of the 'foreseeability' of harm, arising in a relationship, they are not using the concept in a dichotomous, either/or sense. It is not a question of whether, 'in fact', someone could or did foresee harm. Rather it is a qualitative, and thereby to an extent, quantitative concept.

The test for whether the *standard* of care has been broken is qualitative. In cases involving, for example, accidents on the road or in factories, the qualities of the driving, supervision or regulation are the core issues. Just because injury results, it does not follow that the standard of care has been broken. The driver is not liable for injuring the person who jumped into the road in a suicide bid, providing they were driving in a manner, including speed, which was reasonable for the time and other circumstances. Negligence is, largely but not entirely, about determining what is 'reasonable.'

It is *not* being suggested that psychology should become involved in determining what is 'reasonably foreseeable'. The judges are not developing a test of what reasonable people, whomever they may be, might foresee or what most people would foresee when being reasonable, whatever that might be. However, it is suggested that they could assist the elucidation of some of the concepts and tests involved when determining whether a duty of care should be recognized. For example, if a policy objective is to encourage people to think about the consequences of their actions in certain relationships, and to penalize them (by fine or compensation) if they fail, it should be important to consider how often and how readily people can and do perceive cause and effect in such relationships. Such questions are open to empirical inquiry. Are judges right or wrong when assuming or concluding that 'reasonable' people, broadly the mean or mode, would anticipate the type of consequences in question? Are there groups of people who, or particular circumstances when, certain outcomes are particularly unlikely or likely to be predicted? Just as the behavioural sciences have demonstrated a number of ways in which we are poor at making particular kinds of decision, for example when we 'satisfice' (that is, adopt a good enough decision) rather than maximize subjective expected utility (see Chapter 12 by Heilbrun and Erickson), so might they identify and explain barriers to foresight, anticipation and accurate prediction. This would not only be relevant when determining when reasonable people do foresee consequences, but it might provide tests for identifying when foresight actually took place (which would undermine defence arguments).

It could also inform policy debates about when it is appropriate to impose, or not to impose, a duty relationship in terms of whether doing so would make a difference. If, in fact, some or all people do not foresee certain consequences, in particular circumstances, then the moral case for imposing a duty is diminished. If a person cannot foresee the harms that will (or are likely to) occur, not just refuses or fails to exercise their abilities, then any penalty will be on account of their disabilities/incapacities rather than blame for failing to do what they could. In the criminal case of *Elliott* v. *C* ([1983] 2 All ER 1005), the defendant's learning disability prevented her from realizing that pouring inflammable liquid around the wooden hut, where she had sought safety and warmth, would endanger herself as well as damage the shed. Although the meaning of 'recklessness' for the crime of criminal damage in England and Wales has since changed (*G* [2003] UKHL 50), she was convicted because the risk of damage would have been obvious to other people.

What is 'reasonable' behaviour? Whilst the concept includes a judgemental, normative, element it is also descriptive in the sense of what reasonable people would do. Jurors, both in criminal and civil courts where they are used (juries do not determine civil negligence claims in England and Wales but do in Northern Ireland, where insurance premiums are markedly higher), are regularly asked to decide whether behaviour was negligent or dangerous, and to apply the standards of reasonable people, which they are expected to represent (Dolan, 2002). The vagueness of the concepts makes prediction of the jury's, or even a judge's, decision more difficult. There is no system of precedent for decisions of fact rather than law. So a finding of fact, that K's behaviour was found to be dangerous in circumstances L, is not a precedent which can be cited to argue that, since circumstances L have recurred, the decision in K's case ought to be repeated. That is not to deny that there may be a system of 'fact precedent' where experienced lawyers predict judges' or juries' decisions, based on their memories of previous cases. A more scientific articulation of what is 'reasonable,' based on cognitive capacities, psychomotor competence and actual studies of what most people do, for example when driving, could lead to the articulation of standards of 'reasonableness'. These could reflect actual standards, rather than require judges and juries to guess or infer. Such research should make it easier for lawyers to predict outcomes and, by advising their clients, lead to the settlement of claims both earlier and on a fairer basis in that, for example, defendants would have less interest in delaying a settlement offer in order to bargain the claimant, in immediate need of compensation, down. It should also make more explicit the practical implications of policy debates about how to influence public behaviour. For example, it could make clear, to the insurance industry and/or to government, the cost benefit analysis of changing peoples', for example drivers', behaviour.

The same issues equally apply with regard to claims of professional negligence. Here the concern is not with what the reasonable person would do but, according to the fundamental decision in England and Wales, *Bolam* v. *Friern Hospital Management Committee* ([1957] 1 WLR 582), but with what a responsible body of co-professionals would have done in the circumstances of the particular case (Rogers, 2006). Would a 'responsible body' of clinical psychologists have made the same decision? 'Reasonable' has been replaced by 'responsible.' It is unnecessary to demonstrate that most members of the appropriate reference group would make the same decision, or act in the same way. The courts recognize that professional progress, in terms of developing new methods and more appropriate standards, is a product of some individuals developing new approaches and methods, not just technology, which get tested. Some stand the tests and become the new orthodoxy, at least until replaced by the next set of changes. So this test has more to do with the 'rational quality' of the decision, the scientific and professional culture surrounding such decisions. The object is that new methods or standards are not adopted without careful consideration. Adoption of new techniques or treatments in medicine, for example would be inappropriate without appropriate care, for example drug trials and debates in peer reviewed journals. However, it could be appropriate to try a new treatment, on a strictly controlled basis, before it is rolled out for use on a more general basis. The issue is whether the standards adopted are 'defensible' (*Bolitho v. City and Hackney Health Authority* [1988] AC 232).

The same decision, by the UK's highest appeal court, referred to the 'logical' quality of the decision. That may be an unfortunate choice of expression, given its association with deductive reasoning, but the object appears to have been to stress the quality of the decision-making process. That, of course, is very pertinent to psychology and the other behavioural sciences, which have identified forms and causes of poor decision-making. Could psychology contribute to a more rigorous assessment of how the standard of care is established? For example, a working practice may have been adopted by all of a profession, not just a responsible body within it. It may develop the characteristics of a rule which new entrants to the profession are reluctant to challenge. It may be thoroughly inappropriate in terms of how it was initially reached or with contemporary standards in that or cognate disciplines.

An example may help to elucidate some of the issues. However, it is emphasized that this is an example and it is not being contended that the discipline and profession concerned, general medical practitioners, are wrong to adhere to this practice. It is simply argued that behavioural scientists ought to investigate these and similar issue to discover what current standards and practices are, and to inform debates about what they ought to be in terms of their effects.

One evening, a mother phoned her general medical practitioner. She was concerned about her sick child. She had collected him from school as they had reported him to be ill. What, exactly, was said during that phone conversation was disputed at trial but it was agreed that the doctor had only used open questions. He was careful to avoid putting words or ideas into the mother's mouth or head. He did not wish to suggest symptoms, or ways of describing them, which she might adopt and repeat back to him. He did not ask whether the child had a fever, whether it was 'phlegm' or 'vomit.' The mother referred to throwing up phlegm but did not mention the higher temperature when he was at school. The doctor did know that the child had, soon after birth, had a 'shunt' fitted. This was necessary to drain off excess fluid from his brain cavity. He knew that the shunt could get blocked and that, if it did, it would be serious and require immediate attention. The doctor concluded that the boy had an upper respiratory tract infection and decided not to visit him. If he had undertaken a home visit it was accepted that (which is legally crucial for the requirement that any breach of standard must cause the loss), he would have noted that the shunt was likely to have been blocked and had the boy taken to hospital for immediate treatment. Twenty-four hours later the boy had to be taken to hospital, by ambulance, where they discovered that his shunt had become blocked. The young boy had a heart attack and experienced brain damage.

It could not have been disputed that the GP owed a duty of care to the boy. The legal question was whether he had broken the standard of care. To ascertain this issue, the trial judge, there being no civil juries for such cases in England and Wales, heard expert evidence from both the family's side and from the GP's team. *Both* of these expert witnesses agreed that a responsible body of GPs (not necessarily all) would have acted as the particular GP did in this case; they would have avoided the use of leading questions despite the potential for receiving incomplete and ambiguous information. Ordinarily that would have been enough for the court to decide in favour of the GP. All the evidence supported a finding of fact that the standard of care had not been broken; a responsible body of co-professionals would have done the same thing. However, the trial judge appeared unhappy that that should be considered an acceptable standard of care. Citing *Bolitho v. City and Hackney Health Authority* ([1988] AC 232), he decided that the standard of care agreed by the experts for both sides, that it was proper practice only to ask open questions and not to seek to clarify answers which might be vague, ambiguous or incomplete, was illogical and not defensible. So he refused to adopt it and ruled for the family.

The Court of Appeal (*Burne v. A,* [2006] EWCA Civ 24) had to overrule the trial judge's decision, although not without an appearance of regret. The judge was not entitled to go against the clear finding of fact, agreed by both experts, that the GP had acted consistently with current standards in interviewing patients, particularly without giving the experts, and lawyers involved, warning that he was contemplating doing that. If he had heard arguments relevant to his proposal to decide that the professional standards were too low, from the lawyers and the experts, he might have had higher regard for the professed current standard and might have accepted that it was appropriate.

The suggestion is that psychology is especially well placed, as the science of human behaviour, to contribute analytical and descriptive studies of the 'logic' or defensibility of such standards. It is not just that interviewing has become a core topic in legal psychology, that the dangers of closed and advantages of open questions, have been well documented (e.g. Gudjonnson, 2003; Home Office and Department of Health, 2002), but that psychology is also specially placed to assess the appropriateness of such standards. There is the initial empirical question; is an 'open questions only' policy commonplace amongst GPs? (Is it consistent with readers' experience?) Of course, even if it is a minority practice that does not prevent it being an acceptable standard because those who do adopt it might still be regarded as a 'responsible body' within the profession. However, an assessment of the appropriateness (logic or defensibility) of the claimed standard is also appropriate. A cost-benefit analysis might be undertaken. Further, does it discriminate against those who are less assertive and/or have a less extensive vocabulary?

It is understandable that doctors are concerned about suggesting symptoms for patients to repeat back to them but they have to rely on the patient's competence with words in order to make initial decisions. What they are told will determine their initial thoughts and range of possible diagnoses and interventions. GPs have to make very difficult decisions whether to undertake a home visit. They have to exercise a discretion, as a means of managing scarce resources, not just funds and their time, where medical need is only one, albeit the most important, factor. 'Skilful' patients and parents will be reinforced for exaggerating symptoms. Parents and patients could be encouraged or required to be more informative, such as by being given a checklist of things on which to have information prepared, such as temperature, before seeking a home visit. Specialist nurses could triage home visits just as they regularly do in hospital emergency rooms, and in GP practices. A richer understanding of human behaviour will always aid social and political analysis.

The example, of the boy who suffered brain damage as the consequence of a GP's risk-taking process, concerned a civil trial and the law of negligence, whereas this book has focused on the criminal justice system. Yet the ideas are still appropriate. There remains a role for psychology. There are legal differences. A defendant will be guilty of a negligence-based crime, for example dangerous or careless driving, if the standard of behaviour (the *actus reus* rather than the 'standard of care') is seriously negligent, without any debate about the existence of a duty of care. Gross negligence will provide the *mens rea* for certain crimes, such as manslaughter, and lesser degrees will suffice for driving offences.

In both civil and criminal contexts psychologists should have a valuable role to play in analysing how defendants make risk decisions. That could inform assessments of degrees of criminal responsibility valuable when determining the nature and degree of appropriate penalties. For example was the offender's problem that they were antisocially poor at assessing likelihoods and/or degrees of possible loss? The House of Lords has decreed for England and Wales (although the whole area of homicide law is being reviewed at the time of writing) (Law Commission, 2006), that an individual commits manslaughter if:

> ... that breach of duty should be characterised as gross negligence and therefore as a crime. That will depend upon the seriousness of the breach of duty committed by the defendant in all the circumstances in which the defendant was placed when it occurred. The jury will have to consider whether the extent to which the defendant's conduct departed from the proper standard of care incumbent upon him, involving as it must have done a risk of death to the patient, was such that it should be judged criminal. (*R. v. Adomako,* [1995] 1 AC 171).

Note, for example that the House of Lords (who recognized that the test was circuitous but denied that that was problem), referred to 'a' risk. That could relate to either of the key features of a risk, the outcomes or their likelihood. Lord Mackay, who wrote the judgement, went on to specify that, because the charge was manslaughter, the risk had to relate to the one relevant outcome, death. Hence, the qualifier 'a' would seem to relate to the likelihood of that outcome. But should any degree of risk, as 'a' implies, suffice? What of countervailing factors; there is a risk that we will cause someone's death every time we drive somewhere, and yet the social and economic benefits of people getting to their workplaces are quite significant. Such vague tests give juries considerable discretion in how they interpret the test. That the test is comprehensible by a lay juror, as Lord Mackay asserted was the supreme test for legal directions such as these, does not guarantee that the jury will understand how to apply it, let alone ensure consistency between cases. Tests with such vague expressions as 'the seriousness of the breach' and 'a risk' make it easier for juries to be influenced by such extraneous circumstances as how the defendant looks and their impression management skills when answering questions in the witness box or sitting in the dock being observed by judge and jury.

CONTRACT: DEVELOPING REALITY

Very many people, working in criminal justice (including forensic psychiatry), use contracts. As individual employees they have contracts of employment that give both them and their employers a range of rights. Many will have contracts with professional associations that guarantee them certain services, but which can also authorize their expulsion if they break certain rules or standards. The type of contract to be discussed here is that between the employee, as a professional, and a client. An example would be the contract between a psychologist, working in a prison, and an offender. Such psychologists – also probation officers, psychiatrists and others – will negotiate a contract so that, in return for the offender agreeing to do something, for example adopting certain anger management strategies, they will do something else. Experience has led many practitioners to consider contracting with clients to be a very valuable, and practical professional tool for securing progress towards agreed goals.

Unfortunately, no matter how popular and useful they are, they are not contracts, in any legal sense (Treitel, 2003). They do not meet some of the minimum requirements for a contract. There will be an agreement; both sides will have specified or accepted their obligations. This agreement, and the degree of explicitness that is usually involved, are key features in making these 'contracts' attractive to both professionals and clients. People 'know where they stand'. The agreement can be unique; it is for the parties to specify what they agree. They do not have to adopt pro forma terms. Indeed, negotiation of the terms is likely to enhance motivation and commitment to see the contract through. As the terms can be unique, contracts can enhance individuality. Instead of the client just receiving a service 'off the peg,' they can negotiate to have it 'tailor-made'. However, there will be no 'consideration'.

The law of contract requires, except for contracts under seal (which we will not consider), that each party to the contract provides consideration to the other. This does not refer to good manners or thoughtfulness but rather to something of value. You pick up a newspaper and put down the price, marked on it, in front of a shop assistant. It is too early in the morning to say anything so you simply leave the shop with your newspaper. Nevertheless, you have made a binding contract. Your behaviour, and that of the assistant in accepting the money, was enough to evidence the agreement to exchange that money for that paper. The money was consideration for the shop assistant and the newspaper was the same for you. There has to be a quid (or other monetary value) pro quo. The consideration does not have to be fair or equal; if someone is prepared to exchange their car for a sweet then, in the absence of lack of capacity, fraud or similar, it is a binding contract. The courts insist that it is up to the parties, to a contract, to decide for themselves how things should be valued (Treitel, 2003).

The problem is that, whilst the offender can give the prison psychologist some consideration, whatever it is they have agreed the offender will do for their part of the 'bargain', the psychologist does not reciprocate – in law. The psychologist will certainly be doing something valuable, something for which private clients might pay handsomely. Why is the service being provided? The prison psychologist is providing the offender with services because they are paid to do so by the prison service, or under other arrangements, but not by the offender. It is the prison services authority who can dismiss the psychologist. Consideration does not move from one of the parties, the offender or other nonprivate client, to the professional. That prevents it from being a contract. The courts will not enforce it. They could if the offender was, for example, given a voucher which they could choose to give to a psychologist, or other, in consideration for services to be received. The fact that the voucher is just a piece of paper, and/or that there are arrangements for third parties to redeem its value to the psychologist rather than through the client, should not matter because the client is exercising choice to dispose of the voucher.

Does it matter that these 'contracts' are not legally enforceable contracts? Many people might actually be delighted that they are not legally enforceable; the prospect of litigation, with all its attendant costs, is not particularly attractive. However, if that is the case why are they using a legal concept, the contract, when they do not want to acknowledge it as such? (Many contracts now make provision for the use of alternative dispute resolution techniques such as mediation, to reduce the cost and to increase the speed and informality of reaching a resolution. Such arbitration contracts can ultimately find their way to the courts.)

The most significant point would seem to be that 'contracts' have proved a very popular way for many different professionals to work with their clients. The absence of legal enforceability has not been a critical problem. Indeed, research into commercial contracts has shown that they have more to do with finding ways for the parties to relate to each other, on a continuing basis, than in establishing binding rights and obligations (Macaulay, 1963; Beale and Dugdale, 1975). Whilst, of course, the courts will see the cases where the contracting parties are no longer able to work with each other, the norm is, where a breach of such a contract occurs, for the parties to use it as a means of renegotiating the relationship. The contract may be a legal agreement (whether written or oral), which the courts will interpret and enforce if necessary. However, it is also, and in many cases is more valuable as, a tool for managing continuing relationships. Consider, for example, how many publishers have sued academic authors for breach of contract because they did not deliver the manuscript by the agreed date? That date is important, for marketing and printing reasons, but publishers could not – realistically (and this is not an invitation to use this publication as a test case) – expect to succeed in such a business by taking their authors to court.

It is submitted that the law and practice of contracting has enormous potential for psychological insights and research, not least in criminal justice contexts. What are the factors or circumstances – other than the contractual terms – which make it more likely that contracts will be adhered to? Does, for example the quality and/or quantity of negotiation that takes place before contracting affect adherence? Would making the contracts legally enforceable, albeit using informal alternative dispute resolution schemes rather than the full panoply of the courts, facilitate those professionals who use them with clients? Bonnie and Monahan (2005), members of the renowned, US-based, McArthur Research Network on Mental Health, have called for a focus on contract. They suggest it is a more appropriate basis for future developing ideas and research concerned to encourage treatment compliance. Carson (1999) has argued that contract could, and should, become the basis for governing the relationship between patients and treatment providers for the vast majority of patients. That it would not be sufficient where patients, considered to be dangerous, were unwilling to make a contract, or others lacked sufficient capacity to make any contract, it could have many benefits in terms of encouraging patient motivation and withdrawing from the primary associations with 'public safety', 'compulsion' and 'loss of personal control' so enduring with mental health services.

CONCLUSION

This chapter, as well as this book, set out to argue for a broader and richer range of ways in which psychology might be applied to criminal justice and, thereby, to law. The contributors have covered a wide range of topics, including civil law topics in this final chapter. The common theme has been that psychology's contribution could be much greater than it currently is. Hopefully, the case has been made for applying psychology in a much more diverse and imaginative way than heretofore.

REFERENCES

Beale, H. and Dugdale, T. (1975) Contracts between businessmen: Planning and the use of contractual remedies. *British Journal of Law and Society*, **2**, 45–60.

Bonnie, R.J. and Monahan, J. (2005) From coercion to contract: Reframing the debate on mandated community treatment for people with mental disorders. *Law and Human Behavior*, **29** (4), 485–503.

Carson, D. (1999) From status to contract: A future for mental health law? *Behavioral Sciences & the Law*, **17** (5), 645–60.

Dolan, S. (2002) Trial by jury, in *The Handbook of the Criminal Justice Process* (eds M. McConville and G. Wilson), Oxford University Press, Oxford, pp. 379–402.

Her Majesty's Inspectorate of Constabulary and Her Majesty's Crown Prosecution Service Inspectorate (2002) Her Majesty's Inspectorate of Constabulary and Her Majesty's Crown Prosecution Service Inspectorate (2002) *A Report on the Joint Inspection into the Investigation and Prosecution of Rape Offences in England and Wales*, HM Inspectorate of Constabulary & HM Crown Prosecution Service Inspectorate, London. (Downloaded from http://www.hmcpsi.gov.uk/reports/jirapeins.pdf on October 11, 2005.)

Gudjonnson, G.H. (2003) *The Psychology of Interrogations and Confessions: A Handbook*, Wiley, Chichester.

Home Office and Department of Health (2002) *Achieving Best Evidence in Criminal Proceedings: Guidance for Vulnerable and Intimidated Witnesses Including Children*, HMSO, London.

Hoyano, L.C.H. (1999) Policinq flawed police investigations: Unravelling the blanket, *Modern Law Review*, **62**, 912–36.

Hoyle, C. and Young, R. (2002) Restorative justice: Assessing the prospects and pitfalls, in *The Handbook of the Criminal Justice Process* (eds M. McConville and G. Wilson), Oxford University Press, Oxford, pp. 525–48.

Johnstone, G. and van Ness, D. (2006) *Handbook of Restorative Justice*, Willan, Cullompton.

Kelly, L. (2002) *A Research Review on the Reporting, Investigation and Prosecution of Rape Cases*, HM Crown Prosecution Service Inspectorate, London. http://www.hmcpsi.gov.uk/reports/Rapelitrev.pdf (Accessed 23 April 2007).

Law Commission (2006) *Murder, Manslaughter and Infanticide*, TSO, London.

Macaulay, S. (1963) Non-contractual relations in business: A preliminary study. *American Sociological Review*, **28**, 55–67.

Markesinis, B.S., Auby, J.-B., Coester-Waltjen, D. and Deakin, S.F. (1999) *Tortious Liability of Statutory Bodies: A Comparative and Economic analysis of Five English Cases*, Hart Publishing, Oxford.

Ormerod, D. (2005) *Smith and Hogan Criminal Law*, 11th edn, Oxford University Press, Oxford.

Rogers, W.V.H. (2006) *Winfield & Jolowicz on Tort*, 17th edn, Sweet & Maxwell, London.

Treitel, G.H. (2003). Treitel on the Law of Contract, Sweet & Maxwell, London.

Westmarland, N. (2004) *Rape Law Reform in England and Wales*. University of Bristol: School for Policy Studies Working Papers Series, Paper No. 7 http://www.bristol.ac.uk/sps/downloads/working_papers/sps07_nw.pdf (Accessed 11 October 2005).

Winick, B.J. and Wexler, D.B. (eds) (2003) *Judging in a Therapeutic Key: Therapeutic Jurisprudence in the Courts*. Carolina Academic Press, Durham (SC).

Index

10,000 Volts, 217–8
Abduction – *see* inferential reasoning
Accidents, 285
Accreditation, 159
Accuracy, 82
Actuarial tests, 10
   Tools, 203–4
Actuarial v. clinical decision-making, 201–4
Actus reus, 132
Adolescents, 151–2, 155, 174
Adversarial trials, 251–62
Amnesia, 272–4
Analogical reasoning, 104
Anatomically correct dolls, 266
Anchored narratives, 102, 108, 127
Anchoring and adjustment, *see* heuristics
Anti-social behaviour, 150–3
Argumentation schemes, 123
Auld, Lord Justice, Report, 252
Automatism, 139–41
Availability, *see* heuristics
Awareness
   Mens rea, 103–5

Bad character
   Evidence, 98
Bail, 194
Behavioural sciences
   Policing and 39–42
Bias, *see* Prejudice
   Egocentric, 193
Blame, 136
   And, *see* morality

Capacity, 117, 137, 143
Care Programme Approach, 173
Case construction, 118–9
Causation, 133, 136
Charting, 122
Child sexual abuse accommodation syndrome, 271
Civil law concepts, 299–309
Codes, 10–11

Cognition/cognitive, (*See also*) criminal thinking
Cognitive model of offender rehabilitation, 148
Cognitive distortions, 148, 154
Impersonal cognition, 147
Interpersonal cognition, 147
Load, 185
Social information processing, 148–53
Cognitive-behavioural therapies, 175–6
Cognitive neuroscience, 132, 137
Common sense, 134–5
Communication, 60, 286
Communities, 55, 57
   Standards, 132, 143
   Police relations, 212
Confession, 66, 275
Confidence, 193
Consciousness, 104–5, 137–41
Contracts, 3, 14, 307–9
Content Based Credibility Analysis, CBCA, 84–5, 88, 124, 267–8
Control, 131, 147–8
   Over action, 137
Control Question Test, 81, 88–91, 94
Conviction, 21
   False, 21
Corporate
   culture, 16, 292–5
   liability, 284
   manslaughter, 284–94
Counterfactual, *see* heuristics
Courtroom, 35–6
Credibility, 81–94
Criminal responsibility, 131–145
   Causation, 133
   Corporate, 288–94
   Defences, 133, 137, 141, 144
   Mens rea, (*See also* criminal thinking), 16, 131–45
   Strict liability, 133
Criminal thinking, 147–61
Critical thinking, 211–30
Custody, 41

Dangerous Severe Personality Disorder, 172, 178
Daubert v. *Merrel Dow Pharmaceuticals*, Inc. (1993), 86, 90, 92, 107
  See also - expert evidence
Deception, 81–2, 117
Decision making, 183–98, 201–8, 211–230, 233–49, 305
  Abstract communication systems theory, 227
  Actuarial v. clinical, 201–4
  Avoidance, 211, 222–30
  Complexity, 183
  Individuals, 218–24
  Naturalistic decision making theory, 214–5
  Pragmatism, 216–8
  Recognition primed decision making, 215–6
  Traditional decision-making theory, 212–4
  Trials, 251–62
Deduction – *see* inferential reasoning
Defeasible reasoning, 123, 125
Defences to criminal responsibility – *see* criminal responsibility
Detention
  Hospital, 168
Dialectical behaviour therapy, 178
Dichotomies, 7, 9, 105, 120, 140, 233, 240
Diminished responsibility, 137
Directed Lie Polygraph Test, 81, 93
Discipline, 155
'Disease of the mind,' 8
Disenablers to services, 167–80
Dissociation, 137–41
DNA, 21

Enhanced thinking skills, 156
Epistemic imbalance, 42
Evidence, 5, 6, 97–110, 116, 253
  Bad character, 98
  Exclusionary rules, 97, 116
  And fact-finding – *see* fact-finding
  Hearsay, 98
  Identification, 99
  Jury admonitions, 191
  New evidence scholarship – *see* new evidence scholarship
  Opinion, 106–10
  Overconfidence, 192
  Statistical, 185
Executive functions, 139
Experiences, 149
Expert evidence, 6–7, 106–10, 201, 207–8, 265–78
  admissibility, 6, 7, 107–8
  assessing, 108–10
  frontiers of science, 107
  understanding methodology, 7
  identification, 99
  science, 106, 108–9
  syndrome evidence, 108
  witnesses, 119, 257
Expertise, 214, 270
Eyewitness identification, 21–38

Faces
  Computerised facial composite systems, 25
Fact-finding, 5–6, 97–110, 115–28, 265
Falsification, theory of, 266–7
Families, 55
Feedback, 23, 32
Feigning, 272–4
Field studies, 21
Fisher Inquiry, 41
Forensic evidence, 39
Forensic mental health services, 175
Free will, 132, 136, 138, 142–3
  v. determinism, 2, 131, 137
Free proof, 97, 116
Fricker, Miranda, 42–3, 54, 59

General offender behaviour programmes, 156
Genetics, 141–3
Gestalt psychology, 121
Goals, 149
Guilty Knowledge Test, 81, 91–4

Health & Safety
  Executive, 290–1
Heuristics, 104–6, 183, 213–4
  Anchoring and adjustment, 193–5
  Availability, 186–7, 214
  Counterfactual, 195–6
  Hindsight, 190–2, 201, 204–8, 216
  making judgments, 184–6
  representativeness, 187–90
  simulation, 195–196
  unstructured judgement, 201–8
Hindsight, *see* heuristics
Hofstadter, Douglas, 42–43, 59
Homicide
  Corporate manslaughter, 16

Identification evidence, 9, 21–38, 39, 41, 54–5, 99, 117
  Confidence in, 31–32, 99, 193
  Instructions, 31
  Line-ups, 26,-7, 30–1, 276
  Match to description or suspect, 28–9
  Photographs, 33–4
  R.v. Turnbull, 54, 99
  Sequential v. simultaneous, 30
  Show-ups, 26–7

INDEX

Individualism, 15
  Liability, 285
  Self-categorization theory, 224–5
  Social identity theory, 224–5
Induction – *see* inductive reasoning
Inductive reasoning, 118, 120
Inferences, 102–3, 116, 135
Inferential reasoning
  Abduction, 120–2, 124
  Deduction, 119, 123, 126
  Induction, 120
Information overload, 183
Innocence, *see* guilt
Inquisitorial trials, 251–62
Intelligence, 42
Intention, 103–5, 132, 134–5, 143
Interdisciplinarity, 2–4, 40, 201
Interrogation, 41, 45, 53–4
Interventions, 147, 155–9
  General offender behaviour programmes, 156
  Enhanced thinking skills, 156
  Pathfinder, 158, 160
  Think first, 157
Interviewing, 6, 10, 11, 13, 24, 39, 117
  ACPO investigative interviewing strategy, 74–8
  Cognitive, 24, 45, 53–4, 68–72
  Conversation management, 72–3
  Investigative, 65–78
  PEACE, 67–8, 73–4
  Style, 84
Investigations, 39–64, 121
Investigative psychology, 117
Islamic trials, 252–62

Judges, 4, 6
  Cognitive errors, 189–90
Judicial instructions, 97–101
Juries
  Instructions, 100, 197
  Comprehension, 100
  Note-taking, 101
  Structured verdicts, 100–1

Knowing, 134

Laboratory research, 22, 27
Laming Report, 43
Law reform, 8
Learning paradigm, 284
Legal criteria, 8–10
Legal education, 5, 8, 126
Legislation, 7–8
Likelihood, 188

Management sciences, 40
MAOA (monoamine oxidase A), 141
Meanings, 135
Memory, 117, 215
  Guided memory technique, 24
  Selective, 184
Mens rea, 103–5, 131–3, 289
Mental disorder, 141
Mentally disordered offenders, 167–80
Meta-analysis, 206
Miscarriage of justice, 21, 39, 40, 41, 45, 67, 233–5
Morality, 131–2, 134, 137, 143
  Moral capacity, 137
  Moral development, 137
  Moral reasoning. 153–5
Multi-Agency partnerships, 227–9

Negligence, 12, 132, 216, 300–7
  In criminal law, 134
  Duty of care, 12–13
  Standard of care, 13
New Evidence Scholarship, 115–6, 121

OASY, 173
Obstacles to service delivery
  Mental health, 167–180
Offender profiling, *see* profiling
Opinion evidence – *see* evidence
Opinion survey, public, 187
Organisations
  Culture, 211, 286
  Errors, 283–96
  Identity, 225–7
  Learning, 286
  Service design, 288

Parents, 154
  attitudes, 152
  management programmes, 179
  mothers' disciplines, 153
Pathfinder, 158, 160
PEACE, *see* interviewing
Perception, 104, 119
Police and Criminal Evidence Act, 1984 (PACE), 65–8
Policing, 41
  decision-making, 44, 211
  diversity 56–8
  knowledge-led, 42
Polygraph, 86
Political, 7–8
Popper, *see* falsification
Practice statements, 11–2
Practitioners, 4, 5, 15
Pragmatism, 216–8

Prejudice, 55
Prevention, 5
Principles, 67
Problem solving, 253
　Courts, 254–5
　skills, 155
Professional practice statements, 12–13
Profiling, 39, 57, 117
Process, 66
Proof, 5, 116, 233–49, 299–300
　Correspondence v. coherence theories, 120, 125
Psychology and law
　American Psychology-Law Society, 1, 2
　Applied discipline, 2–3
　Australian and New Zealand Association of Psychiatry, Psychology & Law, 1–2, 3
　Developments 1–2
　Differences, 2–3
　European Association of Psychology & Law, 1
　Misapplications, 265–78
Psychopathy, 137
PTSD, 270–1
Punishment, 259

Racism, 55
Rape, 10, 299
Readiness to act, 138
Reality Monitoring, 81, 87–8
Reasonable, 4, 303–4
Relevant-Irrelevant Polygraph Test, 81, 93–4
Representativeness, *see* heuristics
Restorative justice, 4, 15, 252
Resources, 174
Risk
　Assessment, 201
　Decision-making, 13
　Trials, 234, 239–40

Schemas, 122–123, 149, 151, 155
Science – *see* expert evidence
Scientific Content Analysis (SCAN), 81, 87–8
Self-categorization theory, 224–5
Sentencing, 142, 170, 238–9
Sexual abuse, 266–8, 299
Sharia law, 258–62
Silence, 244–6
Simulation, *see* heuristics
Social cognitive defects, 148

Social control, 260
Social identity theory, 224–5
Social information processing, 148–153
Statement Validity Assessment, 81, 83–7, 94, 124–5, 267–8
Story theory, 5, 102, 127, 221
Strategic Use of Evidence technique, 83
Strict liability, *see* criminal responsibility
Syndrome evidence, 106
Systems, 15
　Analyses, 5, 13, 168
　Communication systems theory, 227
　Errors, 283–96
　Failure, 257
　Justice systems, 14–5
　Inquiries into, 43–4

Therapeutic communities, 176–7
Therapeutic jurisprudence, 4, 15, 160
Think first, 157
Thinking styles, 147–8, 159–60
Training manuals, 13–14
Trials, 5
　Criminal, 3, 251–62
Truthful, 81
　Truth-bias, 82
　Truth-finding, 261

Utilitarianism, 131–2, 143

Validity Checklist, 84–85
Variables
　Estimator v. System, 22–3
　System, 23–35
VCL, 267–8
Verbal overshadowing, 25
Victims
　Statements, 256
VIPER, 29
Voice recognition, 99
Voice Stress Analysers, 81, 93–4
Voluntary act, 132, 137, 139–40, 142

Witnesses
　Display of affect, 188
　Vulnerable, 117

XYY syndrome, 141

Young offenders, *see* adolescents